INTERNATIONAL MARKETING

INTERNATIONAL MARKETING

Vern Terpstra
University of Michigan

James Foley
Bradley University

Ravi Sarathy
Northeastern University

Tenth Edition

Naper Publishing Group

Naper Publishing Group
© 2012 all rights reserved

Cover photo: Grant Faint/Getty Images

International Marketing, Tenth Edition

Copyright © 2012 by Naper Publishing Group LLC

Previous edition copyright © 2006 by Northcoast Publishers

13-digit ISBN 978-0-9817293-5-0
10-digit ISBN 0-9817293-5-5

Library of Congress Control Number: 2011932903

Printed in the United States of America by Naper Publishing Group LLC.

10 9 8 7 6 5 4 3 2 1

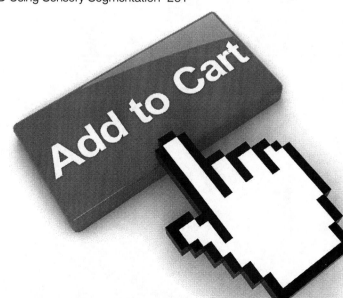

Part 3: Strategy, Planning, Coordination, and Control of Global Marketing

Chapter 14: Global Marketing Strategy 433

LIST OF CASES

Very few international marketing texts have the rich history of scholarship and longevity enjoyed by Terpstra's *International Marketing*. The publication of the tenth edition makes the release all the more significant. The first edition, published in 1972, came at a time when scholars debated the significance of international business as a separate discipline. The reason was partly that at the time the United States still enjoyed a trade surplus (more exports than imports). Given the U.S. was such a strong exporter, surely that meant we already had the skills to compete internationally in business.

That perception started to change in 1976 when U.S. imports exceeded exports, and in every subsequent year, the United States has continued to have a trade deficit. This change was reflected in the preface from Terpstra's fourth edition in 1986:

> It is no longer necessary to argue that students of business need to learn about the world economy and international business. Internationalization of business studies has been accepted almost everywhere and is even a criterion for accreditation of business schools in the United States. International marketing is recognized as one of the most critical skills in international business today. For Americans, this is evident in the huge trade deficits that have plagued the United States in recent years. This deficit results from a combination of foreign firms' success in selling here and American firms' problems in selling abroad.

As colleges and universities continued to embrace the importance of international business through the 1980s and 1990s, publishers responded with an ever increasing number of international business textbooks, including a number of new titles in international marketing. And this textbook continued to serve students and instructors of international marketing as well, culminating with the release of Terpstra's ninth edition in 2006. The ninth edition was translated into Chinese, joining editions previously published for Taiwan, Indonesia, and India.

Just as perceptions of international marketing have evolved, the profession and the needs of students have also evolved. The new tenth edition of this landmark text represents one of the most significant revisions in the nearly 40-year history of the Terpstra text. Beyond being fully updated with regard to all references, data, websites, and other technical information, the text includes significant new features that address the changing needs of faculty and students:

- **The length of the book has been significantly reduced**, offering greater flexibility within course needs. The briefer, more concise format meets the needs of today's students who rely much more heavily on the Internet to supplement their course text. Although the text is more concise, it remains a comprehensive introduction to the field, designed and written as a stand-alone resource for students of international marketing.

- **The text now covers all the international marketing tasks and knowledge statements from the NASBITE Certified Global Business Professional (CGBP) certification**. For students and practitioners seeking the CGBP qualification, this text will also serve as the most useful preparation for the international marketing portion of the exam. Practice questions have been added, which are correlated to knowledge statements in the NASBITE CGBP certification.

- There is a **stronger practical approach to topics and examples**. This is partly due to the alignment with the NASBITE CGBP, but also reflects a stronger demand from students to see how principles and techniques in this text can be directly applied to building and enhancing their international business skills.

* The text has a **new focus on global entrepreneurship**, with greater discussions of the role of the international marketing manager within small- and mid-sized businesses.

* Unique issues associated with **international marketing in emerging markets** have been integrated throughout the text, reflecting the critical importance of effective marketing in markets such as China and India.

* The text includes **a new, ongoing team project: the Global Marketing Plan**. Each chapter incorporates activities and team-based assignments that culminate in the development (and presentation) of a comprehensive international marketing plan for a specific company. This project has been an invaluable teaching tool in both traditional classroom environments and distance-learning environments.

Chapter Structure of Tenth Edition

The chapter structure of the tenth edition of *International Marketing* closely follows the overall structure of the ninth edition. Though the text has been shortened and updated, instructors familiar with previous editions will find a strong correlation between the tenth edition and prior editions.

The tenth edition retains the original chapter groupings from earlier editions. The 15 chapters are grouped into three parts:

> **Part 1:** The Global Business Environment
> **Part 2:** Global Marketing Management
> **Part 3:** Strategy, Planning, Coordination, and Control of Global Marketing

Changes/Additions

The most significant change in the tenth edition is the elimination of the chapter titled "Information Technology and Global Marketing." The IT-related topics from that chapter instead have been integrated, as appropriate, into other chapters.

The tenth edition also has a new chapter, titled "Supply Chain Management and International Marketing." This addition reflects the trend toward emphasizing the role of supply chain and logistics in the field of international business. The chapter also includes some of the NASBITE CGBP topics from the supply chain domain.

A list of the chapter titles in the tenth edition follows, along with the corresponding ninth edition chapter numbers.

Tenth Edition Chapter Title	Ninth Edition Chapter Number
1. Introduction: The Global Marketing Manager	1
2. The Global Economic Environment	2
3. The Political–Legal Environment	4
4. The Cultural Environment	3
5. Ethics and International Marketing	6
6. Global Marketing Research and Data Sources	Part of 7
7. Foreign Market Selection	Part of 7
8. Foreign Market Entry, Partner Selection, and Distribution	Part of 8
9. International Product Policy	Parts of 9 and 10
10. International Branding and Promotion	Parts of 9 and 11
11. Supply Chain Management and International Marketing	None—new chapter
12. International Pricing	12
13. Global Marketing of Services	13
14. Global Marketing Strategy	14
15. Planning, Organization, and Control of International Marketing	15

Tenth Edition Pedagogical Elements

The tenth edition of *International Marketing* contains a number of teaching elements to support student and practitioner learning. The overall goals are to ensure that the practical (application) aspect of each chapter is drawn out for the reader and to support critical learning objectives such as significant theories.

Each chapter contains the following common set of elements:

Learning Objectives: Each chapter begins with a list of the key learning goals for that chapter. This helps instructors to understand the main learning objectives and provides the reader with an overview of what to expect in the chapter.

Key Terms: The key terms in each chapter are set off with bold type and accompanied by marginal definitions. This treatment makes key terms easy to recognize and emphasizes their importance to the reader. An alphabetical list of these key terms appears at the end of each chapter, and the terms and their definitions also are included in the comprehensive Glossary at the end of the book.

Special Topic Boxes: Each chapter contains a number of topic boxes to further illustrate particular issues. These boxes often present specific company examples to help the reader relate to the topic or issue. They also address issues specific to emerging markets such as China.

Chapter Summary: Chapters end with a summary of the key points made in the chapter to reinforce for the reader the chapter's learning objectives.

NASBITE CGBP Topics: A unique feature in each chapter is the list of the six-digit task/knowledge statements (rubrics) from the CGBP Practice Delineation discussed in that chapter. For students or practitioners studying for the NASBITE Certified Global Business Professional, this list

can be used as a guide to which issues within that chapter are particularly important to study. These rubrics are cross-referenced again in the master list at the end of the book in the section "Studying for the NASBITE CGBP Exam." The text addresses all of the CGBP Domain 2 rubrics—International Marketing. In addition, the text also discusses many of the rubrics from the other three domains.

Questions and Research: Each chapter includes a list of questions or research assignments that students can use in class to apply the knowledge included in the chapter. Many of these questions direct the reader to websites or other resources in support of international trade research. These questions and research tasks also work well within a distance-learning environment as either individual assignments or as discussion board topics.

Team Project Assignment: Another unique feature of the book is the team assignment at the end of each chapter. Each chapter assignment takes the team through the steps needed to formulate an international marketing plan for a specific company. (The project also works as an individual assignment.) The specific team assignment for a chapter directly relates to the topic discussed in that chapter. If the semester is shorter than 15 weeks, assignments from more than one chapter can be combined or eliminated.

The team project works well within a facilitated (face-to-face) class. In these situations, the team could potentially develop an international marketing plan for a local company that the team could visit. Then the final marketing plan would be presented to the client both in written and verbal form. The team project also works well within a distance-learning class, in which case the instructor might assign a company that the student could research from Internet resources. In either case, the series of tasks takes the team/ student through the full process of developing an international marketing plan, including:

- initial client and industry SWOT
- political/economic/cultural assessment
- development of foreign market demand and risk indicators
- creation of a foreign market selection matrix (spreadsheet)
- choice of entry mode
- research on possible foreign partners
- competitive assessment
- trade finance issues, including payment method and foreign exchange (fx) issues
- supply chain implication
- product or service selection and development issues
- overall execution of the marketing plan, including strategy, timetable, and implementation issues

Depending on the course requirements and time constraints, instructors can select only a few of the team assignments (such as only doing a foreign market selection matrix) or assign the full range of tasks.

Cases: Each chapter includes one or several cases supporting the learning objectives for that chapter. Some of the cases are quite short and work well for in-class or distance-learning discussion assignments. The longer cases tend to cover multiple learning objectives across chapters and can be used in the same way as shorter cases or for individual reports.

Acknowledgments

As with earlier editions, this edition benefited from the contributions of many people. We thank the hundreds of American, Asian, European, and Latin-American executives whom we consulted, who conducted research, and whom we met at seminars over the years. They provided many practical insights and examples. Our students, both in the United States and abroad, challenged and stimulated us to sharpen our analyses.

Many faculty colleagues provided cases, materials, and constructive suggestions. We gratefully acknowledge them and especially thank the major reviewers of this edition:

Richard Hise, Texas A&M University
Phillip Seder, Portland Community College

As well as the faculty involved in the prior edition:

Andrew C. Gross, Cleveland State University
Attila Yaprak, Wayne State University
Dharma de Silva, Wichita State University
Mohammad Elahee, Quinnipiac University

Special thanks goes to David Williams of The University of Tennessee for his excellent work on the instructor's manual, test bank, and lecture slides, as well as significant research to support this new edition. David built on the previous instructional material developed by Thomas Lloyd of Westmoreland Community College.

Thanks also to Lloyd Russow, Philadelphia University. Lloyd was a member of our prior writing team and made significant contributions to the previous edition.

Our thanks to NASBITE International for developing the Certified Global Business Professional (CGBP) certification. Our hope is that by aligning this text with many of the competencies in the CGBP standard, we can assist with growing the base of students and practitioners receiving their CGBP.

Finally, we want to gratefully acknowledge the dedicated people at Naper Publishing Group for their tireless and patient support. The vision for an up-to-date, practical, CGBP aligned text was given space to germinate and grow into this finished book. Thanks to Jeff Lindblade, Executive Editor, for his motivational skill and technical abilities. Bob McLaughlin and his marketing team have given the book the wide exposure it needs to reach 21st century learners.

We also thank the production team of the tenth edition. The project was skillfully managed by Victoria Putman, Putman Productions, LLC, with the help of her team, especially Charles Hutchinson for copyediting. The interior pages and cover image were creatively produced by Laurie Entringer. Ed Laube provided important editorial consulting. Your patience and outstanding abilities have meticulously refined the text in important ways.

We welcome comments and suggestions from users of this edition. Through such feedback, we can continue to provide an up-to-date and useful product.

Vern Terpstra, James Foley, and Ravi Sarathy, June 2011

chapter

1

Introduction: The Global Marketing Manager

Effective international marketing is a critical task for many companies. Foreign markets represent an increasing portion of the total world market, leading to sizeable international sales and profits. Emerging markets represent exciting new opportunities—and new competitors. As the world becomes increasingly interdependent, companies must recognize these opportunities and risks as they grow their international business.

The main goals of this chapter are to ●●●

1. Distinguish between international and domestic marketing.

2. Describe the global environment in which marketing takes place.

3. Show a variety of ways in which a firm may practice international marketing.

4. Discuss current global trends affecting global marketing.

1

Global Marketing and Domestic Marketing

marketing

The collection of activities undertaken by a firm to assess and satisfy customer needs, wants, and desires.

International marketing is best explained by briefly reviewing marketing in a domestic context. In this book, **marketing** is defined as the collection of activities undertaken by a firm in order to assess and satisfy customer needs, wants, and desires. This broad definition of marketing encompasses both for-profit and not-for-profit organizations, whether public or private. When it discusses products, this book refers not only to manufactured goods, but also to services, ideas, and people (as in political campaigns or movies). A firm's ultimate success depends primarily on how well it performs in the marketplace, requiring knowledge of the market. Marketing involves many responsibilities, including the following:

- A firm must identify and study its consumers: Who are they? Where are they? Who are prospective buyers? Are they similar to or different from current consumers? What factors are important in consumers' decisions to purchase (or not to purchase) a product?

- The firm must develop products that satisfy customer needs and wants.

- The company must set prices and terms on the products so they seem reasonable to buyers and return a fair profit to the company.

- The company must distribute the products so they are conveniently available to buyers.

- The firm must inform the market about its products and service offerings; it must use marketing communications to raise awareness, increase interest, and increase sales. With the Internet, distance and time have become less important, whereas delivery and service have become more important.

- There is an implied warranty of satisfaction with the product. Firms must reassure customers, and they may need to perform a variety of after-sale services. The firm's marketing responsibility does not end with the sale.

- Firms must monitor the marketing activities of their competitors and develop appropriate organizational structure and long-term marketing strategies and competitive responses.

marketing management

The planning and coordinating of activities to achieve a successfully integrated marketing program.

Marketing management, therefore, is the planning and coordinating of all of these activities to achieve a successfully integrated marketing program.

International marketing is marketing across national borders but addressing similar issues as in domestic marketing, including customer identification, product development, product distribution, promotion, and pricing.

Figure 1-1 ● Global Marketing: Moving Products between Countries

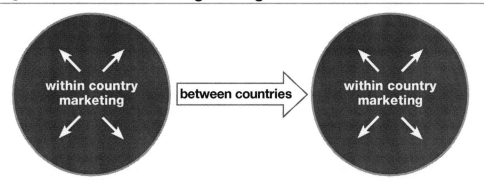

International marketing is, by definition, the act of marketing across national boundaries. One difference between domestic marketing and international marketing is that the latter includes the task of marketing between countries, as well as within each country, as shown in Figure 1-1. That is, the international marketer has another responsibility—moving products across national boundaries—in addition to moving products within each market the company serves.

> **international marketing**
> The act of marketing across borders including marketing between countries as well as within each country.

International Marketing: A Closer Look

The activities just described—market research, product development, distribution, promotion, and pricing—together constitute the essence of marketing. What then is international marketing? International marketing consists of identifying, understanding, and satisfying global customer needs better than the competition (both domestic and international). It also consists of coordinating marketing activities within the constraints of the global environment. Table 1-1 examines this definition in greater detail and breaks down the main components of international marketing into five objectives, which are discussed next.

Identifying and Understanding Global Consumer Needs

Consumer needs can be identified by carrying out international marketing research. Such research helps a firm understand consumer needs in different markets and determines whether those needs are different from those of the customers it currently serves. For example, a firm seeking to sell washing machines in Europe must know that Europeans often wash their clothes with hot water (at

Table 1-1 ● International Marketing: The Essentials

Objectives	Marketing Activities
Identifying and understanding global consumer needs	Carrying out international marketing research and analyzing market segments; seeking to understand similarities and differences in customer groups across countries.
Satisfying customer needs	Adapting manufactured goods, services, and elements of the marketing mix to satisfy different customer needs across countries and regions. Included in manufacturing and technology decisions are the implications of costs and prices, development of global customer information databases, and distribution channel and logistics information.
Being better than the competition	Assessing, monitoring, and responding to global competition by offering better value and developing superior brand image and product positioning; broader product range; low prices; high quality; good performance; superior distribution, advertising, and service. Recognizing that competitors may include state-owned enterprises, other multinationals, and domestic firms, each having different goals, such as market share instead of profits.
Coordinating marketing activities	Coordinating and integrating marketing strategies and implementing them across countries, regions, and the global market, which involves centralization, delegation, standardization, and local responsiveness.
Recognizing the constraints of the global environment	Recognizing that the global environment includes • Complex variation due to governmental, protectionist, and industrial policies. • Cultural and economic differences. • Differences in marketing infrastructure. • Financial constraints due to exchange-rate variation and differences in inflation rates.

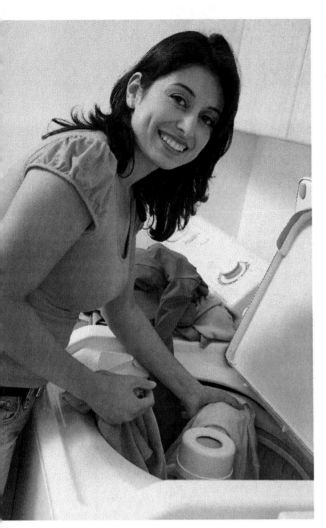

Identifying and understanding global consumer needs are among the international marketing challenges. For example, firms selling washing machines need to recognize differences between countries in water temperatures used for washing.

---

point of sale (POS)

The location at which a transaction occurs between buyer and seller.

---

global environment

A business environment in which business transactions take place between and within different country environments.

---

a temperature of 60 degrees Centigrade/140 degrees Fahrenheit), whereas most washing in the United States is done at lower water temperatures. Companies also need to analyze market segments across countries to be able to position their products appropriately for entry into international markets.

Satisfying Customer Needs

If needs differ across countries and regions, a company must consider how to adapt its products and the various elements of the marketing mix to best satisfy customers. If a company needs to lower prices, it should consider how to reduce manufacturing costs and whether to shift manufacturing to a country where manufacturing costs are lower. Well-developed distribution is needed to make sufficient quantities of goods and services available at the **point of sale (POS)**. Ideally, firms also should develop global customer databases and information systems to be able to understand and respond to customer needs and purchasing decisions.

Being Better Than the Competition

Firms must contend with competitors in their home markets and competitors in the foreign markets in which they operate. Competitors may include large multinationals and state-owned enterprises that are not profit-oriented, as well as small local firms. Multinational companies have a more extensive set of experiences to draw upon and generally have access to resources a domestic-only firm may not. These resources include labor, financing sources, and managers with a broader perspective. Long-term success comes, in part, from assessing, monitoring, and responding to actions by global competitors, especially in the understanding of competitive and comparative advantages that competitors enjoy.

Coordinating Marketing Activities

International marketing creates a new level of complexity because firms must coordinate their marketing activities across countries. These activities may involve staffing and allocating responsibilities across marketing units in different countries and deciding which decisions to decentralize and which to control from headquarters; whether to develop standardized campaigns and plans; and how much local responsiveness is appropriate.

Recognizing the Constraints of the Global Environment

The **global environment** is complex, and this complexity increases as the number of markets served by a firm increases. As firms attempt to market in the international arena, they must cope with cultural and economic differences that exist in the marketing infrastructure. These differences include factors such as the structure and sophistication of the distribution system (people who prefer or have time to purchase food daily tend to rely less on refrigeration and purchase smaller quantities of products than people who purchase on a weekly basis), the financial constraints imposed by exchange-rate changes and varying inflation rates (which, in turn, depend largely on the state of a nation's economy), and the impact of government policies (especially protectionist and other policies that unfairly benefit competitors and create difficulties in market entry).

International Marketing Management ● ● ●

The complexity of international marketing is due largely to two factors: global competition and the global environment. Customer needs vary across countries. Competitors with different strengths now come from all over the world. Likewise, the global environment presents a bewildering variety of national governments, cultures, and income levels. Domestic marketing management is often portrayed as the task of responding to the uncontrollable factors in a firm's environment while manipulating the controllable factors. International marketing management is infinitely more complex.

As depicted in Figure 1-2, the global environment is multifaceted. The controllable elements of the global environment include the **4 P's of marketing**: product, price, place (distribution), and promotion. The uncontrollable elements are those things marketers cannot control, such as the legal environment. However, marketers can exert pressure on and effect change in these "uncontrollable" elements. For example, by introducing products such as computers and the Internet, marketers change how people communicate (a part of culture). The so-called controllable elements are not always totally under the marketers' influence. Governments place price floors on products such as cigarettes (or add to the price of the product through taxes). International marketing management has the same task as that of a domestic marketer, but must view the environment in broader terms. Thus, product, price, place, and promotion vary across countries and regions. Although marketers must consider the laws of a nation when marketing domestically, in the international environment, they must take into account the laws of many nations. Furthermore, they must contend with

> **4 P's of marketing**
> The key aspects of any marketing program: product, price, place (distribution), and promotion.

Figure 1-2 ● Global Environment

The international legal environment is an example of an uncontrollable element complicating the international marketing task.

the possibility that the laws of one country may conflict with those of another.

An added dimension of international marketing management is the need for a firm to coordinate and integrate its many national marketing programs into an effective multinational program. Indeed, a principal rationale of multinational business operations (as opposed to the alternative of independent national companies) is that the division of labor and the transfer of know-how in international operations enable the whole to be greater than the sum of its parts.

A practical result of these differences is that an international marketing manager needs broader competence than domestic marketing managers or managers marketing in a specific foreign country. In other words, the international marketing manager has a dual responsibility: **foreign marketing** (marketing within foreign countries) and **global marketing** (coordinating marketing in multiple markets in the face of global competition).

With all these country differences and challenging issues, what tends to be the main concerns of the international marketing manager? Table 1-2 highlights the results of a survey of mostly European marketing managers (72 percent) working in various industries: industrial products (45 percent), consumer goods (21 percent), pharmaceuticals (14 percent), and services (20 percent). The results help illustrate that their concerns include those of a domestic marketer (developing new products, developing relationships with channel partners, and so on), along with concerns more unique to the international marketing manager (stronger global customers, greater regional integration, and so on).

The Global Marketplace

To provide a sense of the range of activities that constitute international marketing, the following sections include some examples of companies operating in the global marketplace. It is helpful to see how different companies make decisions regarding products, prices charged, distribution channels, countries sold to, and partners chosen—all in an attempt to increase sales and profits.

foreign marketing

Marketing within foreign countries.

global marketing

Coordinating marketing in multiple markets in the face of global competition.

Disney with a Foreign Accent

With Disney characters such as Mickey Mouse having been shown in movies and cartoons all over the world for more than 50 years, Tokyo Disneyland was a logical creation. It began in 1983 as a joint venture between Mitsui Real Estate Development and Keisei Electric Railway companies. The Walt Disney Company, however, had no ownership share; it designed the amusement park and it supplies its managerial expertise, receiving in return royalties of 10 percent of gate and 5 percent of concessions.

With this foreign success, Disney expanded into Europe. Construction of Euro Disney began in the summer of 1988, 20 miles east of Paris, at a cost of $2.8 billion for the first phase. The Paris location was chosen, in part, because 109 million people lived within a six-hour drive and because, as part of the deal, France agreed to build a high-speed train between the theme park and Paris (with travel time estimates of just 30 minutes each way). Unlike its stake in Tokyo Disneyland, Disney owns 49 percent of Euro Disney, the maximum permitted by the French government.

Disney began promoting the Disney characters with French corporate partners such as Renault and Banque Nationale de Paris. Disney also started a Disney Channel on European television in a joint venture with media entrepreneur Rupert Murdoch and aired Disney entertainment specials in Europe. Disney even adapted the park to reflect European culture. Fantasyland focused on the Grimm Brothers' fairy tales and Lewis Carroll's *Alice in Wonderland*. Discoveryland focused attention on European greats such as Jules Verne, Leonardo da Vinci, and H. G. Wells. Signs are in multiple languages, and employees are expected to speak at least two languages.

In its first year of operation, attendance at Euro Disney was about 20 percent lower than targeted. High European admission prices (about 30 percent higher than at Walt Disney World in Orlando), recession in Europe, and roads blocked by protesting farmers have been cited as some reasons for lower-than-planned attendance. Disney also encountered some labor problems because French workers were less willing to comply with stringent Disney standards pertaining to dress, hairstyle, and general appearance.

Euro Disney opened to high hopes in April 1992, but it incurred continual losses for the next three years prior to registering a minuscule profit of 2 million French francs before extraordinary gains on a debt restructuring.

Why did this park perform poorly when Disneyland operations in the United States and Japan were so successful? The reasons include (1) location—a 30-minute train ride from Paris with little else in the area to hold tourists' interest and cold weather much of the year; (2) relatively high prices; (3) a limited number of rides, allowing tourists to go through the park in a day and providing them with little incentive to stay overnight at Disney-owned hotels; (4) little cultural adaptation to familiar childhood characters (Goofy in the United States versus Asterix in France); (5) a ban on wine sales (later rescinded); and (6) a European recession that resulted in a decrease in the number of visitors (attendance dropped from around 9.8 million in the first year to 8.8 million from 1993 to 1994, with about 9 million in the third year of operation). The Disney Corporation also learned that tourists preferred to bring their meals as picnic lunches rather than purchase fast food and that few customers bought souvenirs. This meant that attendees spent less per person at Euro Disney than at the firm's other parks. Competitors also emerged, such as Blackpool Pleasure Beach, Tivoli Gardens in Copenhagen, and Anheuser-Busch's PortAventura in the sunnier climate near Barcelona, Spain.[1]

Table 1-2 • Marketing Managers' Concerns

Concern	Reason
Developing new products	The pace of innovation is so high that every firm must be capable of launching new products in a timely fashion. Time-to-market is a critical variable in determining competitive advantage.
Developing relationships with suppliers, distributors, and customers	The complexity of technology and markets demands that companies develop long-term partnership relations with suppliers to jointly develop products and processes, with distributors to launch detailed marketing campaigns in many countries, and with customers to learn about the utility of their products and to cooperatively develop product modifications and new products.
Fewer but stronger global competitors	The resource and scale needs of global markets are leading to mergers, acquisitions, and greater industry concentration. Larger competitors have greater resources and the ability to implement global strategies over a longer time horizon; this places pressure on firms to grow, seek alliances, and constantly seek partners and acquisition candidates. The alternative is to become a takeover candidate of other companies.
Growing price competition	Products become commodities more rapidly. This, coupled with scale economies, leads to severe price competition. Firms must either reduce costs or innovate constantly to compete on the basis of differentiated products rather than price.
Greater regional integration and government regulation	Increasing regionalization, examples of which include the European Union (EU), NAFTA, and ASEAN trading blocs. Other important influences on strategy include government regulations, such as local content laws and trade barriers (tariff and non-tariff barriers).
Developing a marketing culture	Listening to the customer is paramount; enhancing and using communication capabilities are essential to successful international marketing, as is recognition of other important constituencies, such as the environmental lobby.

Source: K. Kashani, "Marketing Futures: Priorities for a Turbulent Environment," *Long-Range Planning* 28, no. 4 (1995): 87–98.

Euro Disney offers good insights into the challenges of expanding internationally.

For all these reasons, the highly leveraged amusement park, with over $3.4 billion in debt, incurred over $750 million in losses in its first three years and was forced to restructure its operations. Disney had spent heavily on creating a hotel complex around the park outside Paris. However, because the park was only a short train ride away from the center of Paris, many tourists avoided staying at park hotels, opting instead to combine a day trip to the park with a hotel stay in Paris. This is quite unlike Orlando, where Disney is the major attraction and tourists, principally Americans, seem to enjoy planning their holidays around entertainment provided by Disney.

Walt Disney, the parent company of Euro Disney, attempted a variety of cost-cutting strategies in the 1990s and early part of this century, including postponing expansions, deferring royalty payments, lowering admission prices, reducing hotel rates, and cutting costs. Yet French labor laws made it difficult to reduce costs by cutting the workforce. (Plans were to reduce the number of workers from 17,000 to about 12,000.)

In 2002, the $600 million Walt Disney Studio Park opened; but as with the original theme park, attendance figures and profits were much lower than expected. Among other things, Disney had incorrectly forecasted that a large number of Germans would vacation at the park. Moreover, the timing of the grand opening took place just six months after the September 11, 2001, terrorist attacks, which discouraged travel from other European locations. Losses through mid-2004 increased to $134 million, and the firm accumulated $2.7 million in debt. As part of a refinancing deal by Euro Disney creditors, Disney initiated a second round of restructuring in 2004.

Disney has continued to learn from its previous international experiences. In 2005, it opened Hong Kong Disneyland Resort, which has been very well received. Though many of the park's themes and traditions are in common with the other sister parks, the Hong Kong resort has continuously strived to show it has local connections and local impact. It has a particular focus on helping lower income populations and has a strong green and sustainability focus. By its fifth anniversary in 2010, the resort had hosted over 20 million visitors. To celebrate the anniversary, Disney contributed HK$1 million (approximately US$125,000) to a scholarship fund to assist 100 students study hotel and tourism.[2]

Profiting from the Newly Rich—and Extending Beyond: Dickson Poon

To succeed in international marketing, one must understand as well as influence consumers' tastes in different countries. Dickson Poon of Hong Kong has made a fortune estimated at over $1 billion by selling luxury brand-name goods to the newly rich from Japan and the fast-growing countries of Southeast Asia—namely, Hong Kong, Malaysia, Singapore, South Korea, and Taiwan. While working as an apprentice in Geneva at Chopard, a jeweler and maker of fine watches, Poon absorbed the ambience of high-fashion, high-price retailing. Stores were understated, refined, and luxurious, and there was no hard sell. Poon took this style back to Hong Kong, opening a European-type store in Hong Kong's most upscale shopping center. He emphasized attentive service and carefully selected merchandise, concentrating on brands such as Chopard, Rolex, Hermès, and Audemars Piguet. The concept worked. Poon then obtained the Charles Jourdan fashion franchise (adding names such as Polo/Ralph Lauren and Guy Laroche) and, in some cases, obtained licensing rights to manufacture and distribute franchise products in the Far East (and worldwide).

Poon's signature is elegant shops in a prime location. But he has continued his luxury retail focus by extending his reach in the UK. Dickson Concepts

(40 percent owned by Dickson Poon) owns Harvey Nichols, a leading UK retailer. Today, Dickson Concepts operates about 500 stores worldwide with 25 percent of the sales outside Hong Kong and China. His business is vanity, making a profit from it wherever it can be found.[3] See "Dolls for Chinese Children: Marketing in Emerging Markets" as another example of marketing to fast-growing countries.

••• Dolls for Chinese Children: Marketing in Emerging Markets

China has over one billion people, of whom about one-third are between the ages of 3 and 16, totaling about 375 million. Because population-control practices in China typically restricted families to one child, parents and grandparents lavish much love and attention on their only child or grandchild. Among other things, this means they are willing to splurge on toys, despite significantly lower average income compared to developed countries.

Anthony Chirico, who founded Nanuet Entertainment, had been selling U.S. TV shows such as *G.I. Joe* and *Teenage Mutant Ninja Turtles* to China. He saw an opportunity to increase his markets in China by selling Western toys, teaming up with a client who had been marketing the Robotech line of plastic figures in the United States. Chinese children traditionally played with toys made of wood and metal. Chirico speculated the newer, colorful plastic figures priced between $1.60 and $30.00 might be attractive to the Chinese children and their families.

The U.S. toy introduction was accompanied by an 85-episode cartoon series. Chirico began by licensing the TV cartoon show for nominal fees and by persuading the Chinese TV stations to allow his company to insert TV commercials for Robotech toys in the middle of programs. (Chirico also had to overcome the Chinese preference for showing commercials in five-minute blocks at the end of programs.) Those negotiations took three years. The programs also were dubbed in Mandarin Chinese and were attractive to Chinese stations because their themes—family values and world cooperation against aliens—were not in conflict with Chinese values. A Hong Kong–based toy company supervised production of the toys in China and distributed them. Chirico was able to convince the Chinese TV stations to start showing the Robotech cartoon series shortly after the toys went on sale in department stores.

The toys were first introduced into Shanghai and Guangdong, prosperous areas of China, and then into other provinces. As children in Guangdong became exposed to Hong Kong TV, however, their tastes evolved to the likes of Batman. As a result, Robotech toys began to sell better in the distant provinces in northeast China, where newer fads such as Batman had yet to catch on.

Chinese parents' preoccupation with their only child is not limited to buying toys. Chinese parents play English language tapes to their unborn child, hoping to give the child a head start. Later, the child might hear Tang dynasty poetry, music, and the Roman alphabet and numbers, all of which could provide Western marketers with new global marketing opportunities. As China becomes more affluent, Chinese scholars have begun to worry about the possible impact of such lavish attention on their children. A study by Kara Chan notes, with relief, that even young children are not overtly affected by materialism.

Marketing dolls in China was not as straightforward for Mattel, which owns the Barbie doll franchise. Mattel closed its flagship store in 2011, only two years after opening the store in Shanghai. The store was opened amidst giant celebration and included a restaurant and beauty salon so Chinese girls could mimic the Barbie make-up and style. But analysis suggests that Mattel did not adapt the Barbie doll enough. It chose to use clothes designed by Patricia Fields, known for her work on *Sex in the City*. But the clothes style did not resonate with local consumers. Though Mattel remains committed to building the Barbie brand, the store closure was no doubt a setback. Mattel is not the only retailer challenged in China. Home Depot and Best Buy have also closed stores in China.[4]

A Maui Product Goes Global: Maui Jim Sunglasses

Maui Jim is the fastest-growing premium polarized sunglass maker in the world—partly due to its strong international sales. The company was founded in 1980 in Hawaii with a goal to solve the ongoing challenge of eliminating the high-glare of a sunny-weather location, while still being easy to see colors and details through the sunglasses. The company invented PolarizedPlus®—a seven-layer patented process that offers extremely high-quality viewing, yet maximum glare reduction. The concept and the company's sunglasses have been a hit with U.S. golfers, sports pros, and other enthusiasts enjoying the quality and performance of the company's sunglasses. The company has been awarded *Golf Digest's* "Best Sunglass for Golf" and *Advertising Age's* Marketing 50 list of biggest success stories. As the company puts it: "The Aloha Spirit permeates our philosophy at Maui Jim. Our 'ohana' (Hawaiian for family) is passionate about creating the best sunglasses on the planet. Because at the end of the day, we want to see the world at its best—and we know that you do, too, no matter where you live. Aloha, friends!"[5]

But more than U.S. consumers enjoy the performance of Maui Jim sunglasses. The company opened its first international location in Canada soon after moving its world headquarters to Peoria, Illinois, in the mid 1990s. Today, Maui Jim has significant international sales, with offices throughout the world, including France, Australia, Mexico, United Kingdom, Italy, Germany, Spain, Sweden, United Arab Emirates, and India. Its strong export success earned it the U.S. Department of Commerce Export Achievement Certificate, and its CEO, Walter Hester, was awarded the ESA Visionary Award by the European Sunglass Association.[6]

Where the Buyers Are: Iconics, Inc.

Sometimes foreign markets may be the only markets in which a company's products can be sold. Consider water desalination, for instance. About two-thirds of the world's water desalination plants used to convert salt water into freshwater are in Saudi Arabia. These plants use considerable energy and are expensive to run. Saudi Arabia has plentiful energy and high incomes; it is also a country where salt water is plentiful, whereas freshwater is scarce. Ionics, Inc., of Watertown, Massachusetts, has built its business around water desalination, with considerable sales coming from North Africa and the Middle East, not the United States.

Where the Ideas Are—Bringing Foreign Products Home: Gantec, Inc.

Researchers at Michigan-based Gantec, Inc., recognized an interesting characteristic of the Neem trees in sub-Saharan Africa. Other trees struggled during onslaughts of pests and poor weather. But the Neem trees still thrived. Perhaps there was something unique in the properties of the trees that could be utilized to protect other plants from similar stress. Using a proprietary process to extract the biochemical properties from Neem tree seeds, Gantec and related company Organibliss have been able to develop a line of organic plant bionutri-ents and supplements that deliver remarkable performance. Customers are using their products as a substitute for synthetic plant products and find the results are healthier, thicker plants that mature faster—all from natural, plant-based sources. Gantec was selected as one of "Michigan 50 Companies to Watch" and received *Corp! Magazine's* Going Green Award. The company's success helps show the power of combining an overseas product with local technology to develop an entirely new line of products.[7]

Risks and Differences of Foreign Markets: Russia

Getting a product to the consumer can be quite a feat in emerging markets. Ben & Jerry's, the manufacturers of super-premium ice cream in unusual flavors, began a 70 percent joint venture with the company Iceverks, manufacturing and selling ice cream in Karelia, Russia, 700 miles north of Moscow. The companies deliberately waited two years before expanding into Moscow because they did not want quality to suffer because of poor logistics and supply problems. There were shortages of refrigerated trucks, which had to be imported. Franchisees lacked freezers, and Iceverks had to sell or lease equipment to them so that ice cream could be kept frozen. Franchisees and their employees had to be taught to be polite to customers and to restock inventory before completely running out of certain flavors. Franchisees were selected based on personal contacts and trust. Iceverks chose a small Moscow distributor, Vessco, because key managers at the two companies had been classmates. Despite these efforts, continued Russian economic difficulties made profitable operation a distant dream, ultimately leading Ben & Jerry's to divest from its Russian venture and consider U.S. expansion instead.[8]

A somewhat different tack was taken by Mary Kay in selling cosmetics in Russia. With economic liberalization, Russian women began to seek Western cosmetics. At the same time, several Russian state-owned enterprises privatized, and Russian women were often getting laid off in downsizings. These women were seeking new jobs and stable income sources. Mary Kay thus found a ready-made environment for its products—reasonably priced American cosmetics—as well as for its sales approach of multilayered marketing. Relying on women acting as independent representatives, buying cosmetics for themselves at 40 percent off retail and then selling them in small groups of friends and acquaintances, Mary Kay found Russian women eager to take on the job of selling its products. This was particularly true because a Mary Kay representative could earn $300 to $400 a month compared to the average salary for Russian women of a little over $100 a month. Mary Kay has had to train its representatives, of course, with more experienced representatives training new recruits in areas such as understanding the quality and use of products, being well groomed, being polite and complimentary to potential clients, and doing basic bookkeeping. Representatives from more distant locales face further difficulties, having to come to Moscow to replenish their cosmetics supplies.[9] Mary Kay's Russia strategy has paid off: Today it counts Russia as one of its top four largest markets. The other three are China, Mexico, and the United States.[10]

Learning from the Examples   ● ● ●

Companies market their products and services internationally for several reasons:

- They want to take advantage of the potential of world markets. Disney, Dickson Concepts, Ionics, and Maui Jim have all benefited from expanding their foreign market potential.

- They want to diversify geographically.

- They want to use excess production capacity and take advantage of a low-cost position due to experience-curve economies and economies of scale as seen in the Robotech launch in China.

- A product can be near the end of its life cycle in the domestic market while just beginning to generate growth abroad. Dickson Poon's export of brand-name luxury goods to the Far East is an example of taking advantage of the general rise in conspicuous consumption that accompanies prosperity. Selling Robotech toys to China is an example of responding to lagging product cycles in developing countries.

- Sometimes overseas markets are a source of new products and ideas, as seen with Gantec. Companies in foreign markets can become joint-venture partners providing capital and market access.

- Tested market entry methods can work in emerging markets, as shown by Mary Kay in Russia. Emerging markets, however, require patience and sometimes innovative market entry modes, as in the case of Ben & Jerry's in Russia. International marketing can bring expected risks, such as international currency risk, but also unexpected risks.

- One of the most difficult aspects of international marketing is developing products with universal appeal, as illustrated by Disney. Success in one country does not always translate to success in another country, as Euro Disney illustrates.

- There are many ways to enter foreign markets, as the examples suggest, ranging from simple exporting to more complex and risky investments involving manufacturing, marketing, and top management.

Trends in International Marketing

As with most disciplines, the task and challenges for the international marketing manager are continually changing and shaped by trends. Following is a short discussion of some of the most important trends affecting international marketing.

The role of emerging (and emerged) economies as both consumer and competitor has increased. The rising middles classes in China, India, and other emerging countries bring enormous opportunities to companies seeking to expand their global sales. In many cases these countries have larger consumer sectors than the home markets of some companies. Yet these same emerging companies are also generating new global competitors that are and will continue to be strong competitors to companies based in the emerged economies of the West and elsewhere. Examples of these companies are highlighted throughout this book.

The service sector shows continued growth and strength. Too often global sales is associated with the sales of products. As we discuss in Chapter 13, the service sector is actually the fastest-growing segment of internationalization, representing about 20 percent of world trade.[11] And it is a sector in which some countries with long-standing trade deficits in products, such as the United States, actually have a trade surplus.

Franchising offers growth opportunities. Related to the preceding issue—franchising is a fast-growing opportunity for successful companies. Many markets, such as Brazil, are opening up to foreign franchises. Local brands may dominate now, but evidence suggests that foreign franchises have tremendous growth opportunities.[12]

Ongoing change and increasing risk are the new normal. The global business environment continues to change, seemingly faster and faster. Low communication costs, faster product development cycles,

The continued growth of the global service sector is an important trend affecting international marketing.

new competitors each day—all are examples of the changing dynamics in the international marketplace. As we discuss in Chapters 2 through 5, this changing environment puts even greater pressure on the international marketing manager to understand these changes and their potential for increased risk.

Increasing economic integration and cooperation between countries mean opportunity and risk. Countries are signing new free-trade agreements at considerable speed. Countries are also moving toward significant economic and political integration as seen in the enlarging European Union. As we discuss in Chapter 2, this move toward increasing economic integration can be a good thing for global firms because it means lower trade barriers and low costs of doing business. But it can also mean new competitors or increased strengths of local competitors. Companies must recognize these new opportunities, but also the risks.

The global financial crisis of 2008–2009 has undermined any growing support for globalization. Related to the issue of change and risk is the issue that the global financial crisis of recent years has led to a renewed concern about globalization. The crisis has led to significant federal and local government budgets deficits, leading to program cuts and job loss. Naturally, workers question the logic of open borders. This places new stress on politicians to understand the role of globalization and how best to leverage its benefit. Likewise, global firms must recognize and address these concerns. As we discuss in Chapter 5, corporate social responsibility and commitments toward sustainability may be important tools.

Small can be big. As seen with Maui Jim, relatively small companies can be big international players. As discussed in The *World Is Flat* by Thomas Friedman,[13] the presence of various "flatteners" has meant even small companies can act like big multinationals. Probably the single best example is the availability of a company's website to be a tremendous international marketing asset, yet often at very low cost.

New communication technologies and social media are important influences. From Facebook to Twitter, and Skype to the iPad, these new technologies and social media companies are having an important impact on international marketing. Marketers must recognize their growing influence and integrate new technologies into their global business plan. (See "Internet, Social Networks, and Internationalization" box for illustrations of this trend.)

Product life cycles are shortening. In years past, a firm could often leverage a product's life cycle internationally by taking mature or even declining products into new foreign markets where consumption of the same product may be growing. However, due to technology and faster product development cycles, consumers are increasingly demanding the "best and latest" in all global markets. As we discuss in various examples throughout the book, companies can no longer expect to introduce new products only in high-income countries. Indeed, some firms are choosing emerging economies for new product launches even prior to their home-country launch. Similarly, products developed initially for use only in an emerging economy, such as India, are later being released for well-developed countries.[14]

Import and export regulations are increasing. Terrorism concerns and the need to limit weapons of mass destruction and nuclear proliferation mean governments will continue to enforce and likely increase import and export regulations. As we discuss in Chapters 3 and 11, international firms must understand these regulations and ensure they are compliant. Otherwise, they risk significant fines and potential loss of import or export privileges.

Internet, Social Networks, and Internationalization

The Internet has dramatically impacted how companies expand internationally. The Internet allows companies to directly offer their goods globally via their own websites or vendors with a global reach selling their products. Further, the Internet has eased communication between people worldwide with email and voice/video communication such as Skype replacing expensive "snail" mail services, video conferencing, and even foreign travel. These developments make it quicker, easier, and cheaper than ever before to expand internationally.[15]

Networks—personal and business—have always been important facilitators of international expansion. Knowing the right people in foreign markets provides critical foreign market and internationalization process knowledge and provides access to potential partners in foreign markets.[16] Today, the task of building and maintaining networks is easier than ever due to global social networking websites such as Facebook, LinkedIn, Orkut (Brazil), Renren (China), and many other social networking sites.

Social networking also leads to opportunities for companies to market their products and services through social media. In conjunction with the 2012 London Olympics, UK-based Cadbury is using social media as part of a worldwide marketing campaign in which users search for GPS-enhanced balls, upload photos of themselves with a ball to Cadbury's Facebook or Twitter pages, and then pass the ball along to someone else. The ball that travels the farthest and involves the most people will win. This global competition engages Cadbury's consumers, gains attention for Cadbury, and also promotes the upcoming Olympics and Paralympics.[17]

However, using social media is a two-way street that has risks as well as benefits. For example, Nestlé was recently attacked by environmental groups over claims that the palm oil used in its Kit Kat candy bars comes from firms in Indonesia that are destroying the rainforests.[18] Greenpeace International and other environmental groups effectively used social media to spread the word and put pressure on Nestlé, which eventually canceled orders from the problematic suppliers. As a result, those suppliers, such as Golden Agri-Resources Limited (GAR), have begun measures to obtain sustainable sources of palm oil.[19] Thus, while social media helped to save the Indonesian rainforests, it also damaged Nestlé's brand name and brought a problem of social corporate responsibility into the spotlight.

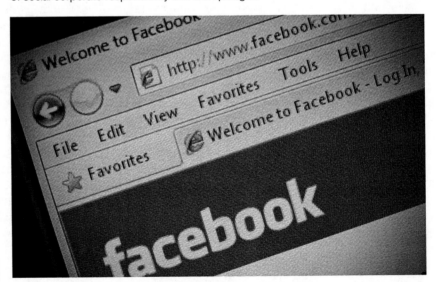

The increased use of social media is an important trend affecting companies as they grow internationally.

The Approach of This Book

This book is divided into three major themes: the global environment in which international marketing is conducted, the implementation of international marketing, and the overall management of international marketing. These themes are reflected in the book's three sections. Part 1 discusses the world environment in which international marketing is practiced, Part 2 analyzes the management and execution of marketing in this multinational context, and Part 3 deals with planning and coordinating the international marketing program.

Part 1, "The Global Business Environment" (Chapters 1–5). In domestic business studies, consideration of the environment plays a critical though somewhat unrecognized role in the behavior of a firm. A number of "environmental" courses deal with topics such as business and society, business and government, business conditions, and business law. In the functional courses, too much attention is paid to the external environment of the firm. Marketing, for example, discusses buyer behavior, demographic trends, competition, laws regulating pricing and promotion, developments in retailing, use of technology, and so on. For the international marketing manager, the global environment involves similar issues, but it is broader and more complex because of interactions among nations. The global environment, its impact on marketing, and the way marketing affects the global environment are the focus of Part 1.

Part 2, "Global Marketing Management" (Chapters 6–13). The various functions of marketing as they are performed in the international environment are discussed in Part 2. An examination of the problems peculiar to international marketing should also help broaden a reader's general understanding of marketing. The foreign environment dealt with in Part 1 is seen as the key variable in international marketing. A large part of the discussion centers on international marketing by manufacturers. However, the specific international marketing problems of service industries are covered in Chapter 13. In addition, Part 2 discusses the critical task of international marketing research and highlights important data sources in support of that research (Chapter 6).

Part 3, "Strategy, Planning, Coordination, and Control of Global Marketing" (Chapters 14–15). A final critical aspect of international marketing management, covered in Part 3, is the task of integrating and coordinating many individual national marketing programs into an effective multinational operation. These chapters in this part discuss and illustrate how firms develop their global strategy and the steps necessary to implement that strategy. Also included is a discussion of the organizational and situational analysis that must be done. Chapter 15 discusses the planning, organization, and control of international marketing. This discussion includes approaches to how a firm conducts its short- and long-term planning, as well as how a firm structures its international operations.

SUMMARY

Marketing involves many responsibilities for the marketing manager, including customer identification (who, where, difference between current and future customers, and so on), product development, pricing, distribution, advertising, and promotion. The international marketing manager also deals with these same responsibilities except within a global context. A considerable challenge is international marketing within the constraints set by the global business environment.

International marketing is, by definition, the act of marketing across national boundaries. One difference between domestic and international marketing is that the latter includes the task of marketing between countries, as well as within each country.

The complexity of international marketing is due largely to two factors: global competition and the global environment. These two factors make the task of international marketing significantly more complex than wholly domestic marketing.

Examples in the text help illustrate why companies expand internationally. Reasons include reaching more consumers in world markets, diversifying, lowering costs of production, taking advantage of product life cycle opportunities, finding new products and ideas in foreign markets, and taking a domestic product or service with global appeal to new markets. These opportunities enhance a firm's long-run profitability.

The tasks and challenges for the international marketing manager are continually being shaped by changes in the global environment and global trends in marketing. These include opportunities in emerging markets; global growth of the service sector, including increased use of franchising; the constant need to adapt to change; increasing opportunities from economic integration; the need to understand the impact of the 2008–2009 global financial crisis; the ability to leverage technology so small and midsized firms can compete with larger firms; the increasing use of social media to support global marketing; the shortening of the product life cycle due to technology advances; and the increased need for firms to be compliant with import and export government regulations.

KEY TERMS

foreign marketing	global marketing	marketing management
4 P's of marketing	international marketing	point of sale (POS)
global environment	marketing	

NASBITE CGBP TOPICS COVERED IN THIS CHAPTER

Note: For full details of the alignment of each chapter with the NASBITE CGBP, be sure to review the information provided in the section "Studying for the NASBITE CGBP Exam."

CGBP Rubric	Topic
01/03/01:	environmental factors affecting international strategies (e.g., political, legal/regulatory, sociocultural)
02/01/01:	internal resources (e.g., export readiness assessment, goals and preferences of senior management, experiences and capabilities of employees, technical and production capabilities)
02/06/01:	customer expectations and cultural requirements
02/06/02:	product life cycle implications (or strategies)
02/06/03:	(new) product development modification process

QUESTIONS AND RESEARCH

1. What is international marketing? How does it differ from domestic marketing?
2. Why is international marketing important to most firms? What are motivations for expanding globally?

3. Consider the examples described in the section "The Global Marketplace." Compare and contrast the international marketing actions of the firms discussed. Focus on their choices in the areas of products, market segments, the sequential choice of countries to sell to, pricing, the growth of and response to competition, and the use of licensing and joint ventures. Discuss your findings.

4. How do large U.S. multinationals compete in the global marketplace? Why do most of them sell more from their foreign subsidiaries than through exports?

5. "Global marketing is a shift in perspective." Explain this statement.

6. Choose a prominent publicly held company in your geographic area. Find out what its total foreign revenues have been for the past five years and how much of its foreign sales come from overseas operations and how much come from exporting from the home market. Also study the comments about international markets made by the chair of the company in its annual report. How important is international marketing to this firm?

7. The book offers a number of trends in international marketing. Pick one of these trends. Explain how it might impact a firm as it grow internationally. Find one or two examples of companies that recognize the trend and have taken action. Discuss your findings.

PROJECT OVERVIEW: TEAM PROJECT ASSIGNMENT

At the end of each chapter, this book incorporates tasks to be completed as part of a team project. It could also be completed individually. The goal is to develop an international marketing plan for a company (called the "client" within the context of this project). Your client will either be a company that is assigned to the team, or you may do this exercise on behalf of your own firm. The assignment within each chapter will take the team through the process of developing the marketing plan.

HERE IS AN OVERVIEW FROM EACH CHAPTER

Chapter 1: Company introduction and international Strengths, Weaknesses, Opportunities, and Threats (SWOT) analysis

Chapter 2: Economic environmental analysis

Chapter 3: Political–legal environmental analysis

Chapter 4: Cultural analysis

Chapter 5: Discussion of ethics and implications for your client

Chapter 6: Initial data research tasks

Chapter 7: Development of the foreign market selection matrix and final market selection

Chapter 8: Selection of foreign entry mode and initial partner identification

Chapter 9: Discussion of product policy for your client

Chapter 10: Discussion of international branding, advertising, PR, and sales implications for your client

Chapter 11: Identification of supply chain issues for your client

Chapter 12: Discussion of pricing and trade finance issues

Chapter 13: If applicable, discussion of unique issues associated with global services

Chapter 14: Initial work on the final plan including strategy

Chapter 15: Completion of the final plan including organizational implications

If this team or individual report is being done as a class project, your instructor will define the specifics of the final report and/or presentation. However, as a suggestion, a typical outline of the international marketing plan would be as follows:

1. Client introduction: product/service description.

2. Client international SWOT analysis. Explain from an internal perspective the strengths and weaknesses for the firm as it grows internationally. From an outside industry perspective, outline the opportunities and threats for the firms as it expands.

3. Foreign market selection matrix. This would include a copy of the spreadsheet developed from Chapter 7 including a list of the initial data, sources, justifications for weights, and a related discussion on issues associated with creating the matrix.

4. Countries for further expansion. Depending on the needs of the client or the parameters of the class project, you are to select the top countries for expansion by your client. This will be followed by the individual international marketing plans for each country.

3. Detailed reports on your selected countries, including the following for each country:

   - Strengths of the country
   - Weaknesses/threats of the country
   - Potential size of the market for your client (as best as can be estimated—perhaps in terms of total number of consumers or dollar value of the market)
   - Proposed entry mode (Chapter 8)
   - Any potential foreign partners (Chapter 8)
   - Product adaptation or standardization policy* (Chapter 9)
   - Branding and promotion strategies* (Chapter 10)
   - Supply chain issues* (Chapter 11)
   - Discussion of pricing and trade finance* (Chapter 12)
   - Possible timetable for international expansion into the markets*
   - Final recommendations, concerns, future issues, and so on that may apply to your client including overall strategy (Chapter 14) and planning, organizational, and control issues (Chapter 15).

If your client is a service company, you would also include a discussion from Chapter 13 of implications for your client.

*Issues that could also be grouped together as one separate section if needed, rather than by country.

 CHAPTER 1 TEAM PROJECT ASSIGNMENT: Client Introduction and Research

For this chapter, your goal is to write an introduction of your client, including company history, product/service overview, competitive position, and discussion of the industry. You should also develop an international SWOT analysis that essentially indicates an internal and external analysis from the perspective of the firm expanding internationally. The internal analysis would be internal strengths that will help the company expand internationally, as well as weaknesses that will be a barrier. The external analysis would include industry threats and opportunities that will impact the client as it expands internationally.

CASE 1.1 IKEA

IKEA, founded in Sweden in 1943, designs and sells inexpensive furniture and accessories. It operates over 300 of its no-frills furniture stores in over 35 countries with 2010 sales exceeding US$30 billion. With stores across Europe, the United States, Canada, Asia, and the Middle East, IKEA hosts over 800 million visitors per year. IKEA's concept is straightforward: Sell functional, well-designed furniture at prices so low that everyone can afford it, thus creating better living for its customers. On the marketing side, IKEA sells inexpensive, ready-to-assemble, well-made furniture to customers who are willing to transport it home. On the manufacturing side, IKEA designs the furniture and then subcontracts manufacturing to low-cost sources around the world that can produce high-quality products. Because the furniture itself is sold in kit form, the pieces actually are made in different locations, with IKEA purchasing from manufacturers offering the lowest prices.

IKEA's furniture comes boxed and must be assembled by the customer at home. Customers pick up the boxed kits from an adjacent self-service warehouse. IKEA stores tend to be located near freeway exits and outside cities, where space is available at low rates. That allows the firm to provide ample parking, and customers can easily get in and out of the store without encountering traffic jams. IKEA also cooperates with local car rental companies to help customers rent small trucks to transport their purchases.

The furniture design is Scandinavian modern, with textiles in pastel colors. The international product line is less varied than that sold within the home markets of Scandinavia. Over the years, IKEA has won design awards, designed furniture based on eighteenth-century Swedish furnishings, and designed special furniture for children. IKEA's market is the "young of all ages." It has a flair for marketing to young couples with children. Its warehouses are festively decorated, it provides day care for children, and it features inexpensive restaurants. The focus on child care and in-store restaurants is to keep people in the stores until they buy something, preventing their exit because of bored and unmanageable children or the desire to get a meal.

The emphasis is on low-priced furniture, priced 30 to 50 percent below the competition's fully assembled furniture. From market to market, prices vary somewhat for the same basic product, but not greatly.

IKEA's founder, Ingvar Kamprad, grew up on a farm in southern Sweden and began a business selling flower seeds and ballpoint pens through mail-order catalogs. He insists that employees be "cost-conscious to the point of stinginess." He has written, "Too many new and beautifully designed products can be afforded by only a small group of better-off people. We have decided to side with the many."

IKEA has always been innovative in selling furniture. When it entered Sweden in the early 1950s, furniture retailers were small, purchasing furniture to customer specifications and placing orders with a manufacturer only after receiving a commitment from customers. Furniture was expensive and bought in sets (for example, a dining room suite), and credit was an important sales tool. IKEA entered the market with large showrooms outside cities, the option to buy one piece of furniture at a time, self-service for cash, and low prices.

When IKEA entered Switzerland with its first store near Zurich, it had to decide whether to rely on the IKEA company name, to position itself as a Scandinavian furniture company (in which case it might be confused with Danish furniture), or to identify IKEA as a distinctive Swedish company. IKEA knew it would have to address Swiss concerns (the Swiss were perceived to be a conservative group) about a Swedish company and its way of selling furniture.

IKEA prepared a set of ads that showcased typical conservative Swiss opinions of and reactions to IKEA. The ads consisted of letters sent by a conservative Herr Bunzli to IKEA, saying what he thought of the company's ideas and way of selling furniture in Switzerland. The aim of the campaign was to joke about the old-fashioned values of the Swiss and appeal to those who wanted to change. The ads exemplified IKEA's philosophy: to take advantage of being a foreigner and to use attention-getting and provocative advertising. Managers in all countries are required to follow that advertising strategy, though they can use local agencies, following guidelines from headquarters.

The first year IKEA was in Switzerland, 650,000 people visited its stores. The next year IKEA entered the huge German market and subsequently France, drawing on its experiences with the German- and French-speaking parts of Switzerland. IKEA continues to open stores at a rapid rate, averaging 15 new stores a year.

IKEA has a special organization structure dedicated to smooth and speedy entry into foreign markets. This foreign-expansion group has several key subunits: a European deco-manager, a manager of construction, and a first-year group whose responsibility is to create and manage new overseas outlets during the first year. The construction manager selects a site and supervises the creation of the new store, overseeing inventories, installation of fixtures, communications networks, and so on. The first-year manager oversees hiring, reassignment of experienced employees from other IKEA locations, training, and advertising campaigns and decides on the "assortment" of product line to be carried. Furniture is typically ordered from a central warehouse in Sweden and starts arriving three months before opening day.

Planning of a new outlet begins about ten months before opening day. Because IKEA has expanded rapidly, the first-year group cannot spend a whole year nurturing new outlets, as originally envisaged. Training has to be speeded up to allow local management to take over sooner. The staff begins working about two months before opening day to familiarize themselves with IKEA's mode of operations and product line, which ensures a smooth opening. Advertising begins at about the same time. The staff generally take a trip to IKEA's outlets in Scandinavia, culminating in a press conference the day before store inauguration.

IKEA AND THE UNITED STATES

IKEA entered Canada in 1976. With nine stores in Canada by 1985, the United States seemed the next logical market. California was its first pick; Boston, its second choice. Executives who set out to study the California market encountered some obstacles, however. California had unique standards for upholstered furniture that would have raised costs by 15 percent. California's system of unitary taxation by which it taxed its "share" of IKEA's worldwide income was unpalatable.

Boston was attractive because of its huge student and young professional populations. However, government regulations and lack of responsiveness on the part of state officials led the company to establish its first warehouse and retail operation in suburban Philadelphia. Local government officials made special efforts to convince IKEA to establish there, with a goal of increasing jobs and tax revenues. Through the Greater Philadelphia International Network, a small-business-backed office that tries to attract foreign investment, IKEA officials were introduced to bankers and real estate brokers, given a helicopter tour of the city, and invited to receptions every evening of their three-day stay.

Location, of course, is critical to this kind of company. The Philadelphia market area, which includes Delaware and southern New Jersey, had large numbers of young middle-income families and relatively inexpensive commercial real estate. The Network helped IKEA find space in a mall next to a turnpike exit in the suburb of Plymouth Meeting. "Pennsylvania Turnpike, Exit 25" is the sort of address it seeks. (Forty percent of its customers were likely to be from out of state.)

Beyond the issue of headquarter location and first store, IKEA recognized it needed to adapt its policies, stores, and products to better suit U.S. consumer needs. Following are examples of the adaptations:

- It had to adapt its furniture to larger American physiques; for example, Americans found its beds too narrow.
- It had to specify product dimensions in inches rather than the metric system.
- It had to develop suites of furniture to cater to the American penchant for buying furniture as a group for the bedroom, dining room, living room, kitchen, and so on.
- It had to redesign its furniture for U.S. use patterns—for example, deeper cabinets to hold larger dinner plates and larger glasses, as Americans preferred.
- Because long queues and out-of-stock items led to disgruntled customers, IKEA upgraded its point-of-sale systems and added more checkout stations to speed up customer processing. It also increased local manufacturing to prevent inventory shortages caused by a lengthy supply chain.
- Exchange rate appreciation could render its imported furniture more expensive and at odds with its marketing message of selling affordable furniture. The solution was to increase its sourcing of locally made furniture, working with and developing U.S. suppliers to the point where they accounted for 45 percent of products sold at U.S. IKEA stores, up from 15 percent formerly.
- It matched U.S. customer service expectations by accepting a more generous returns policy than in Europe and by offering next-day delivery to attract customers who did not want to transport their own furniture, a key aspect of the IKEA model in Europe.

The U.S. expansion has been a strong success with over 35 stores by 2010.

IKEA clearly focuses on customer value. It is concerned with two questions: How can the product be improved? How can we become a better place to work? The company expects all of its employees to be thrifty; even the head of its North American operations flies economy class to Scandinavia. The point is that anything that does not add to customer value is to be avoided.

Questions and Research

1. As discussed in this chapter, international marketing is a complex task, and highly differentiated from domestic marketing. Using Table 1-1 as a guide, discuss the international marketing strategic issues for IKEA as it expanded globally.
2. What is the basis for IKEA's success globally?
3. Discuss the issues IKEA faced when expanding into the United States. How did it address these challenges? What evidence is there today that it continues to incorporate these issues into its U.S. strategy?
4. Of the international marketing trends discussed in this chapter, which are the issues most likely to impact IKEA as it continues its global growth?
5. IKEA expanded into China in the late 1990s. Research IKEA's efforts in China. How has the company's strategy been different from that in other countries? What have been its challenges in China?
6. How does IKEA's experience in China illustrate issues in international marketing?

NOTES

1. "Step Right Up, Monsieur," *New York Times*, August 23, 1995.

2. See "Euro Disney's Fiscal Loss to Spur Study of Woes by U.S. Concern," *Wall Street Journal*, July 9, 1993; "Euro Disney's Loss Narrowed in Fiscal 1994," *Wall Street Journal*, November 4, 1994; "Euro Disney's Prince Charming?" *Business Week*, June 13, 1994; "A Faint 18—International Marketing Squeak from Euro-Mickey," *Economist*, July 29, 1995; "Euro Disney Posts First Annual Profit," *Wall Street Journal*, November 16, 1995; "California; For Struggling Euro Disney, Help from Abroad," *Los Angeles Times*, June 10, 2004; "Disney Gives Plans to Aid European Parks," *New York Times*, July 1, 2004; "Hong Kong Disneyland Resort Celebrates Its 5th Anniversary with the Community," press release September 11, 2010, Hong Kong Disneyland (http://news-en.hongkongdisneyland.com/PressReleases/pressreleases.aspx), retrieved March 3, 2011.

3. Andrew Tanzer. "Keep the Calculators Out of Sight," *Forbes*, March 20, 1989; Louise Lucas, "Dickson Concepts Faces Loss as Recession Bites," *Financial Times*, December 11, 1998. "Dickson Concepts (International) Limited Company Profile," Yahoo Finance (http://biz .yahoo.com/ic/104/104953.html), retrieved March 3, 2011.

4. Andrew Tanzer, "China's Dolls," *Forbes*, December 21, 1992; "Study This, Baby: Chinese Fetuses Bear Heavy Course Loads," *Wall Street Journal*, February 8, 1994; Kara Chan, "Materialism among Chinese Children in Hong Kong," International *Journal of Advertising & Marketing to Children* 4, no. 4 (July 2003): 47–62; Data query: http://devdata.worldbank.org/data-query, accessed January 27, 2004. "Barbie Fails to Charm China Fans as Shanghai's Pink Store Closes," *Financial Times*, March 8, 2011, p. 1.

5. Maui Jim corporate profile (http://www.mauijim.com/about-us), retrieved March 3, 2011.

6. Profile of Walter Hester and Maui Jim, Westminster College (http://www.westminster-mo .edu/news/news/Pages/CEOofMauiJimSunglassestoLecture.aspx), accessed March 3, 2011.

7. www.gantecgreen.com and corporate literature.

8. "Ben & Jerry's Is Trying to Smooth Out Distribution in Russia as It Expands," *Wall Street Journal*, September 9, 1995; The History of Ben & Jerry's Ice Cream (http://www.benjerry .com/our_company/ about_us/ our_history/timeline/index.cfm); Unilever Company History (http:// www.unilever.com/company/unilevertoday).

9. "For Mary Kay Sales Reps in Russia, Hottest Shade Is the Color of Money," *Wall Street Journal*, August 30, 1995; "Mary Kay's Eastern Front," Forbes.com, September 13, 2003; Mary Kay, Russia (http://www.marykay.ru).

10. "MARY KAY: The Company 2010 United States Fact Sheet," corporate website www.marykay .com (http://www.marykay.com/content/company/images/cpk_thecompany.pdf), accessed April 12, 2011.

11. "Services: Rules for Growth and Investment," World Trade Organization (http://www.wto .org/english/thewto_e/whatis_e/tif_e/agrm6_e.htm), accessed November 21, 2010.

12. For a good discussion of a specific example, see the U.S. Department of Commerce "Brazil—Country Commercial Guide" at www.export.gov.

13. Thomas Friedman. *The World Is Flat: A Brief History of the Twenty-First Century* (New York: Farrar, Straus and Giroux, 2005).

14. For an interesting example, visit www.trendsetter.com and view the February 2010 edition for a discussion of a product in India launched elsewhere.

15. S. Tamer Cavusgil. "From the Editor in Chief," *Journal of International Marketing* 2, no. 3 (1994): 4–6.

16. Paul D. Ellis. "Social Ties and Foreign Market Entry," *Journal of International Business Studies* 31, no. 3 (2000): 443–469.

17. Charlotte McEleny. "Cadbury Launches Worldwide Game for Spots v Stripes," *New Media Age*, December 9, 2010, p. 6.

18. Emily Steel. "Nestlé Takes a Beating on Social-Mediasites," *Wall Street Journal*, March 29, 2010, vol. 255, no. 72, p. B5.

19. "Golden Agri Vows to Stop Destroying Forests for Palm Oil," *Jakarta Post*, February 10, 2011, p. 13.

chapter

2 The Global Economic Environment

The international marketing manager encounters a whole new set of challenges when selling and marketing overseas. The global business environment is different from a domestic environment in generally three ways: economic, political–legal, and cultural. These differences also have ethical considerations. In this chapter we discuss the first of these issues: the global economic environment. Later chapters review the political–legal, cultural, and ethical issues. Understanding these important elements of the global business environment helps to highlight the differences in the global business environment for the international marketing manager.

The main goals of this chapter are to ● ● ●

1. Discuss how the global economic environment differs from the domestic economic environment.

2. Analyze different international trade theories and their influence on government policies in support or constraint of trade.

3. Discuss the balance of payments (BoP) as a leading indicator of the international economic health of a country.

4. Describe how the World Trade Organization (WTO), the United Nations Conference on Trade and Development (UNCTAD), and other global organizations influence trade.

5. Detail the five levels of regional economic integration and their implications for the international marketing manager.

Challenging Differences in the Global Economic Environment

It is critical that the international marketing manager recognize and understand the differences in economies of the world marketplace. Misunderstanding the global economic environment can lead to lost opportunities and increased risks. For example, underestimating the impact of tariff and non-tariff barriers could lead to significantly lower sales, or even failure, in a foreign market such as Brazil, which has considerable trade barriers in place to protect its local industries.

Exchange rate instability is another example of how the economic landscape differs for the international marketing manager. The Argentina peso devaluation in the early 2000s illustrates the challenges associated with fluctuating exchange rates. The dramatic change in exchange rates helped firms operating in Argentina and encouraged investment as lower labor costs attracted U.S. firms such as Oracle.[1] However, the peso devaluation hurt foreign firms exporting to Argentina. For example, U.S. exports to Argentina fell from nearly US$4.7 billion in 2000 to US$1.6 billion in 2002.[2] Though specific strategies, such as using a different foreign market entry mode, can mitigate the effects of these economic forces, the first step is recognizing these economic differences.

The key topics associated with the global economic environment are

- **International trade theory.** Firms expanding internationally must appreciate how their international activities match a country's goals for international trade.
- **Balance of payments.** This is a leading indicator of the international economic health of a country and may directly influence a firm's expansion decisions.
- **Government policy and trade.** Firms are directly impacted by government policies in areas such as tariffs and non-tariff barriers.
- **Institutions in the world economy.** Institutions such as the World Trade Organization and the World Bank greatly influence trade policies and ultimately can influence a firm's global strategy.
- **Regional economic integration.** Firms generally benefit from economic integration because costs of doing business are lower. However, economic integration can also lead to stronger competitors.

The next sections look at each of these topics in detail.

The Argentina peso crisis in the early 2000s is a good example of the challenging economic environment a firm may encounter when expanding internationally.

International Trade Theory

As a firm begins to expand internationally, it does so within the constraints (or incentives) that foreign governments impose. Understanding the perspectives that governments may have on trade helps a firm recognize the opportunities and risks it faces when expanding internationally.

International trade theory seeks answers to a few basic questions: Why do nations trade? What goods do they trade? Nations trade for economic, political, and cultural reasons. However, the principal economic basis for international trade is difference in price; that is, a nation can buy some goods more cheaply from other nations than it can make them. In a sense, nations face the same "make-or-buy" decision that firms do. Just as most firms do not seek complete vertical integration but buy many materials and supplies from outside firms, so most nations decide against complete self-sufficiency (or **autarky**) in favor of buying cheaper goods from other countries.

Adam Smith, the eighteenth-century pioneer of political economics, illustrated this point: When discussing the advantages to England in trading manufactured goods for Portugal's wine, he noted that grapes could be grown "under glass" (in greenhouses) in England but that to do so would lead to England's having both less wine and fewer manufacturers than if it specialized instead in manufacturers.

> **autarky**
>
> Self-sufficiency—in this context, in a country's production of goods and services.

Absolute Advantage

Nations—and, in fact, people—have an **absolute advantage** when it comes to making or doing certain things. Florida has a climate that is better suited for growing oranges than Alaska does and, therefore, can grow oranges less expensively. Japan has a workforce that is more skilled in producing highly sophisticated robots than does the Philippines. And although a physician may be able to install a new light fixture, a licensed electrician is likely able to do it better and faster. In fact, Adam Smith's major conclusion was that the "wealth of nations" is derived from the division of labor and specialization.[3] Applied to the international picture, this means trade rather than self-sufficiency.

> **absolute advantage**
>
> A country's ability to produce a good at a lower cost, in terms of real resources, than another country.

Comparative Advantage

It has been said that price differences are the immediate basis of international trade. The firm that decides whether to make or buy also considers price as a principal variable. But why do nations have different prices on goods? Prices differ because countries producing the goods have different costs. And why do countries have different costs? Swedish economist Bertil Ohlin came up with an explanation generally held to be valid: Different countries have dissimilar prices and costs on goods because different goods require a different mix of factors in their production and because countries differ in their supply of these factors.[4] Thus, in Adam Smith's wine example mentioned earlier, Portugal's wine would be cheaper than England's wine because Portugal has a relatively better endowment of wine-making factors (for example, land and climate) than England does.

International trade theories help to explain patterns of trade between countries, such as why a country with a high-tech, skilled workforce would export high-tech products and import low-tech commodities.

This explanation comprises the principle of **comparative advantage**— namely, that a country tends to produce and export those goods in which it has the greatest comparative advantage and import those goods in which it has the least comparative advantage. As Adam Smith suggested, nations maximize their supply of goods by concentrating production where it is most efficient and trading some of those products for imported products where production is least efficient. An examination of the exports and imports of most nations tends to support this theory.

> **comparative advantage**
>
> A country's ability to produce a good at a lower cost, relative to other goods, compared to another country; a country tends to produce and export those goods in which it has the greatest comparative advantage and import those goods in which it has the least comparative advantage.

Product Life Cycle

product life cycle

When referring to international trade and product patterns, a trade cycle that many markets go through wherein one nation is initially an exporter, then loses its export markets, and finally may become an importer of the product.

A refinement in trade theory is related to the **product life cycle**, which in marketing refers to the consumption pattern for a product. When applied to international trade theory, product life cycle refers primarily to international trade and production patterns. According to this concept, many products go through a trade cycle wherein one nation is initially an exporter of a product, then loses its export markets, and finally may become an importer of the product. Empirical studies have demonstrated the validity of the model for some kinds of manufactured goods. This theory is helpful in identifying when a company may want to consider overseas manufacturing, especially as a product matures.

Outlined next are the four phases in the production and trade cycle, with the United States as an example. In this example, assume that a U.S. firm has developed a high-tech product. What follows is

Phase 1: The United States exports the product.

Phase 2: Foreign production starts.

Phase 3: Foreign production becomes competitive in export markets.

Phase 4: Import competition begins.

In Phase 1, a product's innovation is likely to be related to the needs of the home market. A firm usually serves its home market first and also produces the product locally. Local production also provides the firm with easy communication to suppliers and customers, who provide important feedback for a firm as it identifies manufacturing and usage factors related to the new product. As the firm begins to fill home-market needs, it starts to export the new product, seizing its first-mover advantage, and to increase sales. In our example, assume the U.S. firm is exporting to Europe.

product innovation

A new or substantially different way of meeting customers' needs through the development of a new product.

In Phase 2, importing countries gain familiarity with the new product. Gradually, producers in wealthy countries begin producing the product for their own markets. (Most **product innovations** begin in one developed country and then move to other developed countries.) Foreign production will reduce the exports from the home market of the firm that first created the product. In our example, the U.S. firm's exports to Europe will be replaced by production within Europe.

In Phase 3, foreign firms gain production experience, leading to lower per-unit manufacturing costs. If they have lower costs than the innovating firm, which is frequently the case, they export to third-country markets, replacing the innovator's exports there. In our example, European firms will now export to Latin America, taking away the U.S. firm's export markets there.

In Phase 4, the foreign producers now have sufficient production experience and economies of scale to allow them to export back to the innovator's home country. In our example, the European producers will now take away the home market of the original U.S. innovator.

In Phase 1, the product is "new." In Phase 2, it is "maturing." In Phases 3 and 4, it is "standardized." The product may become so standardized by Phase 4 that it almost becomes a commodity. This modification of the theory of comparative advantage provides further insight into patterns of international trade and production and helps the international company plan logistics, such as when it will need to produce—or source—abroad.

Technological advances have changed many aspects of international marketing, and the impact on the product life cycle is the speed at which products move through these stages. Because information is more readily available and ideas are exchanged more rapidly, the time between product introduction in one country and its introduction in other countries has grown much shorter. Competitors are also entering industries more quickly, which means that firms must

Trading Services

According to the World Trade Organization (WTO), trade in services accounted for more than 20 percent of world trade in 2006 and is growing more rapidly than merchandise trade and world production.[5] Four trends will drive the proportion of trade in services to manufactured goods still higher:

1. Continuing mergers and consolidations in key service areas such as accounting (Deloitte Touche Tohmatsu), banking (Credit Suisse First Boston), Internet (Google's purchase of YouTube), and travel (Carnival and Princess cruise lines). These mergers will create global companies that serve their clients and customers wherever they may be. More than half of the world's foreign direct investment is in services.

2. Increased service usage among consumers, particularly among Internet users of e-business. All estimates predict continued phenomenal growth for business-to-consumer (B2C) service e-commerce in the next few years. Using financial services as an example, significant growth continues in use of online payment methods, check clearing, banking, and trading. Business-to-business (B2B) service, although attracting less attention, will continue to dominate Internet activity.

3. Efforts by the WTO and others to reduce trade barriers for services. The goal of the General Agreement on Trade in Services (GATS) is freer trade in such services as accountancy, advertising, architectural and engineering services, education, postal and courier services, sporting services, telecommunications, and tourism.

4. Better measurement. Advances in hardware, software, and data analysis techniques, as well as adoption of

standards such as the Harmonized System (the global standard for classifying products developed by the World Customs Organization), will make it easier to measure the flow of services from nation to nation.

Certain legal factors will negatively affect trade in services. Antitrust laws will target the formation of huge companies that dominate an industry. Antitrade laws will focus on protecting industries that play an important role in a nation's economy or that are considered vital to defense. Consumer protection laws will likely become more elaborate and labyrinthine as countries within the European Union (EU) and other regional groups attempt to coordinate these laws. Finally, intellectual property protection (IPP) is an important topic in most trade negotiations. Piracy of entertainment, such as movies, software, and music, is at the top of stolen intellectual property (IP) lists in nearly every country of the world.

Trade in services is growing more rapidly than trade in products.

seek lower production alternatives more quickly. Thus, movement to Phase 4 occurs more rapidly as well. Finally, some firms, called "**born globals**," internationalize their operations and sales early in their firm's life cycle, skipping many of the stages just described.[6]

born globals

A term used to refer to companies that begin operations with both domestic and foreign sales from the outset.

Balance of Payments

In the study of international trade, the principal source of information is the **balance-of-payments (BoP)** statement of the trading nations. This is a summary statement of all the economic transactions between one country and all other countries over a period of time, usually one year. As an accounting of all transactions between one nation and the rest of the world, the BoP is a double-entry report in which the totals of all payments and receipts are equal.

balance-of-payments (BoP)

Statements of the economic transactions between one country and all other countries over a period of time, usually one year.

deficits

In the context of balance-of-payments, the shortfall that results when country-level spending exceeds country-level saving.

surpluses

In the context of balance-of-payments, an overage that results when country-level saving exceeds country-level spending.

current account

A specific balance-of-payment account that includes transactions in manufactured goods and services as well as unilateral transfers.

capital account

A specific balance-of-payment account that includes flows such as direct and portfolio investments, private placements, and bank and government loans.

Deficits (spending exceeds earnings) or **surpluses** (earnings exceed spending) occur in specific BoP accounts. The accounts most often discussed are the current account and the capital account.

The **current account** includes a list of trade transactions in manufactured goods and services, as well as a list of unilateral transfers. Unilateral transfers, as the term suggests, are one-way transfers. Assume that a firm exports a manufactured good, such as a book, and in exchange gets the value of that book in some currency. Those actions are offsetting parts of the transaction (outflow: book; inflow: money). When someone earns money during the year, purchases a gift, and sends it to a relative in another country, the transaction is only one-way. (The gift is shipped or exported, but no money flows back into the country.) Where there are large numbers of foreign workers, as in Germany and Saudi Arabia, these transfers can be substantial.

The **capital account** includes flows such as direct and portfolio investments, private placements, and bank and government loans. Again, in countries that receive a lot of investment funds (such as those in eastern Europe and in China) or in countries that supply a lot of funds (such as the United States, the Netherlands, and the United Kingdom), the capital account can be a significant component in the total BoP accounting statement.

The international marketer usually is more interested in the details of current account transactions—that is, in the nature of the goods being traded and their origin and destination. Careful examination of the current account can identify the source of competing products as well as potential markets. A more-detailed explanation of the usefulness of balance of payments follows.

Impact on Marketing Decisions

The BoP is an indicator of the international economic health of a country. The data helps government policymakers plan monetary, fiscal, foreign exchange, and commercial policies. The data can also provide information for international marketing decisions. By reviewing import data, marketers can determine the major sources of foreign-made products and, from this, gain some idea of *competitors'* locations. Export data, on the other hand, can be used to identify the places where a nation's products are being shipped and thereby divulge some information about *consumers'* locations. Chapter 7 discusses how trade statistics can be used to identify export market opportunities and competitor activities.

For those companies facing severe import competition, another useful aspect of BoP data is that it may aid a firm in arguing for protection of its industry. This would be the case if imports are rising rapidly and displacing workers or if imports are threatening strategic industries. Companies supplying products to a foreign nation should also review the BoP statistics for warning signs of impending trade legislation. For example, rapidly rising imports might lead to government regulation of trade for that particular product. This means that watching trends in the BoP data over several years is critical.

Financial Considerations

Up to this point, discussion has focused primarily on the current account in the BoP, especially the movement of goods reflected in that account. A look at the capital account is also useful.

A nation's international solvency can be evaluated by checking its capital account over several years. If the nation is steadily losing its gold and foreign exchange reserves, there is a strong likelihood of a currency devaluation or some kind of exchange control. An exchange control means that the government restricts the amount of money sent out of the country as well as the uses to which it can be put. With exchange control, a firm may have difficulty obtaining foreign exchange to repatriate (send home) profits or import supplies needed to manufacture its products. If the firm is importing products that are not considered necessary, the scarce foreign exchange will go instead to goods on which the nation places a higher priority.

The firm's pricing policies also are affected by the BoP problems of the host country. If the firm cannot repatriate profits from a country, it tries to use its intercompany pricing policies to minimize the profits earned in that country, gaining its profits elsewhere where it can repatriate them. If the exporting firm fears devaluation of a currency, it hesitates to quote prices in that currency, preferring to give terms in its home currency or another "safe" currency. Thus, the BoP is an important information source, particularly for international marketing and international finance decision makers. (See the box "Greece's Economic Woes: A Cautionary Tale" for a current example.)

Greece's Economic Woes: A Cautionary Tale

The English word *crisis* derives from the Greek word *krisis*, and the 2010 economic crisis in Greece painted a cautionary picture for countries throughout the world. In May 2010, the European Union (EU) and the International Monetary Fund (IMF) provided €110 billion in assistance for Greece. Up to an additional €650 billion is available for other problematic countries in the eurozone. How did Greece get to this point, and what did it mean for the international marketing manager?

Greece's troubles stemmed from problems with its balance of payments. Greece has chronically run annual BoP deficits with imports of more than twice its exports. It also maintained unsustainable debt levels, with a government deficit that reached 10 to 15 percent of the country's gross domestic product (GDP), despite EU rules stating that government deficits should not be more than 3 percent of GDP.

The caution for firms investing in Greece is to balance financial and political risk with market benefits, as discussed in Chapter 3. Greece's GDP per capita of over $32,000 ranks Greece in the top 20 percent of countries, creating a seemingly strong market for international expansion. However, the 2010 Greek financial crisis presented trouble for firms operating there. For example, Owens-Illinois' stock dropped from $37.53 per share on April 6, 2010, to $27.50 on May 21, 2010, as investors worried about the glassmaker's significant exposure to the European market. Smaller firms, both foreign and domestic, found that getting credit was harder than ever as Greek banks reduced their leverage and foreign banks remained wary about lending to firms with market exposure in Greece. Signs of the impending crisis were there for international marketing managers to see, given that Greece's BoP and debt problems had persisted for years. Identifying the potential economic risk is an important aspect of the international marketer's job.[7]

Government Policy and Trade

International trade differs from domestic trade in that it occurs between different political units, each one a sovereign nation exercising control over its own trade. Although all nations control their foreign trade, they vary in the degree of such control. Each nation invariably establishes laws that favor its citizens and discriminate against traders from other countries. This means, for example, that a U.S. firm trying to sell in Brazil faces certain handicaps from the Brazilian government's control over its trade. These handicaps to the U.S. firm are in addition to any disadvantages resulting from distance or cultural differences. By the same token, a Brazilian firm trying to sell in the United States faces similar restrictions when competing with U.S. firms also selling in the United States.

Commercial policy is the term used to refer to government regulations affecting foreign trade. The principal tools of commercial policy are tariffs, quotas, exchange control, and administrative regulation (the "invisible tariff"). Governments often use trade barriers to protect domestic industries and the jobs they provide, which is why some individuals refer to this intervention as protectionism. For instance, if a government placed a tax (tariff) on all foreign-made cars, making the cars more expensive, simple rules of supply and demand would lead consumers to buy more domestic-made cars than foreign-made cars. This, in turn, leads to more domestic jobs. The next sections review each of these commercial policy tools.

Tariffs

A **tariff** is a tax on products imported from other countries. The tax may be levied on the quantity (such as 10 cents per pound, gallon, or yard) or on the value of the imported goods (such as 10 or 20 percent *ad valorem*). A tariff levied on quantity is called a **specific duty** and is used especially for primary commodities. A tariff levied as a percentage of the value of the goods is called an **ad valorem duty**. *Ad valorem* duties generally are levied on manufactured products.

Governments impose tariffs for two reasons: (1) They may want to earn revenue, and/or (2) they want to make foreign goods more expensive to be able to protect national producers. When the United States was a new nation, most government revenues came from tariffs. Many less-developed countries today derive much of their revenue from tariffs because tariffs are among the easiest taxes to collect.

The protective purpose of tariffs, however, generally prevails over straight revenue collection. One could argue that tariffs penalize a country's own consumers by making them pay higher prices on imported goods. Tariffs also penalize producers that import raw materials or components. The countervailing rationale is that a policy that is too liberal with regard to imports may hurt employment in the country's own industries.

commercial policy

Government regulations dealing with foreign trade.

tariff

A tax on products imported from other countries.

specific duty

A tariff levied based on quantity.

ad valorem duty

A tariff levied as a percentage of the value of the goods.

Governments have long used import duties (tariffs) as a way to reduce imports and protect local industries.

Tariffs affect pricing, product, and distribution policies of the international marketer, as well as foreign investment decisions. If a firm is supplying a market by means of exports, the tariff increases the price of its product and reduces its competitiveness in that market. This necessitates a price structure that minimizes the tariff barrier, such as marginal cost pricing, as discussed in Chapter 12. This examination of price is accompanied by a review of other aspects of the firm's approach to the market. The product may be modified or stripped down to lower the price or to get a more-favorable tariff classification. For example, watches could be taxed as timepieces at one rate or as jewelry at a higher rate. The manufacturer might be able to adapt its product to meet the lower tariff. **Tariff engineering** is the term used to describe this process of minimizing the impact of tariffs by modifying the form in which the product is exported so the importing country imposes a lower tariff. In most cases, tariff engineering results in exporting components rather than final products.

tariff engineering
A process of minimizing the impact of tariffs by modifying the form in which the product is exported.

Another aspect of the debate about using different trade barriers is that the tariff collected goes back to the nation that imposed the duty. This money can be distributed to consumers and others in the home country. Non-tariff barriers (NTBs), described in a later section, raise prices for consumers, but the additional money does not go to the government or other home national parties. Instead, the money flows out of the country and may even go to the exporter in the form of higher profits.

Tariffs used to be the most effective and easiest tool for countries to use in reducing or eliminating foreign-made goods. Over the past 50 years, though, the WTO, bilateral trade agreements, and agreements among nations (such as the **North American Free Trade Agreement [NAFTA]**) have significantly reduced and even eliminated tariffs. Tariffs are easily identifiable as trade barriers and, therefore, are one of the main targets of free-trade proponents.

North American Free Trade Agreement (NAFTA)
A free trade agreement between Canada, the United States, and Mexico.

Protecting local industries remains a goal of many government leaders, which means that innovative ways were—and still are—being invented to stem the tide of imports. Increasingly, as governments agree to reduce tariff barriers, they turn to NTBs, such as quotas, to affect changes in the flow of trade.

Quotas

Other barriers to imports are quantitative restrictions, or **quotas**. Quotas set absolute limits on the amount of goods that may enter a country. An import quota can be a more-serious restriction than a tariff because a firm has less flexibility in responding to it. Price or product modifications do not get around quotas the way they might get around tariffs. A government's goal in establishing quotas on imports is not revenue but the protection of local production and/or the conservation of scarce foreign exchange. About the only response a firm can make to a quota is to assure itself a share of the quota or to set up local production if the market size warrants doing so.

quotas
Quantitative restrictions that limit the amount of goods that may enter a county.

Exchange Control

The most complete tool for regulation of foreign trade is **exchange control**, a government monopoly on all dealings in foreign exchange. Exchange control means that foreign exchange is scarce and that the government is rationing exchange according to its own priorities. A national company earning foreign exchange from its exports must sell this foreign exchange to the control agency, usually the central bank. For example, a Venezuelan company earning U.S. dollars from its exports to the United States must then sell those U.S. dollars to the Venezuelan Foreign Exchange Administration Commission (CADIVI) to obtain Venezuelan bolivars. In turn, a company wanting to buy goods from abroad must buy its foreign exchange from the control agency. Thus, a Venezuelan

exchange control
A government monopoly on all dealings in foreign exchange, often resulting in a government's rationing it out according to its own priorities.

company wanting to import a good priced in U.S. dollars must obtain the dollars by exchanging bolivars through the CADIVI, which can allow or not allow that exchange. Another implication for a firm when foreign exchange is limited is that the government is likely to restrict companies' profit remittances as another way of keeping the country's scarce foreign earnings within its borders.

Non-tariff Barriers

non-tariff barriers (NTB's)

trade barriers that include customs documentation requirements, marks of origin, food and drug laws, labeling laws, antidumping laws, "buy national" policies, and subsidies.

Another form of government trade restriction, **non-tariff barriers (NTBs)**, do not directly impose a duty on imports. NTBs include customs documentation requirements, country-of-origin marking, food and drug laws, labeling laws, antidumping laws, "buy national" policies, subsidies, and many other means. A safety standard, such as the CE mark in Europe, which certifies that a product has met EU consumer safety, health, or environmental requirements, is often considered an NTB because it places additional compliance burdens on exports to Europe. Subsidies are another example of an NTB. (See the box "Subsidies and Retaliation.")

As traditional trade barriers have declined since World War II, NTBs have acquired additional significance. For further examples of what nations are doing to impede trade, review the disputes under consideration by the WTO (www.wto.org).

••• Subsidies and Retaliation

After September 11, 2001, travelers were understandably shaken and reluctant to get back into airplanes. Airlines, already facing poor earnings in a highly competitive industry, faced collapse. In hindsight, one can see the number of passengers actually declined very little. Yet airlines slashed prices dramatically in an attempt to regain customers in the months following the attacks on New York and Washington, D.C.

Drastically lower revenues produced global industry losses of $2.5 billion in 2001, and losses in subsequent years dwarfed this amount. To support the hard-hit airline industry, the U.S. government provided over $15 billion in aid, including subsidies and loan guarantees, to the U.S. airline companies. Even though the EU provided similar, although smaller, subsidies to its industry, it filed a charge with the WTO, stating that U.S. companies were abusing the government aid to unfairly lower prices in Europe to make up for lost revenue at home.

In response, the EU proposed that a surcharge be placed on foreign airline tickets for non-EU companies that were using subsidies to unfairly lower their prices. This action, referred to as a countervailing duty or tariff, caused a reaction among affected firms. The United States threatened to counter the EU surcharge with surcharges on European-carrier tickets. Like two children fighting, this sort of behavior can easily escalate. Given the number of jobs at stake in the global airline industry, these subsidies and related issues were important agenda items at future WTO talks.[8]

Institutions in the World Economy ••••

The global business environment is complex and includes many players: national, regional, and local governments; private and publicly held firms; and innumerable international organizations, special interest groups, and individuals. The next sections look at some of the more widely known institutions and their potential influence on a firm's global strategy.

The World Trade Organization (WTO)
www.wto.org

Because each nation is sovereign in determining its own commercial policy, the danger is that arbitrary national actions will minimize international trade. This was the situation in the 1930s, when international trade was at a low ebb and each nation tried to maintain domestic employment by restricting imports. The economic reality of tariffs is that if one nation erects trade barriers, other nations are likely to follow suit and erect their own barriers, most typically retaliating by imposing duties on products they purchase from the first nation. The fallacy of these "beggar my neighbor" policies was evident in the worldwide depression to which they contributed. This unhappy experience led the major trading nations to seek better solutions after World War II. One outcome of their efforts was the General Agreement on Tariffs and Trade (GATT), now called the **World Trade Organization (WTO)**.

Although GATT's initial membership consisted of only 23 countries, it included the major trading nations of the Western world. Today, the WTO is the world's trading club, accounting for over 90 percent of world trade. It has 153 member countries, with 30 applicants currently negotiating membership.[9] The WTO has contributed to the expansion of world trade. Since 1947, it has concluded eight major multilateral trade negotiations, the latest being the Uruguay Round, which lasted from 1986 to 1994. (The Doha Development Round is the most recent but has not yet been concluded.) As a result of these conferences, the tariff rates for tens of thousands of items have been reduced, and there has been an easing of restrictions on most manufactured goods and many services. (Apparel, textiles, and agricultural products have traditionally involved difficult negotiations.)

Providing a framework for multilateral trade negotiations is a primary reason for the WTO's existence, but other WTO principles further trade expansion. One is the principle of **nondiscrimination**. Each contracting party must grant all others the same rate of import duty; that is, a tariff concession granted to one trading partner must be extended to all WTO members under the most-favored-nation (MFN) clause. In the United States, this rate of duty is also known as normal trading relations (NTR).

Consultation is another WTO principle. When trade disagreements arise, the WTO provides a forum for consultation. In such an atmosphere, disagreeing members are more likely to compromise than to resort to arbitrary trade-restricting actions. All in all, world trade cooperation since World War II has led to a much better trading policy than the world might have expected. The WTO has been a major contributor to this cooperation.

United Nations Conference on Trade and Development (UNCTAD)
www.unctad.org

Although the WTO has been an important force in world trade expansion, benefits have not been distributed equally. Less-developed countries, many of which are members of the WTO, have been dissatisfied with trade arrangements because their share of world trade has been declining, and prices of their raw

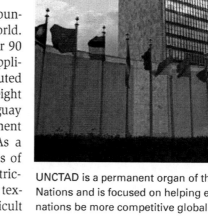

UNCTAD is a permanent organ of the United Nations and is focused on helping emerging nations be more competitive globally.

World Trade Organization (WTO)

An association of over 150 countries focused on cooperation and agreements concerning the trade of goods and services. Its primary goal is to provide a framework for multilateral trade negotiations.

nondiscrimination

A policy such that each contracting party must grant all others the same rate of import duty; a trade concession granted to one trading partner must be extended to all members.

consultation

A stage in the WTO process for managing trade disputes between countries whereby the countries have a chance to talk to each other and attempt to resolve the dispute before it goes to a mediator or a panel of experts.

material exports compare unfavorably with prices of their imported manufactured goods. According to these countries, the WTO has accomplished more to further trade in goods of industrialized nations than it has to promote the primary products produced by developing nations. It is true that tariff reductions have been far more important to manufactured goods than to primary products. The result of the dissatisfaction of these less-developed countries' was the formation of the **United Nations Conference on Trade and Development (UNCTAD)** in 1964. UNCTAD is a permanent organ of the United Nations General Assembly and has over 190 member countries.[10]

The goal of UNCTAD is to further the development of emerging nations—by trade as well as by other means. Under the WTO, trade expanded, especially in manufactured goods, creating a growing trade gap between industrial and developing countries. UNCTAD seeks to improve the prices of primary goods exports through commodity agreements. For example, if the countries with commodities such as oil, minerals, and food products could get together to control supply, higher prices and higher returns would result.

UNCTAD has also worked to establish a tariff preference system favoring the export of manufactured goods from less-developed countries. Because these countries have not been able to export commodities in a quantity sufficient to maintain their share of trade, they want to expand in the growth area of world trade: industrial exports. They believe they might achieve this goal if manufactured goods coming from developing countries faced lower tariffs than the same goods coming from developed countries.

UNCTAD has made modest progress. One achievement is its own formation: a new club for world trade matters that lobbies for the interests of developing nations. Former Tanzanian president Julius Nyerere called it "the labor union of the developing countries." Through UNCTAD, developing countries have also received preferential tariff treatment from the EU, Japan, and the United States, as they requested. Overall, UNCTAD has focused world attention on the trade needs of developing countries and has given them a more-coherent voice. UNCTAD's committees and studies have also contributed to a more-informed dialogue.

The WTO, UNCTAD, and the Firm's Global Strategy

The WTO's success in reducing barriers to trade has meant that a firm's products may be more price competitive in foreign markets. Further, the firm, through its subsidiaries in various markets, can help protect its interest in trade matters through discussions with governments in advance of trade negotiations.

UNCTAD can have a more-direct impact on a firm than the WTO. International firms can play a major role by relating to the tariff preferences granted by the industrialized nations. Developing countries have limited experience in exporting manufactured goods. By itself, elimination of tariffs is not sufficient to help those countries. In these cases, the international firm can be a decisive factor. If the international firm combines its know-how and resources with those of the host country, it can offer competitive exports. Included in the international firm's resources is its global distribution network, which could be the critical factor in gaining foreign market access. Also, the international firm supplies the foreign marketing know-how lacked by most producers in developing countries. For example, if Ford had the choice of importing engines from its plant in Britain or its plant in Brazil, it might choose Brazil if engines from Brazil had a zero tariff and engines from Europe faced a 15 percent duty.

United Nations Conference on Trade and Development (UNCTAD)

The United Nations Conference on Trade and Development; a permenent organ of the United Nations General Assembly with the primary goal to further the development of emerging nations.

International Monetary Fund (IMF)
www.imf.org

The following historical perspective is helpful in understanding why the International Monetary Fund (as well as the World Bank) was formed shortly after World War II. The section on the international financial system provides additional background and clarifies the impact of exchange rate instability.

A BRIEF HISTORY

In the days of the gold standard, exchange rates did not change in value. The stability and certainty of the international gold standard came to an end, however, with the advent of World War I. In the 1930s, the international financial system had no certainty, stability, or accepted rules. Instead, there were frequent and arbitrary changes in exchange rates. This chaotic and uncertain situation contributed to the decline in international trade during that period. The worldwide Depression of the 1930s was reinforced by the added risks in international finance.

> **International Monetary Fund (IMF)**
>
> An organization that acts as a forum for monetary and fiscal discussions that affect the world economy and that supplies financial assistance (loans) and technical assistance (economic consultants).

At the conclusion of World War II, nations met to address some of the problems that were believed to have been contributing factors leading up to the war. In 1944, some of the allied nations met at Bretton Woods, New Hampshire, to design a better international economic system for the postwar world. One element of this system dealt with international trade, resulting in the formation of GATT and the WTO. Another element was concerned with the need for international capital and led to the formation of the World Bank. A third element involved the international monetary system and resulted in the establishment of the **International Monetary Fund (IMF)**.

FORMATION OF THE IMF

The IMF was originally designed to help nations control exchange-rate fluctuations by having members agree on a specific exchange rate (U.S. dollars per British pound, for example) and then using vast stores of gold to buy and sell currencies to maintain those exchange rates. This system worked well. Trade increased dramatically after World War II, in part because currency prices were stable, making it less risky to buy and sell products and services denominated in other currencies.

The system failed in the early 1970s because there was too little gold reserve to offset the tremendous amount of foreign currency being used. In essence, the system fell victim to its success. Since then, many currencies "float" freely in price relative to one another, with prices being determined by supply and demand. The IMF or central banks of various nations intervene only occasionally.

Gold once helped maintain fixed exchange rates between IMF member countries. Since the early 1970s, however, fixed rates have been dropped, and most currencies are allowed to "float" freely, based on supply and demand.

In the new millennium, the IMF plays a slightly different role. The organization and some of its members still occasionally intervene in foreign exchange markets; but this intervention, although it does affect currency prices, cannot control prices to the degree first established under the Bretton Woods agreement. Most often, the IMF acts as a forum for monetary and fiscal discussions that affect the world economy, much as the United Nations (UN) acts as a forum for initiatives designed to promote peace. In addition to providing a forum for discussion, the IMF supplies financial assistance in the form of loans (usually for stabilizing a currency or for balance-of-payment problems) and technical assistance in the form of economic consultants (who provide advice to governments on designing effective economic and financial policies). All these initiatives are designed to support the core IMF goals, which have remained the same since its inception: the promotion of worldwide financial stability and economic growth.

Financial stability and economic growth lead to more customers for the world's products and remove some of the risks associated with international trade. The importance of currency prices is that international marketers must contend with continuously changing exchange rates, which complicates decision making about international pricing and logistics.

INTERNATIONAL FINANCIAL SYSTEM

A major goal of business is to make a profit, so firms pay close attention to financial matters. International companies must be even more concerned with financial matters than national firms because international companies deal with many currencies and many national financial markets where conditions differ. Marketing across national boundaries involves financial considerations, such as exchange rate instability.

EXCHANGE RATE INSTABILITY

International payments are one aspect of the financial side of international trade. In most cases, international transactions occur in different currencies. Dealing with multiple currencies is not a serious problem in itself, but difficulties arise because currencies frequently change in value with regard to each other and in unpredictable ways.

foreign exchange rate

The domestic price of a foreign currency.

A **foreign exchange rate** is the domestic price of a foreign currency. For the United States, this means that there is a dollar rate, or price, for the British pound, the euro, and the Brazilian real, as well as every other currency. If one country changes the value of its currency, firms selling to or from that country may find that the altered exchange rate is sufficient to wipe out their profit or, on the brighter side, to provide a windfall gain. In any case, firms must be alert for currency variations to optimize their financial performance. (See the box "That Will Cost You a Little More, Sir.")

Tourists in a foreign country participate in a foreign exchange transaction nearly every day. They exchange their home (domestic) currency for the currency of the country they are visiting. From tourists' perspective, it is good when their home currency is strong and they can purchase a lot for their (domestic) currency. However, it is bad when their (domestic) currency is weak and they have to spend more for hotels, meals, and other purchases.

It is the opposite perspective for a manufacturer that depends on exports. When its domestic currency is expensive, demand for the manufacturer's products will likely decrease. Supply and demand for goods and services are affected by the price of the currency that people use and by the volatility of the currency. The more a currency changes in value, the greater its volatility, and the harder it is to predict the cost of whatever people buy with that currency. Chapter 12 discusses how a firm can manage this volatility.

Major currency traders include banks and other financial institutions, which trade currencies in the hundreds of billions of dollars every day. Trading is used in business transactions (for example, Dell Computers may need yuan to pay suppliers in China), but also for speculative reasons. Just as traders in stock exchanges seek profits, foreign currency traders gamble on whether the price of a currency will rise or fall.

CANADA	CAD	0.9512	0.8883
CHINA	CNY	7.3169	6.0910
EURO	EUR	0.6644	0.6100
JAPAN	JPY	109.00	102.00
SINGAPORE	SGD	1.3712	1.2630
HONG KONG	HKD	7.0043	6.4072
NEW ZEALAND	NZD	1.1646	1.0675
MYR		3.2536	2.7818

Tourists on international trips encounter foreign exchange on a routine basis as they convert their home currency into the local currency of the country they are visiting.

Currency prices also reflect the overall health of an economy and, in part, explain why people believe a strong currency is good and a weak currency is bad for the consumer. A nation that has a positive balance of trade, or trade surplus, is exporting more products than it is importing. This means that traders need to purchase the nation's currency to pay for those products. The more demand there is for a currency, the higher the price. Countries that are growing or that have a stable economy attract investors. Investors need the local currency to buy property, build factories, and so on, which, in turn, increases demand for the currency and raises its price.

Achieving exchange stability within the EU was a major reason behind the adoption of the euro. This process involved cooperation and coordination of fiscal and monetary policies among the EU member participants, the creation of a European Central Bank, and the loss of substantial national sovereignty on policies that had a direct impact on employment and economic growth.

That Will Cost You a Little More, Sir

Imagine that the $300 stereo equipment you are considering purchasing increases to $400 overnight. Drastic changes in exchange rates might cause such a price increase. Yet when buying products that are made abroad (and so many things are made abroad), you do not usually think about the exchange rate between your currency and that of the manufacturer. Do you own a Toyota or a Volkswagen? Did you look up the exchange rate between the U.S. dollar and the Japanese yen or the German euro? Probably not. If you ever traveled to a country that uses a different currency, you undoubtedly watched the exchange rate, which probably changed a few cents or more between the time you planned your trip and the time you returned. So whether buying a hamburger in Paris or a jacket in Hong Kong, you likely had to calculate the cost in dollars or some other home currency.

When companies manufacture something in another country, even if the item consists of only one of the components of a product, the firm must consider the cost of doing so in the local currency because that is how the locals expect to be paid. Or, if a firm makes something in one country and sells it in another country, the exchange rate is important because the price must be stated in a foreign currency (like the stereo sold in the United States and the hamburger sold in Paris). When the exchange rate changes, costs and prices also change. Sometimes, currency prices relative to one another are very stable and change little over time; at other times, though, changes can be substantial and sudden. Consider the following:

Change in Price Relative to U.S. Dollar

Country/Area	Currency	Change over Three Months (%)	Change over One Year (%)
Eurozone	Euro	−9.52	−11.62
Japan	Yen	−2.42	+5.92
Mexico	Peso	−0.46	+2.99
South Africa	Rand	+1.47	+6.27
Switzerland	Franc	−6.94	−5.86
United Kingdom	Pound	−4.67	−9.30

Source: http://www.ratesfx.com/rates/rate-usd.html (University of Tampere).
Note: May 28, 2010, was used as the end date.

Continued on next page . . .

That Will Cost You a Little More, Sir

Continued

To put this in perspective, imagine that firms making the following products decided to pass along to the consumer the entire 10 or 15 percent increase in their prices.

Change in Price (U.S. Dollar)

Item	Original Price	Price after 10% Increase	Price after 15% Increase
Jeans	$50.00	$55.00	$57.50
Textbook	$110.00	$121.00	$126.50
Computer	$1,500.00	$1,650.00	$1,725.00
Car	$18,000.00	$19,800.00	$20,700.00

Sometimes, that "little bit more" can be a lot. Whether a currency increases or decreases in value relative to another currency is important. For example, when the Canadian dollar is strong or strengthens relative to other currencies, more euros can be purchased for each Canadian dollar. That is good for tourists traveling to the eurozone. It is not good for Canadian manufacturers, though, because Canadians will buy foreign-made goods and services instead of those produced in Canada. When the Canadian dollar is weak or weakens, fewer units of foreign currency can be purchased. That generally means that tourists will spend less time abroad and buy fewer souvenirs. Businesses that use foreign suppliers also have to pay more Canadian dollars for the foreign currency used to pay for their foreign-made components and supplies.

World Bank Group
www.worldbank.org

World Bank

An institution whose goal is to promote economic growth, to provide loans for infrastructure development, and to improve the living conditions of the world's population.

The **World Bank** is another institution conceived at Bretton Woods. Originally called the International Bank for Reconstruction and Development (IBRD), its primary mission was to assist war-torn countries of World War II in rebuilding their cities and infrastructure through loans with very favorable terms.

Like the IMF, the World Bank plays a different role today. The goals of promoting economic growth remain, and the World Bank still provides many loans for infrastructure development. Instead of helping countries such as France and other developed nations, however, assistance goes primarily to developing nations. Today, the World Bank Group includes the IBRD, the International Development Association (IDA), the International Finance Corporation (IFC), the International Centre for Settlement of Investment Disputes (ICSID), and the Multilateral Investment Guarantee Agency (MIGA). The activities of these organizations support the main goal of the World Bank Group, which is to improve the living conditions of the world's population, especially among the poorest countries. Loans for schools, roads, and telecommunication projects create potential consumers and an environment better able to support the needs of businesses.

Organization for Economic Cooperation and Development (OECD)
www.oecd.org

Organization for Economic Cooperation and Development

A membership organization of over 30 countries committed to democracy and market economics, with a focus on research and a sharing of policies and best practices.

Another important institution related to international trade is the **Organization for Economic Cooperation and Development** (OECD). Founded in 1960, OECD members share a commitment to democracy and market economies.

OECD supports this commitment through sharing of policies and best practices. Though its membership remains relatively small with only 33 countries, it has become a respected voice on a variety of issues. They include employment, living standards, financial security, sustainable economic growth, and trade. Of relevance to the international marketing manager is OECD's numerous comparable statistics (stats.oecd.org) and its extensive publications in economics and public policy. OECD provides significant insights into each of its members' economies with up-to-date reports on key issues affecting each country and its industries. Most of this research is available at no cost through its website. To be a member of the OECD, a country must demonstrate its commitment to democracy and a market-led economy. Countries achieving membership often refer to the process as joining the "elite club" of countries in the world. As such, firms expanding internationally can point to membership in the OECD as an important factor in considering expansion in a specific country.

Regional Economic Integration

Another major development since World War II has been the growth of regional groupings. **Regional economic integration** takes place when nations agree to work together to pursue common economic gains. Formal agreements have been signed among nations that are similar in terms of culture and religion (such as La Asociación Latinoamericana de Integración [ALADI]), among neighbors (Economic Community of West African States [ECOWAS]), and among nations that are similar in terms of relative wealth and economic development (Caribbean Community [CARICOM]). Regional economic integration also often follows historical trade patterns as research shows that geographically proximate countries trade more with each other than with geographically distant countries.[11] Two of the best-known (and political) regional economic integration agreements are the North American Free Trade Agreement (NAFTA) and the European Union (EU). Some major regional groupings are shown in Table 2-1.

> **regional economic integration**
> Economic cooperation within geographic regions to pursue common economic gains.

Table 2-1 • Selected Regional Economic Groupings

Name	Details	Member Nations
ALADI	La Asociación Latinoamericana de Integración (Latin American Integration Association [LAIA]); established in 1980; 12 members	Argentina, Bolivia, Brazil, Chile, Colombia, Cuba, Ecuador, Mexico, Paraguay, Peru, Uruguay, and Venezuela
ASEAN	Association of Southeast Asian Nations; established in 1967; 10 members	Brunei, Cambodia, Indonesia, Laos, Malaysia, Myanmar, Philippines, Singapore, Thailand, and Vietnam
CAN	Comunidad Andina (Andean Community); established in 1969; 5 members	Bolivia, Colombia, Ecuador, Peru, and Venezuela
CARICOM	Caribbean Community; established in 1973; 15 members, 5 associates	Antigua and Barbuda, Bahamas, Barbados, Belize, Dominica, Grenada, Guyana, Haiti, Jamaica, Montserrat, Saint Kitts and Nevis, Saint Lucia, Saint Vincent and the Grenadines, Suriname, and Trinidad and Tobago
ECOWAS	Economic Community of West African States; established in 1975; 15 members	Benin, Burkina Faso, Cape Verde, Ivory Coast, Gambia, Ghana, Guinea, Guinea Bissau, Liberia, Mali, Niger, Nigeria, Senegal, Sierra Leone, and Togo
EU	European Union; established as European Economic Community (EEC) in 1957; 27 members	Austria, Belgium, Bulgaria, Cyprus, Czech Republic, Denmark, Estonia, Finland, France, Germany, Greece, Hungary, Ireland, Italy, Latvia, Lithuania, Luxembourg, Malta, the Netherlands, Poland, Portugal, Romania, Slovakia, Slovenia, Spain, Sweden, and the United Kingdom
GCC	Gulf Cooperation Council, founded 1981; 6 members	United Arab Emirates, The Kingdom of Bahrain, The Kingdom of Saudi Arabia, The Sultanate of Oman, Qatar, Kuwait
MERCOSUR	El Mercado Común del Sur (Southern Cone Common Market); established in 1991; 5 members	Argentina, Brazil, Paraguay, Uruguay, and Venezuela
NAFTA	North American Free Trade Agreement; established in 1993; 3 members	Canada, Mexico, and the United States

national sovereignty

A nation's right to govern itself without outside interference.

There are costs to a nation in joining a regional group, the chief one being that the nation must give up some **national sovereignty**—its right to govern itself without outside interference. Nations do this only because they hope the benefits will be greater than the costs. The major benefit sought through economic integration is faster economic growth. By joining together, member nations gain additional resources, larger markets, and economies of scale for their industries. Another objective of regional groupings is countervailing power. For example, the EU seeks a stronger position against the economic power of the United States and Japan.

The reduction of trade barriers within the group adds dynamism to member economies by increasing competition. Sluggish national firms and monopolies lose their protective walls and are forced to change in a more-competitive direction. Furthermore, the group of countries together may be able to support an industry too large for any individual member country. Thus, regional integration can aid industrialization. All of this may mean greater wealth, progress, and self-sufficiency for the region.

euro

The common unit of currency used by members of the European Union.

Forms and degrees of economic integration are summarized in Table 2-2. As controversial as NAFTA was when it became law in 1994 (and it remains so today), it actually represents the least amount of economic cooperation: a free-trade area. On the other hand, the countries that form the eurozone within the EU (those countries within the EU that have adopted the **euro** as their currency) represent one of the highest forms of economic cooperation: economic union. Distinguishing characteristics and examples of the various types of economic integration are discussed next.

Table 2-2 • Forms of Economic Integration

Stage of Integration	Elimination of Trade Barriers among Members	Common Trade Barriers among Members	Free Factor Mobility	Coordination of Economic Policies	Coordination of Political Policies
Free-trade area	Yes	No	No	No	No
Customs union	Yes	Yes	No	No	No
Common market	Yes	Yes	Yes	No	No
Economic union	Yes	Yes	Yes	Yes	No
Political union	Yes	Yes	Yes	Yes	Yes

Free-Trade Area

free-trade area

Member countries that agree to have free movement of goods among themselves, so no tariffs or quotas are imposed against goods coming from other members.

Although all regional groupings have economic goals, the various groups differ in organization and motivation. The simplest is a **free-trade area**, in which the member countries agree to have free movement of goods among themselves; that is, no tariffs or quotas are imposed against goods coming from other members. In contrast to the next form of integration (customs union), member countries of a free-trade area do not have a common trade policy with nonmember countries.

NAFTA, with its members Canada, the United States, and Mexico, is a widely known example of a free-trade area. Under NAFTA, products that qualify as having originated (essentially meaning assembled, manufactured, or grown) in any of the three member countries may be imported duty free. But because NAFTA is a free-trade area and not a customs union, as discussed in the next section, each member country may have separate trade agreements with nonmember countries. Indeed, Mexico has a free-trade agreement with the EU, but the United States does not.

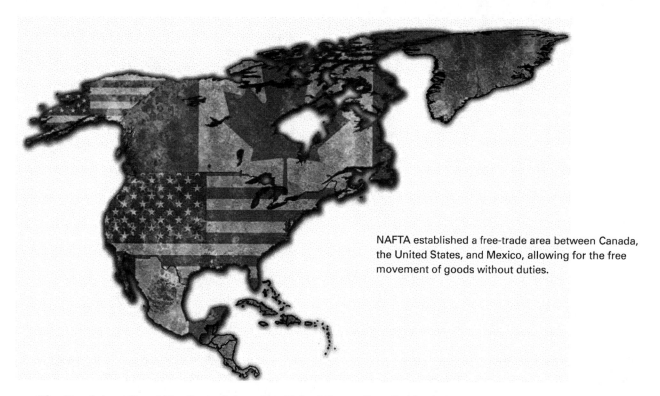

NAFTA established a free-trade area between Canada, the United States, and Mexico, allowing for the free movement of goods without duties.

The Dominican Republic–Central America–United States Free Trade Agreement (CAFTA–DR) created a free-trade area involving seven countries: the United States, Costa Rica, the Dominican Republic, El Salvador, Guatemala, Honduras, and Nicaragua. As with NAFTA, it allows for duty-free trade of products among member countries. CAFTA–DR also includes other provisions, such as access to government procurement opportunities within member countries and the cross-protection of foreign direct investment and intellectual property rights.

NAFTA and CAFTA–DR are examples of **multilateral trade agreements**—trade agreements with more than two members. A **bilateral trade agreement** is an agreement between two countries. The United States has signed many bilateral trade agreements in recent years, including agreements with Australia, Chile, Jordan, Morocco, Singapore, Oman, and Peru. Bilateral trade agreements offer the same primary benefit as a free-trade area: free movement of goods.

> **multilateral trade agreement**
> Trade agreement between more than two countries.

> **bilateral trade agreement**
> Trade agreement between two countries.

Customs Union

Though similar to a free-trade area in that it has no tariffs on trade among members, a **customs union** adds the more-ambitious requirement that members also have a uniform tariff on trade with nonmembers. Thus, a customs union is like a single nation not only in having internal trade, but also in presenting a united front to the rest of the world with its common external tariff.

A customs union is more difficult to achieve than a free-trade area because each member must yield its sovereignty in commercial policy matters—not just with member nations, but with the whole world. Its advantage lies in making the economic integration stronger and avoiding the administrative problems of a free-trade area. For example, in a free-trade area, imports of a particular good would always enter the member country with the lowest tariff, regardless of the country of destination. Special regulations are necessary to avoid this distortion of trade patterns.

The EU was the leading example of a customs union in the years prior to its allowing the free movement of labor. Today, however, the EU is more akin to a common market—and even an economic union—for eurozone members.

> **customs union**
> Similar to a free-trade area, but adds the requirement that members also have a uniform tariff on trade with nonmembers.

Common Market

common market

A type of market that includes the features of a customs union but goes significantly beyond it because it seeks to standardize all government regulations affecting trade.

A true **common market** includes a customs union but goes significantly beyond that because it seeks to standardize or harmonize all government regulations affecting trade. These government regulations include all aspects of government policy that pertain to business—for example, corporation and excise taxes, labor laws, fringe benefits and social security programs, incorporation laws, and antitrust laws. In such an economic union, business and trade decisions are unaffected by the national laws of different members because the laws are uniform. Equally important, a common market allows free flow of all factors of production, meaning products and labor. Achieving common market integration can be quite difficult because it allows workers to take jobs within any member countries. The Southern Cone Common Market (MERCOSUR) is a contemporary example.

Economic Union

economic union

An association that includes the features of a common market but also includes a common currency and the coordination of monetary and fiscal policies.

Economic unions among nations are characterized by a common currency. Underlying this obvious aspect is the coordination of fiscal and monetary policies (establishment of prime lending rates of interest, size of reserves banks must retain, and so on). This form of integration is uncommon because of the impact on inflation and unemployment rates. A review of the discussions surrounding the adoption of the euro among EU members highlights some of these issues and the difficulties in obtaining eurozone consensus. The requirement that members of an economic union adopt harmonized fiscal and monetary policies is a major reason behind some EU members opting out of the eurozone.

Political Union

political union

An association that often includes the features of an economic union but also adopts a governing structure that supersedes individual national or state interests.

The most integrated form of economic cooperation is **political union**. This form requires adoption of the principles behind the other forms of integration, as well as the adoption of a governing structure that supercedes individual national or state interests. One characteristic that indicates a group is moving in this direction is the members of the union agreeing to the jurisdiction of the same governing body. Other characteristics include a common army and common foreign policy related to international issues.

Political unions are actually more common than many might realize. A number of nations in the world today are federations of smaller geographic areas that at one time or another believed they would be better off if they cooperated. Germany, a federation of 16 states, is a good example. The United States is a grouping of what were once independent states, some of which minted their own currency, manned their own militias, and collected tolls or duties at their borders.

Regionalism and the International Marketing Manager

The rise of regional groupings means that fewer but larger economic entities are gradually replacing nearly 200 national markets. When a firm is considering an investment decision, the relevant market area may include five, ten, or even more countries, rather than just one national market. For example, the "United States of Europe" and "Euro-Land" are expressions used to describe the new Europe. The following statistic provides an indication of the importance of the EU to American investors: Over 57 percent of all capital flowing out of the United States in 2008 ($180 of $311 billion) went to Europe.[12] Analysts attribute the amount of and growth in foreign investment flowing into the EU to harmonization of product specifications, lower foreign exchange risk, and other steps taken in the economic integration of the nations that make up the EU. In addition, research shows that managers think in terms of regions and geography when making decisions on which markets to enter, selecting those areas geographically proximate, while also tending to evaluate regions, not countries, as their unit of analysis.[13]

A firm's logistics will be modified by regional groupings. There will be pressures to supply a region from within, rather than to export to it. A firm will have the added incentive of the larger market, but it will also benefit by avoiding the tariff barriers, where it will be able to compete better with local producers and be protected from outside competition. At the same time, these local producers will become stronger competitors, due to economies of scale in the larger market, the alliances they are forming, and the stronger competition in the free-trade area. A firm's operations within a regional group will tend to be more uniform and self-contained than they would be in ungrouped national markets.

In response to global forces and economic integration, a firm's marketing program will be modified over time. As the differences in markets diminish, marketing to member countries will become more uniform. A firm will gain economies of scale in product development, pricing, distribution, and promotion. For example, as member nations harmonize their food, drug, and labeling laws, a firm can eliminate product and packaging differences that were required by different national laws. Similar modifications will occur in other functional areas.

SUMMARY

The international marketing manager needs to understand how the global economic environment differs from the domestic economic environment. These differences increase the risks associated with global expansion, such as foreign exchange risk. But they also offer opportunities, such as regional economic integration lowering barriers to trade, thereby reducing the cost of doing business in those countries.

International trade theory helps in understanding a nation's comparative advantage and is useful for locating supply or production sources. The international product life cycle theory can help a firm know when to source, or produce, abroad.

The balance of payments (BoP) is a summary statement of a nation's economic transactions that can be analyzed to determine market potential and competition in a country.

All countries have regulations on their international trade (commercial policy), usually to protect employment in home industries. Tariffs and quotas are the major tools used by industrial countries to control their trade. These tools affect a firm's pricing, product, and logistics decisions. Exchange control is a more comprehensive and rigid form of trade control.

As the world's trading club, the World Trade Organization (WTO) works to liberalize the exchange of goods and services between countries. To the degree it is successful, the WTO facilitates a firm's international marketing. The United Nations Conference on Trade and Development (UNCTAD) is the lobby for developing countries' interests in trade. Its efforts also can affect a firm's international marketing and influence the firm's logistics.

The major world currencies have been floating since 1973. The resulting instability and uncertainty disrupt the sourcing patterns and pricing decisions. The International Monetary Fund (IMF), though no longer able to maintain stable currencies, is still a force for moderation and stability in international finance. By lending to deficit countries, the IMF helps to keep the markets viable and open to the international marketer.

The World Bank, through its development loans, provides resources to help poor countries strengthen their economies and become more prosperous, thus providing more-attractive markets for international firms. World Bank projects themselves can provide attractive marketing opportunities.

In the growing interdependence of the world economy, many nations are finding economic integration with their neighbors desirable. This integration offers more resources, larger markets, and economies of scale to help the countries compete in the world economy. The European Union (EU) is the major successful integration story. Where integration is successful, it offers opportunities for firms that can operate within the group, but challenges for those on the outside.

KEY TERMS

absolute advantage
ad valorem duty
autarky
balance of payments (BoP)
bilateral trade agreement
born globals
capital account
commercial policy
common market
comparative advantage
consultation
current account

customs union
deficits
economic unions
euro
exchange control
foreign exchange rate
free-trade area
International Monetary Fund (IMF)
multilateral trade agreements
national sovereignty
nondiscrimination

non-tariff barriers (NTBs)
North American Free Trade Agreement (NAFTA)
Organization for Economic Cooperation and Development
political union
product innovation
product life cycle
quotas
regional economic integration

specific duty
surpluses
tariff
tariff engineering
United Nations Conference on Trade and Development (UNCTAD)
World Bank
World Trade Organization (WTO)

NASBITE CGBP TOPICS COVERED IN THIS CHAPTER

Note: For full details of the alignment of each chapter with the NASBITE CGBP, be sure to review the information provided in the section "Studying for the NASBITE CGBP Exam."

CGBP Rubric	Topic
02/01/02:	external environment—economic
02/01/02	external environment—regulatory
02/01/02	external environment—currency fluctuations
02/01/02	external environment—protected industries and sectors
02/01/04:	major trade agreements
02/01/04:	trade law
02/01/04:	customs unions including NAFTA, European Union
02/06/02:	product life cycle implications (or strategies)
02/07/02:	tariff and non-tariff barriers and incentives

QUESTIONS AND RESEARCH

1. What can be learned from studying the composition and patterns of world trade?

2. How can an understanding of international trade theory help the international marketer?

3. What is a BoP? Of what use is it to international marketing?

4. What is the World Trade Organization (WTO), and what does it do for the environment of international marketing?

5. How might the role and actions of the International Monetary Fund (IMF) impact a firm as it expands into a particular country?

6. Why might an exporter feel threatened by the formation of regional economic groupings that include its home (domestic) country? How might the firm react?

7. What economic characteristics would one look for in an emerging potential market?

8. What does the euro mean for U.S. firms already operating in the European Union (EU)? What impact does the euro have on those countries considering entering the EU?

9. What are the potential benefits of World Bank activity for international marketing?

10. As discussed in the box titled "Greece's Economic Woes: A Cautionary Tale," the Greek economic crisis greatly affected businesses operating specifically in Greece, as well as businesses in Europe if the company had exposure to Greece. Research some examples of companies affected, and detail the actions they took.

CHAPTER 2 TEAM PROJECT ASSIGNMENT: The Global Economic Environment

This chapter focused on the global economic environment and discussed how differences in the economic environment can impact a firm as it expands globally.

You have not yet selected foreign markets for your client's international expansion (which will be done in Chapter 7), so you cannot research the specific challenges for your firm in those markets. However, knowing the industry in which your client operates, you can begin some initial research of potential issues your firm may encounter. For example, if your client manufactures a product, it may incur relatively high tariffs when exporting to specific countries. If your client provides a service, other government commercial policies may be a concern, such as controls on what foreign companies are permitted to do or own in a particular country.

For your team research from this chapter, discuss the following issues:

1. Will import tariffs be a concern for your client? You can research the import duties imposed by various countries on products by visiting www.export.gov and search for the section "Find Tariffs and Taxes." You will find details regarding how to classify products (Schedule B) and how to research the import duties for those products in selected countries.

2. If your client is a service provider, tariffs may not be an issue. However, foreign governments still may place restrictions on allowable activities by foreign firms and/or company ownership controls. To better understand these restrictions, visit www.export.gov and go to the section "Market

Research." Then select the "Market Research Library" and from the Industry drop-down box, choose "Services." This tool will provide access to a number of marketing reports regarding U.S. service exports opportunities. Review whether any of those reports relate to your client. Even if none directly relates, read selected reports to better understand how foreign governments place restrictions on the activities of foreign firms.

3. The chapter discussed how emerging markets often encounter economic crisis, as shown in the box "Greece's Economic Woes: A Cautionary Tale." Nongovernmental organizations (NGOs), such as the IMF, often play a critical, though controversial, role in assisting such countries. For your client, select an emerging market that even in these early stages of your research appears to be a good country for international expansion. Research the economic history of that country, and discuss any significant roles of NGOs, including the IMF and UNCTAD.

CASE 2.1 Foreign Exchange Rates

Foreign Exchange Rates

Country	Currency	Exchange Rate (per $U.S., August 2, 1999)	Exchange Rate (per $U.S., August 2, 2004)
Argentina	Peso	2.98	2.981
Brazil	Real	3.047	3.04696
Britain	Pound	0.619819	0.547261
Canada	Dollar	1.50753	1.33103
China	Renminbi/Yuan	8.2772	8.282
Eurozone	Euro	0.938031	0.831032
India	Rupee	43.2917	46.29
Indonesia	Rupiah	6,804.00	9,135.69
Japan	Yen	114.374	111.079
Mexico	Peso	11.4229	11.4266
Philippines	Peso	38.5483	55.82
Russia	Ruble	24.24	29.14
South Africa	Rand	6.17527	6.31468
Switzerland	Franc	1.4983	1.27834
Turkey	Lira	430,375.00	1,470,742.00

Source: http://www.xe.com/ucc/; http://www.xe.com/ict/; http://www.x-rates.com

Questions and Research

1. Find the latest quotations for these currencies.

2. Calculate the approximate changes in the value of these currencies. Show the increase or decrease in relation to the U.S. dollar.

3. Why have these changes occurred? (Give a general explanation.)

4. What are some of the implications of changing exchange rates for marketers?

CASE 2.2 U.S. Pharmaceuticals, Inc. (A)

U.S. Pharmaceuticals (USP) is a U.S. firm with about 30 percent of its sales outside the United States. USP concentrates on the ethical drug business but has diversified into animal health products, cosmetics, and some patent medicines. These other lines account for about one-fourth of USP's $800 million sales.

USP's international business is conducted in some 70 countries, mostly through distributors in those markets. In six countries, however, it has manufacturing or compounding operations. (*Compounding* refers to the local mixing, assembling, and packaging of critical ingredients shipped from the United States.) USP's only Latin American manufacturing/compounding operations are in Latinia, a country with a population of about 30 million. Some products are shipped from Latinia to other Latin American markets.

USP's Latinian plant is operated by the pharmaceutical division. It is engaged in producing and compounding USP's ethical drug line. It does no work for other USP divisions (cosmetics, proprietary medicines, and animal health). All the other divisions, which also sell in Latinia, export their finished products from plants in the United States. The Latinian plant employs 330 people, of whom only two are North Americans—the general manager, Tom Hawley, and the director of quality control, Frixos Massialas.

USP's cosmetics and toiletries business accounts for $150 million in sales and is handled by a separate division—Cosmetics and Toiletries. The division sells in only 38 of USP's 70 foreign markets. One of the division's better foreign markets is Latinia, where it has sales of over $8 million and an acceptable market position. Cosmetics and Toiletries has a marketing subsidiary in Latinia to handle its business there. Jim Richardson, an American, heads the subsidiary. The rest of the staff are Latinians.

Jim Richardson was very disturbed by news received from the Latinian Ministry of International Trade. Tariffs were being increased on many "nonessential products" because of the balance-of-payments pressures the country had been experiencing for the past year and a half. For USP's Cosmetics and Toiletries specifically, this meant a rise in the tariffs it pays—from 20 percent to 50 percent *ad valorem*. The 20 percent duty had posed no particular problem for Cosmetics and Toiletries because of the prestige of the imported product and the consumer franchise it had established, Richardson explained. He believed, however, that the 50 percent duty was likely to be an insurmountable barrier.

Cosmetics and Toiletries' competition in Latinia was about evenly divided between local firms and other international companies from Europe and North America. Jim believed that local firms, which had about 40 percent of the market, stood to benefit greatly from the tariff increase unless the international firms could find a satisfactory response. When Jim received the news of the tariff increase, which was to be imposed the first of October—one week away—he called a meeting to consider what Cosmetics and Toiletries could do. Deborah Neale, manager, Cosmetics Marketing, and Emilio Illanes, manager, Toiletries Marketing, met with Jim to discuss the situation.

Several different courses of action were proposed at the hastily called meeting. Deborah suggested, "We could continue importing, pay the high duty, and change the positioning strategy to appeal to a high-price, premium market." Another idea was to import the primary ingredients and assemble (compound) and package them in Latinia. (Duties on the imported ingredients ranged between 10 percent and 35 percent *ad valorem*.) Emilio suggested asking Cosmetics and Toiletries in the United States for a lower price on the products shipped to Latinia so that the duty would have a lesser impact on the final price in the local market. Jim mentioned the alternative that none of them wanted to think about. "If we can't compete at those high prices, we may have to give up the market."

Questions and Research

1. Evaluate the alternatives that were brought up at the meeting.
2. Are there any other possible courses of action? Explain.
3. Propose and defend a course of action.
4. How would your response differ if, instead of a tariff increase, Latinia had imposed a quota cutting the imports of these products by 75 percent?

NOTES

1. Tony Smith, "Peso's Devaluation Gives Argentina Cost Advantages," *The New York Times*, October 24, 2002, section W.
2. TradeStats Express website, Foreign Trade Division, U.S. Census Bureau (http://tse.export.gov/); accessed May 31, 2010.
3. Adam Smith, *The Wealth of Nations* (Chicago: University of Chicago Press, 1976). First published 1776.
4. Bertil Ohlin, *Interregional and International Trade* (Cambridge, MA: Harvard University Press, 1933).
5. For a good discussion of export of service, see the WTO Publication "Opening Markets for Trade in Services: Countries and Sectors in Bilateral and WTO Negotiations" (Geneva, Switzerland: World Trade Organization, 2009).
6. Gary A. Knight and S. Tamer Cavusgil, "The Born Global Firm: A Challenge to Traditional Internationalization Theory," *Advances in International Marketing* 8 (1996): 11–26.
7. "Euro Trashed; The Greek Debt Crisis Could Be the Beginning of the End of Europe's Answer to the Dollar," *Newsweek*, May 31, 2010, U.S. edition; "World News: The Word on IMF's Task in Greece: Herculean," *The Wall Street Journal*, May 29, 2010; CIA World Factbook website (https://www.cia.gov/library/publications/the-world-factbook/rankorder/2004rank.html), accessed May 31, 2010; "Barron's Daily Stock Alert: Raise a Glass to Owens-Illinois," *Barron's*, May 24, 2010, M4; "European Businesses Hit in Credit Squeeze from Greek Crisis," *The New York Times*, May 18, 2010, New York edition.
8. "EU Ponders Duty on Foreign Airlines," *Financial Post*, March 13, 2002, world edition; "Airlines Face More Heavy Losses," *South China Morning Post*, May 28, 2002, Business Post section; "U.S. Carriers Could Incur Large Costs from EC Tariff Plan," *Airline Financial News*, March 25, 2002 (Note: The reference to EC is the European Commission); Documents on Air Transport Services, the World Trade Organization, Air Transport Services (http://www.wto.org/english/tratop_e/serv_e/transport_e/transport_air_e.htm), accessed September 30, 2010.
9. Understanding the WTO: The Organization (http://www.wto.org/english/thewto_e/tif_e/org6_e.htm); accessed June 3, 2010.
10. Membership of UNCTAD and TDB, (http://www.unctad.org/templates/Page.asp?intItemID = 1929&lang = 1); accessed June 3, 2010.
11. Pankaj Ghemaway, "Distance Still Matters: The Hard Reality of Global Expansion," *Harvard Business Review* 79, no. 8 (2001): 137–47.
12. U.S. Direct Investment Abroad: Balance of Payments and Direct Investment Position Data (http://www.bea.gov/international/di1usdbal.htm); accessed May 25, 2010.
13. Vern Terpstra and Chwo-Ming Yu, "Determinants of Foreign Investment of U.S. Advertising Agencies," *Journal of International Business Studies* 19, no. 1 (1988): 33–46; Kenichi Ohmae, *The End of the National State: The Rise of Regional Economies* (New York: The Free Press, 1995); Paul D. Ellis, "Paths to Foreign Markets: Does Distance to Market Affect Firm Internationalization?" *International Business Review* 16, no. 5 (2007): 573–93.

chapter

3 The Political–Legal Environment

The politics and laws of a nation dramatically influence the practice of international marketing. The political–legal environment of international business has three dimensions: the host country, home country, and international environments. The many laws affecting international marketing fall into three categories: U.S. law, international law, and foreign law.

The main goals of this chapter are to ● ● ●

1. Discuss concepts critical to nations, such as sovereignty and security, in order to understand political risk.

2. Describe the role of firms in the political and legal environment—how firms are shaped by it and how firms shape the laws and politics of a nation.

3. Identify the areas of the home country environment that affect a firm's international marketing.

4. Explain how U.S. export controls, antitrust laws, and tax laws affect the feasibility and profitability of a U.S. firm's international marketing.

5. Discuss the effect of international organizations such as the International Monetary Fund (IMF) and the Word Trade Organization (WTO) and regional groups such as the European Union (EU) on the international legal environment.

6. Describe international conventions designed to protect intellectual property.

The Political Environment

The **political environment** of international marketing includes any national or international political factor that can affect operations of a firm. A factor is political when it derives from the government sector.

Host Country Political Environment

By definition, an international firm is a guest, a foreigner in all of its markets abroad. Therefore, international managers are especially concerned with nationalism and dealings with governments in host countries.

HOST COUNTRY NATIONAL INTERESTS

One way to gain an understanding of the situation in a foreign market is to see how compatible a firm's activities are with the interests of the host country. Although each country has its own set of national goals, most countries share many common objectives. Nationalism and patriotism refer to citizens' feelings about their country and its interests. Such feelings exist in every country. The celebration of a major holiday in recognition of a country's birthday and its achievement of independence or nationhood reinforces the sense of national identity and nationalism.

All countries want to maintain and enhance their **national sovereignty**—control over their own government and internal affairs without external influence. Foreign firms, individually or collectively, may be perceived as a threat to that sovereignty. The larger and more numerous the foreign firms, the more likely they are to be perceived as a threat—or at least an irritant. In times of turmoil, foreign firms and foreign embassies may be targets, such as the 1979 seizure of the U.S. embassy in Iran.[1]

Countries want to protect their national security. Although a foreign firm is not a military threat as such, it may be considered as being potentially prejudicial to national security. Governments generally prohibit foreign firms from involvement in "sensitive" industries such as defense, communications, and perhaps energy and natural resources. For example, when Libya nationalized the service stations of foreign oil companies, the reason it gave was that this commodity was too important to be in the hands of foreigners. When a firm is from a country deemed unfriendly to the host country, the firm may have difficulty operating or may even be denied admission.

Countries also recognize the potential positive impact of foreign firms, in particular the chance to enhance their economic welfare. Generally, this means increasing employment and income in the country. Foreign firms contribute by generating employment. They can contribute further by using local suppliers and having local content in their products. They can contribute further still by exporting from the country and generating foreign exchange. They can contribute in a different way by supplying products, services, and/or training that enhance productivity.

Depending on the current position of a country's government, the country may embrace foreign firms, or it may severely restrict local involvement by foreign firms. Most developed countries, such as the United States or countries in Western Europe, embrace local investments by foreign firms. North Korea is an example of the opposite position; it still maintains a very closed economy. But regardless of their position, all countries utilize some form of host country controls. The goal is to try to ensure desirable behavior by foreign firms—and to prevent undesirable behavior.

ENTRY RESTRICTIONS. If allowed to enter a country, a firm may be restricted in terms of industries it can enter. A firm may be prohibited from acquiring a national firm. It may not be allowed 100 percent ownership, instead being required to enter a joint venture with a national firm. It may be restricted as to the products it can sell. For example, the United Kingdom, Australia, Brazil, and Canada are debating whether to reduce foreign ownership restrictions on media. Post–9/11 United States is not likely to loosen (and may even tighten) current ownership regulations. (A domestically owned free press is viewed as critical for imparting an unbiased view of local and global events.)

QUOTAS AND TARIFFS. A country's quotas and tariffs may limit a firm's ability to import equipment, components, and products, forcing a higher level of local procurement than the firm may want.

EXCHANGE CONTROL. Many countries run chronic deficits in their balance of payments and are short of foreign exchange. They ration its use according to their priorities. Foreign firms may be low on that priority list and have difficulty getting foreign exchange for needed imports or profit repatriation. For example, Venezuela maintains a strict control on the exchange of bolivars, which as seen recently, can have a critical impact on importers and exports. In 2010, as exports decreased due to the global economic crisis, the government agency tasked with exchange control, the Foreign Exchange Administration Commission (CADIVI), seemed to have reduced the number of permits it provided for currency exchange. The number approved in early 2010 was dramatically less than that in 2009. This would have the effect of reducing imports (because importers are unable to buy foreign currency), likely leading to an increase in demand for domestic goods.[2]

(FORCED) ASSET TRANSFER. This type of transfer can take the form of **confiscation** (government seizure of assets with no remuneration), **expropriation** (seizure with some compensation, though typically less than fair market value or a firm's valuation), or **nationalization** (seizure of entire industries, such as banking and railroad, regardless of nationality). Fortunately, expropriation,

confiscation
Government seizure of assets without remuneration.

expropriation
Government seizure of assets with some compensation, usually less than fair market value or the firm's valuation of the assets.

nationalization
Government seizure of entire industries, regardless of nationality.

confiscation, and nationalization are occurring less often as developing countries begin to see foreign direct investment (FDI) as desirable.

Future host country controls will likely focus on the protection of individuals and national security, protection of privacy rights, corporate ethical behavior, and environmental protection. These complicated issues will lead to different, often conflicting laws. Mexico's "opt-in" program is one example of a privacy rights law. In Mexico, direct marketers are required to purchase a list of people who have expressed an interest in receiving direct mail. There are also the European Data Protection Directive and the U.S. anti-spam initiatives.

Political Risk Assessment

As a firm considers its international expansion options, it must balance the commercial opportunities in a country against the risks of that country. As discussed in Chapter 8, if the foreign market entry mode will involve significant foreign direct investment, such as a manufacturing facility, assessing these risks will be critical. Not surprisingly, research shows that managers pay close attention to political risk and seek to minimize political risk when expanding internationally.[3] In addition, the greater the potential political risk, the less commitment managers are willing to make to international markets.[4]

Political risk is the possibility that actions or policies by a government may adversely affect a firm's operations and profits. Political risk encompasses the whole of a country's business environment, including political, economic, and legal conditions. These risks include expropriation, nationalization, terrorism, social unrest, political and economic instability, protection of intellectual property, and government policies concerning business practices and international trade.

> **political risk**
>
> The possibility that actions or policies by a government may adversely affect a firm's operations and profits.

Table 3-1 • The Euler Hermes Global Political Risk Rankings[5]

Euler Hermes has developed a methodology that combines both political and economic analyses when looking at developing and emerging economies. This produces country rankings in six categories, from the safest (AA) to potentially the most risky (D).

Euler Hermes Rating: AA

Number of countries: 35

% of world GDP 2006: 70.8%

Strong economic structure and policy framework (industrialized economy or similar). Negligible risk of external liquidity crisis. Generally sound business environment. Negligible risk of political instability. Strong capacity to respond to economic crisis.

Euler Hermes Rating: A

Number of countries: 44

% of world GDP 2006: 4.4%

Economic structure and policy framework generally adequate. Very low risk of external liquidity crisis. Generally sound business environment. Negligible risk of political instability. Good capacity to respond to economic crisis.

Euler Hermes Rating: BB

Number of countries: 20

% of world GDP 2006: 7.4%

Some signs of structural and policy weakness. External liquidity adequate, some weaknesses in business environment and/or identified but moderate risk of political instability and adequate capacity to respond to economic crisis.

EulerEuler Hermes Rating: B

Number of countries: 27

% of world GDP 2006: 9.2%

A range of structural and policy weaknesses and/or vulnerable external liquidity position, some weaknesses in business environment and/or serious weaknesses in political framework with higher risk of political instability and limited capacity to respond to economic crisis.

Analyzing the political risk of a country is an important but difficult task for the international marketing manager. A firm may rely on in-house skills to estimate political risk but will more likely use outside resources for research and insights into a country's overall risk. One government example is the U.S. Department of Commerce/U.S. Commercial Service, which reports regularly on a country's business environment, especially from the perspective of a U.S. company seeking to do business in that country. This analysis is contained in the Country Commercial Guides available at www.export.gov. The U.S. Commercial Service also has country and regional experts based in Washington, D.C., as well as employees posted around the world. Often their staff specialize in particular industries and can offer assistance in understanding the industry-specific risks for a country.

Private companies also offer political risk assessment. An example is Euler Hermes. Although its primary service is international trade-related insurance (credit insurance), the company also provides global political risk analysis. As shown in Table 3-1, Euler Hermes categorizes countries in one of six grades: from the least risk (AA) to potentially the highest risk (D). Examples of countries rated in 2009 as the least risky include the United States, the countries of Western Europe, and Australia. Those judged most risky include a number of sub-Saharan countries such as Angola and Sudan, a number of countries in the Middle East including Iran and Iraq, and various other countries around the world. Euler Hermes also offers country profiles and bulletins discussing current risk-related events. Other private companies offering political risk assessment include The Economist Intelligence Unit (www.eiu.com), The PRS Group (www.progroup.com), and Moody's (www.moodys.com). For more insights, visit www.countryrisk.com.

Euler Hermes Rating: C

Number of countries: 39

% of world GDP 2006: 5.6%

Deep structural weaknesses and/or strong policy measures required and/or external liquidity risk is high, serious weaknesses in business environment and/or serious weaknesses in political framework with higher risk of political instability and little capacity to respond to economic crisis.

Euler Hermes Rating: D

Number of countries: 76

% of world GDP 2006: 2.6%

Structurally very weak and policy ineffective and/or current/imminent external liquidity crisis, serious weakness in business environment and/or actual or very high risk of political instability. No capacity to respond to economic crisis.

EXTERNAL FACTORS

In its own study of the political environment, a firm can include a preliminary analysis of its political vulnerability in a particular host country. An analysis of external factors should be conducted first, followed by company factors.

Political risk factors external to a firm's control are as follows:

- **Firm's home country.** A firm is usually better accepted in a country that has good relations with the firm's home country.

- **Product or industry.** Sensitivity of the industry is an important consideration. Generally, raw materials, public utilities, communications, pharmaceuticals, and defense-related products are most sensitive.

- **Size and location of operations.** The larger the foreign firm, the more threatening it is perceived to be. This is especially true when the firm has large facilities and is located in a prominent urban area, such as the capital, which serves as a constant reminder of the foreign presence.

- **Visibility of the firm.** The greater the visibility of the foreign firm, the greater its vulnerability. Visibility is a function of several factors, including the size and location of the firm's operations in the country and the nature of the firm's products. Consumer goods are more visible than industrial goods. Finished goods are more visible than components or inputs that are hidden in the final product. Heavy advertisers are more visible than nonadvertisers. International brands are more provocative than localized brands.

- **Host country political situation.** The political situation can affect a firm. The company should thus evaluate a country's political risk. (See the box entitled "Terrorism—Taking Its Toll.")

••• Terrorism—Taking Its Toll

Terrorism takes a terrible toll, not just because of the death and destruction, which is horrific, but also because of the loss of a sense of security that people everywhere feel. Examples include the killing of the Olympic athletes in Munich in 1972; the attacks on the eastern United States on September 11, 2001, when approximately 3,000 people were killed; and the hostage taking in a Moscow school in September 2004 that resulted in over 300 deaths, many of whom were children. As horrific as these events were, they provide only some understanding of terrorism.

Unfortunately, acts of terrorism are an everyday occurrence, and foreign businesses often represent symbolic targets for terrorists. In addition, many terrorist groups focus on "soft" targets such as the hotels, restaurants, and transportation used by tourists and business travelers. Smaller-scale terrorism includes the kidnapping and ransom of business executives, government officials, and others. A recent survey of businesses showed that more than one in three businesses expect their personnel or facilities to be targeted by some form of terrorism, and two-thirds of respondents believe that terrorism is a significant threat to them. International marketing managers need to be aware of the political and terrorism risks wherever their firm has facilities or employees.

Businesses can also help combat global terrorism. The U.S. Customs and Border Protection (CBP) created a program called the Customs-Trade Partnership Against Terrorism, or C-TPAT. C-TPAT is a voluntary program designed to help businesses secure their supply chains by working with government and other entities to provide the highest level of cargo security.[6]

Terrorists often select high-profile business symbols of capitalism as targets. Firms must take steps to protect their facilities and employees.

COMPANY FACTORS

The risk factors listed here are more controllable because firms are the decision makers:

- **Company behavior.** Each firm develops some record of corporate citizenship based on its practices. Some firms are more sensitive and responsive to the situation in the host country than others. Goodwill in this area is a valuable asset, and multinational organizations are increasingly expected not only to be good corporate citizens in the host country but also perhaps be part of the solution to local problems.[7]

- **Contributions of the firm to the host country.** Many of these contributions are objective and quantifiable. How much employment has been generated? How much tax has been paid? How many exports has the firm generated? What new resources or skills has the firm brought in?

- **Localization of operations.** Generally, the more localized a firm's operations, the more acceptable the firm is to the host country. There are several dimensions to localization, including having local equity, hiring local managers and technical staff, using local content in the products (including local suppliers of goods and services, for example), developing local products, and using local brand names.

- **Subsidiary dependence.** This factor somewhat contradicts the preceding point. The more a firm's local operation depends on the parent company, the less vulnerable it is. If a firm cannot function as a separate, self-contained unit but is dependent on the parent for critical resources and/or for markets, it will be seen as a less rewarding takeover target.

Political monitoring and analysis are continuing tasks for a firm. A firm must use the information that these analyses provide to manage its political relations. Table 3-2 suggests some approaches to managing potential political risk, both before and after entering a country. The U.S. Department of State maintains a website focused exclusively on issues associated with foreign travel (http://travel.state.gov). It contains useful reports on most countries, including

Table 3-2 • Managing Political Risk

Pre-entry Planning

1. Perform research; assess potential risks. Review U.S. Department of State travel advisories and warnings.
2. Avoid threatening countries.
3. Negotiate with host government. (Include planned domestication.)
4. Purchase insurance: Government agencies such as ExIm Bank and private providers provide insurance against political risk. Chubb Group offers kidnap, ransom, and extortion insurance.[8]
5. Adjust entry method. Indirect exporting, for example, has little-to-no political risk because a partner company does the exporting.
6. Use local capital, which avoids exposure to foreign banks or foreign stock markets.

Post-entry Planning

1. Have a monitoring system.
2. Develop a corporate communications program.
3. Develop local stakeholders (employees, suppliers, customers).
4. Have appropriate national executives and an appropriate advisory board.
5. Change operations over time as perceived host country cost-benefit ratio changes; for example, new products and processes, more local equity and management, new exports, and local R&D.
6. Have contingency plans.

the well-regarded travel advisories and travel warnings, which provide country-specific insights as to potential issues associated with international travel. Many companies use the guidance provided by the State Department as an important benchmark for internal travel policies.

International Political Environment

The international political environment involves political relations between two or more countries. This is in contrast to the previous concern for what happens only within a given foreign country. An international firm almost inevitably becomes involved with the host country's international relations, no matter how neutral it may try to be. It does so, first, because it is a foreigner from a specific home country and, second, because its operations in a country are frequently related to operations in other countries, on the supply side, the demand side, or both.

One aspect of a country's international relations is its relationship with a firm's home country. U.S. firms abroad are affected by a host nation's attitude toward the United States. When a host nation dislikes any aspect of U.S. policy, it may be the U.S. firm that is bombed or boycotted along with the U.S. Embassy.

A second critical element affecting the political environment is a host country's relations with other nations. If a country is a member of a regional group, such as the EU or ASEAN, that fact influences a firm's evaluation of the country. If a nation has particular friends or enemies among other nations, a firm must modify its international logistics to comply with how that market is supplied and to whom it can sell. For example, the United States limits trade with various countries. Arab nations have boycotted companies dealing with Israel.

Another clue to a nation's behavior is its membership in nongovernmental organizations (NGOs). Besides regional groupings, NGOs also affect a member's behavior. Members of NATO, for example, accept a military agreement that may restrict their military or political action. Membership in WTO reduces the likelihood that a country will impose new trade barriers. Membership in the IMF or the World Bank also puts constraints on a country's behavior. Many other international agreements impose rules on their members. These agreements may affect patents, communication, transportation, and other items of interest to the international marketer. As a general rule, the more international organizations a country belongs to, the more regulations it accepts—and the more dependable its behavior.

HOME COUNTRY POLITICAL ENVIRONMENT

A firm's home country political environment can constrain its international as well as domestic operations. The political environment can limit the countries that an international firm will enter. As discussed in the next section, the U.S. has sanctions in place that partially or totally prohibit trade with specific countries.

The best-known example of the home country political environment affecting international operations used to be South Africa. Home country political pressures induced more than 200 American firms to leave that country in the latter decades of the twentieth century. After U.S. companies left South Africa, the Germans and the Japanese remained as the major foreign presence. German firms did not face the same political pressures at home that U.S. firms did. However, the Japanese government was embarrassed when Japan became South Africa's leading trading partner. As a result, some Japanese companies reduced their South African activity. Matsushita closed an office there; Sanyo and Nissan reduced their exports to South Africa; NEC and Pioneer Electronics agreed to suspend exports.

Another example is PepsiCo and Myanmar. Pressure from American human rights groups induced some U.S. firms to leave Myanmar. PepsiCo pulled out of a joint venture even though it held 85 percent of the soft drink market there.

legal environment

A nation's laws and regulations pertaining to business that also influence the operations of a foreign firm.

One challenge facing multinationals is that they have a triple-threat political environment. Even if the home country and the host country pose no problem, multinational firms can face threats in third markets. Firms that do not have problems with their home government or the host government, for example, can be bothered or boycotted in third countries. An example is the lengthy Nestlé boycott in the late 1970s, which centered around the issue of Nestlé promoting breast milk substitutes. The boycott against the Swiss firm started in the United States and quickly spread to other countries.

The Legal Environment

In addition to the political environment in a nation, the **legal environment**—that is, the nation's laws and regulations pertaining to business—also influences the operations of a foreign firm. A firm must know the legal environment in each market because those laws constitute the "rules of the game." At the same time, a firm must know the political environment because it determines how the laws are enforced and indicates the direction of new legislation. The legal environment of international marketing is complicated, possessing three dimensions. For a U.S. firm, these are (1) U.S. laws, (2) international law, and (3) domestic laws in each of the firm's foreign markets.

U.S. Law and International Trade

U.S. firms are familiar with domestic regulations affecting domestic business, such as the truth-in-advertising laws and the Uniform Commercial Code. These are not the U.S. laws that affect international marketing, however. Numerous other laws are relevant to international marketing and relate to exporting, antitrust, and organization and ownership arrangements.

EXPORT CONTROLS

A priority of the U.S. government has long been to control "what" and "where" U.S. companies may export. The "what" includes military goods or technologies for which the U.S. government wants to restrict exports for reasons of national security. The "where" is controlling which countries are allowed to receive some—or indeed any—U.S. exports, again for national security concerns or political reasons. Export controls refer to a broad range of U.S. laws that govern what products may be exported and to which countries. Understanding these controls has become significantly more important post 9/11 as the U.S. government has increased its surveillance of U.S. companies (see Table 3-3). The fines and penalties for non-compliance have also been increased.

It is relatively clear why some products would be subject to export controls. Examples are ammunitions; sophisticated aircraft; biological, nuclear, or conventional weapons; and nuclear technologies. Other products appear less evident. In particular are products classified as **dual-use goods**— products that have both commercial and military or proliferation applications. Examples are high-precision instruments, advanced textiles (for example, those that can change color to mimic surroundings), and sophisticated encryption

Table 3-3 • U.S. Government Departments and Agencies with Export Control Responsibilities[9]

- **Department of State, Directorate of Defense Trade Controls (DTC).** The DTC licenses defense services and defense (munitions) articles.

- **Department of the Treasury, Office of Foreign Assets Control (OFAC).** OFAC administers and enforces economic and trade sanctions against targeted foreign countries, terrorism-sponsoring organizations, and international narcotics traffickers. The OFAC website provides information on these sanctions as well as the complete list of Specially Designated Nationals and Blocked Persons list (the "SDN list").

- **Nuclear Regulatory Commission, Office of International Programs.** The NRC licenses nuclear material and equipment.

- **Department of Energy, Office of Arms Controls and Nonproliferation, Export Control Division.** The DOE licenses nuclear technology and technical data for nuclear power and special nuclear materials.

- **Department of Energy, Office of Fuels Programs.** The DOE also licenses natural gas and electric power.

- **Defense Technology Security Administration.** The DTSA administers the development and implementation of Department of Defense (DoD) technology security policies on international transfers of defense-related goods, services, and technologies.

- **Department of the Interior, U.S. Fish and Wildlife Service.** The FWS manages import and export of wildlife and endangered and threatened species.

- **Drug Enforcement Administration, Office of Diversion Control, Import-Export Unit.** The DEA oversees the export of controlled substances and the import and export of listed chemicals used in the production of control substances under the Controlled Substances Act.

- **Food and Drug Administration, Office of Compliance.** The FDA regulates the export of unapproved medical devices

- **Food and Drug Administration, Import/Export.** The FDA also licenses drugs for import and export.

- **Patent and Trademark Office, Licensing and Review.** The PTO oversees patent filing data sent abroad.

- **Environmental Protection Agency, Office of Enforcement and Compliance Assurance.** The EPA regulates hazardous waste exports.

> **dual-use goods**
>
> Products that have both commercial and military or weapons proliferation applications.

software. These products are widely available within the United States for domestic sale. Although they have commercial use (use by ordinary businesses and individuals), they also have the potential for use in military or terrorism applications, which is why the United States controls their export.

How do exporters know what and to whom they may ship? There are many agencies in the U.S. government with trade oversight responsibilities, as shown in Table 3-3. However, the four most significant are

- **U.S. Department of Commerce, Bureau of Industry and Security (BIS).** This agency has responsibility for controlling dual-use goods and technology that could threaten U.S. security if improperly exported. BIS also maintains directories of individuals and companies (parties) that have been identified by BIS as having engaged in activities that threaten U.S. national security or for which BIS has been unable to verify their status.

- **U.S. Customs and Border Protection (CBP).** As related to the trade of goods, the CBP's mission is to keep the United States safe by preventing the illegal entry of goods and to ensure the appropriate duties and fees are paid. CBP also ensures counterfeit goods are not illegally imported. On the export side, CBP maintains the Automated Export System (AES) in partnership with other federal agencies. AES allows for electronic submission of the Electronic Export Information (EEI) record (previously known as the Shippers Export Declaration) and for filing export licenses.

- **U.S. Department of the Treasury, Office of Foreign Assets Control (OFAC).** The role of OFAC is to enforce U.S. economic and trade sanctions with specific countries such as Cuba and Iran, as well as individuals. The basis of the sanctions may be political or national security.

- **U.S. Department of State, the Directorate of Defense Trade Controls (DDTC).** This agency regulates the exports of defense articles and services, including guns, ammunition, explosives, military-related products such as tanks and training equipment, and protective personal equipment. The DDTC controls these products under the guidelines of the *International Traffic in Arms Regulations (ITAR)*.

It is important to note that U.S. export controls are not an absolute ban on exports, nor are sanctions. The role of the preceding agencies is to regulate the export of involved goods. This means that U.S. companies may very well be able to export products such as guns or dual-use goods. To legally do so, however, the U.S. company must receive authorization, typically an export license, from the appropriate agency. For example, not all exports are prohibited to Cuba. Shipments of certain products are permitted, such as agricultural products, medicines, and medical supplies.

There are fines and other penalties for those firms that do not adhere to the export control regulations. In one case, a New Jersey firm paid $30,000 because it violated U.S. regulations by shipping chemicals through the United Arab Emirates to Iran. The company also violated Arab antiboycott rules by verifying that the goods did not originate in Israel. In another case, a fine of $52,500 was imposed on a firm for illegally selling sophisticated measuring devices used in constructing military hardware to Singapore, Taiwan, and Thailand. In yet another example, a $2.12 million penalty was imposed on McDonnell Douglas for allegedly exporting machine tools to China, while the Chinese firms that accepted shipment of the tools were slapped with a $1.32 million penalty and a denial of export privileges order. And in yet another example, the Department of Commerce imposed a fine of $30,000 on Hans Wrage & Co. for re-exporting nearly $500,000 worth of shotguns from Germany to Poland. Although Hans

U.S. exporters must obtain an export license prior to shipping any goods under export controls of the U.S. government. Failure to obtain such a license can result in significant fines.

Wrage is a German firm, the guns originated in the United States, and the company shipped them to Poland without the required U.S. authorization. The U.S. Department of Commerce, through BIS, administers and enforces export controls. Violations of Export Administration Regulations may result in fines, as in the examples provided (typically being settled rather than going to court), but can also lead to criminal penalties and administrative sanctions. Chapter 11 discusses best practices in compliance with export controls and the required documentation. See Case 3.2 for more examples of export violations.

ANTITRUST CONTROLS

It might seem strange that U.S. antitrust laws would affect the foreign business activities of U.S. companies. However, that is a fact. The opinion of the U.S. Justice Department is that even if an act is committed abroad, it falls within the jurisdiction of U.S. courts if the act produces consequences within the United States. Many activities of U.S. businesses abroad have repercussions on the U.S. domestic market. The question arises primarily in three situations: (1) when a U.S. firm acquires a foreign firm, (2) when it engages in a joint venture with a foreign firm, or (3) when it enters into an overseas marketing agreement with another firm.

The two agencies in the U.S. government that have jurisdiction over antitrust regulations for most industries are the Department of Justice (DOJ) and the Federal Trade Commission (FTC). There are many antitrust regulations, but perhaps the most familiar are the Sherman Antitrust Act passed in 1890 and the Clayton Antitrust Act from 1913. When a U.S. firm expands abroad or when a foreign corporation enters the U.S. market by acquiring an existing company, the DOJ and FTC are concerned about the possible impact on competition in the United States. If it is determined that the activity is anticompetitive, it will not be approved; or if the activity is already underway, it may be halted. As shown in the following examples, there are civil and criminal penalties, including officer liability, for corporate violations. Government action is more likely when the firms are in the same industry.

The acquisition of the Princess Cruise Line (United Kingdom) by American rival Carnival had to be brought before the FTC. Although the European Commission approved a takeover bid, the FTC initially had not decided how to classify the market in which these firms operate—as "holiday industry" or "high-end cruise industry." If it had been the latter, approval was unlikely because that classification is more specialized and has fewer firms. Subsequently, the acquisition was approved.

Companies must receive governmental approvals when business activities impact international business between countries. An example was the Carnival Cruise Line's acquisition of the Princess Cruise Line.

Joint venturing, alliances, and other forms of cooperation among firms can lead to government intervention, too. The reasoning by the government is the same: Competition in the U.S. market will be reduced by a particular marriage of a U.S. and foreign firm, regardless of location.

Laws in the United States can reach foreign countries and affect the international marketing of U.S. and foreign firms. These laws also affect international marketing by foreign firms operating in the United States; foreign firms are also subject to U.S. antitrust regulation.

Three of the world's largest dynamic random access memory (DRAM) chip makers were part of an industrywide investigation into anticompetitive **predatory pricing**, which is the practice of pricing a product at a very low price (perhaps below cost) to gain market share and take business away from competitors. Micron Technology (United States), Samsung Electronics (Korea), and Infineon Technologies (Germany) were suspected of keeping prices artificially low in order to drive smaller competitors out of the industry. The commodity-like price for 128 megabit chips rose from $1 to over $2, but it was still considerably less than the estimated $4 it cost to manufacture them.

The 2009 movie *The Informant!* detailed the real-life story of Mark Whitacre, a past employee of Illinois-based Archer Daniels Midland (ADM). Whitacre confessed to the FBI that he and other ADM employees were involved in a global price-fixing scheme of lysine, which is a food additive used in the cattle industry. With Whitacre's help, the FBI secretly taped the price-fixing conversations of ADM and its competitors during various meetings around the world. The U.S. Department of Justice eventually found ADM guilty of price fixing. Three senior executives were given prison sentences, and ADM was fined $100 million.

Businesses must contend with U.S. laws that are applied both in the United States and in firms' foreign markets. Companies must also be aware of the counterparts to the FTC and DOJ in other parts of the world, which may have their own perspective on the importance of competition and what might be viewed as anticompetitive behavior (see the box entitled "Government: Friend or Foe?"). A dramatic example of this was the attempted merger of General Electric (GE) and Honeywell in 2001. The proposed $43 billion acquisition of Honeywell by GE had been approved by the U.S. government, but it was blocked by the European Commission antitrust division. In other cases, companies face different penalties or requirements in different markets. For example, as part of the settlement in its antitrust cases, in 2005, Microsoft was fined $650 million and had to unbundle its Media Player software and Windows operating systems for the European market, but not in the United States or elsewhere.

OTHER U.S. LAWS

Examples of other U.S. laws affecting international trade include laws against bribery by U.S. firms, antiterrorism initiatives, and laws against the support of Arab boycotts.

FOREIGN CORRUPT PRACTICES ACT (FCPA)   As a result of public outcry in the late 1970s about the ethical behavior of firms and bribery, the U.S. government passed the Foreign Corrupt Practices Act (FCPA) to prohibit U.S. firms from paying bribes to foreign officials for the purpose of obtaining or keeping business. (Under the FCPA, "grease payments" are still allowed, defined as small payments to facilitate actions of a routine manner such as obtaining a permit.) At first, the problem for U.S. firms was that their competitors from Japan and Western Europe were not forbidden to use bribes. U.S. firms complained that the act put them at a serious competitive disadvantage because bribery has often been the most effective form of persuasion in business and government markets abroad. Fortunately, in December 1997, the members of the Organization for

---

predatory pricing

The practice of pricing a product at a very low price, sometimes below cost, to gain market share and take business away from competitors.

National governments play dual roles—both helping and hindering businesses in their international expansion.

In general, national leaders and lawmakers believe that trade is good for the economy and that exports mean more jobs and a better chance of getting reelected. In 2010, President Obama stated a goal of doubling U.S. exports and supporting two million U.S. jobs via exports within the next five years. In the United States, governments at the local, state, and federal levels have various programs to encourage exports. These programs include market research, trade missions, trade-lead matching, as well as programs to identify partners in international markets. Many U.S. states and the U.S. Commercial Service have offices throughout the world to help U.S. businesses and promote U.S. products.

On the other hand, governments also enact legislation to limit trade to protect consumers against certain products (genetically modified foods, for example), as well as to support specific ideas. U.S. presidents since 1962 have supported a continued embargo against Cuba because of the Communist regime in that country. Annual votes in the UN show that most other nations around the world do not support the 50-year-old embargo, and many other countries openly trade with Cuba. One recent report indicated that the embargo costs U.S. businesses between $1 billion and $2 billion each year in travel-related industry alone.[10]

Government: Friend or Foe?

Economic Co-operation and Development (OECD), a group of 33 industrialized nations, and five nonmember countries signed the Convention on Combating Bribery of Foreign Public Officials in International Business Transactions. All participants have ratified the agreement, and all except Turkey adopted legislation to implement enforcement of the convention's articles.

Although the FCPA specifically prohibits bribes to foreign officials, bribes within the private sector are not illegal. However, multinational companies in the United States and elsewhere are taking an increasingly tougher stand against corruption of any kind. Often, this is reflected in a firm's "core values" statements. One example is that of the Carlsberg Group, one of the world's largest breweries. Carlsberg follows the United Nations Ten Principles, of which Principle Ten states that "businesses should work against corruption in all its forms, including extortion and bribery."[11] Firms are taking these strong stands against corruption in light of increases in corruption in particular countries, especially those with recently relaxes economies, such as Russia.

These policies do not mean the end of bribery or corruption. Transparency International, which researches public corruption around the world, publishes the Corruption Perceptions Index. Table 3-4 shows the scores of selected countries. Each country's score relates to perceptions of the degree of public corruption as seen by business and country analysts. Countries that rank high (for example, New Zealand, Denmark) are judged to have little public corruption—for example, bribery of government officials or embezzling of government funds. Countries that rank low, such as Somalia, are seen to have more corruption.

ANTITERRORISM REGULATION   After September 11, 2001, the United States and other governments became aware of the need to monitor and halt financing of terrorism. An example of an initiative to address this growing problem is the Uniting and Strengthening America by Providing Appropriate Tools Required to

The Carlsberg Group is an example of a growing number of companies adopting standards set by the United Nations for ethical behavior.

Table 3-4 • Transparency International Country Ranking of the Corruption Perceptions Index[12]

Rank	Country	CPI
1	New Zealand	9.4
2	Denmark	9.3
3	Singapore	9.2
3	Sweden	9.2
5	Switzerland	9.0
6	Netherlands	8.9
8	Australia	8.7
8	Canada	8.7
8	Iceland	8.7
19	United States	7.5
79	China	3.6
106	Argentina	2.9
111	Indonesia	2.8
146	Ecuador	2.2
168	Iran	1.8
180	Somalia	1.1

Intercept and Obstruct Terrorism Act of 2001 (USA PATRIOT Act). It expands reporting requirements by financial institutions and those businesses that conduct financial transactions with clients that might attract criminals or terrorists (a broad spectrum that includes banks, casinos, mutual fund investment houses, real estate agencies, travel agents, and jewelry dealers). Activities that are illegal or suspicious (for example, transferring large funds or purchasing many money orders in small amounts) must be reported to the government. This means that smaller transactions and more kinds of transactions will come under scrutiny and will require customers to give up privacy that many associate with firms in financial industries. Failure by businesses to comply with reporting these transactions can result in million dollar fines and other penalties.[13] Yet disclosure requirements in which one nation (for example, the United States) requests information on transactions that took place in another nation (for example, Switzerland) are a challenge to national sovereignty (Swiss in this example) and would undoubtedly raise issues of extraterritoriality.

ANTIBOYCOTT RULES   Antiboycott laws were enacted to prohibit U.S. firms from participating in foreign boycotts that the United States did not sanction. Although the Arab League boycott of Israel is the principal foreign economic boycott that U.S. companies must be concerned with today, the laws apply to all boycotts imposed by foreign countries that are unsanctioned by the United States. The oil wealth of the Arab states has given them power that they use in several ways. One way is to try to force companies that sell to lucrative markets not to have any dealings with Israel. In other words, the Arabs boycott firms that sell to Israel. Because the Arab markets are much larger collectively than the Israeli market, many firms are tempted to drop the Israeli market and sell to the Arabs. This is counter to U.S. foreign policy. An example of a request to violate the antiboycott rules is provided by BIS: "Importation of goods from Israel is strictly prohibited by Kuwait import regulations; therefore, certificate of origin covering goods originating in Israel is not acceptable."[14]

Companies found to be violating the antiboycott regulations must desist and may be subject to civil penalties. The penalties are often in the $5,000 to $50,000 range but can be larger. In 1993, Baxter International (medical equipment) agreed to pay a civil suit that exceeded $6 million for violating the anti-Arab boycott rules. In 2005, Maine Biological Labs received a $500,000 penalty for various charges, one of which was antiboycott violations.[15]

International Law and International Trade

No international lawmaking body corresponds to the legislatures of sovereign nations. What, then, is international law? For this discussion, it is defined as the collection of treaties, conventions, and agreements between nations that carry, more or less, the force of law. International law in this sense is quite different from national laws that have international implications, such as the U.S. antitrust laws. The international extension of U.S. law is on a unilateral basis. International law involves some mutuality, with two or more countries participating in the drafting and execution of laws or agreements.

Discussion of the impact of international law begins here with those international agreements having a general effect on international business and then addresses those dealing with more specific marketing questions. Then, the legal implications of regional groupings will be presented.

Tax and Other U.S. Treaties

Tax treaties that the United States has signed with a number of nations are generally bilateral and can have a significant impact on doing business internationally. One purpose of such treaties is to avoid double taxation; that is, if a company has paid income tax on its operations in a treaty nation, the United States will tax the firm's income only to the extent that the foreign tax rate is less than the U.S. rate. Thus, if the corporate income tax rates are equal in the two countries, there is no tax to pay in the United States on income earned in the other country. Obviously, tax treaty nations are, in general, better places for a subsidiary than countries that do not have such a treaty.

The Wassenaar Arrangement on Export Controls for Conventional Arms and Dual-Use Goods and Technologies is a multilateral treaty that the United States and 39 other nations have signed. The purpose of the agreement is to deny transfer of goods that could be used for military purposes and that might threaten the security of the participating nations.

Many other treaties exist between the United States and other nations. The examples provided here emphasize the need for careful evaluation of opportunities and the recognition that home rules as well as foreign regulations may have an impact on how, what, and where business is conducted.

IMF and WTO

The IMF and the WTO were discussed in Chapter 2, but both agreements are part of the limited body of effective international law. Both agreements identify acceptable and unacceptable behavior for member nations. Their effectiveness lies in their power to apply sanctions. The IMF can withhold its services from members that act "illegally," that is, contrary to the agreement. The WTO allows injured nations to retaliate against members who have broken its rules.

International marketers are interested in the IMF and WTO because of a shared concern in the maintenance of a stable environment conducive to international trade. These firms are concerned about the IMF's ability to reduce restrictions on international finance, and they support the WTO's efforts to free the international movement of goods.

The legal reach of the WTO and IMF does not extend to an international marketer's behavior, but rather to the behavior of the nations to which the firm is marketing. The environment for international marketing is more dependable and less capricious because of these two organizations.

The United Nations (UN), OECD, and Other International Organizations

Many other nongovernmental organizations do not have legislative rights or responsibilities over nations, but they are concerned about the behavior of firms and the impact their activities have on the economic and social well-being of the world. Examples are the UN, the OECD, and the World Health Organization (WHO). They also recognize that multinational businesses make a large contribution economically and socially and that an environment conducive to conducting international business is essential. To address these concerns, these bodies have developed codes of conduct, or guidelines, for ethically and socially responsible corporate behavior that promote the fair treatment of corporate entities. Although these international bodies do not formally coordinate or consult with one another in developing these guidelines, it is safe to assume that the people in each organization do review one another's work. Emphasis should be placed on the word *guidelines* because these do not constitute any form of international law.

CE mark

A product safety standard of the European Union.

Product safety standards, such as the UL, CE, and ISO marks, indicate a company has met the required standards. Meeting these requirements is often the only way a firm may sell its products into specific markets.

Standards Organizations

Numerous other NGOs have a semilegal influence on international marketing. One group of special interest is the International Organization for Standardization (ISO). The ISO is a nongovernmental organization that is a network of the national standards institutes of nearly 150 countries. ISO specifications are system standards about materials, products, processes, and services used in manufacturing products and supplying services. Industry groups in most of the major industrial countries participate in the work of the ISO, and many firms require that their partners be ISO-certified.

Perhaps the most recognized ISO standard adopted in the United States is ISO 9000, which helps ensure companies follow well-documented internal procedures to better ensure consistency throughout a firm's operations. Although ISO 9000 initially was a requirement enforced by European buyers, it has become a commonplace requirement even for domestic sales within the United States.

Product safety standards are another example of multinational standards that impact trade. The **CE mark** used within the European Union is one example. For particular products to be sold within the EU, such as medical products, machines, or toys, they must be certified to the CE mark standard. The UL mark in the United States and CCC in China are other examples.

Protecting Intellectual Property Rights

Intellectual property (IP) is the creative and technical output from individuals. It includes thoughts and ideas that are turned into new technologies, software, music, painting, books, and architectural designs. Four types of IP are protected by international law:

intellectual property (IP)

Abstract property created in the human mind. IP includes thoughts and ideas that are turned into paintings, music, software, and architectural designs, and the processes used to create products.

patents

Intellectual property protection for products, technology, and inventions.

trademarks

Intellectual property protection for words, phrases, symbols, and designs that distinguish one product from another.

copyrights

Intellectual property protection for artistic or literary works such as books, paintings, music, and software.

- **Patents.** Patents protect technology, inventions, and products.
- **Trademarks.** A trademark is a word, phrase, symbol, design, or combination of these. Trademarks are used to distinguish one product from other similar types of products, such as a brand name.
- **Copyrights.** Copyrights protect an original artistic or literary work and the expression of an idea. Copyrights are for books, paintings, and music.
- **Trade secrets.** Trade secrets protect company information that is highly secret to the company but otherwise not a patent, trademark, or copyright. Examples are competitive pricing and marketing activities strictly confidential to one firm. Another is the formula for the Coca-Cola Company's Coke® soft drink recipe.

Why is IP protection necessary? One problem is that rather than purchase a product from the producer, many consumers merely copy the product (for example, download music and DVDs from the Internet or copy software) or buy the product, sometimes unknowingly, from individuals who have copied the product without the permission of the IP owner and are selling unlicensed, counterfeited, or pirated copies. Lost revenue for the companies owning the IP is substantial. Estimates vary considerably, but the projected loss for software companies because of piracy was over $50 billion in 2009.[16]

Lost revenue is not the only justification for protecting IP. When the owners of IP are not paid for their inventions and other creations, they have little incentive to invest more time, effort, and money into creating and commercializing other new ideas. In the end, the consumer has fewer choices. Having fewer choices may not be so important when it comes to the latest video games or style of automobile, but it may be an issue for, say, the development of a cure for a deadly disease. In addition, countries with weak IP protection attract less foreign direct investment as international marketing managers choose not to enter or invest in countries that cannot protect their intellectual property.[17] This hurts the host country in addition to removing a potential market for the multinational business.

INTELLECTUAL PROPERTY PROTECTION (IPP)

IP without intellectual property protection (IPP) is not worth much because others could take and use a product, and there would be no need to compensate the inventor. Registration of trademarks and patents is a common method used to protect a firm's IP. The U.S. Patent and Trademark Office (USPTO) tracks information on applications filed in the United States and makes this information available, as do other national agencies in other countries. The USPTO received 485,500 patent applications and 411,818 trademark applications in 2009.[18] The World Intellectual Property Organization (WIPO) and other international organizations provide similar data. Most patents, trademarks, and copyrights are granted to companies and individuals in developed countries, except for the notable exception of China. For example, in 2007, of the 428,997 patents granted worldwide to local companies, the four countries with the most were Japan (145,040), South Korea (91,645), the United States (79,527), and China (36,003).[19] The importance of protection can be seen in "Pirates at Large."

PATENT AND TRADEMARK PROTECTION SYSTEMS

Many firms have patented and trademarked products to sell. When selling outside their home market, they want to protect their intellectual rights in those markets as well. Generally, applications for patents and trademarks must be filed separately in whatever country the firm wants protection. This can be a time-consuming and expensive process.

Because of the expense and inconvenience of applying for patents and trademarks in multiple countries, various efforts have been made to develop a multilateral approach. The main feature is a simplified application system, which can be a major convenience for firms wanting protection in many countries, although individual national filing fees generally must still be paid. The benefit is the elimination of duplicate procedures. Developing countries tend to accept the preliminary search and evaluation findings of industrialized countries.

Several efforts include global and regional agreements and conventions that are designed to eliminate some duplication in applying for IPP. There are also some multinational bodies whose mission encompasses IPP.

The most significant of the conventions is the **Paris Union** (officially called the Paris Convention for the Protection of Industrial Property) because of the broad scope of protection and the number of contracting member nations. The Paris Union includes 173 nations and allows a six-month protection period in the case of trademarks and a one-year period for patents. That is, registration of a trademark in one member country gives the firm six months in which to register in other member countries before it loses its protection in those countries. There are many other conventions, such as the **Berne Convention** that focuses on literary and artistic works and currently has 161 members.[20]

---

trade secrets

Proprietary company information that is highly secret to the company but not officially registered with a patent, trademark, or copyright.

Paris Union

A multilateral agreement offering trademark and patent protection among member countries. The agreement offers extended time in which to file for IPP in a member country.

Berne Convention

A multilateral agreement offering protection of literary and artistic works among member countries.

••• Pirates at Large

Piracy on the high seas still takes place, as indicated by the news headlines " Shipping Insurance Sky-rockets as Pirate Attacks Increase" and "Somalia: Pirates Attack Fishing Boats." This type of piracy is a serious commercial risk.

However, another type of piracy involves the illegal copying of trademarks and the manufacturing of fake products for resale. Many companies fall victim to piracy of IP and counterfeiting of their products, hurting their bottom line and their brand's image. With over one billion people, China is an attractive market for companies, but it is also a market in which a large percentage of trademarked goods are counterfeited. Procter & Gamble estimates that 15 percent of its soaps and detergents bearing the brand names Tide, Head & Shoulders, and Vidal Sassoon that are sold in China are fake (cost: $150 million per year). For Gillette, the situation is even worse: As many as 25 percent of all Gillette razors, Duracell batteries, and Parker pens are bogus. Anheuser-Busch representatives walked into a store to make an initial sales call only to find their beer on the shelves—identical in package, but not in taste. Pirates of Microsoft software have become so sophisticated that even experts have a difficult time telling what is real from what is fake.

Yamaha, recognizing the enormous potential in the Chinese market, entered into a joint venture with a state-owned motorbike manufacturer, investing $93 million to update three plants. Not only was the excess plant capacity used to produce copies of the Yamaha motorbikes, but the latest engine technology used in new products quickly showed up in the products of Yamaha's competitors. It is believed that as many as five of every six "Yamaha" motorbikes in China are fakes.

There are thousands of examples of piracy all over the world, including the United States. All one needs to do is walk down a crowded city block, where he or she is likely to see peddlers selling "Rolex" watches, "Kate Spade" handbags, and videos or DVDs of new movie releases. A store in a major Atlanta mall was even busted for selling counterfeit jewelry and handbags.

Piracy is a serious problem with potentially serious consequences beyond lost income. The International Chamber of Commerce (ICC) has reported on fake eyedrops that contained untreated tap water rather than sterile solution and contraceptive pills made from flour. According to the WHO, 10 percent of all pharmaceuticals are fake and may contain harmful ingredients or little or no medication at all.[21]

Counterfeit goods are a huge concern to companies as they expand internationally.

Madrid Agreement

A multilateral agreement offering a single international application for trademark protection.

Patent Cooperation Treaty (PCT)

A cooperative union for the filing of patents among member countries.

Another important convention is the Madrid Agreement Concerning the International Registration of Marks, or simply the **Madrid Agreement** (not to be confused with the Madrid Agreement for the Repression of False or Deceptive Indications of Source on Goods, which was signed in 1994). This treaty, originally signed in Madrid in 1891, focuses on trademark registration and protection among the 83 countries that have signed the Madrid Protocol, which allows for a single international application for trademark protection.[22]

In addition, the **Patent Cooperation Treaty (PCT)** (or International Patent Cooperation Union) signed in Washington, D.C., in 1970 is a cooperative union for the filing of applications for the protection of inventions among 142 member nations.[23] The significant number of patents filed under this treaty indicates its popularity and member nations' belief in the enforcement of IPP when disputes arise, as specified in the treaty. International protection of IP is critical for the expansion of world trade and investment.

There are many other conventions and agreements, the goal of which is to bring some order to IPP. The World Intellectual Property Organization (WIPO) is an agency of the UN, which coordinates the protection of IP on a global scale

Holograms were an early high-tech solution used to prevent piracy and counterfeiting. They appeared on credit cards, CD and DVD packages, and on some currencies (the euro paper money). Now, though, the machines used to produce the prototypes have fallen in price to about $2,500—well within the reach of serious counterfeiters.

Businesses are responding with new high-tech solutions to combat piracy. Bsecure, an Israeli firm, offers a variety of products that can tell what is genuine and what is fake. The company manufactures inks that contain signature chemicals, microwires thinner than a human hair, and unique polymers with embedded codes used to coat identification badges and packaging—all of which can be detected with special scanners to make sure the products are genuine. Bsecure also makes tamper-proof packaging substances that prevent counterfeiters from opening product packages and substituting imitations. Bsecure's clients include New Balance Athletic Shoe, Inc.; Intel; Seagram's; and the motor vehicle departments in Israel and Belarus.

Authentix manufactures nanotechnology isotags. These unique and identifiable single molecules can be added to a variety of products (including cosmetics, gasoline, and pharmaceuticals) to help firms distinguish real from counterfeit. Since 2005, Authentix claims to have saved its clients over $5 billion in lost revenues in the petroleum, pharmaceutical, and consumer goods industries alone. What's the best part? Isotags cost less than 1 cent per unit.

There are other product defense techniques: ink that becomes visible when copied (the word *counterfeit* appears), tamper-evident glue, self-destruct technologies for sound and video recordings, and activation and deactivation codes for software. Bsecure estimates that the amount of counterfeit products sold annually totals $1 trillion, and the market for products to prevent counterfeiting is booming![24]

through information services and administration of many of the international IPP conventions. The mission of WIPO is "the maintenance and further development of the respect of intellectual property throughout the world" and "that the acquisition of the protection and its enforcement should be simpler, cheaper, and more secure."[25] This must be balanced with the needs of developing nations, though. Because the vast majority of patents originate in industrialized countries, less-developed nations argue that for them, patents mean high prices for products, import monopolies rather than local manufacturing, and high royalty payments for the use of patents. Those nations are expected to attempt to change the patent system to give them less-expensive access to technology.

The WTO, within its Agreement on Trade-Related Aspects of Intellectual Property Rights (TRIPS), contains a most-favored nation (MFN) clause regarding trademark registration. This agreement includes WTO members, some of which are not Paris Union members, thereby extending protection to other nations.

Regional counterparts provide similar protection, registration, and information. The European Patent Office (which includes the EU members and other European nations) and the Office for Harmonization in the Internal Market (which provides a single system for trademark registration throughout the EU, called Community Trade Mark or CTM) are European examples. The Inter-American Convention for Trademarks and Commercial Protection (also known as the Pan-American Convention) and the Buenos Aires Convention for the Protection of Trade Marks and Commercial Names are examples in the western hemisphere.

When marketing products abroad, firms must pay attention to IPP and the agencies and conventions that provide assistance and information. The most interesting question in brand and trademark protection concerns the countries that are not members of one of these arrangements. (See "Pirates at Large: Fighting the Pirates.")

common law

A form of law English in origin and found in the United States and other countries that have had a strong English influence. Also called "case law," it is tradition-oriented and based on the interpretation of what the law means on a given subject and is influenced by previous court decisions, as well as by usage and custom.

civil or code law

A form of law based on an extensive and comprehensive set of laws organized by subject matter into a code. The intention in civil law countries is to spell out the law on all possible legal questions rather than rely on precedent or court interpretation.

Islamic law

Law of the religion of Islam. Although it has harsh penalties for adultery and theft, it is not dramatically different from other legal systems with regard to business.

Islamic law is practiced in countries such as Saudi Arabia.

Local Laws and International Trade

U.S. laws play a dominant role in U.S. business practices. The laws of other nations play a similar role with regard to the activities of businesses within their boundaries. The importance of foreign laws to a marketer lies primarily in domestic marketing in each foreign market. Problems arise when the laws in each market are somewhat different from those in every other market.

DIFFERING LEGAL SYSTEMS

Before considering national peculiarities in marketing law, this section provides a brief discussion of the predominant legal systems that underlie individual national law. Legal systems are most often based on common law, civil or code law, or Islamic traditions. When categorizing nations, one must exercise care because many nations are best classified as a mixture of one or more types of legal systems. For example, Quebec province uses both civil and common law traditions, whereas in Nigeria, Islamic law is applied in the northern, predominantly Muslim areas, but common law is used in other parts of the country.

Common law is English in origin and is found in the United States and other countries that have had a strong English influence, usually a previous colonial tie (about 40 nations). Common law, often called "case law," is tradition oriented; that is, the interpretation of what the law means on a given subject is heavily influenced by previous court decisions, as well as by usage and custom. If there is no specific legal precedent or statute, common law requires a court decision. To understand the law in a common law country, one must study the previous court decisions in matters of similar circumstance, as well as the statutes.

Civil or **code law** is based on an extensive and, presumably, comprehensive set of laws organized by subject matter into a code. The intention in civil law countries is to spell out the law on all possible legal questions rather than rely on precedent or court interpretation. The "letter of the law" is very important in code law countries. However, this need to be all-inclusive may lead to some rather general and elastic provisions, permitting application to many sets of facts and circumstances. Because code law countries do not rely on previous court decisions, various applications of the same law may yield different interpretations. This can lead to some uncertainty for a marketer. Code law is a legacy of Roman law. It is predominant in Europe and in nations of the world that have not had close ties to England. Thus, code law nations are more numerous than common law nations. Many civil code systems are influenced by the French, German, and Spanish systems because of previous colonial or other relationships. For example, the German code has had an influence on the Teutonic and Scandinavian countries. There are about 90 civil law countries.

Islamic law represents the third major legal system. About 35 countries follow Islamic law in varying degrees, usually mixed with civil, common, and/or indigenous law. The Islamic resurgence in recent years has led many countries to give Islamic law, Shari'a, a more prominent role. Shari'a governs all aspects of life in areas where it is the dominant legal system, as in Saudi Arabia. Rules not defined by Shari'a are decided by government regulations and Islamic judges. Although it has harsh penalties for adultery and theft, Islamic law is not dramatically different from other legal systems with regard to business. In Saudi Arabia, for example, the Committee for Settlement of Commercial Disputes operates in a manner that would not be uncongenial to a Westerner.

The differences in legal systems are important to international marketers. They must study the legal systems and seek appropriate local legal advice when necessary. The following section merely alerts the international marketer to some of the variations in legal systems abroad.

Foreign Laws: Challenges for the International Marketing Manager

Just as in the United States, other countries have numerous laws that impact sales and marketing. Companies seeking to do business in foreign countries must understand and comply with these laws. A convenient way to group these foreign laws is by product, pricing, distribution, and promotion.

PRODUCT

If product is everything the consumer receives when making a purchase, the international marketer will find many regulations affecting it. The physical and chemical aspects of a product are affected by laws designed to protect national consumers with respect to its purity, safety, and performance. Product safety is one of the most problematic issues, and safety concerns are often reasons cited by foreign governments to prohibit the imports of certain goods—for example, the EU's ban on food with genetically modified organisms (GMOs). Product labeling is another example. Countries have differing requirements as to what must be included on a product label, including language (such as English and French in Canada), weights (must be metric in some countries), country of origin marking indicating where the product was produced, and consumer safety warnings such as on cigarettes and alcohol. Brands and trademarks for products also face different national laws. Differences exist between code law countries (ownership by priority in registration of a brand—known as "first to file") and common law countries (ownership by priority in use—known as "first to use") in their treatment of a brand or trademark.

PRICING

Price controls are pervasive in the world economy. **Resale price maintenance** (RPM) is a common law related to pricing. Many nations have some legal provisions for RPM but with numerous variations. Another variable is the fact that some countries allow price agreements among competitors.

Another law in many nations is that of government price control. The price controls may be economywide or limited to certain sectors. For example, France has had a number of economywide price freezes. At the other extreme, Japan controls the price on only one commodity: rice. Generally, price controls are limited to "essential" goods, such as foodstuffs. The pharmaceutical industry is one of the most frequently controlled, sometimes taking the form of controlled profit margins.

> **resale price maintenance (RPM)**
> The effect of rules imposed on manufacturers, wholesalers, or retailers on their own products to prevent them from competing too fiercely on price and thus driving profits down from the reselling activity.

DISTRIBUTION

Distribution is an area in which an international marketer has fewer constraints. A firm has a high degree of freedom in choosing distribution channels from among those available in the market. Of course, one cannot choose channels that are not available. For example, France had a specific prohibition against door-to-door selling, but the Singer Company received a special exemption from this law. One major question is the legality of exclusive distribution. Fortunately, this option is allowed in most markets. In fact, the strongest legal constraint does not apply to firms managing their own distribution in foreign markets, but rather to exporters who are selling through distributors or agents.

Careful selection of an agent or a distributor is critical for two reasons. First, the quality of the distributor helps determine a firm's success in the market. Second, the contract with the distributor may bind the exporter to a commitment that is difficult and costly to terminate. The challenge for the exporter is to be aware of national laws concerning distributor contracts to avoid potential problems. It is much easier to enter an agency agreement than to end one. (See "Distributor Divorce: Including an Escape Clause.")

PROMOTION

Advertising is one of the more controversial elements of international marketing, and it tends to be subject to more control than product, price, and distribution. Most nations have some law regulating advertising, and advertising groups in many nations have self-regulatory codes. Advertising regulation takes several forms. One pertains to the message and its truthfulness. In Germany, for example, it is difficult to use comparative advertising and the words *better* or *best*. In Argentina, advertising for pharmaceuticals must have prior approval of the Ministry of Public Health. Even China has brought foreign firms to court over their advertising claims.

Another form of restriction relates to control over the advertising of certain products. For example, Britain allows no cigarette or liquor advertising on television. Finland is more restrictive and allows no newspaper or television advertising of political organizations, religious messages, alcohol, undertakers, diet drugs, immoral literature, or intimate preparations. Another restriction is through the taxation of advertising. For example, Peru once implemented

Distributor Divorce: Including an Escape Clause

Escape clauses are designed to protect the parties of an agreement in the event a disagreement or circumstance arises that prevents completion to the expectations of those involved. In the case of hiring sales representatives in other countries, the desire to get out of a contract is most commonly due to the salesperson not meeting the company's goals. The U.S. Department of Commerce and an American export compliance firm, Unz & Co., have formulated some advice about sales representative agreements.

In international contracts, escape clauses may be limited by local laws, regardless of what the parties agreed to, whether verbal or written. Therefore, one should learn as much as possible about appropriate commercial laws and seek local legal advice. When talking to a lawyer, one should consider asking the following questions:

- What is the required advance notice for termination? (possibly 180 days or more)
- What is "just cause" for termination of a contract? (Not meeting a sales objective may be insufficient grounds.)
- What compensation is due on termination? (Depending on the country, laws may dictate some compensation is paid.)
- Which country's laws would apply in the case of a dispute? (Even with a written contract, some nations do not allow the salesperson [or the firm] to waive the nation's jurisdiction.)
- What happens to proprietary property upon termination (including sales records, customer data, patents, trademarks, and similar materials)?
- Are the host country laws in conflict with home country laws? (Sales exclusivity, labeling, and other components may be in violation of antitrust regulations, antiboycott laws, or other home country regulations.)[26]

an 8 percent tax on outdoor advertising; Spain taxed cinema advertising. Some markets institute greater restrictions on sales promotion techniques than what is found in the United States. In the United States, there is often no constraint on contests, deals, premiums, and other sales promotion gimmicks. The situation is quite different in other countries. As a general rule, participation in contests must not be predicated on purchase of the product. Premiums may be restricted with regard to size, value, and nature. A premium may be limited to a certain fraction of the value of the purchase and may be required to relate to the product it promotes; that is, steak knives cannot be used as a premium with soap or a towel with a food product. Free introductory samples may be restricted to one-time use of the product rather than a week's supply.

ENFORCEMENT OF FOREIGN LAWS

A firm needs to know how foreign laws will affect its operations in a market. It is not sufficient to know only the laws; a firm must also know how the laws are enforced. Most nations have laws that have been forgotten and are not enforced. Other laws may be enforced haphazardly, and still others may be strictly enforced.

An important aspect of enforcement is the degree of impartiality of justice. Does a foreign subsidiary have as good a standing before the law as a national company? Courts have been known to favor national firms over foreign subsidiaries. In such cases, biased enforcement means that a law is interpreted one way for the foreigner and another way for a national. Knowledge of such discrimination is helpful in evaluating the legal climate.

Advertising tends to be one of the marketing mix options most affected by local law, including restrictions on promotions and contests.

Contract Considerations: Whose Law, Whose Courts?

Firms that have little experience with international transactions may not realize that there may be little recourse when another party in a contract does not pay for goods or services received, the product received is defective, or the service is not up to agreed-upon standards. Whatever the resolution of a contracted dispute, the time it takes to reach that point is often much longer and more costly than expected.

WHOSE LAW? WHOSE COURTS?

Domestic laws govern marketing within a country. Questions of the appropriate law and the appropriate courts may arise, however, in cases involving international marketing.

When commercial disputes arise between principals of two different nations, each would probably prefer to have the matter judged in its own national courts under its own laws. By the time the dispute has arisen, however, the question of jurisdiction has usually already been settled by one means or another. One way to decide the issue beforehand is by inserting a **choice of law clause** in a contract, naming a specific country's laws. Then, when the contract is signed, each party agrees that the laws of a particular nation (or state in the case of the United States) govern the content of the contract.

choice of law clause

A specific section added to contracts that specifies which country's laws govern the content and enforcement of a contract.

The decision as to which nation's courts will try the case depends on who is suing whom. The issue of which courts have jurisdiction is separate from the issue of which nation's laws are applied. Suits are brought in the courts of the country of the person being sued. For example, a U.S. company might sue a French firm in France. This kind of event often leads to the situation in which a court in one country tries a case according to the laws of another country; that is, a French court may apply the laws of New York State. This would happen if the parties had included a choice of law clause stating that the laws of New York State govern.

ARBITRATION OR LITIGATION?

An international marketer must be knowledgeable about laws and contracts. Contracts identify two things: (1) the responsibilities of each party and (2) the legal recourse to obtain satisfaction. Actually, however, international marketers consider litigation a last resort and prefer to settle disputes in some other way. For several reasons, litigation is considered a poor way of settling disputes with foreign parties. Litigation usually involves long delays, during which time inventories may be tied up and trade halted. Further, it is costly—not only in money, but also in customer goodwill and public relations. Firms also frequently fear discrimination in a foreign court. Thus, litigation is seen as an unattractive alternative, to be used only when all else fails.

More peaceful ways to settle international commercial disputes are offered by conciliation, mediation, and arbitration. Conciliation and mediation are informal attempts to bring the parties to an agreement. They are attractive, voluntary approaches to the settlement of disputes. If they fail, however, stronger measures (such as arbitration and litigation) are needed. Because of the drawbacks of litigation, arbitration is used extensively in international commerce.

arbitration

The use of a neutral third party to resolve contract disputes.

Arbitration is the use of a neutral third party to resolve a dispute. Arbitration generally overcomes the disadvantages of litigation. Decisions tend to be faster and cheaper. Arbitration is also less damaging to goodwill because of the secrecy of the proceedings and its less hostile nature.

For international arbitration, firms may want an arbitrator located in a neutral country, not in the same country as any of the firms signing the contract. The International Chamber of Commerce (ICC) in Paris is one of the leading, more well-established and well-respected centers in the world, receiving more than 500 arbitration cases every year. The ICC also supplies samples of arbitration clauses, but in a variety of languages, and allows users to access an "arbitration cost calculator" to estimate the cost of pursuing a claim. All of those resources are available on the ICC website at www.iccwbo.org. Estimates are that fewer than 10 percent of the ICC decisions are challenged.

Another resource is the International Centre for Dispute Resolution (ICDR), a division of the American Arbitration Association (AAA). The ICDR has cooperative arrangements with more than 62 arbitral agencies in 44 countries, including the Permanent Court of Arbitral Awards at The Hague.[27] Many resources and agencies for ADR are helpful in reducing the costs and other problems often associated with litigation, but the following offer a starting point. China created its own arbitration tribunal in 1989, and Beijing is now one of the busiest arbitration centers in the world. Even with this tribunal's problems, foreign firms find it far superior than going into a Chinese court.

Legal Considerations in Cyberspace

E-commerce is not new, but it certainly becomes more pervasive every year. New opportunities and challenges face businesses and marketers, whether they are considering new methods of distribution for software, videos, and reading material; advertising using the Internet; dealing with transparent pricing; developing new products such as Internet security; or developing interactive gaming software or website consultant services.

E-commerce also introduces new legal issues. Marketers must deal with topics such as privacy. Examples of risks include the theft of customer records and subsequent threat of release unless a ransom is paid, spy software capable of snooping competitors' records, and virus attacks that destroy vital records or close websites—all becoming common. Laws establishing punishments for those crimes and the way perpetrators are to be prosecuted must also cross national boundaries if they are to be effective.

Governments are particularly interested in the issue of taxation. With billions of dollars in transactions taking place on the Internet, governments are losing money because of uncollected sales tax and value-added tax (VAT). Attempts to regulate or control sales and taxes have not been successful, but the United States and the EU are at the forefront of designing and implementing new regulations. It may become the responsibility of firms such as eBay to collect the sales taxes and distribute them to the appropriate authorities.

Whether a firm is marketing products through e-mail, offering promotions on its website, or making statements about its products, a firm's after-sales responsibilities and liability are issues being debated in the press, in courts, and in international agencies around the world. The topics mentioned here are only a few of those likely to occupy lawmakers for years to come, but marketers must keep abreast of new developments and the regulatory impact those developments can have on marketing.

The Marketer Is Not a Lawyer

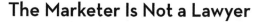

What are the implications for the international marketer of all the legal parameters discussed in this chapter? There are methods to reduce political and legal risks, some of which were shown in Table 3-2. Hiring an expert is usually a good idea. One should keep in mind, however, that many lawyers do not have detailed knowledge about all the domestic, international, and foreign legal aspects involved in international marketing. Although international marketers cannot know all the relevant laws, they do need to know what decisions are affected by the laws. A firm can bring in legal counsel when special expertise is needed. Expertise includes not only the domestic legal staff, but also legal representatives from the firm's foreign markets.

A firm's need for legal expertise is related to its international involvement. If a firm only exports or licenses, it has fewer legal needs than if it has foreign subsidiaries and joint ventures. Where it operates through licenses or distributors, these parties relieve the firm of some of its legal burden. When a firm has subsidiaries, however, it needs local legal counsel.

With the growth of international business and the proliferation of national and international regulation, the international legal function is becoming more complex. Firms need an international legal staff at headquarters and local lawyers in foreign subsidiaries. In host countries, the task will be largely decentralized because of local practices. However, some coordination and exchange of experience will be necessary to optimize performance of a firm's international legal function.

SUMMARY

A host country's behavior is guided by its national interests, such as security, sovereignty, prestige, and economic welfare. To achieve its goals, a country uses a variety of controls over a firm, such as entry restrictions, price controls, quotas and tariffs, exchange control, and even expropriation. These national interests and controls constitute the political environment of an international firm.

A firm needs to evaluate the host country environment and assess the political risk in every country in which it enters into business transactions. Then the firm needs a plan for managing host country relations, both before and after entering the country.

An international firm often becomes involved in international relations, usually against its will. It needs to know how a given host country relates to its own country and to other nations as well. Also, a firm's home country may restrict its international marketing activities.

Many U.S. laws affect U.S. firms. These laws relate to the regulation of exports and to antitrust implications of overseas ventures. A priority of the U.S. government has long been to control "what" and "where" U.S. companies may export.

Still other U.S. laws concern the behavior of U.S. firms abroad. The FCPA prohibits bribery, and antiboycott provisions are meant to prevent U.S. firms from cooperating with the Arab boycott of Israel.

International patent conventions help international firms protect their most valuable IP.

Each foreign country has its own legal system, which is shaped by the common law, by civil law, or by Muslim law tradition. These foreign laws affect all aspects of product policy, including the physical product, package and label, brand name, and use of warranty.

Pricing and promotion programs are generally more strictly regulated in foreign markets than in the United States.

In cases of legal disagreements, each party usually prefers its own country's courts. A jurisdictional clause should be included in all international marketing contracts in case a problem arises. However, rather than litigate in a foreign court, many international firms prefer to settle differences by arbitration. Arbitration is often more efficient, more equitable, and less damaging to continuing relations.

E-commerce is causing lawmakers to review current laws about privacy, liability, and taxation.

KEY TERMS

arbitration
Berne Convention
CE mark
choice of law clause
civil (or code) law
common law
confiscation

copyrights
dual-use goods
expropriation
intellectual property (IP)
Islamic law
legal environment
Madrid Agreement

nationalization
national sovereignty
Paris Union
Patent Cooperation Treaty (PCT)
patents
political environment

political risk
predatory pricing
resale price maintenance (RPM)
trademarks
trade secrets

NASBITE CGBP TOPICS COVERED IN THIS CHAPTER

Note: For full details of the alignment of each chapter with the NASBITE CGBP, be sure to review the information provided in the section "Studying for the NASBITE CGBP Exam."

CGBP Rubric	Topic
01/03/01:	environmental factors affecting international strategies—political, legal/regulatory
01/05/01:	country risk (e.g., political risk, economic risk, expropriation)
01/05/03:	risks and sources (e.g., Department of State) associated with travel and expatriate activities
01/06/01:	general legal liability issues (e.g., product, international contractual disputes, governance issues, export license compliance)
01/06/02:	intellectual property rights (e.g., patent, trademark, copyright), international agreements (e.g., Paris Convention, Madrid System) and practical enforcement levels
01/06/03:	issues related to and sources of information (e.g., Bureau of Industry and Security, United Nations) for offshore regulatory/legal concerns (e.g., bribery/corruption, antitrust, customs, import/export permits, licenses, labor law, currency regulations)
02/01/02:	external environment—economic
02/01/02:	external environment—regulatory
02/01/02:	external environment—currency fluctuations protected industries and sectors
02/01/02:	external environment—protected industries and sectors
02/01/04:	major trade agreements, trade law
02/01/04:	export control regulations, antiboycott regulations (Foreign Corrupt Practices Act)
02/01/05:	product certifications and standards (e.g., CE mark)
02/02/01:	laws and regulations that impact the marketing plan (e.g., entity law, promotional restrictions, distributor requirements, corruption)
02/03/02:	how to find laws and regulations that impact the market selection (e.g., entity law, promotional restrictions, distributor requirements)
02/06/08:	legal/regulatory requirements for pricing
02/06/09:	trade assistance resources in support of providing products and services
02/09/03:	contractual issues related to market entry (e.g., common elements found in most distributor agreements)
03/03/05:	U.S. legal and regulatory requirements regarding documentation for goods/services (export/import control regulations)
03/04/03:	international conditions of contract—arbitration
04/01/01:	political and economic risks causing late and/or nonpayment from overseas markets (e.g., cancellation/failure to grant U.S. export license, civil unrest, foreign currency delays/shortage)
04/01/02:	cultural issues of buyer's country which may impact payment methods—corruption issues
04/04/02:	commercial, economic, and political risks of buyer and buyer's country

QUESTIONS AND RESEARCH

1. Explain the threefold political environment of international marketing.
2. Discuss the various kinds of host country controls over an international firm.
3. How might a firm analyze its own political vulnerability in a particular host country?
4. What can a firm do to help manage its host country relations?
5. Identify the elements of the international political environment.
6. Explain the foreign policy concerns with regard to U.S. export controls.
7. Discuss the various aspects of international marketing that can be affected by U.S. laws.
8. Give examples of the kinds of international laws that can influence a firm's international marketing.
9. Explain a firm's concerns relating to international patent and trademark law.
10. Explain how foreign laws can affect the four Ps of marketing.

CHAPTER 3 TEAM PROJECT ASSIGNMENT: The Political–Legal Environment

This chapter focused on the global political and legal environment and discussed how differences in the political and legal systems can impact a firm as it expands globally.

The assignment for this chapter builds on the work done in the preceding chapter regarding the global economic environment. Knowing the industry in which your client operates, begin some initial research of potential issues your firm may encounter as regards to political risk and legal challenges. For example, might there be restrictions on the export of your client's products? If your client provides a service, are there any indications such services are restricted in particular countries? The goal is to think through what some of the political or legal issues may be for your client as it expands internationally.

For your team research from this chapter, discuss the following issues:

1. Do you anticipate that your client will need to own significant assets overseas as part of its international expansion? Manufacturing facilities or retail stores would be good examples of substantial investment that may lead to high political risk.
2. Although you have not yet selected foreign markets, are there initial indications that higher-risk countries may be important markets for your client? If so, are there some initial thoughts about how those risks might be mitigated?
3. Review Table 3-3. Are there any early signs that your client may encounter export controls in order to sell its products overseas?

CASE 3.1 U.S. Pharmaceuticals, Inc. (B)

U.S. Pharmaceuticals (USP) is a U.S. firm with about 30 percent of its sales outside the United States. USP concentrates on the ethical drug business but has diversified into animal health products, cosmetics, and some patent medicines. Those other lines account for about one-fourth of USP's $800 million sales. USP's international business is conducted in some 70 countries, mostly through distributors in those markets. In six countries, however, USP has manufacturing or compounding operations. (Compounding refers to the local mixing, assembling, and packaging of critical ingredients shipped from the United States.) USP's only Latin American manufacturing/compounding operations are in Latinia, a country with a population of about 30 million. Some products are shipped from Latinia to other Latin American markets.

Recently, USP ran into a problem in Latinia with its newest drug, Corolane 2. This drug is effective in treating certain intestinal diseases and infections. The drug has been under development for several years. Three years ago, when it showed considerable promise in the extensive testing process, USP registered the name Corolane 2 in the United States and several other major world markets. Last year, USP introduced Corolane 2 in the United States and several large foreign markets. Its early promise was confirmed by its quick acceptance by the medical profession in those countries.

Because of Corolane 2's initial success, USP planned to introduce the drug in all its foreign markets. It planned to both manufacture and market the drug in Latinia. A problem arose, however, because Jorge Rodriguez, a Latinian citizen, had already registered local rights to the name Corolane 2. Though a questionable procedure, this is perfectly legal, because Latinia is a code law country that gives exclusive rights to trade names according to priority in registration rather than to priority in use, which is the basis for exclusive rights in the United States.

The problem for USP was that it could not sell Corolane 2 under that name in Latinia because Rodriguez owned the rights. Of course, Rodriguez was quite willing to sell his rights to the Corolane 2 name for $20,000.

Registering foreign brand names was Rodriguez's way of supporting himself. He made a good living by subscribing to foreign trade and technical publications (especially in the medical field) and registering all the new names he found. Not all the names would be exploited in Latinia, but enough of them were to make it profitable for him. Corolane 2 was an atypical case. Early in the drug's development process, journal articles told of successful tests and applications. As soon as the name Corolane 2 was mentioned in one of the articles, Rodriguez registered it in Latinia, beating USP lawyers by just two weeks.

USP had encountered problems like this before in Latinia and other countries. It conducted R&D on many projects, most of which never reached the market. Some company officials believed it was not profitable to register every new product name in every market.

Questions and Research

1. Identify and evaluate the alternatives open to USP in Latinia.
2. What variables are important in this decision?
3. How could this kind of problem be avoided?

CASE 3.2 U.S. Export Controls

The following are real-life examples of export control violations taken directly from the U.S. Bureau of Industry and Security (BIS) publication "Don't Let This Happen to You."

ACE SYSTEMS INC.

The Violation: In July 2006, Ace Systems Inc. (Ace), located in Gainesville, Georgia, attempted to violate the General Order Concerning Mayrow and Related Entities by acting to export dialogic voice cards to Mayrow General Trading (Mayrow) in Dubai, United Arab Emirates, without the required license. Ace tendered the ten cards to its freight forwarder with instructions to export them to Mayrow. BIS special agents intervened, and the cards never reached their destination.
The Penalty: Ace agreed to pay an administrative penalty of $36,000.

SPARESGLOBAL, INC.

The Violation: SparesGlobal, Inc., of Pittsburgh, Pennsylvania, and company president, Om Sharma, conspired to falsify documents and make false statements about a 2003 illegal export of graphite products to a trading company in the United Arab Emirates that ultimately ended up in Pakistan. The graphite products can be used in nuclear reactors and in the nose cones of ballistic missiles. After the shipment, the company attempted to mislead federal investigators when questioned about the shipment and the documents.
The Penalty: On October 4, 2007, SparesGlobal, Inc., was sentenced to a $40,000 criminal fine.

SCP GLOBAL TECHNOLOGIES, INC.

The Violation: Between May 2003 and January 2005, SCP Global Technologies, Inc. ("SCP") made 45 exports of controlled pumps and valves to Taiwan, China, and Israel, without the required export licenses. The items are controlled for their potential use in chemical and biological weapons and would have required a license for shipment to Taiwan, China, or Israel. SCP had previously received a warning letter for the unlicensed export of controlled pumps.
The Penalty: SCP agreed to pay a $264,000 administrative penalty.
Mitigating Circumstances: SCP voluntarily self-disclosed these violations and cooperated fully in the investigation.

NING WEN AND HAILIN LIN

The Violation: Ning Wen and Hailin Lin used a business called Wen Enterprises, which they operated from their home in Wisconsin, to ship semiconductors and other controlled electronic components with radar and satellite applications, both military and civilian, to Jian Guo Qu and Ruo Ling Wang at Beijing Rich Linscience Electronic Company in China. For most of these transactions, Lin obtained the restricted components from a United States manufacturer or supplier based on a request from Wang or Qu, falsified shipping documents by concealing the true nature of the shipments and stating that a license was not required for the shipments, and then shipped the product to Wang and/or Qu in China without obtaining the required export license.
The Penalty: In 2005, Qu was sentenced to 46 months' imprisonment (later reduced to 22 months based on his cooperation in prosecution of codefendants), a $2,000 criminal fine, and two years' supervised release. Lin was also sentenced in 2005 to 42 months in prison and a $50,000 fine for her role in these unauthorized exports. In 2006, Wen was sentenced to five years in prison, a $50,000 fine, and two years' supervised release. Additionally, the court ordered the forfeiture of Wen and Lin's home and over $329,000 in cash.

WORLDWIDE SPORTS & RECREATION, INC. / BUSHNELL CORPORATION

The Violation: Between September 1995 and December 1997, Worldwide Sports & Recreation, Inc., which does business as Bushnell Corporation, exported Night Ranger night vision devices to Japan and 14 other countries without the required BIS export licenses. Bushnell sold the cameras to a Japanese company but transferred them to a U.S. company in Florida, knowing that they were going to be exported to Japan. The foreign company and the domestic intermediary pled guilty and cooperated.

The Penalty: In the criminal case, Bushnell was sentenced to a $650,000 criminal fine and five years' probation. In the related administrative case, Bushnell agreed to pay an administrative penalty of $223,000 and to a one-year suspended denial of export privileges.

Source: U.S. Department of Commerce, Bureau of Industry and Security; 2008, "Don't Let This Happen to You!" Full version available at www.bis.doc.gov.

Questions and Research

1. What are common mistakes made by companies and individuals as shown in the preceding examples?
2. Research the web to find recent examples of companies that have violated U.S. export controls.
3. What are best practices a firm should follow to better ensure compliance with U.S. export controls?
4. What are examples of export controls enforced in other countries?

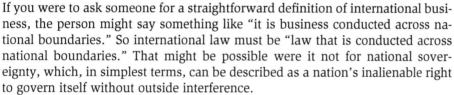

CASE 3.3 What Is International Law?

If you were to ask someone for a straightforward definition of international business, the person might say something like "it is business conducted across national boundaries." So international law must be "law that is conducted across national boundaries." That might be possible were it not for national sovereignty, which, in simplest terms, can be described as a nation's inalienable right to govern itself without outside interference.

National sovereignty was at the heart of the Gulf War in the 1990s and the dispute between Iraq and the UN about weapons inspection. The allied coalition (the United States, France, the United Kingdom, Saudi Arabia, and other countries) defended Kuwait because Iraq sent in troops, which was a violation of Kuwait's sovereignty. The rationale for the Iraqi invasion, to some extent, was that Kuwait had been taking oil from Iraq's Rumaila field (theft of Iraqi property and a violation of Iraqi national sovereignty). Iraq stated that the subsequent weapons inspections were a violation of its national sovereignty—that it had the right to do whatever it wants within its own borders.

China, France, and Mexico enact laws to which they hold their corporate and individual citizens responsible. Perhaps the best or truest form of international law takes place in the EU. The EU is a group of nations, each with its own national sovereignty; but the nations have agreed to policy making and legal restrictions that supersede national laws in certain circumstances and areas. No other international entity has the right to govern the activities of citizens from different nations.

Controversy over the use of child labor, poor working conditions, and exploitation in manufacturing products around the globe are issues raised by nations and consumers alike. Response may take the form of product boycotts, demonstrations, or government-imposed sanctions. The response from the offending nation is that these actions violate national sovereignty. It is an important issue that has consequences for everyone—consumers, CEOs, wage earners, policy makers, marketers, and responsible global citizens.

Much to the dismay of American firms, however, lawyers representing foreign claimants have been using an arcane 1789 U.S. statute to sue American companies. The Alien Tort Claims Act was originally intended to reassure Europeans that the new United States of America would not provide protection to pirates and assassins. However, the law was used in a suit brought by Burmese citizens against Unocal, a southern California energy giant. In essence, the complaint was that Unocal was "vicariously responsible" for the Burmese government's use of peasants (forced at gunpoint, some of whom were tortured and killed) to build a pipeline to be used by Unocal to transport natural gas. Even though Unocal did not participate in building the pipeline, it was being held accountable for "providing practical assistance or encouragement" to the Burmese government. The terms were not disclosed, but the case was settled out of court in April 2005. Had the case gone to trial and Unocal lost, the amount of monetary award would have been enormous and, more importantly, would have laid the foundation for similar claims against multinationals. More disturbing to American firms is that U.S. law is based on precedence; therefore, if this law had been successfully applied in the Unocal case, it would have been used in other cases as well. It is estimated that over 1,000 American and foreign firms could be facing similar suits. The awards would be in the trillions of dollars, likely forcing some firms into bankruptcy.

What does this mean for international marketers? If someone breaks a contract with them in their own nation, marketers can often sue for restitution. Between parties of different nationalities, though, this may be difficult or impossible because of national sovereignty and the refusal of one nation to allow its citizens to be subjected to the laws of another nation. In essence, it means that any contract involving parties from different nations requires careful scrutiny and that all methods of reducing commercial and political risk should be considered—from using forward exchange contracts, arbitration clauses, and political risk insurance to withholding proprietary information and being a good corporate citizen.

Source: "Making a Federal Case of Overseas Abuses," *Business Week*, November 25, 2002, p. 78

Questions and Research

1. Identify an EU law that has an impact on marketers. Discuss how it might best be addressed.

2. Review ways in which contract disputes can be managed.

NOTES

1. The U.S. Department of State provides excellent insights into the political environment of countries. See its report on Iran, which also discusses the 1979 U.S. embassy seizure at http://www.state.gov/r/pa/ei/bgn/5314.htm.
2. "Venezuela Currency Controls Tightened as Economic Clouds Gather," *Latin America Herald Tribune*, June 3, 2010 (http://www.laht.com/article.asp?ArticleId = 332348&Category Id = 10717), accessed June 3, 2010.
3. Simon Collinson and John Houlden. "Decision-Making and Market Orientation in the Internationalization Process of Small and Medium-Sized Enterprises," *Management International Review*, 45, no. 4 (2005): 413–36.
4. Sanjeev Agarwal and Sridhar Ramaswami. "Choice of Foreign Market Entry Mode: Impact of Ownership, Location, and Internationalization Factors," *Journal of International Business Studies*, 23, no. 1 (1992): 1–27.
5. Country Risk Rating; Euler Hermes 2009 (http://www.eulerhermes.us/en/country-risk-rating/country-risk-rating.html), accessed August 21, 2010.

6. U.S. Department of State, Patterns of Global Terrorism, 2003 (http://www.state.gov/s/ct/rls/pgtrpt/2003); U.S. Customs and Border Protection, Customs Trade Partnership Against Terrorism (http://www.cbp.gov/xp/cgov/trade/cargo_security/ctpat/); Rand Corporation and the Financial Times (http://www.rand.org/news/press.04/05.10.html).

7. Ans Kolk and Rob van Tulder. "International Business, Corporate Social Responsibility and Sustainable Development," *International Business Review*, 19, no. 2 (2010): 119–25.

8. See: http://www.chubb.com/businesses/csi/chubb979.html

9. U.S. Department of Commerce, Bureau of Industry and Security (http://www.bis.doc.gov/about/reslinks.htm), accessed July 1, 2010.

10. "Lifting Travel Ban to Cuba Would Generate $1.18 Billion to $1.61 Billion for U.S. Economy," PR Newswire, July 15, 2002; "U.N. Again Condemns U.S. Embargo against Cuba," CNN, U.S. Edition, October 28, 2009; "U.S. Exports Rise 16.7% in the First Quarter; On Track to Meet President's Goal of Doubling Exports over the Next Five Years," News Release, U.S. Export-Import Bank, May 18, 2010 (http://www.exim.gov/pressrelease.cfm/AD452E0C-97D9-503D-97595B2DD89B38DD/).

11. Carlsberg Group (http://www.carlsberggroup.com/csr/ourfocusareas/2009COP/Pages/default.aspx), accessed June 2, 2010; United Nations Global Compact—The Ten Principles (http://www.unglobalcompact.org/AboutTheGC/TheTenPrinciples/index.html), accessed June 2, 2010.

12. Corruption Perceptions Index 2009; Transparency International (http://www.transparency.org/policy_research/surveys_indices/cpi/2009/cpi_2009_table), accessed June 3, 2010.

13. John J. Ensminger, "September 11 Brings New Anti-Terrorism and Anti-Money Laundering Responsibilities to Financial Institutions," *Review of Business*, 23, no. 3(Fall 2002): 29–34. In the United States, the agency responsible for coordinating activities among the 25 or so other federal bodies and enforcing the regulations is the Financial Crimes Enforcement Network (FinCEN).

14. U.S. Department of Commerce, Bureau of Industry and Security, Office of Antiboycott Compliance (http://www.bis.doc.gov/antiboycottcompliance/oacantiboycottrequestexamples.html), accessed June 2, 2010.

15. BIS has a number of publications discussing export violations, including antiboycott charges. For more details, see "Major Cases List" at the BIS homepage (www.bis.doc.gov).

16. "BSA Reports $51 Billion Worth of Software Theft in 2009" (http://www.bsa.org/country/News%20and%20Events/News%20Archives/global/05112010-globalpiracystudy.aspx), accessed June 4, 2010.

17. Balay Seyoum, "Patent Protection and Foreign Direct Investment," *Thunderbird International Business Review*, 48, no. 3 (2006): 389–404.

18. "USPTO Annual Reports" (http://www.uspto.gov/web/offices/com/annual/2009/oai_05_wlt_02.html), retrieved June 1, 2010.

19. World Intellectual Property Organization. "Total Number of Patent Grants (1985–2007) by Resident and Non-Resident, and Patent Grants by Patent Office (1883–2008) by Resident and Non-Resident" (http://www.wipo.int/ipstats/en/statistics/patents/), accessed June 4, 2010.

20. World Intellectual Property Organization, "Members of WIPO Bodies" (http://www.wipo.int/treaties/en/ShowResults.jsp?lang=en&search_what=B&bo_id=7), accessed June 4, 2010.

21. "New Service Will Help Firms Fight Fake Drugs," International Chamber of Commerce (http://www.iccwbo.org/home/ news_archives/2002/stories/drugs.asp), accessed November 26, 2002; International Chamber of Commerce website (http://www.iccwbo. org); "China's Piracy Plague," *Business Week*, June 5, 2000, pp 44–48; "In Wooing Brazil's Teens, Converse Has Big Shoes to Fill," *Wall Street Journal*, July 18, 2002, pp B1–B2; "Shipping Insurance Sky-Rockets as Pirate Attacks Increase," DW-World.DE (http://www.dw-world.de/dw/article/0,,4278642,00.html) accessed October 2, 2010; "Somalia: Pirates Attack Fishing Boats," *New York Times*, April 21, 2010, p. 9; "Counterfeit Jewelry, Handbags Seized at Two Discover Mills Stores," *Atlanta Journal Constitution*, March 30, 2010 (http://www.ajc.com/news/gwinnett/counterfeit-jewelry-handbags-seized-418503.html), accessed October 2, 2010.

22. Madrid System for the International Registration of Marks, World Intellectual Property Organization (http://www.wipo.int/madrid/en/members/), accessed October 2, 2010.

23. Patent Cooperation Treaty Contacting Parties, World Intellectual Property Organization, (http://www.wipo.int/treaties/en/ShowResults.jsp?lang=en&treaty_id=6), accessed October 2, 2010.

24. "Forgery Fighters," *Jerusalem Report*, October 7, 2002, p. 36; "Tech Goes Undercover," *Optimize*, November 1, 2002, p. 15; "Beam Me Up Some Ivory Soap," *Fast Forward*, October 2002, Issue 12 (http://www.optimizemag.com/issue/012/fast.htm), accessed December 6, 2002; Authentix site (http://www.authentix.com), accessed June 02, 2010.

25. World Intellectual Property Organization, "What Is WIPO"; (http://www.wipo.int/about-wipo/en/what_is_wipo.html), accessed October 2, 2010.

26. "U.S. Department of Commerce International Trade Administration, *A Basic Guide to Exporting*, 1998 and 2008.

27. American Arbitration Association, "About the International Centre for Dispute Resolution" (http://www.adr.org/about_icdr), accessed June 4, 2010.

4 The Cultural Environment

As discussed in the preceding chapter, economic factors are important in determining a consumer's ability to purchase a product. Whether a purchase actually occurs, however, depends largely on cultural factors. Therefore, to understand markets abroad, the international marketing manager must have an appreciation for the cultural environment of buyer behavior. This chapter presents the major elements of that cultural environment.

The main goals of this chapter are to ●●●

1. Distinguish characteristics among different values and attitudes that influence purchasing decisions.

2. Explore the subject of a society's aesthetics —its sense of beauty, proportion, and appropriateness—in connection with a firm's products and communications.

3. Explain the role of a culture's language and communication style in shaping the marketing task.

4. Discuss the effect of religion on consumer behavior.

5. Describe how the local educational system can impact a firm's marketing and staffing situation.

6. Explain how the social organization in a given country (family, age group, class, etc.) affects consumer behavior.

7. Show how a country's material culture and technology determine whether a firm's products fit in with the way of life for a group of people and, if not, what adaptation may be necessary.

8. Look at cultural frameworks that help to clarify the impact of cultural differences in the international marketplace.

A common theme in previous chapters was the increased challenge for the international marketing manager in dealing with a complex and diverse international marketplace versus, perhaps, the domestic market. This challenge is particularly acute within the context of cultural differences. Because an understanding of marketing is culture bound, the international marketing manager must acquire knowledge of diverse cultural environments to be successful.

It is equally important to remove one's cultural perspective to study foreign markets. This means not judging other cultures against one's own cultural background. **Ethnocentrism** is a belief that one's culture is superior to other cultures. The international marketing manager needs to avoid ethnocentric bias in marketing decisions.

The growing use of anthropology, sociology, and psychology in marketing is clear recognition of the noneconomic factors of marketing behavior. It is not enough to say that consumption is a function of income. Consumption is a function of many other cultural influences as well. Furthermore, only noneconomic factors can explain the different patterns of consumption of two individuals with identical incomes—or, by analogy, of two different countries with similar per capita incomes.

A review of consumer durables ownership in European Union (EU) countries shows the importance of noneconomic factors in determining consumption behavior. For example, comparing penetration levels of home appliances (white goods) among EU members, Slovakians, relatively recent members of the EU, have a high percentage of households with refrigerators (83%), but one of the lowest levels of clothes dryers (2%) and dishwashers (10%). Austrians, with a higher per capita income than Slovakians ($49,599 versus $18,212), also have a high percentage of households with refrigerators (99%), but a higher level of clothes dryers (24%) and a much higher level of dishwashers (80%). This seems to indicate a strong relationship between income and the purchase of white goods perhaps seen as convenience products such as dishwashers and clothes dryers versus items that might be considered more of a necessity, such as refrigerators.[1]

ethnocentrism

A belief that one's culture is superior to other cultures.

The different pattern of consumer purchases of white goods among EU members helps highlight the importance of noneconomic factors in determining consumption behavior.

Nevertheless, consumptions patterns of white goods among EU members does not necessarily follow income levels. The United Kingdom and Germany have similar per capita income at $43,541 and $44,446, respectively. Both have high levels of household ownership of refrigerators, with both at 99%. Yet only 38% of households in the United Kingdom have dishwashers, compared with nearly twice that level in Germany at 63%.[2] As such, differences in consumption patterns for these and other consumer products cannot be explained by different levels of income alone. They can be better explained when cultural differences are taken into account.

What Is Culture?

Culture is too complex to define in simple terms. It seems that each anthropologist has a definition. Anthropologist John Bodley succinctly brought together the major points of agreement in his description of the term: "Culture is learned behavior; a way of life for any group of people living together in a single, related and interdependent community."[3] One fundamental aspect is that *culture is a total pattern of behavior that is consistent and compatible in its components*. It is not a collection of random behaviors, but behaviors that are related and integrated. A second fundamental is that *culture is learned behavior*. It is not biologically transmitted. It depends on environment, not heredity. It can be called the man-made part of the environment. The third fundamental is that *culture is behavior that is shared by a group of people, a society*. It can be considered as the distinctive way of life of a people. The following sections discuss the elements of culture, along with their implication for international marketing.

Elements of Culture

Varying definitions exist pertaining to the elements of culture, including one that counts 73 "cultural universals." This text uses a simpler list that encompasses seven major areas: (1) attitudes and values, (2) aesthetics, (3) language, (4) religion, (5) education, (6) social organization, and (7) material culture and technology. The discussion of culture here is not definitive and perhaps would not satisfy anthropologists. Nonetheless, this material should contribute to an understanding of the cultural environment as it affects a firm's foreign marketing.

Attitudes and Values

People's **attitudes and values** help determine what they think is right or appropriate, what is important, and what is desirable. People have attitudes and values about work, money, time, family, age, men, women, and a host of other topics that have an impact on marketing.

> **attitudes and values**
>
> An element of culture that clarifies what people in that culture think is right or appropriate, important, and desirable.

WEALTH, MATERIAL GAIN, AND ACQUISITION

The United States has been called the "affluent society," the "achieving society," and the "acquisitive society." These somewhat synonymous expressions reflect motivating values in society. In the United States, wealth and acquisition are often considered signs of success and achievement and are given social approval. In a Buddhist or Hindu society, where nirvana or "wantlessness" is an ideal, people may not be so motivated to produce and consume. Marketers obviously prefer to operate in an acquisitive society. However, as a result of rising expectations around the world, national differences in attitudes toward acquisition seem to be lessening. For example, Buddhist Thailand is proving to be a profitable market for many consumer goods firms.

Work may be an end unto itself for some people, and one's position with a particular organization may be an important measure of a person's social status. For others, family, leisure time, and friends take precedence over money and position. German and French workers have gone on strike, even rioted over plans to extend their workweek beyond 35 hours, to cut paid vacation time, or to raise the age that one becomes qualified for retirement benefits.[4] Similar protests took place in Greece as government officials suggested changes to address the financial problems discussed in Chapter 2.

CHANGE

When a company enters a foreign market, it brings change by introducing new ways of doing things and new products. In general, North Americans accept change easily. The word *new* has a favorable connotation and facilitates change when used to describe techniques and products. Many societies are more tradition oriented, however, revering their ancestors and traditional ways of consuming. The marketer as an agent of change has a different task in traditional societies. Rather than emphasize what is new and different about a product, the marketer might relate the product to traditional values, perhaps noting that it is a better way of solving a consumer problem. In seeking acceptance of its new product, a firm might try to get at least a negative clearance—that is, no objection—from local religious leaders or other opinion leaders. Any product must first meet a market need. Beyond that, however, to be accepted, the product must also fit in with the overall value system.

The Campbell Soup Company met this kind of obstacle when it introduced its canned soups into Italy. In conducting marketing research, the company received an overwhelmingly negative response to the question, Would you marry a user of prepared soups? Campbell had to adjust its marketing accordingly.

RISK TAKING

Consumers take risks when they try a new product. Will the product do what they expect it to do? Will purchasing or using the product prejudice their standing or image with their peers? Intermediaries handling the untried product may also face risks beyond those associated with their regular line. In a conservative society, there is a greater reluctance to take such risks. Therefore, a marketer must seek to reduce the risk perceived by customers or distributors in trying a new product. In part, this can be accomplished through education, guarantees, consignment selling, and other marketing techniques.

CONSUMER BEHAVIOR

The attitudes just discussed are relevant to understanding consumer behavior in the markets of the world. International managers must have such an understanding to develop effective marketing programs. Because of the impossibility of gaining intimate knowledge of a great number of markets, they must rely not only on company research, but also on help from others. Those who can assist managers in understanding local attitudes and behavior include personnel in the firm's subsidiary, the distributor, and the advertising agency. Although a firm is interested in changing attitudes, most generally it has to adapt to them. As Confucius said, "It is easier to move mountains than to change the minds of men."

Aesthetics

aesthetics

An element of culture that reflects what that culture considers beautiful and in good taste. Aesthetics are expressed in the arts and in the appreciation of color and form.

Aesthetics refers to the prevalent ideas in a culture concerning beauty and good taste, as expressed in the arts—music, art, drama, and dance—and the appreciation of color and form. International differences abound in aesthetics, but they tend to be regional rather than national. For example, Kabuki theater is exclusively Japanese, but Western theater includes at least all of Western Europe in addition to the United States and Canada in its audience.

Musical tastes, too, tend to be regional rather than national. In the West, many countries enjoy the same classical and popular music. In fact, due to modern communications, popular music has become truly international. Nevertheless, obvious differences exist between Western music and music of the Middle East, Africa, or India. Likewise, the dance styles of African tribal groups or the Balinese are quite removed from Western dance styles. Architecture is another expression of aesthetics. Each culture appreciates architecture differently. The beauty of India's Taj Mahal is different from that of Notre Dame in Paris or the Chrysler Building in New York City.

COLOR

The significance of different colors also varies from culture to culture. In the United States, for instance, people use colors to identify emotional reactions: People "see red," they are "green with envy," and they "feel blue." Black signifies mourning in Western countries, whereas white is often the color of mourning in Eastern nations. Green is popular in Muslim countries, whereas red and black have a negative connotation in several African countries. Red is an appealing and lucky color in China, blue sometimes suggests evil, and yellow is often associated with authority. Certain colors have particular meanings because of religious, patriotic, or aesthetic reasons. The marketer needs to know the significance of colors in a culture when planning products, packages, and advertising. For any market, the choice of colors should be related to the aesthetic sense of the buyer's culture, rather than that of the marketer's culture. Generally, using the colors of the country's flag is safe. Japan has a Study Group for Colors in Public Places; it wages war on "color pollution." Its mission is "to seek out better uses for color," to raise the issue of colors.

DESIGN

In the design of its plant, product, or package, a firm should be sensitive to local aesthetic preferences. This may run counter to the desire for international uniformity, but the firm must be aware of the positive and negative aspects of its designs. Generally, Asians appreciate complex and decorative styles, particularly when it comes to gift wrapping, for instance.

BRAND NAMES

The choice of brand names is also affected by aesthetics. Frequently, the best brand name is one in the local language, pleasing to local taste. This leads to a multiplicity of brand names, which some firms try to avoid by searching out nonsense words that are pronounceable everywhere but have no specific meaning anywhere. Kodak is one example. In other cases, local identification is important enough that firms seek local brand names. For example, Procter & Gamble has 20 different brand names for its detergents in foreign markets. Interestingly, P&G also uses a number of English brand names in foreign countries as shown in the example from Poland in Table 4-1.

The aesthetics of a culture influence a firm's marketing abroad, often in ways that marketers are unaware of until they make mistakes. A firm needs

Table 4-1 • Procter & Gamble Brand Names in Poland

Following are brand names sold in Poland by P&G. Note how many are in English or use an English foundation with Polish extensions.

Beauty and Healthcare/Hygiene Products

Olay	Braun Silkepil Xelle	Mexx
Pantene Pro-V	Braun SatinHair	xx by Mexx
Head & Shoulders	Braun Pulsonic	Puma
Herbal Essences	Braun Series	Bruno Banani
Wella	Braun Cruzer	Tom Tailor
Shockwaves	Braun Moja Golarka	Gabriela Sabatini
Shamtu	Braun Blendery	Naomi Campbell
Londa	Serwis Braun	Christina Aguilera Pampers
MAX Factor	Gillette Champions	Instytut Pampers
Old Spice	Gillette Fusion	Blend-a-Med
Secret	Valentino	Instytut Blend-a-Med
Always	Dolce & Gabbana	Blend-a-Dent
Naturella	Gucci	Oral-B
Discreet	Escada	Wick
Tampax	Dunhill	Pringles
Braun	Boss by Hugo Boss	Eukanuba
Braun Silkepil Xpressive	Hugo by Hugo Boss	Iams
	Boss Skin	

Household Products

Ariel	Lenor	Braun
Vizir	Fairy	Gillette
Bonux	Ace	Duracell

Source: P&G Global Operations. Poland website (http://www.pg.com/pl_PL/products.shtml), accessed July 2, 2010.

language

An element of culture that includes the spoken and written word—how a culture communicates verbally and in writing.

Firms often use the influence of aesthetics in selecting a different brand name to use in foreign markets.

local input to avoid ineffective or damaging use of aesthetics. This input may come from local marketing research, local nationals working for the firm, and local advertising agencies or distributors.

Language

Language is perhaps the most obvious difference between cultures. Inextricably linked with all other aspects of a culture, language reflects the nature and values of that culture. For example, the English language has a rich vocabulary for commercial and industrial activities, reflecting the nature of the English and U.S. societies. Many less-industrialized societies have only limited vocabularies for those activities but richer vocabularies for matters important to their culture. (Table 4-2 shows various languages and the number of people that speak that language as their first language.)

An Indian civil servant, Nabagopal Das, commented on the important role of the English language in India's development. He said it would be a serious error for India to replace English with Hindi or other Indian languages because none of them gives adequate expression to the modern commercial or technical activities necessary for India's development. On the other hand, these other languages are more than adequate, indeed rich, for describing the traditional culture. Similarly, Eskimo has many words to describe snow, whereas English has one general term. This is reasonable because the difference in forms of snow plays a vital role in the lives of Eskimos. The kinds of activities they can engage in depend on the specific snow conditions. Of course, in the United States, the subculture of skiers has a richer vocabulary for snow than that of nonskiers.

Because language is such an obvious cultural difference, everyone recognizes that it must be dealt with. It is said that anyone planning a career in international business should learn a foreign language. Certainly, if a person's career involves dealing with a particular country, he or she will find learning the country's language to be very useful. However, learning German or Japanese is not a great help to those people whose careers do not involve Germany or Japan. Because it is usually impossible to predict to which countries a career will lead, it is best to study a language spoken by many people (Mandarin) or a language that is commonly used as a first or second language in many nations (English, French, and Spanish). Whether or not it is a primary language of the parties involved, English is frequently used in negotiations, legal documents, and business transactions. Some companies consider English so important it is mandatory. This is the case with Rakuten, Inc., Japan's biggest online retailer. Rakuten has mandated that by 2012, all employees must be able to speak English or they will be fired![5]

Language differences within a country may indicate social as well as communication divisions. In both Canada and Belgium, linguistic groups have occasionally clashed to the point of violence, such as the 1970 violence over French-speaking Quebec wanting to secede from Canada. Angola, Nigeria, and India are examples of less-developed countries where differing linguistic groups have also engaged in hostilities.

The United States is not exactly a linguistic melting pot either. Spanish accounts for over half of all of the foreign-language speakers, but several of the other groups provide segmentation for marketing and media purposes, such as African Americans and Asian Americans. Although the United States is more homogeneous than the EU, the melting pot is not complete.

Even in China, where over a billion people "speak Mandarin," more than ten sociolinguistic groups exist. Among the Han Chinese, there are many Sinitic sublanguages and dialects, whose speakers are often unable to understand one another. These linguistic variations are related to cultural differences.

Many former colonies have some linguistic unity in the language of the former colonial power, but even this is threatened in certain countries. For example, in India, Hindi is an official language along with English. Hindi has the advantage of being an Indian language, but also the drawback of belonging to just one segment of India's population. When it was declared an official language, riots broke out due to the disapproval of other language supporters such as Tamil and Malayalam.

It is said that a language defines a cultural group—that nothing distinguishes one culture from another more than language. But what does it mean when the same language is used in different countries? French, for example, is the mother

Table 4-2 ● World Languages (First-Language Speakers)

Language	Speakers (millions)
Chinese, Mandarin	1,213
Spanish	329
English*	328
Arabic (all)	221
Hindi	182
Bengali	181
Portuguese	178
Russian	144
Japanese	122
German	90
Javanese	85
Lahnda (all)	78

*The figures for English are misleading because for almost every country, English is the first choice as a second language.

Source: Ethnologue: Languages of the World (http://www.ethnologue.com/ethno_docs/distribution.asp?by=size), accessed June 28, 2010.

Different languages are not the only challenges in doing business around the world. There are also differences in communication style.

---

tongue not only for the French, but also for many Belgians and Swiss. Spanish plays a similar role in Latin America. Anthropologists, however, stress the spoken language as the cultural distinction. The spoken language changes more quickly than the written language and reflects the culture more directly. Although England, the United States, and Ireland use the same written English, they speak somewhat different dialects. These three cultures are separate yet related, as are the Spanish-speaking cultures of Latin America.

Even where a common language is spoken, different words signifying the same meaning are occasionally used, as are different pronunciations. In Latin America, for example, the word for tire is not the same as that used in other Spanish-speaking countries. In England, people say "lorry," "petrol," and "biscuits," but in the United States, people say "truck," "gasoline," and "cookies." Incidentally, even within one country—for example, the United States, where almost everyone speaks "American" English—there are different cultural groups, or subcultures, among which the spoken language varies. A simple example is the use of "y'all" versus "you guys."

COMMUNICATION STYLE—UNSPOKEN WORDS

Related to the issue of language is communication style, especially what is often not said in a conversation. Some cultures tend to be quite explicit in their communications—for example, Americans. In other cultures, lots of assumptions are built into any conversation—for example, the French. Edward T. Hall described these differences as "low context" versus "high context."[6] **Low-context cultures** have a very direct communication style in which the message is clear, logical, and specific. An easy way to think of a low-context culture is as a group of passengers in an airport where signs and directions must be explicit so everyone understands important communications. Examples of cultures that tend toward low context are those in North America, Scandinavia, and Germany. **High-context cultures** place less importance on the actual verbal communication and more on the relationship. For high-context cultures, communication style is less direct and more respectful and considerate. As contrasted with passengers in an airport, a high-context example would be a family reunion in which social rules are understood and communication is polite. Examples of cultures that tend toward high context are the Chinese, Japanese, and Koreans. The impact goes beyond communication style. In low-context cultures, relationships are more casual, and less emphasis is put on prior business relationships or the background of individuals. In high-context cultures, personal relationships are valued, and notions such as trust, honor, and obligation are important. Not recognizing these differences could have an important impact on communication style, just as with differences in languages.

LANGUAGE AND COMMUNICATION AS A PROBLEM

In advertising, branding, packaging, personal selling, and marketing research, marketing is highly dependent on communication. If management is not speaking the same language as its various audiences, it is not going to enjoy much success. In each of its foreign markets, a company must communicate with several audiences: its workers, its managers, its customers, its suppliers, and the government. Each of these audiences may have a distinctive communication style within the common language. The number of language areas in which a firm operates approximates the number of countries in which it sells. Any advantage gained by the fact that one language may be used in more than one

low-context culture

Culture with a very direct communication style in which the message is clear, logical, and specific.

high-context culture

Culture that places less emphasis on actual verbal communication and more on the relationship and nonverbal communication.

country is partly offset by the fact that in many countries, more than one language is spoken. In fact, research shows that the "language distance" between the home and host country is a major factor when managers select markets for international expansion. All other things being equal, managers prefer to expand to countries that speak the same language, or at least a language with a similar linguistic root.[7]

Language diversity in world markets could be an insurmountable problem if managers had to master the languages of all their markets. Fortunately, that is not the case. To be effective, however, any person assigned to a foreign operation for a period of a year or more should learn the local language.

Similarly, a good understanding of the culture's tendency toward high- or low-context communication would be critical with such tasks as contract negotiations. In high-context business negotiations (less direct style), a manager needs to understand that the negotiations may take time, with participants wanting to establish trust and understanding prior to actual negotiations. In a low-context culture (direct style), one can expect the opposite: Negotiations are very efficient, ending with clear, specific contractual agreements.

To navigate these differences, one needs to take advantage of cultural bridges available in many markets. In countries where a firm is operating through a distributor, the distributor may act as the bridge between the firm and its local market. At least some distributor employees likely speak the marketing manager's language, especially if the firm communicates principally in English. For example, the Dutch firm Philips uses English as the official company language, even though it is domiciled in the Netherlands. Because of its widespread operations, the company finds English to be the most useful language for its markets. In the Chrysler/Daimler-Benz merger, American English was made the corporate language. As previously discussed, Rakuten in Japan made English mandatory. Another cultural bridge would be the use of a local marketing or advertising agency.

As has been suggested, there are ways to circumvent the language or communication problem. However, these are critical factors. It is the key to understanding and communicating with the local cultures around the world. An international firm needs language and communication capabilities not only among its distributors and other collaborators, but eventually also among its own personnel. (See the following box "When Marketers Go Wrong.")

••• When Marketers Go Wrong

Culture and language differences can challenge even the largest companies and the smartest marketing managers. One of the mostly widely known examples is the time General Motors introduced the Chevrolet Nova into Latin American markets, but the car did not sell well because "no va" roughly translates to "doesn't go" or "no go" in Spanish. However, this example (even included in many marketing textbooks) is not true, as the car sold well and the name was never changed from Nova in Spanish-speaking markets. Although this example is an urban legend, marketers

do sometimes make these kinds of mistakes. For example, the Braniff Airlines slogan "fly in leather" was improperly translated to "fly naked" in Spain; a company selling razors into Qatar found that its brand name "tiz," which meant "sharp" in Persian, loosely translated to "passing wind" in Arabic slang; and a firm selling laundry detergent in French-speaking Quebec found that its labels contained the term "les parts de sale," which is similar to "private parts" in American English.

Meanings of colors and consumer behaviors also differ by culture. In the 1950s, PepsiCo sales suffered in Southeast Asia when it changed the color of its vending machines from a regal blue to a light ice blue. In Southeast Asia, light blue is associated with death and mourning, creating a different brand image than Pepsi was hoping for! Avon had trouble adapting to different cultural conditions when it introduced its direct sales force in Japan. Japanese women had difficulty selling the products to people they did not know, and potential buyers were equally uncomfortable inviting strangers into their homes. Eventually, Avon overcame this problem by hiring local sales representatives who knew the customers in their area.[8]

Religion

religion

An element of a culture that provides insight into the culture; in general, religion is a set of beliefs about the cause, nature, and purpose of the universe.

Some of the elements of culture already discussed, such as aesthetics and language, are in effect, outward manifestations of a culture. To gain a full understanding of a culture, however, one needs to become familiar with the internal behavior that gives rise to the external manifestations. Generally, it is the **religion** of a culture that provides the best insights into this behavior. Therefore, although an international company is interested primarily in knowing how people behave as consumers or workers, management's task will be aided by an understanding of why people behave as they do.

Numerous religions exist in the world. This section presents brief overviews of some major worldwide religions, including Judaism, Christianity, Islam, Hinduism, Buddhism, and animism. These religions were selected on the basis of their importance in terms of numbers of adherents and their impact on the economic behavior of their followers. Adherents to these religious beliefs account for a majority of the world's population. Estimates for the largest religions in 2010 were as follows: Christianity, 2.1 billion; Islam, 1.5 billion; Hinduism, 900 million; and Buddhism, 376 million. There are also those people who are described as "secular" (including agnostic, atheist, and nonreligious), which includes approximately 1.1 billion people, and followers of "Chinese Traditional Religion" (a combination of Confucianism, Buddhism, and Taoism), which has approximately 394 million adherents. The number of animists, described as various forms of primal-indigenous religions (tribal, ethnic, etc.), is difficult to determine—with the reported number of adherents varying from 100 to 245 million. (Most estimates are in the range of 150 million followers.)[9]

JUDAISM

One of the oldest religions in the world, Judaism has roughly 14 million followers worldwide.[10] Jewish ancestry is traced to the Biblical patriarchs Abraham, Isaac, and Jacob, and many suggest that Judaism was the first religion to believe in a single God. Central to Judaism is the Torah, which is the body of the Jewish sacred writings coming from the first five books of the Bible. Proper Jewish practice (principles regarding how one lives one's life) is tied directly to the Torah.

Interpreting the role of the Torah and its impact on daily life has led to differences in the way the Jewish faith is practiced. The U.S. based Jewish Outreach Institute classifies four types (denominations) of Judaism. **Orthodox Judaism** (or "fully observant") is the traditional practice of Jewry that upholds the traditional (Halakhic) way of life as detailed in the Torah. Not all Jewish people are orthodox. For example, although the majority of the population of Israel is Jewish (roughly 75 percent), about 12 percent are Orthodox. The other denominations include **Reform Judaism**, which is seen as more liberal and supports the notion that how ones lives in accord with the Torah may change over time; **Conservative Judaism**, which is the largest group worldwide and attempts to maintain tradition while applying new methods of study; and **Reconstructionism**, which is the most recent denomination and rejects the assertion that Moses received the Torah at Mount Sinai.[11]

This long and rich history of Judaism is of particular significance in understanding Judaism and its impact on beliefs, traditions, and the daily routine of the Jewish people. It also has particular importance to the international marketing manager because these traditions impact a range of product and service issues. For example, some foods are banned, such as pork and shellfish. Airlines, restaurants, and hotels need to offer kosher meals, which are foods that meet dietary laws. The Sabbath begins at sundown on Friday and continues until sundown on Saturday, which means employees will need that time off work. There are other important religious observances central to the Jewish faith, and employers need to recognize their importance and remain flexible.

CHRISTIANITY

Christianity is a major religion worldwide. The emphasis within international marketing is the impact of the different Christian religious groups (Roman Catholic and Protestant) on economic attitudes and behavior. Of interest are two studies that have dealt with this subject: Max Weber's *The Protestant Ethic and the Spirit of Capitalism* and R. H. Tawney's *Religion and the Rise of Capitalism*. The Eastern Orthodox churches are not discussed in this section, but their impact on economic attitudes is similar to that of Catholicism.

Roman Catholic Christianity traditionally has emphasized the church and the sacraments as the principal elements of religion and the way to God. The church and its priests are intermediaries between God and human beings, and apart from the church, there is no salvation. Another element is the distinction between the members of religious orders and the laity, with different standards of conduct applied to each. An implicit difference exists between the secular and the religious life. The Protestant Reformation, especially Calvinism, brought about some critical changes in emphasis but retained agreement with Catholicism on most traditional Christian doctrine. The Protestants, however, stressed that the church, its sacraments, and its clergy were not essential to salvation: "Salvation is by faith alone." The result of this thinking was a downgrading of the role of the church and a consequent upgrading of the role of the individual. Salvation became more an individual matter.

Although it is useful to recognize the separate thrust of Roman Catholic and Protestant Christianity, it is also important to note the various roles Christianity generally plays in different nations. Some nations reflect varying mixtures of

Orthodox Judaism

One of four types (denominations) of Judaism; orthodox adherents uphold the traditional way of life as detailed in the Torah.

Reform Judaism

One of four types (denominations) of Judaism; reformists tend to be more liberal and support the notion that how one lives in accord with the Torah may change over time.

Conservative Judaism

One of four types (denominations) of Judaism; conservatives attempt to maintain tradition while applying new methods of study.

Reconstructionism

One of four types (denominations) of Judaism; this most recent denomination rejects the assertion that Moses received the Torah at Mount Sinai.

Catholicism and Protestantism, and the resulting ethic may be some combination of both doctrines. Of course, within Christianity (as with Buddhism, Hinduism, and Islam), wide variations exist in the degree to which adherents follow the teachings. In all groups, segments range from fundamentalist to conservative to casual.

ISLAM

Islam dates from the seventh century AD. It has over 1.5 billion adherents, mostly in the northern half of Africa, the Middle East, and throughout parts of Asia to the Philippines. Islam is usually associated with Arabs and the Middle East, but non-Arab Muslims outnumber Arab Muslims by almost three to one. Although there are two major groups in Islam (Sunni, 85 percent, and Shi'ite, 15 percent), they are similar enough on economic issues to permit identification of the following elements of interest to marketers.

Muslim theology, *Tawhid*, defines all that one should believe; whereas the law, Shari'a, prescribes everything one should do. The Koran (Qur'an) is accepted as the ultimate guide. Anything not mentioned in the Koran is likely to be rejected by the faithful. Introducing new products and techniques can be difficult in such an environment. An important element of Muslim belief is that everything that happens, good or evil, proceeds directly from the Divine Will and is already irrevocably recorded on the Preserved Tablet. This belief tends to restrict attempts to bring about change in Muslim countries; to attempt change may be a rejection of what Allah has ordained. The name *Islam* is the infinitive of the Arabic verb meaning "to submit." *Muslim* is the present participle of the same verb; that is, a Muslim is one submitting to the will of Allah.

The Five Pillars of Islam, or the duties of a Muslim, include (1) the recital of the creed, (2) prayer, (3) fasting, (4) almsgiving, and (5) the pilgrimage. The creed is brief: There is no God but God, and Mohammed is the Prophet of God. Muslims must pray five times daily at stated hours. During the month of Ramadan, Muslims are required to fast from dawn to sunset—no food, no drink, no smoking. Because the Muslim year is lunar, Ramadan sometimes falls in midsummer, when the long days and intense heat make abstinence a severe test. The fast is meant to develop self-control and sympathy for the poor. During Ramadan, work output falls off markedly, which is attributable as much to the Muslims' loss of sleep (from the many late-night feasts and celebrations) as to the rigors of fasting. The average family actually spends more money on the food consumed at night during Ramadan than on the food consumed by day in the other months. Other spending rises also. Spending during Ramadan has been said to equal six months of normal spending, corresponding to the Christmas season elsewhere. Sales increases of 20 to 40 percent for furniture, cars, jewelry, and other large or expensive items are common. One firm stated that between 35 and 40 percent of all auto sales take place during Ramadan.[12]

By almsgiving, Muslims share with the poor. It is an individual responsibility, and there are both required alms (zakat) and freewill gifts. The pilgrimage to Mecca is a well-known aspect of Islam. The thousands who gather in Mecca each year return home with a greater sense of the international solidarity of Islam. Spending for the pilgrimage is a special form of consumption directly associated with religious behavior.

There is a relationship between religion and culture, as is discussed here, but there is also a relationship between culture and laws, which will be discussed later in the text. Behavior deemed acceptable or not acceptable is often reflected in the laws of a nation or group of people. The tie between religion and law is perhaps most clear in Islam. With respect to business, Muslims are not allowed to consume pork or alcohol. Furthermore, people are not allowed to invest in firms whose primary business involves alcohol, defense, entertainment, gambling, or the manufacture of or processes using pork products. Under

Shari'a law, investors are not allowed to hold any stake in conventional banks or insurance companies because these institutions are believed to engage in usurious practices that are illegal. Even the ability to own stock or shares in companies with large amounts of debt or that make annual interest payments is being called into question. Although there is some tolerance for investing in these companies, devout Muslims point out that this is a breach of Shari'a rules against usury. Some marketing implications of Islam are noted in Table 4-3.

Table 4-3 • Islam and Marketing

Islamic Element	Marketing Implication
1. Daily prayers	Work schedules; hours of peak/off-peak customer traffic; timing of sales calls
2. Prohibition on usury and consumption of pork and alcohol	Prohibition of or difficulty in selling certain products (insurance, banking, and financial services); processes used in manufacturing of food and other products for human consumption or use; inappropriateness of layaway and other credit tools
3. Zakat (mandatory alms)	Spending patterns; attitude toward charity; social consciousness; excessive profits used for charitable purposes
4. Religious holidays (e.g., Ramadan) and other religious or sacred periods	Sales and special promotions; lavish gift periods; food distribution and restaurant hours; Muslim "weekend" is Thursday and Friday
5. Public separation of sexes	Access to female customers; direct marketing to women; mixed gender focus

HINDUISM

There are over 900 million Hindus in the world, most of them in India. In a broad sense, about 80 percent of India's population is Hindu; but in the sense of strict adherence to the tenets of Hinduism, the number of followers is smaller. A common dictum is that Hinduism is not a religion, but a way of life. Its origins go back approximately 3,500 years. It is an ethnic, noncreedal religion. A Hindu is born, not made; so a person cannot become a Hindu or convert to Hinduism, although he or she may become a Buddhist, for example. Modern Hinduism is a combination of ancient philosophies and customs, animistic beliefs, legends, and more recently, Western influences, including Christianity. A strength of Hinduism has been its ability to absorb ideas from outside; Hinduism tends to assimilate rather than exclude.

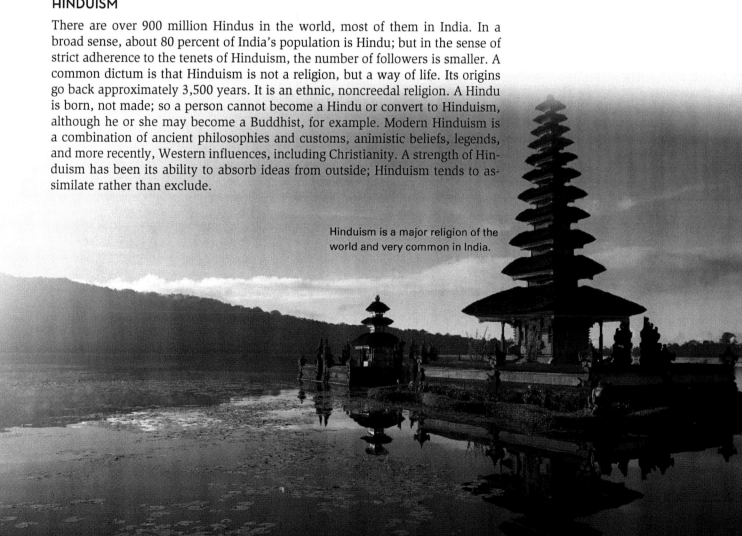

Hinduism is a major religion of the world and very common in India.

Despite this openness, many in India are unhappy about marriages between Hindus and Christians or Muslims because such relationships are viewed as a threat or dilution of Hindutva (Hindu-ness) of the culture. Much violence has occurred between the Hindu and Muslim populations, with one instance of over 500 people killed in Gujarat in early 2002.[13] Because Hinduism is an ethnic religion, many of its doctrines apply only to the Indian situation. However, they are crucial in understanding India and its people.

Sikhism is a religion also practiced in India that represents a combined form of Hinduism and Islam, featuring a much debated aspect: the caste system. Although the Indian government officially abolished this system over a half century ago and instituted quotas and job-preferment policies, there are still examples of separate gurdwaras (houses of worship) for Sikhs and the Dalit, or scheduled caste (formerly called "untouchables"), some of whom are converting to Buddhism, Christianity, and Islam to escape the caste system.[14,15]

Another element—and a strength of Hinduism—is baradari, or the "joint family." After marriage, the bride goes to the groom's home. After several marriages in the family, there is a large joint family for which the father or grandfather is chief authority. In turn, the older women have power over the younger. The elders give advice and consent in family council. The Indian grows up thinking and acting in terms of the joint family. If a member goes abroad to a university, the joint family may raise the funds. In turn, that member is expected to remember the family if he or she is successful. Baradari is aimed at preserving the family.

Veneration of the cow is perhaps the best-known Hindu custom: Gandhi called this the distinguishing mark of the Hindu. Hindu worship of the cow involves protecting it, but eating the products of the cow is also considered a means for purification. Another element of traditional Hinduism is the restriction of women, following the belief that to be born a woman is a sign of sin in a former life. Some marriages are still arranged by relatives. Traditionally, a man may remarry if widowed, but a woman may not. But traditions and beliefs are changing, especially among the younger generation, and as seen years ago when India elected a woman, Indira Gandhi, to its highest office.

Nirvana is another important concept, one that Hinduism shares with Buddhism. This topic is discussed in the following section.

BUDDHISM

Buddhism springs from Hinduism, originating about 2,600 years ago. Buddhism has approximately 376 million followers, mostly in South and East Asia from India to Japan. There are, however, small Buddhist societies in Europe and America. Buddhism is, to some extent, a reformation of Hinduism. It did not abolish caste but declared that Buddhists were released from caste restrictions. This openness to all classes and both sexes was one reason for Buddhism's growth. While accepting the philosophical insights of Hinduism, Buddhism tried to avoid its dogma and ceremony, stressing tolerance and spiritual equality.

At the heart of Buddhism are the Four Noble Truths:

1. The Noble Truth of Suffering states that suffering is omnipresent and part of the very nature of life.

2. The Noble Truth of the Cause of Suffering cites the cause of suffering to be desire—that is, desire for possessions and selfish enjoyment of any kind.

3. The Noble Truth of the Cessation of Suffering states that suffering ceases when desire ceases.

4. The Noble Truth of the Eightfold Path that leads to the Cessation of Suffering offers the means to achieve cessation of desire. This is also known as the Middle Way because it avoids the two extremes of self-indulgence and self-mortification. The eightfold path includes (1) the right views, (2) the right desires, (3) the right speech, (4) the right conduct, (5) the right occupation, (6) the right effort, (7) the right awareness, and (8) the right contemplation. This path, though simple to state, is a demanding ethical system.

Nirvana is the reward for those who are able to stay on the path throughout their lifetime or, more probably, lifetimes. Nirvana is the ultimate goal of the Hindu and Buddhist; it represents the extinction of all cravings and the final release from suffering. To the extent that such an ideal reflects the thinking of the mass of the people, the society's values would be considered antithetical to such goals as acquisition, achievement, and affluence. This is an obvious constraint on marketing. Of course, not all Buddhists are so nonmaterialistic.

ANIMISM OR NONLITERATE RELIGION

Animism is the term used to describe the religion of indigenous peoples. It is often defined as spirit worship, as distinguished from the worship of God or gods. Animistic beliefs have been found in all parts of the world. With the exception of revealed religion, some form of animism has preceded all historical religions. In many less-developed parts of the world today, animistic ideas affect cognitive behavior. Magic, a key element of animism, is the attempt to achieve results through the manipulation of the spirit world. It represents an unscientific approach to the physical world. When cause-and-effect relationships are not known, magic is given credit for the results. The same attitude prevails toward many modern-day products and techniques.

Other aspects of animism include ancestor worship, taboos, and fatalism. All of them tend to promote a traditionalist, status quo, backward-looking society. Because such societies are more interested in protecting their traditions than in accepting change, marketers face problems when introducing new products, ideas, or methods. Marketers' success in bringing change depends on how well they understand and relate to the culture and its animistic foundation.

RELIGION AND THE ECONOMY

Religion has a major impact on attitude toward economic matters and, therefore, an impact in international marketing, as in the following examples.

• Religious holidays vary greatly among countries—not only from Christian to Muslim, but also from one Christian country to another. In general, Sundays are a religious holiday where Christianity is an important religion. In the Muslim world, however, the entire month of Ramadan is a religious holiday for practical purposes. A firm must see that local work schedules and marketing programs take into account local holidays, just as American firms plan for a big season at Christmas.

- Consumption patterns may be affected by religious requirements or taboos. Fish on Friday for Catholics used to be a classic example. Taboos against beef for Hindus or pork for Muslims and Jews are other examples. The Muslim prohibition against alcohol has been a boon to companies such as Coca-Cola. Heineken and other brewers sell a nonalcoholic beer in Saudi Arabia. On the other hand, dairy products find favor among Hindus, many of whom are vegetarians.

- The economic role of women varies from culture to culture, and religious beliefs are an important cause. Women may be restricted in their capacity as consumers, as workers, or as respondents in a marketing study. These differences may require major adjustments in the approach of a management conditioned to the U.S. market. Procter & Gamble's products are used mainly by women. When the company wanted to conduct a focus group in Saudi Arabia, however, it could not induce women to participate. Instead, it used the husbands and brothers of women for the focus group.

- The Hindu joint family has economic effects. Nepotism is characteristic of the family business. Staffing is based more on considerations of family rank than on any other criteria. Furthermore, consumer decision making and consumption in the joint family may differ from those in the U.S. family, requiring an adapted marketing strategy. Pooled income in the joint family may lead to different purchase patterns.

- Religious institutions themselves may play a role in economic matters. The church, or any organized religious group, may block the introduction of new products or techniques if it sees the innovation as a threat. On the other hand, the same product or technique can be more effectively introduced if the religious organization sees it as a benefit. The United States has seen the growing role of religious groups. The box entitled "Marketers Get Religion" provides some examples from other countries.

- Religious divisions in a country can pose problems for management. A firm may find that it is dealing with different markets. In India, Muslim–Hindu clashes led to the formation of the separate nation of Pakistan, but the animosity continues. In the Netherlands, major Catholic and Protestant groups have their own political parties and newspapers. Such religious divisions can cause difficulty in staffing an operation or in distributing and promoting a product. Religious differences may indicate market segments that require separate strategies and media.

Clearly, an international firm must be sensitive to religious differences in its foreign markets and be willing to make adaptations. To cite one example, a firm that is building a plant overseas might plan the date and method of opening and dedicating the building to reflect the local religious customs. In particular, a firm's advertising, packaging, and personal selling practices need to take local religious sensitivities into account.

••• Marketers Get Religion

The U.S. Post Office sells stamps for Christmas, Chanukah, Kwanzaa, and a host of other holidays and events. On September 1, 2001, it released the first Islam-themed American stamp. The first-class postage EID stamp commemorates the end of Ramadan and the end of the pilgrimage to Mecca.

In Germany, The Land of Genesis is set to open in 2012, offering 40 Bible-related attractions, including a life-size version of Noah's Ark surrounded by water. The park's roller coasters aim to take visitors through the great flood as well as heaven and hell. The Scriptorium, a $25 million Christian Foundation theme park, opened in Florida in 2002. Included in the park is a re-creation of ancient Jerusalem, animatronic robots that "talk" about the Bible, and a fiber-optic finger of God that writes the Ten Commandments on a rock. Similar theme parks have been discussed or planned in other U.S. states, Russia, and China.

Coca-Cola and PepsiCo have held special promotions for Ramadan in Turkey. PepsiCo offered free 600-milliliter bottles of soda with the purchase of larger 2.5-liter bottles so customers could "get through iftar and sahur in one purchase." (Iftar is the meal at the start of the day before the fast begins, while sahur is taken in the evening to end the fast.) Coca-Cola offered special commemorative Ramadan plates for consumers who sent in bottle caps and began selling special cans during Ramadan just as Coke does for Christmas in other countries.

McDonald's agreed to pay $12 million to settle a class action suit filed by Hindus, Sikhs, and Jews for not disclosing that beef flavorings were used in the McDonald's French fry recipe. American Muslims also wanted a portion of the funds because the use of beef likely violated the halal food code (which specifies how the beef is to be prepared).

There are banks, mortgage companies, and other financial institutions in Muslim nations, despite the prohibition on earnings through interest payments (riba). If someone wants to purchase a car, a typical deal might go something like this: The person buying the car would go to the local Jaguar dealer and pick out the model and features. Then, through a transaction referred to as murabaha, the buyer would ask his bank to purchase the car (for, say, $50,000), which would then resell the car to the buyer for $55,000, paid in monthly installments.

There are many other examples of how marketers have attempted to address religious-based opportunities, as well as many cases where they have failed to do so.[16]

Education

In developed nations, **education** usually means formal training in school. In this sense, those people without access to schools are not educated; that is, they have never been to school. However, this formal definition is too restrictive. Education includes the process of transmitting skills, ideas, and attitudes, as well as training, in particular disciplines. Even so-called "primitive" peoples have been educated in this broader sense. For example, regardless of formal schooling, the Bushmen of South Africa are well educated in relation to the culture in which they live.

One function of education is to transmit the existing culture and traditions to the new generation. (The role of women in Afghan society—particularly their access to formal education under Taliban rule—and the subsequent changes instituted when President Hamid Karzai was elected illustrate the role of education in the process of cultural change.) Education plays an important role in cultural change in the United States, as it does elsewhere. For example, in the past, developing nations' educational campaigns were carried out with the specific intent of improving techniques used in farming and in reducing the population explosion. In Britain, business schools were originally established to improve the performance of the economy. Researchers attributed the rapid economic development of Singapore to formal apprenticeship programs.[17]

> **education**
> An element of culture that includes formal training in schools and the process in that culture for transmitting skills, ideas, and attitudes.

INTERNATIONAL DIFFERENCES IN EDUCATION

When looking at education in foreign markets, the researcher is limited primarily to information about the formal process—that is, education in schools. This is the only area for which the United Nations Educational, Scientific and Cultural Organization (UNESCO), the World Bank, and others have been able to gather data. Traditionally, literacy rates have been used to describe educational achievement; recently, however, international agencies have been measuring inputs as well as educational system outputs other than literacy. For example, the World Bank still includes adult and youth illiteracy rates in its reports. (Now it has begun measuring participation in education, which includes enrollment ratios in primary, secondary, and tertiary levels of education; and education efficiency, which includes completion rates at different levels of education and average number of years of school.) The World Bank also reports on inputs such as expenditures per student, teachers' compensation, number of faculty with appropriate qualifications, and pupil-teacher ratios. Perhaps most importantly, the goals of the World Bank have changed—from activities aimed merely at increasing literacy rates to measures designed to ensure that "all children complete a full course of primary education," a target it hopes is achieved by 2015. (See Table 4-4.)

Table 4-4 • World Education*

Country by Income Group	Primary School Teacher-Pupil Ratio	Secondary School Enrollment (%)	Adult Literacy Rate	Adult Literacy Rate
			Male	Female
Low Income	42	41	67	50
Lower-Middle Income	29	62	85	73
Upper-Middle Income	22	90	99	99
High Income	15	100	99	99
World Average	24	66	88	79

*Notes: All data for 2007 except Lower-Middle Income Primary School Teacher-Pupil Ratio, where the latest data is for 2003; also, all literacy data for the period 2005–2008.

Source: World Bank World Development Indicators Online, accessed June 28, 2010; UNESCO Institute for Statistics, Online Statistics Centre, accessed June 28, 2010.

The education information available on world markets refers primarily to national enrollments in the various levels of education: primary, secondary, and college or university. This information can give an international marketer insight into the sophistication of consumers in different countries. There is also a strong correlation between educational attainment and economic development. Hanushek and Kimko argued that qualitative measures such as math and science scores on international achievement tests should also be used as indicators of human capital development and long-term economic prospects. Because U.S. students consistently score lower on these exams than students in other countries, researchers warned that the United States may lose its technological edge in the future.[18]

Because only quantitative data are available, there is a danger that the qualitative aspects of education might be overlooked. Furthermore, in addition to the limitations inherent in international statistics, the problem exists of interpreting them in terms of business needs. For example, a firm's needs for technicians, marketing personnel, managers, distributors, and sales forces must be

Different levels of education between countries have an important impact on a marketing plan that must be adapted to reflect these differences.

met largely from the educated population in the local economy. When hiring people, the firm is concerned not only with the level, but also with the nature of the applicants' education.

EDUCATION AND INTERNATIONAL MARKETING

The international marketer must also be something of an educator. The products and techniques a firm brings into a market are generally new to that market. The firm must educate consumers about the uses and benefits. Although a firm may not make use of a formal educational system, its success is constrained by that system because its ability to communicate depends in part on the educational level of its market. The international marketing manager is further concerned about the educational situation because it is a key determinant of the nature of the consumer market and the kinds of marketing personnel available. Some implications for businesses include the following:

- When consumers are largely illiterate, existing advertising programs, package labels, instructions, and warranties need to be adapted to include fewer words and more graphics and pictures.

- When women are largely excluded from formal education, marketing programs may differ from those aimed at female segments in developed nations. When a firm is targeting women audiences with less education, messages need to be simple, perhaps with less text and more graphics.

- Conducting marketing research can be difficult, both in communicating with consumers and in getting qualified researchers. If few people are able to read, written surveys would be an ineffective tool in gathering data. Personal interviews, although more costly, would tend to increase response rates and accuracy. See Chapter 6 for more details.

- Cooperation from the distribution channel depends partly on the educational attainments of members in the channel and of other partners and employees. When overall levels of education are low, finding and hiring local qualified marketing employees for certain service or managerial positions may be difficult and very competitive. Long-term training programs and commitments to employee education may raise local operating costs.

Social Organization

social organization

An element of culture that describes the roles and expectations a group of people place upon themselves and others within the group.

The **social organization** of a group of people helps define their roles and the expectations they place upon themselves and others in the group. Concepts such as family vary from group to group, which becomes evident when talking about these concepts to people from other cultures. The nature of people's friendships with others—how quickly the relationships develop, how the friendships are nurtured, and how long they last—also reflects on the social organization within the culture or group. Social organization is formally defined in the government and the laws that proscribe certain behavior among people. The nature of social organization and the impact on marketing are discussed next.

KINSHIP

kinship

A form of social organization that is based on a shared origin, often the same family.

common territory

A form of social organization based on geography as in a neighborhood, city, or tribal grouping.

special interest group

A form of social organization in which group members come together as a result of a common cause, interest, or idea.

Kinship includes the social organization or structure of a group—the way people relate to other people. This relationship differs somewhat from society to society. The primary kind of social organization is based on kinship. In the United States, the key unit is the family, which traditionally included only the father, mother, and unmarried children in the household. Of course, the definition is changing, as is reflected in each census. The family unit elsewhere is often larger, including more relatives. The large joint family of Hinduism was discussed previously. A large extended family is also common in many other less-developed nations. Those who call themselves brothers in Congo, for example, include cousins and uncles.

In developing countries, the extended family fulfills several social and economic roles. The family unit is not prescribed or defined by a specific religious restriction, as does the baradari of Hinduism. The extended family provides mutual protection, psychological support, and economic insurance or social security for its members. In a world of tribal warfare and primitive agriculture, this support was invaluable. The extended family, still significant in many parts of the world, means that consumption decision making takes place in a larger unit and in different ways. Pooled resources, for instance, may allow larger purchases. (For this reason, per capita income may be a misleading guide to market potential.) The marketer may find it difficult to determine the relevant consuming unit for some goods. Is it a household or a family? How many members are there?

Table 4-5 helps to illustrate the differences in the sizes of households around the world. As expected, countries that embrace an extended family, such as India, have a higher average number of occupants per home than those that don't, such as the United States and Sweden.

Table 4-5 ● Average Number of Occupants per Household

Country	Number of Occupants
Pakistan	7.2
Kuwait	6.9
Saudi Arabia	5.4
India	5.3
Mexico	3.9
Brazil	3.6
China	3.4
Israel	3.5
USA	2.6
Japan	2.5
Czech Rep.	2.3
Sweden	2.0

Source: Euromonitor International GMID. "Occupants per Household at January 1st." (2009). (http://www.portal.euromonitor.com/Portal/Statistics.aspx), accessed July 1, 2010.

COMMON TERRITORY

In the United States, common territory can be a neighborhood, suburb, or city. In many countries of Asia and Africa, **common territory** is the tribal grouping. The tribe is often the largest effective unit because the various tribes do not voluntarily recognize the central government. Nationalism has not generally replaced tribalism. Tribalism and religious or ethnic divisions often lead to bloody conflict, shown by such examples as Congo, Ireland, Israel and Palestine, Pakistan, the Philippines, Rwanda, and Sudan. For marketing purposes in some countries, groupings based on common territory may be a useful way to segment the potential market.

SPECIAL INTEREST GROUP

A third kind of social grouping, the **special interest group** or association, may be religious, occupational, recreational, or political. Special interest groups can also be useful in identifying different market segments.

For example, in the United States, the American Association of Retired Persons (AARP), Sierra Club, and National Rifle Association (NRA) represent market segments for many firms.

OTHER KINDS OF SOCIAL ORGANIZATION

Some kinds of social organizations cut across the three categories just discussed. One is caste or class groupings. These groupings may be detailed and rigid, as in the Hindu caste system, or they may be loose and flexible, as in U.S. social classes. The United States has a relatively open society, but there is still concern about social standing and status symbols. Although social class is more (or less) important and rigid in comparing countries, each country has its own social and ethnic groupings that are important for its society and the economy. These groupings usually mean that some groups are discriminated against and others are favored. A firm needs to know this social organization because it will affect the company's marketing program. Different groups may require different marketing strategies, for example.

Other groupings based on age occur especially in affluent industrialized nations. Senior citizens usually live as separate economic units with their own needs and motivations. They are a major market segment in industrialized countries. And although teenagers do not commonly live apart from their families, they still compose a significant economic force to be reckoned with. (See "Teens: Truly Global Consumers.") Children are another important market segment, and understanding local influences and conditions would provide important insights for the local manager. For example, research shows that in China, the television has become the most important source from which Chinese children learn about new products. This finding runs against prior assumptions that the role of family and interpersonal relationships would have been more significant.[19]

As noted in the discussion of the extended family, much less separation between age groups exists in less-developed areas. Generally, strong family integration occurs at all age levels, as well as a preponderant influence of age and seniority, which is in contrast to the youth motif prevalent in the United States. Of course, Baby Boomers, Generation X, and Millennials are important age groupings in the United States.

A final aspect of social organization concerns the role of women in the economy. Women seldom enjoy parity with men as participants in the economy, and their participation is related to the economic development of nations—the poorer the nation, the fewer women seen in jobs outside the home. The extent to which women participate in the money economy affects their role as consumers and consumption influencers. Even developed countries exhibit differences in attitude toward female employment. For example, significant differences in female employment exist between the United States, several European countries, and Japan. These differences are reflected both in household income levels and in consumption patterns. In spite of the constraints noted, the economic role of women is undergoing notable change in many countries.

The role of women in business is changing in many countries, with women increasingly active in business.

SOCIAL ORGANIZATION AND INTERNATIONAL MARKETING

The impact of social organization on international marketing is quite broad. It molds the message conveyed in advertising, such as including large, extended families in media campaigns for countries that define families as such. Social organization impacts the product design. Countries that typically have a high average number of occupants per house yet relatively small dwellings, such as Japan, require goods that use less space than their counterparts in countries with fewer constraints, such as the United States. The role of women is a critical distinction among countries and impacts the whole of the marketing function. Examples include promotion (how women are portrayed in advertising) and sales management (hiring women for sales positions). In various ways, the social organization of a country must be recognized as the international marketing plan is developed and implemented.

Material Culture and Technology

material culture

An element of culture that includes the tools and artifacts (physical things) in a society.

Material culture includes the tools and artifacts—the material or physical things—in a society, excluding those physical things found in nature unless they undergo some technological transformation. For example, a tree, as such, is not part of a culture, but the Christmas tree is. **Technology** refers to the techniques or methods of making and using that which surrounds us. Technology and ma-

Teens: Truly Global Consumers
• • •

technology

Techniques or methods of making and using that which surrounds us.

technology gap

Differences in the ability of two societies to create, design, and use that which exists in nature or to use that which has been transformed in some way.

One article comparing teenagers in the United States and Korea finds that different cultures worldwide are converging. The authors look at many attitudes of young people in those two nations and come to the same conclusion that many others have. The findings of many cross-cultural studies are that young people, because of their exposure to new ideas and to one another through television and the Internet (as well as their willingness to take risks and try new things), are similar in those respects that are not confined to a particular geographic area or culture. That is, certain characteristics, beliefs, attitudes, and behaviors are common to teenagers; and consequently, marketers can get teenagers' attention in similar ways. Something else marketers do not miss is the fact that teenagers are more affluent than in the past. Those factors were also highlighted by Parmar, who referred to a "homogeneous global youth customer segment."

Look in teens' bedrooms in cities around the world—Des Moines, Los Angeles, Jakarta, Mexico City, Paris, Santiago, Singapore, and Tokyo. You will find an amazing similarity of items: Nikes and Reeboks, Levis, MP3 players, laptops, and NBA jackets. Teens everywhere watch MTV and the World Cup, and most of them shop in malls that look amazingly alike.

These developments are promising for international consumer goods marketers. Caution is necessary, however, before firms implement a one-size-fits-all strategy. Many seasoned observers note that cultural differences persist. For example, one survey found that American teenagers prefer to eat on the run, whereas teens elsewhere prefer meals they can savor. The same survey showed that American teenagers use fewer features on their cell phones than their European and Japanese counterparts. Yet another study found that teenagers in China, Japan, and the United States view clothing brands differently. So despite similarities among teenagers around the world, marketers are unable to use identical practices to reach teenagers in all markets and must remember to take culture into account, no matter how old the target market is.[20]

terial culture are related to the way a society organizes its economic activities. The term **technology gap** refers to differences in the ability of two societies to create, design, and use that which exists in nature or to use that which has been transformed in some way.

When referring to industrialized nations, developing nations, the nuclear age, or the space age, one is referring to different technologies and material cultures. One can also speak of societies being in the age of the automobile, the bicycle, or foot transportation—or in the age of the computer, the abacus, or pencil-and-paper calculation. The relationships between technology, material culture, and the other aspects of life are profound but not easily recognized because people are the products of their own culture. It is primarily as people travel abroad that they perceive such relationships.

How people consume and what people consume are also heavily influenced by the technology and material culture. For example, the car has helped to create the conditions that made suburban living possible, with the accompanying lifestyle and consumption patterns. Television has a wide-ranging impact on consumer and voter behavior. Cell phones with Internet and video have impacted how we communicate and interact. Buying behaviors have been significantly altered by online retailing, leading to greater consumer awareness and buyer power. Technology has impacted consumer behavior and expectations in the home, at work, and at school.

The wide-ranging impact of these products on U.S. culture highlights the potential future cultural impact in countries with much lighter penetration of such products and technologies. For example, the number of cars in use in 2009 ranged from 430 per 1,000 people in the United States to 148 in Mexico, 30 in Egypt, 20 in China, 15 in India, 11 in Nigeria, and 2 in Vietnam.[21]

MATERIAL CULTURE, TECHNOLOGY, AND INTERNATIONAL MARKETING

It is equally important for marketers to understand the material culture in foreign markets. In large diversified markets such as the United States, almost any industrial product can find a market. In developing nations, however, industrial goods marketers find increasingly limited markets in which they can sell only part of their product line—or perhaps none of it.

Consumer goods marketers are also concerned with the material culture in foreign markets. Such simple considerations as electrical voltages and use of the metric system must be taken into account. Product adaptations may also be necessitated by the material culture of the family. Does the family have a car to transport purchases? Does the family have a stove to prepare foods or a refrigerator in which to store food? If electrical power is not available, electrical appliances will not be marketable unless they are battery-powered. To those people who wash clothes by a stream or lake, detergents and packaged soaps are not useful; the market is for bar soaps only.

Large multinationals are learning from entrepreneurs in developing countries that the key to success in markets where income is low is to market products that come in small sizes, are relatively cheap, and are easy to use. Unilever packages its shampoo in single-use sizes, selling it for a few cents in India. Other examples include 3-inch square packages of margarine in Nigeria that don't need refrigeration and an 8-cent tube of Close-Up with enough toothpaste for about 20 brushings. Unilever's commitment to emerging markets is a critical part of its international growth strategy. Emerging markets now account for about 50% of its total sales, which is higher than its competitors such as Procter & Gamble.[22]

Multinationals are finding new ways to access markets while helping to develop **bottom of the pyramid (BOP)** markets, which represent the consumers at the lowest level of per capita income in a country. BOP markets may have a large aggregate purchasing power, even if individual purchasers do not. Recent estimates place the global BOP consumer market at $5 trillion. Firms access these markets by involving local partners and helping to develop the local economy. For example, Telenor AS of Norway, in partnership with the Grameen Bank, undertook the Village Phone Programme (VPP) in Bangladesh, where individuals could purchase mobile phones and services and rent out use of the phone to others to offset the overall cost.[23]

Other parts of the marketing program are also influenced by the material culture. For instance, the promotional program is constrained by the kinds of

bottom of the pyramid (BOP)

A group of people within a country (or other geographic, political, economic, or cultural entity) with the lowest level of per capital income.

media available. Advertisers want to know the availability of television, radio, magazines, and newspapers. How good is the reproduction process in newspapers and magazines? Are there advertising and research agencies to support the advertising program? The size of retail outlets affects the use of point-of-purchase displays. The nature of travel and the highway system affect the use of outdoor advertising.

Modifications in distribution may also be necessary. These changes must be made on the basis of the alternatives offered by the country's commercial infrastructure. What wholesale and retail patterns exist? What warehouse or storage facilities are available? Is refrigerated storage possible? What is the nature of the transport system—road, rail, river, or air? What area does it cover? Firms that use direct channels in the United States, with large-scale retailers and chain-store operations, may have to use indirect channels with a multitude of small independent retailers elsewhere. These small retailers may be relatively inaccessible if they are widely dispersed and transportation is inadequate.

If local storage facilities are insufficient, a firm may have to supply its own packaging or provide special packaging to offer extra protection. Whereas highways and railroads are most important in moving goods in the United States, river transport is a major means in other countries. And in still other countries, air is the principal means of transport. Thus, in numerous ways, management is concerned with the material culture in foreign markets. (See "Material Culture Matters.")

••• Material Culture Matters

The per capita income in Mexico in 2008 was $9,990. Fewer Mexicans own cars, trucks, telephones, and personal computers than people in the United States and other developed nations own. Because of this fact, it's difficult and expensive to ship goods, to travel, and to communicate with customers and suppliers.

Over 17 million cars are on the roads of Mexico. Approximately 38 percent of roads are paved, and although they are expensive to use, the best of these roads are the toll roads (las cuotas). Outside these toll roads, transportation is difficult and costly. Some estimates suggest that 8 to 15 percent of total product costs in Mexico are related to logistics, roughly twice the cost of developed markets.

Telephone service was privatized in 1990 and opened to competition in 1997. However, there are still only about 19 telephone lines for every 100 people, and installing a new line may take a month or two. Mobile phone usage is considerably higher, with 71 cellular phones for every 100 people. Local telephone service is still unreliable in some areas, and in general, the cost of making calls is expensive because of high government taxes on phone services.

Independent messenger services should be used to deliver important correspondence because mail service is slow and, at times, unreliable. Sending mail electronically is an option in some areas, but it reaches only the relatively wealthy segment of the population who own computers. Only 15 million computers are in use in Mexico, or an average of 7 people for every computer. Twenty percent of the population of 106 million people were classified as Internet users in 2008.[24]

Implications for International Marketing   •••

Analyzing the various elements of culture, such as language, religion, education, and so on, is a helpful way to understand the basis of cultural difference primarily within an anthropological context. Many studies have been conducted to understand cultural difference within primarily a business context. One of the most important cultural frameworks developed for this purpose is the Hofstede cultural dimensions, which is discussed next.

Table 4-6 • The Hofstede Cultural Dimensions

Country	Power Distance	Individualism	Masculinity	Uncertainty Avoidance	Long-Term Orientation
Australia	36	90	61	51	31
Bangladesh	80	20	55	60	40
Brazil	69	38	49	76	65
Canada	39	80	52	48	23
China	80	20	66	30	118
Czech Republic	57	58	57	74	13
India	77	48	56	40	61
Norway	31	69	8	50	20
United States	40	91	62	46	29

Source: Geert Hofstede Cultural Dimensions (http://www.geert-hofstede.com/hofstede_dimensions.php), accessed June 28, 2010.

Hofstede Cultural Dimensions

Over 40 years ago, the psychologist Dr. Geert Hofstede studied cultural characteristics in individuals from around the world. This landmark study involved over 100,000 people. In essence, the study attempted to classify people and define cultural characteristics that shaped work-related values and impacted the work environment. Originally, there were four dimensions: power distance, individualism, masculinity, and uncertainty avoidance. In a subsequent study, Dr. Hofstede added long-term orientation as a fifth dimension.[25] Table 4-6 shows the cultural dimensions for selected countries.

Power distance is the degree to which power in a group is shared and is the relative distance between the "most" and "least" powerful people. In cultures with low power distance, there is a tendency toward egalitarianism and group decision making. In cultures characterized as high power distance, rank and title are more important, and authority is accepted rather than questioned.

Societies that score high on the Hofstede **individualism** dimension tend to place more emphasis and importance on individuals than on collectivistic cultures. Praise and blame are placed on the individual, and family ties and friendships tend to be weak. Independence is a trait associated with high individualism. Collectivists, on the other hand, place much importance on family and friends and having many long-term relationships and an extended notion of family. (When asked "How large is your family?" an individualist would tend to provide a small number [4—that includes parents, brother, and sister], whereas a collectivist would respond with a larger number [20—that includes grandparents, cousins, and many other family members].)

Masculinity versus femininity recognizes that some societies are male-dominated and that a large separation exists between men and women. Gender roles in a masculine society are very different; they are often more structured. Manifestations of this separation can be seen in education levels (women do not attend school at the same rate and level as men), in upper-level government posts held by women (women hold no or few positions of power), and in the wage gap that exists between women and men performing the same job (and in the fact that men and women do not hold the same jobs). This dimension also helps identify what the culture values as relates to achievement and success (high masculinity scores) versus nurturing and taking care of society (low masculinity scores).

power distance

The degree to which power in a group is shared and is the relative distance between the "most" and "least" powerful person.

individualism

The degree to which a culture places emphasis on the individual as opposed to a group of people.

masculinity

The recognition that some societies are male-dominated.

Cultures that have a high masculinity score on the Hofstede cultural dimension tend toward an emphasis on achievement and success.

uncertainty avoidance

A cultural index that measures a nation's tolerance for risk.

Whether a person or group can be characterized as high or low in terms of **uncertainty avoidance** is a matter of how entrepreneurial he or she is, whether the culture generally can be referred to as risk takers, or whether the group avoids change or prefers structured, lock-step instructions. Those who are entrepreneurial, who gamble, who embrace change, and who appreciate diverse opinions but don't like to follow rules are low on the Hofstede uncertainty avoidance scale. On the other hand, when a person or a group of people is likely to avoid uncertain situations, that person or group is less likely to gamble or try new things but is apt to follow instructions.

long-term orientation

People's beliefs that wisdom comes from age or longevity, that traditions and elders are to be valued, and that rewards come to those who make long-term commitments.

In studying Chinese managers, Hofstede also identified a fifth cultural dimension or characteristic he called **long-term orientation**. People who believe that wisdom comes from age or longevity, that tradition and elders are to be valued, and that rewards come to those who make long-term commitments are classified as having a long-term orientation. Those who "live for today," have little savings, and focus on short-term gains and ill-defined plans are ranked low on this dimension. For example, cab drivers in the Czech Republic shortly after the fall of Communism often charged tourists double, sometimes triple, the fare they charged locals because the tourists were unlikely to return, were rich, and could afford it.[26]

Hofstede's work has been expanded, duplicated, tested, and contested in a wide body of research that spanned a large portion of the last century. His work is important to international business because it laid the groundwork for viewing the role of culture in the work environment. Hofstede helped explain how to motivate people in the work world and why people react differently to the same circumstances or objects. In marketing, people are often classified on the basis of demographics—income levels, size of family, and geographic location. When marketers refer to baby boomers, Generation Xers, and Millennials, they use psychographics (age, certainly, but also people's interests, values, and beliefs) to classify people into those groups. Taking the step from demographics to psychographics takes research like that conducted by Hofstede to identify characteristics that are commonly held across international boundaries. The influence of Hofstede's research is seen in the profusion of scholarly articles that identify his characteristics in today's research (see box entitled "Using the Hofstede Dimensions to Target Online Buyers").

••• Using the Hofstede Dimensions to Target Online Buyers

Recent research has applied the Hofstede cultural dimensions to better understand the buying behavior of online shoppers. Higher levels of individualism and long-term orientation lead to greater adoption of Internet shopping, whereas higher levels of power distance, uncertainty avoidance, and masculinity relate to less adoption of Internet shopping. As a result, international Internet marketers may find more success in countries with higher levels of individualism and lower levels of uncertainty avoidance.

The Hofstede cultural dimensions can also help marketing managers configure and maximize the effects of online advertising. Cultures with low individualism tend to prefer group consensus appeals, whereas emotional appeals (as opposed to rational appeals) tend to be preferred by high-context cultures.

Finally, culture influences how consumers view your company's website. A recent study found that Chinese Internet users focused on power distance aspects of websites, such as website ownership information and pictures, whereas American users attended to aspects related to uncertainty avoidance, such as guided navigation and customer service.[27]

SUMMARY

Culture is an integrated pattern of behavior and the distinctive way of life of a people. The various dimensions of culture influence a firm's marketing.

Attitudes and values greatly affect consumer behavior. Attitudes about wealth and acquisition, change, and risk taking are especially important for the international marketer who may be introducing innovation to a society in the form of new products and new lifestyles.

Each society has its own ideas about beauty and good taste—its own aesthetics. When a firm is considering the design and color of its products and packaging, is advertising, and is selecting music and brand names, it must try to appeal to those tastes.

Communication is a major part of the marketing task, so a firm must communicate in the languages of its markets. This may require adaptation in packaging and labeling, advertising and personal selling, and marketing research. Fortunately, national employees, distributors, and advertising agencies can help with the language barrier.

Religion is a major determinant of attitudes and behavior in a society. Each country has its own religious profile, but major world religions such as Buddhism, Christianity, Hinduism, Islam, and secular groups (agnostic, animism, atheist, and nonreligious) include approximately 85 percent of the world's population. Each religion has its own impact on the attitudes and behaviors of consumers who follow it. For example, a traditional animist might be reluctant to accept new products, and a devout Buddhist who is seeking an absence of desire, or a state of wantlessness, is not a strong potential consumer. Other religious impacts on marketing include religious holidays and product taboos, the role of women in the economy and society, and the caste system. Finally, religious divisions in a country may indicate market segments that require different marketing programs and sales forces. Even Japan's composite religious tradition has affected the economy of that country.

Differences in literacy and consumer skills, as a result of a country's educational system, determine what adjustments in products and marketing communications are necessary. The quality of marketing support services (advertising and marketing research) in a country is also affected by the output of the educational system there.

Social organization refers to the way people relate to one another and to the various groups and divisions in a society. The size and nature of the family, tribalism and ethnic divisions, and different roles for women or age groups (such as senior citizens) can all influence a marketing program.

A country's worker behavior and consumer behavior are shaped by the technology and material culture. The kinds of products a firm can sell and its distribution and promotional programs are constrained by the country's infrastructure. This includes not only the country's transportation and communications systems, but also factors such as the availability of media and advertising agencies.

Hofstede's cultural dimensions provide a useful framework in understanding cultural differences within the context of the workplace. The five dimensions are power distance, individualism, masculinity, uncertainty avoidance, and long-term orientation.

KEY TERMS

aesthetics	ethnocentrism	masculinity	social organization
attitudes and values	high-context cultures	material culture	special interest group
bottom of the pyramid (BOP)	individualism	Orthodox Judaism	technology
common territory	kinship	power distance	technology gap
Conservative Judaism	language	Reconstructionism	uncertainty avoidance
education	long-term orientation	Reform Judaism	
	low-context cultures	religion	

NASBITE CGBP TOPICS COVERED IN THIS CHAPTER

Note: For full details of the alignment of each chapter with the NASBITE CGBP, be sure to review the information provided in the section "Studying for the NASBITE CGBP Exam."

CGBP Rubric	Topic
01/02/01:	business ethics as perceived and practiced in the U.S. and in other countries—cultural relativism
01/02/02:	culturally appropriate techniques for international business settings (e.g., adaptive behavior, response, and verbal/written language to correspond with local business culture, group vs. individual, ethnocentric vs. monocentric, high context vs. low context)
01/03/01:	environmental factors affecting international strategies—sociocultural
02/01/02:	external environment—cultural
02/01/06:	cultural issues related to marketability of product, translation issues
02/06/01:	customer expectations and cultural requirements
03/05/02:	cultural considerations affecting supplier/buyer relationships
04/01/02:	cultural issues of buyer's country which may impact payment methods

QUESTIONS AND RESEARCH

1. What is culture?

2. Give examples of cultural concepts used in U.S. marketing.

3. How can a nation's technology and material culture affect a firm's marketing in that country?

4. Discuss the role of the international marketer as an agent of cultural change. Is this role legitimate? Explain.

5. Why are international marketers interested in the linguistic situation in their markets?

6. How can an international firm deal with the language challenges in its foreign markets?

7. How can the aesthetic ideas and values of a society influence a firm's marketing in that country?

8. How is international marketing constrained by the educational level in a market?

9. What, if anything, does a country's religious situation have to do with a firm's marketing in that country?

10. Discuss the marketing implications of the following religious phenomena: (a) religious holidays, (b) taboos, (c) religious institutions (church and clergy), and (d) nirvana.

11. Identify some constraints in marketing to a traditional Muslim society.

12. What is the marketing significance of these aspects of social organization: (a) the extended family, (b) tribalism, (c) the role of women in the economy?

13. Convenience Foods Corp. has asked you to do a cultural analysis of a South American country in which it is considering operations. How would you go about completing this task?

14. Detail the five Hofstede cultural dimensions, and clarify their importance for the international marketing manager.

15. Assume a culture scores high on the Hofstede uncertainty avoidance index. What are examples of how the international marketing plan for that culture would be adapted?

CHAPTER 4 TEAM PROJECT ASSIGNMENT: The Cultural Environment

This chapter focused on the cultural environment in which a firm operates as it expands internationally.

The assignment for this chapter builds on the work done in previous chapters. Knowing the industry in which your client operates, begin some initial research of potential issues your firm may encounter regarding cultural differences. For example, will your client's products or services need to be adapted to meet cultural differences in Europe, Asia, or other parts of the world? Are there some cultural aspects that would lend well to your client's marketing methods? Your client may offer a product or service that appeals primarily to individuals aspiring for wealth and recognition. In this case, potentially a culture with a high individualism score on Hofstede index would be a good market for your client. The goal is to think through what some of the cultural issues may be for your client as it expands internationally.

For your team research from this chapter, discussion the following issues:

1. Will your client's product or service require any significant adaptation to meet cultural differences? As an example, what adaptations would be required for the United Kingdom, China, India, Brazil, or South Africa?

2. Are they any indications your client has already made such modifications to its product or service?

3. Research the Hofstede cultural indicators for a country of your choice in Asia, Europe, Central and South America, and Africa. For each of the five countries, identify the Hofstede score for the four dimensions:

   - Power distance
   - Uncertainty avoidance
   - Individualism
   - Masculinity

   To find the score, visit: www.geert-hofstede.com/hofstede_dimensions.php

   Compare each country to the Hofstede cultural indicators for the home country of your client—for example, the United States if your client was Starbucks. Describe how the Hofstede indicators for each country could provide guidance on international marketing challenges (or opportunities) for your client in each country. If your client relies on marketing messages that emphasize the individual, this may be a challenge in a culture with a low individualism score. Discuss your findings. Include specific recommendations on how your client may have to adapt its marketing due to these cultural differences. For example, if your selected company was Rolex watches (retail store) and one country was the Netherlands, you would first identify the Individualism score as 80 (which is quite high). For Rolex, this would mean

   - Salespeople should be rewarded individually, not as a team.
   - Advertising should focus on individual achievement, perhaps showing a Rolex as a reward for someone in the workplace as opposed to a family birthday.

4. Based on this research, which of the five countries looks to be the best prospect for your firm for *strictly cultural reasons*. Of course, a firm would never choose a country for expansion based solely on cultural reasons. But in thinking through the challenges and opportunities discovered through your research, see whether one country stands out as a particularly good cultural fit for your firm. Discuss why.

CASE 4.1 Bottled Spirits

The Hopi are the westernmost tribe of Pueblo Indians, located in northeastern Arizona. There are fewer than 10,000 of them. They typically live in terraced pueblo structures of stone and adobe and are clustered into a number of small, independent towns. Like all Pueblo Indians, the Hopi are peaceful, monogamous, diligent, self-controlled, and very religious.

The most conservative tribe in the Southwest, the Hopi want no tourists to photograph, sketch, or record their dances. They do, however, allow visitors to observe their ceremonies where masked Kachina dancers impersonate Hopi gods. The Hopi also invite tourists into their homes to buy Kachina dolls and Hopi pottery.

Kachinas are the Hopi Indians' holy spirits. They are sometimes personified by masked dancers and sometimes represented by wooden dolls. There are roughly 250 different Kachinas. Although the Hopi will sell Kachina dolls to tourists, they are sensitive to how others may use the Kachina costume or idea. For example, in 1987, Miss New Mexico won the costume competition in the Miss USA competition, wearing a Kachina costume. Hopi religious leaders complained that its use was sacrilegious.

In another incident, the Hopi protested when Kentucky's Ezra Brooks distillery began marketing its bourbon in bottles shaped like Kachina dolls. As a Christmas promotion, the Brooks distillery had planned to distribute 5,000 of the Kachina doll bottles in Arizona and the Southwest. It had already shipped 2,000 bottles when it learned of the Hopi complaint. Reflecting the Hopis' anger, a tribal leader asked, "How would a Catholic feel about putting whiskey in a statue of Mary?" The Hopi not only complained but also received assistance from the Arizona senator to have production halted.

Questions and Research

1. What options did the distillery have to address the situation? What courses of action would you have recommended to the distillery management, given so many bottles had already been shipped?

2. Propose and defend your solution to this problem.

CASE 4.2 AFLAC

AFLAC became the official name of the American Family Life Assurance Company in 1989. It entered the Japanese market in 1975 and soon became one of the most successful foreign companies in any industry operating in Japan. By 1982, 1 in 20 Japanese households was an AFLAC policyholder. By 1988, the ratio was 1 in 6. And by 1995, about 1 in 4 Japanese households had an AFLAC policy, which is still true today. AFLAC is the second largest insurance company in Japan and the number one foreign life insurance company. It is the second most profitable foreign company operating in an industry in Japan. In 2001, Japan accounted for 78 percent of the total company sales of $9.6 billion.

Founded in the United States in 1955, AFLAC specializes in cancer insurance (about 54 percent of its policies are in this field). Although AFLAC was the second foreign insurance company to enter the Japanese market, it was the first company, either Japanese or foreign, to introduce a policy for cancer protection in Japan. Two Japanese firms also issued independent health insurance coverage, but they had a much smaller number of policies outstanding.

Cancer insurance is a controversial product in the United States because consumer advocates argue that disease-specific policies are an inefficient, costly form of coverage. Bans on the sale of these policies were lifted in Connecticut and New York only in the late 1990s. Attitudes in Japan are somewhat different, however. When AFLAC hired Nomura Research to see what its customers wanted, the answer was more coverage. On the government side, then-company president John Amos had developed a strong relationship with the powerful Japanese bureaucracy. Indeed, in 1988, John Amos was named by *Forbes* magazine as the insurance industry's most innovative executive for his success in penetrating the Japanese market. (The company has won many other prestigious awards since then, too.)

Japan is one of the largest insurance markets in the world. About 90 percent of Japanese households carry life insurance with a relative contract value much higher than that in either Europe or the United States. Japan also has rather comprehensive national health insurance, so private company plans supplement the government program in such areas as private rooms, costly major disease, and lost income. AFLAC's cancer insurance sales grew rapidly, in part because cancer is the major cause of death in Japan and because cancer is usually associated with costly treatment and long stays in the hospital. Thus, the Japanese perceive cancer as the most threatening and the most expensive disease they can encounter, wanting to provide for it as best they can.

Most Japanese insurance companies use homemakers as a part-time sales force for door-to-door sales. Amos came up with another idea: use retired

Japanese workers to sell to their former colleagues. "Their retirement benefits weren't good enough to last them forever, so AFLAC became a little like their social security," he said. AFLAC uses different methods for distributing its products, which also helps to reduce operating costs.

Japanese corporations agreed to encourage their workers to buy the insurance and to deduct the premiums from their monthly paychecks. Retired executives from each corporation are often enlisted to do the actual selling. Over 17,000 such payroll groups have been established. Over 92 percent of the corporations listed on the Tokyo Stock Exchange use AFLAC's payroll deduction plan, although less than half of their employees subscribe to it. Even Nippon Life and Dai-ichi Mutual Life, two of Japan's largest life insurance companies, offer AFLAC's cancer policies to their employees. Another part of AFLAC's approach is "bank set sales." With this program, a bank automatically deducts the annual premium from the accumulated interest on a policyholder's savings account and transfers it to AFLAC's account. Some 250 banks participate in this program, serving about 500,000 policyholders. The Japanese have a favorable attitude toward saving, and this program appeals to their orientation to save and to their strong desire for insurance coverage. Because the banks enjoy a good reputation, AFLAC's insurance program gains further credibility by this association with them.

AFLAC has not relied on advertising in Japan, depending instead on its strong sales network and full-time sales force. Because the company innovated cancer insurance and because of the company's different marketing approach, however, it received a lot of publicity in various media.

In 1994, AFLAC expanded its product line with Super Care, a policy for nursing home care, and Super Cancer, an upgrade on its original policy. Super Cancer allows for a cash payment when cancer is first diagnosed. Nursing home costs are another major concern in Japan because the population has a very long life expectancy.

One indicator of AFLAC's success is a first-year renewal rate of 90 percent—and 94 percent after the second year. Both of those figures are higher than in either the Japanese or U.S. life insurance industries. AFLAC views those figures as corroboration of its product and marketing program.

Some changes have taken place. In 2000, sales of accident/disability policies surpassed those for cancer policies in the United States. As a result of an aggressive marketing program, the current CEO, Dan Amos, is on his way to meeting his goal of increasing U.S. sales as a percentage of total sales. (In 2001, 70 percent of the firm's earnings and 80 percent of its assets were Japanese.) Deregulation in the Japanese insurance industry has led AFLAC to form an alliance with the largest Japanese insurer, Dai-ichi Mutual Life, and noncancer products now account for 60 percent of new sales. AFLAC also uses newer technologies, such as processing claims on the Internet, to increase profitability. It costs the firm about $72 to write and process new policies, versus a cost of $120 for Japanese insurance firms, giving AFLAC a big advantage over its competitors.

Source: AFLAC corporate website (http://www.aflac.com); Hoover's Company Profile Database, 2002; "How AFLAC Laid a Golden Egg in Japan," *Business Week*, November 11, 2002, p. 56.

Questions and Research

1. Describe AFLAC's marketing program in Japan: product policy, pricing, promotion, and distribution.

2. Explain how this marketing program relates to the Japanese culture and economy and why it is so successful.

3. Research the AFLAC website (www.aflac.com) to get an update on current activities of AFLAC in Japan and to view the latest Duck Campaign commercial. (More commercials are available on YouTube.) Has AFLAC in Japan remained successful? Discuss the results of your research.

1. Passport Reference and Markets, Household Ownership of Durable Goods by Income (2009), (http://www.portal.euromonitor.com/Portal/Statistics.aspx), retrieved October 5, 2010. GDP Per Capita (Current US$), World Development Bank Indicators (http://data.worldbank.org/indicator/NY.GDP.PCAP.CD), accessed October 5, 2010.
2. Ibid.
3. John H. Bodley, *Cultural Anthropology: Tribes, States, and the Global System* (Mountain View, CA: Mayfield, 1994).
4. "Longer Workweeks Likely in Europe," *USA Today*, Tuesday, July 27, 2004, p. 4B.
5. "English Gets the Last Word in Japan," *Wall Street Journal*, August 6, 2010, p. B.1.
6. Edward T. Hall, *Beyond Culture* (New York, NY: Anchor Books, 1976).
7. Douglas Dow and Amal Karunaratna, "Developing a Multidimensional Instrument to Measure Psychic Distance Stimuli," *Journal of International Business Studies* 37, no. 5 (2006): 578–602; Nicholas Alexander, Mark Rhodes, and Hayley Myers, "International Market Selection: Measuring Actions Instead of Intentions," *Journal of Services Marketing* 21, no. 6 (2007): 424–34.
8. Gary A. Knight, "Educator Insights: International Marketing Blunders by American Firms in Japan—Some Lessons for Management," *Journal of International Marketing* 3, no. 4 (1995): 107–29; Tevfik Dalgic and Ruud Heijblom, "Educator Insights: International Marketing Blunders Revisited—Some Lessons for Managers," *Journal of International Marketing* 4, no. 1 (1996): 81–91; D.W. Helin, "When Slogans Go Wrong," *American Demographics* 14, no. 2, (1992): 14; David A. Ricks, Jeffery S. Arpan, and Donald Patton, "International Business Blunders," *Academy of Management Proceedings* (1972): 356–57.
9. "Major Religions of the World Ranked by Number of Adherents" (http://www.adherents.com/Religions_By_Adherents.html), accessed June 30, 2010.
10. "Major Religions of the World Ranked by Number of Adherents" (http://www.adherents.com/Religions_By_Adherents.html); accessed June 30, 2010.
11. For further details, visit the Jewish Outreach Institute's website at http://joi.org.
12. "Oman's Auto Distributors Gearing Up for Ramadan," *Times of Oman*, September 1, 2002.
13. "Religious Violence in India Ebbs after 4 Days of Killing," *Wall Street Journal*, March 4, 2002, Section A, p. 12.
14. "Caste in India, Still Untouchable," *Economist* 359, no. 8226 (June 16, 2001): 42.
15. "Quitting Hinduism," *Christianity Today*, December 9, 2002, pp. 22–23.
16. "Banking on Allah," *Fortune* 145, no. 12 (June 10, 2002): 154–64; "Holy Robots Give Bible Buzz in Pond's 8m Theme Park," *Sunday Times*, August 18, 2002, p. 18; "Muslims Making Push to Join McDonald's Fries Settlement," *Dallas Morning News*, July 5, 2002; "Sale of Islamic-Themed Stamps Shouldn't Be Affected by September 11 Attacks," *Patriot News*, November 27, 2001; "Businessmen to Build China's First Bible Theme Park," *Agence France Presse*, November 23, 2009; "Biblical Theme Park Planned in Germany," *France 24 International News*, June 4, 2008; "Drink Giants in Ramadan Battle," *Arabian Business*, August 28, 2008.
17. Kenneth Hall and Stanley Petzall. "The Making of Technicians for a High-Technology Future: The Singapore Apprentice," *Journal of Asian Business*, 16, no. 4 (2000): 39–56.
18. Eric A. Hanushek and Dennis D. Kimko. "Schooling, Labor-Force Quality, and the Growth of Nations," *American Economic Review* 90, no. 5 (2000): 1184–1208.
19. James U. McNeal and Mindy F. Ji, "Chinese Children as Consumers: An Analysis of Their New Product Information Sources," *Journal of Consumer Marketing* 16, No. 4 (1999): 345–64.
20. Mark Mitchell, Barbara Hastings, and Faruk Tanyel, "Generational Comparison: Xers in the United States and Korea," *International Journal of Commerce and Management* 11, no. 3/4 (2001): 35–53; Arundhati Parmar, "Global Youth United; Homogeneous Group Prime Target for U.S. Marketers," *Marketing News*, October 28, 2002, pp. 1, 49; Stephen Parker, Charles Hermans, and Allen Schaefer, "Teens' Attitudes Towards Clothing Brands in General: A Cross-Cultural Exploration," *Journal of International Business and Economics*, 8, no. 2, (2008): 110–16.
21. Euromonitor International GMID. "Passenger Cars in Use per 1000 Population" (2009). (http://www.portal.euromonitor.com/Portal/Statistics.aspx), accessed July 1, 2010.
22. "Emerging Markets Exposure Makes Unilever One to Feast On," *Sunday Times*, August 7, 2008 (http://business.timesonline.co.uk/tol/business/columnists/article6742164.ece), accessed October 7, 2010.
23. Ahmed Rashid and Mizan Rahman, "Making Profit to Solve Development Problems: The Case of Telenor AS and the Village Phone Programme in Bangladesh," *Journal of Marketing Management* 25, no. 9/10 (November 2009): 1049–1060.
24. World Bank, "World Development Indicators Online" (http://data.worldbank.org/indicator), accessed June 28, 2010; Mexico Country Commercial Guide, 2009; U.S. Department of Commerce, International Trade Administration (http://www.buyusainfo.net/docs/x_2817461.pdf), accessed June 28, 2010.
25. Although Hofstede's research was published in multiple books, a good overview of the history of his research and a listing of each indicator may be found on his research website: http://www.geert-hofstede.com.

26. Slavenka Drakuliç, *Café Europa: Life After Communism* (New York, NY: Penguin Books, 1999).

27. Sujana Adapa, "Adoption of Internet Shopping: Cultural Considerations in India and Australia," *Journal of Internet Banking and Commerce* 13, no. 2 (2008): 1–17; Hairong Li, Ang Li, and Shuguang Zhao, "Internet Advertising Strategy of Multinationals in China: A Cross-Cultural Study," *American Academy of Advertising Conference Proceedings* (2008): 8–9; Gennadi Gevorgyan and Lance Porter, "One Size Does Not Fit All: Culture and Perceived Importance of Web Design Features," *Journal of Website Promotion* 3, no. 1/2 (2008): 25–38.

5 Ethics and International Marketing

High-profile events of recent years have highlighted dramatic instances of firms' unethical, irresponsible, and illegal activities. This behavior is not beneficial for the firms; their constituents, which include customers and stockholders; or the public at large. This chapter explores how ethical standards should govern firms as they expand globally. It discusses ethical principles and how they affect the development of moral standards. The chapter then discusses the variety of ethical dilemmas that impact international marketing and ways international firms have attempted to resolve them.

The main goals of this chapter are to ● ● ●

1. Identify recent instances of unethical behavior and the consequences of that behavior.

2. Identify the rationale behind why firms need to establish standards that will govern their corporate behavior internationally.

3. Detail moral principles that may help guide firms as they develop such standards.

4. Identify efforts under way by international agencies to address the need for morally responsible behavior.

5. Discuss the variety of ethical dilemmas that firms may encounter internationally.

6. Discuss the debate of corporate social responsibility and sustainability and its implications for the international marketing manager.

7. Introduce the United Nations Global Compact as a model that firms may use for global ethical behavior.

The Effect of Ethical Behavior on Global Business

Consider the following instances:

- World renown hedge fund manager Raj Rajaratnam (as shown in the opening chapter photo), is convicted on all 14 counts of securities fraud charges in one of the highest profile insider trading convictions.

- Bernard Madoff is convicted to 150 years in prison for managing a Ponzi scheme that defrauded thousands of companies, charities, and individuals around the world of billions of dollars of investments.

- A firm increases its sales of cigarettes in countries such as Indonesia because of growing restrictions and liability issues placed on them in markets such as the United States.

- A firm markets its Internet gambling services to U.S. citizens and fights attempts to regulate such activities, taking its case to the World Trade Organization (WTO).

- The European Commission begins investigating Apple after receiving complaints from consumers that downloading songs from the iTunes music service in the United Kingdom is more expensive than in other parts of Europe.

- Activists accuse toy and clothing manufacturers of sourcing their products from suppliers who do not respect labor rights and protest against such practices.

- Two Chinese executives in the mining industry are jailed in China after being found guilty of leaking commercial secrets to employees of Anglo-Australian miner Rio Tinto.

- In the United States, there are many well-documented cases of unethical behavior on the part of individuals and corporations that lead to the Sarbanes-Oxley Act of 2002, as well as the antifraud actions being pursued by the European Commission, the Organization for Economic Cooperation and Development (OECD), and the International Federation of Accountants. Names such as Enron, Adelphi Communications, Parmalat, Nortel Networks, Ahold NV, and WorldCom are forever associated with unethical, unscrupulous, and illegal behavior.

Multinational corporations can have significant power and influence in foreign markets. They must be careful to use such influence ethically.

Although the Madoff conviction is a clear case of unethical (and illegal) behavior, the challenge for the international marketing manager is that ethical dilemmas are not always so clear-cut. Legal, cultural, and religious differences are just a few examples of the way the international business environment contains much more complex ethical issues than in a firm's domestic market.

Multinational corporations (MNCs) may have more power and influence compared to local firms, local consumers, and perhaps local governmental authorities. They also have accumulated more knowledge about products, markets, consumer behavior, and societal consequences of their actions. Therefore, multinationals must be careful to use this power ethically.

Culture and local context influence local values and local moral standards. MNCs may find that they have to balance conflicting local values and corporate values. They must judge, then, when to adapt to local standards and when to hold on to their own moral standards—which may be Western, but they consider to be universal.

Another issue is one of accountability. MNCs in international markets have a multitude of executives and employees carrying out actions on behalf of their corporations. Corporations need to ensure that a firm's corporate moral standards are followed by their employees in these markets.

Economic ideology may also play a part in affecting the ethical standards of a firm. Capitalism elevates the role of consumption, wealth accumulation, and the right to private property. This, in turn, influences how firms in a capitalist system view their social responsibility and affects how much they believe they should concern themselves with social justice, environmental pollution, and the like. Capitalism also assumes perfect competition, and the lack thereof may lead to a higher level of unethical behavior. There are no or few competitors who can gain from being more ethical, and collusion is possible when an oligopoly exists. In such a situation, governmental regulation to promote competition and antitrust regulations may be a necessary complement to gradually enhancing ethical behavior.

Firms, therefore, must make a diligent effort to understand moral principles from which to draw ethical standards. Those standards will govern their behavior and help them bridge the gap between profit-oriented actions and greater corporate social responsibility. For a company conducting international business, implementing these ethical standards can be challenging.

Developing Ethical Standards

Corporations need to be ethical. Unethical behavior hurts society, consumers, suppliers, workers, and the general social welfare (for example, consider the consequences of pollution). Unethical behavior will result in a gradual erosion of society's acceptance of and patience with corporations. It is in the long-term self-interest of corporations to practice ethical behavior. Firms have to obey the law, and legal compliance may be seen as satisfying society's expectations of ethical behavior. In many cases, however, legal compliance represents a bare minimum, a floor for ethical behavior (see the box entitled "Beyond Compliance"). Hence, firms need to explore and establish for themselves the ethical standards that will govern their behavior. Questions typically arise over what is ethical behavior and how far ethics must govern corporate behavior. Developing ethical standards is a gradual process. It can develop over time through a process of learning, dialogue, and reflection with workers and customers, with other businesses, and with other societal institutions.

In judging whether corporate actions meet an ethical standard, firms may need to assess legal compliance in light of their own ethical standards. A firm that is in compliance with the law may decide that it does not need to concern itself further with ethics. However, in the international arena, local laws may be at odds with universally accepted moral principles—apartheid laws previously in South Africa being an egregious example. Hence, firms seeking to develop and uphold ethical standards may find it necessary to go beyond legal compliance and assess whether their actions meet ethical standards. Firms may want to pay particular attention to the consequences of their actions and how the outcomes of their actions affect various individuals and groups. (This perspective is further explored in the next section in a discussion of rights and justice as moral principles governing ethical actions.)

To conduct business activities in an ethical manner, a firm needs to develop moral standards that will serve as a foundation for all its behavior. Several moral principles can help shape ethical standards for a firm. Those principles include utilitarianism, justice, human rights, and caring for others.

••• Beyond Compliance

In light of widespread, well-documented lapses in corporate ethical behavior at the outset of the twenty-first century, more and more firms and nonprofits are beginning to realize that it is necessary to manage and conduct corporate affairs "beyond mere compliance" with legal norms. Alfred Marcus and Sheryl Kaiser, authors of *Managing Beyond Compliance: The Ethical and Legal Dimensions of Corporate Responsibility*, defined managing beyond compliance as follows:

> In the continuum of ethics (political consciousness) law, this gap where the law ends or does not yet speak to regulate conduct is the area "beyond compliance." For corporations to function in an ethically responsible manner, business managers must recognize that the technical limits of law do not set a moral floor for behavior. Operating beyond compliance requires recognition that, though some moral obligations to others may not be codified, yet that does not make their observance any less imperative. Managing beyond compliance requires the members of an organization to progress beyond the at-any-cost corporate culture of previous decades. It will require a move beyond the gamesmanship of hypertechnical parsing and the what-can-be-gotten-away-with mentality by business managers, their attorneys, accountants and other professionals guiding and advising the corporation.[1]

Furthermore, given legal decisions that have traced corporate liability back two, three, or more decades, managing beyond compliance is a pragmatic stance for twenty-first century corporations. As Marcus and Kaiser stated:

> The advantages of such progressive leadership will be myriad. The risk that unethical behavior poses to the vitality and perpetuity of a company cannot be overestimated. Pushing the legal envelope into arguably unethical territory at various stages in the process or levels in the entity invariably produces a cumulative end result well outside of the legal obligations of compliance. This approach was the cause of many of the financial disasters that beset some of the largest and oldest U.S. firms in the beginning of this century. Further, given that the law is continually evolving, mere compliance with the letter of the law can be dangerous. Unless a company has its finger on the precise pulse of where the law is going, it can get stung by mere compliance, particularly where personal harm is caused by corporate action or inaction. Tobacco companies did not violate any legal regulation when they failed to warn the public of the known health risks posed by cigarettes. Nonetheless, they now face billions of dollars in punitive damage judgments for their negligence. Companies that dispose of toxic waste in water or soil in a manner that causes personal injury or property damage can be held legally liable for such harm regardless of the legality of the original dumping. Examples abound of situations where a company's activities result in financial liability that far exceeds the cost-benefit calculation factored into corporate decision making.[2]

There is also an apparent trend toward conferring legal reward for companies operating beyond compliance. Principles of organizational accountability impose indirect vicarious liability on a corporation for the actions of its agents (managers, employees). Increasingly, organizations are held accountable for the actions of their agents whether or not management knew of the misdeeds. To alleviate some of the harshness of such strict liability on the entity, some statutes and court decisions have recognized that a company's financial damages may be mitigated to the extent that the organization affirmatively attempted to prevent the illicit behavior—that is, to the extent that it operated the entity beyond the bare floor of legal compliance.

Utilitarianism

The first principle, **utilitarianism**, judges behavior in terms of the costs and benefits to society; it suggests choosing actions that result in the greatest net benefit or the lowest net cost. Such judgment also results in efficient behavior in using resources efficiently. Implementing utilitarianism means being able to measure costs and benefits. The measurement may be subjective in that the benefit of a meal or job may have different values for different people; hence, two people may not agree on the precise cost and benefit of an action. Some of the most important aspects of life (quality of life, for example) are also the most difficult to measure. Another difficulty involves trade-offs—that is, how much of a certain cost to accept in return for other benefits. Further, the costs may fall disproportionately on certain segments of society while the benefits accrue to other (distinct) segments of society. Utilitarianism does not easily accommodate the impact of these costs on a segment that may be disadvantaged. That is, the distribution of costs and benefits is not a paramount consideration under the utilitarian perspective. The eventual distribution of costs and benefits that results may conflict with the notion of an individual's rights and with the concept of justice for an individual or group. Hence, moral principles built on rights and on justice are equally important.

Rights and Justice

Theories based on rights and justice have many roots. Immanuel Kant's categorical imperative is a useful starting point, stating that people should not be treated as means, but as ends. This is to say that people are beings whose existence as free, rational individuals should be promoted, that everyone should be treated as a free person equal to everyone else.[3] The possibility arises, however, that individual rights will conflict. In such cases, society must decide whose rights take precedence. Hence, justice and fairness become important in determining ethical behavior. But a society's view of justice and fairness varies based on many factors, including economic history. A socialist society may have a quite different view of these issues than a capitalist society. Views of individuals' needs and their ability to work would also impact a society's view of justice and fairness.

John Rawls attempted to develop a theory of justice that takes into account equality, needs, ability and effort, minimum standards of living, and preservation of freedom.[4] He asserted that the distribution of benefits and burdens in a society is just if

A society's view of justices and fairness is impacted by a number of factors, including economic history. With China's history of communism, its views may be different from those in the West.

1. Everyone has the same degree of liberty; that is, one's liberties are protected from infringement by others—the Principle of Equal Liberty.

2. There are inequalities in society, efforts are made to improve the position of the most needy members of society—the Difference Principle.

3. Everyone has the same opportunity to qualify for the most privileged positions in society's institutions—the Principle of Fair Equality of Opportunity.

Caring for Others

One characteristic of the ethical principles discussed thus far is that they are impartial; they do not take into account specific individuals. However, most individuals assess their acts partly in terms of the impact their acts have on people they know—their family, friends, coworkers, neighbors, community, and even city, state, and nation. The question arises, should individuals show special consideration for those with whom they have a close relationship—that is, parents, children, spouses, relatives, and close friends? Is showing favoritism ethical? Cultural differences may play a part here, with cultures that favor collectivism over individualism, for example, accepting and requiring special consideration for others with whom one has a close relationship.

Figure 5-1 • Developing Ethical Standards

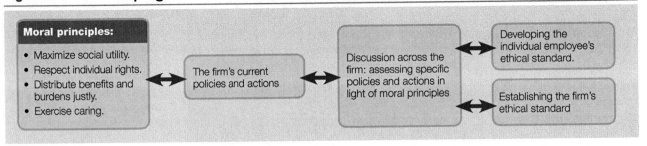

Moral principles:
- Maximize social utility.
- Respect individual rights.
- Distribute benefits and burdens justly.
- Exercise caring.

The firm's current policies and actions

Discussion across the firm: assessing specific policies and actions in light of moral principles

Developing the individual employee's ethical standard.

Establishing the firm's ethical standard

Integrative Social Contracts and Hypernorms

Integrative Social Contracts

Implicit social contracts between companies and stakeholders whereby local ethical expectations guide the relationship.

hypernorms

Manifest, universal norms that represent principles so fundamental to human existence that they are reflected in a convergence of religious, philosophical, and cultural beliefs.

As suggested in the previous discussion, cultural differences can be a source of ethical conflicts because of the underlying multiple value systems. An effort to reconcile such conflicts is Donaldson and Dunfee's **Integrative Social Contracts** theory and their **hypernorms** approach.[5] They suggested that in the context of most local cultures, managers can apply ethical standards derived from the local context, principally from domestic firms, industries, professional associations, and other organizations. However, there will be instances when hypernorms take precedence. Hypernorms are manifest, universal norms that represent principles so fundamental to human existence that they are reflected in a convergence of religious, philosophical, and cultural beliefs.[6] These norms represent standards that are in some sense universal, most likely negative injunctions against murder, deceit, torture, oppression, and tyranny.[7] An example of a hypernorm, suggested by Donaldson and Dunfee, is informing employees about dangerous health hazards, a universal ethical standard that should override any local practice that contradicts this ethical injunction.

Given these different approaches to developing moral principles, how should a firm incorporate such principles as it seeks to develop its own ethical standards? One approach might be to accept that different ethical principles have arisen because of drawbacks in one of the approaches. Thus, a pragmatic approach may require drawing on the implications of all these theories as specific policies and actions are tested. Further, discussion of the ethicality of a firm's policies and actions in light of the various principles is necessary to arrive at reasoned moral judgments shared across a firm, thus helping to derive moral standards.

In the international arena, why does unethical behavior happen? Job pressures, lack of personal ethics, flawed corporate culture and leadership, a complaisant government and national culture, poor governance processes, lack of sanctions, ease of using intermediaries and hiding one's tracks, large stakes (size of orders, profits)— all of these can create a breeding ground for unethical behavior. And as previously discussed, differences in society's view on what is right and just, especially if they are in conflict with the home country society's views, may lead to challenging ethics decisions that must be made by the international marketing manger.

Hence, internal discussion is essential to help develop a firm's ethical outlook because the ethical standards of a firm are nothing but the collective acting out of the ethical beliefs of all the employees of the firm. Thus, examining and debating ethical principles can result in a firm's shared ethical outlook and a high moral standard underpinning collective ethical actions. Such a discussion might embrace the model shown in Figure 5-1, which illustrates that such discussions should be in both directions: management to employees and employees to management. Firms may also find adoption of the Balanced Scorecard in its strategic planning as a useful tool in supporting ethical behavior. The **Balanced Scorecard**, as developed by Kaplan and Norton, adds to a firm's traditional financial measures three additional areas for performance evaluation: a company's relationship with its customers, its key internal processes, and its learning and growth. Each of these nonfinancial areas would have important insights in developing a firm's ethical standards.[8]

Balanced Scorecard

Method of evaluating firm performance that adds non-financial measures (relationship with customers, internal processes, and learning and growth) to financial measures of performance.

Types of Ethical Conflicts

In this section, a variety of ethical dilemmas that face the international marketing manager are presented, using a firm's supply chain as an outline. Table 5-1 summarizes these dilemmas and how they can be used to develop ethical standards.

Global Strategy: Bribery and Corruption

Part of global strategy is deciding which markets to compete in and then developing strategies and actions to win market share in those markets. An ethical problem arises when bribery is used to win business and market share and to influence public officials and co-opt consumer agencies and consumer rights watchdogs.

For example, in 2005 Monsanto agreed to pay fines of $1.5 million to settle bribery charges. The company had made $750,000 in payoffs to Indonesian officials to get permission to sell its genetically modified seeds (permission that it ultimately did not receive).[9] The bribes were paid by local executives and lobbyists working for Monsanto but were apparently done without the knowledge of Monsanto's top management. Upon learning about the transgression, Monsanto voluntarily informed U.S. authorities and accepted sanctions, though prosecutors did attribute the occurrence of the bribes to careless oversight by the company. In another example, the U.S. firm Fidelity National Financial was accused by its Taiwanese competitor of paying bribes through its Alltel Information Services subsidiary (which it had recently acquired) to secure software contracts worth around $176 million.[10] (See Table 5-2.)

Table 5-1 • Ethical Conflicts in the Value Chain

Value Chain Activity	Example
Global strategy: competing for market share	Bribery to obtain contracts
International marketing research	Testing new drugs in emerging markets
New product and service development	Ignoring low-income segments and populations in need of the new products or services
Global manufacturing; supply chain and logistics and linkage to international marketing	Supply chain manufacturing outsourcing partners who exploit local labor, negatively affecting the reputation of the company
International pricing	Price discrimination across markets
Global branding	Accusations that brands charge premium prices, create barriers to entry, shut out local competitors, and create cultural homogeneity
International distribution	Exclusive distributors that raise prices and reduce competition
Staffing international marketing positions; control and incentive systems	Hiring family members to fill supervisory positions
International advertising	Inappropriate appeals that clash with cultural values
Multiple stakeholders and societal consequences	SUVs and their impact on global warming

Table 5-2 • Antomy of a Bribe: Fidelity National and the China Construction Bank

Year	Month	Event
2001	June	Alltel Information Services (AIS) and Grace & Digital Information Technology (GDIT) agree to help sell Fidelity National Financial (FNF) software to China Construction Bank (CCB).
	July	CCB and AIS sign an interim software licensing agreement.
	December	CCB and AIS sign a long-term licensing agreement.
2002	January	The chairman of CCB, Wang Xuebing, is fired and replaced by Zhang Enzhao; the contracts with AIS are suspended.
	March	AIS terminates its agreement with GDIT.
	May	AIS hosts the new CCB chairman Zhang Enzhao and others at a golf outing at Pebble Beach.
2003	April	FNF takes over AIS and renames it Fidelity Information Services.
	September	CCB agrees to license FNF's software.
2004	October	Fidelity announces that CCB will use its software to process loans.
2005	March	China news media report that a Chinese company filed a lawsuit accusing CCB chairman Zhang Enzhao of accepting a $1 million bribe from AIS. The report also accuses AIS of helping to pay for educational expenses in London for Mr. Zhang's son.
	One week later	CCB chairman Zhang Enzhao resigns for "personal reasons."
2006	November	Zhang Enzhao is jailed for 15 years by a Beijing court after pleading guilty to taking bribes to arrange loans.

Sources: "Alltel Board Looks into Alleged Chinese Bribery Case," *Arkansas News*, May 3, 2005 (http://arkansasnews.com/search/josie/page/2/), accessed October 7, 2010; "Former CCB Head Jailed for 15 Years," CHINAdaily.com, November 3, 2006 (http://www2.chinadaily.com.cn/china/2006-11/03/content_724071.htm), accessed August 27, 2010.

Firms may encounter expectations to pay bribes in any number of countries, especially those in which such payments are more culturally the norm. Yet beyond the direct cost of the bribe, such payments have indirect costs, which include unfair competition, misallocation of resources, inefficiency, the long-term impact on slowing growth, and reduced entrepreneurial drive. If seen as pervasive and arbitrary, bribery and corruption can reduce the motivation to set up business and enter new markets. How should firms respond? A number of recommendations have been discussed. They range from avoiding such markets to changing entry mode (using joint ventures, licensing, arms length distribution), developing and adhering to corporate codes of conduct against bribery (a concern being that local firms might refuse to join such an agreement, thus gaining a temporary advantage), and being thoroughly trained and educated about bribery, as well as by developing laws and agreements governing such behavior.[11]

U.S. LAW AND CORRUPTION

As discussed in Chapter 3, the Foreign Corrupt Practices Act (FCPA) specifically bans payments to foreign government officials to gain or retain business, although it does allow facilitating "grease" payments. The difficulty in allowing some level of bribery is that it may become a slippery slope leading to larger and more frequent payments. Hence, corporations may prefer to ban all such payments. For example, Sealed Air Corporation (manufacturer of Bubble Wrap® cushioning and other packaging products) has developed a code of conduct, sections of which are provided here:

> Sealed Air Corporation has a reputation for conducting its business on a highly ethical level. It is important that we continue this record of integrity in the future.

Each and every employee of the Company and its subsidiaries throughout the world is responsible for the maintenance of our fine reputation. We expect that each employee will support the Company's principles of business ethics and behave in a manner consistent with these high standards. No employee in a supervisory position has the authority to instruct a subordinate to violate the ethical guidelines of the Company.

Each of our employees is expected to comply with the law, but our standard of business ethics goes beyond compliance with law. No list of rules can substitute for the exercise by anyone who represents our Company of basic morality, common decency, high ethical standards and respect for the law. If an employee is in doubt about the acceptability of a particular course of action, the following test should be applied: Assuming full public disclosure of the action, would both the employee and the Company feel comfortable from a moral, ethical and legal standpoint? If the answer is "Yes," then the action is very probably consistent with our corporate philosophy. If not, then the action should be reviewed with the employee's manager or with the Company's Law Department before proceeding.[12]

Sealed Air's code of conduct is clear in stating the company's explicit ethical standard that "goes beyond compliance with law." It further suggests an easy-to-understand generalizable test: "Assuming full public disclosure of the action, would both the employee and the Company feel comfortable from a moral, ethical and legal standpoint?" Such unequivocal and clear statements from top management help create a climate of regard for ethical standards and a strong desire to comply with them. Such a commitment is the necessary first step to developing ethical standards that pervade a company.

GLOBAL EFFORTS AGAINST CORRUPTION

National and supranational laws and regulations may clarify what constitutes minimal ethical behavior and may constrain the range of legal actions that a firm can undertake in its international operations. As stated in Chapter 3, attempts to forge supranational laws governing business conduct are counter to traditional legal notions and respect for national sovereignty. National sovereignty means that a country can conduct its own affairs without interference from other governments or the laws of any other country. Thus, when the European Union (EU) was formed, individual European nations had to agree to accept European laws and pass enabling legislation to mirror those laws. The alternative is to create voluntary associations such as the OECD, the UN, and the WTO and to voluntarily agree to accept and abide by their rules and guidelines, such as those against bribery and corruption.

The UN, as part of its **Global Compact**, announced in June 2004, "Businesses should work against corruption in all its forms, including extortion and bribery."[13] (The UN Global Compact is discussed in detail later in the chapter.) The UN Convention against Corruption stresses that corruption is damaging to national economic growth. It has recommended codes of conduct for public officials, transparency of public procurement, the prevention of bribery to influence public officials, and generalized anticorruption crime-fighting efforts. Although the UN stops short of policing efforts, it does recommend the sanctioning of such unethical behavior. Transparency International, a supranational NGO that seeks to eradicate corruption in international trade and business, similarly notes in its "Business Principles for Countering Bribery" that "The enterprise shall prohibit bribery in any form whether direct or indirect. The enterprise shall commit to implementation of a Programme to counter bribery."[14]

> **Global Compact**
> United Nations (UN) effort listing ways in which businesses should fight against corruption.

International Research

An issue with international research, particularly in emerging markets, is that a firm or its agencies may be working with research samples and with underlying populations whose members may be less informed, less educated, and less powerful when compared with the foreign firm. Hence, ethical standards dictate that a firm insists that permission of the research subjects, informed consent, confidentiality, and restrictions on using and sharing information gathered from research be in place before the research begins. As with the issue of corruption, a good general rule for a firm would be: If the research methods were published, would the company or individual be embarrassed by the revelations?

As in the home country, a firm needs to be especially attentive when using children as subjects for its international research effort. Pharmaceutical drug testing in emerging markets is an example of the kind of ethical issue that firms need to take into account when conducting international market research. Newly developed drugs require extensive testing for toxicity, effectiveness, side effects, and interactions with other drugs before they can be certified by the FDA and other drug certification agencies worldwide. Drug companies have begun testing new drugs among populations in regions of Africa, Asia, and Eastern Europe. The attraction for researchers is a larger pool of patients to draw from who have not received much medical treatment involving new drugs (they are "drug-naïve"), as well as the low costs of administering the drug trials. For instance, Covance, one of the world's largest drug development service companies, has considerably expanded its clinical trials services in Central and Eastern Europe. To find potential recruits for its new drug studies, Covance draws on a population of over 470 million people in 20 countries in this region. In return, the countries and their health-care systems gain access to advanced medical treatments and new drugs under development. The drug companies and Covance clients benefit from "high patient recruitment rates and excellent data quality." The Central European region also has well-trained medical investigators, and the drug trials can be done at a low cost, which may explain the five-fold increase in clinical trials in the Czech Republic, Poland, and Hungary since the 1990s. Another attraction is the "high incidence of many of the diseases most targeted by the pharmaceutical industry." For example, Bulgaria has one of the highest rates of cardiovascular disease and strokes.[15]

Ethical conflicts can arise when the only access to health care for low-income patients is through participation in such clinical trials. One of the difficulties of conducting these trials includes recruiting patients for whom English is not a native language. Their understanding of English is often limited. In such a case, questions can be raised about their giving informed consent when signing a liability release in English. In India and other countries with a patriarchal culture, women may be pressured by male relatives to sign releases and enter new drug trials. To be sensitive to possible exploitation, the contract research organization should use local and regional ethics committees at the hospitals and local facilities to evaluate patient recruitment practices and the proposed features of the clinical trials. Joseph Herring, then-president and current CEO of Covance, noted that certain principles govern such collaboration, with the most important principle being the dictum "Aspire to a good that is greater than the individual or the group."[16]

New Product Development

New product development (NPD) for foreign markets usually involves product adaptation and segment identification. Firms have to decide how to adapt their products, which segments they will adapt products for, and whether to develop entirely new products for those markets and segments.

Product development focusing on the needs of low-income populations can be a controversial choice within a firm. Making such a choice has particular significance in the global pharmaceutical industry. Diseases such as AIDS and malaria are scourges that have a huge effect in Africa, in India, and in other tropical countries—with lives lost and debilitating effects on the ability to work.[17] Merck's work on a drug for river blindness in the highlands of Africa illustrates an ethical dilemma.[18] This disease affects about 20 million people, primarily poor, in remote parts of Africa. The disease is transmitted by black flies whose habitat is swift-flowing water. Merck spent over $100 million of its R&D funds on developing a potential treatment for this disease but would not be able to market it commercially, given the low purchasing power of the affected population. The company decided to make its treatment for river blindness, Ivermectin, available free of charge for distribution by numerous agencies, including the UN.[19]

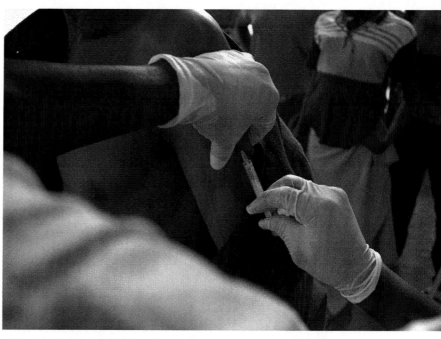

Global Public Goods (GPG) are important for the development of poor economies and poverty reduction. Vaccines are an example of such GPGs and have contributed to reduction of AIDs and malaria in Africa.

Merck's development and subsequent donation of a treatment for river blindness is an example of **Global Public Good (GPG)**. The World Bank defines GPGs as "commodities, resources, services and systems of rules or policy regimes with substantial cross-border externalities that are important for development and poverty reduction, and that can be produced in sufficient supply only through cooperation and collective action by developed and developing countries."[20] With regard to pharmaceutical drugs, given the low level of drug development efforts directed toward affordable drugs for diseases such as river blindness, private philanthropies have often stepped up their efforts. For example, the Global Alliance for Vaccines and Immunization (GAVI) has donated over a billion U.S. dollars to promote the development of vaccines for malaria, AIDS, tuberculosis, influenza, and hepatitis. By the end of 2009, donations by the GAVI led to preventing over five million deaths.[21]

> **Global Public Good (GPG)**
>
> Commodities, resources, services and systems of rules or policy regimes with substantial cross-border externalities that are important for economic development and poverty reduction, and that can be produced in sufficient supply only through cooperation and collective action by developed and developing countries (World Bank definition).

Global Manufacturing and the Supply Chain

Many companies manufacture the bulk of their products in China or Asian countries. By doing so, they can take advantage of low-cost labor and an efficient logistics system that allows them to raise or lower procurement quantities as demand increases or decreases. It allows them to rapidly design and manufacture new products in response to competitors' successes. It also allows them to quickly adapt their products to changing tastes among consumers. Thus, overseas manufacturing is critical to their global procurement strategy.

These companies have come under attack from public interest groups for not paying enough attention to the welfare of their overseas workers, particularly when those workers are employed by subcontractors in China, Vietnam, and elsewhere. An example of a specific response to these concerns is the toy company Mattel. It developed a set of Good Manufacturing Practices (GMP) that govern its overseas manufacturing practices and provide an overarching ethical framework for such decisions. The elements of the company's GMP are as follows:

Mattel Good Manufacturing Practices (GMP) Highlights (The firm must comply with local laws as a minimum standard.)

Management Systems. Facilities must have systems in place to address labor, social, environmental, health, and safety issues.

Wages and Working Hours. Employees must be paid for all hours worked. Wages for regular and overtime work must be compensated at the legally mandated rates, and all overtime must be voluntary.

Age Requirements. All employees must meet the minimum age for employment as specified by country and Mattel requirements.

Forced Labor. Employees must be employed of their own free will. Forced or prison labor must not be used to manufacture, assemble, or distribute any Mattel products.

Discrimination. The facility must have policies on hiring, promotion, employee rights, and disciplinary practices that address discrimination.

Freedom of Expression and Association. Each employee must have the right to associate, or not to associate, with any legally sanctioned organization.

Living Conditions. Dormitories and canteens must be safe, sanitary, and meet the basic needs of employees.

Workplace Safety. The facility must have programs in place to address health and safety issues that exist in the workplace.

Health. First aid and medical treatment must be available to all employees.

Emergency Planning. The facility must have programs and systems in place for dealing with emergencies such as fires, spills, and natural disasters.

Environmental Protection. Facilities must have environmental programs in place to minimize their impact on the environment.[22]

To obtain widespread adoption of its GMP principles, Mattel has to be persuasive in motivating its suppliers to implement such practices and must be willing to accept the higher procurement costs that follow. Mattel can feel comfortable knowing it is following ethical principles in its procurement only when its far-flung supply network can be swayed to adopt such principles. Mattel's actions, if unsuccessful, could damage its reputation in the eyes of parents and children. Setting a high ethical standard within its supplier network will also raise the bar for the rest of the industry. Those corporations will become aware of Mattel's sourcing principles and may be expected to follow similar ethical principles. One possible consequence is the improvement of working conditions worldwide for workers in similar factories in a variety of industries beyond toys and apparel.

Pricing

A generalized problem is one of high prices relative to incomes in specific markets. An extreme example is the cost of the AIDS "cocktail" of drugs, which arrests the progress of AIDS. This course of treatment can average thousands of dollars a year (far beyond the reach of most Africans), and Africa has one of the highest rates of AIDS infections. One response has been the development by Indian pharmaceutical companies of copycat drugs, which are sold for less than one-tenth the price of regular drugs. This development was made possible because India recognized process patents only until 2005, allowing Indian firms to legally manufacture similar drugs using noninfringing processes, thus underpricing Western competitors in the markets of Africa.

Other pricing problems may include price fixing, unfair discounts, discriminatory discounts, and premium pricing in poor neighborhoods (such as offering high-interest payroll loans). All those practices are possible because of a lack of competition, allowing the foreign firm to exercise market power through pricing control. Another factor is the desire to maximize profits from the higher margins that result from higher prices, without much concern for affordability. In the long run, those practices can be self-defeating, as the higher prices create an umbrella that allows for the emergence of competitors who can develop and offer products suited to local needs at affordable prices.

Global Branding

Corporations develop global brands as one of the bases for product differentiation in the global marketplace. The intent is for consumers to learn to trust the brand and purchase it with the confidence that the company behind the brand will deliver quality and value. Firms build brands by extensive advertising and promotion. Extensive investment in a brand is often rewarded with premium prices and brand loyalty, resulting in repeat purchases and higher long-term income. Brand loyalty also translates into increased sales volume and sustainable market share, creating a barrier to entry.

Companies generally want to grow at the expense of their competitors, and that alone is not unethical. However, these very qualities of a global brand—namely, premium prices, barriers to entry, and brand loyalty—may also be held against the company and the brand as negative consequences that prevent smaller local companies from competing and winning market share. The argument is that brands delude customers into believing that consuming certain brands provides a superior lifestyle. Furthermore, the emotional attachment to a brand promotes a "banal lifestyle" and an increasingly consumerist economy. Brand power is also seen as allowing companies behind the brand to use low-cost labor in developing economies, to ignore workers' rights, and to use materials and create consumption habits that are harmful to the environment (for example, the SUV).[23] The No Logo movement, which first gained prominence in the United Kingdom and Europe, is the foremost proponent of such an argument, blaming global brands for creating cultural homogeneity and creating "a Barbie world for adults."[24]

Local policymakers and international executives both need to consider whether strong global brands crowd out local brands (for shelf space and mind space) and whether global brands represent a battle between unequals (between large global brand companies and smaller, underfinanced competitors from developing countries). At the same time, a company that makes massive investments in building and sustaining global brands is likely to want to safeguard its reputation with vigor and avoid unethical actions, such as selling shoddy quality and dangerous products, harming the environment, or exploiting workers in poor countries. The company has to worry that consumers will take their business elsewhere if it undertakes such actions. Enlightened, long-term self-interest may, in fact, motivate a company with a global brand to behave more ethically, if only because it is more in the global limelight.

Global Promotion

A general problem in global promotion is a lack of cultural sensitivity that results in offending local mores and values. One example is the controversial series of Benetton clothing ads from 2000 that featured interviews with convicted killers. The campaign was called "We, on Death Row." With respect to this and other campaigns, Benetton sees such campaigns as an expression of the times.[25]

Beyond the themes and content of ad campaigns, other treacherous areas are false advertising, advertising to children, and not respecting religious and other cultural values. Unethical sales promotion is another concern, such as selling a product known to be harmful to consumers but that local government has not yet regulated. A larger question is the power of advertising to influence consumption, a point referred to earlier as part of the No Logo movement. One can indeed question the long-term consequences of advertising that promotes consumption at the cost of ever-increasing indebtedness and personal bankruptcy. But it would be difficult for a marketing executive to question whether promoting conspicuous consumption and a throwaway culture is ethically suspect.

Coca-Cola has signed onto the UN Global Compact indicating its support of the compact's ten universally accepted principles relating to human rights, labor, environment, and anticorruption.

corporate social responsibility (CSR)

A firm's commitment and policies regarding global social and ethical behavior.

UN Global Compact, Corporate Social Responsibility, and Sustainability

Given the great variety of ethical dilemmas facing a multinational firm, it is important that a corporate ethics policy is developed. Yet, this could be quite difficult, given the seemingly high variability in each society's views on rights, justice, and caring for others. Thus, firms are seeking a global standard against which a corporate policy might be developed. Increasingly, firms turn to the UN Global Compact as just such a global standard.

In 2000, the UN launched the UN Global Compact, a practical framework (as well as a policy platform) for firms committed to responsible business practices and sustainability. It seeks to align businesses with ten principles of corporate social responsibilities in the areas of human rights, labor, environment (sustainability), and anticorruption. The compact also seeks greater support and actions toward the UN Millennium Development Goals (MDGs) of ending poverty and hunger, universal education, gender equality, child health, maternal health, combating AIDS/HIV, environmental sustainability, and global partnership. The ten universally accepted principles within the UN Global Compact for responsible business practices are listed in Table 5-3.

The Coca-Cola Company is one of the most high-profile firms adopting the UN Global Compact. As discussed by Muhtar Kent, president and chief operating officer during the 2009 World Economic Forum in Davos, Switzerland, Coke has fully embraced the compact.[26] The company was attracted to the compact based on the premise that unless the company "played a meaningful role in creating sustainable communities where the firm operates, Coke's business would not be sustainable." One of the benefits of a firm adopting the compact, as Mr. Kent saw it, is that it offers consistent language, principles, protocols, and measurements. He also believed Coke benefits from its association with the UN brand, which brings credibility, responsibilities, and accountability that are important to Coke's overall corporate mission. Coke's support of the UN Global Compact is an important endorsement from a firm that operates in 200 countries.

As seen from the Coke example, the UN Global Compact may provide a firm with a global standard against which to develop a firm's ethical outlook. **Corporate social responsibility (CSR)** is a term that is often used to describe a firm's commitment to global ethical behavior.[27] It has become such an important

Table 5-3 ∘ The Ten Principles of the UN Global Compact

The UN Global Compact asks companies to embrace, support, and enact, within their sphere of influence, a set of core values in the areas of human rights, labor standards, the environment, and anti-corruption:

Human rights

1) Businesses should support and respect the protection of internationally proclaimed human rights; and

2) make sure that they are not complicit in human rights abuses.

Labor

3) Businesses should uphold the freedom of association and the effective recognition of the right to collective bargaining;

4) the elimination of all forms of forced and compulsory labor;

5) the effective abolition of child labor; and

6) the elimination of discrimination in respect of employment and occupation.

Environment

7) Businesses are asked to support a precautionary approach to environmental challenges;

8) undertake initiatives to promote greater environmental responsibility; and

9) encourage the development and diffusion of environmentally friendly technologies.

Anti-corruption

10) Businesses should work against corruption in all its forms, including extortion and bribery.

Source: United Nations; UN Global Compact (http://www.unglobalcompact.org/AboutTheGC/TheTenPrinciples/index.html), accessed April 12, 2010.

issue that firms have created positions such as Director of Corporate Social Responsibility to help incorporate CSR into the company's strategies, objectives, and activities. An example is Intel, which produces an annual corporate social responsibility report and created a blog to publicize its CSR efforts (see http://blogs.intel.com/csr/).

Linked to corporate social responsibility is the issue of **sustainability**—pursuing corporate goals that lessen the environmental impact of a firm's business. The goal of sustainability is also captured in the three environmental principles of the UN Global Compact detailed in Table 5-3.

Sustainability goals have an important impact on the international marketing manager. For a pet foods supplier, achieving this goal may mean using farmers in foreign markets as suppliers, rather than exporting the same food goods from its home market. For a manufacturer, achieving this goal could mean using more stringent pollution controls in a foreign factory than otherwise required by the local government. For international promotional materials, it may mean using soy ink or reducing paper-based marketing materials in exchange for a more web-based presence.

CSR and Greenwashing

Are these goals of corporate social responsibility and sustainability good for a firm's profitability, or just a public relations ploy? Some criticisms of a company's stance on sustainability are that the company promotes being committed to green issues but in fact the commitment is more "talk" than "action." Critics refer to this as **greenwashing**—when a company publically claims to be committed to sustainability and environmental issues, but its actual business practices do not support the claim.[28]

> **sustainability**
> Pursuing corporate goals that lessen the environmental impact of a firm's business.

> **greenwashing**
> When a company publically claims to be committed to sustainability and environmental issues but its actual business practices do not support the claim.

CSR has been an important issue during the recent global financial crisis beginning in 2008. The concern was that the crisis would lead to firms reducing or abandoning their social responsibility commitments. Muhtar Kent of Coca-Cola believed otherwise. In his remarks at the World Economic Forum, Mr. Kent not only endorsed Coke's commitment to the UN Global Compact but added that Coke does so not because the company sees the compact as philanthropic; rather, it is "doing well by doing good and touches every part of our sustainability framework." But not everyone necessarily sees it that way.

Dame Anita Roddick, founder of The Body Shop, worried for some years that corporate social responsibility had been hijacked by large multinationals seeking more influence and control. Her contention was that their motivation is less philanthropic and more to influence governments. Dame Roddick argued that the foundation of the business responsibility movement, which included leading companies such as Ben and Jerry's, could be traced back to much of the thinking from the 1960s, including the antiwar movement. She believed that the key issues were "How do you make business kinder?" "How do you embed it in the community?" and "How do you make community a social purpose for business?" What failed, in her opinion, was the lack of measuring a firm's commitment to responsible business beyond economic measures. They must also measure "human rights, social justice, and workers' justice, and the environmental movement." Lacking these, she believed we are still left with greedy businesses, too close to governments, being judged by their economic success only, not also social and environmental successes.[29]

Roddick's concerns about firms not fully committing to the ideals of CSR have some merit. Researchers find that firms tend to ignore the most difficult regions (e.g., sub-Saharan Africa) and the most difficult developmental goals of the UN Global Compact (e.g., anticorruption and labor rights).[30] Further, firms tend to view the UN Global Compact as a code of conduct but often fail to implement CSR as part of their active business strategies. Nike is a good example of a firm that has moved beyond CSR as a code of conduct and has implemented—and monitors—CSR actively throughout its supply chain to ensure that bad behavior is not "outsourced" to third parties. Of course, Nike's motivation for these changes stems from global criticism in the 1990s about the working conditions in factories making shoes for Nike under contract manufacturing.[31]

Thus, the debate continues. Nevertheless, companies do seem to be taking these issues seriously, and certainly the number of companies adopting the UN Global Compact is increasing. As of 2010, more than 7,700 organizations were involved with the compact, including some of the most well-known global brands. From Accenture to Volvo, companies are embracing the principles supported by the compact. Further research will be helpful to see its overall impact on corporate ethical behavior.[32]

SUMMARY

Ethical dilemmas abound in international business, ranging from dealing with expectations of bribery to wages paid to workers in developing countries. Because they are societal institutions that exist with the permission of the various societies and markets they serve, firms need to act ethically across international markets. Firms also have to consider cultural differences and how they may reflect different ethical standards. Firms need to factor those differences into their own behavior.

Several moral principles are useful in arriving at ethical standards. These moral principles include utilitarianism, theories of rights and justice, Kant's categorical imperative, the notion of caring for significant others, and the Integrative Social Contracts theory.

In addition, a recent perspective includes the notion of "managing beyond compliance"—the recognition that a gap exists where the law ends or does not yet speak to regulate corporate conduct. Operating beyond compliance means that although some moral obligations to others may not be codified, that fact does not make their observance any less imperative.

To develop ethical standards, a firm must apply the moral principles to its policies and actions, discuss them among its employees, and then arrive at its (mutually agreed-upon and enforceable) ethical standards. At the same time, individual employees should use the moral principles and discussion of the firm's policies and actions to develop their own ethical standards.

Ethical dilemmas pervade a firm's international marketing value chain. Major problems include bribery to compete for business and market share, market research, assurance that subcontractors manufacturing products marketed globally adhere to working standards that safeguard worker welfare, international price discrimination, consequences of global branding and the backlash against global brands as contributing to high prices and a consumerist culture, problems in international distribution and advertising, and pressures from multiple stakeholders (the Green lobby, for example) over the environmental consequences of a firm's products and marketing.

Given the variety of ethical dilemmas facing a firm as it grows internationally, it is important a corporate ethics policy is developed. One model increasingly adopted is the UN Global Compact. The compact is a set of ten universally accepted principles for responsible business practices in the areas of human rights, labor, environment, and anticorruption.

Corporate social responsibility (CSR) and sustainability may also play a role as a firm develops its corporate ethics policy. Critics of CSR argue firms may hide behind strong statements of good corporate behavior while their actions are less convincing. For example, *greenwashing* is a term for this behavior when applied to the issue of sustainability.

KEY TERMS

Balanced Scorecard	Global Compact	hypernorms	sustainability
corporate social responsibility (CSR)	Global Public Good (GPG)	Integrative Social Contracts	utilitarianism
	greenwashing		

NASBITE CGBP TOPICS COVERED IN THIS CHAPTER

Note: For full details of the alignment of each chapter with the NASBITE CGBP, be sure to review the information provided in the section "Studying for the NASBITE CGBP Exam."

CGBP Rubric	Topic
01/02/01:	business ethics as perceived and practiced in the U.S. and in other countries (e.g. cultural relativism, labor laws)
01/06/03:	issues related to and sources of information for offshore regulatory/legal concerns-bribery/corruption
02/02/01:	laws and regulations that impact the marketing plan—corruption
02/03/01:	impact on market selection of product, price, place, and promotion (the four P's)
02/06/03:	(new) product development modification process
02/06/10:	environmental concerns
02/07/05:	how local market conditions could impact pricing
04/01/02:	cultural issues of buyer's country which may impact payment methods—scorruption issues

QUESTIONS AND RESEARCH

1. How can concerns over ethical behavior affect global business practices? Provide examples.

2. Why should a firm be concerned about ethics in international marketing activities?

3. What are some fundamental moral principles that are relevant to assessing global business actions?

4. How can a firm connect moral principles to the development of ethical standards that would govern its international activities?

5. Describe some ethical conflicts that can arise along the value chain, such as in pricing, research, or branding.

6. How can ethical standards help overcome problems associated with bribery and corruption in international markets?

7. Discuss Sealed Air Corporation's code of conduct described in the text. How can such codes of conduct be implemented? How can other firms learn from Sealed Air Corporation?

8. How do ethical issues affect the clinical testing of new pharmaceutical drugs in emerging markets?

9. How can a multinational firm be affected by unethical manufacturing practices among its suppliers? How has Mattel handled such conflicts?

10. What is the UN Global Compact? Research the UN's website (www.unglobalcompact.org) and provide examples of companies around the world that have adopted the compact. What are some companies that are on the compact's "noncommunicating" list?

11. How could the UN Global Compact be used as a framework for developing a firm's corporate ethics policy?

12. Do further research on the issue of greenwashing. What are some examples from around the world?

13. Watch the video referenced in Dame Roddick's remarks about corporate social responsibility. Do further research in support of or in contradiction to her statements. What is your opinion and why?

CHAPTER 5 TEAM PROJECT ASSIGNMENT: Ethics and International Marketing

This chapter focused on ethics in international marketing and how a firm might develop its own ethical standards. It also discussed corporate social responsibility and issues of sustainability.

All firms will face some ethical challenges as they expand internationally. Your client research for this chapter is to think about what ethical challenges your firm may encounter as it expands internationally. The goal is also to research any current activities of your client that will support global ethical conduct and corporate social responsibility.

For your team research from this chapter, discuss the following issues:

1. Does your client currently have a corporate statement regarding its ethical conduct? Research the firm's website or annual report. Discuss your findings.

2. Does your client currently have a corporate statement regarding its commitment to corporate social responsibility? Discuss your findings.

3. What is your client's public statement regarding sustainability? Does it have a corporate officer responsible for its sustainability program? Discuss your findings.

4. Has your firm signed the UN Global Compact? Have any of its competitors signed the compact?

5. Based on your research, do you feel confident your client has a strong foundation to expand internationally in an ethical manner? Discuss why or any concerns you have.

CASE 5.1 Walmart and Its Critics

Walmart is the world's largest retailer. It had 2010 fiscal year sales of over $400 billion and employs two million employees in 8,500 stores worldwide. Economists would consider retailing a fragmented industry, as Walmart, the biggest firm in the industry, accounts for less than one-tenth of the industry. However, Walmart exercises a global influence on retailing. It has pioneered the concept of providing a wide variety of low-priced, quality goods to its customers. It is responsible for pushing its competitors to lower their prices and match the value that Walmart provides its customers. It is in the forefront of a movement to use overseas sourcing of goods, particularly from China, in an effort to lower the cost of goods sold in retail stores. And it has pioneered the spread of superstores, with more than 3,700 stores in the United States, dwarfing football fields in size and offering a large assortment of goods and services.

As Walmart has continued to grow, it has attracted several critics. Robert Greenwald's documentary, *Walmart: The High Cost of Low Prices*, is an example of such criticism. Critics focus on its antiunion stance; the low wages it pays; its increasing use of foreign sourcing, contributing to job losses in U.S. manufacturing; and its impact on small retailers, often driving them out of business. Finding itself the target of negative publicity, Walmart may have to reassess how it balances achieving corporate goals with the impact it has on the United States and other countries in which it does business.

THE WALMART FORMULA FOR SUCCESS

The key points of Walmart's retailing strategy include the following:

- Everyday low prices. Customers are attracted to Walmart because it has built a reputation for low prices.

- Superstores. Very large stores are usually located on the outskirts of town. They offer ample parking and the space to carry a wide assortment of products.

- An emphasis on listening to the consumer. Walmart emphasizes listening to and pleasing the customer.

- An emphasis on keeping costs low and continually cutting costs. This allows Walmart to sustain and continually lower prices.

- Low wages that help keep labor costs low. Walmart indicated that its average hourly wage for U.S. full-time employees was $9.68 an hour and about a dollar higher in major urban areas such as Chicago and Atlanta.

- No unions. Walmart believes that "only an unhappy associate would be interested in joining a union." Thus, Walmart actively sought to prevent unions from being formed.

- An emphasis on volume sales, with low margins per unit compensated for by the high volume of units sold.

- The importance of a wide and expanding assortment of goods and services.

- A constant search for lower-cost suppliers. This put pressure on suppliers to constantly lower prices; otherwise, they could be supplanted.
- A growing reliance on overseas sourcing to lower procurement costs.
- Low overheads, almost spartan in its general and administrative (G&A) spending—spare offices, simple furniture, shared hotel rooms, and economy-class travel.
- Entrepreneurial store managers and limited bureaucracy at headquarters, which allows individual managers greater autonomy.
- State-of-the-art supply-chain management. This allows Walmart to manage a global widely dispersed supply chain and ensure that goods arrive just in time at warehouses and stores across the United States and around the world.
- Excellence in information technology. This allows Walmart to gauge consumer demand and shifts in demand and to manage inventories, pricing, and sourcing.
- Expansion overseas. This ensures that Walmart can maintain growth rates as the U.S. market nears saturation, thereby exporting the Walmart retailing and management model (though with mixed results).

Walmart is a major U.S. employer, with over 1.2 million workers in the United States. It describes itself as a leading employer of Hispanic Americans, with more than 139,000 Hispanic employees. It is also one of the leading employers of African Americans, with more than 208,000 African American employees. Of its 1.2 million U.S. workers, over 220,000 are 55 or older. It sees itself as providing jobs for minorities, new immigrants, and older employees. Based on the company's policy of promoting from within, low-paying entry-level jobs can be a stepping stone for promotion if workers exhibit drive and performance.

Walmart also asserts that it helps improve the living standards of lower-income consumers by allowing them to buy goods they could not otherwise afford.

ETHICS AND GLOBAL MARKETING

Walmart stresses that its relentless drive to lower costs and to lean on suppliers helps increase productivity in the U.S. economy. Walmart also suggests that the savings from low prices reduce U.S. inflation and that the savings consumers incur from shopping at Walmart allows them to use the money in other ways, such as saving for home ownership and making mortgage and car payments.

COMPLAINTS ABOUT WALMART

Walmart's critics point to several negative consequences of the company's policies. Critics have asserted that

- Walmart's volume-based, low-price strategy makes it difficult for mom-and-pop retailers to compete, driving them out of business.
- By creating large superstores on the outskirts of cities, Walmart hollows out inner cities and despoils the environment, gobbling up land for its stores, creating the need for parking lots and highways.
- Walmart pays low wages to keep costs down, making it difficult for workers to support a family. In its desire to keep overheads low, the company offers limited health care and requires copayments that make health care unaffordable to low-paid employees. The company has been accused of exploiting its workers. It has also been the target of lawsuits over its treatment of workers, accusing it of requiring employees to work "off the clock," not paying overtime to workers, hiring illegal immigrants (indirectly through a floor-cleaning subcontractor), and discriminating against female workers.

- Walmart is antiunion. In response, unions have joined together in an attempt to organize Walmart workers and move Walmart to recognize and accept unions. The Union Network International, a federation of 900 unions in 150 countries, has focused on Walmart. It has tried to influence Walmart workers in Germany who are unionized to initiate sympathetic work stoppages and has tried to organize workers in South Korea, where Walmart has 16 stores. It is also trying to convince teachers who belong to unions to boycott Walmart as a source of back-to-school supplies.

- Walmart has contributed to manufacturing activity moving out of the United States. This has resulted from the company's continued pressure on U.S. suppliers to lower costs, forcing them to manufacture overseas in order to get access to low-wage labor, thus being able to meet Walmart's demands for low prices.

- Walmart's suppliers follow lax labor policies, such as using child labor, paying substandard wages, conducting business in hazardous factories and workplaces, and not respecting workers' rights. Walmart, like other corporations, has responded with codes of conduct for suppliers, conducting internal audits to ensure compliance with their rules for fair treatment and employment of workers. However, Walmart has not used outside independent agencies to audit the workplaces and labor practices of its overseas suppliers.

One consequence of the criticisms has been opposition to Walmart's expansion in areas such as California and the eastern states. Walmart has been able to expand rapidly and successfully in some parts of the United States, such as the southwest. Opposition to and support for Walmart seems somewhat divided along geographic lines within the United States.

WALMART OVERSEAS

In its recent expansion into China, Walmart has been enthusiastically received. When it opened a store in Chongqing, it had over 120,000 customers the first day. Customers asked the managers why they waited so long to open a store. Shoppers avidly purchased the merchandise on display, marveling at the quality, the assortment, the low prices, the freshness of the produce, and the eye-catching displays of wares. Most of what Walmart sold in China was also sourced in China. Walmart took care to adapt to Chinese cultural needs. The store increased the amount of space devoted to food and produce; allowed customers to touch the goods and to examine open packages; and sponsored cultural activities at the stores for all age groups, including the elderly. Walmart has attempted to ensure that it develops a positive image in China. It faces considerable competition in China from local state-owned retailing chains and from Carrefour, the French superstore retailer, which has twice as many stores and has partnerships with local governmental and state-owned firms.

Walmart has had somewhat mixed results in its expansion into Europe, where it attempted to acquire existing retail chains in Germany (Walmart has since pulled out of Germany) and the United Kingdom. Most of its overseas success has come from the United Kingdom, Canada, and Mexico. It has been less successful with its expansion into Brazil and Argentina and with its one-third ownership of the Seiyu Japanese retail chain. It has aggressively moved into China and, within a few years of opening, has become a major retailer there.

WALMART'S FUTURE

As complaints about Walmart mount, it cannot afford to ignore them, hoping they will disappear. The issue is whether the complaints are justified and whether Walmart can respond to them without sacrificing some of its commercial success.

But Walmart needs to develop an effective response to its critics if it wants to preserve its reputation and continue to grow around the world.

Questions and Research

1. What is Walmart's impact on customers, suppliers, competitors, workers, communities, and the overall economy in the United States?

2. What is the impact of Walmart on the global economy and on individual countries where it sources from and where it has stores (China, for example)?

3. What should Walmart's goals be with regard to its different constituencies—customers, suppliers, employees, shareholders, and society at large?

4. In your view, how well has Walmart fulfilled its social responsibilities in the United States? In the world as a whole?

5. What changes might you recommend to Walmart? What are your reasons for recommending such changes?

Sources: "Labor Leaders Say Multination Effort Targets Wal-Mart," *Wall Street Journal*, August 23, 2005; Clay Chandler, "The Great Wal-Mart of China," *Fortune*, July 25, 2005; "Special Report: Wal-Mart: How Big Can It Grow?" *The Economist*, April 17, 2004; "Learning to Love Wal-Mart," *The Economist*, April 17, 2004; "Wal-Mart," *Forbes* 2000, April 12, 2004; Abigail Goldman and Nancy Cleeland, "An Empire Built on Bargains Remakes the Working World," three-part series, *Los Angeles Times*, November 23, 24, and 25, 2003; http://www.walmartfacts.com/newsdesk/wal-mart-fact-sheets.aspx#a22. "Walmart Stays Strong in China, Brazil and Mexico," *Financial Times*, August 17, 2010 (http://blogs.ft.com/beyond-brics/2010/08/17/walmart-stays-strong-in-china-brazil-and-mexico/), accessed October 7, 2010. "Wal-Mart's New Market: Small Town China," *The Huffington Post*, October 18, 2008 (http://www.huffingtonpost.com/2008/10/18/wal-marts-new-market-smal_n_135842.html), accessed October 7, 2010.

(Walmart Corporate website: http://walmartstores.com/)

Case prepared by Professor Ravi Sarathy, for use in classroom discussion. Copyright 2006 (Revised 2010) Professor Sarathy.

CASE 5.2 Nutriset and Plumpy'nut

Starvation is unpleasant to think about. As the body starves, it turns on itself, beginning to consume muscle and tissue. Starvation is agonizing for the crying child and for his or her mother who is frantically trying to save her child. Starvation follows war and famine in places such as Darfur, Sudan, where thousands of families have been attacked by Arab militias and driven away from their arable lands in what the U.S. government has termed genocide. How can a company help in such a situation? Nutriset, a French company, is focused on humanitarian nutrition programs. It seeks to develop products that can help children and adults recover from malnutrition and starvation.

Nutriset is a small company based in Normandy, with $15 million in sales. Its founder and managing director, Michel Lescanne, had worked in a French aid agency, attempting to develop an enriched chocolate bar for malnourished children. However, the taste was not pleasant. The chocolate bar melted quickly in warm weather, a climate common in much of Africa and other tropical locations. It was also costly to produce and unlikely to suit straitened budgets of aid agencies. When Lescanne founded Nutriset, he continued to work on food products for humanitarian relief.

The traditional approach to countering starvation was to give patients enriched milk powder drinks. A UN formula, F-100, was mixed with water to give to a child or an adult. This approach presented several difficulties. Water, clean water, was scarce in famine-ridden areas. If the milk powder was not mixed with clean water, it could become contaminated and cause other diseases. If the milk was not consumed immediately, bacteria could form in the warm temperatures.

Getting the milk powder often meant making a trip to a refugee camp, which sometimes meant leaving other children behind with no adult to care for them. Refugee camps were possible vectors for disease, and a weakened child could easily be infected. Aid workers who had to administer the milk and water mixture were often overwhelmed by the number of children and families seeking treatment and help.

Andre Briend, Lescanne's colleague and a consultant to Nutriset, had also been working on the problem of finding foods for the treatment of starvation. At breakfast one day, he noticed a jar of Nutella and immediately called Lescanne to ask, "Why not a spread?" As a result, Plumpy'nut was born.

Plumpy'nut is a peanut butter-based spread, a peanut butter paste that comes in small packets, each weighing 92 grams and costing an aid agency 35 cents. Diets to combat starvation are dependent on the weight of the child, as the overtaxed digestive system cannot handle too much rich food. The packets are small enough to ensure that the correct amount can be given to a child over the course of a day. Three to four packets a day for several weeks can overcome severe malnutrition and nourish starving children back to health.

Peanuts are common in much of Africa and a regular part of the diet; hence, few children are allergic to peanut products. Because the paste comes in a sealed sachet, it can be torn open and given to a child immediately without risk of contamination or the need for clean water. Aid workers are not needed to mix the food, as was the case with the enriched milk powder. A mother can take care of the child herself, does not need to visit a refugee camp or aid station, and does not need to leave her other children behind or expose her children to the risks of infection at the camp.

Nutriset has distributed over 300 tons of Plumpy'nut in Darfur and in places such as Ethiopia, Sudan, and Malawi. It is not "big business," with relatively small orders. An exception is a big customer such as the United Nations High Commissioner for Refugees (UNHCR), which placed ten orders for Plumpy'nut, totaling $400,000. Since its "customers" reside in remote places that are difficult to access, Nutriset has to pay attention to logistics. It needs to be able to respond to emergencies, shipping the requisite quantities as quickly as possible. Nutriset, wary of being seen as profiting from tragedy, does not seek to develop commercial products such as energy bars. Its other products include a 20 mg zinc tablet for use in treating acute diarrhea in infants and young children under the age of 5. It also makes Vitapoche, an enriched food that has been used by the French government in helping homeless people. Its R&D also focuses on improving Plumpy'nut. For example, its research helped develop a version of Plumpy'nut with a longer shelf life. The company has developed the ability to give Plumpy'nut a two-year shelf life, with new packaging and a new formula. Longer shelf life is important, as it may take several months to ship products to reach remote famine and treatment sites. Plumpy'nut may also be stored for use in possible emergencies, which cannot be forecast. And longer shelf life helps optimize scarce aid agency funds. The Plumpy family of products is covered by an IRD/Nutriset patent. Nutriset has also been considering the development of similar nourishing foods using corn or wheat as a base.

Plumpy'nut's success, the difficulties in delivering it to famine-torn countries, and the need to conserve aid agency funds have resulted in requests to manufacture Plumpy'nut locally. In response, Nutriset has helped some aid workers to source local peanut ingredients and combine them locally, using vitamins and nutrients supplied by Nutriset. Nutriset plans to set up a network of franchisees to help ensure quality, optimal production levels, and lower costs, while earning a fee for its advice. Those initiatives have led to local production in places such as Dakar and the Democratic Republic of Congo. An aid worker rhapsodized that the most beautiful thing about Plumpy'nut was that it puts the mother in charge of feeding the child.

Nutriset is an interesting example of a company that can balance commercial activity while having a social conscience. Its challenge is to continue to grow while being socially responsible.

Questions and Research

1. What lessons could other companies learn from the experience of Nutriset and Plumpy'nut?

2. Visit the corporate website at http://www.nutriset.fr/en/homepage-nutriset.html. What current information on international activities do you find? Discuss the results of your research.

3. Research the web for other examples of companies that have successfully combined their commercial interests with a social conscience. Discuss your findings.

Sources: Roger Thurow, "Famine Relief," *Wall Street Journal*, April 12, 2005; Andre Briend, "Highly Nutrient-Dense Spreads: A New Approach to Delivering Multiple Micronutrients to High-Risk Groups," *British Journal of Nutrition* 85, Supplement 2 (2001): S175–S179; Nutriset website (http://www.nutriset.fr; in English: http://www.nutriset.fr/en_index.php).

Case prepared by Professor Ravi Sarathy, Northeastern University, for use in class discussion. © 2005, all rights reserved.

NOTES

1. A. Marcus and S. Kaiser, *Managing Beyond Compliance: The Ethical and Legal Dimensions of Corporate Social Responsibility* (Garfield Heights, OH: NorthCoast Publishers, 2006): vi.
2. Ibid., vi–vii.
3. Manuel Velasquez, *Business Ethics*, 5th ed. (Upper Saddle River, NJ: Prentice Hall, 2002): 97–99.
4. John. A Rawls, *Theory of Justice* (Cambridge: Harvard University Press, 1971), Revised Edition (Cambridge: Harvard University Press, 1999); Manuel Velasquez, *Business Ethics*, 5th ed. (Upper Saddle River, NJ: Prentice Hall, 2002): 116–20.
5. T. Donaldson and T. W. Dunfee, "Towards a Unified Conception of Business Ethics: Integrative Social Contracts Theory," *Academy of Management Review*, 19 (1994): 252–84.
6. Ibid., 265.
7. A. Spicer, T. W. Dunfee, and W. J. Bailey, "Does National Context Matter in Ethical Decision Making? An Empirical Test of Integrative Social Contracts Theory," *Academy of Management Journal* 47, no. 4 (2004): 610–20.
8. For more details of the Balanced Scorecard, see Robert S. Kaplan and Daniel P. Norton, "Using the Balanced Scorecard as a Strategic Management System," *Harvard Business Review*, January–February 1996.
9. "Seed Money: In Indonesia, Tangle of Bribes Creates Trouble for Monsanto," *Wall Street Journal*, April 5, 2005, p. A1.
10. "Suit Alleges US Firm Paid Bribes for China Contracts," *Wall Street Journal*, March 21, 2005.
11. Jonathan P. Doh, Peter Rodriguez, K. Uhlenbruck, J. Collins, and L. Eden, "Coping with Corruption in Foreign Markets," *Academy of Management Executive* 17, no. 3 (2003): 114–129.
12. Sealed Air Corporation Code of Conduct (http://www.sealedair.com/corp/conduct.html), accessed April 7, 2005.
13. United Nations; UN Global Compact (http://www.unglobalcompact.org/AboutTheGC/TheTen-Principles/index.html), accessed April 12, 2010.
14. "Business Principles for Countering Bribery," *Transparency International*, 2009 (http://www.transparency.org/global_priorities/private_sector/business_principles), accessed October 7, 2010.
15. Milan Vrabevski, "Clinical Trials in Bulgaria, Parts 1 and 2," *European Pharmaceutical Contractor* (Summer 2002 and Autumn 2002) (http://www.samedanltd.com/magazine/11/issue/21/article/1062) and (http://www.samedanltd.com/magazine/11/issue/22/article/1112), accessed October 7, 2010.
16. Joseph L. Herring, "A Winning Prescription for Drug Development Outsourcing," *European Pharmaceutical Contractor* (Autumn 2004) (http://www.samedanltd.com/magazine/11/issue/12/article/782), accessed October 7, 2010.
17. "The Menace of AIDS," *The Economist* (July 8, 2002); "Four Horsemen of the Apocalypse," *The Economist*, 367, no. 8322 (May 3, 2003): 85.
18. LaRue Tone Hosmer, "Merck Corporation and the Cure for River Blindness: Case 5-3," in *The Ethics of Management*, 4th ed. (Boston: McGraw-Hill, 2003): 132.

19. *World Development Report*, 2000/2001, Box 10.1 (Washington, DC: The World Bank, 2001): 182.

20. Inge Kaul, Pedro Conceicao, Katell Le Goulven, and Ronald U. Mendoza, eds., *Providing Global Public Goods* (New York: Oxford University Press, 2003); Inge Kaul, Isabelle Grunberg, and Marc Stern, *Global Public Goods—International Public Cooperation in the 21st Century* (New York: Oxford University Press, 1999).

21. "GAVI Alliance 2009 Progress Report," GAVI Alliance (http://www.gavialliance.org/media_centre/features/GAVI_Progress_Report_2009.php), accessed July 15, 2010.

22. Mattel Inc.'s Corporate Social Responsibility Report, 2004, p. 18 (http://www.mattel.com/about_us/Corp_Responsibility/csr_final.pdf), accessed April 7, 2005.

23. "The Case for Brands," *The Economist* 360, no. 8238 (September 2001): 9.

24. Naomi Klein, *No Logo: Taking Aim at Brand Bullies* (New York: Picador USA, 2000).

25. "Benetton Death Row Ads Outrage America," *The Independent*, April 2, 2000 (http://www.independent.co.uk/news/world/americas/benetton-death-row-ads-outrage-america-719129.html), accessed July 14, 2010.

26. Remarks at the World Economic Forum Annual Meeting 2009, "The Global Compact and the Corporate Citizen," Muhtar Kent, President and Chief Executive Officer, the Coca-Cola Company, Davos, Switzerland, January 29, 2009; video; (http://www.thecoca-colacompany.com/presscenter/viewpoints_kent_davos_video.html), accessed July 14, 2010.

27. For a good overview of many of the issues associated with corporate social responsibility (including quite critical ones), visit SourceWatch's CSR page: www.sourcewatch.org/index.php?title = Corporate_Social_Responsibility.

28. A number of websites discuss the issue of greenwashing. For an example, visit www.greenwashingindex.com.

29. "Corporate Social Responsibility?" video interview with Dame Anita Roddick, September 15, 2006 (http://www.globalissues.org/video/733/anita-roddick-corporate-social-responsibility), accessed April 12, 2010.

30. R. Barkemeyer, "Beyond Compliance—Below Expectations? CSR in the Context of International Development," *Business Ethics: A European Review* 18 (2009): 273–89.

31. S. Lim and J. Phillips, "Embedding CSR Values: The Global Footwear Industry's Evolving Governance Structure," *Journal of Business Ethics* 81 (2008): 143–56.

32. United Nations, UN Global Compact Participants (http://www.unglobalcompact.org/ParticipantsAndStakeholders/index.html), accessed July 14, 2010.

chapter

6 Global Marketing Research and Data Sources

Previous chapters discussed the significant differences in the global landscape versus a strictly domestic market. Differences in cultural, political, economic, and legal environments mean international marketing decisions are more complex than wholly domestic decisions. The international marketing manager must learn how to conduct effective international marketing research upon which to make crucial decisions such as which countries to enter and how to develop an effective marketing plan for each foreign market. Marketing decisions cannot be made intelligently without knowing the specific environment and characteristics of each foreign market. This chapter addresses the goals of international marketing research, barriers to such research, and data sources for the international marketing manager.

The main goals of this chapter are to ● ● ●

1. Discuss the types of information required for global marketing research.

2. Detail the differences in the marketing environment and how marketing research can be used to understand those differences.

3. Evaluate how international research may be used to impact marketing mix decisions.

4. Review the range of tasks involved in international marketing research by outlining the problems

encountered in conducting research overseas and discussing ways to solve those problems.

5. Present techniques, such as analysis of demand patterns and estimation by analogy, for dealing with problems with primary data, as well as incomplete data or market indicators.

6. Review various sources of data and how each can be used to find data on countries, industries, trade statistics, and companies.

Global Marketing Research: What Information Is Needed?

The information gathered for global marketing is used to support a wide range of important decisions for a firm as it expands internationally. At the most basic level, a firm needs data to make the initial decision to expand (or not expand) beyond its domestic market and which products or services to offer. Another key early decision would be which world markets to enter. Data from marketing research would be used to rank markets according to their attractiveness (as discussed in the next chapter). This requires an investigation of each market's sales/profit potential, growth rates, and the local competitive situation.

Having selected the target foreign markets, a firm must decide how to serve those markets: by exporting, licensing, or perhaps producing locally. Once a decision has been made to market in a particular country, standard marketing questions arise—questions regarding product, pricing, and channel. Those decisions can be further broken down until, eventually, a specific local issue is resolved—the kind of package and label that should be used for a firm's floor wax in the Philippines, for example. (See Table 6-1.)

What types of information would need to be gathered to support these critical decisions? Essentially, the international marketing manager would be seeking six categories of information: an internal assessment of the firm's corporate environment; understanding the marketing environment, the competitive landscape, consumer behavior, and marketing mix options; and firm-specific historical data. (In addition, researchers would be looking for specific market indicators (e.g., gross national income) for use in the critical task of selecting international markets for expansion. This aspect of international marketing research will be discussed in Chapter 7.

Table 6-2 provides a summary of the task of global marketing research with specific examples of the preceding research goals.

Table 6-1 • Information for Marketing Decisions

Marketing Decisions	Intelligence Needed
1. Go international or remain a domestic marketer?	Assessment of global market versus domestic market (demand and competition) and internal assessment of company readiness to go international
2. Which markets to enter?	Assessment of individual market potential (e.g., demand, local competition, political environment)
3. How to enter target markets?	Market size, trade barriers, transportation costs, requirements and standards, and political environment
4. How to market in target markets?	Buyer behavior, competitive practices, distribution channels, promotional media, market experience, and company expertise

International marketing research is used to support critical marketing decisions, such as which countries in the world to enter.

Understanding the Marketing Environment

As discussed in earlier chapters, the international business environment is very different from a domestic market. For a better understanding of these differences, marketing research would be used to provide insights into a country's political, economic, and other market-related dimensions.

The political dimensions of marketing research include data on the *political structure and ideology*. What does the political leadership of the country seek? What roles do major institutions such as business, labor, the educational sector, and religion play in shaping national goals? How do legal systems and differences affect markets? The political

Table 6-2 • The Task of Global Marketing Research

The Firm's Corporate Environment	The Marketing Environment	The Competition	The Product	Marketing Mix	Firm-Specific Historical Data
Internal strengths to expand internationally	Political context: leaders, national goals, ideology, and key institutions	Relative market shares	Industrial and consumer buyer characteristics	Channels of distribution: evolution and performance	Sales trends by: • product and product line • sales force • customer
Internal weaknesses regarding international expansion	Economic growth prospects and business cycle stage	New product introductions	Size, age, sex, and segment growth rates	Relative pricing, elasticities, and pricing tactics	Trends by country and region
Level of current international expertise	Per capita income levels and purchasing power	Pricing and cost structure	Purchasing power and intentions	Advertising and promotion: choices and impacts on customers	Contribution margins
Management commitment to internationalize	End-user industry growth trends	Image and brand recognition	Customer response to new products, price, and promotion	Service quality, perceptions, and relative positioning	Innovation, experience, and results
Employee commitment to internationalize	Government: legislation, regulation, standards, and barriers to trade	Quality: its attributes and positioning relative to that of competitors	Switching behavior	Logistics, networks, configuration, and change	Customer retention
		Competitors' strengths and favorite marketing strategies	Role of credit and purchasing	Marketing mix used and marketing response across countries and regions	
			Future needs		
			Impact of cultural differences		

Analyzing the Findings: Answering Questions from the Market Research Information

- What are our internal strengths we can leverage to expand internationally?
- Which markets are attractive in the short and long run?
- How do we attract customers?
- What do customers think of our product and that of the competition?
- What do we do about competition? Cooperate or compete? With whom?
- What new products should we introduce?

- What internal weaknesses must we address before expanding internationally?
- What should the price be?
- Which distribution channels should we use?
- How much advertising and promotion are necessary?
- Which countries should we target next?
- How should we overcome barriers to entry?

dimensions also include the *national objectives*. What are the country's goals for specific industries; the defense sector; its fiscal, monetary, and investment policy; and the foreign trade sector? What are its social policies, including health care and education? Depending on the specific product or service to be globalized, these political dimensions could have a significant impact on the firm.

Another aspect of the marketing environment is the *economic dimension of information gathering*. It includes obtaining data on economic performance, covering indicators such as GDP, per capita income levels and growth rates, stage of the business cycle, balance of trade and balance of payments, productivity, labor costs and capital availability, capacity utilization, inflation rates, savings and investment, employment levels, educational attainment, population demographics, age distribution, public health, and income distribution.

Marketing infrastructure is also of interest, including the structure of wholesaling and retailing, laws concerning pricing and promotion, the physical distribution infrastructure, and the extent of development of consumer protection. All these issues help determine the attractiveness of the market, as well as obstacles to entry and marketing of goods and services and the long-term profit potential.

Technology and culture form part of the market environment. Thus, a firm should note how the use of technology, the level of technology available, and cultural differences affect the environment and influence market growth and attractiveness.

Government regulation is another area for market research, particularly with regard to product and safety standards, barriers to entry (affecting foreign companies and their products), and controls over managerial and marketing autonomy. Does the government implement industrial policies that benefit domestic companies and industries at the expense of foreign firms?

Competitive Landscape

As a firm expands internationally, the international marketing manager would likely want to know as much as possible about its competitors' activities. Some companies may trust their own competitive advantages and take the stance that their firm is uniquely positioned apart from competitors. In such a case, knowledge of competitors may be seen as less useful. Competitors may also be making mistakes, such as selecting markets that result in poor demand for their product or services.

Most companies, regardless of their competitive strengths, still seek to understand the competitive landscape of a foreign market prior to entering that market. This would be particularly true if local (domestic) competition in the market is strong and the competitors are otherwise unknown to the foreign firm entering the market. But getting good information on the competitive landscape of foreign markets is often difficult, though increasingly becoming easier. On a country level, sources such as the World Economic Forum's *Global Competitiveness Report* can give insight into the overall competitive intensity in a country.[1]

However, industry-and firm-level data for countries is critical for the international marketing manager to understand the competitive landscape in potential international markets. The first step is to identify as many competitors as possible and then research their activities via traditional data sources. Chapter 8 discusses in more detail a variety of online databases that may be used to identify competitors. They include Kompass and OneSource. After the international marketing manager has identified the competitors, research of the competitor's websites at the very least would confirm their product or services offering, offices in the country, and perhaps even some important marketing details. Local and international news sources (such as Factiva) also provide useful insights. (Table 6-5, later in this chapter, provides a summary of these data sources.)

Some of the most useful competitive information would be aggregated industry data. Such data would provide information on the total size, strength, and perhaps growth projections for specific industries. Every nation has a way of classifying firms by the products they produce or by the things they use in the production process. The United States uses the North American Industry Classification System (NAICS). Other nations use different industry and product classifications systems; for instance, the European Union (EU) collects product data using Classification of Products by Activity (CPA). The CPA is also related to the EU's Common Procurement Vocabulary (CPV). But these differences lead to an oft-cited complaint that data from one source is not comparable to data from another entity.

Government export agencies address these deficiencies by conducting their own research and report on global industry opportunities. Examples are the Country Commercial Guides produced by the U.S. Commercial Service and the Market Analysis Tools produced by the World Trade Centre, Geneva, which is a joint agency of the World Trade Organization and the United Nations. Private companies also provide extensive industry information that is both specific to individual countries and comparative across markets. Examples include Euromonitor International (www.euromonitor.com), which has a variety of consumer, industrial, and service market reports. More data sources are cited later in this chapter.

Consumer Behavior

A firm must understand users—users of its product or services and users of the firm's competitors. A paramount consideration is documenting and understanding cultural differences as they affect customer needs, products demanded, and purchasing behavior. Analysis and market research can focus on end-user industry categories and, if relevant, on unique characteristics of consumers. Information to help in *market segmentation* should be gathered, using parameters such as age, sex, size, income levels, growth rates of consumption, regional differences, purchasing power, influence over purchasing and purchasing intentions, and the role of credit granting in purchasing behavior. Another major area of research is product benchmarking (or quality comparisons), which enables a firm to obtain objective comparisons of its products with those of its competitors. A firm can use that information to understand its competitors' product positioning issues within the industry. The information also is helpful to the firm in determining its positioning across countries, customer response to new product introductions, and the likelihood

Part of understanding the international marketing environment is understanding consumer behavior in foreign markets. Locating data on consumer behavior is an important goal of marketing research.

that customers will purchase its brands instead of competitors' brands. Finally, research should identify market trends for the medium and long term, rather than providing information for decision making only on immediate marketing plans and actions. Frequently, this type of very specific consumer behavior data would be available only through primary research, likely conducted using an international market research company. But industry reports, as discussed previously, may also provide useful insights.

Marketing Mix Options

A company can standardize or adapt its product as well as its marketing mix to different country markets. Hence, it is also necessary for a firm to research its choice of marketing mix in international markets. A firm should investigate the following areas:

- **Distribution channels.** Their evolution and the firm's and its competitors' comparative performance in different channels.

- **Comparative pricing strategies and tactics.** The price positioning by all competitors, price elasticity, government regulations on pricing, and customer response to differential pricing behavior.

- **Advertising and promotion.** The range of choices available, differences in the allocation of promotion expenditures, delineation of the advertising response function in different markets, government regulation of advertising and promotion, and comparison of competitor choices in advertising and promotion.

- **Media research.** Research that is useful in determining where to advertise in order to reach target audiences; major market research firms such as Arbitron and the Kantar Group (part of WPP) provide media research and media measurement services.

- **Service quality issues.** Issues relative to positioning by competitors and customers' reactions to higher levels of service.
- **Supply chain.** A firm may rely on very close relationships with vendors as part of its business model, but those same vendors may not be available. A country's infrastructure would impact the logistics network available to a firm to supply products and services. Chapter 11 discusses this issue in more detail.

In all the preceding elements of the firm's marketing mix, it is important to analyze how each is similar to or different from what the firm currently uses in the domestic market or other international markets. For example, can the firm apply the same distribution strategy in the international market as it uses in its home market? Academic research suggests that the greater the similarities between the home country and the potential international market, the more likely the firm is to select that market, and the firm is more likely to enter similar markets more quickly.[2]

Firm-Specific Historical Data

Marketing research using outside resources should also be augmented by data the firm collects internally. Useful data could include sales history by product and product line, by customer and sales force, by distribution channel, and within a country and across countries. The data could also be used to analyze trends across countries and regions; to derive and analyze contributions by product, product line, customer, and region; to develop market response functions across countries for comparing past marketing mix decisions; and for suggesting future mix decisions that differ from country to country, within a country, or across regions.

Marketing Research and the Firm's Global Strategy

Beyond influencing specific marketing discussions, marketing research can also play a role in helping a firm formulate its global strategy. While strategy sets a path for how a firm should interact with its customers, competition, and environment, market research can provide information and analyses on environmental trends, changes in competitive behavior and government regulation, and shifting consumer tastes. In other words, market research can provide strategic information by focusing on future research and scenario development.

Global marketing research can influence strategic planning issues such as:

- Determining the firm's mission, scope, and long-range objectives.
- Anticipating environmental changes and their effects—and the resulting opportunities and threats that they pose.
- Understanding the firm's capabilities versus the strengths and weaknesses of competitors.

Problems in International Marketing Research

Because of the complexity of international marketing research, the international marketing manager will likely encounter data challenges that are less common in domestic marketing research. One problem is that research must be gathered for many markets—dozens of countries in some cases—and each country poses a unique challenge. A second problem is the frequent absence of **secondary data** (data from published and third-party sources). Even when such data is

secondary data

Data from published and third-party sources, often quantitative in nature.

available, it may be outdated or difficult to accurately compare across countries. A third problem is the challenges and costs of gathering **primary data** (data gathered firsthand through interviews and field research).

primary data

Data gathered first hand through interviews and field research.

Problems of Numerous Markets

Multiplying the number of countries in a proposed research project multiplies the costs and problems involved, although not in a linear manner. Because markets are not identical from one country to another, the research manager must be alert to the various errors that can arise in replicating a study on a multinational basis. Five kinds of errors to look for in multinational research are:

- Definition error, which is caused by the way the problem is defined in each country.
- Instrument error, which arises from the questionnaire and the interviewer.
- Frame error, which occurs when sampling frames are available from different sources in different countries. (A frame is the list of the population of elements or members from which the survey sample is selected.)
- Selection error, which results from the way the actual sample is selected from the frame.
- Nonresponse error, which results when different cultural patterns of nonresponse are obtained. Response rates can vary significantly by age or gender. For example, if selected randomly, car buyers in the United States who are asked why they purchased a car will include a large percentage of women. If one asks car buyers in Argentina the same question, a large percentage of respondents will be men. This difference will have an impact on the responses that researchers obtain.

Using Secondary Data

A research manager would likely first seek information on a foreign market through secondary data sources. Such data sources, as found on numerous websites, are available on-demand and often at low to no cost. However, such data is often not available for all foreign markets and is less reliable. As discussed in the next section, even when this data is available, it may not be comparable across several markets. Fortunately, secondary data is becoming increasingly timely and complete. The Internet has helped tremendously in disseminating secondary data. United Nations trade data used to be in print format only and lagged by at least a couple of years. Such data today, through the UN's free website, is much more complete and current.

It should be noted that most secondary data is **quantitative data**—information expressed as a number or statistics. The population, GDP, or import statistics of a country are all examples of secondary data. **Qualitative data** is information that represents opinions, preferences, or behaviors. Consumers' preferences for a particular color, taste, or purchasing habits are examples of qualitative data. Often qualitative data can be obtained only through conducting primary research projects focused on the specific information needed to be obtained. Increasingly, though, the results of past primary research yielding qualitative information are then released on the Internet as secondary data.

quantitative data

Information expressed as a number or statistics.

qualitative data

Information expressed as words often representing opinions, preferences, or behaviors.

Comparing Several Markets

When data for several markets are compiled, the researcher may find that many gaps exist. For example, current data on the number of automobile registrations may be available only for a few countries in the group of interest—and often, not for the same time period. Data quality may vary, and the estimates may not be reliable. The underlying definitions may not be the same. Some countries exclude light trucks from automobile registrations, whereas others include them, for example. Many countries lack specialized firms that develop industry data for specific industries such as automobiles and air conditioners. Fortunately, specific websites such as www.nationmaster.com are helping increase the comparability of data across several markets. And when such data is unavailable, research techniques, as will be discussed later, may help fill such gaps.

Problems with Primary Data

Marketing research involves getting information from people about their perceptions, intentions, and actual behavior concerning a company's products, brands, prices, or promotion. People differ from country to country in income levels, culture, attitudes, and understanding of business issues, including specific items on surveys and questionnaires. Hence, skilled interviewers are needed to conduct personal interviews.

A fundamental problem in doing international marketing research is making sure that the same construct is being studied across cultures. For example, does the word *quality* mean approximately the same thing to consumers in different countries and cultures? Different types of equivalence are outlined in Table 6-3.

Telephone surveys may work poorly and give biased results in countries with low rates of telephone penetration, such as Bangladesh, Cameroon, or Haiti, which have less than one telephone line per 1,000 people.[3] (It should be noted that countries in many cases are going directly to cell phones rather than land lines; for example, in China, cell-phone growth is outpacing land-line growth.) Mail surveys require a developed postal system, good mailing lists, and an educated population. Accurate and complete street addresses are necessary to provide representative samples for mail questionnaires.

Often mail and telephone surveys are not practical, in which case the researcher is left with personal interviewing as an alternative. With a largely rural population in developing countries, the problem then becomes one of physically reaching the people. Poor roads and lack of public transportation may make interviewing people economically unfeasible. Privacy considerations are important, with Europe generally having stricter privacy protection laws than the United States. Respondents may feel pressure to respond with answers they perceive to be "socially correct." Speed, cost, and control for bias also affect the choice of technique.

Table 6-3 • Types of Cross-National Equivalence

Construct	The construct must exist and be meaningful in all cultures studied.
Functional	Similar activities/products must have similar functions in different cultural settings.
Conceptual	The meaning of what is studied must be comparable across cultures.
Category	The category in which objects, stimuli, and behaviors are grouped is the same across cultures.
Instrument	The instrument used must measure the same phenomenon uniformly across cultures.
Item	Each item of an instrument should mean the same thing across the cultures studied.
Translation	The wording of the instrument must mean the same thing to respondents in every culture studied.
Sample	Comparability and representativeness of samples exist across countries.
Contextual	The relationship and expectations between experimenter and subject are the same across countries.
Temporal	This determines whether different times at which studies were conducted across countries affects the results.
Measurement/ Measure	The same measurement model must hold across countries—that is, the relationship between observed scores and latent constructs.
Calibration	Comparable measurement units and correct conversion exist from one domestic norm to another.
Scalar / Metric	The same distance between scales and rank orders is maintained; that is, individuals with the same score have the same value on a construct and this relationship.

Source: Derived from Anne Smith and Nina C. Reynolds, "Measuring Cross-Cultural Service Quality," *International Marketing Review* 19, no. 5 (2002): 450–81.

Languages

Language, as discussed in Chapter 4, is an obvious cultural difference affecting primary research in foreign markets. Language difference poses problems of

Language is one of the most important cultural differences affecting primary research in a foreign market.

communication, and solutions to those problems may be expensive. The research design and specifications must be translated twice, first from the operating language of the firm to the language of each country where the study is to be conducted. Then, upon completion of the study, the results must be translated back into the original language. More important than translation expense is the communication problem. Concepts and phrases widely understood in one language may be incomprehensible in others; for example, concepts such as *net worth, well-being,* or *value for the money.*

Social Organization

Much of marketing research involves gaining insight into buyers' decision processes. That research is predicated on the assumption that the decision makers and influencers have been identified. In foreign markets, a researcher usually finds that the social organization is different enough to warrant identifying anew the decision makers and influencers. This difference may be due to a bigger emphasis on family business and a greater emphasis on relationships in other countries.

Obtaining Responses

Consumers may be reluctant to respond to marketing research inquiries. This reluctance may be, in part, the result of a general unwillingness to talk to strangers. Individuals in a particular culture may also be reluctant to discuss personal consumption habits and preferences. In contrast to the reluctant respondent is the cooperative respondent who feels obliged to give responses that will please the interviewer rather than state his or her true opinions or beliefs. This type of response bias is called **acquiescence bias**. In some cultures, this is a form of politeness, but it obviously does not contribute to effective research. An additional problem is the **social desirability bias**, whereby respondents answer questions based on what makes them look good, rather than their actual feelings on the matter.[4]

Another challenge is that respondents may be unable to cooperate effectively because they are asked to think in a way that is foreign to their normal thought patterns. They may be asked to react analytically rather than intuitively. Whatever the cause of a respondent's inability to respond, it is basically a translation

acquiescence bias

Occurs when respondents feel obliged to give responses that will please the interviewer rather than state their true opinions or beliefs.

social desirability bias

Occurs when respondents answer questions based on what makes them look good, or is socially acceptable, rather than state their true opinions or beliefs.

problem. The research designer must be able to translate not only the words, but also the concepts. The cultural gap must be bridged by the research designer.

Incomplete and Old Data

During the task of researching foreign markets, firm- and industry-specific data is often not available for all countries, in particular emerging markets. If the data is available, it may be significantly out of date. This creates the challenge of how to best approximate market potential in countries with missing data rather than just ignoring the gaps.

A number of techniques are commonly used when incomplete or old data prevents a good understanding of market potential, including (1) analysis of demand patterns, (2) multiple-factor indexes, (3) estimation by analogy, (4) regression analysis, and (5) cluster analysis. Some of these techniques mirror techniques discussed in Chapter 7 for analyzing market potential and selecting foreign markets.

Analysis of Demand Patterns

Although data at the industry level (or micro level) may not be available for particular industries in some countries, macro-level data is often available for nearly every country in the world. In many industries, consumption and production levels in a country vary by the country's level of per capita income, and there are often similarities in production and consumption levels between countries at similar levels of economic development. For example, poorer nations tend to have a larger proportion of the population involved in agriculture, consumption of energy tends to be directly related to the country's level of economic development, and richer nations tend to trade more services than poorer countries. By using macro-level indicators of demand as substitutes for micro-level indicators of demand, the international marketing manager can get a rough idea of the country's current consumption profile as well as the trend in economic development over time. Though relatively crude, that information helps a firm identify possibilities for export or for local production in the market.

Multiple-Factor Indexes

The analysis of demand pattern approach just described can be improved when more data is available on the country or countries of interest. Instead of using only macro-demand statistics (e.g., per capita income) as described in the "Analysis of Demand Patterns" section, the multiple-factor index uses more variables and more fine-grained measures of potential market demand. A **multiple-factor index** indirectly measures market potential by using multiple variables that the international marketing manager finds are closely correlated with the potential market for the product in question. For example, a manufacturer of modular housing may look at the following variables:

- The rate of household formation.
- Population demographics to gauge the percentage of the population in the age bracket from 20 to 30 years, a prime household-forming segment.
- Income-level segments, with some minimum per capital household income, such as $2,000 per year, being used to gauge purchasing power.

Each of the preceding variables is then weighted according to its importance for estimating market demand, and all the variables are analyzed together to determine the overall market potential of different international markets. When historical data is available, smoothing out those numbers over several time

multiple-factor index

Indirectly measures market demand by using multiple variables that are closely correlated with the actual market potential.

periods and relating them to historic house sales and new housing construction may provide useful estimates of potential market size for the modular housing construction industry. Chapter 7 further discusses the use of multiple variables for estimating market demand and selecting foreign markets.

Estimation by Analogy

One technique for countries with limited data is estimation by analogy, which is done in two ways: (1) through cross-section comparisons and (2) through the displacement of a time-series trend to a different time period.

The **cross-section comparison approach** involves taking the known market size of a product in one country and relating it to some economic indicator, such as disposable personal income, to obtain a ratio. That ratio (in the example, product consumption to disposable personal income) is then applied to another country (where disposable personal income is known) to derive the market potential for the product in the country. Assume that a firm was attempting to gauge demand for do-it-yourself retailers in a potential market. It found that in Germany, the average annual per capita purchase for do-it-yourself projects was the equivalent of $1,200 and that the average per capita disposable income was $19,000. The company's proposed expansion into Poland, where the disposable income average is $5,500, would lead the researcher to believe that the average per capita purchases for do-it-yourself projects in Poland would be approximately $350.

The **time-series approach** estimates the demand in the second country by assuming that it has the same level of consumption that the first country had at the same level of development (or per capita income). This technique assumes that product usage moves through a cycle. The product is consumed in small quantities (or not at all) when countries are underdeveloped and in increasing amounts when economic growth is occurring. Thus, a researcher could gather data of the meat and egg consumption in Taiwan in 1970 (which is known) to provide a rough estimate of the demand for meat and eggs in mainland China in 1990 (perhaps unknown) as Chinese incomes were similar to those prevalent in Taiwan 20 years earlier.

Both approaches have limitations. The cross-section method assumes a linear consumption function. Both assume comparable consumption patterns among countries. When those assumptions are not true, the comparisons are misleading. When more sophisticated techniques are not feasible, however, estimation by analogy is a useful first step.

Knowing the demand level of a product in a given country at a known level of economic development may be used to predict the demand for the same product in another country when it reaches the same level of economic development. This technique is call the time-series approach.

Regression Analysis

Regression analysis is often used with the preceding techniques to provide a quantitative method for sharpening estimates derived by the estimation methods just discussed. Regression analysis provides researchers with additional evidence—beyond statistical correlation—of which variables are most closely associated with demand for the firm's product or service. Regression analysis is simply an equation in which the international marketing manager plugs in data expected to predict demand. The results of this statistical analysis show which of the data (e.g., per capita income, percentage of population between 20 and 30, and/or meat and egg consumption) predicts demand and how strongly each piece of data predicts demand. By providing international marketing managers with a more accurate picture regarding which data predicts demand and how strongly each predicts demand, regression analysis allows the international marketing manager a more refined means by which to estimate demand using the techniques described here.

cross-section comparison approach

Takes the known market size of a product in one country and relates it to some economic indicator, such as disposable income, to obtain a ratio that can be applied to another country.

time-series approach

Estimates the demand in the second country by assuming that it has the same level of consumption that the first country had at the same level of development.

Table 6-4 • Country Segment Options

Segmentation Using Macroeconomic Data	Segmentation Using Product Diffusion
Production and transportation variables	Long-term series product sales data
Personal consumption data	Macroeconomic data
Health and education statistics	Lifestyle data

Cluster Analysis

Before moving to a full-scale data collection effort, international marketing managers often want to first generate a short list of potential markets that they can then analyze more intensively. Cluster analysis is a favored technique for identifying similar markets with the assumption that markets similar to the domestic market also represent potentially good international markets for a firm. Research shows that increases in similarity between the domestic market and potential international markets increases international marketing managers' propensity to select that market.[5] For example, researchers commonly use indicators such as per capita income, life expectancy, population, and air passenger traffic to identify similarities among countries. A more in-depth use of cluster analysis to screen markets will be presented in Chapter 7.

Clustering Countries by Product Diffusion Patterns

A problem with clustering countries on the basis of macroeconomic variables is that international marketers may not find the resulting markets helpful. Acceptance and diffusion of new products may in practice vary within the proposed countries. An alternative is to segment countries based on how similar they are in the rate at which new products are adopted (the product diffusion rate). (See Table 6-4.) If such segments could be derived, managers might use information from the lead market about variables such as growth in market size when sales reach a peak to make inferences on the same variables for lagging markets. This allows a country to belong to more than one segment at the same time. For example, the United States could be in the leading markets segment for a product such as advanced personal computers while lagging in the use of products such as smart cards or high-speed trains.

Macroeconomic data, such as standard of living, is important in explaining the readiness of a country's market to accept innovation. In addition, a diffusion-based segmentation approach uses data about factors such as lifestyle (use of phones per capita, for example) and cosmopolitanism (tourist expenditures and receipts). One study included an examination of the relationship between country-level variables and sales growth over a 14-year period for three consumer durables—televisions, videocassette recorders (VCRs), and compact disc (CD) players—for 12 advanced industrial nations from Europe, Japan, and the United States.[6]

The study showed that segments based on product adoption rates did not agree with segments derived from broad macroeconomic data alone. Those results suggest that countries that look similar from a broad macroeconomic perspective may differ in the rate at which they are willing to adopt and buy new products. Cultural factors such as language and religion, which were not specifically included in the study, may play an important role in explaining differences in the product diffusion rate. Numerous studies have noted that culture, mobility, and sex roles are important factors in explaining differences in product adoption rates,[7] and academic researchers strongly advocate that international marketing managers include cultural and political factors in their cluster analyses along with economic and commercial factors.[8]

Market Segmentation and Marketing Research

The international marketing manager will naturally view international opportunities in terms of countries, such as expanding to China or Germany. However, market opportunities for some firms will be less defined by political borders (countries) and better defined by other methods of grouping consumers or businesses. This alternative grouping may be within a country (such as a single city) or a collection of countries (such as the European Union). **Market segmentation** is a technique in which a subset of consumers who share common characteristics or common needs is identified. Common ways to define the subset would be geographic (city, region), demographic (age, income), psychographic (behaviors, value), and behavioralistic (brand loyalty, first adopters).

market segmentation
Technique in which a subset of consumers who share common characteristics or common needs is identified.

The key benefit of market segmentation is to better define the marketing task so it is targeted to a more focused group of potential buyers. Market segmentation helps to identify the most profitable or easiest sales opportunities. For example, entering the whole of China would be a daunting task, but using the concept of market segmentation would mean developing a market plan to enter Shanghai or Beijing, which would likely be more achievable than the entire country. Similarly, a firm may develop a marketing plan in which only high-income individuals are defined as the market, regardless of their country of residence.

Though market segmentation is an important concept when developing the international marketing plan, it can create challenges during international marketing research. Most international data, as discussed in the next section and Chapter 7, is collected at the country level. Examples are import statistics or lifestyle indicators such as computer usage. Indicators are sometimes available at levels other than just country, such as the population of a city or the per capita income across a region. But for the most part, marketing research data is collected at the country level. The implication for the international marketing manager is that although the international marketing research may be initially at the level of country, major marketing decisions should also incorporate market segmentation analysis. Examples of applying market segmentation will be included in subsequent international marketing tasks, such as foreign market selection (Chapter 7) or international product policy (Chapter 9).

Data Sources

Generally speaking, the two basic sources of foreign market data and information are (1) secondary data from published information and (2) primary data gathered through empirical research in foreign markets or discussions with knowledgeable individuals within the markets and industries.

Secondary Data

Secondary data is data and information obtained from existing published sources. Most secondary data is obtained through the Internet and often at no cost. Secondary data has become more current as statistics and reports move from print form to the Internet. In recent years information on emerging markets has also increased considerably in accuracy and currency due to efforts of nongovernmental organizations such as the World Bank and the United Nations. Now that such data is much more up-to-date and complete, secondary data has become a critical source of information for the international marketing manager.

Secondary data can be grouped into four categories: country or market information, industry information, trade statistics, and company information.

All four types are used for a variety of international marketing tasks such as selecting markets, analyzing markets, selecting partners, and developing a marketing strategy. In addition to the websites discussed here, Table 6-5 summarizes the most important websites by four types of data: country, industry, trade statistics, and company.

Table 6-5 • Key Websites for International Marketing

1) Sources for Country or Market Information

Use these sites to answer questions such as

- What is the population of a country?
- What is the GDP per capita income?
- What are the top export opportunities for U.S. products or services into a particular country?
- What is the number of Internet users in a country?
- How many hospitals are in a country?
- What is the economic growth projection for a country?
- How much pollution does a country emit?
- How many McDonald's restaurants are there per country?
- How are cultural differences measured between countries?
- Is a country competitive with other countries?

Sources	Cost	Types of Data Available	Comments
Export.Gov www.export.gov	Free	Very specific data on key export markets for U.S. products and services as well as insights on how to conduct business in the country.	Outstanding resource for research, updated annually. Not suitable for downloading data, since each country has an individual report. Country Commercial Guides are particularly important reports.
The World Bank—Open Data http://data.worldbank.org	Free	One source for key economic and demographic data including GDP, per capita, population, and over 100 other indicators; profiles for over 200 countries.	Authoritative site since the World Bank originates the data. Best source for comparable and current country-specific data. All downloadable.
NationMaster www.nationmaster.com	Free	One source for key economic and demographic data including a number of hard-to-find lifestyle indicators.	Also links to some industry reports and detailed country-competitiveness reports.
CIA World Factbook https://www.cia.gov/library/publications/the-world-factbook/	Free	One source for key economic and demographic data all in comparable format.	Another alternative to preceding sites—easy to use. Use the "country comparison" section to download data.
OECD Statistics Portal www.oecd.org/statsportal/ http://stats.oecd.org/	Free—also for-fee site	Offers indicators for both OECD countries and many nonmembers; also has detailed country reports and economic analysis.	Good companion site to the World Bank. Excellent on economic and country development issues.
Global Edge http://globaledge.msu.edu/	Free	A source for key economic and demographic data and also a good site to find other websites related to each country.	Easy to use, continually updated. Also see the "Academy" section for training videos and a glossary.
World Economic Forum's Global Competitiveness Reports www.weforum.org	Free	Offers comparable indicators measuring a country's competiveness, including innovation, infrastructure, health, and primary education; also has classified economies into one of five levels of economic development.	Also links to some industry reports and detailed country-competitiveness reports.
Hofstede Cultural Dimensions www.geert-hofstede.com/	Free	Official home page for the Hofstede cultural dimensions discussed in Chapter 4.	Though not directly related to demand, these indicators are helpful in understanding marketing challenges based on cultural differences.
Psychic Distance Stimuli Indicators www.mbs.edu/home/dow/research/	Free	Statistical approximations of the "distance" between countries on language, religion, and political systems.	Covers 120 countries and helps to understand potential barriers to communications between a firm and the market, especially as perceived by the firm's management.

Table 6-5 • (continued)

2) Sources for Industry Data and Insights

Use these sites to answer questions such as

- How strong is the retail sector in a country?
- What percent of sports equipment is purchased from local suppliers versus imports?
- What would be growing markets for electronic consumer goods?
- What is the value of dog food purchases in a country?
- What is the percent of Internet purchases versus total retail purchases?
- What are the fastest-growing markets for footwear?
- What are the eating and drinking habits of the people in a country?

Sources	Cost	Types of Data Available	Comments
Export.Gov www.export.gov	Free	Insights into specific industries as long as the industry is a top opportunity for U.S. exporters.	Database also includes specific trade opportunities such as large government projects.
The World Bank—Open Data http://data.worldbank.org	Free	One source for key economic and demographic data, including GDP, per capita, population, and over 100 other indicators. Profiles for over 200 countries.	Authoritative site since the World Bank originates the data. Best source for comparable and current country-specific data. All downloadable.
Global Edge http://globaledge.msu.edu/	Free	Has profiles on 20 industries, including apparel, consumer products, health care, travel, retail.	Easy to use, continually updated. Also see the "Academy" section for training videos and a glossary.
Euromonitor International www.euromonitor.com/	For-fee database—can purchase individual reports	Very in-depth reports on many industries with a particular strength on consumer goods.	Uses over 600 analysts to provide unique research on many areas. Schools often subscribe to the database.
Full-Text Newspaper and Industry Journal Databases	For-fee database	Examples are LexisNexis and Factiva.	Excellent source of insights from newspapers around the world. Schools and public libraries all have some type of online access.

3) Trade Statistics

Use these sites to answer questions such as

- Which countries import the most computers and from which countries?
- Where are the largest buyers of U.S. exports of medical equipment?
- Which country exports the most apples?
- What is the total value of U.S. imports of automobiles?

Sources	Cost	Types of Data Available	Comments
United State International Trade Commission (USITC) http://dataweb.usitc.gov/	Free	U.S. import and export data at the 10-digit harmonized code level as well as NAICS.	Similar to USA Trade Online with different functionality. U.S. trade data only.
USA Trade Online www.usatradeonline.gov/	Fee based: $25/day; $75/month; $300 year	U.S. Census Bureau version of U.S. import and export data at the 10-digit harmonized code level.	Easy to use, very current data. U.S. trade data only. U.S. Census Bureau is the official U.S. government source of U.S. trade data.
International Trade Administration (ITA) Trade Stats Express http://tse.export.gov/tse/	Free	U.S. import and export data at a broader level than above two options—good for patterns of trade.	Good source for state trade data and industry-level trade patterns.
United Nations Commodity Trade Statistics Database (UN Comtrade) http://comtrade.un.org/ http://data.un.org	Free	Offers global trade statistics (country-level imports and country-level exports) at the six-digit harmonized code.	Useful to understand trading patterns between non-U.S. countries. Both sites have the same data, but the first has a more rigorous search engine. The second is easier to use.
Global Trade Information Services, Inc. (GTI) www.gtis.com	Fee based	Offers country-level import and export data for over 50 countries, often at the 10-digit harmonized code level.	Can provide more specific data than UN Comtrade since deeper level harmonized code.

(continued)

Table 6-5 • (continued)

For trade data from non-U.S. countries, visit:

- Association of South East Asian Nations (ASEAN): www.aseansec.org/
- Canadian Data: http://strategis.ic.gc.ca/sc_mrkti/tdst/engdoc/tr_homep.html
- Caribbean Community (CARICOM): www.caricomstats.org/
- EU Europa Trade: http://europa.eu.int/comm/trade
- Free Trade Area of the Americas (FTAA): www.ftaa-alca.org/Alca_e.asp

4) Sources for Company Information

Use these sites to answer questions such as

- Which companies in France are sellers of medical equipment?
- Which companies in China manufacture children's apparel?
- What are the foreign subsidiaries of a major multinational?
- What company in Germany supplies products to a particular company in the United States?

Sources	Cost	Types of Data Available	Comments
Kompass http://kompass.com/	Fee based, but basic searching free	Worldwide directory of companies categorized by producer, importer, distributor.	Easy to use, free searching including by harmonized code; detailed company information requires subscription.
OneSource/Infogroup www.thereferencegroup.com	Fee based	Worldwide directory of companies with parent/subsidiaries linkages and financial data.	Very large company database with significant in-depth details for many entries. Searchable by SIC and other industry classification.
Alibaba www.alibaba.com/	Free	Directory of companies for a limited number of countries.	Good business-to-business platform such as finding suppliers in China.

Other sites—often available at libraries. All are private databases based on subscriptions:

- Hoovers: www.hoovers.com/
- Mergent Online: www.mergentonline.com
- D&B: www.dnb.com

Also refer to the industry sources (such as Euromonitor) because company information is also included in those sources.

Web Portals

The first websites to use in international marketing are the large mega-websites, often referred to as web portals. These sites include not only significant data and information across many countries and industries, but also links to websites for further research.

WWW.EXPORT.GOV

The Export.gov web portal is the primary Internet depository for U.S. government–sponsored reports and training to assist U.S. companies expand their exports. It is maintained by the International Trade Administration of the U.S. Department of Commerce. The site offers insights into all significant global markets and overviews of key industry sectors in which U.S. firms hold a competitive advantage. The site also links users to many other government resources such as tariff databases and assistance with export barriers. Country Commercial Guides (CCGs) for over 100 countries are published on this site. CCGs are in-depth reports discussing each country from the perspective of a U.S. firm seeking to enter that country. These reports help answer questions such as how risky a country is, how best to develop a market-entry strategy, and what the important contacts are.

WWW.FAS.USDA.GOV

The Foreign Agricultural Service site focuses exclusively on assisting food and agricultural exports expand. As with www.export.gov, the site offers insights into foreign markets and training on how to enter markets, but all within the context of food or agricultural products.

GLOBALEDGE.MSU.EDU

GlobalEdge is one of the best examples of an international marketing web portal because this one site links users to hundreds of other websites. The site is organized by areas of interest such as country, industry, or training. All the links on the site are frequently checked by Michigan State University. The site includes a glossary of international trade terms. There is also a Training Academy, which include no-cost presentation on a variety of trade topics, including international marketing, trade financing, and logistics.

Non–U.S.-Centric Websites and International Organizations

The websites described in the preceding sections are in some cases U.S. centric in that the information provided is from the perspective of a U.S. firm seeking to expand internationally. Many countries and regions have their own national/regional web portal that contains useful reports and marketing insights regardless of the home country of the firm seeking to expand. Many nongovernmental organizations also offer websites containing a wealth of information and statistics. Some relevant examples of these websites are

- **Canada:** Industry Canada (www.ic.gc.ca)
- **Japan:** Japan External Trade Organization (www.jetro.org)
- **European Commission:** Eurostat (http://epp.eurostat.ec.europa.eu)
- **OECD:** Organization for Economic Cooperation and Development (www.oecd.org)
- **UN:** United Nations (www.un.org)
- **WHO:** World Health Organization (www.who.int)
- **WTO/UNCTAD:** International Trade Centre (Geneva) (www.intracen.org/)
- **Southeast Asia:** Association of Southeast Asian Nations (www.aseansec.org)
- **Africa:** African Development Bank Group (www.afdb.org)
- **Latin America:** Inter-American Development Bank (www.iadb.org)

The preceding sites can be viewed at no cost and offer English-language versions.

A final non–U.S.-centric site to highlight is the World Bank's World Development Indicators (WDI), which offer a source of significant indicators across more than 200 countries (http://data.worldbank.org/indicator). This site is one of the most important authoritative sources for over 1,000 separate country-level measures. Many of these indicators could be used as part of an international marketing plan. They are especially helpful when creating a foreign market selection screening, as discussed in Chapter 7. The WDI data is part of a larger database of economic and demographic indicators published by the World Bank through its World dataBank portal (http://databank.worldbank.org/). Table 6-6 illustrates some of the more important indicators available from the World Bank WDI and dataBank portal.

Table 6-6 • Selected Indicators Available from the World Bank World Development Indicators Website

Adolescent fertility rate (births per 1,000 women ages 15–19)

Agricultural irrigated land (% of total agricultural land)

Agricultural land (% of land area)

Agricultural machinery, tractors per 100 sq. km of arable land

Agricultural methane emissions (% of total)

Agricultural nitrous oxide emissions (% of total)

Agriculture value added per worker (constant 2000 US$)

Agriculture, value added (% of GDP)

Air transport, registered carrier departures worldwide

Alternative and nuclear energy (% of total energy use)

Annual freshwater withdrawals, total (billion cubic meters)

Arable land (% of land area)

Average number of times firms spent in meetings with tax officials

Bank capital to assets ratio (%)

Bank nonperforming loans to total gross loans (%)

Birth rate, crude (per 1,000 people)

Births attended by skilled health staff (% of total)

Cash surplus/deficit (% of GDP)

Central government debt, total (% of GDP)

Cereal yield (kg per hectare)

Children out of school, primary, female

Children out of school, primary, male

Claims on governments, etc. (annual growth as % of M2)

Claims on private sector (annual growth as % of M2)

CO_2 emissions (kt)

CO_2 emissions (metric tons per capita)

Combustible renewables and waste (% of total energy)

Container port traffic (TEU: 20 foot equivalent units)

Contraceptive prevalence (% of women ages 15–49)

CPIA economic management cluster average (1 = low to 6 = high)

CPIA policies for social inclusion/equity cluster average (1 = low to 6 = high)

CPIA public sector management and institutions cluster average (1 = low to 6 = high)

CPIA structural policies cluster average (1 = low to 6 = high)

Credit depth of information index (0 = low to 6 = high)

Crop production index (1999–2001 = 100)

Current account balance (BoP, current US$)

Daily newspapers (per 1,000 people)

Death rate, crude (per 1,000 people)

Deposit interest rate (%)

Documents to export (number)

Documents to import (number)

Domestic credit provided by banking sector (% of GDP)

Domestic credit to private sector (% of GDP)

Ease of doing business index (1 = most business-friendly regulations)

Economically active children, female (% of female children ages 7–14)

Economically active children, male (% of male children ages 7–14)

Economically active children, study and work, female (% of female economically active children, ages 7–14)

Economically active children, study and work, male (% of male economically active children, ages 7–14)

Economically active children, total (% of children ages 7–14)

Economically active children, work only, female (% of female economically active children, ages 7–14)

Economically active children, work only, male (% of male economically active children, ages 7–14)

Electric power consumption (kWh per capita)

Employees, agriculture, female (% of female employment)

Employees, agriculture, male (% of male employment)

Employees, industry, female (% of female employment)

Employees, industry, male (% of male employment)

Employees, services, female (% of female employment)

Employees, services, male (% of male employment)

Employment in agriculture (% of total employment)

Employment to population ratio, 15+, total (%)

Energy imports, net (% of energy use)

Energy production (kt of oil equivalent)

Energy related methane emissions (% of total)

Energy related nitrous oxide emissions (% of total)

Energy use (kg of oil equivalent per capita)

Energy use (kt of oil equivalent)

Expenditure per student, primary (% of GDP per capita)

Expenditure per student, secondary (% of GDP per capita)

Expenditure per student, tertiary (% of GDP per capita)

Expense (% of GDP)

Export value index (2000 = 100)

Export volume index (2000 = 100)

Exports of goods and services (% of GDP)

External debt stocks (% of GNI)

External debt stocks, private nonguaranteed (PNG) (DOD, current US$)

External debt stocks, public and publicly guaranteed (PPG) (DOD, current US$)

External debt stocks, short-term (DOD, current US$)

External debt stocks, total (DOD, current US$)

Fertility rate, total (births per woman)

Fertilizer consumption (kilograms per hectare of arable land)

Firms using banks to finance investment (% of firms)

Fish species, threatened

Fixed broadband Internet subscribers (per 100 people)

Food production index (1999–2001 = 100)

Foreign direct investment, net inflows (BoP, current US$)

Forest area (% of land area)

Forest area (sq. km)

Fossil fuel energy consumption (% of total)

GDP (current US$)

GDP growth (annual %)

GDP per capita (current US$)

GDP per person employed (constant 1990 PPP $)

GDP per unit of energy use (constant 2005 PPP $ per kg of oil equivalent)

GEF benefits index for biodiversity (0 = no biodiversity potential to 100 = maximum)

GNI per capita, Atlas method (current US$)

GNI per capita, PPP (current international $)

GNI, Atlas method (current US$)

GNI, PPP (current international $)

Grants, excluding technical cooperation (current US$)

Gross capital formation (% of GDP)

Gross intake rate in grade 1, female (% of relevant age group)

Table 6-6 ● (continued)

Gross intake rate in grade 1, male (% of relevant age group)

Gross savings (% of GDP)

Health expenditure per capita (current US$)

Health expenditure, public (% of total health expenditure)

Health expenditure, total (% of GDP)

Highest marginal tax rate, corporate rate (%)

Highest marginal tax rate, individual (on income exceeding, US$)

Highest marginal tax rate, individual rate (%)

High-technology exports (% of manufactured exports)

High-technology exports (current US$)

Households with television (%)

IBRD loans and IDA credits (DOD, current US$)

ICT goods exports (% of total goods exports)

ICT goods imports (% total goods imports)

ICT service exports (% of service exports, BoP)

IDA resource allocation index (1 = low to 6 = high)

Immunization, DPT (% of children ages 12–23 months)

Immunization, measles (% of children ages 12–23 months)

Import value index (2000 = 100)

Import volume index (2000 = 100)

Imports of goods and services (% of GDP)

Improved sanitation facilities (% of population with access)

Improved sanitation facilities, urban (% of urban population with access)

Improved water source, rural (% of rural population with access)

Improved water source, urban (% of urban population with access)

Incidence of tuberculosis (per 100,000 people)

Income share held by fourth 20%

Income share held by highest 10%

Income share held by highest 20%

Income share held by lowest 10%

Income share held by lowest 20%

Income share held by second 20%

Income share held by third 20%

Industry, value added (% of GDP)

Inflation, consumer prices (annual %)

Inflation, GDP deflator (annual %)

Informal payments to public officials (% of firms)

Information and communication technology expenditure (% of GDP)

Interest rate spread (lending rate minus deposit rate, %)

International Internet bandwidth (bits per person)

International migrant stock, total

International voice traffic (minutes per person)

Internet users

Internet users (per 100 people)

Investment in energy with private participation (current US$)

Investment in telecoms with private participation (current US$)

Investment in transport with private participation (current US$)

Investment in water and sanitation with private participation (current US$)

ISO certification ownership (% of firms)

Labor force, total

Labor participation rate, female (% of female population ages 15+)

Labor participation rate, male (a% of male population ages 15+)

Labor participation rate, total (% of total population ages 15+)

Land area (sq. km)

Land under cereal production (hectares)

Lead time to export, median case (days)

Lead time to import, median case (days)

Lending interest rate (%)

Life expectancy at birth, total (years)

Listed domestic companies, total

Literacy rate, adult total (% of people ages 15 and above)

Literacy rate, youth female (% of females ages 15–24)

Literacy rate, youth male (% of males ages 15–24)

Literacy rate, youth total (% of people ages 15–24)

Livestock production index (1999–2001 = 100)

Logistics performance index: Overall (1 = low to 5 = high)

Long-term unemployment (% of total unemployment)

Long-term unemployment, female (% of female unemployment)

Long-term unemployment, male (% of male unemployment)

Malnutrition prevalence, weight for age (% of children under 5)

Mammal species, threatened

Marine protected areas (number)

Market capitalization of listed companies (% of GDP)

Market capitalization of listed companies (current US$)

Maternal mortality ratio (modeled estimate, per 100,000 live births)

Merchandise trade (% of GDP)

Methane emissions (kt of CO_2 equivalent)

Military expenditure (% of central government expenditure)

Military expenditure (% of GDP)

Mobile and fixed-line telephone subscribers

Mobile cellular prepaid tariff (US$ per month)

Mobile cellular subscriptions (per 100 people)

Money and quasi money growth (annual %)

Mortality rate, infant (per 1,000 live births)

Mortality rate, under 5 (per 1,000)

Motor vehicles (per 1,000 people)

Net barter terms of trade index (2000 = 100)

Net flows on external debt, long-term (NFL, current US$)

Net flows on external debt, total (NFL, current US$)

Net migration

Net ODA received (% of GNI)

Net ODA received per capita (current US$)

Net official development assistance and official aid (current US$)

Net official development assistance received (current US$)

New businesses registered (number)

Nitrous oxide emissions (thousand metric tons of CO_2 equivalent)

Organic water pollutant (BOD) emissions (kg per day)

Other greenhouse gas emissions, HFC, PFC and SF6 (thousand metric tons of CO_2 equivalent)

Out-of-pocket health expenditure (% of private expenditure on health)

Passenger cars (per 1,000 people)

Patent applications, residents

Permanent cropland (% of land area)

Persistence to last grade of primary, female (% of cohort)

Persistence to last grade of primary, male (% of cohort)

Personal computers (per 100 people)

Plant species (higher), threatened

PM10, country level (micrograms per cubic meter)

Population ages 0–14 (% of total)

Population ages 15–64 (% of total)

Population ages 65 and above (% of total)

Population covered by mobile cellular network (%)

(continued)

Table 6-6 • (continued)

Population growth (annual %)

Population in the largest city (% of urban population)

Population in urban agglomerations of more than 1 million (% of total population)

Population, female (% of total)

Population, total

Portfolio investment, equity (BoP, current US$)

Poverty gap at $1.25 a day (PPP) (%)

Poverty gap at $2 a day (PPP) (%)

Poverty gap at national poverty line (%)

Poverty gap at rural poverty line (%)

Poverty gap at urban poverty line (%)

Poverty headcount ratio at $1.25 a day (PPP) (% of population)

Poverty headcount ratio at $2 a day (PPP) (% of population)

Poverty headcount ratio at national poverty line (% of population)

Poverty headcount ratio at rural poverty line (% of rural population)

Poverty headcount ratio at urban poverty line (% of urban population)

Pregnant women receiving prenatal care (%)

Prevalence of HIV, total (% of population ages 15–49)

Primary completion rate, total (% of relevant age group)

Private credit bureau coverage (% of adults)

Progression to secondary school, female (%)

Progression to secondary school, male (%)

Proportion of seats held by women in national parliaments (%)

Public credit registry coverage (% of adults)

Public spending on education, total (% of GDP)

Public spending on education, total (% of government expenditure)

Pump price for diesel fuel (US$ per liter)

Pump price for gasoline (US$ per liter)

Pupil-teacher ratio, primary

Rail lines (total route-km)

Ratio of female to male enrollments in tertiary education

Ratio of girls to boys in primary and secondary education (%)

Real interest rate (%)

Refugee population by country or territory of origin

Renewable internal freshwater resources, total (billion cubic meters)

Repeaters, primary, female (% of female enrollment)

Repeaters, primary, male (% of male enrollment)

Research and development expenditure (% of GDP)

Researchers in R&D (per million people)

Revenue, excluding grants (% of GDP)

Rigidity of employment index (0 = less rigid to 100 = more rigid)

Risk premium on lending (prime rate minus treasury bill rate, %)

Road sector fuel consumption (% of total consumption)

Roads, paved (% of total roads)

Royalty and license fees, payments (BoP, current US$)

Royalty and license fees, receipts (BoP, current US$)

Rural population

Rural population (% of total population)

S&P Global Equity Indices (annual % change)

School enrollment, preprimary (% gross)

School enrollment, primary (% gross)

School enrollment, secondary (% gross)

School enrollment, tertiary (% gross)

Scientific and technical journal articles

Secure Internet servers (per 1 million people)

Services, etc., value added (% of GDP)

Share of women employed in the nonagricultural sector (% of total nonagricultural employment)

Start-up procedures to register a business (number)

Stocks traded, total value (% of GDP)

Stocks traded, turnover ratio (%)

Strength of legal rights index (0 = weak to 10 = strong)

Tax payments (number)

Tax revenue (% of GDP)

Technical cooperation grants (current US$)

Technicians in R&D (per million people)

Teenage mothers (% of women ages 15–19 who have had children or are currently pregnant)

Telecommunications revenue (% GDP)

Terrestrial protected areas (% of total surface area)

Terrestrial protected areas (number)

Time required to start a business (days)

Time to prepare and pay taxes (hours)

Time to resolve insolvency (years)

Total businesses registered (number)

Total debt service (% of exports of goods, services and income)

Total reserves (includes gold, current US$)

Total tax rate (% of profit)

Trade in services (% of GDP)

Trademark applications, direct nonresident

Trademark applications, direct resident

Trained teachers in primary education (% of total teachers)

Transport sector diesel fuel consumption per capita (liters)

Transport sector gasoline fuel consumption per capita (liters)

Unemployment, female (% of female labor force)

Unemployment, male (% of male labor force)

Unemployment, total (% of total labor force)

Unemployment, youth female (% of female labor force ages 15–24)

Unemployment, youth male (% of male labor force ages 15–24)

Unmet need for contraception (% of married women ages 15–49)

Urban population

Urban population (% of total)

Use of IMF credit (DOD, current US$)

Value lost due to electrical outages (% of sales)

Vehicles (per km of road)

Vulnerable employment, female (% of female employment)

Vulnerable employment, male (% of male employment)

Vulnerable employment, total (% of total employment)

Water pollution, chemical industry (% of total BOD emissions)

Water pollution, food industry (% of total BOD emissions)

Water pollution, metal industry (% of total BOD emissions)

Water pollution, paper and pulp industry (% of total BOD emissions)

Water pollution, textile industry (% of total BOD emissions)

Water pollution, wood industry (% of total BOD emissions)

Workers' remittances and compensation of employees, received (current US$)

Source: The World Bank, "World Bank Open Data Indicator Listing" (http://data.worldbank.org/indicator), accessed July 19, 2010.

Newspapers, Magazines, and Journals

Some of the most in-depth international marketing insights are from journalists, industry professionals, and academic researchers. These sources are generally written in newspapers, magazines, industry publications, and academic journals. Often these insights and research are available on the Web. Research projects should fully utilize these sources to answer specific international marketing topics. Some reports may require a fee, but their specific market or industry insights could be of particular importance to a firm as it develops its international marketing plan.

Another option to find these reports is to use any number of full-text retrieval services from online databases. An example is LexisNexis, in particular its Academic & Library Solutions (http://academic.lexisnexis.com) as well as Factiva (http://factiva.com), which is part of Dow Jones. Both offer complete versions of newspaper articles, industry reports, and academic journals from around the world. These reports can be helpful and may even offer competitive insights, such as an interview with the CEO of a company talking about its international expansion plans. Although these resources are not free, they are often available at public libraries, colleges, and universities.

Primary Research ●●●

Secondary data will not always be sufficient to fulfill all the marketing research goals. To fill in gaps unanswered through secondary sources, a firm may need to conduct primary research. Although primary data (custom data, not previously available, and obtained through primary research) is typically more expensive than secondary data (data already developed and available), its attractiveness is that primary data answers very specific questions needed to develop the international marketing strategy. Primary research is also the most likely research technique needed for qualitative data, such as color or tastes preferences.

In-House Primary Research

The primary research may be conducted in-house without contracting with an outside research firm. Examples follow.

VISITS TO POTENTIAL COUNTRIES

Staff could visit targeted markets to meet with potential customers or partners. Travel to a city or region can accomplish a lot in answering critical questions, such as competitor market share, pricing of competitive products, and distribution channel issues. Meetings could also be held with industry experts, the media, or industry associations. Government officials can also be very helpful in understanding local market conditions. For example, the U.S. Department of Commerce Foreign Commercial Service maintains consulates throughout the world, each staffed with industry experts focused on assisting U.S. companies expand into foreign markets. Other governments, from Argentina to Sweden, maintain similar offices. Leveraging these contacts can be a cost-effective way for a firm to understand issues unresolved through secondary data sources.

Trade shows can be a useful venue to conduct small primary research projects. Many trade shows have significant numbers of international visitors.

reverse trade missions

Meetings and seminars for in-bound international visitors at a trade show.

focus groups

A group of individuals gathered together to answer specific research questions.

TRADE SHOWS

A significant amount of primary research can be conducted at trade shows—even shows in the home market of a firm. Trade shows are increasingly very international in the profile of participants who exhibit and attend. The 2010 International Consumer Electronics Show (CES) in Las Vegas had nearly 25,000 international visitors as part of its total 126,641 attendees.[9] The international visitors came from more than 130 countries. Such a large international group provides an easy forum in which to meet with potential buyers and industry experts from international markets. These trade shows have become such an important venue to conduct international business that local governments in the trade show's host country arrange for **reverse trade missions**—meetings and seminars for in-bound international visitors. During the 2010 CES show, for example, the U.S. Commercial Service set up meetings between U.S. firms and international visitors to help facilitate the exports of the U.S. firms.

SURVEYS

A firm might also conduct a limited survey of potential international buyers to answer basic questions, such as current brand preferences, buying habits, or service expectations. Online survey tools make this task increasingly affordable and easy. However such ad hoc surveys should be used with care. Given the considerable cultural, technological, and communication style differences between countries, the results of these surveys are likely not statistically valid.

FOCUS GROUPS

A **focus group** is a group of individuals gathered together (by a company or by an outside contractor) to answer specific research questions. One example is a group of students being asked about their cell phone habits. Another would be a group of recent automobile purchasers being asked about their brand and quality opinions. Using focus groups is an excellent way to obtain primary research because they can be relatively inexpensive, feedback is received quickly, and very specific questions can be asked. However, international focus groups would generally require outside expertise to ensure cultural and communication issues are handled appropriately.

Outside Marketing Research

As discussed earlier, there are considerable challenges in conducting international primary research. Examples discussed were language differences, acquiescence bias, and social desirability bias. These significant challenges may dictate that a firm seek outside professional research assistance. Companies such as VNU, Arbitron Inc., and Information Resources Inc. all conduct significant international research. Each has foreign subsidiaries to assist with such projects. The majority of the income from these large research firms often is derived from outside their home country. Table 6-7 details the top market research firms as identified in the Honomichl Global 25 published by *Marketing News*.

Table 6-7 ∗ Top Market Research Firms

Rank 2005	Rank 2004	Organization	Headquarters	Parent Country	Website	Number of Countries with Subsidiaries/Branch Offices[1]	Global Research Revenue (U.S. $, in millions)[2]	Revenue from Outside Home Country (U.S. $, in millions)	Percent of Global Revenue from Outside Home Country
1	1	VNU NV	Haarlem	Netherlands	www.vnu.com	81	$3,537.9	$3,502.5*	99.0*
2	2	Taylor Nelson Sofres plc	London	U.K.	www.tns-global.com	70	1,802.7	1,513.5	84.0
3	3	IMS Health Inc.	Fairfield, Conn.	U.S.	www.imshealth.com	76	1,754.8	1,120.5	63.9
4	—	GfK AG	Nuremberg	Germany	www.gfk.com	60	1,311.3	955.9	72.9
	5	GfK Group	Nuremberg	Germany	www.gfk.com		917.3	—	—
	9	NOP World	Nuremberg	Germany	www.gfk.com		394.0	—	—
5	4	The Kantar Group	Fairfield, Conn.	U.K.	www.kantargroup.com	61	1,237.2	798*	64.5*
6	—	Ipsos Group SA	Paris	France	www.ipsos.com	44	964.6	836.2	86.7
	6	Ipsos	Paris	France	www.ipsos.com	44	871.7	—	—
	19	MORI	London	U.K.	www.ipsos-mori.com	2	92.9	—	—
7	7	Information Re-sources Inc.	Chicago	U.S.	www.infores.com	8	624.0	409	34.5
8	8	Synovate	London	U.K.	www.synovate.com	51	602.9	494.2	82.0
9	10	Westat Inc.	Rockville, Md.	U.S.	www.westat.com	1	420.4	—	—
10	11	Arbitron Inc.	New York	U.S.	www.arbitron.com	2	310.0	12.4	4.0
11	12	INTAGE Inc.**	Tokyo	Japan	www.intage.co.jp	2	261.4	1.9	0.7
12	13	Harris Interactive Inc.	Rochester, N.Y.	U.S.	www.harrisinteractive.com	4	210.5	42.5	20.2
13	14	Maritz Research	Fenton, Mo.	U.S.	www.maritzresearch.com	4	207.1	42.9	20.2
14	16	J.D. Power and Associates	Westlake Village, Calif.	U.S.	www.jdpower.com	8	198.2	46.0*	23.2*

(continued)

Table 6-7 • (continued)

Rank 2005	Rank 2004	Organization	Headquarters	Parent Country	Website	Number of Countries with Subsidiaries/Branch Offices[1]	Global Research Revenue (U.S. $, in millions)[2]	Revenue from Outside Home Country (U.S. $, in millions)	Percent of Global Revenue from Outside Home Country
15	15	Video Research Ltd.**	Tokyo	Japan	www.videor.co.jp	3	$183.0	$0.2	0.1
16	18	The NPD Group Inc.	Port Washington, N.Y.	U.S.	www.npd.com	13	161.1	32.6	20.2
17	17	Opinion Research Corp.	Princeton, N.J.	U.S.	www.opinionresearch.com	5	150.6	56.4	37.5
18	22	IBOPE Group	Sao Paulo	U.S.	www.ibope.com.br	15	82.1	18.3	22.3
19	20	Lieberman Research Worldwide	Los Angeles	U.S.	www.lrwonline.com	2	75.7	9.9	13.1
20	21	Dentsu Research Inc.	Tokyo	Japan	www.dentsuresearch.co.jp	1	61.1	0.2	0.3
21	23	Nikkei Research Inc.	Tokyo	Japan	www.nikkeiresearch.com	5	53.1	—	—
22	25	Abt Associates Inc.	Cambridge, Mass.	U.S.	www.abtassociates.com	1	52.2	—	—
23	—	comScore Networks Inc.	Reston, Va.	U.S.	www.comscore.com	3	50.5	5.6	11.1
24	—	Market Strategies Inc.	Livonia, Mich.	U.S.	www.marketstrategies.com	2	44.5	1.5	3.4
25	24	Burke Inc.	Cincinnati	U.S.	www.burke.com	1	42.8	5.7	13.3
						Total	$14,399.70	$9,711.80	67.4%

* Estimated by Top 25

** For fiscal year ending March 2006

[1] Includes countries that have subsidiaries with an equity interest or branch offices, or both

[2] Total revenue that includes nonresearch activities for some companies are significantly higher.

This information is given in the individual company profiles.

Source: "Honomichl Global Top 25," *Marketing News,* August 15, 2006, p. H4.

International market research firms can be contracted to conduct any number of marketing research projects to address a firm's needs. Generally, the projects would be used to address (1) market and competition decisions and (2) product and marketing mix decisions. For example, each of the following issues would be suitable research projects conducted through outside marketing research:

- Understanding how customers rate the company compared to the competition.
- Determining the company's chances to attract customers.
- Deciding whether to compete or cooperate with the competition.
- Choosing which products to introduce, which distribution channels to use, and how to advertise and promote the product (product and marketing mix).
- Identifying barriers to attractive markets and finding ways to overcome them.

As previously detailed in Table 6-2, the task of global marketing research is quite broad. The use of an outside market research firm can significantly contribute to completion of this task and may even play a role in helping a firm formulate its global strategy. Such research might be used to provide information and analysis on environmental trends, changes in competitive behavior and governmental regulation, and shifting consumer tastes. Most importantly, market research firms have localized knowledge to be able to tackle the primary research obstacles that might otherwise undermine the effectiveness of in-house marketing research.

SUMMARY

International marketing research is complex primarily because of the difficulty of gathering information about multiple different foreign environments. The first step is to determine what information to gather. The data would be used for critical marketing decisions such as which foreign markets to enter, how to enter, and how to market in selected markets.

The marketing environment is quite different from the domestic marketing environment. Differences exist in political structure and ideology, economic dimensions, marketing infrastructure, technology and culture, and government regulations.

As a firm develops its international marketing plan, it must standardize or adapt its products as well as its marketing mix to different country markets. The firm needs to investigate distribution channels, comparative pricing strategies and tactics, advertising and promotion choices, media availability, service and quality issues, and the impact on the firm's supply chain.

Marketing research also plays a role in developing the firm's global strategy. This research helps with defining the firm's mission, scope, and long-range objectives.

Problems in international marketing research include the availability and quality of primary and secondary data, the comparability of data on different markets, and challenges in gathering information about areas such as social organization and culture.

Quantitative techniques for market research include analysis of demand patterns, use of multiple-regression models, estimation by analogy, use of time-series approach, and use of cluster analysis.

Sources for secondary data are numerous and include web portals such as www.export.gov, as well as large, multicountry databases of comparable indicators used for international marketing research. A leading example is the World Bank's Open Data site.

Primary research is an effective method to go beyond data available through secondary sources. Firms may choose to obtain such primary data in-house, such as attending a trade show or traveling to selected markets. Alternatively, the firm may contract with market research companies. Such companies have subsidiaries in foreign countries with local experts to assist with the marketing challenges.

KEY TERMS

acquiescence bias	focus group	qualitative data	social desirability bias
cross-section comparison approach	market segmentation	quantitative data	time-series approach
	multiple-factor index	reverse trade missions	
	primary data	secondary data	

NASBITE CGBP TOPICS COVERED IN THIS CHAPTER

Note: For full details of the alignment of each chapter with the NASBITE CGBP, be sure to review the information provided in the section "Studying for the NASBITE CGBP Exam."

CGBP Rubric	Topic
01/04/01:	basic research concepts and techniques (e.g., primary vs. secondary data, basic research methodologies/processes, surveys) and data analysis/evaluation processes (statistical evaluation, quantitative and qualitative analyses)
01/04/02:	data sources for international market data (e.g., U.S. Dept. of Commerce, IMF, World Bank, UN agencies, Country Desks, and private firm data)
02/01/03:	public and private sources of data and assistance including electronic and print
02/01/07:	assessing technological infrastructures in target markets
02/01/09:	how to research competitor activities internationally (e.g., PIERS, UN Comtrade, Kompass Directory, STAT-USA, USA Trade Online)
02/02/02	public and private marketing resources (e.g., International Trade Administration, U.S. Commercial Service and the Country Commercial Guides, freight forwarders)
02/03/02:	how to find laws and regulations that impact the market selection (e.g., entity law, promotional restrictions, distributor requirements)
02/03/03:	market segmentation and demand analysis
02/06/09:	trade assistance resources in support of providing products and services
03/02/06:	databases available to search for intermediaries
03/02/07:	resources available in support of intermediary selection (e.g., WTCs, local trade associations, state and federal government)

QUESTIONS AND RESEARCH

1. Explain the following statement: International marketing research is more comprehensive than domestic marketing research.

2. Can domestic marketing research techniques be used in researching foreign markets? Explain.

3. Compare and contrast qualitative data versus quantitative data, and primary data versus secondary data. What are examples of each type of data and how might they be used in international marketing research?

4. Why is it often more difficult to get responses to marketing research in other countries than it is in the United States?

5. Explain how the economic and commercial infrastructure in a country can affect the marketing research task there.

6. Define the "data problems" in international marketing research.

7. How can international marketing researchers deal with the problems encountered in their task?

8. Give examples of the kinds of international laws that can influence a firm's international marketing.

9. Detail two methods for dealing with incomplete or old data. Show an illustration using each technique.

10. Provide two examples of sources of country-level data. Research the data for five countries. Compare the results and what they may indicate about the attractiveness of the country for international expansion.

11. Assume an exporter of medicines for veterinary use is looking for potential buyers or partners in Japan, Germany, India, and Argentina. Using the resources identified in this chapter, find potential buyers in each country. What difficulties were there in finding information on companies?

12. How should a firm decide whether to gather its own research or to buy it?

13. How could a trade show be used for primary research?

CHAPTER 6 TEAM PROJECT ASSIGNMENT: International Marketing Research and Data Sources

This chapter focused on the task of conducting international marketing and introduced important resources for secondary data research. Chapter 7 contains additional data resources that will be used for your team project.

The goal with this chapter is to begin thinking about the market research challenges for your client as it expands internationally. Firms want to know as much as possible about the markets they enter. However, as discussed in this chapter, international marketing research can be time consuming and expensive. Firms have to balance the cost of international research versus the need. For your team research from this chapter, discuss the following issues:

1. What are some key international marketing questions your firm is likely to want answered prior to entering a foreign market?

2. Of the questions raised in question 1, which could be answered through secondary data, and which would likely require primary research?

3. To identify what data is already available that will assist in your team project, visit the websites shown in Table 6-5. What reports or data are included in those sites that may be useful for your project? Discuss your findings.

4. Trade statistics are an important part of the international marketing process. You will be using trade statistics as part of your foreign market selection matrix in Chapter 7. For this chapter, visit the following website to understand their functionality:

    http://dataweb.usitc.gov/   Use this site for U.S. exports and imports.

    http://comtrade.un.org/db/   Use this site for all countries' imports and exports. (Express Selection may be easiest as a start.)

5. Classify a product sold by your client. The ten-digit Schedule B number is used for export statistics. You can find help searching for your Schedule B number at the U.S. Census website (www.census.gov/foreign-trade/schedules/b/index.html).

If your client is a service export, you'll need to search for a product used by customers of your client. For example, if your client provides financial services to banks, you could track the exports/imports of automated teller machines (ATM) under Schedule B 8472.90.1000: "Automatic teller machines."

Having found the Schedule B, use the USITC website to find the top 20 countries importing that product from the United States. Then use the first six digits of the Schedule B at the Comtrade database to find which 20 countries in the world buy the most of that product. Report your findings.

CASE 6.1 Whirlpool: The European Market

Whirlpool is a major U.S.–based appliance manufacturer. The company moved aggressively into Europe when it purchased a 53 percent interest in the Philips major home appliance line. In 1990, Whirlpool bought out the remaining 47 percent, thus obtaining a wholly owned home appliance subsidiary in Europe. However, Europe experienced a recession shortly thereafter, and European operating margins were disappointing, at 3.3 percent in 1991, about 4 percent below comparable U.S. levels. Table 6-8 presents Whirlpool sales and operating profits.

Table 6-8 ● Whirlpool Corporation Revenues ($ millions)

	1991	1990	1989
Revenues			
North America	$4,236	$4,165	$4,116
Europe	2,540	2,456	2,269
Operating Profits			
North America	326	277	311
Europe	83	73	101

Table 6-9 ● Market Share in Europe (percent)

Electrolux	19%
Bosch-Siemans	13%
Whirlpool	10%
Miele	7%
Temfa	6%
AEG	5%
Merloni	4%
General Domestic	4%
Candy	4%
Other	28%

To improve its European business, Whirlpool needed to gather additional information about the European home appliance market. Table 6-9 summarizes 1990 market share for Whirlpool and its major competitors, a useful starting point. What else is needed to develop appropriate and comprehensive plans for European marketing?

THE WISH LIST

The following represents a wish list of information that managers might find useful in preparing European marketing plans. It is based on information typically gathered in the United States.

- **The European economy.** A recovery from recession in Europe will stimulate economic activity in many fields, including the market for home appliances. Within European countries, the macroeconomic growth rates vary. Beyond the EU, growth rates in the Eastern European countries are also important.

- **Housing starts.** In the U.S. market, information on housing starts is useful in predicting the demand for major home appliances. However, given the large base of installed appliances, only about 25 percent of appliances are sold directly to builders. Whirlpool would find it useful to understand how European housing starts can help predict appliance sales.

- **Replacement demand.** Approximately 75 percent of U.S. sales are through the retail channel, representing primarily replacement sales. Brand loyalty is an important consideration in determining whether a company such as Whirlpool can increase its sales by taking away customers from competitors. Different from appliance to appliance, the length of the replacement cycle also affects when and how often the appliance is replaced.

- **Appliance-specific information.** Major home appliances include clothes washers and dryers, refrigerators, dishwashers, and kitchen ranges (stoves). This category also includes microwave ovens. On the horizon is the microwave clothes dryer. For each appliance, a different set of product features may affect market size, competition, market share, and profits. Table 6-10 summarizes the relative penetration rates for major household appliances in Europe and the United States. The market for each appliance may be growing at different rates. Each appliance has its own price point, representing high-, medium-, and low-priced appliances. Understanding how prices are evolving in a segment of the appliance market is useful to Whirlpool, helping the company decide how to price its appliances, whether to lower prices, and at what rate. Different competitors have different strengths in each area of major home appliances, and profit margins can be significantly different from appliance to appliance. Cost structure can also differ among appliances, although in general, home appliances are raw materials- and parts-intensive. About 70 percent of cost of goods sold is in materials: steel, plastics, motors, timers, and so on; another 10 percent is in labor; and the rest is in fixed overhead costs.

- **Distribution channels.** In the United States, retail sales are evenly split between Sears (33 percent), major national and regional dealers (33 percent), and smaller local shops (the remaining 33 percent). In the United States, by the early 2000s, there was a move to free retail dealers from the need to carry inventories. Instead, a retailer relays an order to the company, which ships the appliance directly to the customer within a few days. Whirlpool was experimenting with a Quality Express program that would supply customers within 48 hours. When such an innovation was tried by Shaw Industries in the carpet business, low-inventory, cut-to-order retailers took 50 percent of the distribution channel. The advantages to the manufacturer are higher margins, more information about customer preferences, and the possibility of stealing competitors' customers.

- **Competition.** The European industry is fragmented, as shown in Table 6-10. Understanding competitors' plans in areas such as price setting, cost structure, and plans for product introduction is important. Some competitors are having financial difficulties. They are experiencing problems with quality or with dealer networks who are dumping their brands on the market, representing both a threat and an opportunity. Such short-term discounting by weak competitors is relevant to setting short-term marketing responses and long-term marketing plans. Acquisitions and consolidations continue to be important in Europe. By using such information, Whirlpool can grow by "buying" market share through the acquisition of competitors that may have specific strengths; for example, a strong local brand or significant market share in one or two European countries.

Table 6-10 ◦ Appliance Market Penetration (percent)

	Europe	United States
Dishwasher	25%	54%
Range	92%	104%
Refrigerator	97%	100%
Washer	88%	75%
Dryer	18%	66%

OPPORTUNITIES IN EUROPE

European markets have the potential to grow faster than U.S. markets. The main reason is that the level of penetration of some major appliances, such as dishwashers and dryers, is far lower than in the United States (see Table 6-10). There may also be opportunities for trading up as European incomes grow, houses become more spacious and energy-efficient, and multiple features and ease of use become driving considerations in replacement purchase decisions.

However, the European market differs from the U.S. market. Design differences exist between European countries; the features that make a model a top-selling item in one country may leave customers in another country feeling quite indifferent. Currently, there are local brands specific to each country, while pan-European advertising is increasing. Whirlpool faces a special problem: ensuring that current Philips brand users switch to Whirlpool brand appliances when Whirlpool's rights to the Philips brand name end. Whirlpool's competition may not be the same company in every European country market. Whirlpool needs to design and carry out marketing research that provides the information necessary for the company to compete successfully in the more competitive EU.

Questions and Research

1. What market research information does Whirlpool typically gather in the U.S. market?

2. Should Whirlpool be gathering the same information for Europe? Explain.

3. Design a marketing research plan for the major home appliance market in Europe. Specifically, how should Whirlpool identify differences between European countries that are germane to product design and marketing mix choices?

4. Try to obtain some information you listed in your answer to question 3. What difficulties exist in gathering information about the European market?

5. Looking beyond Europe, for what other countries or regions should Whirlpool be gathering information? Why? How should it go about gathering that information?

6. Increasingly, European consumers have become concerned with environmental matters, giving rise to green parties and green products. Is this fact relevant to the marketing of home appliances? If so, how could Whirlpool incorporate environmental considerations in its marketing research? If not, explain your reasoning.

7. What success has Whirlpool had in Europe since this case was written?

8. Discuss the results of your research.

NOTES

1. World Economic Forum, *The Global Competitiveness Report 2009–2010* (www.weforum.org/en/initiatives/gcp/Global%20Competitiveness%20Report/index.htm), accessed July 20, 2010.
2. David W. Williams, "Why Do Different New Ventures Internationalize Differently? A Cognitive Model of Entrepreneurs' Internationalization Decisions" (unpublished dissertation, Georgia State University, Atlanta, Georgia, 2010).
3. World Bank Development Indicators, "Telephones per capita 2007" (databank.worldbank.org/), accessed September 19, 2010.
4. Norman Bradburn, Seymour Sudman, and Brian Wansink. *Asking Questions: The Definitive Guide to Questionnaire Design for Market Research, Political Polls, and Social and Health Questionnaires* (San Francisco: Jossey-Bass, 2004).
5. W. H. Davidson, "Market Similarity and Market Selection: Implications for International Marketing Strategy," *Journal of Business Research* 11, no. 4 (1983): 439–56; J. Johanson and J. E. Vahlne, "The Internationalization Process of the Firm—A Model of Knowledge Development and Increasing Foreign Market Commitments," *Journal of International Business Studies* 8, no. 1 (1977): 25–34.
6. K. Helsen, K. Jedidi, and W. S. DeSarbo. "A New Approach to Country Segmentation Utilizing Multinational Diffusion Patterns," *Journal of Marketing* 57 (October 1993): 60–71.
7. See, for example, Sengun Yeniyurt and Janell D. Townsend, "Does Culture Explain Acceptance of New Products in a Country? An Empirical Investigation," *International Marketing Review* 20, no. 4 (2003): 377–97.
8. S. Tamer Cavusgil, Tunga Kiyak, and Sengun Yeniyrt. "Complementary Approaches to Preliminary Foreign Market Opportunity Assessment: Country Clustering and Country Ranking," *Industrial Marketing Management* 33, (2004): 607–17.
9. Consumer Electronics Association, "Final Audit to the 2010 International CES" (http://cesweb.org/docs/Final_Audit_Summary_-_with_TWICE.pdf), accessed July 22, 2010.

chapter

7 Foreign Market Selection

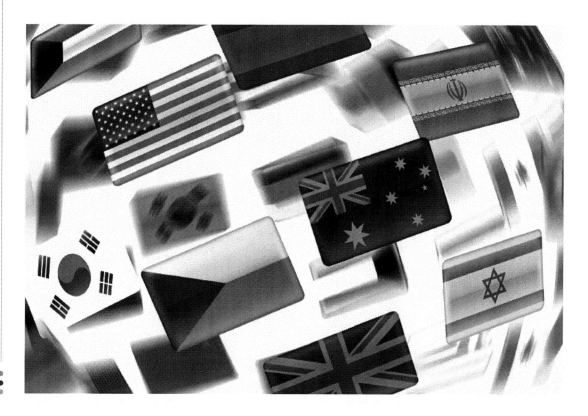

One of the most important decisions a firm will make as part of its international growth strategy is selecting which foreign markets to enter. Firms are often reactive in their foreign market selection process and follow competitors or choose markets based on "perceived" demand. A better approach is to research foreign market demand, growth opportunities, and risks to be able to rank foreign market opportunities. A firm would then set a timetable for entering those markets.

The main goals of this chapter are to •••

1. Discuss the characteristics of a country or market that would be useful indicators to predict demand for a particular product or service.

2. Identify other market conditions that would impact profitability, such as political and economic risk factors.

3. Detail a model for screening suitable foreign markets to rank market opportunities.

4. Discuss the importance of primary research in fully understanding the opportunities and risks in a foreign market.

Why Foreign Market Selection Is Critical

As a firm develops its global expansion strategy, it must address a number of issues. Identification of the firm's export readiness, adaptation of the firm's products or services for international usage, and development of country-specific marketing plans are a few examples of these issues. But all these steps may be of little help if targeted to a market that has poor demand, that is overly risky, or in which the firm is not competitive.

Developing a list of top foreign markets and ranking those opportunities would seem an obvious task for the international marketing manager. Yet, as frequently seen with both large and small companies, this is not always the case (See "When Market Selection Goes Wrong" for the examples of eBay and Amway.)

How is it that firms often get their foreign market selection wrong? The easy answer is that with so many foreign markets to choose from and with many seemingly endless opportunities (such as China or India), firms simply don't do enough research before making their decision. But a better answer is that firms are often reactive rather than proactive in their foreign market selection. Understanding the difference between a reactive and proactive foreign market selection helps highlight the role of each.

Reactive Market Selection

reactive market selection

When a firm enters a foreign market mostly based on opportunities presented to the firm or following the activities of competitors.

A **reactive market selection** is one in which a firm enters a foreign market mostly based on "reacting" to opportunities presented to the firm or following the activities of competitors. For example, an overseas distributor may approach a firm with an offer to represent the firm in the distributor's home market. If

When Market Selection Goes Wrong

The large market of China holds vast appeal for the international marketing manager. However, looking at only population or potential market size data (as will be discussed later in this chapter) can lead to selecting the wrong market. eBay and Amway found this out when each company entered China.

Despite the large market potential and fast-growing online auction market in China, eBay shut down its China operations in late 2006 after spending millions trying to establish eBay China from 2002 to 2006. eBay's current presence in China involves a joint venture with TOM Online, with TOM Online taking majority ownership (51 percent) despite eBay's funding about two-thirds of the venture. Today, analysts estimate eBay's market share in China is about 7 percent. When selecting China, eBay focused too heavily on market potential while underestimating differences in consumer preferences, political and regulatory issues, and competitors.[1]

Amway established operations in China in 1992 with the beginning of construction on a manufacturing facility to pair with its direct marketing force. Amway thought it was playing by the rules by manufacturing in China, which the Chinese government demanded as a condition for market entry. However, in 1998, the Chinese government became concerned about "pyramid" selling schemes and banned all forms of direct selling, effectively eliminating Amway from the Chinese market. Amway responded by opening retail outlets that "employed" its direct sales force. Amway continues to build its success in China but only through major, expensive, and unforeseen adaptations to its business model—specifically, local manufacturing facilities and retail outlets.[2]

the firm currently has no sales in that country, it may be persuaded to act on the distributor's offer. Similarly, a firm may become aware that its competitors have entered a particular foreign market. Not wanting to be outdone, the firm follows its competitors and enters the market. Both illustrations are examples of a reactive strategy—one in which the "market" chooses the firm rather than the firm choosing the market.

A reactive market selection may be a successful strategy. The distributor in the first example may indeed be an excellent partner for the firm, leading to strong sales in the market. Following a competitor into a market may also prove successful, especially if a firm knows it competes well with its competitors. However, a reactive market selection can also be a poor strategy due to loss of first-mover advantage and to opportunity costs, both of which mean the best country to expand to next may not be selected.

LOSS OF FIRST-MOVER ADVANTAGE

Following competitors into a foreign market means a firm's competitor is in the market first. This gives the competitor **first-mover advantage**—the advantage associated with being first to market to a particular group of consumers. Such advantages include establishing a brand, developing strong relationships with buyers, establishing expectations of consumers such as customer service or quality issues, and developing competitive market intelligence. These advantages can lead to significant barriers for firms following a competitor into a market.[3] Recent research also highlights the fact that first-mover advantages can be particularly important in emerging markets.[4]

> **first-mover advantage**
>
> The advantage associated with being first to market to a particular group of consumers, such as establishing a brand and developing strong relationships with buyers.

OPPORTUNITY COSTS

A firm generally cannot enter all possible foreign markets simultaneously. This is particularly true if the foreign market entry method involves foreign direct investment because there would be resource constraints. In any given year, a firm must add foreign markets within certain constraints—financial and human resources being two important ones. There is a limit as to how much money and time a firm can allocate to its international expansion. There is an opportunity cost associated with each foreign market entry. The opportunity cost is the potential lost revenue of entering one market over another that might have been more successful.

Proactive Market Selection

A more planned approach is to develop a list of potential markets, establish a time frame to enter the market, and incorporate those decisions into the international marketing plan. Such a process is considered proactive market selection—anticipating demand in various countries or markets and then ranking those opportunities. A firm using a proactive approach is less focused on what competitors are doing and wants to be a leader to reap first-mover advantages.

A firm with a proactive approach may still incorporate "reactive" measures. There may be changes economically, politically, or financially that were missed during the firm's initial analysis. A firm may indeed be contacted by a foreign distributor or potential buyer, and the opportunity may justify deviating from the originally planned markets. But in general, a firm should develop a list of potential markets, set a time frame for entry, and incorporate those decisions into the international marketing plan.

The following section discusses the research goals of finding suitable data to make better foreign market selection decisions. Later sections show how to incorporate this data into a decision model.

Research Goals: What Data Is Important?

Chapter 6 introduced the topic of global marketing research and data sources, which are applied here to identify and select potential international markets. A firm would want to know a number of factors about a potential foreign country before judging how attractive the country may be to enter. Generally, the concerns of a firm are potential demand, entry barriers, and market risks.

Potential Demand: Size of the Market

Estimating the market size (demand) for any given product or service is a function of various market indicators, many of which can be researched from secondary sources. The specific product or service to be sold internationally will impact the importance of each indicator. For many products and services, two types of market indicators (metrics) are particularly important: (1) population—in particular, growth rates and distribution, and (2) income, especially distribution, income per capita, and gross domestic product (GDP).

Population Indicators

People (consumers) are needed to make a market. Other things being equal, the larger the population in a country, the better the market. Of course, other things are never equal, so population figures in themselves are not usually a sufficient guide to market size. Nevertheless, the consumption of many products is correlated with population figures. For many "necessary" goods, such as pharmaceutical drugs, health-care items, some food products, and educational supplies, population figures may be a good first indicator of market potential. For other products that are low in price or that meet particular needs, population also may be a useful market indicator. Products in these second categories include soft drinks, ballpoint pens, bicycles, and cell phones.

Population figures are among the first considerations in analyzing foreign economies. One striking fact is the tremendous differences in the size of the nations of the world. The largest nation in the world has about 10,000 times the population of the smallest countries. Well over half the people of the world live in the ten countries that have populations of more than 100 million. On the other hand, as many as one-half of the countries have populations of fewer than 10 million, and more than 50 have fewer than 1 million people. (See the box "New Markets in China.")

••• New Markets in China

Many people would argue that China, with a per capita income (PPP) of less than $8,000 per year,[5] is not a good market for high-technology merchandise. As in many other nations, though, income in China is not evenly divided among its people. According to Simon Leung, chairman and chief executive of Microsoft Greater China, China is the world's second largest market for personal computers (after the United States) with a bigger market size than the combined market sizes of Britain, Japan, Germany, and India.[6]

This is good news for companies like Microsoft and for any companies targeting China for their technology products. Sim Wong Hoo is the CEO of Creative Technology of Singapore. His firm developed Prodikeys, which combines a special keyboard and software that allows people to learn to play music at the computer. The plan was to introduce the product in China first, then Japan, South Korea, Taiwan, Hong Kong, and Singapore. Originally priced at $175 per unit, the Prodikey also requires that the user have a computer with a high-end sound board and speakers. Again, given the per capita income in China, trying to sell this product there may not seem to have been the best strategy. Yet Mr. Sim relied on the projections for computer sales and the overall size of the Chinese market. He also relied on acceptance because Creative Technology developed the product in China for the Chinese, and he expected the high value placed on education to carry over into learning to play music.[7]

POPULATION GROWTH RATES

The international marketing manager must be concerned with population trends as well as the current population in a market. The reason is that many marketing decisions will be affected by future population developments. Although most countries experience some population growth, the rates among the world's richest nations are typically low.

Companies often use population as an indicator of possible demand for their product or service.

The World Bank projects that global population will exceed seven billion people by 2015, even though population growth rates are expected to decline further, to an average of 1 percent per year. The populations of high-income nations are expected to grow by an average of 0.3 percent annually, whereas low-income nations are expected to grow by approximately 1.5 percent. As the most populous nations, China and India are expected to grow at a slower rate but will still add almost 300 million people to their combined populations. Population growth rates are provided in Table 7-1. The data in the table reflects the strong correlation between level of economic development and population growth. The richer countries have more stable populations; the poorer countries are growing rapidly.

DISTRIBUTION OF POPULATION

Understanding population figures involves more than counting heads. The population figures should be classified by age group, gender, education, or occupation, for example, or in other ways that show the relevant segments of the market. Two important population characteristics are age and density.

AGE People in different stages of life have different needs and present different marketing opportunities. Many firms recognize different market segments related to age groupings. Each country has a somewhat different profile as to age groupings. Generally, however, there are two major patterns: one for developing countries and one for industrialized countries.

Table 7-1 • Population (2003, 2008), Life Expectancy, Population Growth, and Projected Population (2015)

Income Group or Country Name	Population (2003) millions (1)	Population (2008) millions (2)	Life Expectancy at Birth, Total (years) (2)	Population Growth (annual %) (2)	Population 2015 (1)
Low-income Countries	2,311.9	976.2	58.96069796	2.1	2,794.9
Lower-middle-income Countries	2,305.8	3,703.0	67.81883853	1.1	2,918.3
Upper-middle-income Countries	333.1	949.3	71.39949995	0.9	380.6
High-income Countries	887.2	1,068.7	79.80832518	0.7	1,007.0
World	6,272.5	6,697.3	68.94744707	1.2	7,100.9
China	1,280.4	1,324.7	73.12456098	0.5	1,389.5
India	1,048.6	1,140.0	63.71765854	1.3	1,231.6
United States	228.4	304.1	78.43902439	0.9	319.9
Indonesia	221.7	227.3	70.79329268	1.2	245.5
Brazil	174.5	192.0	72.40212195	1.0	201.0

(1) *Source:* World Bank, *2004 World Development Bank Indicators,* Table 2.1, "Population Dynamics," pp. 38–41.

(2) *Source:* World Data Bank, "World Development Bank Indicators and Global Development Finance" (http://databank.worldbank.org/ddp/home .do?Step=1&id=4), accessed September 3, 2010.

Developing countries are experiencing population growth, and their people have relatively short life expectancies. This means that in developing economies, there is a much greater percentage of the population in the 0–14 age group than in the 65-year or older group, whereas in developing economies, the opposite age profile may be true. The international marketing manager needs to know the age profile of a market to be able to understand the potential demand for the company's product or service and what adaptations may be required. The World Bank, Organization for Economic Cooperation and Development (OECD), and NationMaster are all good sources of a country's age segmentation. (See Chapters 2 and 6.)

DENSITY AND URBANIZATION The concentration of population is important to the marketer in evaluating distribution and communication problems. The United States, for example, had a population density of 33 people per square kilometer in 2008, which was only a small fraction of the population density in the Netherlands (487 people per square kilometer) or in Singapore (6,943 people per square kilometer).[8] Even with a modern transportation network, distribution costs in the United States are likely to be higher than in the Netherlands. Promotion is facilitated where population is concentrated, but land prices, and consequently, rent for office space, will be higher in denser markets.

Even when the density figure for a given country is used, careful interpretation is necessary. For example, Egypt is listed as having 82 people per square kilometer. That number is very misleading because Egypt's population is among the world's most concentrated, located almost entirely along the Nile River. The rest of the country is desert. Canada provides a similar example. It has a density of 4 people per square kilometer, but most of the population is concentrated in a narrow band along the U.S. border, leaving the major portion of the landmass unoccupied. In such cases, the population is more concentrated and reachable than the statistics indicate.[9]

Density is often closely linked with urbanization, the number of people living in cities rather than rural locations. Numerous cultural and economic differences exist between people in cities and people in villages or rural areas. Those differences are reflected in the attitudes of the people. Modern transportation and communication have greatly reduced the differences between urban and rural populations in the United States, but in much of the world, the urban–rural differences persist. Because these differences are important determinants of consumer behavior, the international marketing manager needs to be aware of each market's particular situation.

People living in rural communities tend to be more self-sufficient (because trading is often more difficult and time consuming). They also tend to rely more heavily on agriculture for income, rather than manufactured goods or services. Several reasons exist for the contrasting behavior of urban and rural populations. Research shows that products aimed at rural markets in developing countries require more adaptation than products sold in urban markets.[10]

Cities are the places in an economy where communications media are most developed. Cities also offer more possibilities for formal and informal education, which affect the literacy, skills, and attitudes of their inhabitants. Urbanites, therefore, tend to be less conservative and less tradition-oriented than rural dwellers. There is a stronger demonstration effect of new products and consumption patterns in urban areas, which leads to stronger markets in those locations.

The international marketing manager must study the relationship of urbanization to the consumption of the firm's product. Several factors may favor the urban markets: income and consumption patterns, distribution facilities, and communications possibilities. Cities such as Bangkok, Istanbul, and Shanghai, for example, possess a highly disproportionate share of their countries' consumption of many consumer goods.

gross domestic product (GDP)
Measure of the total domestic value created by resident producers plus any product taxes and minus any subsidies.

gross national income (GNI)
Measure of a country's wealth by summing the value added of all resident producers, plus any product taxes (less subsidies) not included in the valuation of output plus net receipts of primary income (compensation of employees and property income) from abroad.

There is a strong correlation between degree of urbanization and the level of economic development. A relationship between the level of economic development of a nation and the agrarian nature of its economy also exists. Poorer nations tend to earn more income from agriculture than rich nations.

Developing countries are generally less urbanized, especially the low-income nations. Combined with low incomes in these regions, the lack of urbanization makes these markets unattractive to many marketers of consumer goods. These poor markets are not only small, but also difficult to reach when most of the population is rural. Thus, the degree of urbanization is an indicator of the size of the market and the nature of the marketing task. Although this kind of data is especially significant for marketers of consumer goods, even companies that produce industrial goods find a correlation between their market potential and urbanization.

Income

Income is also a factor firms use when selecting markets. Wages and wealth are not related to the size of a market. Norway, Singapore, and Switzerland are wealthy but small nations, yet firms want to identify even small markets or segments of markets that are willing and able to buy their goods or services. Firms use measures of income (both at the national level and individually) to select potentially good markets, as well as to develop strategies to meet the needs of people with different incomes.

MEASURING NATIONAL INCOME: GROSS DOMESTIC PRODUCT (GDP) AND GROSS NATIONAL INCOME (GNI)

An important indicator to measure the income of a nation is gross domestic product, or GDP. As defined by the World Bank, **gross domestic product (GDP)** is a measure of the total domestic value created by resident producers plus any product taxes and minus any subsidies.[11] Essentially, the GDP measures the total market value of goods and services created by individuals and businesses within the country. It is an important indicator for the international marketing manager because a large GDP implies a large economy needing lots of goods and services. Indeed, countries with a large GDP, such as the United States, are big importers. Table 7-2 shows the countries with GDP of over $300 billion, along with each country's total imports and world share of imports. The top 15 countries on the chart alone account for over 60 percent of the worlds imports.

Directly linked to GDP is a country's gross national income, or GNI (formerly GNP). The World Bank defines **gross national income (GNI)** as the sum of value added by all resident producers, plus any product taxes (less subsidies) not included in the valuation of output, plus net receipts of primary income (compensation of employees and property income) from abroad.[12] It is the "net receipts of primary income (compensation of employees and property income) from abroad" that

Table 7-2 • Countries with Gross Domestic Product over $300 Billion

Country	GDP ($U.S. billions)* 2008	Percent of World Total GDP 2008	Total Imports 2007	Percent of World Imports 2007
United States	14,093	23.3	2,370	13.9
Japan	4,911	8.1	698	4.1
China	4,327	7.1	1,035	6.1
Germany	3,649	6.0	1,322	7.8
France	2,857	4.7	736	4.3
United Kingdom	2,674	4.4	835	4.9
Italy	2,303	3.8	618	3.6
Russian Federation	1,679	2.8	281	1.7
Spain	1,604	2.6	478	2.8
Brazil	1,575	2.6	162	1.0
Canada	1,501	2.5	468	2.8
India	1,159	1.9	291	1.7
Mexico	1,088	1.8	306	1.8
Australia	1,015	1.7	179	1.1
Korea	929	1.5	424	2.5
The Netherlands,	871	1.4	515	3.0
Turkey	735	1.2	178	1.1
Poland	528	0.9	186	1.1
Indonesia	511	0.8	110	0.6
Belgium	504	0.8	393	2.3
Switzerland	492	0.8	199	1.2
Sweden	479	0.8	203	1.2
Saudi Arabia	469	0.8	145	0.9
Norway	452	0.7	116	0.7
Austria	414	0.7	199	1.2
Greece	356	0.6	105	0.6
Denmark	341	0.6	156	0.9
Argentina	328	0.5	53	0.3
Venezuela	314	0.5	56	0.3
World	60,557	100.0	17,021	100.0

*current U.S.

Sources: World Development Bank Indicators, GDP, 2008, "Imports Goods and Services (2007)" (http://data.worldbank.org/indicator), accessed September 7, 2010.

are critical in understanding the difference between GNI and GDP because GNI reflects foreign income. GNI is GDP plus income derived from other countries, such as income or dividends, whereas GDP is the value produced strictly within the borders of a country.

In practice, the difference in a country's GDP versus GNI is not materially different for the purpose of determining market potential. For example, in 2008, the United States' GDP was $14.093 trillion and the GNI was $14.574 trillion, a difference of about 3 percent. But both figures are very large national incomes, regardless of which number is used. Further discussions in the text about national income will primarily use GDP.

MEASURING NATIONAL INCOME: WHICH EXCHANGE RATE?

Another issue in measuring income is deciding on which exchange rate to use. To analyze incomes between countries, one converts each country's income measure to a common currency so the figures are comparable. For example, Table 7-2 would be less useful in understanding relative difference in income if each country's GDP was expressed in its local currency, such as the yen for Japan. The World Bank and other data sources routinely use the U.S. dollar as a common currency. In selecting an exchange rate, the World Bank offers the **Current U.S. method**, in which the U.S. dollar figures are calculated by converting each foreign currency using a single-year official exchange rate. The World Bank also uses the **Atlas method**, which uses an exchange rate averaged over three years.

An alternate method to determine exchange rate is to use purchasing power parity (PPP).[13] **Purchasing power parity** utilizes an exchange rate that takes into account the relative difference in purchasing power between countries. Price differences can be seen in emerging economies where goods and services are generally priced lower than developed economies. For example, one would expect a U.S. dollar converted in India or Vietnam to purchase more food than a dollar would purchase in the United States or Japan. The PPP exchange rates attempt to take into account these pricing differences and more accurately reflect the "real" purchasing power in a country. As shown in Table 7-3, use of the PPP exchange rate method generally leads to a higher PPP income level for lower-income countries and a lower PPP income level for high-income countries. When conducting international marketing research, one needs to know which method was used to restate figures in a common currency.

PER CAPITA INCOME

Another measure for income in a country is the GDP **per capita income**, defined as the gross domestic product (GDP), converted to U.S. dollars, divided by the midyear population.[14] (Refer to Table 7-3.) This figure is often used as a shorthand expression for a country's level of economic development because it is commonly available and often a good indicator of the size or quality of a market.

The per capita income figures vary widely among the countries of the world. Many nations of the world have an average annual per capita income below $500, the poorest of which are in Africa (Burundi, the Democratic

Current U.S. method

Exchange rate calculation in which the U.S. dollar figures are calculated by converting each foreign currency using a single-year official exchange rate.

Atlas method

Exchange rate calculation in which the exchange rate is averaged over three years.

purchasing power parity

Calculation that utilizes an exchange rate that takes into account the relative difference in purchasing power between countries.

per capita income

A measure of income in a country where a measure of national wealth (e.g., GDP or GNI) is divided by the midyear population of that country.

Republic of Congo, and Liberia—all with an annual per capita income of less than $200 in 2008).[15] To put that amount in perspective, it takes the average Liberian one year to earn what a U.S. lawyer who charges $400 per hour earns in 30 minutes. People in high-income countries have average annual per capita income nearly 70 times that of the average person in low-income countries, with European nations being among the richest. In Luxembourg, per capita income (2008/Current U.S.) was $109,903; and in Norway, $94,759.

The World Bank categories of "upper-middle income" and "high income" nations account for 30 percent of the population, but they accounted for 85 percent of the world's GDP in 2008. This emphasizes the need for managers to not only identify those people who are willing to purchase their products, but also to recognize that potential customers must also have the ability to pay for the products. As shown in Table 7-3, per capita income may be expressed using either the current U.S. or PPP exchange rate. The PPP per capita income leads to a higher income figure for emerging countries such as China and India. (See the box "Rolls Royce Targets Major Chinese Cities.")

PURCHASING POWER NOT NECESSARILY REFLECTED IN PER CAPITA INCOME
Notwithstanding the widespread use of per capita income as a potential indicator of the attractiveness of a market, per capita income is not useful in a number of instances. As previously discussed, per capita income figures are expressed in a common currency through an exchange rate conversion. The resulting dollar figure for a country's per capita income is accurate only if the exchange rate reflects the relative domestic purchasing power of the two currencies. Use of alternate methods attempts to provide more accurate conversions, such as the Atlas and PPP methods. However, accuracy still depends on a number of interdependent factors that can be difficult to accurately quantify. Exchange rates are predominantly determined by the demand for and supply of a country's imports and exports, plus speculative demand. A country's external supply and demand have quite a different character from supply and demand within the country. Thus, it is not surprising that the external value of a currency (the exchange rate) may be different from the domestic value of that currency, all of which can undermine the accuracy of per capita income figures.

Table 7-3 • Total and Per Capita Income in 2008

Income Group or Country Name	GDP, Current U.S. (U.S. $ billions)	GDP, PPP, Current International (U.S. $ billions)	Population, Total	GDP per Capita, Current U.S. (U.S. $)	GDP per Capita PPP, Current International (U.S. $)
Low income (43 countries)	565	1,320	976,219,534	578	1,352
Lower middle income (55 countries)	8,278	17,115	3,702,965,676	2,235	4,622
Upper middle income (46 countries)	8,442	11,869	949,342,883	8,893	12,502
High income (66 countries)	43,310	39,676	1,068,725,947	40,525	37,124
World (210 countries)	60,557	69,609	6,697,254,041	9,042	10,394
China	4,327	7,909	1,324,655,000	3,267	5,971
India	1,159	3,359	1,139,964,932	1,017	2,946
United States	14,093	14,093	304,060,000	46,350	46,350
Indonesia	511	908	227,345,082	2,246	3,994
Brazil	1,575	1,978	191,971,506	8,205	10,304

Source: "World Development Bank Indicators, 2008" (http://data.worldbank.org/indicator), accessed September 7, 2010.

Rolls Royce Targets Major Chinese Cities

As discussed earlier in this chapter, total per capita income in China is less than $8,000, suggesting weak markets for luxury goods makers such as Rolls Royce. However, when one looks at the major cities of China, the per capita income numbers change dramatically due to the concentration of wealth in a few major cities. Rolls Royce has targeted this wealth with showrooms in Shanghai, Hong Kong, Beijing, Guangzhou, and Chengdu. China now ranks as the third largest market in the world for Rolls Royce, after the United States and the United Kingdom.[16]

The trend in China mirrors trends throughout the world, where the per capita incomes of major cities are growing at astronomical rates. International marketers may want to pay attention to cities that *Forbes* magazine calls "future world capitals": Shanghai, Beijing, Moscow, Mumbai, Sao Paulo, Dubai, and Perth (as well as Calgary, Houston, and Dallas in North America).[17]

The strong success of Rolls Royce in China helps show how a country's per capita income may not be a good indicator of demand.

LACK OF COMPARABILITY Another limitation of the use of per capita income figures is that there is a lack of comparability for two reasons. First, many goods entering into the national income totals of developed economies are only partially accounted for in less-developed countries. A large part of a North American's budget, for example, goes for food, clothing, and shelter. In many less-developed nations, those items may be largely self-provided and, therefore, not reflected in national income totals. Second, many goods that figure in the national income of developed nations do not figure in the national incomes of poorer countries. For example, a significant amount of U.S. national income is derived from such items as snow removal, heat for buildings and homes, pollution control, military and space expenditures, agricultural support programs, and winter vacations in Florida or other warm states. Many less-developed nations are in tropical areas, and their citizens are not necessarily poorer for not having the aforementioned items of consumption. However, their national income figure is lower because of the absence of these items.

SALES NOT RELATED TO PER CAPITA INCOME A third limitation to using per capita income figures to indicate market potential is that the sales of many goods show little correlation with per capita income. Many consumer goods sales correlate more closely with population or household figures than with per capita income. Some examples include jeans, bicycles, computers, cell phones, soft drinks, and increasingly, cars. Industrial goods and capital equipment sales generally correlate better with the size of the manufacturing sector or total national income than with per capita income. For example, the airport and office buildings in Mumbai, India, are equipped in much the same way as similar structures in London. Manufacturing facilities tend to use similar equipment wherever they are located. Where governments manage health and education programs, per capita income is not necessarily a useful guide to the national potential of goods supplied to the health and education industries.

PER CAPITA VERSUS GDP   It is helpful to contrast the GDP approach to measuring market potential with the per capita income approach. For example, in 2008, Iceland's per capita income was $52,479, and India's was $1,017. Adjusting those figures for purchasing power narrows the gap to $36,902 for Iceland and $2,946 for India. When per capita income is used alone, Iceland is over 50 times as attractive economically as India. However, that same year, India's GDP was nearly 70 times as large as Iceland's ($1,159.2 billion versus $16.6 billion), or using GDP PPP, India's GDP was nearly 300 times that of Iceland's (3,358.8 billion versus 11.7 billion). India's population is over 3,000 times as large as Iceland's (1.14 billion versus 317,414). This illustration helps demonstrate why per capita income alone is likely not an adequate indicator of a market's potential for a firm's product or service.[18]

DISTRIBUTION OF INCOME

A final way of understanding the size of a market is to look at distribution of income. Per capita income figures are averages, and they are meaningful, especially when most of the population is near the average. Frequently, however, this is not the case. Few nations have an equal distribution of income among their people, though the high-income economies are somewhat better in this respect than the other country categories. Researchers must be attentive to differences in income levels if their product is at all income sensitive.

Most countries have an uneven distribution of income. For example, the poorest 40 percent of the people in the Russian Federation account for less than 15 percent of the income generated. The richest 20 percent generate over 50 percent of the income. This pattern of uneven income distribution is common across many countries, both developed and developing. Of recent significance is the growth of the middle class in developing economies such as China and India, which is actually contributing to the challenge of income inequality. A common indicator to measure income distribution is the **Gini index**, also known as the Gini coefficient. The higher the number, the greater the income inequality. Between 2000 and 2010, the index has increased the most in China. It was estimated to reach 51.3 in 2010, up from 40.2 in 2000. Other countries showing significant increases are Indonesia, Malaysia, and India.[19]

Income inequality is a significant issue for the international marketing manager. The more skewed the distribution of income, the less meaningful the per capita income figure. The analysis of a market may require researching two economies within that market: The poor group must be studied separately from the wealthy group. One might find, for example, that the two groups are not different segments of the same market but are actually different markets. Brazil, India, and Mexico are examples of countries with sizable groups of affluent consumers living alongside a sizable segment of the population who live in poverty. As was already mentioned, income is not evenly distributed in industrial markets, either. Products designed for affluent consumers in developing nations can be marketed to these upper-income groups as well as to industrial nations. This characteristic is a major reason why firms should pay less attention to national or geographic borders and more attention to consumers' needs and desires.

Gini index

Also known as the Gini coefficient, this is a common indicator of income distribution such that the higher the number, the greater the income inequality between people in a country.

Nature of the Economy

In addition to their size and market potential, foreign economies have other characteristics, including those produced by the nation's physical endowment, the nature of their economic activity, their infrastructure, and their degree of urbanization—all of which affect a marketing program.

PHYSICAL ENDOWMENT

A nation's resources play a major role in economic development. Countries with large land mass tend to have more natural resources, both in terms of quantity and breadth. Australia, China, Russia, Canada, Mexico, and the United States are among the world's largest in terms of land mass, and they also have a wealth of natural resources. Smaller nations such as Japan must buy much of the raw materials they consume and must buy much of what goes into the production of goods and services. Although there are exceptions, generally, the richer and more diverse the endowments, the higher the country's potential for favorable economic development.

NATURAL RESOURCES

A nation's natural resources include its actual and potential forms of wealth supplied by nature—for example, minerals and water power—as well as its land area, topography, and climate. The international marketing manager needs to understand the economic geography of a nation in relation to the marketing task at hand. Land area is not typically important, except as it figures in population density and distribution problems. Local natural resources can be important to a firm in evaluating a country as a source of raw materials for local production. Significant natural resources can also be an indirect indicator of future economic prospects.

TOPOGRAPHY

The surface features of a country's land, including rivers, lakes, forests, deserts, and mountains, are its topography. These features interest the international marketing manager as they may indicate possible physical distribution problems.

Flat country generally means easy transportation by road or rail. Mountains are barriers that raise transportation costs. Mountains also may divide a nation into two or more distinct markets. For example, the Andes Mountains divide many South American countries into entirely separate areas. Although these areas are united politically, a firm often finds them to be separate markets culturally and economically. Deserts and tropical forests also separate markets and make transportation difficult. Data on the topography, population, and transportation systems may be used to anticipate marketing and logistical problems.

Navigable rivers are desirable because they enable economical transportation. The Mississippi River and the St. Lawrence Seaway are North American examples. In Europe, river and canal transportation are more important than anywhere else in the world. Even landlocked Switzerland can ship by river barge to Atlantic ports. The accessibility of a market should also be determined by its ports and harbors and contact with sea transportation.

CLIMATE

Another dimension of a nation's physical endowment is its climate, which includes not only the temperature range, but also wind, rain, snow, dryness, and humidity. The United States is very large and has great climatic variations within its borders. Smaller nations have more uniform climatic patterns. Climate is an important determinant of a firm's product offerings. An obvious example is the heater or air conditioner in an automobile. Climate also affects a whole range of consumer goods—from food to clothing and from housing to recreational supplies. Even medical needs in the Tropics are different from those in temperate zones. Extremes of climate may dictate modifications in product, packaging, or distribution. For example, electric equipment and many packaged goods need special protection in hot, humid climates. There is great international variation in climate; for example, in July, on average, New Delhi has 8 inches of rainfall, New York City has 3, and Cairo has none.[20]

Infrastructure of the Nation

A manufacturing firm generally divides its activities into two major categories: production and marketing. These operations depend on supporting facilities and services outside the firm. These external facilities and services are called the *infrastructure* of an economy. They include paved roads, railroads, energy supplies, and other communication and transport services. The commercial and financial infrastructure includes advertising agencies and media, distributive organizations, marketing research companies, and credit and banking facilities. The more adequate these services are in a country, the better a firm can perform its production and marketing tasks. Where these facilities and services are not adequate, a firm must adapt its operations (or avoid the market altogether).

When considering the potential profitability of operations in a given country, an international marketer must evaluate the infrastructure constraints as well as the market potential. As might be expected, tremendous variation exists internationally. Generally, the higher the level of economic development, the better the infrastructure. Case 7.1, "The Lifeblood of the World's Economies: Electricity," provides an indication of the variation in energy supplies available. The box titled "Infrastructure: Building Bridges to Close the Digital Divide" highlights the importance of infrastructure and its many components in the development of a truly World Wide Web as opposed to a developed-country web.

Climate is an important factor impacting what a firm sells in a foreign market. Cold climates have different product and service needs than hot, tropical climates.

ENERGY

The statistics on energy production per capita serve as a guide to market potential and to the adequacy of the local infrastructure. Marketers of electrical machinery and equipment and consumer durables are concerned about the extent of electrification throughout the market. In countries with low energy consumption, a firm will find that power is typically available only in the cities, not in the villages or countryside where most of the population lives. Energy production is also closely related to the overall industrialization of an economy and thus is correlated to the market for industrial goods there. Finally, energy production per capita is probably the best single indicator as to the adequacy of a country's overall infrastructure.

TRANSPORTATION

Transportation capabilities, infrastructure, and modes vary significantly from country to country, depending on the topography and level of economic development. The transportation infrastructure is vital to a firm that must move people, components, services, and finished goods to another country or within a nation's borders. Information on railways (miles and gauge), highways (paved and unpaved), waterways, pipelines, airports, and seaports is available from

••• Infrastructure: Building Bridges to Close the Digital Divide

For the digital divide to shrink, technology must be made available to those people who currently do not have it. There are three requirements for e-commerce to take place, whether B2B (business to business) or B2C (business to consumer): content, income, and infrastructure. All transactions require that the parties involved be willing and able to participate in the exchange process. Content (music, videos, e-mail, telephony, and information, for example) is what drives people to want to have an Internet connection; income and infrastructure are the "capability" components that enable people to participate in e-commerce. With literally billions of websites and the addition of more every hour, content exists. Its access is limited only by entities that charge for the material or by governments and other interested parties who want to protect consumers from fraud and subversive or obscene information.

Income, as previously discussed, is still very low in some nations, which means that even old technology—three- or four-year-old computers and software that may cost only $100 for a complete PC and the software necessary for an Internet connection—is beyond the reach of many, such as the average Ethiopian, who earns $900 per year. [21]

This is a small part of the picture, however, when one considers the time and money needed to build the infrastructure required to connect to other computers, the financial infrastructure that must be in place to allow people to enter into transactions on the Web (worldwide is a bit premature), and the ability to deliver manufactured goods once they are purchased.

Infrastructure at a basic level requires roads for delivering goods, computers and software, and electricity to power the connecting electronics (even if going wireless, power is needed to recharge power packs). Very often financial institutions are needed to complete a transaction—transferring funds from one account to another and sometimes supplying credit (in the form of a credit card, for example). If the parties live in different countries, banks may also provide the service of exchanging currencies. Without a commercial infrastructure, many transactions would not take place. [22]

Perhaps most important, though, is a connection to the Internet. If the industry standard remains land-connected, using traditional telephone lines, coaxial cable, or fiber optics for dedicated service line (DSL) or cable connections, large amounts of capital and labor are needed to build the infrastructure to link computers in cities and nations with the rural populations prevalent in so many areas of the world. [23] If the standard becomes wireless, scores of additional satellites and transmission towers must be built. Different compression software would also be needed to send pictures, sound, and gigabytes of other data between wireless components. [24]

There are some encouraging signs of people finding solutions to these problems. In Laos, for example, the head of the Jhai Foundation, Mr. Lee Thorn, distributed sturdy PCs that had no moving parts and cost around $400, including all the hardware and wireless capabilities needed to connect to the Internet. Farmers could check the prices they would get for their crops before making a long trek to the nearest sales office. The PCs also helped farmers make decisions about future crop allocations. [25] Even with these encouraging statistics and isolated signs of improvement, much needs to be done in terms of building infrastructure and providing the tools needed to reduce the digital divide.

the U.S. Central Intelligence Agency's *The World Factbook*. The International Institute for Management Development publishes a competitiveness ranking for 60 nations that includes a comparison of the basic infrastructure as well as scientific and technological infrastructures across nations. [26] Transportation companies and associations are other good resources for such data.

COMMUNICATIONS

In addition to being able to move its goods, a firm must be able to communicate with various audiences, especially workers, suppliers, and customers. Communications with those outside the firm depend on the communications infrastructure of the country. Intracompany communications between subsidiaries or with headquarters depend on local facilities. As discussed in Chapter 10, there are significant differences in communications infrastructure and media availability among countries. These differences will have an important impact on a firm as it expands internationally. The international marketing plan will likely need to be adapted, such as modifying the advertising strategy to reflect the market's communication infrastructure.

Market Barriers

As discussed in Chapter 2, governments establish policies to support national interests and protect their economy. As relates to government policy and trade, the commercial policy may include barriers to trade that will impact a firm seeking to enter that market. It would be important to include an analysis of these barriers when researching opportunities in foreign markets.

TARIFFS AND QUOTAS

Significant barriers are tariffs (taxes on imports) and quotas (limits on imports of specific products). Identifying them is important because they will directly affect the competitiveness of the products after a firm enters a country. Both tariffs and quotas will likely lead to higher prices paid by buyers, potentially making the products less competitive. There is less concern if all competitors are foreign, meaning all competitors will have the same level of tariffs or quotas applied. But that is not always the case. More often than not, locally supplied products will be available and not have to bear the costs of the import duties or limits on their sales due to quotas. Or, foreign competitors may be located in countries that have free trade agreements with the target countries; for example, products made in Argentina and selling in Brazil would likely have no import duties, due to Mercosur, making those products more competitive.

Tariffs and quotas can also be mitigated by selecting an entry mode that utilizes some foreign assembly or foreign manufacturing. These factors will be discussed in Chapter 8. Tariffs and quotas are also not as important for licensing arrangements because little to no products may be exported, such as a pizza company establishing a chain of restaurants in a country through licensees.

NON-TARIFF BARRIERS

Non-tariff barriers (NTBs), as discussed in Chapter 2, are another form of government trade restriction that could have an impact on the attractiveness of a country for foreign expansion. Although there are many forms of NTBs, some are more of a concern when evaluating countries. The first is product quality and safety standards. These are product-specific standards that products must meet to be legally sold in a country. Governments impose these standards as a way of protecting consumers, but they also act as barriers for some products because meeting these standards may require significant engineering or manufacturing changes. Because these changes could be costly, product standards are important considerations for a firm when selecting countries for expansion. An example is the **CE mark** in the European Union. CE marking on a product indicates the manufacturer has certified that the product conforms to safety, environmental, and other standards as prescribed in the specific standard for that product. The standards are published in directives for groups of products, such as toys or medical devices directives. Without a CE mark on a product, many items may not be sold in Europe.

> **CE mark**
> A product safety standard of the European Union.

Another NTB of significant concern is the partial or complete ban countries impose on the importation of particular products. Egypt bans the importation of chicken parts. Canada prohibits imports of fresh or processed fruits and vegetables if the packages exceed certain standard package sizes, although exceptions may be allowed. Genetically modified crops and foods have long been a contested issue among countries, with some countries prohibiting their importation. Through the World Trade Organization, governments continue to work on reconciling these product bans, but they remain a concern for affected firms. Related to the ban on products, certain services may also be restricted. China has previously had significant barriers for foreign financial and insurance services companies, although the restrictions have been considerably loosened, partly as a result of China's joining the WTO. Similar constraints and liberalization can be seen, particularly in emerging economies.

The political and economic risk of a country will have an impact on a firm's market selection strategy. A firm may avoid high-risk countries or select a foreign market entry mode that helps reduce its exposure to market risks.

A final NTB is lack of intellectual property protection in a country. As discussed in Chapter 3, if a country does not adequately protect against the theft of patents, trademarks, or other intellectual property, firms may hesitate to sell their products in that country. The risk may be high enough to take a country out of consideration for expansion. But if the potential demand is strong enough, such as in China, firms may still enter a market but take steps to further protect its intellectual property.

Market Risks

Due to political, economic, and legal differences between countries, some countries are more risky than others. As discussed in Chapter 3, these risks arise from the possibility that due to government actions, a firm's operations and profits will be adversely affected. Examples of these risks are confiscation, expropriation, nationalization, economic factors (such as inflation, currency devaluations), and political and social instability. These risks could have a significant impact on a foreign firm operating in a country and must be considered as part of a firm's marketing strategy. There are strategies to manage these risks, such as those highlighted in Table 3-2. It is also important to recognize that market risks are directly tied to foreign market entry mode. As will be discussed in Chapter 8, a firm may select an entry mode that reduces the market risks if the country is judged to be too risky. An example is direct exportation of products with no foreign direct investment in the country. This minimizes the holdings of foreign assets (inventory, buildings), which greatly reduces risks associated with international expansion in that country.

Ranking Foreign Market Opportunities ● ● ●

market screening

Means of identifying and ranking foreign market opportunities by using selection criteria to reduce the total number of countries under consideration.

With so many types of data available to help indicate potential demand for products and services, what is a reasonable way to organize the data as part of an international marketing strategy? A common technique, called **market screening**, uses a selection criteria to reduce the total number of countries or markets under consideration. Such a process reduces the global market of 200-plus countries to a more manageable list. The process may involve more than one step. For example, the initial selection criteria may include only two market indicators, perhaps population and GDP, resulting in the selection of the top 30 countries. These countries would then be further ranked based on a much more rigorous selection criterion involving multiple indicators. (The researcher, however, should always keep in mind pitfalls to using only one or two indicators, as previously discussed in the income section.) The indicators are then put into a spreadsheet, converted into a common scale (generally 1–10), weighted, and then the points calculated for each country.

Market screening would be conducted prior to in-depth market research of potential countries. The benefit of using market screening first is that it helps prioritize which countries or markets should be researched. Because in-depth research is likely time consuming and possibly expensive, it would best be conducted, on markets that appear to offer stronger demand, or fewer barriers and less risk, than other countries. Such in-depth research may ultimately include travel to the market or perhaps contracting for primary research, both of which require time and investment. Such expenditures are best if the market initially shows good potential.

Market Screening Steps

Regardless of how many rounds of market screening are conducted, the process generally involves identifying the selection criteria, researching the data and equating the results to a common measure, weighting each indicator, and reviewing the final results. These four steps are discussed in detail next.

STEP ONE: IDENTIFYING INDICATORS FOR THE SELECTION CRITERIA

The first and most important step is to develop a list of indicators that form the selection criteria. This list is critical because it has significant implications for the validity of the final outcome. If the indicators don't accurately indicate demand for the specific product or service being researched, the results will not be dependable and will be of little help in ranking foreign market opportunities. Results could be misleading and identify markets that actually have little demand.

When one is selecting potential indicators, particular effort should be put on demand indicators, as opposed to market barriers and risk. The reason is that of most importance to a firm is researching if there is significant demand for its products or services overseas and which markets hold greater potential demand than others. Market barriers and risks, such as tariffs and political risk, will influence the final marketing strategy but not play a significant role in ranking market opportunities. As previously discussed, there are methods to mitigate market risks and ways to work around market barriers. These concerns would be addressed in the international marketing plan, such as selecting an entry mode that avoids significant political risk. (There would, of course, still be some examples in which market barriers and risks would be of greater or equal significance to demand. The earlier discussion of product bans with food and agricultural products, or limitations on financial services, are good examples illustrating where market barriers or risks are critical because they otherwise would keep the foreign firm from entering the market.)

Well-performing selection criteria would incorporate five to ten market indicators. The following categories should all be considered:

* **Product-specific indicators:** Trade statistics, trade barriers, past sales.
* **Industry indicators:** Projected industry growth rates, level of competition.
* **Demand indicators:** Population, population growth rates, population density, number of households.
* **Income, political, and economic indicators:** GDP, per capita GDP, income distribution, projected GDP growth rates, political risk.
* **Nature of the economy:** Climate, natural resources, size of the country.
* **Infrastructure of the country:** Number of facilities linked to demand (manufacturers, hospitals, hotels, airports), number of paved roads, access to the Internet.

As previously discussed, an initial market scan may be done using one or two indicators to identify the 30–50 top countries. The full selection criteria of five to ten indicators would then be used for the remaining 30–50 countries. There should also be consideration of putting cities rather than just countries into the model. Some cities (Mumbai, Shanghai, or London) represent sales opportunities more significant than entire countries. However, it is often difficult to get city-level data (such as import statistics), which means data will be incomplete. City analysis may be better as part of the in-depth marketing research.

Table 7-4 highlights some tips when selecting indicators for the selection criteria.

STEP TWO: CONVERTING THE DATA INTO COMPARABLE INDICATORS

After the indicators are selected, the data for each indicator is put into a spreadsheet. The next step is to convert the data into a comparable number. For example, it would be difficult to evaluate population data for various countries against import statistics. Population is a measure of people. Imports are measured in currency. The two are not comparable.

Table 7-4 • Tips for Selecting Market Indicators

Find indicators that relate to the total size of the market: Any list of indicators must include at least one indicator that, it is hoped, predicts the total size of the market. An example for a firm that sells auto insurance would be "total number of automobiles." For a company that produces wine, the indicator might be "total population of legal drinking age." For a medical device manufacturer, it may be "total number of clinics and hospitals."

Use a single source for each indicator: Because the indicator must be comparable across all countries, the same data source should be used for all countries. This ensures the definition and measure are the same for all countries.

Incorporate trade statistics: The level of imports into a country of a specific product may be a good indicator of demand. Import statistics are particularly useful if there is not a strong local industry. For example, high-tech medical equipment is primarily manufactured in a few countries (United States, Japan, Germany, Netherlands), so the level of imports in other countries would be a good indicator of demand.

Research demand for comparable products: A firm may manufacture a product that is not specifically defined in the trade statistics and instead is classified with allied products. This could mean import statistics are misleading because they are not for the specific product. In these cases, a comparable product could be substituted. For example, refrigerated wine coolers to store wine bottles for the purpose of trade statistics are classified under the Harmonized System as HS 8418.50: "Other furniture (chests, cabinets, display counters, showcases and the like) for the storage and display, incorporating refrigerating or freezing equipment."[27] Because import statistics for 8418.50 would include lots of other unrelated refrigerators (such as retail showcases), the data would likely be misleading. Imports of wine could be substituted because consumers of wine coolers also purchase wine.

Avoid general or vague indicators; quantitative indicators are best: Indicators used for the selection criteria have to be numbers. It is problematic to use qualitative indicators because they are difficult to compare across multiple countries. "Cultural attitude toward technology" may be an important concept to a manufacturer of high-tech gadgets, but perhaps better would be "Internet users per 1000 population." Important qualitative indicators should be examined in the post-screening market research phase.

Determine foreign market entry mode: The entry mode a company is planning to use can have an important impact on the suitable indicators. Generally speaking, if a company is only exporting and does not anticipate any overseas assets, then political and economic risk indicators are not as important. However, if the entry mode will include foreign direct investment (sales office, distribution warehouse, manufacturing facility), political and economic risks are much more important.

Investigate tariff and non-tariff barriers: When considering market barriers as suitable indicators, a firm also should consider the level of local production of the particular product. If, generally speaking, most consumption of a product is imported (for example, fresh fruit in Canada, where there is some local production, but the majority is imported), market barriers are not as important.

A simple method to make the data comparable is to convert the raw data for each indicator into a scale from 1 to 10. This is done by dividing each indicator by the value of the top-performing country. The result is then multiplied by 10. An example is shown in Table 7-5, which converts data from five countries for the GNI per capita and the import statistics for HS 901812 (ultrasonic scanning apparatus). For the GNI per capita, each indicator is divided by \$35,190 because Japan has the highest per capita income among the five countries. Similarly, for the import statistics, each is divided by \$456,398,008, since China is the largest buyer of such equipment. The result for the first indicator is that Japan receives 10 points (as the top per capita income country of the list), while China receives 1.7. The 1.7 point indicator is reasonable, given the per capita income in China is only 17 percent of Japan's.

This method essentially allocates points based on the relative performance of each indicator against the top indicator. A country with 50 percent the size of the top country will get 5 points. For many indicators, this is a reasonable way to convert the data. However, if the top country is considerably larger than all other countries, the results may be very skewed. As shown in Table 7-6, if the

Table 7-5 • Converting per Capita Income and Import Data into Comparable Indicators

Country	GNI (PPP) per Capita		
	Raw Data	Formula to Convert	Result
China	$6,010	= 6010 / 35190 × 10	1.7
Colombia	$8,430	= 8430 / 35190 × 10	2.4
Japan	$35,190	= 35190 / 35190 × 10	10.0
Spain	$ 30,830	= 30830 / 35190 × 10	8.8
Thailand	$7,770	= 7770 / 35190 × 10	2.2

Country	Imports of 901812 (Ultrasonic Scanning Apparatus)		
	Raw Data	Formula to Convert	Result
China	$456,398,008	= 456398008 / 456398008 × 10	10.0
Colombia	$12,514,568	= 12514568 / 456398008 × 10	0.3
Japan	$126,861,998	= 126861998 / 456398008 × 10	2.8
Spain	$82,889,192	= 82889192 / 456398008 × 10	1.8
Thailand	$5,523,515	= 5523515 / 456398008 × 10	0.1

Sources: World Bank Development Indicators (2008), "GNI per capita, PPP (current international $)" (http://data.worldbank.org/indicator/NY.GNP.PCAP.PP.CD), accessed July 10, 2010. United Nations Commodity Trade Statistics Database (2008), "Imports of 901812 (Ultrasonic scanning apparatus)" (http://comtrade.un.org/db/dqBasicQueryResults.aspx?cc=901812&px=H3&y=2008&p=0&rg=1&so=1001), accessed July 10, 2010.

Table 7-6 • Converting Population into a Comparable Indicator

Country	Population	Formula to Convert	Result
China	1,324,655,000	= 1324655000 / 1324655000 × 10	10.0
Colombia	45,012,096	= 1139964932 / 45012096 × 10	0.3
Japan	127,704,000	= 1139964932 / 127704000 × 10	1.0
Spain	45,555,716	= 1139964932 / 45555716 × 10	0.3
Thailand	67,386,383	= 1139964932 / 227345082 × 10	0.5
Average without China	71,414,549		

Source: World Bank Development Indicators (2009), "Population, Total" (http://data.worldbank.org/ddb), accessed July 10, 2010.

same method is used for population, the result for all countries other than China is one or less. This result may seem reasonable, given the significantly larger population for China, and other indicators (such as per capita income) may mitigate this skewing. However, it may not be reasonable, depending on the product or service being researched.

An alternate approach would be to still award 10 points to China as the "outlier" but compare other countries to the average of all others. For the population example, this would mean calculating the average population of Colombia, Japan, Spain, and Thailand (which is 71,414,549) and dividing that figure into the population for the four countries. The result would then be multiplied by some factor. For example, if a factor of five is used in this example, it would result in points as follows: Colombia, 3.2; Japan, 8.9; Spain, 3.1; and Thailand, 4.7. A lower factor could be used if it is not reasonable that the results are so close to China and its 10 points. Alternatively, instead of an average, the next best-performing country could be used to set the benchmark against which the others are judged. This approach was used in Table 7-8 for the GDP indicator and total imports of video games.

A final approach is to use a five-point scale and allocate points based on judgment of the performance of each country in that indicator. The scale could be

1. Very inadequate
2. Inadequate
3. Adequate
4. Good
5. Excellent

For population, the points could then be allocated as follows: 5 points for China; 4 points for Japan; and 3 points for Colombia, Spain, and Thailand because each country represents a sizable market.

One method is not necessarily better than another. The goal is to be sure the points a country receives are in some ways relative to other countries and that the results are reasonable. The methods may also be changed after the final outcome is reviewed for reasonableness.

STEP THREE: WEIGHING EACH INDICATOR

After the indicators are converted into a comparable scale, each set of indicators would also be weighed as to their relative importance. The weight should depend on a couple of factors. First is the criticality of the indicator. If the indicator is directly related to demand, for example, it may be weighted more heavily than other indicators. Second is the accuracy and dependability of the data. An indicator that relied on suspect data or that is out of date would be left neutral (weight of 1) or even weighted below 1, which would mean points are reduced. An example is provided in Step four.

As with the method for converting data to a comparable scale, the selection of weights is a judgment call. The model may be first calculated using a neutral weight of 1 for all indicators and reviewing the resulting ranking of countries. Then one recalculates the ranking, applying weights and reviewing results. Of importance are countries that continue to rank high, regardless of the weights. This ranking indicates that these markets should be very attractive versus other countries.

STEP FOUR: ANALYZING THE RESULTS

Tables 7-8 and 7-9 show the results of a foreign market selection screening for 20 countries, along with the United States as a benchmark. The screening uses as an example a firm that manufactures video games. Table 7-8 includes the raw data for eight indicators and the resulting score for each country after converting the data to a scale of one to ten. In most cases, the first method discussed was the one used: each indicator divided by the top-performing country times 10.

In a couple of exceptions, the top indicator was set to 10, and the second-best country was also set to 10; then the value of the second country was used for all further calculations. For example, the United States and China had significantly larger GDPs than all other countries considered. Both were given 10 points, and China's GDP was used for the remaining calculations. (Per capita GDP [PPP] for Luxembourg is not shown, but was $78,921, which was the amount used for all calculations, resulting in no countries scoring 10 points.)

In reviewing the results of a market screening model, the most important point to remember is that the top-ranking country in no way indicates that, for sure, this is the first market for a firm to enter. As seen in previous discussions, the results of the model are based on decisions that potentially have a significant impact on country ranking yet may not in practice be related to final demand for a firm's product or service. Rather, top-performing countries should be seen as likely candidates for expansion, but more research will be needed.

When one looks at the results, the ranking should be matched against the current level of international experience of the firm and its international expansion goals. If the firm is relatively inexperienced and new to international expansion, it may be important to select markets that show good potential but are also attractive for factors beyond potential demand. Examples are countries that are close to the home country of the firm, countries that share a common economic trade agreement, or countries in which the culture is more aligned with the home country culture. A firm in the United Kingdom may prefer to expand to the Netherlands (which is close geographically and part of the European Union) or Australia (which is close culturally) before India, even if India shows the potential for greater sales. A U.S. firm making video games and reviewing the results in Table 7-9 is more likely to select Canada or Mexico (ranked 2 and 5, respectively) than China (ranked 1), due to membership in NAFTA, close proximity, and somewhat similar cultural connections.

Table 7-7 ● Assumptions Used in Calculating Results for Tables 7-8 and 7-9

Indicator	Weight	Reasoning
GDP (PPP)	0.5 (not important)	GDP needed to be included, but purchases of video games are more a personal decision. Even low GDP countries will have some part of the population that wants video games. A weight of 0.5 reduces the point value by 50 percent.
GDP per capita (PPP)	3.0 (critical)	Per capita income is a good differentiator between individuals who can afford video games versus a population that may want them but cannot afford them. (It would be good to also research per capita incomes of large capital cities.)
Internet subscribers	1.0 (neutral)	This number is a potentially good related indicator of demand. Data is reliable.
Number of TVs	1.0 (neutral)	This number is a potentially good related indicator of demand. Data is reliable.
Total imports (of video games)	3.0 (critical)	This number indicates level of demand for the product being researched as purchased from all countries. It is an important indicator assuming demand has been developed.
Exports from the U.S. (of video games)	3.0 (critical)	This number indicates level of demand for the product being researched as purchased from the United States. Because the United States is a strong competitor, this is also a good indicator of receptivity to U.S. video games versus those from other countries. This is an important indicator assuming demand has been developed.
Population, ages 10–29	2.0 (important)	Because this is the target population of video games, this number is quite an important indicator, and data is reliable.
Market size, toys and games	3.0 (critical)	This number shows total size of the toy and game industry. It is an excellent indicator, especially for countries that are still developing their demand for video games but have an established base of toys.

Table 7-8 • Foreign Market Selection Matrix (Video Game Manufacturer): Raw Data and Points

Country	GDP, PPP (current international U.S.$)	Points	GDP per Capita, PPP (current international U.S.$)	Points	Fixed Broadband Internet Subscribers	Points	Number of TVs	Points
Australia	$831,219,786,824	1.05	$38,784	4.91	5,140,000	0.62	10,150,000	0.25
Belgium	$377,346,412,448	0.48	$35,238	4.46	2,962,450	0.36	4,720,000	0.12
Brazil	$1,978,138,970,799	2.50	$10,304	1.31	10,097,986	1.21	36,500,000	0.91
Canada	$1,301,737,037,289	1.65	$39,078	4.95	9,842,303	1.18	21,500,000	0.54
China	$7,909,260,741,265	10.00	$5,971	0.76	83,366,000	10.00	400,000,000	10.00
France	$2,121,724,118,950	2.68	$33,058	4.19	17,691,000	2.12	34,800,000	0.87
Germany	$2,904,556,833,703	3.67	$35,374	4.48	22,600,000	2.71	51,400,000	1.29
Greece	$329,876,693,494	0.42	$29,356	3.72	1,506,614	0.18	2,540,000	0.06
India	$3,358,870,979,310	4.25	$2,946	0.37	5,280,000	0.63	63,000,000	1.58
Italy	$1,871,708,684,494	2.37	$31,283	3.96	11,283,000	1.35	30,300,000	0.76
Japan	$4,358,471,927,570	5.51	$34,129	4.32	30,107,328	3.61	86,500,000	2.16
Mexico	$1,549,489,806,853	1.96	$14,570	1.85	7,596,545	0.91	25,600,000	0.64
Netherlands	$673,634,234,114	0.85	$40,961	5.19	5,807,000	0.70	8,100,000	0.20
Russian Federation	$2,260,202,409,579	2.86	$15,923	2.02	9,280,000	1.11	60,500,000	1.51
Singapore	$238,684,793,287	0.30	$49,321	6.25	1,003,100	0.12	1,330,000	0.03
South Korea	$1,344,360,373,783	1.70	$27,658	3.50	15,474,931	1.86	15,900,000	0.40
Spain	$1,442,935,677,507	1.82	$31,674	4.01	8,995,411	1.08	16,200,000	0.41
Sweden	$340,769,813,354	0.43	$36,961	4.68	3,791,000	0.45	4,600,000	0.12
Turkey	$991,715,150,480	1.25	$13,417	1.70	5,749,891	0.69	20,900,000	0.52
United Kingdom	$2,178,205,068,968	2.75	$35,468	4.49	17,276,000	2.07	30,500,000	0.76
United States	$14,093,309,949,468	10.00	$46,350	5.87	73,123,368	8.77	219,000,000	5.48

Country	Total Imports (U.S. $)	Points	Exports from United States (U.S. $)	Points	Population, Ages 10–39	Points	Market Size, Toys & Games (U.S.$ millions)	Points
Australia	$627,547,079	1.445	$3,677,923	0.04	8,871,972	0.14	$2,963.8	3.02
Belgium	$174,970,667	0.403	$1,148,636	0.01	3,842,013	0.06	$1,130.7	1.15
Brazil	$13,524,393	0.031	$38,951,677	0.40	99,827,786	1.57	$1,603.7	1.63
Canada	$1,331,703,208	3.066	$925,760,250	9.50	13,088,302	0.21	$3,128.7	3.18
China	$321,124,738	10.000	$78,405,971	0.80	636,946,267	10.00	$9,263.8	9.42
France	$1,345,091,646	3.096	$2,498,917	0.03	24,653,472	0.39	$8,589.1	8.74
Germany	$2,468,935,000	5.684	$6,616,284	0.07	28,521,612	0.45	$5,812.4	5.91
Greece	$110,944,963	0.255	$1,714,824	0.02	4,041,250	0.06	$443.3	0.45
India	0	0.000	$669,054	0.01	600,786,093	9.43	$903.3	0.92
Italy	$385,761,160	0.888	$1,586,403	0.02	20,593,170	0.32	$4,867.1	4.95
Japan	$1,441,828,719	3.319	$18,399,381	0.19	45,309,118	0.71	$8,731.6	8.88
Mexico	$1,669,194,482	3.842	$974,491,680	10.00	57,767,529	0.91	$2,890.2	2.94
Netherlands	$2,812,178,932	6.474	$8,360,827	0.09	6,359,915	0.10	$2,326.8	2.37
Russian Federation	$75,331,360	0.173	$1,969,418	0.02	58,884,116	0.92	$785.1	0.80
Singapore	$434,702,884	1.001	$23,784,615	0.24	1,996,029	0.03	$272.7	0.28
South Korea	$71,781,689	0.165	$329,751	0.00	21,660,490	0.34	$1,060.3	1.08
Spain	$964,981,269	2.221	$624,377	0.01	18,610,941	0.29	$3,369.1	3.43
Sweden	$269,925,938	0.621	$411,641	0.00	3,405,217	0.05	$906.7	0.92
Turkey	$23,907,416	0.055	$70,878	0.00	39,340,717	0.62	$304.7	0.31
United Kingdom	$2,112,115,625	4.862	$23,122,254	0.24	24,186,259	0.38	$9,829.5	10.00
United States	$8,516,209,326	10.000	N/A	10	125,155,633	1.96	$46,923.1	10.00

Sources: GDP, GDP per capita, and Internet subscribers: World Development Indicators, World Bank, 2008 (http://databank.worldbank.org/ddp/home.do?Step=12&id=4&CNO=2), accessed August 27, 2010.
Number of TVs: NationMaster (http://www.nationmaster.com/red/graph/med_tel-media-televisions&int=-1), accessed August 27, 2010.
Total imports: UN Comtrade, Annual Imports, 2008, Commodity "950410 Video Games of a Kind Used with a Television Receiver" (http://comtrade.un.org), accessed August 27, 2010.
Exports from U.S.: USA Trade Online, Annual Exports, 2009, Commodity "9504100000 Video Games Used with TV Receiver, Parts & Access" (http://data.usatradeonline.gov), accessed August 27, 2010. *Note:* The United States would not import its own product, so data is unavailable. However, the United States is the largest importer of such products, so it is also awarded 10 points as a benchmark.
Population ages 10–39: U.S. Census Bureau, Population Division, International Data Base, 2009 (www.census.gov/ipc/www/idb/informationGateway.php), accessed August 27, 2010.
Market size toys and games: Euromonitor International Passport Reference; Toys and Games: Euromonitor from Trade Sources/National Statistics; Market Sizes, Historic Retail, Value RSP US$ mn, Current Prices, Fixed 2009 Exchange Rates (www.portal.euromonitor.com/Portal/Statistics.aspx), accessed August 27, 2010.
Note: Historic regional/global values are the aggregation of local currency country data at current prices converted into the common currency using fixed exchange rates.

Tables 7-8 and 7-9 are examples of a market screening model for a company that manufacturers video games.

Table 7-9 • Foreign Market Selection Matrix: Final Ranking (Video Game Manufacturer)

Rank	Country / Indicator	GDP, PPP (current international US$)	GDP per Capita, PPP (current international US$)	Internet Subscribers (fixed broadband)	Number of TVs	Total Imports	Exports from U.S.	Population, Ages 10–39	Market Size, Toys & Games	Total
	Weight	0.50	3.00	1.00	1.00	2.00	3.00	2.00	3.00	Points
	United States	5.00	17.62	8.77	5.48	20.00	30.00	3.93	30.00	120.80
1	China	5.00	2.27	10.00	10.00	20.00	2.41	20.00	28.27	97.96
2	Canada	0.82	14.85	1.18	0.54	6.13	28.50	0.41	9.55	61.99
3	United Kingdom	1.38	13.48	2.07	0.76	9.72	0.71	0.76	30.00	58.89
4	Japan	2.76	12.97	3.61	2.16	6.64	0.57	1.42	26.65	56.78
5	Mexico	0.98	5.54	0.91	0.64	7.68	30.00	1.81	8.82	56.39
6	France	1.34	12.57	2.12	0.87	6.19	0.08	0.77	26.21	50.16
7	Germany	1.84	13.45	2.71	1.29	11.37	0.20	0.90	17.74	49.48
8	Netherlands	0.43	15.57	0.70	0.20	12.95	0.26	0.20	7.10	37.40
9	Italy	1.18	11.89	1.35	0.76	1.78	0.05	0.65	14.85	32.51
10	Spain	0.91	12.04	1.08	0.41	4.44	0.02	0.58	10.28	29.77
11	Australia	0.53	14.74	0.62	0.25	2.89	0.11	0.28	9.05	28.47
12	India	2.12	1.12	0.63	1.58	0.00	0.02	18.86	2.76	27.09
13	Singapore	0.15	18.75	0.12	0.03	2.00	0.73	0.06	0.83	22.68
14	Sweden	0.22	14.05	0.45	0.12	1.24	0.01	0.11	2.77	18.96
15	Belgium	0.24	13.39	0.36	0.12	0.81	0.04	0.12	3.45	18.52
16	South Korea	0.85	10.51	1.86	0.40	0.33	0.01	0.68	3.24	17.87
17	Brazil	1.25	3.92	1.21	0.91	0.06	1.20	3.13	4.89	16.58
18	Russia	1.43	6.05	1.11	1.51	0.35	0.06	1.85	2.40	14.76
19	Greece	0.21	11.16	0.18	0.06	0.51	0.05	0.13	1.35	13.66
20	Turkey	0.63	5.10	0.69	0.52	0.11	0.00	1.24	0.93	9.22

In addition, the international marketing manager should evaluate key firm-specific factors regarding international market selection. For example, the firm's current networks and level of foreign market knowledge play a key role in which markets firms select.[28] Further, the ability to transfer the firm's strategy and sources of competitive advantage to a particular market are hard to quantify with numerical indicators but should be strongly considered when selecting international markets and developing the international market entry plan.[29] The key is to balance demand with firm-specific factors that should also influence foreign market selection.

Assessing Local Market Potential and Barriers • • •

After the completion of foreign market screening and selection of countries that show good potential while also matching the needs and strategy of the firm, the final step is to conduct detailed market research. The goal of the research is to confirm demand, quantify sales potential, better understand competitor activities, and identify possible risks and barriers. Some of these issues were researched in the market screening process. However, given the importance of selecting the right markets that balance risk with reward, further research will likely still be required to confirm any prior assumptions.

Primary Research and Foreign Market Selection

One option prior to making final market selections is to conduct primary research in selected foreign markets. The goal of primary research is to answer any remaining questions that need to be considered prior to confirming the market is suitable for expansion. The issues may be related to demand, such as asking potential buyers their opinion of a product or service. The issues may also be related to market barriers, such as product standards or government regulations. As first identified in Table 6-1, there are many issues of importance to the international marketing manager as the marketing plan is developed. Any of these issues may be the goal of primary research.

Often, these questions may be answered by working with trade assistance organizations, such as the U.S. Export Assistance Centers (www.export.gov), that can work with the many overseas U.S. consulates to gain better market information. They can also be answered by traveling to the market. Such travel could include meeting with potential buyers, as well as industry experts such as industry associations, government agencies, or the media.

This task may also require hiring a research firm to conduct specific primary research projects in the markets. This would be the case if detailed market knowledge is required about consumer behavior and preferences, which can really be answered only through primary research. As discussed in Chapter 6, a marketing research firm with in-country expertise would need to be used so the barriers to primary research are adequately addressed.

Further In-Depth Research

The remaining research questions may also be answered through more detailed secondary research resources. For example, any U.S. firm considering its final selection of foreign markets would want to review the "County Commercial Guides" published by the U.S. Commercial Service. These are free and available at www.export.gov. They contain very useful insights to countries, including industry analysis and market barriers.

As discussed in Chapter 6, there are also many online research databases that have very detailed industry and country analyses. For example, Euromonitor (www.euromonitor.com) has a variety of research reports, all available on demand for a fee. These reports contain very detailed analyses of a variety of industries, from consumer appliances and electronics to retailing and consumer health. As seen in Figure 7-1, the information contained in these reports is very detailed and otherwise quite difficult to find.

When the research is complete, the firm can make its final market selection decisions, including prioritizing countries and setting a timetable against the expansion. The research would also be used when developing the country-specific marketing plan.

Figure 7-1 • Euromonitor World Retail Data and Statistics—Slovakia Report

Sales in Retailing by Sector: % Value Growth 2000–2005			
% current value growth	**2004/05(%)**	**2000–05 CAGR(%)***	**2000/05 TOTAL(%)**
Grocery retailers	3.9	6.5	37.1
Non-grocery retailers	1.9	2.1	10.9
Store-based retailing	2.8	3.9	21.1
Vending	4.9	8.5	50.4
Home shopping	5.7	6.0	33.7
Internet retailing	42.1	73.6	1,478.1
Direct selling	6.4	9.1	54.6
Non-store retailing	8.4	9.4	56.4
RETAILING	**3.0**	**4.1**	**22.1**

Sales of Grocery vs. Non-Grocery Sales in Retailing 2000–2005						
% retail value rsp excl sales tax**	**2000**	**2001**	**2002**	**2003**	**2004**	**2005**
Grocery	40.6	40.3	40.1	40.0	39.9	39.7
Non-grocery	59.4	59.7	59.9	60.0	60.1	60.3
TOTAL	**100.0**	**100.0**	**100.0**	**100.0**	**100.0**	**100.0**

*CAGR: Compound annual groth rate

**rsp: retail sales price

Euromonitor Source: Official statistics (Statistical Office of Slovakia), trade associations (Slovak Chamber of Commerce & Industry), trade press (*Moderni Obchod, Slovak Spectator, Slovensky Vyber*), company research, trade interviews, Euromonitor International Estimates.

Report Source: Euromonitor World Retail Data and Statistics (www.euromonitor.com/World_Retail_Data_and_Statistics), accessed July 10, 2010.

SUMMARY

One of the most critical tasks of the international marketing manager is to develop a list of the top foreign markets, rank those opportunities, and then conduct further research to confirm demand for the firm's products or services and to better understand market risks and barriers.

Firms sometimes take a more reactive market selection approach to identifying foreign market opportunities. Following a competitor is one example. Although such a method can be fast and affordable, the firm loses first-mover advantages and other benefits related to a proactive market selection.

A more planned approach is to develop a list of potential markets, establish a time frame to enter the market, and incorporate those decisions into the international marketing plan. This proactive method anticipates demand in various countries as well as identifies risks and barriers.

When a firm is researching foreign markets, its top priorities are a market's potential demand for particular products or services, the entry barriers into that market, and local risks.

To estimate market demand, the two main areas of research for a company are (1) the size of the market and (2) the nature of the economy. Population is one of the primary indicators of market size. Two-thirds of the world's countries have fewer than ten million people and represent small markets, especially compared to China, India, or the United States. Growth rates vary widely and are generally inversely correlated with the attractiveness of a market.

The international marketing manager is concerned with the distribution of the population among different age groups with different purchasing power and consumption patterns. Population density is important for evaluating distribution and communication problems.

Markets are "people with money," so income figures on a country are necessary for market evaluation. One dimension is the distribution of income among the members of a society. Countries with a bimodal distribution of income represent dual economies with two major market segments, generally one rich and one poor. Countries with a more even distribution of income or a large middle class represent more of a mass market.

Total GDP gives an idea of the total size of a country's market and is a helpful indicator of potential for some kinds of products. Countries with a large GDP tend to also be large importers of products and services.

Per capita income is also a widely used indicator of market potential. Per capita income figures can vary, based on the method used to convert local currencies into a common currency such as the U.S. dollar. The World Bank uses the Current U.S. method, which is based on a single-year official exchange rate; the Atlas method, which uses a three-year average; and the purchasing power parity (PPP) method, which attempts to take into account pricing differences, especially between emerging and developed economies.

Actual purchasing power in many poor countries is three to eight times as high as that indicated by the per capita income figure expressed in dollars. Per capita income figures are a useful indicator of potential for some consumer goods but misleading for other consumer goods and for industrial goods.

Per capita income can also be problematic in measuring a market's potential because purchasing power may not be accurately measured, comparability between countries is difficult to determine due to differences in accounting for national income totals, actual sales potential may not indeed be linked to per capita income, and the distribution of income may be heavily varied, resulting in misleading analysis.

A country's physical endowment affects the nature of its economy. Its natural resources are one indicator of its economic potential and raw material availability. Its topography helps identify physical distribution problems and market accessibility. Its climate influences the kinds of products offered and the kinds of packaging needed.

The transportation and communication facilities in a country affect a firm's ability to get its goods to consumers and to communicate with customers, suppliers, and the home office. Energy availability affects the kinds of products that can be sold to consumer and industrial markets. A country's commercial infrastructure (ad agencies, wholesalers, etc.) constrains a firm's marketing task and capability. Generally, major differences exist between urban consumers and rural consumers. Countries differ greatly in their degree of urbanization, with the number of city dwellers declining with the level of economic development. The marketing task varies between the city and the countryside.

Market barriers of importance to the international marketing manager include tariffs, quotas, and non-tariff barriers such as product standards or product prohibitions.

Market risks of importance to the international marketing manager include political, economic, and legal risks. Such risks can be mitigated through choice of entry mode and other techniques.

A common technique to rank foreign market opportunities is market screening, which uses a selection criterion to reduce the total number of countries or markets under consideration to a more manageable list. The screening may be done in more than one step, using increasing amounts of research as the list is reduced.

Creating a market screening matrix, as demonstrated in the chapter, requires four steps: (1) identifying indicators for the selection criteria, (2) researching the indicators and then converting them into comparable indicators, (3) weighing each indicator, and (4) analyzing the results. When one is reviewing the results of a market screening model, the most important point to remember is that the top-ranking country in no way indicates that, for sure, this is the first market for a firm to enter. Rather, top-performing countries should be seen as likely candidates for expansion, but more research will be needed.

A final step in assessing local market potential and barriers is primary research, which typically includes travel to the foreign markets. It may also include contracting for a primary research project. There is also significant in-depth industry information available through marketing research firms.

KEY TERMS

Atlas method	Gini index	gross national income	per capita income
CE mark	gross domestic	(GNI)	purchasing power parity
Current U.S. method	product(GDP)	market screening	reactive market selection
first-mover advantage			

NASBITE CGBP TOPICS COVERED IN THIS CHAPTER

Note: For full details of the alignment of each chapter with the NASBITE CGBP, be sure to review the information provided in the section "Studying for the NASBITE CGBP Exam."

CGBP Rubric	Topic
01/04/01:	basic research concepts and techniques (e.g., primary vs. secondary data, basic research methodologies/processes, surveys) and data analysis/evaluation processes (statistical evaluation, quantitative and qualitative analyses)
01/04/02:	data sources for international market data (e.g., U.S. Dept. of Commerce, IMF, World Bank, UN agencies, Country Desks, and private firm data)
02/01/02:	external environment (e.g., economic and physical geography, competitive analysis, regulatory, cultural, technological issues, currency fluctuations, and protected industries and sectors)
02/01/03:	public and private sources of data and assistance including electronic and print
02/02/01:	laws and regulations that impact the marketing plan (e.g., entity law, promotional restrictions, distributor requirements, corruption)
02/02/02	public and private marketing resources (e.g., International Trade Administration, U.S. Commercial Service and the Country Commercial Guides, freight forwarders)
02/03/01:	impact on market selection of product, price, place, and promotion (the four P's)
02/03/02:	how to find laws and regulations that impact the market selection (e.g., entity law, promotional restrictions, distributor requirements)
02/03/03:	market segmentation and demand analysis
02/06/09:	trade assistance resources in support of global promotion

QUESTIONS AND RESEARCH

1. Discuss the advantages and disadvantages of using a proactive market selection strategy. What types of companies might still use a reactive strategy instead?

2. Assume a company creates software applications for the Apple iPhone. What research goals would the firm likely have to develop its international growth strategy?

3. Income is one of the most important factors a firm uses in selecting foreign markets. Discuss how income indicators would be important for a company that sells expensive clothing. How would these income indicators be different for a company that sells air conditioners?

4. What is the difference between per capita income (Current U.S.) or per capita income PPP? What is an example of a company that would likely use PPP rather than Current U.S.?

5. How does the infrastructure of a nation impact foreign market selection?

6. Describe a company in which foreign import tariffs would not be an issue in selecting foreign markets.

CHAPTER 7 TEAM PROJECT ASSIGNMENT: Foreign Market Selection

This chapter focused on the task of selecting foreign markets. It included a discussion of using selection criteria to create a market selection spreadsheet as shown in Table 7-9.

For your team research from this chapter, the goal is to create a spreadsheet for your client similar to the one in Table 7-9. Use the same steps as outlined in the chapter: (1) identify the indicators; (2) get the indicators from the data sources in Chapters 6 and 7; (3) convert into comparable indicators (Table 7-5); (4) weight each indicator; and then (5) create the final table in the format shown in Table 7-9.

When your foreign market selection matrix is complete, discuss the following issues:

1. Why did you select each indicator? What did you hope to measure?

2. Were there any indicators you wanted to use but could not find through secondary sources?

3. Explain the basis for assigning the weights to each indicator. Did you try running the model with different weights? How did it impact the final ranking?

4. Based on the final ranking, pick the top three markets you believe would be the best markets for your client. They do not necessarily need to be the top three ranking markets. Explain your decision.

CASE 7.1 The Lifeblood of the World's Economies: Electricity

Electricity is a critical part of any nation's infrastructure. Without it, people would not have computers, telephones (even wireless phones need to be recharged), televisions, and (perhaps most importantly) electric lights and refrigeration—all of which are important parts of people's lives. There is also, of course, the electricity needed to run the machines for industries. Businesses need electricity to function, so researching a nation's ability to provide electricity is important.

Consumption of electricity also gives some indication of a nation's wealth. Assuming that the electricity consumed goes toward powering appliances in homes as well as in manufacturing, the higher the consumption, the larger the middle class—those who can afford electric appliances. The following table provides some statistics on average energy use around the world. (Consider that an average energy-efficient refrigerator requires approximately 600 kilowatts of energy per year.)

These data tell only part of the story, though. In the United States and other developed nations, on rare occasions, the ability to supply electricity still does not meet local demand. On a particularly hot day, when people are running air conditioners and fans in addition to using electricity for other needs, the population may be subject to a brownout (when lightbulbs grow dim because they and other electrical devices are not getting sufficient power to run at designed levels). California, among other places, has experienced rolling blackouts, where power is available only to a specific area at certain times of the day. Total blackouts are also possible when a storm or another unexpected occurrence completely cuts power to a region.

In India, the problem of getting enough power to run trains, manufacturing plants, and home appliances is becoming severe in some areas. Power outages may last only an hour; even more common, though, are power outages that last five or ten hours (sometimes even longer). In the town of Purnea, for instance, power was out on one occasion for 34 days. Although the problems in India have existed for decades, they are becoming acute as more people can afford to purchase computers, refrigerators, televisions, and air conditioners. The shortages are blamed not only on the inability of the power companies to generate enough electricity, but also on the theft of electricity. India's then-Power Minister, Suresh Prabhakar Prabhu, estimated that half of all power generated is subsequently stolen by people who illegally tap overhead power lines. (Do not attempt this at home!)

Comparing populations and power consumption provides intriguing bases for discussions about major environmental issues facing the world. The United States has a large middle class and uses a lot of electricity. America, with a population that is one-fourth that of India, consumes more than 30 times the electricity. Access to electricity may be as high as 40 or 50 percent in urban areas of India, but available only to between 3 and 10 percent of people living in rural locations. Comparing India or China to Norway, with only five million people, is even more dramatic.

China, projecting a rapid increase in demand for electricity, built the second largest dam in the world, the Xiaolangdi Dam. It is just one of ten dams planned for the Hongshui River. Where is the largest dam? The largest dam, the Three Gorges Dam, is also located in China. Behind this dam sits a lake, created by damming the Yangtze River, that is 400 miles long and nearly 600 feet deep. The dam is capable of generating 18,200 megawatts of power. The average middle-income electric consumption is approximately 1,400 KwH per person. With a population of 1.3 billion, China would need 1,820 gigawatts (billion watts) of power to satisfy the demand of an average middle-income nation. On the bright side, the Chinese also hope that the dam will allow them to control flooding and the associated loss of life: In the last century, approximately 300,000 people died due to floods.

Across the globe in Costa Rica, the government is eager to sell electricity to neighboring countries as a source of income. As a result, it has been studying the feasibility of building a dam in the Boruca territory. The estimated yield of the plant would be 1,500 megawatts, most of which would be exported to Mexico and the United States (because Costa Rica is already meeting the demands of its population). Preliminary plans call for a dam over 800 feet tall that would result in the flooding of more than 50,000 acres. Local residents would be displaced. The property destined to be flooded is home to flora and fauna that, if not endangered, are certainly rare. Unique wildlife and plants attract tourists, and building this dam would hurt the tourism industry, one of Costa Rica's major "exports."

Although hydroelectric power is seen as a cleaner alternative than coal-burning or nuclear plants, it also presents unique problems. Flooding large tracts of land requires that many people and companies move or be displaced. If the land that is flooded contains dangerous chemicals or byproducts from industries, waste treatment plants, and abandoned vehicles (with oil and gasoline left inside), the pollutants must be cleaned or cleared; otherwise, the water will be contaminated. New water treatment plants, factories, roads, housing, and other

Annual Electric Consumption, 2007

Country or Income Group	(KwH/person)
Low income	324
Cambodia	94
Kenya	151
North Korea	764
Vietnam	728
Zimbabwe	898
Lower middle income	1310
China	2332
Guatemala	558
India	542
Indonesia	566
Ukraine	3529
Upper middle income	3052
Brazil	2171
Mexico	2036
South Africa	4986
Turkey	2238
High income	9753
Canada	16995
Germany	7184
Norway	24980
South Korea	8502
Spain	6296
United States	13652
World	2846

Sources: World Bank Development Indicators, "Electric Power Consumption (kWh per capita)," 2007 (http://databank.worldbank.org/ddp/home.do?Step=2&id=4&hActiveDimensionId=WDI_SERIES), accessed September 17, 2010.

construction must occur to take the place of the submerged properties. There is also the ecological impact of plant and animal life within the flooded region and the impact on support infrastructure (transmission towers, for example).

Whatever the solutions, as nations develop and people want more power-driven products, economic and ecological consequences will result. Companies that provide the plans for these projects and build them, as well as the firms that produce energy-consuming products (from automobiles to refrigerators), have a responsibility to take these important issues into account when they design, build, and market their products.

Sources: "China Builds Second Biggest Dam," July 1, 2001, BBC News; "China's Three Gorges Dam—Eco-Boon or Cesspool?" November 4, 1997, CNN Interactive, CNN.com, accessed August 14, 2002; "Costa Rica: Indigenous Territory Threatened by Hydroelectric Dam," World Rainforest Movement (www.wrm.org.uy/bulletin/4/CostaRica.html), accessed July 15, 2002; "Indians Can Only Wait on Government as Blackouts Strike," August 2, 2002, *Philadelphia Inquirer*, p. A21; The World Bank, Data Query, 2002 World Development Indicators (http://devdata.worldbank.org/data-query), accessed August 14, 2002; The World Bank, 2002 World Development Indicators, p. 130.

Questions and Research

1. Why would frequent brownouts or prolonged blackouts have an impact on after-sales service costs for electrically powered products?

2. How much power will India need in five years (consider current population, population growth rates, and current electricity/power consumption)?

3. How would intermittent power access like that in India and other parts of the world affect sales of electrically powered products?

4. There are vast opportunities for many companies in developing markets. What can companies do to help developing nations plan for the infrastructure needs associated with economic development? What implications does a country's electricity infrastructure have on a firm's foreign market selection strategy? Which industries would be most sensitive to electricity supply and demand issues in a country?

5. What implications does a country's electricity infrastructure have on a firm's foreign market selection strategy? Which industries would be most sensitive to electricity supply and demand issues in a country?

CASE 7.2 Unicola

Unicola is a medium-sized beverage and snack-food company based in the United States. Annual sales are $450 million. The firm has developed some special enriched beverage and snack foods that offer high nutritional value as well as convenience and refreshment. Unicola is interested in foreign markets for these new products. (Its present business is confined to the United States and Canada.) The company believes that these products should not be promoted as "health foods" but as traditional soft drinks and snacks because consumers do not like to buy products just because "they are good for you."

Because promotion is so important to the successful introduction of these products, George Horton, Unicola's advertising manager, has been looking at promotional possibilities in various foreign markets. One of these areas is Southeast Asia. His preliminary screening includes four variables: (1) newspaper circulation per capita, (2) radio receivers per capita, (3) television receivers per capita, and (4) population. The markets being investigated have already been screened on the basis of political criteria. After the political screening, the following Southeast Asian nations remain on the list for further screening on the basis of promotional possibilities: Bangladesh, Hong Kong, India, Indonesia, Malaysia, Pakistan, the Philippines, Singapore, South Korea, Sri Lanka, Taiwan, Thailand, and Vietnam.

Questions and Research

1. Prepare a table showing the scoring for these 13 countries on the four criteria suggested.

2. Which five countries would you choose as offering the best possibilities for promoting Unicola's products? Explain and defend your choices.

3. What other information would you need about these countries? How would you get it?

NOTES

1. "EBay Is Expected to Close Its Auction Site in China," *New York Times*, December 19, 2006, Section C, p. 1.

2. "Amway Learns Key Lessons on Direct-Sales Obstacle Course," *South China Morning Post (Hong Kong)*, August 13, 2002, p. 3.

3. Yigang Pan, Shaomin Li, and David K. Tse. "The Impact of Order and Mode of Market Entry on Profitability and Market Shares," *Journal of International Business Studies* 30, no. 1 (1999): 81–103.

4. Takehiko Isobe, Shinge Makino, and David B. Montgomery, "Resource Commitment, Entry Timing, and Market Performance of Foreign Direct Investments in Emerging Economies: The Case of Japanese International Joint Ventures in China," *Academy of Management Journal* 43, no. 3 (2000): 468–84.

5. World Development Bank Indicators, 2008 (http://data.worldbank.org/indicator), accessed September 7, 2010.

6. "Microsoft Steps Up Mainland Push; Partners Stand to Gain as Software Giant Plans Rollout of Flagship Products," *South China Morning Post*, August 11, 2009, p. 6.

7. "Creative to Pitch Keyboard Combo at China Market," *Business Times Singapore*, Monday, April 29, 2002.

8. World Bank Development Indicators, "Population Density (People per sq. km)," 2008 (http://databank.worldbank.org/ddp/home.do?Step = 2&id = 4&hActiveDimensionId = WDI_SERIES), accessed September 7, 2010.

9. Ibid.

10. See, for example, John S. Hill and Richard R. Still, "Effects of Urbanization on Multinational Product Planning," *Columbia Journal of World Business* (Summer 1984): 62–7. See also Martin S. Roth, "Effects of Global Market Conditions on Brand Image Customization and Brand Performance," *Journal of Advertising* 24, no. 4 (Winter 1995): 55–75.

11. Full definition of GDP (current US$) from the World Bank: "GDP at purchaser's prices is the sum of gross value added by all resident producers in the economy plus any product taxes and minus any subsidies not included in the value of the products. It is calculated without making deductions for depreciation of fabricated assets or for depletion and degradation of natural resources. Data are in current U.S. dollars. Dollar figures for GDP are converted from domestic currencies using single year official exchange rates. For a few countries where the official exchange rate does not reflect the rate effectively applied to actual foreign exchange transactions, an alternative conversion factor is used." World Bank national accounts data and OECD National Accounts data files (http://data.worldbank.org/indicator/NY.GDP.MKTP.CD), accessed July 7, 2010.

12. Full definition of GNI, Atlas method (current US$) from the World Bank: "GNI (formerly GNP) is the sum of value added by all resident producers plus any product taxes (less subsidies) not included in the valuation of output plus net receipts of primary income (compensation of employees and property income) from abroad. Data are in current U.S. dollars. GNI, calculated in national currency, is usually converted to U.S. dollars at official exchange rates for comparisons across economies, although an alternative rate is used when the official exchange rate is judged to diverge by an exceptionally large margin from the rate actually applied in international transactions. To smooth fluctuations in prices and exchange rates, a special Atlas method of conversion is used by the World Bank. This applies a conversion factor that averages the exchange rate for a given year and the two preceding years, adjusted for differences in rates of inflation between the country, and through 2000, the G-5 countries (France, Germany, Japan, the United Kingdom, and the United States). From 2001, these countries include the Euro area,

Japan, the United Kingdom, and the United States." World Bank national accounts data, and OECD National Accounts data files (http://data.worldbank.org/indicator/NY.GNP .ATLS.CD), accessed July 7, 2010.

13. World Bank definitions: "PPP GDP is gross domestic product converted to international dollars using purchasing power parity rates. An international dollar has the same purchasing power over GDP as the U.S. dollar has in the United States. GDP is the sum of gross value added by all resident producers in the economy plus any product taxes and minus any subsidies not included in the value of the products. It is calculated without making deductions for depreciation of fabricated assets or for depletion and degradation of natural resources. Data are in current international dollars. Total population is based on the de facto definition of population, which counts all residents regardless of legal status or citizenship—except for refugees not permanently settled in the country of asylum, who are generally considered part of the population of their country of origin. The values shown are midyear estimates; GDP per capita is gross domestic product divided by midyear population. GDP is the sum of gross value added by all resident producers in the economy plus any product taxes and minus any subsidies not included in the value of the products. It is calculated without making deductions for depreciation of fabricated assets or for depletion and degradation of natural resources. Data are in current U.S. dollars; GDP per capita based on purchasing power parity (PPP)." World Development Bank Indicators (http://databank.worldbank.org), accessed September 7, 2010.

14. Full definition of GNI per capita from the World Bank: "GNI per capita (formerly GNP per capita) is the gross national income, converted to U.S. dollars using the World Bank Atlas method, divided by the midyear population. GNI is the sum of value added by all resident producers plus any product taxes (less subsidies) not included in the valuation of output plus net receipts of primary income (compensation of employees and property income) from abroad. GNI, calculated in national currency, is usually converted to U.S. dollars at official exchange rates for comparisons across economies, although an alternative rate is used when the official exchange rate is judged to diverge by an exceptionally large margin from the rate actually applied in international transactions. To smooth fluctuations in prices and exchange rates, a special Atlas method of conversion is used by the World Bank. This applies a conversion factor that averages the exchange rate for a given year and the two preceding years, adjusted for differences in rates of inflation between the country, and through 2000, the G-5 countries (France, Germany, Japan, the United Kingdom, and the United States). From 2001, these countries include the Euro area, Japan, the United Kingdom, and the United States." World Bank national accounts data and OECD National Accounts data files (http://data.worldbank.org/ indicator/NY.GNP.PCAP.CD), accessed July 8, 2010.

15. World Bank Development Indicators (2008), "GNI per Capita, Atlas method (current US$)" (http://data.worldbank.org/indicator/NY.GNP.PCAP.CD), accessed July 8, 2010.

16. "Rolls Royce Expands in China," *Automotive News*, June 11, 2007, p. 36.

17. "World Capitals of the Future," *Forbes*, September 2, 2009.

18. World Bank Development Indicators (2008), "GDP per Capita (current US$)" (http://data. worldbank.org); "GDP per capita, current US$" (http://data.worldbank.org); "GDP, current US$" (http://data.worldbank.org); "Population, total" (http://data.worldbank.org), accessed July 8, 2010.

19. "Emerging Focus: Rising Middle Class in Emerging Markets," *Euromonitor Passport Reference and Markets*, March 29, 2010 (http://www.portal.euromonitor.com), accessed July 8, 2010.

20. WorldClimate, "Average Rainfall" (http://www.worldclimate.com/), accessed October 9,2010.

21. CIA *World Factbook* entry on Ethiopia (https://www.cia.gov/library/publications/the-world-factbook/geos/et.html), accessed August 25, 2010.

22. Joanne E. Oxley and Bernard Yeung, "E-Commerce Readiness: Institutional Environment and International Competitiveness," *Journal of International Business Studies* 32, no. 4 (2001): 705–23.

23. "High-Speed Internet Access; Broadband Blues," *Economist* 359, no. 8227 (June 23, 2001): 62.

24. Srilata Zaheer and Shalini Manrakhan, "Concentration and Dispersion in Global Industries: Remote Electronic Access and the Location of Economic Activities," *Journal of International Business Studies* 32, no. 4 (2001): 667–86.

25. Making the Web World-Wide," *Economist* 364, no. 8292 (September 28, 2002): 76.

26. Further details on their research and *World Competitiveness Yearbook* is at the institute's website at http://www.imd.ch/research/publications.

27. Chapter 11 discusses in more detail the Harmonized System for classifying products and its role in international trade documentation and statistics.

28. Jan Johanson and Jan-Erik Vahlne, "Business Relationship Learning and Commitment in the Internationalization Process," *Journal of International Entrepreneurship*, 1, no. 1 (2003): 83–101.

29. Denis A. Grégoire, David W. Williams, and Benjamin M. Oviatt. "Early Internationalization Decisions for New Ventures: What Matters?" In A. Zacharakis et al. (eds.), *Frontiers of Entrepreneurship Research 2008* (Babson Park, MA: Babson College) (http://www.babson.edu/ entrep/fer/2008FER/chapter_18/paper_xviii_2.html), accessed October 9, 2010.

8 Foreign Market Entry, Partner Selection, and Distribution

After a firm chooses which markets to enter abroad, the question arises as to the best way to enter those markets. This chapter presents the major entry methods and the criteria for selecting them. Once in a market, a firm also must identify and manage the internal distribution channels to ensure that its products are delivered when and where they are needed. This chapter discusses techniques for finding partners and managing foreign channels.

The main goals of this chapter are to •••

1. Understand how the foreign market entry mode selected by a firm will vary by market, industry, maturity of the firm, and other issues specific to the firm and market.

2. Explore types of indirect exporting, including piggybacking, and provide information on the role of selected export intermediaries.

3. Discuss the advantages and disadvantages of direct exporting, contract manufacturing, licensing, joint ventures, and wholly owned operations as ways of entering foreign markets.

4. Discuss ways in which wholesalers and retailers differ internationally, requiring adjustment by the international marketer.

5. Identify methods to find suitable foreign partners and how to motivate them to be successful marketing partners.

How to Enter Foreign Markets

A firm has a number of options on how to enter a particular foreign market. Some entry modes require little to no direct contact with the foreign market, such as indirect exporting. Other modes require more sustentative interaction with the foreign market, but no overseas employees or offices. The entry mode may or may not involve foreign manufacturing. In selecting the entry mode, the firm must balance its needs (market control, financial, management) with those of the market and consumers.

Market Entry Modes Defined

The range of alternatives is wide enough that almost any company in any product or service area can find an appropriate way to reach foreign markets. The nature of entry ranges from indirect exporting to wholly owned production in foreign markets. When one is contrasting entry modes, it is useful to distinguish those entry modes that involve foreign direct investment as opposed to those that do not, and likewise, those that keep production in the home market versus those that utilize some form of foreign production. (See Figure 8-1 for selected major methods of market entry.)

Before exploring these alternatives, a firm should consider management expertise and desired level of involvement and control in the market. The higher the expertise and/or the more important the market is in relation to other global markets, the more direct the level of involvement and the greater likelihood some foreign direct investment may be required.

Decision Criteria for Market Entry Method

Selection of the method of entry to foreign markets depends on factors specific to the firm and its industry. Highlights include

- Company goals and global strategy regarding the volume of international business desired, geographic coverage, and the time frame for expansion.
- Size of the company in sales and assets.
- Prior international experience of the firm and personnel.
- Risk tolerance (entry modes vary in the amount of risk).
- Financial and management resources available toward international expansion.
- Product line and the nature of the products (industrial or consumer, high or low price, technological content).
- Level of competition in a particular market.

Figure 8-1 • Entry Mode Strategies

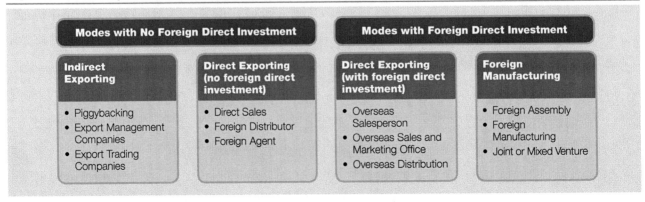

Other criteria also affect the choice of entry method. Some are industry-specific (for example, power generation) and therefore require some form of financial investment that is typically substantial. At times, the choice of entry mode is also dependent on the geographic environment and the potential market's level of economic development.[1,2] Following are further considerations of the firm.

EXPANDING TO MULTIPLE FOREIGN MARKETS

Most firms will seek to expand to more than one foreign market. To obtain the international market coverage it wants, a firm may have to combine different entry methods. In some markets, it may have wholly owned operations; in others, marketing subsidiaries; and in yet others, local distributors served by direct exporting. Different entry methods offer markedly different results in market risks and rewards. For example, wholly owned foreign operations are not permitted in some countries, licensing may be impossible in other markets because a firm cannot find qualified licensees, or a trading company might cover certain markets quite well but have no representation in other markets. A firm should not assume that it will select the same entry mode for all markets it enters.

MARKET FEEDBACK REQUIREMENTS

To be competitive, a firm may need to know what is going on in its foreign markets. In other circumstances, a firm may be satisfied with less-direct market feedback, relying on intermediaries instead. A firm must choose an entry mode that matches its need for market feedback. The more-direct entry mode generally offer better market information. Foreign direct investment should also enhance market feedback.

Foreign market entry mode is sometimes dictated by industry. For example, companies in power generation are likely to use some type of foreign direct investment given the capital needs of power generation.

CONTROL

Management control over foreign marketing ranges from none at all—for example, selling through a trading company— to complete control, as in a wholly owned subsidiary. A firm may want a voice in its foreign marketing, such as pricing and credit terms, promotion, and servicing of its products. The extent to which such control is critical to a firm bears heavily on the firm's choice of entry method.

INCREMENTAL MARKETING COSTS

Costs are associated with international marketing, no matter who does it. However, a producer's incremental marketing outlays and working capital requirements vary with the directness of the channel. For example, with indirect exporting, a producer has practically no additional outlays.

INVESTMENT REQUIREMENTS

Investment requirements are highest in wholly owned foreign operations. Plant investment, however, is not the only consideration. Capital also may be required to finance inventories and to extend credit. A sales, marketing, and distribution center overseas would require capital to purchase or lease office space and required equipment and infrastructure. Because the amount of capital required varies greatly by method of entry, this financial need can be an important determinant of what entry method a firm selects.

ADMINISTRATIVE REQUIREMENTS

The administrative burdens and costs of international marketing vary by entry method. They include documentation and red tape, as well as management time. For example, indirect exporting or licensing may involve little additional burden on management.

PERSONNEL REQUIREMENTS

Personnel needs also vary by market entry mode. Generally, the more-direct kinds of involvement require a number of skilled international personnel. If a firm is short of "internationalists," it is constrained in its alternatives.

LEGAL AND POLITICAL ENVIRONMENT

The more directly a firm is involved in foreign markets, the more management must deal with new kinds of legislation, regulation, taxes, labor problems, and other foreign market peculiarities. If a firm is unable or unwilling to deal with those problems, it must choose an entry method that lets someone else handle them.

RISK

Foreign markets are usually perceived as being riskier than domestic markets. The amount of risk a firm faces is not only a function of the market, but also of the firm's method of involvement in that market. In addition to its capital investment, a firm risks inventories and receivables. A firm must perform a risk analysis of the market and its method of entry. Exchange rate risk is another variable, as discussed in Chapters 2 and 12.

Besides economic risks, there are also political risks. A firm's political vulnerability may differ from market to market. The firm's level of involvement is one factor in that variability. Generally, the more direct and visible the entry, the more vulnerable a firm is politically. (See "Edible Arrangements: A Fresh Taste Goes Global.")

Aligning Entry Mode with Internal and External Factors

Before selecting an entry mode, the firm must evaluate internal and external factors. The internal factors will likely influence the overall international strategy of the firm and be less country-specific. External factors will be global and country-specific.

INTERNAL FACTORS

The firm must first address internal issues that will affect its selection of entry mode. A top consideration is the company's export readiness: the organization's ability to conduct international trade. This includes experience of management, prior experience producing and marketing international products or services, the overall commitment of management to international expansion, and financial strength. Two types of knowledge strongly influence a firm's export readiness and entry mode decisions: foreign market knowledge and internationalization process knowledge (i.e., how to internationalize). Firms without these types of knowledge face great uncertainty when expanding internationally. Therefore, research shows that firms with less knowledge select less committed entry modes (e.g., indirect modes) and progressively select more committed modes (e.g., foreign direct investment) as the firm decreases uncertainty by gaining foreign market knowledge and internationalization process knowledge.[3, 4] Accordingly, a firm with relatively low export readiness would be much more likely to utilize indirect exporting or direct exporting without foreign direct investment. A firm with higher export readiness would not be as limited in its entry mode selection. Clearly, a larger, experienced multinational firm would be less likely to use indirect exporting and more inclined to embrace foreign direct investment as it enters new markets. The firm's international expansion strategy would also impact its entry mode selection. This would include issues such as how fast the company wants to grow internationally and its market share goals.

The level of economic and political risk in a market may affect a firm's selection of entry mode to help mitigate that risk.

••• Edible Arrangements: A Fresh Taste Goes Global

Brothers Tariq Farid (CEO) and Kamran Farid (COO) founded Edible Arrangements with a single store in East Haven, Connecticut, in 1999. Two years later, they opened a second store. By 2010, Edible Arrangements had 958 locations worldwide with locations in the United States, Asia, Europe, and the Middle East. The firm also received numerous accolades from the public press including awards from both *INC* and *Entrepreneur* magazines.

Edible Arrangements opened its first international location in 2003 in Toronto, Canada. Three years later, in 2006, the company expanded to Nottingham, U.K., for its first international expansion outside the United States and Canada. Then, in 2007, Edible Arrangements opened a location in Dubai. Italy and Hong Kong followed in 2009 and 2010, respectively.

When reviewing the internal and external conditions influencing Edible Arrangements, the international marketing manager can better understand why the firm uses direct entry modes and partnerships to expand internationally. First, it is clear that the company's business model required some level of control, especially over product quality to ensure the "wow" effect for each and every customer. Second, the firm was growing fast in the United States, requiring additional financing and taking up significant management time and attention that limited the time, energy, and resources available for international expansion. Third, each store can serve only a limited geographic market to be able to maintain the product's freshness, suggesting that many stores are required for expanded market coverage. Finally, risks increased as the firm expanded beyond markets with similar language, culture, political, and legal systems.

According to the Edible Arrangement's website, the firm operates its U.S., Puerto Rico, Canada, and U.K. operations directly from the corporate office in the United States. These culturally similar and economically developed markets have minimal risk and demand less time and attention from management and fewer specialized personnel.

However, as the firm expanded beyond these markets, it looked to local partners to help develop these new international markets. The further the firm expanded culturally from the United States, the greater the firm's need for partners, especially in markets with different legal and political systems. This explains why Edible Arrangements signed an exclusive partnership agreement with Al Braik Investment LLC of Dubai for all Edible Arrangement locations in the United Arab Emirates and uses partnerships for its locations throughout the Middle East.[5]

EXTERNAL FACTORS

The firm must equally evaluate external factors, starting with its competitive position. A firm that already dominates in its home market would be in a much stronger position to pursue a more aggressive entry mode when expanding internationally. Similarly, a strong brand that already has some global recognition would justify a more aggressive entry mode. "More aggressive" in this context means the greater likelihood the firm would utilize some foreign direct investment or, at the least, direct exporting rather than indirect.

Beyond competitive issues, macro issues that affect the industry in which the firm operates must be considered. This includes government policies such as product certifications and standards (the CE mark in Europe or CCC mark in China, for instance). It also includes government regulations on foreign ownership and allowable activities. The more difficult the political and economic environment, the greater is the justification to utilize local partners such as distributors or joint venture partners.

Table 8-1 • **Advantages and Disadvantages of Selected Market Entry Strategies**

Entry Modes						
	Indirect Exporting	Direct Exporting	Direct Exporting with FDI	Foreign Manufacturing / Foreign Sales & Distribution	Licensing	Joint Venture / Strategic Alliances
Advantages	No experience required	Greater control	Greater control	Full control	Low investment requirements	Can have some control and feedback depending on contract
	Faster to market	Greater feedback	Greater feedback	Greater feedback	Fast market entry	Access to local knowledge and market expertise
	Low cost	Gain market knowledge	Better meet customer needs	Keep all profits	Use local partner	Shared risks
Disadvantages	Limited control	More costly	More complex	Most expensive	Limited control	Actual control may be constrained by foreign partner
	Limited feedback	More time and effort	More time and effort	Most time and effort required	Potentially less profits compared to other modes	May lead to lower profits due to shared risk
	No gained market knowledge	More risk	More risk	Most risky	May be creating future competitor	Can be difficult or expensive to disengage from partner
Likely stage in a firm's globalization	Early stage or never	Early stage	Maturing	Mature firm with strong international experience	Depends on industry and market. Firms must have IP to license.	Depends on industry and market. May be early or mature.

Finally, the firm evaluates the current and future potential of international markets. The greater the market potential, the more likely the firm will want to be involved in this market, and the more likely the firm is to select entry modes that could create a potential competitor such as contract manufacturing and licensing. Further, the firm is more likely to want to learn and understand markets with greater potential. In this way the entry mode decision is highly influenced by external factors.[6]

Table 8-1 provides a summary of some of the key advantages and disadvantages with each of the entry modes discussed in the next section. It also shows that in the early stage of a firm's globalization, the firm will likely choose a less-risky entry mode (indirect exporting, or no FDI) until it gains more international experience. However, this is a generalization. As previously discussed, many factors influence a firm's selection of its entry mode. The selection is also likely country-specific.

Indirect Exporting

Exporting is manufacturing a product in one nation and shipping it to another for sale to a final consumer. Parts or components can also be exported for use in producing another good or service. In those transactions, the nation of origin and the manufacturing firm are referred to as the "exporter," while the nation of destination and the foreign intermediary or buyer are referred to as the "importer." **Indirect exporting**, as a market entry mode, takes place when the manufacturer is not the exporter. Instead, the manufacturer relies on a third party to conduct the exporting. The third party is often located in the home country of the manufacturer.

Types of Indirect Exporting

Piggybacking as a form of indirect exporting is a viable alternative for many firms that do not have a high level of export readiness or prefer to avoid the risks associated with a specific foreign market. As the term implies, one product "rides" on the back of another from one national market to another. For example, a construction firm that already builds dams internationally may team up with a firm that manufactures industrial rakes used to clean the debris that inevitably collects at the base of a dam. The construction firm offers its customers a more complete project without getting into heavy equipment manufacturing or adding to its financial commitment. The benefit to the rake manufacturer is that it piggybacks on the international success of the construction company with little effort. The carrier is generally the larger entity and tends to have more of the human and financial resources needed for a specific market. The rider is the firm that makes a complementary product. The carrier and rider tend to be in the same or complementary industry. They would likely not be competitors.

Export management companies (EMCs) undertake the whole of the export process on behalf of the manufacturer. As contrasted with a piggyback partner, an EMC is not a manufacturer or global service provider. It is a company in which the sole purpose is to export products manufactured by other companies. The services provided by the EMC cover the full range of export development, including appointing foreign representation, conducting foreign marketing, selling the product to foreign distributors or agents, and handling the export transactions. The scope and breadth of EMCs vary but may focus on a particular geographic region, industry, or service. In most cases, the EMC is located in the home market of the manufacturer. As such, the sale from the manufacturer to the EMC is domestic. The EMC takes all risks associated with exporting, including getting paid for the sale. This removes all risks to the manufacturer. Use of an EMC would be attractive to firms that have limited sales or that are inexperienced in a market. Most EMCs require an exclusive contract to represent the manufacturer. The contract may be global, regional, or limited to a single country.

In practice. EMCs are occasionally confused with **export trading companies (ETCs)** and may even be cross-listed in export directories. True ETCs, though, tend to be large, vertically or horizontally integrated entities. The most sophisticated ETCs can be found in Asia, particularly in Japan and South Korea, and are sometimes referred to as sogo shosha or keiretsu. ETCs generally prefer long-term alliances under less-flexible terms than an EMC. They are also more likely to import as well as export products and may even own or control the transportation methods.

Pros and Cons of Indirect Exporting

Using indirect exporting may be an attractive entry mode when a firm essentially is not able or does not wish to directly participate in exporting. Indirect exporting offers the benefit that the manufacturer does not have to have any prior international experience. Instead, the firm relies on the experience of the piggyback partner or EMC. The manufacturer is also not distracted by the exporting

---

indirect exporting

A foreign market entry mode in which the manufacturer is not the exporter; instead, a third party conducts the export transaction.

piggybacking

A form of indirect export in which one product "rides" on the back of another from one national market to another.

export managment companies (EMCs)

Companies that specialize in exporting and handle the export transaction on behalf of the manufacturer.

export trading companies (ETCs)

Companies that specialize in international trade, generally organized as vertically or horizontally integrated entities.

process and may focus entirely on its core activities. As indirect exporting utilizes the existing trading relationships of the indirect partner, the manufacturer may expand its exports faster than if the company utilized an alternative entry mode. The company also has no increased financial costs because all export costs are generally incurred by the indirect partner. Given the low financial commitment and management distraction, indirect exporting may be seen as less risky than other entry modes.

The use of indirect exporting has its drawbacks, however. The manufacturer has very little control of the export process, including foreign market selection, partner selection, and most marketing decisions such as pricing and promotional strategies. All these decisions are instead taken by the indirect partner. The manufacturer is also less likely to receive adequate feedback from the international market. An EMC may withhold information to keep the manufacturer more dependent on the EMC. A piggyback partner may not have the mechanism or inclination to provide substantive feedback to the manufacturer. And because the manufacturer has such little control and feedback, the company really cannot know if it is reaching its full export potential for a particular market. Further, the lack of control and feedback also prevents the firm from gaining internationalization process knowledge and foreign market knowledge, both of which help firms reduce uncertainty and increase market commitment when making current and future entry mode decisions.[7]

This lack of control and feedback is a very real concern when considering indirect exporting. In practice, firms that have the commitment and capacity to export directly avoid indirect exporting. It would be a viable option for a firm that is not in a strong position to export. Indirect exporting is also a suitable entry mode on a selective basis when a firm considers a particular country too risky and would rather hand-off this risk to a piggyback partner or EMC.

Direct Exporting

direct exporting
A foreign market entry mode in which the manufacturer is the exporter and directly sells to an importer in another country.

Direct exporting takes place when a manufacturer conducts the export transaction selling directly to an importer in another country. The foreign importer may be the final consumer or, more likely, an intermediary such as an agent or distributor. Direct exporting through distributors abroad is the major form of foreign market entry. In most countries, it is the primary method used by smaller firms that lack the resources for a greater commitment to reach foreign markets. It is also an important entry mode for large multinationals that do not have their own marketing presence in all of their global markets, and many do not.

Types of Direct Exporting

agent
An individual or organization located in the foreign market that makes the international sale on behalf of the manufacturer.

distributor
An organization located in the foreign market that takes title (ownership) of the manufacturer's product and sells the product.

Direct exporting varies by the type of foreign partner utilized. **Agents** and **distributors** are both examples of intermediaries used to sell in a foreign market. These intermediaries complete the sale to the final consumer or end user, which may be an individual or another company that uses the product. The distinction between agents and distributors can vary from country to country. The essential difference is that agents generally make the sale on behalf of the manufacturer, and the product is shipped by the manufacturer directly to the foreign buyer. In this fashion, agents could be viewed as a manufacturer's representative. They generally do not determine foreign pricing but simply quote prices as directed by the manufacturer for a specific sale. Agents derive their income as a commission on the sale. They generally do not hold inventory of the product in the foreign country.

Distributors sell directly to other buyers in their country or region. The manufacturer ships the product to the distributor, which then takes title (ownership) of the product. The distributor later sells the product either to another reseller, as in the case of a retail store or manufacturer, or to an end user, such as an individual, a government, or a business. As contrasted with an agent, the distributor generally handles all local marketing decisions, including pricing, promotion, customer support, and perhaps even warranty repairs. The distributor makes its income on the margin (difference) between the cost of the product from the manufacturer and the price it charges to the buyer. Distributors hold inventory of products, which means transportation costs are lower because products can be shipped in quantity.

Historically, exporters had to rely on either an agent or distributor to conduct sales in a foreign country. That is no longer the case due to falling trade barriers and technology, specifically the Internet. (See "The Internet Opens Doors Worldwide.") Manufacturers increasingly have the opportunity to sell direct to foreign buyers, thus avoiding agents and distributors. This is commonly termed **direct sales** or B-to-C (or B2C, business to consumer). This type of direct exporting may be attractive to a manufacturer seeking to retain the profit otherwise earned by the agent or distributor or perhaps to sell to consumers at a lower price. However, with no local presence in the foreign market to handle the marketing and sales, the full potential from the country may not be realized. Sales may also not be as efficient as it places a heavy burden on the manufacturer to handle many or all aspects of the transaction, including logistics, training, payment, and repairs.

> **direct sales**
> Occurs when a manufacturer sells direct to foreign buyers; also called B-to-C (B2C).

Choosing which types of direct exporting depends on the particular product, industry, and needs of the buyer. One important consideration is local inventory. High transportation costs may require that the product be shipped in quantity. Foreign buyers may not want to wait to buy the product. In either case, some level of inventory would be required in the foreign market. That would indicate use of a distributor. The product may require significant interaction with the potential buyer prior to the sale, such as a complicated piece of machinery. That would favor an agent or distributor over direct sales. Significant training or post-sales support would also favor agents or distributors. Each of these issues needs to be addressed prior to the firm's selecting a direct exporting method.

Pros and Cons of Direct Exporting

Direct exporting is attractive for companies because it offers much greater control and feedback. The manufacturer is directly involved with the foreign market, even if through an intermediary. This means the manufacturer makes or participates in key marketing decisions such as partner selection, marketing policies, and public relations. Even if the intermediary handles most of these marketing issues, it would typically be in consultation with the manufacturer. This offers greater control than use of indirect exporting. Feedback is also much higher because the manufacturer is in direct contact with a foreign importer and can ask questions about product acceptance and competition and can solicit suggestions of how to improve.

This capability also places a heavier burden on the manufacturer than selecting indirect exporting as an entry mode. Risks are higher. Travel to the foreign market is likely required. The manufacturer must be comfortable handling the export transaction and logistics, as discussed in Chapter 11. Still, most companies with long-term international expansion goals accept this extra risk and elect to use direct exporting over indirect.

The Internet Opens Doors Worldwide

In 2010, more than 1.6 billion people worldwide had Internet access, representing opportunities for firms to sell to international customers directly through the Internet. Further, smart consumers across the globe can use foreign firms' international websites to take advantage of changes in foreign exchange rates. For example, when the Canadian dollar strengthened against the U.S. dollar by 18% in 2007, Canadian consumers responded by increasing their online purchases of U.S. goods over the Internet by 45% to roughly C$ 15.7 billion.

Major players in business-to-consumer (B2C) selling internationally include well-known companies such as Amazon and eBay, both of which have international websites to help them sell across the globe. Amazon has country-specific websites for Canada, China, France, Germany, Japan, and the United Kingdom, and international sales comprise nearly 50% of Amazon's total net sales.

The Internet is not just a playground for big firms, however. Small- and medium-sized businesses also use the Internet to advertise and sell their products worldwide. Swimman, Inc., a company based in Camarillo, California, sells waterproofed personal audio players and accessories that allow users to listen to music underwater. Swimman sells its products exclusively over the Internet to consumers in the United States and throughout the world.

Advances in communication and transportation technology make it easy for companies, large and small, to sell their products directly to consumers all around the world. In addition to the ubiquitous website, firms can talk to foreign customers inexpensively through e-mail, Internet calling programs such as Skype, and voice-over-IP (VOIP) telephone services. Firms can ship goods worldwide with international shipping companies such as UPS, FedEx, and DHL. Firms can even get paid online using credit cards and online payment services such as PayPal. The Internet has opened the doors to worldwide commerce, and firms throughout the world are taking advantage.[8]

Crossing the Line: Foreign Direct Investment

The entry modes discussed thus far do not involve any foreign direct investment (FDI). This means a firm has made no financial investment in the foreign market. It owns no foreign assets. It has no foreign offices nor employees overseas. In the long run, this approach is not practical. As a company grows its international business, it will likely have to cross the line between not having any FDI and making investments overseas.

Factors Forcing FDI

Firms choose to invest overseas for many reasons. For some, the reason is to increase control of the marketing activities or to get closer to the customer. It could be to improve distribution by owning a warehouse overseas. It may be to lower costs by assembling or fully producing the product in the foreign market. The factors influencing a firm to make foreign direct investment include barriers to exporting, need for increased control and feedback, and sales or customer needs.

BARRIERS TO EXPORT SUCCESS

For some foreign markets, the cost of transportation or local import barriers may prevent exporting as a viable long-term option. Even if a company wants to pursue exporting to avoid the cost and risks associated with overseas investments, it may not be possible. If the product has a relatively low value versus its weight, some overseas manufacturing may be required. Similarly, significantly high import tariffs may require at least some local assembly in the foreign market. In these cases, a company may be forced to make a foreign direct investment.

NEED FOR INCREASED CONTROL AND FEEDBACK

As a company gains experience exporting to a particular foreign market, it may become evident that to really achieve success, more control of and feedback from the foreign market is necessary. Compared to the issue of import barriers and transportation costs, which are challenges that exist from the time the firm enters a market, the need for increased control and feedback may only become apparent over time.

Generally, most companies find that the initial effort of their foreign buyers (agents and distributors) leads to a particular level of success. Over time, as the agent or distributor gains more experience with the product and continues to invest in the local marketing efforts, sales will continue to expand. As the manufacturer receives feedback from its foreign distributor, it adapts its product and marketing strategy to enhance sales in that market.

A firm may find that over time, however, there is increased pressure for it to become more involved in the foreign market. This involvement may initially take the form of a foreign sales and marketing office but could eventually lead to a distribution center, customer support/repair center, or foreign manufacturing. The point at which this pressure becomes significant enough to warrant the manufacturer's investing in the foreign market will vary by company, industry, and even product.

SALES AND CUSTOMER NEEDS

A firm may also determine that rather than rely on an intermediary, it is in the best position to sell its own product. Or it may be the best one to service customer needs, such as training or warranty repairs. In each case, this decision could justify opening a foreign sales office staffed by employees of the firm or a customer support facility. Such offices also could take on marketing roles generally done by the intermediary, such as trade shows and public relations.

Increased Risk through FDI

Crossing the line from no prior FDI to making overseas investments comes with increased risk. When a firm makes an investment in another country, it may acquire foreign assets, hire foreign employees, and incur foreign income taxes. All these actions increase the economic and political risks for the firm and open a whole range of new issues such as transfer pricing, international accounting and taxation rules, and translation of financial statements. Nonetheless, firms continually choose to make investments overseas to reap the considerable benefits.

Overseas Offices for Marketing and Sales

Direct exporting was previously highlighted as a market entry mode. The success of direct exporting through overseas distributors relies heavily on selecting suitable and quality partners. It also relies on ongoing effective management of the distributors and distribution channel by the exporter.

To maximize its effectiveness in managing overseas marketing and sales, a firm may elect to open an overseas office. The goal of the office may initially be to conduct marketing activities to support the sales efforts of the distributors. Having a local office would mean the exporter could more frequently participate in trade shows, selling seminars, and training events. The firm could actually take on most of the marketing efforts for the selected markets, including advertising and public relations.

This investment does not necessarily have to be extensive. Exporters often begin with a single employee or contractor working out of his or her home. This approach minimizes expenses and investment outlays yet still achieves greater control of the marketing activities. As exports grow, a formal office with dedicated staff would be justified.

Not only would marketing activities be conducted from these foreign offices, but also sales. Although the exporter may continue to use distributors in each foreign market managed by the overseas office, selling will be more effective because sales staff are located in the market. If staff are local-nationals, they will understand the culture and speak the language. This would allow for much more effective control of the distributors and feedback from the market. The exporter would also better understand the whole of the distribution channel in the foreign market. These offices may also fill a customer support role for training or warranty repairs. This use of FDI combined with direct exporting is a popular method of market entry, especially after a firm has achieved some initial export success in a market. Later in this chapter, we discuss foreign partner selection and management of the distribution channel.

Overseas Distribution

A second rationale to make foreign direct investment is to open a distribution facility. The purpose of such a facility would be to warehouse products centrally, for further distribution to one or more countries. A distribution center in Rotterdam, Holland, to serve all of Europe would be an example. This center would allow the exporter to ship larger quantities to the warehouse than might otherwise be justified to single distributors, resulting in lower freight costs. In such a case, the exporter is less reliant on distributors, a fact that may be particularly important when distributor relationships are not exclusive. Ownership of a distribution facility offers more significant inventory control and the possibility to make light modifications to the product to adapt to local needs. There is a growing use of "outsourced" distribution in which the warehouse facility is not owned by the exporter, but by a third-party logistics firm in the foreign country. This approach offers many of the same benefits but without the exporter making the foreign investment. See Chapter 11 for more details on overseas distribution and its role in supply chain management.

A firm may use either company-owned or outsourced overseas warehouses as a way to reduce transportation costs and make products more readily available to buyers.

Foreign Manufacturing as Foreign Market Entry ...

So far the assumption has been that a firm entering foreign markets is supplying the markets from domestic plants. This is implicit in any form of exporting. However, sometimes a firm may find it impossible or undesirable to supply all foreign markets from domestic production.

Several factors may encourage, or even force, a firm to use **foreign manufacturing** if it wants to sell in foreign markets. For example, transportation costs may render heavy or bulky products noncompetitive. Tariffs or quotas can prevent entry of an exporter's products. In many countries, government preference for national suppliers can also shut the door to goods produced outside the country. (See Chapter 2.) When such preferences exist, a firm that sells to governments must produce locally. Any of those conditions could force a firm to manufacture in foreign markets to be able to sell there.

Other factors may also encourage a firm to produce abroad. Because they are so large, regional groupings such as the European Union (EU) and populous nations such as India, China, or Brazil warrant entry via investment in local production facilities. In addition, local production allows better understanding of customer needs concerning product design, delivery, and service. Sometimes foreign production costs are lower, especially when transportation and tariff savings are added. A firm might undertake foreign production to gain any of those advantages even though it has the option of serving the market, at least partly, by exports. Britain's chemical firm ICI gave all of these reasons for beginning production on the European continent. As discussed in Chapter 2, due to the product life cycle, a firm may also choose to move offshore the production of a product that can be manufactured at a lower cost than in the firm's home country and then import back into the home market or export to other markets.

After a firm has decided to enter certain markets by manufacturing in them, it has several alternatives. Foreign production may range from assembly plants, contract manufacturing, licensing, or joint ventures to wholly owned plants. In each approach, foreign manufacturing is the source of a firm's product in the market, but the extent of the company's involvement in production and marketing varies with the approach it chooses.

> **foreign manufacturing**
> A foreign market entry mode in which the manufacturer produces a product or service in a foreign market rather than exporting it to that market.

Foreign Assembly

In **foreign assembly**, a firm produces domestically all or most of the components or ingredients of its product and ships them to foreign markets for assembly. Assembly operations involve less than full-scale manufacturing but still require that significant value be added in the local market. Notable examples of foreign assembly are the automobile and farm equipment industries. When transportation costs on a fully assembled vehicle or piece of equipment are high, a firm might be more competitive by shipping **completely knocked down (CKD)** and assembling in the market. Another reason for local assembly is the tariff barrier. Many countries have much lower tariffs on unassembled equipment; by forcing local assembly, governments increase local employment.

The pharmaceutical industry also uses extensive assembly operations, although they should be called compounding or mixing operations. Again, because of transportation or tariff barriers, a firm ships key ingredients to foreign markets and adds bulky liquids or other ingredients (and the capsule and packaging) locally. In a similar fashion, Coca-Cola ships its syrup to foreign markets, where local bottlers add the water and the container. The assembly or mixing plants abroad represent partial local manufacturing; they are a compromise between exports and local production.

If an assembly plant involves foreign investment, a firm must make an investment decision as well as a decision on how to enter the market. However,

> **foreign assembly**
> Occurs when a firm produces domestically all or most of the components or ingredients of its product and ships them to foreign markets for assembly.

> **completely knocked down (CKD)**
> A method of foreign assembly where the product is shipped in components and then assembled in the foreign market.

Overseas manufacture is an important option for firms seeking to avoid duties or transportation costs, or to access lower cost structures overseas.

---

contract manufacturing

When a firm's product is produced in a foreign market by another producer under contract with the firm.

---

the investment commitment is not necessarily included in a decision to assemble abroad. A firm can assemble its products in foreign markets through licensing arrangements without making a capital outlay. For example, Jeep licensed Renault to assemble its cars in Belgium.

Contract Manufacturing

Foreign manufacturing by proxy abroad can be accomplished through **contract manufacturing**. That is, a firm's product is produced in a foreign market by another producer under contract with the firm. Because the contract covers only manufacturing, marketing is handled by the firm. Contract manufacturing is feasible when a firm can locate foreign producers capable of manufacturing its product in satisfactory quantity and quality. In some markets, that capability cannot be found.

Contract manufacturing may be attractive when a firm's competitive advantage lies in marketing rather than production. For example, in Italy, Procter & Gamble had several products manufactured under contract; Unilever did the same thing in Japan for some products. Both firms concentrated on marketing the products. Contract manufacturing obviates the need for plant investment, something a firm may want to avoid if the market is politically uncertain or if the firm is short of capital.

With contract manufacturing, a firm can avoid labor and other problems that may arise from its lack of familiarity with the country. At the same time, the firm gains the advantage of advertising its product as being locally made. That fact may be useful in public relations or for government procurement purposes. If a market proves too small or risky for a firm, it is easier and less costly to terminate a manufacturing contract than to shut down a plant. Other advantages include transportation savings (compared to direct exporting), occasionally lower production costs abroad, and possible exports of components or supplies to the contract manufacturer.

Drawbacks to the contract manufacturing approach may limit its application. For one, the manufacturing profit goes to the local firm rather than to the international firm. That is not serious if sufficient profit remains in marketing activities. For another, finding a satisfactory manufacturer in a foreign market may be difficult. Quality control, too, is usually a greater problem when production is done by another firm.

Wholly Owned Foreign Production

The greatest financial commitment to foreign markets is wholly owned foreign production. In principle, wholly owned means 100 percent ownership by an international firm. In practice, a firm usually achieves the same results by owning 95 percent or even less. The chief practical criterion for wholly owned ventures is not the completeness of ownership, but the completeness of control by the international company.

ACQUISITION OR GREENFIELD?

A firm can obtain wholly owned foreign production facilities in two ways: (1) buy out a foreign producer—the acquisition route, or (2) develop its own facilities from the ground up. As a variation on the acquisition route, a firm can buy out a joint-venture partner. The acquisition route is especially popular, and it offers certain advantages.

Acquisition is a quicker way for a firm to get into a market than building its own facilities. Acquiring a going concern usually means acquiring a qualified

---

acquisition

Buying a foreign producer or firm.

labor force, national management, local knowledge, and contacts with local markets and government. In some markets, acquisition may be the only way to enter if the industry has no room for a new competitor.

Rubbermaid was having trouble in Europe, where it had entered through a joint venture with a Dutch chemical firm. Finally, in 1998, it decided to acquire French and Polish plastics producers and the Dutch chemical firm. That acquisition gave Rubbermaid the existing products and markets of those firms, in addition to the ability to integrate their European marketing.

Buying brands is another way to break into a new market. To gain entry into the U.S. market, BP purchased Amoco (but waited a few years to incorporate BP signage) and Philips of the Netherlands purchased Magnavox. In some parts of the United States, Russian Lukoil signs are replacing signs at Mobil stations, and China's bid for American brands has included Unocal (unsuccessful), TLC's purchase of RCA, and Haier's bid for Maytag (which owned the Hoover, Jenn-Air, and Amana brands). This last example was unsuccessful, and Maytag was eventually purchased by Whirlpool.[9, 10]

The alternative to acquisition is the establishment of a new facility from the ground up—known as a **greenfield** investment. A greenfield investment may be desirable or necessary in certain circumstances. For example, in some markets, a firm will not be able to find a national producer willing to sell, or the government will not allow a firm to sell to the international company. In other markets, producers may be willing to sell, but they lack the caliber of facilities needed by an international firm.

> **greenfield**
> Establishment of a brand new facility built from the ground up.

For its part, an international firm may prefer a new facility over an acquisition. If the market has no personnel or management shortages, a firm feels less pressure for acquisition. Furthermore, if a firm builds a new plant, it can not only incorporate the latest technology and equipment, but also avoid the problems of trying to change the traditional practices of an established concern. A new facility means a fresh start and an opportunity for an international company to shape the local firm into its own image and to meet its requirements.

EVALUATING THE WHOLLY OWNED APPROACH

Evaluating the sole ownership approach is easier, having considered the other alternatives. The advantages of wholly owned ventures are few but powerful. Ownership of 100 percent means 100 percent of the profits go to the international firm, eliminating the possibility that a national partner gets a "free ride." Complete ownership also gives a firm greater experience and better market feedback.

With no national partner, no problems arise from conflicts of interest. Perhaps the overriding argument for complete control, however, is the possibility of integrating various national operations into a synergistic international system. Lesser degrees of involvement are more likely to lead to suboptimization because national partners have goals that conflict with those of the international firm. For those reasons, complete control was important for Rubbermaid, as described previously.

The limitations to the 100 percent ownership approach are several. First, it is costly in terms of capital and management resources. The capital requirements prevent many firms from practicing a complete ownership strategy. Although large firms do not often find capital availability a constraint, they may face a shortage of management personnel. Research has shown that internationalizing improves firm performance, up to a point. After a specific point, firm performance begins to decline with further internationalization due to the complexity of managing so many different international markets.[11] Always using 100% ownership marginalizes the relationship between internationalization and performance as managers spend more and more of their time dealing with complex international issues.

Another drawback to 100 percent ownership is the probable negative host-government and public relations effect. Most nations believe that their participation in the venture should not be limited to supplying just labor or raw materials. Some governments go so far as to prohibit 100 percent ownership by an international firm, demanding licensing or joint ventures instead. A further risk occurring from such nationalistic feelings is outright expropriation, which is more likely and more costly with wholly owned operations.

Finally, 100 percent ownership may deprive a firm of the local knowledge and contacts of a national partner. A local collaborator often serves as a buffer between the international firm and its various national audiences. This role of the national partner as a cultural bridge can be its major contribution, helping a firm avoid mistakes in its encounters with nationals in business and government. By taking the acquisition route, a firm has more chance of getting such nationals than it does in setting up a new operation. The same applies to a wholly owned operation developed from a joint venture. With a new establishment, a firm can develop nationals who become a cultural bridge, but the process is slower.

Licensing

licensing

Arrangement wherein the licensor gives something of value to the licensee in exchange for specified performance and payments from the licensee.

Another way a firm can establish local production in foreign markets without capital investment is through **licensing**. Licensing differs from contract manufacturing in that it is usually for a longer term and involves greater responsibilities for the national party. A licensing agreement is an arrangement wherein the licensor gives something of value to the licensee in exchange for specified performance and payments from the licensee. The licensor (the international company with something of value) may give the licensee (the national firm) one or more of the following: (1) patent rights, (2) trademark rights, (3) copyrights, or (4) know-how on products or processes. Any of those may be given for use in a particular foreign market, or a licensee may have rights in several countries or on a whole continent.

In return for the use of the know-how or rights received, the licensee usually promises (1) to produce the products covered by the rights, (2) to market the products in an assigned territory, and (3) to pay the licensor some amount related to the sales volume of the products. The licensee assumes a much greater role than the contract manufacturer, taking over marketing in addition to production. Thus, the licensee is the complete foreign market presence of an international firm for the products covered.

Benefits of Licensing

Several features of licensing are attractive. First, it requires no capital and, thus, need not deter even small companies. Second, it is often the quickest and easiest way to enter a foreign market. Even a firm that has capital may face a slow process establishing local production and distribution. Third, a firm immediately gains local knowledge.

A fourth advantage is that many governments favor licensing over direct investment because licensing brings technology into the country with fewer strings and costs attached. Thus, licensing may gain government approval more quickly than direct investment. And from a licensor's viewpoint, there is no investment to be expropriated. Finally, the general advantages of foreign production also apply to licensing: savings in tariff and transport costs, local production where national suppliers are favored, and so on.

Disadvantages of Licensing

The disadvantages of licensing are less numerous, but they may carry greater weight. The biggest fear about licensing is that the licensor may establish its own competitor. During the five or ten years of the licensing agreement, the licensor may transfer enough expertise that the licensee can go it alone. Thus, the licensor may lose that market, and perhaps neighboring markets, to the former licensee. That is less likely to occur where strong brands or trademarks are involved. A related issue is piracy. In countries with weak intellectual property rights protection, a company may lose its technology or other intellectual property (IP) to firms that illegally copy that IP. This issue was discussed in Chapter 3.

Another reason for hesitancy about licensing is the limited returns it provides. Although no capital outlay is necessary, royalties and fees from licensing are not cost-free to the licensor, which must invest management and engineering time. A direct investment approach to the foreign market requires much effort and many resources, but it may yield greater profits. Licensing returns are limited primarily to a percentage of licensee sales, commonly 3 to 5 percent. Indeed, less-developed countries are trying to reduce even further the royalties and fees paid to licensors.

Yet another possible drawback is the problem of controlling the licensee. Although the contract should spell out the responsibilities of each party, misunderstandings and conflicts can arise in its implementation. Frequent areas of conflict are quality control, the marketing effort of the licensee, and interpretation of the exclusiveness and extent of territorial coverage.

Firms that are successful at licensing have developed certain techniques for minimizing the pitfalls of licensing and accentuating its potential benefits. Following are some of those techniques:

- Have a deliberate policy and plan for licensing; that is, give it proper attention.
- Fix licensing responsibility in the firm by means of a licensing manager or department. Pfizer had nine licensing directors, one for each major business unit.
- Select licensees carefully.
- Draft an agreement carefully and review it with the licensee. Some items to include are territorial coverage, duration, royalties, trade secrets, quality control, and a minimum-performance clause.
- Supply the licensee with critical ingredients.
- Obtain equity in the licensee.
- Limit product and territorial coverage.
- Keep patent and trademark registration in the licensor's name.
- Be a reasonably important part of the licensee's business. Canon deliberately chose a smaller firm for its copier licensee in India in order to get better performance.

International licensing can be an important part of company strategy; U.S. firms receive over $10 billion a year from licensing agreements. It should be noted that licensing income is not limited to royalties, but also includes such items as (1) technical assistance fees, (2) sale of materials or components to the licensee, (3) lump-sum payments for transfer of rights or technology, (4) technology feedback, (5) reciprocal license rights, (6) fees for engineering services, (7) sales of machinery or equipment, and (8) management fees. The typical company receives five different types of return on its licensing agreements, but most of the income tends to be from royalties.

Joint Ventures and Strategic Alliances

In selecting an entry mode, a firm may decide that it needs a partnership with another firm located in the targeted market. This may be the case if the foreign market is considered highly complex or difficult to enter. A local partner may also be required due to foreign government regulations that do not allow 100% ownership of a local company by a foreign company, as was the case for many years in China. When such partnerships are deemed necessary, the two most common forms are joint ventures and strategic alliances, as discussed next.

Joint Ventures

Generally speaking, in a joint venture, the international firm has equity (ownership) and a management voice in the foreign firm. The equity share of the international company can range from 1 to 99 percent but generally is between 25 and 75 percent. Instead of our seeking a technical definition of a joint venture, however, a practical one is used:

> A **joint venture** is a foreign operation in which the international company has enough equity to have a voice in management but not enough to completely dominate the venture.

joint venture

Foreign operation in which the international company has enough equity in a new company to have a voice in management but not enough to completely dominate the venture.

mixed ventures

Joint ventures with foreign government entities as opposed to foreign firms.

Note that the only joint ventures considered are those between an international firm and a firm that is native to the country in which the venture is located. **Mixed ventures**, on the other hand, are joint ventures with government entities.

The goals of international joint ventures may include more than just gaining access to a foreign market. Joint ventures also include cooperative research and development to develop new products and coordinated efforts to bid on large government procurement opportunities such as building a new airport or to solve supply chain challenges such as a distribution joint venture to more effectively get products to consumers.

Advantages and Disadvantages of Joint Ventures

The joint-venture approach must be compared with both the lesser commitments of contract manufacturing and licensing and the greater commitment of wholly owned foreign production. Whatever benefits are derived from foreign manufacture will, of course, be obtained in the joint-venture approach. As compared with a lesser commitment, joint ventures have the following advantages: (1) potentially greater returns from equity participation as opposed to royalties, (2) greater control over production and marketing, (3) better market feedback, and (4) more experience in international marketing. Disadvantages include a need for greater investment of capital and management resources and a potentially greater risk than with a nonequity approach.

When joint ventures are compared with wholly owned foreign production, a different picture emerges: (1) A joint venture requires less capital and fewer management resources and, thus, is more open to smaller companies. (2) A given amount of capital can cover more countries. (3) The danger of expropriation is less when a firm has a national partner than when the international firm is sole owner. As a result, research shows that small firms increasingly use joint ventures and strategic alliances to mitigate the resources required to expand internationally. The use of these entry modes is even greater among "born global" firms that use joint ventures to help them internationalize early in their firm's life cycle.[12, 13]

Many governments prefer or even demand joint ventures. They believe that their nations receive more of the profits and technological benefit when nationals have a share. Also, finding a national partner may be the only way to invest in some markets that are too competitive or crowded to admit a new operation. This latter point is important for many Japanese firms in the U.S. market.

Joint ventures compare unfavorably with wholly owned operations on only a few, but critical, points. The interests of one partner may conflict with those of the other. The interests of the national partner relate to the operation in the local market. The international firm's interests relate to the totality of its international operations; actions it takes to further global operations may not appear beneficial to the national partner. Some points of potential conflict are (1) transfer pricing, (2) earnings—payout or plowback, and (3) product-line and market coverage of the joint venture.

Shared equity may also involve an unequal sharing of the burden. Occasionally, international companies participating in 50–50 joint ventures believe they are giving more than 50 percent of the technology, management skill, and other factors that contribute to success but are receiving only half the profits. Of course, the national partner contributes local knowledge and other intangibles that may be underestimated. Nevertheless, some companies believe that the local partner gets too much of a "free ride."

Compared to 100 percent ownership, the major complaint about joint ventures is the difficulty of integrating them into a synergistic international operation. When an international firm wants to standardize product design, quality standards, or other activities, its various national partners may not agree. Thus, when standardization, international exchange, and integration are important to a company, the joint-venture approach can be a hindrance. Conversely, when national operations present different product lines and localized marketing—as in packaged foods—joint ventures pose less of a problem.

Lack of knowledge about a market is a frequent reason for partnering with local firms. Although the domestic firm brings knowledge about the product, the foreign firm brings its experience with local consumers.

Strategic Alliances

Almost every entry method involves an alliance with a partner. It may be an export management company, a distributor, a licensee, or a joint-venture partner. In the 1980s, however, a new term arose to describe a different kind of international cooperative venture. **Strategic alliance** has no precise definition but covers a variety of contractual relationships. Those agreements may involve competitors and usually do not involve equity. The global auto industry provides numerous examples of firms that have formed strategic alliances, some of which later developed into mergers and acquisitions (Ford–Mazda; GM–Toyota). In those and many other examples, competitors from different countries contract together to meet a strategic need of each party. Because the relationship often does not fit the definition of a licensing arrangement or a joint venture, the looser term *strategic alliance* is used. (See "A Look at Strategic Alliances.")

Alliances among firms have advantages similar to those that accrue to firms that license or franchise their name, products, and processes. A company can expand into new markets more quickly and offer its customers a broader array of products and services (all with less financial and time commitment than trying to undertake those activities on its own).

> **strategic alliance**
>
> Broad term used to describe a relationship formed by a firm and another partner that covers a variety of contractual relationships, may involve competitors, and usually does not involve equity.

A Look at Strategic Alliances

Samsung Electronics teamed up with XM Satellite Radio so Samsung could offer its customers MP3 players with satellite radio reception, thereby giving its customers a single device that combines what Samsung considered the "two most popular forms of digital audio entertainment introduced over the past 20 years." XM Radio subscribers can download music and other content for "on-demand listening." XM Satellite is available in over 100 car, SUV, and truck models, thanks to agreements the firm has with 19 major auto and motorcycle manufacturers such as Volkswagen and General Motors.

Citibank and China Union Pay (CUP) formed an alliance that allows Chinese customers to get cash in the local currency as they travel around the world. With Citibank

The strategic alliance between XM Radio and Samsung was a critical international partnership leading to the growth of XM Radio.

branches and ATMs in more than 50 countries, with one stroke of a pen, CUP is able to provide nearly worldwide customer service.

Li & Fung began as an export trading firm in China more than 100 years ago. Today it is one of the most sophisticated supply chain and sourcing management companies in the world. It orchestrates the manufacturing and delivery of apparel, toys, and electronic goods worldwide. Li & Fung formed a strategic alliance with Daymon Worldwide, a global leader in the private-label food industry. The deal was expected to yield an additional $1 billion annually for Li & Fung. The idea was that Li & Fung would market its products within a new retail setting—grocery stores. Daymon, with its reputation and established networks, would provide the leverage Li & Fung needed to break into this traditionally difficult retail market.[14]

Cross-border strategic alliances take many forms. They have become the most popular method of international expansion as firms face internationalization pressures and find that they need foreign help. The Chinese have been very active in alliance formation, as have firms that want to enter the Chinese market. Firms are finding that in most cases, if they want to enter world markets, frequently the best (and sometimes the only) way is through an alliance. Examples exist in industries ranging from cars to computers to communications.

Strategic alliances have a variety of objectives; a frequent one is market entry. Many firms find that a contractual arrangement with a foreign competitor is a better way to enter a market than the traditional distributor, licensee, or joint-venture approach.

Why would a firm help a competitor enter its home market? The answer is that the local firm is getting a new product, one that is complementary rather than directly competitive. In effect, market entry strategic alliances are a form of piggybacking. Stated differently, piggybacking is an early form of strategic alliance. Finally, although these alliances are called strategic, every entry method a firm uses should be equally strategic.

Partner Selection

When a firm enters a new foreign market, its partner selection is commonly the most critical decision in the process. Partner selection is particularly important when selecting a distributor for direct exporting. The stakes are perhaps even higher when seeking a partner for a more in-depth relationship such as licensing or strategic alliance.

Figure 8-2 • **Key Issues to Consider When Selecting Foreign Partners**

Indicator	Issue for the Company
Company Size	Most manufacturers will want to match their own size and scale with that of their partners. The cultures of each company will probably then be a better match. Size is also an indicator of many other factors such as experience, depth, breadth of market experience, etc.
Product Lines Currently Represented	One of the best indicators will be the product lines (brands) the potential partner already represents. This reveals a great deal about its experience, strengths, and focus. There may be some lines that would be competitive with the manufacturer's product and preclude any potential for a representation agreement. This is particularly important for exclusive representation agreements. Manufacturers want to avoid Line Collectors—companies that try to represent as many product lines as possible in hopes that ultimately one or two will be huge successes.
Industry Focus and Technical Knowledge	Most agents and distributors focus on particular industries, and though their focus may not be a perfect match, it can be used as a guide. If particular technical knowledge is required, such capabilities will need to be identified.
Years of Experience	Manufacturers are sometimes attracted to relatively new agents and distributors that may be more aggressive given their relative need to grow and succeed versus other competitors in the market.
Sales Structure	This is a critical indicator. It describes how the foreign company sells and to whom. For example, does the distributor only sell to retail locations, but never to the end user? Does the distributor sell to large accounts?
Current Customers	If research has determined that particular customers are crucial, such as government agencies, some clarification by the company needs to be made to ensure such accounts will be contacted.
Customer Support	If training, parts distribution, or product repairs will be necessary, the customer support functions the company is able to provide need to be determined.
Office Locations	The location of the main office and any other offices will dictate the geographical sales focus of the company. It will help determine what part of the territory it can effectively cover.

Source: James Foley, *The Global Entrepreneur*, 2nd edition (La Vergne, Jamric Press International, 2004). Used with permission.

Issues to Consider

Figure 8-2 identifies key issues to consider when selecting a foreign partner. Although these indicators are particularly suitable when selecting an overseas agent or distributor, many apply for other entry modes such as licensing. These factors help to identify the potential strengths and weaknesses of each potential partner, as well as the opportunities and threats partners face in the country and industry in which they operate. These same strengths and weaknesses need to fit with the strengths and weaknesses of the exporter, and the opportunities and threats need to match with the international goals of the exporter. This is, of course, difficult to achieve, which is why the selection of a foreign partner is most commonly selecting the "best" partner among a list of considerations rather than finding the "ideal" partner.

The exporter must begin by detailing what it wants from the foreign partner. How much of the sales and marketing burden will be pushed on to the partner? As discussed earlier, if the exporter is planning to open a distribution facility, then much of the logistics issues will be handled by the exporter rather than the partner. Similarly, if the exporter is planning an overseas sales/marketing office, there are considerably fewer expectations of the partner. Following is a discussion of some of the most critical issues when choosing a partner.

FINANCIAL AND PRICING CONSIDERATIONS

A distributor wants to maximize profits and to work as efficiently as possible. A firm's use of financial and pricing variables will affect a distributor's ability to reach those goals. For example, a firm must determine what *margins or commissions* are needed. Should the firm just match the competition, or are higher margins needed to break into the market or to overcome competitive disadvantages? Conversely, a firm may offer lower margins because of competitive strengths in its total offering—a form of nonprice competition. The same questions apply to credit terms. Does a firm need to be generous on credit or merely competitive?

A second aspect of export pricing is *choice of currency* for the quotation. A distributor generally prefers a quote in the currency of its own country rather than a quote in U.S. dollars. This facilitates accounting and eliminates foreign exchange exposure for the distributor.

One other financial consideration is the payment terms specified. For example, the use of open account terms shows trust in the distributor—and saves the several hundred dollars required to open a letter of credit. An exporting firm must balance its need for financial security with its need to satisfy the distributor.

MARKETING SUPPORT CONSIDERATIONS

A number of other considerations will encourage distributor performance. A well-established brand name and customer franchise will make a distributor's marketing task easier. Names such as Coca-Cola, IBM, Philips, and Sony mean that the product is partially presold. Heavy advertising and promotional support by a producer also make a distributor's job easier. In addition, there may be cooperative advertising with a distributor. Another kind of support is participation in trade fairs, preferably in cooperation with distributors in the region.

Exporters usually train a distributor's sales force as a necessary aid to marketing. That would be done at the beginning of the relationship and as new products are added to the line. Distributors should be supplied on a timely basis with product and promotional materials from the home office or through an overseas distribution facility, as discussed earlier.

Regional meeting of a firm's foreign partners is an efficient tool to increase communication and build unity within a firm's international sales channels.

COMMUNICATIONS

If a distributor is to be an effective member of a firm's international network, communication is important. Firms should be in frequent contact with their overseas partners, sending e-mail, making phone calls, and keeping their websites up-to-date. In addition, visits to the partners allow the face-to-face contact that humanizes a long-distance relationship.

Regional meetings of foreign partners can further encourage communications and unity, in addition to providing economies of scale for training or motivation sessions. Toro held its first international sales conference in Switzerland. The conference was attended by Toro distributors from 13 Western European countries. Those distributors had previously attended annual meetings in the United States but thought the meetings were not oriented to their particular needs. The face-to-face contact between Toro personnel and European agents helped the company gain better insight into the marketing problems of each country represented. The language problem was solved by the use of simultaneous translations.

MARKET EXCLUSIVITY

Giving a distributor an exclusive territory means that the distributor will be motivated to actively market and sell in that territory since all its efforts will be returned to the distributor, not a competitor. But caution should be used in granting exclusivity since it may be overoptimistic and exceed a distributor's capabilities. Fully achieving the sales potential of a particular market may demand more than one distributor, perhaps focused on specific customer segments of the market. If a distributor is granted exclusivity, it should be backed with a strong contract that includes some performance guarantees (minimum sales), as discussed in a later section. And as highlighted in Chapter 3, canceling distributor contracts can be problematic.

Finding Foreign Partners

Finding suitable partners is a two-step process. The first is to identify as many potential partners as possible through research and government resources. The second step is a visit to the country to meet with potential partners for final selection. These meetings could be at a trade show or during a trade mission, although preferably they would include a visit to the partner's facility.

IDENTIFYING POTENTIAL PARTNERS

There are a number of ways to find potential partners. The easiest are online databases that allow search terms by industry and country. (See Table 6-5, Section 4.) One example is Kompass (www.kompass.com), which allows free searching although a subscription allows for advanced searches and retrieves more details on the companies. OneSource (www.thereferencegroup.com) is another very large database of companies around the world; it includes significant financial details and shows linkages between parent companies and their subsidiaries. Another site is Alibaba (www.alibaba.com), which bills itself as the largest B2B website.

Another effective method is to find distributors that already represent manufacturers of products that are complementary to the firm seeking partners. For example, a manufacturer of women's clothing may seek to find distributors of men's clothing. Or a manufacturer of jewelry could refer to distributors of watches. A firm would generally avoid a potential partner carrying competing products simply because initial distribution relationships tend to be exclusive. But distribution lists of competitors can also be helpful even just to know which partners to avoid.

Trade associations are another great resource because their leaders and members have significant contacts within the industry. The American Society of Association Executives website (www.asaecenter.org) allows users to search for industry associations worldwide. The World Trade Centers Association and its worldwide network of World Trade Centers (http://world.wtca.org) are a huge networking engine hosting numerous partnering events in most countries.

A firm's current or potential customer base may also be a valuable source of potential partners. Buyers in foreign markets know the successful distributors and agents and can make recommendations. Often distributors in one country know their colleagues in adjoining (one hopes, noncompeting) countries.

Trade shows and missions are also useful to find foreign partners. Each industry tends to have one or more worldwide **trade shows** in which hundreds of exhibitors introduce their products and services to potential buyers and partners. Although the United States has many of these leading shows, many are held outside the U.S. The Medica show for medical products (www.mdna.com) draws over 135,000 health-care professionals to Germany, and the Foodex Exhibition in Japan draws over 90,000 visitors from the food and beverage

trade show

Industry- or country-specific events in which many exhibitors introduce their products and services to potential buyers and partners.

trade mission

Group travel to a foreign market, sometimes led by state or federal officials, to explore business opportunities in that market.

vertical trade show

Trade shows focused within a single industry.

vertical trade mission

Trade mission focused within a single industry.

horizontal trade show

Trade show focused across a wide spectrum of industries but typically within a single market or region.

horizontal trade mission

Trade mission focused across a wide spectrum of industries but typically within a single market or region.

The Key to Export Opportunities

International Partner Search (IPS)

A service provided by the U.S. Commercial Service that connects firms with potential foreign partners.

Gold Key

A service provided by the U.S. Commercial Service whereby the USCS prequalifies companies and sets up appointments with potential foreign partners.

industries. An online directory of trade shows may be found at www.biztrade-shows.com. **Trade missions** are group travel to a foreign market, sometimes led by state or federal officials, to explore business opportunities in that market. These opportunities are very effective ways to find partners because a delegation tends to have a higher profile visiting the market than does a single firm. **Vertical trade shows** and **vertical trade missions** are primarily focused within a single industry, and **horizontal trade shows** and **horizontal trade missions** are focused across a wide spectrum of industries but typically within a single market or region. As discussed in Chapter 10, trade shows are also an effective sales promotion tool.

Finally, government agencies are directly involved in finding suitable partners for exporters. For U.S. exporters of products and services, the primary federal agency is the U.S. Department of Commerce's Commercial Service (www.export.gov). For agricultural products, it is the U.S. Department of Agriculture's Foreign Agricultural Service (www.fas.usda.gov). Both offer extensive services linking exporters with potential partners and buyers overseas. See "The Key to Export Opportunities" for details of services from the U.S. Commercial Service. State governments often have similar services—often at no cost. An association representing such state agencies is State International Development Organizations, or SIDO (www.sidoamerica.org).

The U.S. Department of Commerce, in cooperation with the International Trade Administration (ITA) and the U.S. Commercial Service (USCS), offers several services to American firms that want to expand operations internationally. The type of assistance is broad—identifying markets, performing market research, arranging meetings with industry and country specialists, assisting with travel, providing access to interpreter service and clerical support, resolving commercial disputes, and helping with regulatory or technical standards. If a firm cannot find the time or money to participate in a trade show, U.S. government representatives will present the company's materials at the show.

The USCS can be particularly helpful in finding potential partners overseas through two programs. The **International Partner Search (IPS)** connects firms with potential joint venture partners, licensees, agents, and distributors. After conducting the IPS, the USCS will forward a list of prequalified companies in a particular market that have expressed an interest in the firm's products or services. Another program is helpful when a firm is planning to visit a foreign market. Under the **Gold Key** program, the USCS will prequalify companies that have expressed an interest in the firm's products or services and set up appointments for the firm to visit the potential partners. The USCS can also provide assistance with travel and translation assistance. If the firm cannot travel to the foreign market in person, video conferences can be arranged instead.

These services are available through Export Assistance Centers located in over 100 U.S. cities and throughout the globe in nearly 80 countries abroad. International assistance offices at the state and local levels also offer similar services. Finding partners with help from the government is not foolproof and still requires careful assessment of the partners' capabilities, needs, and reliability. Yet these matching programs do perform much of the prospecting for potential partners—a very time-consuming part of the process.[15]

Contract Negotiations

A dispute between two companies located in the same country may be solved through a quick visit. Although a domestic dispute could still result in a lawsuit, such a dispute is easier to resolve than an international dispute. Domestic disputes occur within the same culture and legal system. International disputes involve different cultures, legal systems, and expectations. Also, travel may not be a viable option. When conducting business internationally, firms use contracts to help mitigate the challenges associated with future disputes. The following sections discuss the cultural considerations on contract negotiation and the use of distributor agreements.

> trattativa
> **negotiation**
> 交涉
> verhandlung
> negociación
> onderhandeling

CULTURAL CONSIDERATIONS

Individuals involved in international negotiations may have different perspectives, depending on their cultural background. As discussed in Chapter 4, cultures vary greatly around the world. Differences in religion, language, attitudes, and other elements of cultures are widespread. These differences impact the contract negotiations.

EXPECTATIONS OF EACH PARTNER

An important difference is the expectations of each partner. Americans are often known to expect fast, quick-to-the-point negotiations. Asians are frequently characterized as placing less emphasis on getting the deal done quickly and more on understanding both positions and getting the right deal. Expectations of the negotiation process itself will also vary in terms of style and process. The issue of high- and low-context cultures described in Chapter 4 also could play an important role on the process.

WIN-WIN OR WIN-LOSE?

Successful international contracts are a win-win for both parties. International business generally requires long-term commitments and dealing with unforeseen circumstances within different cultures and legal systems. This places a heavy burden on both partners. The contract should be fair to both parties to support a long-term partnership. A win-lose contract that favors only one partner will likely lead to poor business results.

> **distributor agreement**
> Legal document that spells out the responsibilities and interests of both the exporter and the distributor.

DISTRIBUTOR AGREEMENTS

The most common international contract for exporters is the **distributor agreement**. The distributor agreement is a legal document that should spell out the responsibilities and interests of each party, protecting both. Carefully preparing the agreement and reviewing it with the distributor should help minimize later misunderstandings. But the exporters should not simply use an existing domestic distributor agreement for its international distributors. As discussed in Chapter 3, legal differences are significant between countries and must be considered in all distributor contracts. Experienced lawyers should be involved in creating distributor agreements. Some of the most common issues to be negotiated are included in Table 8-2. Nearly all contracts would also specify which countries are covered by the contract and provide sales expectations. Poor sales performance is often linked to the termination clause, giving the exporter a mechanism to end the relationship should the distributor fail to purchase enough product to justify the relationship.

Table 8-2 • Common Issues in Distributor Agreements

Issue	Details
Term of the Agreement	One year is quite common for such agreements although distributors will likely want a longer term.
Choice of Law	This part of the agreement establishes what law governs the contract in cases of dispute.
Dispute Resolution Provision	There is a growing use of arbitration (use of a third party) to resolve conflicts because it is faster and less expensive than litigation.
Duties of Each Party	This critical part of the agreement establishes which tasks are done by the seller versus the buyer.
Termination Clause	This clause clarifies what situations would trigger canceling the contract.

EXCLUSIVE VERSUS NONEXCLUSIVE AGREEMENTS

Traditionally, exporters use exclusive contracts with distributors when first entering a market. An exporter agrees not to appoint another distributor in the same country or region. In exchange, the distributor agrees not to carry a competing product. Such exclusive agreements can be very powerful in motivating the distributor because all the marketing and sales efforts will benefit the distributor and not a competitor. Exclusive agreements should include performance targets (sales requirements) for the distributor to protect the exporter from a poor-performing distributor.

A firm may elect to use a nonexclusive distributor agreement as it becomes more established in a foreign market. As an exporter grows stronger and more experienced, nonexclusive agreements offer greater flexibility. This allows the firm to appoint multiple distributors in the same country or region. However, companies choosing nonexclusive contracts must be willing to take on more of the marketing responsibilities because their distributors will not invest as much into the product given the risk that such efforts may simply assist the sales of another competing distributor.

Distribution Environment and Strategy

sales channel
Means by which a manufacturer gets a product to market.

The ways products are distributed and sold vary by country. A country's **sales channel** is the customary ways products in that country are distributed to the marketplace. The sales channel may involve multiple layers, such as wholesalers, distributors, and retailers. It also may be very flat, as in the case of a manufacturer or distributor selling directly to the final consumer. Within a particular country, the typical sales channel can also vary by industry. The international marketing manager must be familiar with a market's distribution environment to be able to develop an effective strategy. The manager should also be aware of distribution trends in world markets. These trends are summarized in Figure 8-3.

Wholesaling in Foreign Markets

merchant wholesalers
Firms that perform the traditional role of buying products and selling to retailers.

single-line wholesalers
Firms that focus on a specific product line.

specialty wholesalers
Firms that carry a very narrow line of products, often to an equally narrow retail market.

Wholesalers are distribution companies that typically buy products from manufacturers and then sell the products to retailers. As such, wholesalers are intermediaries. There are different types of wholesalers although their functions are similar. **Merchant wholesalers** are the most common and perform the traditional role of buying products and selling to retailers. When generically speaking about wholesalers, one is likely referring to merchant wholesalers. **Single-line wholesalers** focus on specific product lines, such as industrial goods, foods, or clothing. **Specialty wholesalers** carry a very narrow line of products, often to an equally narrow retail market. They often provide a higher level of service to retailers than other wholesalers. Examples include niche food products, specialized building supplies, and electrical components.

Figure 8-3 • Distribution Trends in World Markets

There are five major distribution trends in world markets:

The growth of large-scale retailing

The continuing internationalization of retailing

The growth of direct marketing

The spread of discounting

Electronic distribution

The wholesaling functions (inventory, consolidating shipments, distributing to retailers) are performed in all countries but with varying degrees of efficiency. Differences in the economy, its level of development, and its infrastructure all cause variation in the wholesaling function.

SIZE

One notable difference in international wholesaling is the size and number of wholesalers from country to country. Generally, industrialized countries have large-scale wholesaling organizations serving a large number of retailers; developing countries are more likely to have fragmented wholesaling—firms with a small numbers of employees serving a limited number of retailers. Finland and India illustrate this generalization. Finland has one of the most concentrated wholesaling operations in the world. Four groups account for most of the wholesale trade. The largest, Kesko (the Wholesale Company of Finnish Retailers), with a market share over 20 percent, services over 11,000 retailers. India, on the other hand, has thousands of companies acting as wholesalers serving hundreds of thousands of small retailers. Because of the large number of small wholesalers, manufacturers frequently use agents to sell to the wholesalers, adding an extra step in the channel.

Some industrialized countries have small-scale wholesaling much like some developing countries. Italy and Japan are examples. Because of Italy's fragmented distribution system, Procter & Gamble had to use an intermediary to reach the wholesale level, much like firms in India have to do. Japan is notorious for its fragmented distribution system, with wholesalers selling to other wholesalers. Half of Japan's wholesalers have fewer than four employees. Japan has almost as many wholesalers as the United States does, with only half the population. Wholesaler sales are five times retailer sales in Japan, four times the U.S. ratio.

SERVICE

The most important differentiating factor in wholesaling abroad is in the services offered to a manufacturer. The quality of service usually relates to the size of operations. Smaller operators generally have limited capital and less know-how, as well as small staffs, meaning they are unable to give the same service as large wholesalers. In some markets, manufacturers are tempted to bypass wholesalers because of their costs or inefficiencies. Although doing so might lead to more efficient distribution, the feasibility of this approach needs to be carefully evaluated. Various factors—such as the power of wholesalers or the critical functions they perform—may preclude bypassing them.

In markets with fragmented wholesaling, a firm must resign itself to incomplete market coverage or try to overcome the weakness by using a **pull strategy**, by company distribution, or by other means. (A pull strategy involves heavy consumer advertising to "pull" products through the channel. This is in contrast to a **push strategy**, which involves incentivizing the channel directly through discounts or promotion to help motivate channel partners to "push" the product to consumers.) When facing fragmented wholesaling in Italy, Procter & Gamble took a twofold approach. It emphasized its traditional pull strategy and inserted an extra level in the channel, using a master wholesaler that reached smaller wholesalers that contacted the retailers. In Japan, Procter & Gamble uses no fewer than 17,000 wholesalers, a great challenge in distribution management.

Many of the considerations discussed here also apply to industrial goods, but a producer's need for know-how and service are greater than with consumer goods. This might keep industrial marketers out of certain countries or force them to seek other solutions. For example, Unisys uses United Africa Company in several African nations and piggybacks with Plessey, a British electronics firm, in Southeast Asia.

pull strategy

A strategy that attempts to gain business by bringing consumers to the manufacturer, often through heavy consumer advertising.

push strategy

A strategy that attempts to gain business by incentivizing the channel (wholesalers, retailers) to "push" the product to buyers. This strategy often uses incentives and promotions aimed directly at the wholesalers or retailers.

Retailing in Foreign Markets

International differences in retailing are as extensive and unpredictable as they are in the case of wholesaling. A marketer must study retail patterns in each market. Some of the major differences will be noted in the following sections.

GREATER NUMBERS, SMALLER SIZE

The major variable in retailing in world markets is the great difference in numbers and size of retail businesses. The U.S. and other advanced industrial countries tend to have larger retail outlets and a smaller number per capita than the developing countries do. That means the industrialized nations enjoy greater economies of scale and efficiency. Some industrialized countries do not have an extensive modern retail sector, however. Among them are Japan, Italy, Belgium, and France. Japan has more retailers than the United States, with only half the population. In Germany, 75 percent of retailing is done by large units; whereas in Italy, over 75 percent is done by small independents. Italy has four times as many retailers as Germany. These differences in a country's retail sector are often the result of local laws that discourage or even prohibit large-scale retailing.

An important international retail trend is the move toward large, retail outlets, as already seen in the United States for many years.

Visiting just the capitals or largest cities of developing nations does not give a true picture of the retailing structure of those countries. The cities may have department stores and supermarkets like those a tourist sees at home. Such evidence in the small, modernized sector of the economy, however, is not typical of the nation as a whole. Rather, the infrastructure and amenities present in the larger cities represent one side of the "dual economy" phenomenon. That is, the same country has two different economies: one that includes the majority of the population in the villages and rural areas and the other that includes the large cities where some industrialization and commercial development has taken place.

RETAILING SERVICES

Another variable in world markets involves the services provided by a retailer to the manufacturer. A producer might want a number of services from a retailer, including stocking, displaying, and selling the product; promoting the product (by word of mouth, by display, or by advertising); extending credit to customers; servicing the product; and gathering market information.

CARRYING INVENTORY

Stocking products is a basic function of retailers in every country. The services offered, however, are not identical. Small retailers carry limited inventories and frequently may be out of stock of certain items. That is lost business for the manufacturer. Limited inventory means a limited line of products. New entrants to the market can have difficulty getting their products accepted by retailers. Because they are financially weak, small retailers may carry certain products only if they do not have to invest in them; that is, these retailers carry the inventory physically, but the wholesaler or manufacturer carries it financially. That is a problem even in Japan, where small dealers may receive credit up to ten months. Consignment sales are one possible answer to this retailer inventory problem. An American firm selling prepared foods partially dealt with the problem by changing from 48-can cases supplied in the United States to 24-can and 12-can cases distributed in other markets.

PRODUCT DISPLAY

When the package plays a role in persuading consumers, display is important. The kind of display a product has in a retail outlet depends on the physical facilities (space, shelves, and lighting). The producer will find great international variations in these facilities. At one extreme, an African duka may have less than

200 square feet of store space, no electric lighting, one door and one window, a few shelves, and one or two tables. A seller in an open market or a bazaar would have equally limited facilities. Retail facilities range from those examples all the way up to a 250,000-square-foot hypermarket.

Merchandising skills correlate somewhat with the level of economic development, although many retailers in poorer countries have a flair for product display. Few firms in the United States rely on retailers for the display of their products, except for shelf space. Representatives of manufacturers arrange the displays themselves. However, that is not possible in many markets because of the small size and dispersion of retail businesses and because the firm may have a narrower line in a market, offering too small a base over which to spread its costs. Cooperation is also affected by a retailer's overall relationship with the producer, as in the case of Kimberly-Clark. It was distributing Kotex in France through the *pharmacie*, which differs from a U.S. drugstore in that it is limited to dispensing medicines and related items. The company wanted to add Kotex to supermarket outlets, as in the United States. The supermarkets were willing to handle the product, but the *pharmaciens* were angry about the competition. As a result, the *pharmaciens* put all Kimberly-Clark products under the counter and refused to display them.

PROMOTION OF A PRODUCT

Product display is frequently all that a manufacturer can expect. Occasionally, however, retailers might do some personal selling or advertising. That is more likely when retailers have a favorable attitude toward a product and it is an important part of their sales. Use of point-of-purchase materials is another form of retailer promotion, but the small size of retail outlets makes most of those displays impractical. Product advertising by retailers is a form of promotion that also tends to be limited in many markets because of the small resources of retailers. These limitations force a manufacturer to rely on its own advertising.

TYPES OF RETAILERS

How retailers sell to consumers varies based on their type. The traditional type is **vending retailers** (also known as store retailers), which maintain brick-and-mortar retail stores. Consumers visit the stores to make their purchases. Examples include Walmart, IKEA, Macy's, and Lowe's. **Mail-order retailers** sell through catalogs and the Internet. Examples are L.L. Bean, Hammacher Schlemmer, and Overstock.com. Most vending retailers also incorporate mail-order retailing given the increasing popularity of online shopping. **Direct-selling retailers** bypass brick-and-mortar stores and perhaps even the Internet. Direct retail sellers use a sales force to make their sales directly to the consumer. The sales force is often organized as a multilevel or network marketing structure in which one person recruits another, who recruits another, and so on. The salespeople are likely not employees of the retailers and earn their profits solely based on commissions. Examples of direct-selling retailers include Amway and Mary Kay cosmetics.

Most countries have each of the preceding types of retailers. There may be constraints on certain retail models given lack of infrastructure, however. An inadequate mail system would not support mail-order retailers. Cultural barriers may limit the success of direct-selling retails. Nonetheless, all three retail types tend to have some type of presence in most countries.

vending retailers
Firms that maintain traditional brick-and-mortar retail stores.

mail-order retailers
Firms that sell through catalogs and the internet.

direct-selling retailers
Firms that use a sales force to make their sales directly to consumers.

Distribution Strategy

Because the preceding sections considered some of the principal constraints on distribution in foreign markets, the focus turns now to strategic decisions facing the international marketer:

- Should a firm extend its domestic distribution approach to foreign markets or adapt its distribution strategy to each national market?
- Should a firm use direct or indirect channels in foreign markets?
- Should a firm use selective or widespread distribution?
- How can a firm manage the channel?

STANDARDIZATION OR ADAPTATION?

The important question is not whether a firm should have uniform distribution patterns in foreign markets, but which channels in each market are most profitable. A few factors may favor a standardized approach, particularly the possibility of economies of scale. Although economies of scale are not as easily attainable in distribution as they are in production, there may be some. For example, an international marketing manager may work more efficiently when tasks are similar in different markets. The more similar the conditions, the more easily experience in one country can be transferred to another country.

It can be argued that channels used in one market should be tried in another because they have been tested. Although success in one market does suggest trying the same thing elsewhere, that success is not a sufficient reason for using the same strategy in every market. Market analysis should be done before deciding on local channels. Numerous pressures deter a firm from standardized distribution. One is the distribution structure in a country—that is, the nature of wholesale and retail operations. Because distribution structure varies from country to country, a firm's alternatives also vary. Storage and transportation possibilities in addition to the market's dispersion also help to determine channel alternatives. For example, Pepsi-Cola uses similar channels all over the world—that is, local bottler to truck driver/sales representative to retailer. However, in sparse areas, the truck driver/sales representative is too expensive, forcing the company to find another method.

Another channel determinant is the market. Consumer income and buying habits are important considerations in deciding on distribution, as are the strength and behavior of competitors. On the one hand, competitors may force a firm to use the same channel they are using because they have educated the market to that channel. On the other hand, competitors may effectively preempt that channel and force a newcomer to find some other way to the market.

Finally, differences in a manufacturer's situation might suggest channel differences from market to market. An important determinant is a firm's level of involvement in a market. Where a firm supplies a market through an importer-distributor, the company has less freedom than it does in places where it has a local sales office or plant. Similarly, working through a licensee or joint venture is more restrictive of channel selection than a wholly owned operation. Even where the level of involvement is the same in two markets, a firm's product line and sales volume may differ. The smaller the line and volume of sales, the less direct the channels a firm can afford to use.

DIRECT VERSUS INDIRECT CHANNELS

Because direct channels are usually more effective than indirect channels, firms like to be as direct as they can. The major determinant is the volume of sales attainable. Where volume is large, a firm can afford to go direct. When a U.S. firm considers foreign markets, it usually finds less possibility of going direct than in the United States. Many elements, such as lower incomes, a firm's narrower product line, and fewer large-scale buying organizations, combine to make most other markets smaller.

When foreign markets are small, many firms accept indirect distribution as the only feasible alternative. In India, for example, Unilever and other consumer goods companies sell through agents, who reach the wholesalers, who reach the retailers. Procter & Gamble in Italy used a similar three-stage channel. Channels in Japan may be even more indirect than those in India and Italy. In such cases, fragmented wholesaling and retailing force a firm to go less direct than it would like. Those conditions characterize most world markets.

Some firms, however, insist on trying for more-direct distribution as the best way to get a strong market position. That is especially true of consumer durables and industrial goods producers. Goodyear established its own franchised dealers in Europe, just like its dealers in the United States.

SELECTIVE VERSUS INTENSIVE DISTRIBUTION

Intensive distribution refers to the policy of selling through any retailer that wants to handle the product. **Selective distribution** means choosing a limited number of resellers in a market area. A firm usually wants to offer its product in as wide a market as possible. However, the company may need to select a limited number of distributors to make it worthwhile to carry inventory and provide service and promotion. For shopping or specialty goods, retailers may demand selective distribution, which protects their market by limiting competition. For industrial goods or consumer durables, selective distribution may be the only way to induce intermediaries to cooperate in providing service.

Marketing abroad, manufacturers usually give exclusive franchises to importers or wholesalers at the national level. However, selectivity at the retail level depends on local market conditions. With a multiplicity of small retailers, a firm might have difficulty locating retailers that can handle its product effectively. Low consumer mobility also limits the value of selective distribution.

In countries with uneven income distribution, a firm might use selective distribution if it sells only to a group above a certain income level. For consumer durables or industrial products, the distribution in smaller markets might be more selective because of the thinness of the market and its relative concentration. The channel follows the market.

> **intensive distribution**
> Policy of selling through any retailer that wants to handle the product.

> **selective distribution**
> Policy of choosing a limited number of resellers in a particular market.

Working with the Channel

When a firm sells directly to a retailer or to consumers, the costs of direct distribution bring the benefits of control as well as the flexibility to respond to market conditions and better market feedback. When a firm cannot afford to go direct, it must deal with independent intermediaries. The problem then becomes one of getting cooperation rather than maintaining control. Although that problem is not peculiar to foreign markets, a firm's situation and market conditions will vary from country to country, making channel management a somewhat different task in each market. A firm's success in a market often depends on how well independent intermediaries do their job. Thus, helping them to do their job becomes a major responsibility of the marketer. (See "Motivating the Channel" for tips on how a firm can help foreign partners be more successful.)

Selecting a Strategy

All the preceding issues must be considered when a firm sets its distribution strategy for a particular country or region. A firm must match its international goals and capabilities against key distribution decisions such as standardizing its strategy versus adapting to local conditions. The strategy may also change over time as the firm becomes more established in a market or local conditions change. Technology can also trigger a need to change the firm's strategy. Over time, a firm must continually address its distribution strategy and keep that strategy current with market requirements.

••• Motivating the Channel

After a firm has selected an agent or distributor and begun a contractual relationship, there is still work left to do. Firms need to continuously motivate their channel partners to maximize sales and ensure a successful international expansion. Manufacturers have developed many techniques for motivating members of an international sales channel. They include

- **Margins.** These incentives include special discounts or lower pricing.
- **Exclusive territories**. Manufacturers might agree not to appoint another channel member, which protects the marketing and sales efforts of the exclusive member.

- **Valuable franchise or brand.** A firm with a globally recognized franchise or brand is in a stronger position to encourage channel members
- **Advertising support.** Firms often use advertising or co-operative advertising (shared costs) to support international sales.
- **Direct sales support.** Sales staff from the manufacturer can work with channel staff on training or joint sales calls.
- **Marketing support.** The firm may provide channel members with industry marketing information such as competitive positioning.

SUMMARY

Firms have a number of foreign market entry mode options. Some require little to no foreign market involvement; others require significant involvement. Selection of the entry mode should match with the firm's management expertise, commitment to expand globally, and specific requirements of the firm's industry.

Firms with limited resources can find quick and easy entry into foreign markets through indirect exporting. Small firms can make domestic sales to companies with buying offices in their home country. EMCs are one form of indirect exporting. They are specialized intermediaries who sell their export marketing services. Use of EMCs is a low-cost way to obtain an export department without setting one up in a firm. Piggybacking is a form of cooperation between two producers wherein one carries the other's product(s) to export markets. This is a popular form of exporting because the rider gets instant, inexpensive export marketing while the carrier gets a complementary product to round out its line.

Direct exporting, in which a firm does the whole exporting job in-house, is more demanding than indirect exporting. There are greater personnel, administrative, and financial requirements.

A firm must choose its foreign markets, find representatives in those markets, arrange the logistics, and then try to manage its foreign marketing by working with independent distributors.

Product assembly in foreign markets is a blend of exporting and local production, as a firm ships parts or ingredients from home, which are then processed locally. Foreign assembly maintains current production facilities but may allow more favorable tariff treatment, lower shipping costs, lower labor costs, or some combination. Contract manufacturing allows a firm to produce abroad without plant investment by contracting to use a local firm's production facilities. This approach saves on transport and tariff costs and avoids local investment and labor problems. It is useful when governments and/or customers favor local supply.

Working with a licensee means a firm does not have to make a major commitment to a foreign market. A local licensee produces and markets a firm's product. Working with a licensee provides the advantage of local supply at a low cost, but a disadvantage is that it limits the control and returns of a firm. What is more, it may mean training a competitor.

Joint ventures—producing and marketing abroad with a local partner—can be an effective market entry. In addition to the advantages of local production, a firm may gain local market knowledge and contacts as well as potential conflicts. Joint venturing is more costly than other forms of entry except for wholly owned operations.

Wholly owned operations can start with a new establishment or with the acquisition of a local firm. Acquisitions allow quicker entry and an established market position. They may also be necessary in markets that have no room for new entrants.

Exporters can influence foreign distributors' marketing in several ways. The first step is careful distributor selection. That requires a job specification and evaluation of a distributor's track record according to an exporter's criteria. The second step is writing the distributor agreement to recognize the interests of both parties. The third step is making suitable financial arrangements. An exporter must choose margins, price quotes, currency, and payment terms to satisfy both parties. The fourth ingredient is marketing support, which may include a strong brand, advertising support, distributor sales force training, promotional materials, and the establishment of a regional warehouse. The fifth dimension is effective communication, including regional partner meetings.

Wholesalers around the world differ greatly in size and capability. Wholesaling efficiency generally rises with the level of economic development, but there are many exceptions to that trend. When wholesaling is fragmented and small in scale, it constrains a firm's local marketing by increasing transaction costs and credit requirements and by limiting the product line and geographic coverage and services offered.

Retailing shows great international variation, with a majority of countries having large numbers of small retailers. In those markets, a firm may find it difficult to secure retailer cooperation in carrying inventory, displaying the product, promoting the product, and providing market feedback.

An international marketer must monitor distribution trends. As economies develop, their distribution structures change as wholesaling and retailing become modernized and the channel members become more powerful.

A firm would like to use the same channels in every market, but exact duplication is never possible. Differing wholesale and retail structures and consumer income and buying behaviors force adjustments. Also, a manufacturer's situation varies from market to market. Finally, in deciding on selective or intensive distribution coverage, a firm may find that what it wants is overruled by political or economic conditions.

KEY TERMS

acquisition	export management	intensive distribution	sales channel
agents	companies (EMCs)	International Partner	selective distribution
B-to-C or B2C	export trading companies	Search (IPS)	single-line wholesalers
completely knocked	(ETCs)	joint venture	specialty wholesalers
down (CKD)	foreign assembly	licensing	strategic alliance
contract manufacturing	foreign manufacturing	mail-order retailers	trade missions
direct exporting	Gold Key	merchant wholesalers	trade shows
direct sales	greenfield	mixed ventures	vending retailers
direct-selling retailers	horizontal trade missions	piggybacking	vertical trade missions
distributor agreement	horizontal trade shows	pull strategy	vertical trade shows
distributors	indirect exporting	push strategy	

NASBITE CGBP TOPICS COVERED IN THIS CHAPTER

Note: For full details of the alignment of each chapter with the NASBITE CGBP, be sure to review the information provided in the section "Studying for the NASBITE CGBP Exam."

CGBP Rubric	Topic
01/08/01:	industry, trade, and investment associations
01/08/02:	government support agencies—U.S. government agencies
02/01/01:	internal resources (e.g., export readiness assessment, goals and preferences of senior management, experiences and capabilities of employees, technical and production capabilities)
02/02/02	public and private marketing resources—International Trade Administration, U.S. Commercial Service
02/04/01:	foreign market entry methods (e.g., licensing, agency/distributor, sales subsidiaries, international joint venture)
02/06/01:	customer expectations and cultural requirements
02/06/09:	trade assistance resources in support of providing products and services
02/09/01:	types and roles of distribution channels (e.g., resellers, agency/distributor, joint ventures)
02/09/02:	impact of local market distribution characteristics and implementation issues, gray marketing

Note: The CGBP standard does not specifically mention "foreign partner identification" but it is implied in 02/04/01 and that topic is also covered in this chapter.

QUESTIONS AND RESEARCH

1. Identify the ways to reach foreign markets by making a domestic sale.

2. Why might a small, new-to-export company be interested in using an EMC?

3. Identify and contrast the differences between indirect exporting and direct exporting as foreign market entry methods. Identify the type of company that would be suitable for each.

4. What procedures should a firm follow when selecting a distributor?

5. What are the benefits of local manufacturing as a form of market entry? What are the costs?

6. When is contract manufacturing desirable?

7. What are the pros and cons of licensing as a form of market entry?

8. How do successful licensors manage their licensing program?

9. Why is acquisition often the preferred way to establish wholly owned operations abroad?

10. Discuss the financial and pricing techniques for motivating foreign distributors.

11. What are some of the international differences in wholesaling?

12. Many markets have relatively large numbers of small retailers. How does this constrain the local marketing of an international firm?

13. Discuss the implications for the international marketer of the trend toward larger-scale retailing.

14. Why do U.S. firms tend to have somewhat different distribution channels abroad?

CHAPTER 8 TEAM PROJECT ASSIGNMENT: Foreign Market Entry and Partner Selection

This chapter focused on the critical task of selecting the foreign market entry mode for a particular country. It discussed the range of options available to a firm and that firms have to balance their need to control and get feedback from a market with the risks associated with each entry mode. It also discussed the types of foreign partners, ways to find suitable partners, and channel distribution issues.

For your team research for this chapter, you will make a decision as to which entry mode you recommend for each of the three countries selected from the team project in Chapter 7. The entry mode does not need to be the same for each country. You will also research potential foreign partners.

For your team research from this chapter, discuss the following issues:

1. For each country, identify your recommended market entry mode. Explain why you selected that mode and why other modes for that country are not recommended for your client.

2. Depending on the entry mode you recommend for each country, there will be a level of risk associated with that entry mode and that particular country. Discuss what you see as the top two or three most important risks for each country. Highlight some initial ways to potentially mitigate that risk.

3. Review the issues highlighted in Figure 8-2 regarding partner selection. What would be important considerations in looking for a foreign partner for your client in each country? What type of partner do you recommend for each country?

4. Using the resources identified in this chapter, such as Kompass, try to identify potential partners in each country. Using the Internet, find as much information as possible on each potential partner. Discuss your findings.

CASE 8.1 Metro Corporation Alliance Negotiation, by Professor Farok J. Contractor*

INTRODUCTION: A KEY ISSUE IN ALLIANCE AGREEMENTS

We live in an era of corporate alliances where one firm often transfers knowledge, or a capability, to its partner. A key aspect in negotiating alliance agreements is the issue of compensation. This requires two steps (1) Placing a value on the technology or knowledge to be shared with an ally, (2) Devising a compensation formula (e.g., a royalty rate, or an equity share in the case of an equity joint venture) whereby the knowledge-supplying partner is recompensed. Alliances come in many forms, licensing, equity joint ventures, or some combination of the two. In this case, the alliance is a licensing agreement.

In this case, the knowledge was encapsulated, or codified, in software developed by Metro Corporation. This was in the form of a CAD (Computer-Aided Design) software package that gives the user enhanced design capabilities in designing petroleum storage tanks.

The software is available on four CDs or compact disks. The marginal cost of the final step, of writing the software on the CDs, was below $5. But how much should Metro charge a licensee for use of this valuable knowledge and design capability?

Metro Corporation began negotiations with Impecina Construcciones S.A. of Peru, for the licensing of the software. (The events described below are close to real life. However, some facts and numbers have been disguised at the request of the company. This does not greatly distort the essential facts, or detract from the learning value of this case).

THE LICENSOR FIRM

Metro Corporation is a diversified steel rolling, fabricating, and construction company based in the U.S. Midwest and considers itself to be in a mature industry. Innovations are few and far between in the basic steel-making process. With high labor costs, transport and tariff barriers, and the support given by many governments to their own companies, exporting as a means of doing foreign business is limited. Similarly, given the large investment, modest return and political sensitivity of the industry, direct foreign investment is not a very strong international business option for Metro Corporation. In a global strategic sense then, Metro has more frequently focused on licensing as a foreign market entry method, with technologies confined to (1) processes and engineering *peripheral* to the basic steel making process—for example, mining methods, coke oven door designs, galvanizing, and so on, and (2) *applications* of steel in construction and other industries, for example, petroleum tank design, welding methods, thermo-adhesion, and so on.

All Metro's licensing is handled by its international division, International Construction and Engineering (ICE), which is beginning to develop a reputation in Western Europe and South America as a good source for specialized construction technology and design.

THE PROPOSED LICENSEE

Impecina, a private firm, is the largest construction company in Peru and operates throughout Latin America. Impecina has a broad range of interests including residential and commercial buildings, hydraulic works, transportation, and maritime works. Employing several thousand personnel, engineers, and technicians, its sales had doubled in the last five years. It was still primarily a Peruvian business with most turnover in Peru, but was in the process of expanding into Colombia, the North African Mediterranean countries, and Argentina, Brazil, and Venezuela. Impecina has advanced computer capacity at their head office and branches.

At the time of the license negotiation, Impecina's experience was limited to the smaller fixed cone roof designs under 150 feet diameter. Metro's software would enable them to effectively bid on the construction of larger tanks, as well as floating-roof tanks in which they had no experience, so far.

THE TECHNOLOGY

National Tank Inc., a fabrication division of Metro, had developed a CAD or computer-aided design software package for floating-roof oil storage tanks, which minimized the use of steel within American Petroleum Institute or any other oil industry standards. Particularly for the larger tanks, for instance, over 150 feet in diameter, this would confer upon the bidding contractor a significant cost advantage. National Tank had spent one labor year at a direct cost of $2,250,000 just to write the computer program. Patents were involved—in an incidental manner—only for the seals on the floating-roof. Metro had not bothered to file for this patent except in the United States.

THE MARKET

Peru's indigenous oil output is one hundred thousand barrels per day, and it imports two hundred thousand barrels per day. This requires large storage capacity. As part of its infrastructure planning, the Peruvian government announced a program to augment Peru's oil-storage capacity. Impecina's representatives at a preliminary meeting with ICE in U.S. headquarters said their government planned $200 million expenditures on oil-storage facilities over the next 3 years (mostly in large sized tanks). Floating-roof tanks are also considered more environmentally friendly as they have lower evaporation rates. Additional construction beyond the first three years appeared very likely. However, the government's plans were announced only three years at a time. Of this, Impecina's representatives said their "ambition" was to capture a one third market share. This appeared to be a very credible target, as illustrated by Impecina's existing 30 percent share of the market for the fixed cone, under 150-foot diameter tanks. Additionally, they claimed that private sector construction value over the next three years would total $40 million.

Neighboring Colombia was building a 12 million ton refinery, but the tank installation plans of other South American nations were not known, according to the Impecina representative.

Approximately half of a storage system's construction cost goes for the tank alone, the remainder being excavation, foundation, piping, instrumentation, and other ancillary equipment. Impecina's engineers were very familiar with civil construction other than floating-roof tanks.

Each of Impecina's competitors in Peru for this business was affiliated with a prominent company: Umbertomas with Jefferson Inc. in the United States, Zapa with Philadelphia Iron & Steel, Cosmas with Peoria Duluth Construction Inc., and so on. Thus, association with Metro, as a well-known American company, would help Impecina in the bidding process.

THE FIRST MEETING

Metro's National Tank division had in the past year bid jointly with Impecina on a project in southern Peru. Though that bid was unsuccessful, Impecina had learned about Metro's computerized design software and initiated a formal first round of alliance negotiations, which were to lead to a licensing agreement. The meeting took place in the United States. Two Impecina executives of subdirector rank were accompanied by an American consultant they had hired. Metro was represented by the vice president of ICE, the ICE attorney, and an executive from the National Tank division.

Minutes of this meeting show it was exploratory. Both genuine and rhetorical questions were asked. Important information and perceptions were exchanged and the groundwork laid for concluding negotiations. Initial meetings often include maneuvers and claims which may sometimes be inaccurate. Metro's experienced negotiators knew that prospective licensees will often exaggerate the potential market size of the licensee (in order to make the proposal look attractive to a prospective licensor), try to write as many exclusive territories into the agreement as possible, demand use of a licensor's global brand name, while trying to minimize their payment. Following is a bare summary of important issues that were discussed in the somewhat circular discussion:

1. **Licensee Market Coverage:** Impecina tried to represent itself as essentially a Peruvian firm. This was done in the hopes of paying low royalties for an emerging-country market, and not to appear to have overly-large international ambitions. Yet throughout the meeting, there kept cropping up the issue of the license also covering Libya, Algeria, Morocco, Colombia, Argentina, Brazil, and Venezuela. The discussions also reviewed the Peruvian government's expenditure plans and Impecina's hoped for market share of the floating-roof tank market.

2. **Territory and Exclusivity:** For Peru, Metro negotiators had no difficulty conceding exclusivity. They mentioned that granting exclusivity to a licensee for any territory was agreeable in principle—provided a

minimum performance guarantee was given. Metro's mention of a minimum performance guarantee seems to have sobered the territorial ambitions of Impecina representatives, and the question of territory was deferred for future discussion. At one point a Metro executive remarked, "We could give Impecina a nonexclusive license for some countries—and say, for example, we wouldn't give another (licensee) a license in those nations for one year," proposing the idea of a trial period for Impecina to generate business in a territory. There was no comment from Impecina on this suggestion either.

3. **Agreement Life:** Impecina negotiators very quickly agreed to a 10-year term suggested by Metro Corporation. Metro's representatives recall being surprised that Impecina agreed to this somewhat long license term so readily. (A long agreement locks the parties in to making payments over the long term, whereas a short agreement may conclude without the licensee agreeing to renew).

4. **Trade Name:** The Impecina negotiators placed great emphasis on their ability to use Metro's name in bidding, explaining how their competition in Peru had technical collaboration with three U.S. companies (as noted previously). Metro's negotiators asked half-jokingly, "Did that mean Metro's National Tank Division could compete with Impecina in Peru?" (Actually both sides seem to have tacitly agreed that it was not possible for Metro to do business directly in Peru, because infrastructure contracts were typically awarded by governments to their own local companies.)

5. **Licensee Market Size in Peru:** Attention turned to the dollar value of the future large (floating-roof) tank market in Peru. Impecina threw out an estimate of $200 million government expenditures and $40 million in private sector spending, over the next three years, of which they targeted a one third share. Metro's representatives felt that this was an exaggeration. Later, a more realistic market size estimate of $150 million over three years (government *and* private) with a share of $50 million received by Impecina over three years, was arrived at. (Memories are not clear on how the market-size estimates were revised, or how more realistic estimates were concluded).

   Besides the issue of the *total* market for large tanks, a critical variable is the prospective licensee's *share* of the market. Impecina negotiators insisted that they would have a one-third share of the market. Metro's representatives were initially skeptical: "Will Impecina *guarantee* us they will obtain one third of the market?" Impecina responded, "That's an optimistic figure but we hope we can realize it." Impecina offered as evidence their existing one third share of the "fixed-roof under 150 feet" market. This was an undeniable and proven fact, a record based on Impecina's good relations with the Peruvian government—a relationship that was expected to continue.

6. **Product Mix Covered by License:** It became clear that Impecina wanted CAD software for floating-roof technology for *all* sizes, as well as fixed roof over 100 feet diameter. However they suggested that the royalty agreement only cover floating-roof tanks over 100-feet in size; after all, they said they already had the technology for fixed-roof and smaller tanks. Impecina was asked if, in order to simplify royalty calculation and monitoring, it would pay royalties on all tanks (of any size). After considerable discussion, Metro compromised with Impecina, to have the royalties based on both floating *and* fixed-roof types, but for sizes over 100 feet. This was based on consensus over three points: a. Impecina's competition probably does not pay (its licensors) on small tanks and, therefore, Impecina would be at a disadvantage if it had to pay on small tanks also. b. The market in floating-roof tanks was usually over 100 feet. c. Impecina claimed that customers normally dictate the dimensions of the tanks, i.e., Impecina could not reduce tank size in order to avoid paying a royalty to Metro.

7. **Compensation Formula:** Metro proposed three compensation elements: An initial lump sum payment (when the agreement is signed), plus a *per diem*

rate for engineers and executives sent to Peru for bid assistance, plus a royalty on successful bids based on the barrel capacity installed by Impecina.

This would be a function of Peru's market size and oil demand. Impecina representatives spoke glowingly of huge volumes. Impecina's American consultant broached the idea of royalties on a sliding scale, lower with larger-capacity tanks. He talked grandly about "1 million barrel capacity tanks" and a huge potential. Metro's negotiators threw cold water on this and brought the discussion down to earth. Both sides took a long lunch break and mentally regrouped.

On returning, the issue of what to base the royalty on, was again taken up for discussion. Impecina executives ventured that, as a rule of thumb, their profit markup on a turnkey job was 6 percent. However, since excavation, piping, and ancillary equipment, typically constitute half of the total construction value, Metro's representative said this was equivalent to a profit margin of 12 percent on the tank alone.

Impecina negotiators' counter-proposal included no lump sum and only royalties (preferably sliding) and per diem fees at $500 for bid assistance from Metro executives and engineers. Impecina claimed it would be too big a risk to pay Metro a large up-front, or lump sum, fee on technology that was not proven. "What if we do not get a single order, and have paid a large sum to Metro?" Metro countered by pointing out that, as far as they were concerned: a. Lump sums should cover more than their initial technology-transfer costs, and b. that per diem fees of $500 plus travel costs did not amount to even a recovery of costs, let alone profit. The compensation design question was left unfinished at this stage, deferred for later negotiation, the broad outlines having been laid. Metro's starting formal offer, which would mention specific numbers, was to be e-mailed to Lima in a week.

8. **The Royalty Basis:** Metro agreed to the idea that Impecina engineers were very familiar with excavation, piping, wiring, and other ancillary equipment. Metro was transferring technology for *the tank alone*, which typically comprised half of overall installed value. Hence the royalty formula should be based on the tank value alone.

9. **Government Intervention:** Toward the end of the discussions, Impecina brought up the question of the Peruvian government having to approve of the agreement. This led to their retreat from the idea of a 10-year term agreed to earlier, and Impecina then mentioned five years. No agreement was reached. (Incidentally, Peru had regulations indicating a "guideline" of five years for foreign licenses.)

INTERNAL DISCUSSION IN METRO LEADING TO THE FORMAL OFFER

The advantages derived by the licensee would be acquisition of floating roof technology, time and money saved in attempting to generate a computerized design procedure in house, design capabilities for floating-roof tanks which they did not currently possess, a cost and efficiency advantage in bidding on larger tanks, and finally the use of Metro's name.

It was estimated that National Tank had spent $2,250,000 (one labor-year = equivalent to two software engineers or executives for six months, plus other costs) in developing the computer program. Additionally, it may cost $40,000 to convert the program into Spanish, the metric system, and another $ 25,000 to adapt it to the material availability and labor cost factors peculiar to Peru. Simultaneously, there would be semiformal instruction of Impecina engineers in the use of the program, petroleum industry codes, and Metro fabrication methods. All this had to be done before the licensee would be ready for a single bid.

It was visualized that Metro would then assist Impecina for two labor-weeks for each bid preparation, and four labor-weeks on successful receipt of a contract award. Additionally, if Metro's specialized construction equipment were used, three labor-months of on-site training would be needed.

As the licensee's personnel moved along their learning curve, assistance of the type just described would diminish until it was no longer needed after a few successful bids.

Additional considerations that went into a determination of the initial offer were:

1. Metro obligations (and sunk costs) in development and conversion were fairly determinate, whereas their obligations to assist Impecina in bidding depended on the technical sophistication and absorptive capacity of the licensee's engineers, their success rate in bidding, and so on.

2. If Impecina's market estimates were used, they would generate large tank orders totaling $50 million over the next three years, on which they would make a profit of $3 million (at 6 percent on $50 million, or 12 percent on the tank portion of the jobs).

3. The market beyond three years was an unknown, but may continue the same rate.

4. Exclusive rights might be given to Impecina in Peru and Colombia, with Metro perhaps reserving the right of conversion to nonexclusive if a minimum market share was not captured by Impecina.

5. While Impecina's multinational expansion plans were unknown, their business in the other nations was too small to justify granting them exclusivity. They may be satisfied with a vague promise of future consideration as an exclusive licensee in those territories.

6. Metro would agree to a term of 10 years.

7. It was felt that Impecina computer and engineering capability was strong enough so they would not need Metro assistance after a few bids.

Surprisingly, the discussions reveal no explicit consideration given to the idea that Impecina may emerge some day as a multinational competitor. "It all depends on whether governments begin to award construction jobs to foreign bidders," said one Metro negotiator. "But wait! That's not the end of potential competition from Impecina," his colleague added, "They have their own computer capabilities and can compete with us in software licensing." After some discussion in Metro, their representatives concluded that the day when governments would award construction jobs to foreign firms was still in the future, for most of the nations served by Metro or Impecina. Hence the likelihood of such competition was small for the next several years. As far as Impecina's internal computer capabilities, they were good. Impecina could at least improve on Metro's software, and write new versions, and license them in other nations. "To avoid this risk Impecina should have the right to sublicense only to its controlled subsidiaries," observed Metro's lawyer.

In view of the uncertainty about how successful the licensee would actually be in securing orders, and the uncertainty surrounding the Peruvian government's attitude, a safe strategy seemed to be to try and get as large a front-end fee as possible. Almost arbitrarily, a figure of $400,000 was thrown up. (This would more than cover the initial costs of transferring the technology to the licensee. In fact, $400,000 amounted to 16 percent of the software development costs. The latter calculation was not really not meaningful because the software was initially written for the U.S. petroleum tank market and moreover, licenses have been set up in other nations as well, from which amortization of development costs have already begun to occur). With $400,000 there would be sufficient margin for negotiations and to cover uncertainties. In order that the licensee's competitiveness not be diminished by the large lump sum fee, a formula as described later may be devised whereby the first five years' royalties could be reduced.

THE FORMAL OFFER

The formal offer communicated by e-mail a week later called for the following payment terms:

* $400,000 lump sum fee.

* A 2 percent royalty on any tanks constructed of a size over 100 feet in diameter, with up to one half of royalties owed in each of the first 5 years reduced by an amount up to $40,000 each year, without carryovers from year to year. The royalty percentage would apply to tanks alone (i.e. the total contract value less excavation, foundation, dikes, piping, instrumentation, and pumps).

* Agreement life of 10 years.

* Metro to provide services to Impecina described earlier in consideration of the lump sum and royalty fees.

* For additional services, as described earlier, Metro would provide on request personnel paid up to $1500 per day, plus travel and living costs while away from their place of business. The *per diem* rates would be subject to escalation based on a representative cost index. There would be a ceiling placed on the number of labor-days Impecina could request in any year.

* All payments to be made in U.S. dollars, net, after all local withholding, and other taxes.

* Impecina would receive exclusive rights for Peru and Colombia only, and nonexclusive rights for Morocco, Libya, Algeria, Argentina, Venezuela, and Brazil. These could be converted to an exclusive basis on demonstration of sufficient business in the future. For Peru and Colombia, Metro reserves the right to treat the agreement as nonexclusive if Impecina fails to get at least 20 percent of installed capacity of a type covered by the agreement.

* Impecina would have the right to sublicense only to its controlled subsidiaries.

* Impecina would supply free of charge to Metro all improvements made by it on the software during the term of the agreement.

* Impecina would be entitled to advertise its association with Metro in assigned territories on prior approval as to wording, form, and content.

THE FINAL AGREEMENT

Metro executives reported that the Peruvians "did not bat an eyelid" at their demands, and that an agreement was soon reached in a matter of days. The only significant change was Metro agreeing to take a lower lump sum of $300,000 (still a large margin over incremental agreement costs). In return, the provision for reducing one half of the royalties up to $40,000 per year was *dropped*. The final agreement called for a straight 2 percent royalty payment (on tank value alone, as before). Other changes were minor: Impecina to continue to receive the benefit of further R&D; Metro to provide at cost, a construction engineer if specialized welding equipment was used; the per diem fee fixed at $1000 per day (indexed by an average hourly wage escalation factor used by the U.S. Department of Labor); and the $300,000 lump-sum fee to be paid in three installments over the first three months after agreement signing.

In other respects such as territory, royalty rate, exclusivity, travel allowances, and so on, the agreement conformed with Metro's initial offer.

A LAST-MINUTE UNANTICIPATED UPSET

The Peruvian ministry disallowed a 10-year agreement life. By then, both parties had gone too far to want to reopen the entire negotiations and Metro appears to have resigned itself to an agreement life of five years, with a further extension of another five years subject to mutual consent. "Don't worry," said the Impecina representative. "Even if our government does not allow ten years, we will still be friends. After five years friends can shake hands again." Metro appears to have been content with this vague assurance. But given Impecina's in-house engineering and computer capability, extension of the agreement life was a very open question.

Questions and Research

Analyze the negotiations from each party's perspective:

1. List what each party is offering and what it hopes to receive.
2. Identify the elements in each list that are "musts" and those where flexibility may be shown, and state why.
3. Describe negotiating tactics or ploys each party used, or could have used.
4. Compute net cash flows for each party under several scenarios. For example:
   a. SCENARIO 1 (Very pessimistic) Licensee fails to get a single order.
   b. SCENARIO 2 (Conservative Scenario) Licensee gets one third market share in Peru for three years, no orders thereafter, and no orders in any other nation.
   c. SCENARIO 3 (Optimistic Scenario) Licensee gets one third share in Peru for ten years and half again as much in business in other nations.
5. Compute the share of net present value of profits that each of the two parties will capture under various market scenarios. (Use a 10% discount rate for your NPV calculations).
6. What do you think of the "rule of thumb", encountered in licensing literature, that licensors should settle for roughly one-quarter to one-half of the licensee's incremental profit?
7. a. Are sunk costs relevant here?
   b. What, if any, are the opportunity costs to Metro?
   c. In computing the licensor's cash flows, remember that in addition to the direct costs of implementing an agreement, there are sometimes substantial indirect costs. What are they?
   d. How would you apply the licensor's development costs to this exercise?
8. Why did the licensee accept the offer (with small changes) without "batting an eyelid"? (Hint: Calculate break-even sales for both parties.).
9. Should the licensor have threatened to pull out when the government limited the agreement life to five years? (Hint: Recalculate question 5 under a five year limit.)
10. Do you think the licensee knew this all along?
11. Discuss the role of government intervention in licensing negotiations in general.
12. In general, what costs should a technology-owning company consider when opening a negotiation with a prospective ally? Are development costs relevant? If so, how does one calculate them. (It took only $2.5 million to write the software. But what about the over hundred year experience of the company in the steel and construction business which was distilled into the software? Should that be considered? There is no clear answer, but consider this as a long-term competitive strategy issue).

NOTES

1. Enrique Claver and Diego Quer, "Choice of Market Entry Mode in China: The Influence of Firm-Specific Factors," *Journal of General Management* 30, no. 3 (Spring 2005): 51–71.

2. Sumon Kumar Bhaumik and Stephen Gelb, "Determinants of Entry Mode Choice of MNCs in Emerging Markets: Evidence from South Africa and Egypt," *Emerging Markets Finance & Trade* 41, no 2 (March/April 2005): 5–24.

3. Jan Johanson and Jan-Erik Vahlne, "The Internationalization Process of the Firm—A Model of Knowledge Development and Increasing Foreign Market Commitments," *Journal of International Business Studies* 8, no. 1 (1977): 25–34.

4. Jan Johanson and Jan-Erik Vahlne, "The Mechanism of Internationalism," *International Marketing Review* 7, no. 4, (1990): 11–24.

5. Edible Arrangements website (www.ediblearrangements.com/), accessed June 10, 2010; "Edible Floral Arrangements Maker to Expand Business," *New Haven Register*, April 6, 2005; "Edible Arrangements Set to Launch and Expand Its Foray in the UAE," *The Middle East & North Africa Business Report*, Jordan edition, December 6, 2007.

6. V. Kumar and Velavan Subramaniam. "A Contingency Framework for the Mode of Entry Decision," *Journal of World Business* 32, no. 1 (1997): 53–72.

7. M. Krishna Erramilli and C.P. Rao. "Choice of Foreign Market Entry Modes by Service Firms: Role of Market Knowledge," *Management International Review* 30, no. 2 (1990): 135–50.

8. *CIA World Factbook* (https://www.cia.gov/library/publications/the-world-factbook), accessed June 10, 2010; "Canada B2C E-Commerce Report Analyzes the Factors Driving the Canadian Internet Consumer Market to Record Heights," M2PressWIRE, February 18, 2008; Amazon website (www.amazon.com), accessed June 10, 2010; Swimman, Inc website (www.swimman.com), accessed June 10, 2010.

9. Frederik Balfour, "The State's Long Apron Strings," *Business Week*, Issue 3948, August 22, 2005, p. 74.

10. Geoffrey A. Fowler, "Buying Spree by China Firms Is a Bet on Value of U.S. Brands," *Wall Street Journal*, June 23, 2005, p. B.1.

11. Michael A. Hitt, Robert E. Hoskisson, and Hicheon Kim. "International Diversification: Effects on Innovation and Firm Performance in Product-Diversified Firms," *Academy of Management Journal* 40, no. 4 (1997): 767–98.

12. Benjamin M. Oviatt and Patricia McDougall, "Toward a Theory of International New Ventures," *Journal of International Business Studies* 25, no. 1 (1994): 45–64.

13. S. Tamer Cavusgil, "A Quiet Revolution in Australian Exporters," *Marketing News* 28, no. 11 (1994): 18.

14. "Samsung Introduces the First Complete Line of Portable XM Satellite Radios with MP3 Capability," Samsung Press Release (www.samsung.com/us/news/newsRead.do?news_seq = 3244), July 18, 2006; "Samsung Electronics Partners with XM Satellite Radio to Offer Samsung's First MP3 Players with XM Satellite Radio," PR Newswire Association LLC, July 26, 2005; "Citibank, China Union Pay Tie Up to Allow Chinese Access to Forex Abroad AFX," News Limited AFX—Asia, September 13, 2005; "Li & Fung Links Up with Daymon Retail," *Financial Times*, August 12, 2005; Li & Fung website (www.lifunggroup.com), accessed September 15, 2005.

15. For further details of the programs from the U.S. Department of Commerce, visit the website

chapter

9 International Product Policy

International marketing involves satisfying consumers' needs in foreign markets. The question often asked is, "Can I sell my product in international markets?" A better question would be, "What products should I be selling in international markets?" International product policy should be the cornerstone around which other aspects of the global marketing mix are designed and integrated.

Two main questions should be addressed:

- **Existing products.** Should existing products be adapted or standardized to best meet global buyer needs?
- **New products.** How can new products be developed for global markets?

This chapter looks specifically at how companies develop their international product policy, including new product development (NPD) and product-line policies.

The main goals of this chapter are to ● ● ●

1. Delineate the influences that lead a company to standardize or adapt its products.

2. Discuss the product attributes that are considered, in addition to the basic product itself, in formulating international product policy.

3. Discuss the various strategies companies use in new product development for international markets.

4. Discuss how companies manage their new product development.

5. Show examples of international product development to highlight best practices, including customer involvement and cooperation in product development.

6. Discuss global research and development activities and associated key issues, including the location of research and development (R&D) activities and coordination techniques.

251

What to Sell Abroad: Product Policy for International Markets

Swatch is a good example of a firm that was able to expand through primarily a single product concept.

Developing a product policy for a firm as it grows internationally is not an easy process. The firm must take into account a number of factors that will be discussed in this chapter, including consumer needs, governmental influences, and competitive pressures. A firm would, of course, hope to simply extend the product range (policy) used in its domestic market to its foreign markets. But this may or may not be possible.

An interesting product policy example is the Swatch watch company SMH, the largest watch manufacturer in the world. Inexpensive and mass-produced in Switzerland, the watches are plastic fashion items selling for about $40 worldwide. The product concept involves manufacturing and marketing a striking, low-cost, high-quality watch. The watch is designed to appeal to the low-end segment of the market. SMH decided to enter this segment where Swiss companies had zero market share, making and selling an "emotional" product that would allow the wearer to convey an image, a fashion statement.[1]

New Swatch collections are launched each year to add to its over 350 models. A team of approximately 20 designers from Europe, the United States, Japan, Australia, and elsewhere develop designs that are then culled and presented to a management committee, which selects the items for each season's line. The watches have become collectors' items and are inexpensive enough that an individual can own several; in fact, the average customer in Italy owns six watches.

Though Swatch was able to take a standard product global, it nonetheless must continually address the issue of how much adaptation should be made to its product to meet local needs. This is an ongoing challenge for all companies as they expand globally. Standardizing saves money but may not specifically meet local needs. Adapting can be costly. This dilemma is discussed next.

Adaptation versus Standardization of the Product

The easiest product policy for a firm just beginning to go international is to sell in foreign markets the same products designed for its home market. This would be a standardization policy. Standardization is appropriate when customers are similar overseas or share common needs to those in the home market. However, due to a number a factors, standardization may not be possible, and the firm may be forced to use at least some form of product adaptation. Such an adaptation policy may result in new products or simply modified products.

Table 9-1 summarizes the main factors that influence a firm to pursue standardization or adaptation strategies when introducing products into new international markets. The goals of reducing costs and complexity lead companies to consider standardization. The goals of meeting customer needs lead companies toward product adaptation. Depending on the industry and market, the importance of one goal may outweigh that of the other.

Factors Encouraging Standardization

The attractions of standardization are obvious. It can result in lower costs and economies of scale in manufacturing, product development, and marketing. Managerial complexity is reduced, and export marketing is facilitated when the same product is exported to several countries.

Table 9-1 • Factors Favoring Product Standardization versus Adaptation

Standardization	Adaptation
• High costs of adaptation • Primarily industrial products • Convergence and similar tastes in diverse country markets • Predominant use in urban environments • Marketing predominantly to countries similar to the firm's home country • Centralized management of international operations when mode of entry is mainly direct exporting • Strong country-of-origin image and effect • Scale economies in production, marketing, and R&D • Standardized products marketed by competitors	• Differences in technical standards • Primarily consumer and personal-use products • Variations in consumer needs • Variations in conditions of use • Variations in ability to buy—differences in income levels • Fragmentation, with independent national subsidiaries • Strong cultural differences, language, and so on, affecting purchase and use • Local environment-induced adaptation: differences in raw materials available and government-required standards and regulations • Adaptation strategy successfully used by competitors

HIGH COSTS OF ADAPTION

Adaptation costs can be significant. Beyond the required R&D necessary for the modification, manufacturing costs (retooling, training, quality, new technology) can also be high. If sales volumes of the modified product are low, per unit costs are even higher. These added costs may lead to difficulties selling the product at a reasonable price (that covers costs and that is still attractive enough to gain market share and ultimately profits). In the case of washing machines and dryers, Whirlpool found that the colder Scandinavian countries required more powerful heating elements to dry clothes compared to Italy, where it was common to hang clothes out to dry, especially in good weather. Adding a different drying module raised costs and made the dryers less competitive, especially when European economies experienced a slowdown in their economic growth.

Industrial products tend to be standardized globally due to common use regardless of location.

INDUSTRIAL PRODUCTS

Products for which technical specifications are critical tend to be uniform internationally. In general, industrial goods are more standardized than consumer goods. Even when industrial goods are modified, the changes are likely to be minor—an adaptation of the electric voltage or the use of metric measures, for example. Of course, differences may be forced on a company by distinct and different national standards in areas such as environmental protection. (photo)

CONVERGENCE AND SIMILAR TASTES IN DIVERSE COUNTRY MARKETS

As countries obtain similar income levels and develop at the same pace economically, their consumption patterns are likely to converge. Europe is a good example of this trend, with the creation of the EU and the euro resulting in a single large market with growing similarity of tastes and incomes. This convergence of consumption patterns allows firms to sell products that are standardized for much of Europe. To succeed, of course, the standardized products must offer value beyond that available from the competition. A strong driver of globalization is the appeal of lower prices coupled with world-standard technology, quality, and service—all of which persuade consumers to drop local preferences. Global competition spells the end of domestic territoriality. When a global producer offers lower costs internationally, patronage expands exponentially. The producer not only reaches into distant markets, but also attracts customers who previously held to local preferences and now capitulate to the attractions of lower prices.[2] For an example of balancing standardization and local adaptation, see "Washing Machines around the World."

••• Washing Machines around the World

An example of convergence in tastes comes from the history of the European washing machine industry. When Hoover, a major producer of washing machines, researched expanding into the European market, its research showed that consumers from various European countries had distinct preferences. At that time, Italians wanted a shorter machine, whereas most others wanted a 34-inch height. The French, Italians, and British opted for a narrow machine and enamel drums, but Germans and Swedes wanted a wide machine and stainless steel drums. The British wanted a top-loading feature, but the others preferred front-loading washing machines. With regard to washing machine capacity, Italians wanted 4 kilos, the British and French wanted 5 kilos, and Germans and Swedes expressed a need for 6 kilos. Spin speed ranged from a preference for 60 rpm in France to medium speed (400 rpm) in Italy to high speed (700 to 850 rpm) in Britain, Sweden, and Germany. The French and British preferred an agitator washing action; the others wanted a tumble washing action. Each country also had a distinct preference with regard to external styling: British respondents wanted an inconspicuous appearance, Italians wanted brightly colored machines, Germans wanted an indestructible appearance, the French opted for elegance, and the Swedes preferred a "strong" appearance.[3]

However, for the company to satisfy national preferences, implementing changes to the machine produced in the United Kingdom would have dramatically increased cost per unit, as well as required an investment of additional capital. Research also showed that both the heavily promoted top-of-the-line German washing machine and the inexpensive Italian machine at half the price were bestsellers. In fact, the Italian machine was selling well to the German market. An inference from this data is that an aggressively promoted, low-priced washing machine with standard features could be acceptable to a broad market. That means the low price can convince customers to accept the absence of certain features. Low price alone is not enough, however. Aggressive promotion, quality, and service are equally important ingredients of the marketing mix.

Building on these observations, Whirlpool launched its "people's washing machine" project with the goal of developing an affordable washing machine for low-income consumers in developing countries. The price had to be between $150 and $200, with initial markets of focus being Brazil, India, and China. At the time, only about 25 percent of Brazilian households had a washing machine, with penetration rates in China and India of 8 and 4.5 percent, respectively. Whirlpool decentralized its operations to produce components and assemble the washing machine in the most efficient global locations. The machine was designed in Brazil and manufactured in Brazil, India, and China. To make the machine affordable, it used a single-drive system whereby clothes are washed and spun without switching gears and had a smaller capacity of 9 pounds. Although this required more frequent washing and damper clothes, these trade-offs were acceptable to consumers who could never before afford to buy a washing machine. Modifications were also made to customize the machine for each market. Brazilians preferred a machine that sat on legs, had a long soak cycle, and included a transparent acrylic lid so they could see the machine operate. In China, designers incorporated folding lids so the Chinese user could hang shelves above the washer, added a grease removal option to remove bicycle grease from clothes, and customized the colors such as gray and green because it was often kept in living areas and had to look appealing. For the Indian market, the machine had a sari cycle with the ability to wash 6 yards of delicate fabric and casters so the machine could be wheeled from the living area to the washing area.[4]

Hoover's and Whirlpool's experiences with washing machines suggest that standardization can work as part of a well-thought-out marketing mix. Judicious adaptation is sometimes necessary due to local market considerations, but the standardization of the core product is still possible.

PREDOMINANT USE IN URBAN ENVIRONMENTS

Research has shown that products targeted to urban markets in developing countries required only minimal changes from those products marketed in developed countries. Products targeted for semi-urban markets required more changes. Products targeted for national markets in developing countries needed even further adaptation to accommodate the requirements of the poorer, more culturally diverse population. These three levels of product adaptation were identified through a study of 61 subsidiaries operating in 22 less-developed countries.[5] This suggests that urban environments are similar across countries. It also suggests that products such as compact cars, which are designed to be used primarily in large cities, could be standardized across groups of countries that share similar levels of income and economic development.

MARKETING TO PREDOMINANTLY SIMILAR COUNTRIES

As discussed in Chapter 7, one initial strategy for a firm is to sell to countries that are similar to its home market, such as a British firm selling to Australia, Canada, or the United States. Given similar cultures, consumer behavior, income, degree of urbanization, and so on, the need for product adaptation may be lower than selling products into much more diverse markets.

CENTRALIZED MANAGEMENT AND DIRECT EXPORTING

If a firm markets overseas principally through direct exporting, it is likely to sell standardized products. There are two reasons a firm might choose export markets that are more likely to accept standardized products: the costs of adaptation and the lack of detailed knowledge about differences between consumers in the export markets. This is especially true of smaller firms that may not have the financial ability for significant product adaptation. However, as a company expands and becomes more financially secure, it may tend toward more product adaptation in order to more successfully meet consumer needs.

COUNTRY OF ORIGIN EFFECTS

Often firms want to stay with a standardized product to stress its link back to their home market, which is part of the product's appeal to foreign consumers. Wrigley's chewing gum, Coca-Cola, and Levi's are examples, as are French products such as perfumes and women's fashion clothing. In those cases, firms may experience real gains from selling standardized products the same way they sell the products in their home markets.

ECONOMIES OF SCALE IN PRODUCTION

Standardizing a product allows a firm to gain scale economies in manufacturing. By spreading more products across a fixed-cost base, the firm decreases the per unit costs. Having a standard product also means the firm may have lower costs because it has learned how to produce the same product cheaper and with better quality.

ECONOMIES OF SCALE IN RESEARCH AND DEVELOPMENT COSTS

If a firm offers an identical product around the world, it gets more mileage out of its R&D efforts. Less research is directed toward the individual desires of national markets, allowing efforts to be focused on the development of the next-generation product. Thus, standardized products yield an advantage in product-development costs and may shorten the time to develop new products.

ECONOMIES OF SCALE IN MARKETING

Even when marketing is done on a national basis, economies of scale are possible with standardized products. Sales literature, sales force training, and advertising may vary somewhat from country to country; they will be more similar when the product is uniform than when it must be adapted for different national markets. Satisfying after-sales service requirements and stocking spare parts inventories are easier with a standardized product. When a promotional carryover from one market to another occurs because of common language and media spillover, the carryover is not wasted, but it is an extra return on the advertising.

Factors Encouraging Adaptation

The greatest argument for adapting products is that by doing so, a firm can better meet customer needs, increase sales, and realize higher profits. Modifying products for national or regional markets may raise revenues by more than the costs of adaptation. Specific factors encouraging product adaptation include differences in technical standards, products intended for consumer and personal use, variations in consumer needs and consumer use conditions, different income levels, and government regulations.

DIFFERENCES IN TECHNICAL STANDARDS

Firms must meet technical standards to sell in different national markets. For example, agricultural products sold into the United States must meet guidelines for maximum levels of chemical additives and fertilizers used in growing the products. Europe has restrictions on the sale of beef from cows treated with growth hormones. Europe also has the CE mark, which requires specific product safety standards. Many products may not be sold in Europe if the product does meet specific product standards.

CONSUMER AND PERSONAL USE PRODUCTS

Products sold for personal use are likely to be successful when adapted to local markets. Products such as food, clothing, and entertainment cater to highly individualistic tastes and, hence, must be adapted to the differing needs of local populations. For example, Coca-Cola found itself losing market share in Japan to companies marketing a variety of new soft drinks: sugarless blended Asian teas, fermented milk drinks, and fruit-flavored noncarbonated drinks with less sugar. Rather than stick with its cola soft drinks, Coca-Cola began imitating its Japanese competitors. It offered its own version of Asian tea under the brand name Sokenbicha and its fermented milk drink called Lactia to compete against Calpis Co.'s Calpis Water. As a result, Coca-Cola's newer drinks outsold traditional cola drinks by a 3:2 margin. Coca-Cola was able to push its late-entry competing drinks in Japan because it controlled over 40 percent of Japan's vending machines, which are found on nearly every street corner and train platform. It could stock its drinks in the vending machines, bypass Japan's inefficient and tightly controlled traditional hierarchical distribution system, and use its advertising and marketing clout to win back younger customers who had been forsaking cola drinks for the newer variety of beverages.[6]

VARIATION IN CONSUMER NEEDS AND DIFFERING USE CONDITIONS

Although a given product can fulfill a similar functional need in various countries, the conditions under which the product is used may vary greatly from country to country. Climate, for instance, has an effect on products sensitive to temperature or humidity, making it necessary to modify those products. Another factor is the difference in the skill level of users, especially between consumers in industrialized nations and those in less-developed countries. Differing use conditions also

Products such as soft drinks tend to need some adaptation to meet local consumer tastes and preferences.

drive product adaptation, such as refrigerators, washing machines, and micro-waves, all of which are used in varying degrees between countries.

VARIATIONS IN ABILITY TO BUY—DIFFERENT INCOME LEVELS

The income per capita of the world's nations ranges from over $100,000 to under $200.[7] This range affects the demand not only for consumer durables, but also for inexpensive consumer products. Product features may have to be adapted to make a product affordable at lower income levels. In countries with high incomes, bicycles are leisure products, and consumers look for advanced features such as lightweight alloys, a large number of gears, and detachable wheels. All those features add to the cost of the bicycle, making many bikes quite expensive ($500 to $1,000). In contrast, bicycles are used as basic transportation in countries such as China. Bicycles there are heavy, rugged machines, with an average selling price of under $50. Similar pressures to offer low-cost options are seen in the automobile industry. As discussed in "Tata Motors and Target Pricing" in Chapter 12, the goal was to offer a car with a target price of 110,000 rupees (roughly $US 2,500).

MARKET'S LEVEL OF ECONOMIC DEVELOPMENT

Related to the issue of different income levels is the level of overall economic development of a country. The level of economic development often affects the choice of products to be sold there. Established firms usually have a domestic product line that ranges from mature products to advanced, higher technology products. Demand for higher technology products tends to be linked to other advanced technologies. For example, there would be a demand for fiber-optic switches used for controlling Internet traffic only if the market used fiber-optic lines for communications (as opposed to old copper telephone lines). As the level of economic development is often linked to the country's level of advanced technologies, so would be the demand for particular products. Thus, firms from industrialized countries may find that the products offered in their home market may not find a similar demand in countries with lower levels of economic development.

It is worth noting that the opposite may be true: An emerging economy may have demand for higher technology products than otherwise available in the home market of a firm located in a developed country. This would be the case where the federal or local government of a country decides to move directly into the latest technology within an industry, rather than wait for the country to catch up. Examples include nuclear power generation, cell phone technology, or transportation infrastructure. For example, China has the world's fastest train—faster than the better-known trains in Japan and Europe.[8]

ENVIRONMENTALLY INDUCED ADAPTATION: THE INFLUENCE OF GOVERNMENTS

Nations may forbid certain goods from being imported or manufactured in their country. Conversely, they may require that a product be manufactured locally, not imported. Demand for local production or a high degree of "local content" in a product will often lead an international firm to modify the product. A government's taxation policies also can affect the nature of products offered in the market. An example is the European tax on car and engine size that has been a predominant influence on European car design. There have been related moves to attach higher car fees in Europe with vehicles that emit high CO_2 emissions.[9]

Product adaptations may be required by local market regulations. Islam, for example, prohibits the consumption of alcohol. European and U.S. firms have been attempting to sell nonalcoholic beer in the Middle East, targeting Saudi Arabia, a hot, dry desert country. Whereas Western nonalcoholic beer typically contains about 0.5 percent alcohol, nonalcoholic beer sold in Saudi Arabia must be totally alcohol free; this requires reformulation and special manufacturing. To avoid using the word *beer,* firms call the drink a *malt beverage,* and they cannot advertise it. Therefore, marketers must rely on in-store promotions and contests. The target market segment is younger Saudis who have traveled and perhaps lived abroad.[10]

Government regulations on products, packaging, and labeling are an important cause of product variation among countries, especially in food and drugs. Italy, for example, allows only spaghetti made from durum wheat to be called pasta. Government specifications affect some industrial goods, too. Trucks, tractors, and tires often must meet different government specifications in different markets.

New Product Development (NPD) Strategies

new product development (NPD)

The process of bringing a new product or service to market, including research and development, technology commercialization, and product testing. NPD also includes modification of existing products. (See also *product-line extension*.)

Both domestic and global companies need a strong **new product development** strategy to remain competitive. However, the task is particularly complicated for global companies. They must take into account the global business environment, market characteristics, and varying consumer needs. This section discusses NPD strategies within a global context.

At its core, developing a firm's NPD strategy is centered on two major tasks: (1) understanding consumer needs, conditions of use, and their ability to buy the products; and (2) leveraging the firm's R&D expertise, experience, and intellectual property to develop products that can satisfy consumer needs in different countries. The first task essentially takes into account market characteristics and their impact on product-line strategies, as discussed next. The second task impacts the process a firm takes to develop new products, as discussed later. NPD is also dependent on the mode of entry a firm uses for its international expansion, as discussed in "Product Selection and Foreign Market Entry."

Product Selection and Foreign Market Entry

The nature of a firm's involvement in foreign markets is another product-line determinant. Theoretically, if a firm enters a market through exports only, it has the freedom to choose as many or as few products as it wants in each market. Other modes may have a more direct influence on product-line offerings.

Licensing offers less freedom in product selection. Appropriate licensees may not be available for all products a firm wants to enter in a market. Licensees may not have satisfactory technology, or the best candidates may be licensed to competitors. Even if a firm finds suitable licensees, the firm may be producing products that compete with those of the licensor. Therefore, the licensee's product line can limit the licensor's product line in the market. Occasionally, a firm can overcome such limitations by using different licensees in a country. The feasibility of doing that depends on the availability of licensees and the divisibility of the licensor's product line. If the licensor's products are competitive, the licensee would not want another firm in the country to be involved.

The joint-venture approach can restrict a firm's foreign product line, too. Most joint ventures of international firms bring together two companies, each with a particular product line, just like licensing does. When the national partner has complementary products, the product-line possibilities of the international partner are confined.

Wholly owned foreign operations offer the greatest product-line flexibility. A firm can initially produce products in its foreign plants—products deemed best suited to the local market needs, use conditions, competitive situation, and purchasing power. With initial success and market evolution, the firm can introduce and adapt additional products for the foreign market.

Market Characteristics and Product-Line Strategies

Product-line strategies in foreign markets must reflect the local market characteristics: consumer needs, conditions of use, and ability to buy. These characteristics must be balanced against the market characteristics of the home market in which the product was first developed. As shown in Table 9-2, the product-line strategy is directly linked to these similarities or differences. If the needs, use, and ability to buy are the same, a firm can simply extend its current product offerings into that market, as well as its communication (promotion) strategy. But as shown in the table, when one of these issues is not the same, some adaptation to either the product or communication is required.

Table 9-2 ● Market Characteristics and Product-Line Strategies

If consumers need:	If conditions of use are:	If ability to buy:	Then the product-line strategy would be:
Same	Same	Exists	Product and communications extension
Different	Same	Exists	Product extension and communications adaptation
Same	Different	Exists	Product adaptation and communications extension
Different	Different	Exists	Product and communications adaptation (with new products in the future)
Same	Not applicable	Low to none	New products and communications

Source: Warren J. Keegan, "Multinational Product Planning: Strategic Alternatives," *Journal of Marketing* 33(1): 58–62.

These market comparisons result in either a strategy of product extension that does or does not have significant product adaptation, new products for specific foreign markets, or design of a global product for all markets. In companion with developing the product-line strategy, these market comparisons also impact the promotion strategy.

When consumer needs and conditions of use are not taken into account, failure is the result. For example, Heinz was attracted by the size of the Brazilian market. As a result, it set up a joint venture with Citrosuco, an orange juice exporter, to launch its first product, Frutsi, a fruit drink that had been successful in Venezuela and Mexico. Every street corner in Brazil, however, has a small store selling freshly squeezed orange juice at low prices. Although Heinz could keep pure fruit juice content at 10 percent in most countries, Brazilian regulations set a minimum of 30 percent. This restriction raised prices and made Frutsi uncompetitive with the fresh-squeezed variety. To complicate matters, the additional fruit juice shortened shelf life, necessitating new packaging.

To penetrate the market, Heinz gave cases of Frutsi to retailers on consignment, to be paid for after the product was sold. This approach led to overstocking, and many cases of spoiled product had to be returned. (Brownouts and electric supply interruptions are common in Brazil, and the hot climate hastened product deterioration when refrigeration failed). Then Heinz spent $200,000 on television advertising featuring a robot character that was not considered friendly enough. Although a name change to Suco da Monica, based on a popular Brazilian cartoon character, helped to increase sales, Heinz decided to pull out. All three of the factors in Table 9-2—customer need, conditions of use, and ability to buy—were unfavorable to Heinz in Brazil.[11]

Core Competencies and Product Platforms

Another perspective of NPD strategy development extends the relationship between a company's core competencies and new products.[12] It suggests that effective product development has distinct layers, with a bedrock of core competencies upon which are built **product platforms** and then **product families** marketed to customers. The concept of a product family built on a platform rising out of core competencies suggests a clear product development path for next-generation products. It also stresses new product compatibility with the product family and the constant need for innovation and strengthening of the underlying core competencies.

> **product platform**
>
> A common technology, design, architecture, or formula base on which a line of products is developed. (See also *product family*.)

> **product familiy**
>
> A collection of products built on a common platform of technology, design, architecture, or formula. (See also *product platform*.)

Figure 9-1 ● A Framework to Integrate Markets, Platforms, and Competencies

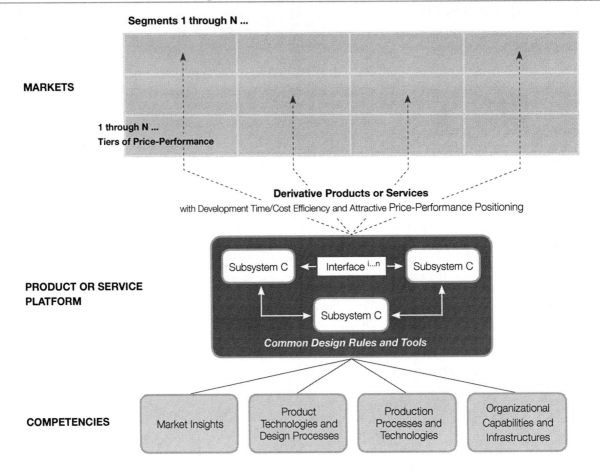

The diagram in Figure 9-1 illustrates this product platform concept. This approach must also take into account the risks and problems connected with the development and management of platforms and product families that emerge from them.[13] Costs and time are associated with developing a platform. Platform thinking requires the formation and collaboration of multifunctional groups. It also requires deliberate planning for the sequence of products that will emerge from the existing platform and planning for platform regeneration and next-generation platforms. Generating additional products from an existing platform may be easiest, even though the platform may be nearing architectural obsolescence, which creates a barrier to architectural innovation.

European firms provide a good illustration of companies taking the platform strategy to NPD: ASML, a leading supplier of semiconductor manufacturing (microlothography) tools; Skil, a division of Bosch and a manufacturer of power tools; and Stork Digital Imaging, a supplier of digital print and preprint applications to the graphic arts and textile printing markets. The three companies had a similar understanding of the complexities and application of the product platform approach. All three focused on product architecture rather than process as the basis for defining and creating their platforms. They resorted to platform approaches to gain increased flexibility in product design, greater efficiency in product development and realization, and improved effectiveness in market positioning and communication.

Table 9-3 provides a summary of how the three companies viewed their experience using platform approaches to product development. The table provides a practical window on the difficulty, costs, and benefits of implementing the

Table 9-3 • Risks and Lessons Learned from Platform-Based Product Development

	ASML	Skil	Stork Digital Imaging
Risks:	• Development time and costs of platform • Rigidity in design • Restrictions on the integration of new technologies • Incorrect forecast of future user needs • Change from one platform to another	• High cost and time for integration of existing elements • Platform development easily becomes a goal in itself • Mistakes made in the beginning have a high impact • Failure to forecast customer needs correctly	• Development time and costs to meet specifications of all target markets • Development process becomes more complex • Restrictions for all market segments • Selection of the right platform
Lessons Learned:	• Definition of a platform requires choosing from alternatives. • Development of a platform is a strategic decision. • Understanding of market requirements is necessary.	• Development of a product family needs a clear concept. • A product family makes communication clear. • Customer needs have to be identified early.	• Having one platform for two markets is difficult for the stability of the platform. • Market requirements have to be tested before platform development.

Source: Johannes I. M. Halman, Adrian P. Hofer, and Win van Vuuren, "Platform-Driven Development of Product Families: Linking Theory with Practice," *Journal of Product Innovation Management* 20 (2003): 149–162, Tables 4 and 5.

product platform concept. Some of the trade-offs from using platforms included platform-constraining flexibility in product development, higher initial time and cost to develop platforms, and lower differentiation resulting from sticking to a common platform. Choosing the wrong platform can negatively affect an entire product family and reduce market success. Interestingly, the common lesson the three companies derived from their experience with product platforms was the necessity—first and foremost—of focusing on consumer needs.[14]

NPD Using Sensory Segmentation

Another strategy to international product development is **sensory segmentation**, which divides customers according to their responses to sensory product characteristics. Such cross-country segments allow the development of a limited range of products within a product line to satisfy a large number of product needs across countries. This approach is most useful in consumer product development, as discussed next.

A multinational marketer of various fruit-flavored sodas in over 50 countries found that the sheer number of flavors led to problems in sourcing; quality control; variable acceptance criteria; and, consequently, lower product-line profitability. The company characterized sensory perceptions along the following dimensions: flavor type, flavor level, color, use of a sweetener, acidity, and cloud. The company had to choose sensory variables that could be controlled through changes in product formulation and in the manufacturing process. That way, the company could respond to consumer preferences with product modifications or new products. Products were chosen or specially blended to conform to the different sensory packages desired. When the product was tested against competitors' products in different countries, consumer panel preferences yielded three sensory segments: "low-impact" seekers who wanted mild products, "medium-impact" seekers, and "high-impact" seekers who wanted robust products with the sweetest taste and the darkest color. Developing products to meet the needs of each sensory segment across countries allowed the company to reduce the number of products marketed internationally while still meeting the needs of large numbers of customers in each country.[15]

> **sensory segmentation**
>
> Segmenting consumers based on their likes and dislikes, especially as related to sensory factors such as taste and smell.

••• NPD at Silicon Graphics

Silicon Graphics (SGI) is a leader in high-performance computing, visualization, and storage technologies. The company's approach to NPD, for example, is based on six fundamentals:[16]

1. Form product development teams focused on specific customer segments. Base the teams on their needs; then let the engineers design new products in cooperation with customers. Market research is useless in that context. Instead, the best technology and R&D staff must work with leading-edge customers, sometimes referred to as lead users. Those users constantly "push the envelope" of the capabilities of current products, suggesting an NPD direction for the company.[17]

2. If new products cannibalize existing products that are still growing, so be it. The paralysis caused by fear of cannibalization of existing product lines can be deadly to long-term growth.

3. Use new technology and capabilities to address high-end frontier customers in a rapidly changing technology environment. Use older technology to develop cheaper, low-end, mass-market products.

4. To create chaos, build on core capabilities, which SGI defined as
   - Advanced microprocessors.
   - Intuitive interfaces, requiring less customer training.
   - Symmetric multiprocessing, allowing SGI supercomputers to use microprocessor arrays to manipulate vast volumes of graphics data at high speeds.
   - A shared architecture and operating system across all SGI machines. Proprietary but open architecture allows a company to set technical standards for an entire industry and consolidate its market share.[18]
   - Bright technological people; the fortunes of SGI, as a technology company, are determined by its people. The technical merits of ideas rather than hierarchy or status should determine new product directions.

5. Alliances are essential to maintaining an accelerated pace of innovation.

6. Financial targets provide control over the NPD process, such as insisting on gross margins of 50 percent, R&D at 12 percent of sales, and 15 percent growth in sales per employee.

Ironically, SGI's deviation from its own NPD philosophy sowed the seeds of the company's ultimate demise. SGI's management got distracted by other markets outside the firm's core competencies in hardware and software to create graphics (such as the dinosaurs in the hit movie *Jurassic Park*) and failed to bring new products to market quickly enough to keep pace with competitors like Hewlett-Packard (HP) and Dell. Today, SGI, now owned by Rackable Systems Inc., focuses on computing-heavy applications such as modeling new drugs and climate simulations.[19]

Technology companies such as Apple often accept the fact that the release of a new product will hurt the sales of an existing product.

NPD and Technology Upheavals

Companies in high-tech industries face the certainty that current-generation technology will become obsolete. Their dilemma is balancing incremental improvements to the current technology-based product line while focusing on next-generation technology that will make their current products obsolete, dramatically reducing sales. Companies cannot avoid next-generation technology because their competitors will innovate and, inevitably, cause the company's current markets to vanish. Hence, the challenge is how to manage new technologies in product development. For global firms, this is especially important given the higher number of competitive pressures versus a wholly domestic firm.

Technology companies have emphasized the need to cannibalize products. That is, they deliberately seek to supplant their products (even if the products are still selling well) with newer products and product lines. Otherwise, a company's mature technology products will become commodities, and with shrinking margins, the company will not be able to spend on R&D and on changing customer needs. Compressing the time it takes to develop new products allows companies to start NPD initiatives later and thus factor in the latest customer perceptions and wants. For an illustration of the influence of technology upheavals and NPD, see "NPD at Silicon Graphics."

Table 9-4 • The Pros and Cons of Product-Line Extension

Advantages	Negative Aspects
• Extension allows narrow customer segments to be satisfied; for example, offering a cereal formulated with added bran and a low-fat, healthy oil might attract health-conscious older consumers.	• Having too many items in the product line muddies the image, leading distribution channels to unilaterally decide what items in the product line they will stock.
• Making minor product modifications to add a "new" product allows firms to claim that they are innovative and to target customers who are looking for something new.	• Extension reduces brand loyalty by encouraging customers to experiment and switch.
• Extension allows a firm to cover high and low price points, putting out both premium-priced products and a lower-priced, bare-bones product.	• Extension crowds out genuine new product ideas.
	• It cannibalizes demand from other items in the product line and does not enhance overall demand.
• Multiple and similar products allow excess capacity to be used without costly setup and product changeover costs.	• As total products in the line grow faster than shelf space, retailers control what is displayed; disappointing performance may give impetus to a private label usurping the company's brand.
• Extension allows additional sales, at least in the short run, and is also cheaper than launching and establishing a new brand, which could cost as much as $30 million.	• Increased complexity leads to higher costs, inventory challenges at the retail level, manufacturing problems, errors in forecasting demand, material shortages, and less management and R&D attention to new product efforts.
• Extension permits additional shelf space, which can keep out a competitor's products.	
• Distribution channels often demand unique variations on the basic product line so that they can differentiate themselves, such as a larger package or added features to attract customers.	• Customers and retailers may be turned off by too many product-line items and opt, instead, for brands with one or two all-purpose offerings.
• Extension allows response to competitive threat—for example, "me-too" products to match the success of hybrid vehicles or of whitening toothpaste.	

Product-Line Extensions

Related to the issue of NPD strategy is the use of **product-line extensions**—using one product upon which to develop further, closely related products. A review of the various corporate examples cited suggests that firms use product-line extension to broaden their appeal to customers and to offer additional products to domestic and international markets. At the end of this chapter, Case 9.1, "Boeing and Airbus: Competing Product Lines," notes that product-line extensions, termed derivative aircraft, have been the mainstay of the aircraft industry over the past decade. However, product-line extensions do have a downside. Research found that at one company, "filler" products were 65 percent of the line but only 10 percent of sales.[20] Reducing the number of those items could increase shelf space for core products in the line. Of course, the company must plan to drop customers of "filler" products, attempting to move them to core products, perhaps through special incentives. Table 9-4 summarizes the positive and negative aspects of a policy of product-line extension.

> **product-line extensions**
>
> The process of developing a new product (or model) primarily based on an existing product that offers new or enhanced characteristics or benefits.

Managing New Product Development ● ● ●

Regardless of the overriding strategy associated with NPD for global companies, the process must be managed to avoid excessive costs. This section looks at a number of best practices in NPD management. One illustration shows the use of a step-wise screening process to ensure that only viable projects receive continued funding. A second example, Canon in Japan, offers a number of insights, including the use of product champions and the importance of involving suppliers. This section also describes how to determine when an NPD project needs to be terminated and how companies often cooperate on a joint NPD. The section ends with a discussion of product testing and NPD.

A Step-Wise Approach to Manage NPD

Companies need a formal process to control the number of new products in development. Such a process would determine whether a project continues or is canceled. One option is a step-wise approach. It utilizes a project approval team (PAT) composed of employees from multiple departments, including manufacturing, quality assurance, finance, R&D, and marketing.[21] The PAT evaluates projects in several phases:

1. Idea generation begins with pilot funding for a project generated by any R&D scientist. The results of the initial investigation are documented in an idea-evaluation report and screened by the PAT. If deemed promising, the idea is investigated further with additional funding. Then another report is generated with a proposal suggesting a feasibility study and possible product development. That report is screened by the PAT. The following factors might be considered:[22]
   - Potential for patent-protected market position
   - Long-term market potential and long-term impact on the company
   - Possibility of alliances and external funding
   - Estimated financial returns
   - Fit with company core competencies and with manufacturing, marketing, and distribution capabilities
   - Probability of technical success

2. The feasibility study, resulting in product definition, includes specifications, market potential, and estimates on return on investment. It is reviewed by the PAT.

3. Product development includes a specifications stage that establishes components used, packaging, fitness testing, and hazard and stability evaluation. Cost estimates and sales forecasts are used to refine rates-of-return calculations, and test marketing is conducted. If PAT approval is positive at this stage, final optimization begins. An initial batch or trial of the product is made with attention to documentation, quality assurance specifications, regulatory compliance, and final design. Marketing is called in to develop product promotion and advertising.

4. Product launch occurs as the product is handed off to the operating divisions.

The step-wise process illustrates a good balance of technological, financial, and marketing issues. Though coordination within a global firm may be difficult if the team is spread out geographically, the process does ensure a broad spectrum of input into the NDP process.

Japanese Model

Studying the NPD process in Japan is interesting, given the capture of significant market share in global markets by Japanese industries. An example from Canon provides useful insights into the Japanese approach.

CANON AND THE PERSONAL COPIER

In the mid-1990s, Japanese company Canon decided that its goal would be to develop a copier for offices with fewer than five employees who did not currently use copiers. Utilizing existing technology, however, the cheapest copier would still be too expensive for such a small office and would need service by professional engineers. Contributing to the high price would also be the selling method: through dealers and manufacturers' direct sales force. For those reasons, existing copiers were too expensive for the small-firm market.

With all that in mind, Canon came up with its Personal Copier Product Concept:[23]

Goal. A copier priced under $1,000.

Issues. Defining the target market segment, quality level required for personal use maintenance, target price and cost, size and weight, and new functions to be added.

Product Concept. Compact, lightweight, priced less than $1,000, maintenance through exchange of disposable parts, and added functions for ease of use and versatility.

Approach. While incorporating cost and reliability issues, study disposable photoreceptors, development apparatus, instant toner fuser, and new materials and components. Study other electronic consumer products, such as fans and televisions, to learn about cost versus reliability. Obtain compactness through the outer structural design, using foam plastics, a piston-motion mechanism utilizing a mechanical clutch, and a small diameter (60-mm) photoreceptor drum.

Organizational Structure. Task Force X for prototype model; engineering model inspired by Team X for AE-1 camera. (The AE-1 was a highly successful camera developed by Canon that quickly became one of the most popular cameras ever developed; it was highly respected for many of its unique features.) The task force included personnel from a variety of departments, including development, design, manufacturing, assembly, legal (patents), user groups, and marketing.

Slogan. "Let's make the AE-1 of copiers."

Canon attributed its success in developing the personal copier to several factors:

* Senior management's vision of an under-$1,000, maintenance-free copier.
* Company-wide cooperation as exemplified by the setting up of Task Force X.
* Use of young engineers, average age 27.
* Designation of a product champion, Hiroshi Tanaka (Director of Reprographics Products Development Center), who acted as a bridge between top management and young engineers.
* Balance of cost versus reliability, leading to invention of cartridge-based technologies.
* A well-structured development process, allowing chronology of product concept through sales launch to be completed within three years.

Canon provides a useful example of NPD, including its use of target pricing, product champions, and a well-managed process.

Additional factors specific to Japanese product development are discussed in a comparison of Sony and Canon. Pertinent factors include job rotation of engineers, direct transfer of R&D teams to production as their products reach commercialization, and the role of centers of excellence.[24]

SUPPLIER RELATIONSHIPS IN JAPAN

Supplier relationships are a critical element of Japanese approaches to NPD. Japanese companies such as Toyota and Nissan make complex products that require mass production, assembly, and integration of several subsystems and thousands of parts. Typically, the companies (1) work with few suppliers; (2) develop long-term partnerships with suppliers; (3) require continuous improvement from suppliers in quality, speed, and time to supply; (4) require lower prices and fewer numbers of parts; and (5) most important, involve a limited number of key suppliers early in the design and development of new products. Large companies such as Toyota have several tiers of suppliers. Those companies deal directly only with tier-one suppliers, who, in turn, work with the next tier, and so on.[25]

Not all suppliers are capable of being full-fledged partners. They may lack the necessary people skills, technology, prototype-building capability, and knowledge base. Hence, some first-tier companies may not be equal partners. Instead, they may have considerable responsibility for developing a complex assembly to meet customer specifications. Other companies with lesser skills may execute instructions from clients, even building commodity parts on a per-order basis. A supplier firm cannot be a partner to every client, and it may be better off serving as order taker and supplier for some clients.

An example of the supplier-partner approach to NPD comes from Nippondenso, a major supplier of parts to the global auto industry. (Toyota is one of Nippondenso's principal customers.) In developing a new line of alternators, Nippondenso used several years of basic research and a survey of customer preferences toward size and performance. Different alternator housing types, wire specifications, regulators, and terminals added up to 700 variations from which a customer could choose. After the customer chose its variations, Nippondenso would work with the customer to customize certain product aspects, such as where the alternator mounts would be located. In this way, Nippondenso took over all the alternator research and product development function, supplying Toyota and other major auto manufacturers on a global basis.

New Product Project Termination

Related to the issue of NPD strategy is recognizing when to stop new product development. Over a two-year period, researchers studied 80 NPD projects in four divisions of a U.S. chemical firm. Interviews were repeated every six months to gauge changes in the project's progress and in project evaluation. The goal was to understand what factors influenced decisions to terminate a project. The findings are interesting. They emerged from a study of NPD projects while the projects were being carried out, not after the projects were completed or terminated. The study found the following variables to be influential:[26]

- **Management advocacy.** If management does not champion or diminishes support for a project, increases pressure on project personnel, and deems the project to be of low priority, the project may not receive resources and, thus, will be terminated.

- **Performance.** This is the likelihood that a project will meet technical and commercial objectives in a timely fashion, be manufactured at a reasonable cost, and achieve desired market share.

- **Innovation context.** Innovation encompasses (1) the nature of the underlying technologies, whether they are established or new or even radical; (2) the firm's or division's technical background, capabilities, and experience with the technology; (3) the firm's or division's business experience with the technology; and (4) the level of investment in the project, including human as well as physical capital and monetary investments.

- **Performance threshold.** The assumption is that different types of projects have unstated but different performance thresholds they must exceed in order to continue. It is possible that new projects in emergent technologies will excite scientists and managers and be allowed to continue for longer periods, implicitly meeting lower thresholds.

Customer Involvement in Joint Product Development

A growing trend is the involvement of customers in designing next-generation products. Lead users often understand best the features they would like in a next-generation product. Hence, firms have begun involving customers in NPD. Firms now provide toolkits that allow customers to design products. The customers return the toolkits to the firm for prototype manufacture. That process cuts development time and increases the likelihood that customers will readily accept the new products.

Customer-oriented product development toolkits should

- Allow users to carry out complete cycles for trial-and-error learning. This process involves building, simulating, testing and evaluating, and ultimately choosing between alternative trials to arrive at the best design.
- Provide users with a solution space (constrained by the manufacturer's capabilities and production system) from which users can create the designs they want.
- Provide user-friendly toolkits so that little time is invested in learning and training.
- Allow users to supplement libraries of standard solution modules with their own add-ons, an approach that leads to unique and customized solutions.
- Ensure that user-designed solutions following the rules of the toolkits can be "translated"; that is, they can be easily manufactured by the toolkit supplier without additional engineering intervention and modification.[27]

Product Development for Global Markets: Where to Locate?

Where a global product is developed and who participates in developing it are both important. Product development may be centered in one country, perhaps at headquarters. Because a product is to be a global one, it is important to acquire information from key markets around the world. Hence, involving foreign subsidiaries at the early stage of product concept development is crucial to success. That way, features of importance to a variety of consumers in different markets can be considered.[28]

Firms must recognize, however, that development teams tend to "own" products. The teams are reluctant to accept designs from other teams, even when the designs originate within the company. In theory, a firm should assign central responsibility for the design of a particular product to a particular team in a particular country. The assumption is that that team's design will then be adopted globally. Organizational conflicts can undermine that plan, however. In that case, a company may be forced to compromise and accept two versions of what was meant to be a global product.

Firms must decide between retaining product development in their home market or decentralizing it to multiple international locations.

BENEFITS OF DECENTRALIZED PRODUCT DEVELOPMENT

Companies with well-established foreign subsidiaries usually encounter demands for increased local autonomy. Those demands may be reinforced by the nationalistic feelings of subsidiary personnel, most of whom are probably citizens of the local country. Participation in the fundamental corporate activity of developing new products is a forceful way of showing employees that they have "a piece of the action." In that situation, a firm must weigh the payoff in improved morale against any loss of efficiency in product development.

In industries in which product development is slow and costly, companies may be forced to go outside for new products. The pharmaceutical industry serves as a good illustration. Although most firms in the industry are research intensive, none can derive a complete product line from internal research only. It takes too many years and vast financial resources to bring a new drug to market, for instance. Therefore, in the pharmaceutical industry, a four-fold approach to product development is seen:

1. Internal R&D
2. Acquisition of firms with new products
3. Licensing of new products from firms that developed them for markets where the firm is not represented
4. Joint venturing with a firm that has complementary products

Unilever is one international company that deliberately seeks the advantages of international research development. The company has development activities in four European countries, as well as close research liaisons with its associated companies in the United States and India. Unilever gains a number of benefits: By locating research and development activities in a number of countries, it takes advantage of its unique capability to do research in a variety of national environments; this should lead to a higher probability of success given the strong relationship between the laboratories; and it may also lead to creating new ideas otherwise missed by a single R&D location.

Table 9-5 ● Concurrent Headquarters and Local Market Influences on Product Development

Headquarters Influences	Local Market Influences
• Recognition by marketing unit of the need for a new or modified product	• Suggestion by local manager of customer need for a new or modified product
• Initiation of product development process, including cost and market (sales) analysis and lab tests	• Suggestion by preliminary market analysis of further development
• Test marketing in local market	• Contact with headquarters to receive information on and permission to develop modified or adapted version of existing product
• Local market product launch	• Ensuing development, with help from headquarters' labs as necessary
	• Test marketing to decide whether to proceed
	• Approval from headquarters for new product launch, with standards for quality, brands, and packaging

LOCAL MARKET NEEDS

Another encouragement to decentralized product development is local market need. Some products require continuous local testing during the development process, when they are being designed primarily to meet market specifications (tastes, use conditions, and so on) rather than technological standards. Development close to the market is practical because use conditions usually cannot be simulated in a firm's domestic laboratories. According to that reasoning, one would expect to find consumer goods developed locally more often than industrial goods. Furthermore, when demand for a product is limited to one market, the product is usually developed in that market.

Given the importance of local market considerations, firms often use bidirectional approaches, whereby both headquarters/local market issues and personnel help shape NPD. The outline of such a concurrent bottom-up and top-down process is described in Table 9-5.

Cooperation in Developing Products

As the costs of developing new products rise and diverse technologies are needed, consortium approaches have increased in appeal. Consortium partners typically have complementary assets in design or technology, and the alliance is initiated to develop new products more speedily. For example, because IBM and Toshiba had complementary technologies, they began collaborating on the design of lightweight computer screen displays used in laptop computers. Because small color screens that use low energy are essential for the next generation of laptops, IBM joined Toshiba. IBM's goal was to learn from Toshiba's expertise in manufacturing. Ultimately, IBM used the color screens in its laptop computers. Over time, IBM's strategic priorities changed, and the company divested its personal computer business to a Chinese company, Lenovo. IBM may no longer need Toshiba's computer screen technologies, but that fact does not negate the initial impetus that led to their collaboration several years ago.

Using consortium in NPD can result in benefits beyond creating a new product. It may help support the creation of a common standard—such as the consortium that supported the Blu-ray Disc standard. The development of this standard was led by the Blu-ray Disc Association (BDA), whose international membership includes Apple, HP, LG (Life's Good), Philips, and Samsung. Cooperation can also lead to the formation of a new company, such as the creation of Airbus—a collaboration between the national governments of France, Germany, Spain, and the United Kingdom. This consortium was originally formed in 1972 to develop a new commercial aircraft for the European market, thus competing with Boeing. It is still in business as a consortium, having successfully developed several commercial aircraft models. It has resulted in a highly successful competitor to Boeing, at times earning about half the global market for commercial jets. (See Case 9.1 for more details on Boeing and Airbus.)

The creation of the Blu-ray DVD standard is an example of industry cooperation in new product development.

Product Testing

As part of the product development process, a product must be tested under realistic use conditions. For a global firm, this may mean testing in multiple countries. Testing is also used to ensure products meet national requirements on product specifications and performance. For example, in the case of food products, drugs, and electrical or transportation equipment, some local testing may be necessary to receive government authorization to sell. In the case of pharmaceuticals, there is often a special factor. Obtaining FDA approval of new drugs is a time-consuming process. Drug manufacturers often test and certify their drugs in other markets. They begin marketing there before getting final approval in the United States, thus expediting international introduction of the product.

Finally, local product testing may be advisable for promotional reasons. Although a firm must test its products vigorously, there may be advantages in having local testing done outside the firm. Such testing may improve the firm's public relations locally by using national testing organizations. That certification may be valuable to an international firm in its efforts to demonstrate adaptation to local market conditions.

For example, Abbott Laboratories develops new drug products and then sends them to universities and hospitals around the world for testing. Findings are reported in various national medical journals. Those actions have the dual advantages of extensive international testing under different conditions in addition to publicity value when findings are reported.

Global Research and Development

New product development and product-line extension decisions require research and development support. Most multinationals are increasing the amount of R&D they carry out at multiple locations around the world. One reason is that a firm's ability to innovate globally contributes to its overall international competitiveness.[29] Conducting global R&D also helps a firm meet host-country interests as it facilitates technology transfer. Multinational foreign R&D is possible because of the increased availability of skilled scientific talent and technology resources in other countries, enhanced intellectual property protection, and better communication capabilities that allow integration and supervision of a dispersed global R&D effort. Comparative advantage comes into play in the sense that different countries may have world-class capabilities. For example, top-notch scientists in specific areas of expertise such as the development of robotics or pharmaceutical drugs might be found in Japan or Switzerland, respectively.

Government incentives may also make it cheaper to conduct overseas R&D when specific program funding exists for technologies deemed to be in the national interest. One example is the ESPRIT project, which promotes advanced technology computing in Europe. Availability of low-cost, high-quality research personnel, such as Russian research scientists, as well as the success of some multinationals with foreign R&D, may motivate other multinationals to attempt the same. Conducive government regulation and a hospitable climate to specific kinds of R&D may also play a part in deciding where to locate R&D effort.

Key Issues in Developing a Global R&D Capability

Linking product development for international markets to a global R&D network raises several critical issues for management.

LOCATION OF FOREIGN R&D

Relevant factors in selecting overseas R&D sites include integration with existing manufacturing and sales operations; host government regulations and requirements; and the quality of local research infrastructure, including availability of scientists and the level and sophistication of the research efforts of local universities.

LEVEL OF AUTONOMY FOR FOREIGN R&D

The level of autonomy determines, to some extent, who decides what research is carried out at overseas R&D facilities. Whether operations are centralized may depend on the overall orientation of the firm, its tendency to centralize authority in most areas of multinational management, and the competency of local R&D facilities, as well as their previous history of contributing research to the firm. Criticality of the underlying technologies being investigated, the amount of resources committed, and the time constraints in completing the research may also influence the degree of centralization. Whether the research is creative and groundbreaking or more an extension and diffusion of previous research may also contribute to the decision of using central control or granting greater autonomy.

For example, a study of R&D labs of multinationals in the United Kingdom showed that most of the labs had a limited role in carrying out basic research. However, they played a major role in developing new products and in adapting existing products and processes for their markets.[30] One approach sets up

Figure 9-2 • International R&D at Kao Corporation

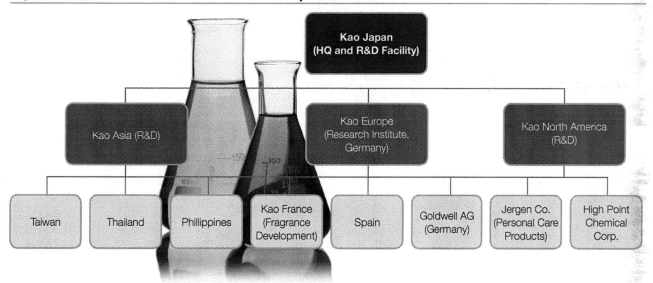

specific research mandates for major overseas labs, with a specific lab functioning as a global clearinghouse for the multinational's research efforts in that area. An example of that approach is shown in Figure 9-2, illustrating Kao Corporation's organization of global R&D.

COORDINATION TECHNIQUES

A major goal of global R&D is the sharing of information. Information communication among scientists and engineers is critical to enhanced research productivity. Measures include periodic meetings and presentations, milestone achievement monitoring systems, travel and telephone contacts, the creation of multinational project teams, job rotation across R&D labs in different countries, and a company culture that fosters open cross-national research communication.

Also relevant to coordinating global R&D is whether a scientific culture prevails across a company (overcoming national culture differences) or whether local cultural norms prevail in affecting operations and the effectiveness of overseas R&D labs. A research project studied communication within the global R&D operations of 14 multinationals that together manage several thousand R&D employees. Following is a summary of the communication and coordination mechanisms used:[31]

- **Socialization efforts** to create a corporate-wide R&D culture, using activities such as temporary assignments in other labs, relatively constant traveling to facilitate face-to-face meetings, clear rules and procedures for matters such as documentation of work and training programs.

- **Formal communication** procedures emphasizing meticulous reporting and documentation, databases of findings to facilitate researcher access to results in distant locations, and planning procedures involving researchers and managers from multiple sites.

- **Boundary-spanning roles** through the identification and use of talented individuals who can facilitate transfer of information across R&D labs. Those people do so through travel, presentations, and special conferences. The individuals are technologically able as well as experienced. They rank relatively high in the hierarchy so they know what informal channels to use and who has information or should receive it.

- **Organizational structures** that include the use of central coordination staff and a network organization facilitated by electronic communication.

- **Electronic communication** that includes the use of videoconferencing, e-mail, and shared databases. (However, researchers suggest that periodic face-to-face meetings are essential to supplement the use of electronic communication technologies.)

ORGANIZATIONAL STRUCTURE OPTIONS

How should a firm organize its foreign R&D operations? Approaches include using matrixes, subordinating overseas R&D to headquarters R&D, and making R&D part of existing product-line or geographic divisions as discussed in Chapter 15. The decisive factor should be whether the organizational structure contributes to effectiveness and efficiency.

STAFFING AND PERSONNEL ISSUES

How are people chosen for the overseas R&D labs? Who is the R&D manager? How important are criteria such as the ability to manage multicultural research

SUMMARY

Developing a product policy for a firm as it grows internationally is not an easy process. As a firm develops its product policy for international markets, it must take into account a number of factors including consumer needs, governmental influences, and competitive pressures.

The most straightforward and cost-effective product policy would be for the firm to extend the product range (policy) used in its domestic market to its foreign markets. Due to differences between foreign markets, this often is not possible. The challenge for a firm is to decide when products can be standardized for global markets versus adapted.

Many factors support product standardization, including the high cost of adaptation; the tendency of products for industrial use to be standardized; convergence of similar tastes around the world; growing use of similar products in urban markets; the sale of products primarily to markets with similar cultures; the need to keep the country of origin of the product; and economies of scale in product, R&D, and marketing.

Factors that support adaption are as follows: There are differences in technical standards between markets, products are for consumer use rather than industrial, the needs of the consumer vary by market, consumer ability to buy varies by market, there are different levels of economic development between markets, and government policies dictate a need for adaptation.

Developing a new product development strategy begins with addressing the market characteristics of foreign markets selected for entry versus the home market for which the firm's existing products were developed. To the extent these characteristics are similar, little to no modification may be required. However, when conditions are quite different, the product (and marketing communications) will likely need adapting.

Another NPD strategy utilizes product platforms that leverage the firm's core competencies. This strategy suggests that effective product development has distinct layers, with a bedrock of core competencies upon which are built product platforms and then product families marketed to customers.

Another strategy of international product development is sensory segmentation, which divides customers according to their responses to sensory product characteristics.

There are particular NPD concerns for firms in industries with fast-changing technology. Their dilemma is balancing incremental improvements to the current technology-based product line while focusing on next-generation technology that will make their current products obsolete, dramatically reducing sales. Companies in such industries often accept that new products will cannibalize sales of existing products.

The product-line extension strategy uses one product upon which to develop further, closely related products. An illustration is the various lines of jets developed by Boeing and Airbus.

Companies employ various techniques to manage NPD. They include a stepwise approach in which a multidiscipline team within the firm continually addresses the viability of NPD projects and uses a common evaluation tool.

Canon in Japan provides other useful insights into NPD management. Key findings include involvement of senior management in NPD vision, company-wide cooperation, designation of product champions, and a focus on achieving NPD against a demanding schedule so the product can be launched within three years. Japan also stresses strong relationships with suppliers in support of effective NPD.

Knowing when to end an NPD project is an important management issue. Key factors may include management advocacy, predicted performance of the new product, the level of innovation, and the level of product performance.

Customers are increasingly asked to be involved in joint product development. Examples include product trials, design involvement, toolkits to learn about new products, and solution "libraries."

Where a global product is developed and who participates in developing it are both important. Product development may be centered in one country, perhaps at headquarters. Because a product is to be a global one, it is important to acquire information from key markets around the world.

Companies with well-established foreign subsidiaries usually encounter demands for increased local autonomy. Those demands may be reinforced by the nationalistic feelings of subsidiary personnel, most of whom are probably citizens of the local country.

Decentralized product development is also related to local market need. Some products require continuous local testing during the development process, when they are being designed primarily to meet market specifications (tastes, use conditions, and so on) rather than technological standards. Development close to the market is practical because use conditions usually cannot be simulated in a firm's domestic laboratories. Given the importance of local market considerations, firms often use bidirectional approaches, whereby both headquarters/local market issues and personnel help shape NPD.

Firms may cooperate with other firms in their NPD. Consortium partners typically have complementary assets in design or technology, and the alliance is initiated to develop new products more speedily. Beyond creating new products, such consortia may result in creating a common technical standard for the industry, such as the Blu-ray Disc, or even a new company, such as Airbus.

As part of the product development process, a product must be tested under realistic use conditions. For a global firm, this may mean testing in multiple countries. Testing is also used to ensure products meet national requirements on product specifications and performance.

As a company develops its global research and development strategies, it must consider a number of factors, including the location, level of autonomy, ways to coordinate, the implications on its organizational structure, and staffing and personnel issues.

KEY TERMS

new product development   product-line extensions   sensory segmentation
product family   product platform

NASBITE CGBP TOPICS COVERED IN THIS CHAPTER

Note: For full details of the alignment of each chapter with the NASBITE CGBP, be sure to review the information provided in the section "Studying for the NASBITE CGBP Exam."

CGBP Rubric	Topic
02/01/05:	product certifications and standards (e.g., CE mark, ISO 9000)
02/01/06:	cultural issues related to marketability of product
02/03/01:	impact on market selection of product
02/06/01:	customer expectations and cultural requirements
02/06/02:	product life cycle implications (or strategies)
02/06/03:	(new) product development modification process
02/06/04:	technical compatibility and product standards (e.g., CE marking)

QUESTIONS AND RESEARCH

1. Discuss the implications of Table 9-1. How might the information in this table be used to guide a firm's product policy?
2. Which company is most likely to pursue a standardized product policy: Starbucks or Apple? Why?
3. Research examples of convergence and similar tastes in a particular industry. What evidence is there that firms in that industry adopt a standardized product policy?
4. Discuss the implications of Table 9-2 for a firm as it expands globally.
5. Explain how consumer needs, conditions of use, and ability to buy affect NPD.
6. How does competition affect product-line composition?
7. How and where should new product screening be done? What should be the role of the foreign subsidiary in this process?
8. How are marketing and production considerations used in screening new products for international markets?
9. Product testing must be done locally even when product development is centralized. Discuss.
10. How does the nature of a firm's involvement in foreign markets affect the composition of its product line? Contrast the product-line alternatives open to an exporter with alternatives available to a licensor.
11. Where should NPD activity be located? What are the advantages and disadvantages of decentralization?
12. Discuss the decision to add or drop products to or from a product line in international markets. Research an example of a firm that recently dropped a product. Were international sales a factor?
13. What are the key issues in developing a global R&D capability? How might a firm decide which are the most important?

CHAPTER 9 TEAM PROJECT ASSIGNMENT: International Product Policy

This chapter's main focus is on product policy and its relation to a firm's international expansion. As discussed in the opening sections of the chapter, the most basic decision a firm must make is to what extent its existing product needs to be adapted to meet consumer needs in the foreign markets it has selected. This is the issue to address for your client.

For this chapter's team project, discuss the following:

1. Using Table 9-1, identify which factors are the most relevant for your client. For example, would you argue that mostly there are factors that favor standardization? If so, which factors and why? Alternatively, do you believe the factors favor adaptation?

2. Based on the results of your analysis in question 1, what is your recommended product policy for your client? How much standardization or adaptation do you recommend?

3. Also, discuss to what extent any new products may need to be developed.

CASE 9.1 Boeing and Airbus: Competing Product Lines

In 2004, Airbus received 370 orders (for $34.4 billion) for its aircraft, giving the company 57 percent of the market. Airbus's leadership in market share was not a temporary phenomenon. In 1994, Airbus received 125 aircraft orders compared to 120 orders for Boeing, the first time in postwar history that Boeing did not have the leading market share. Over the next ten years, Airbus continued to gather orders from the world's leading airlines.

Airbus has received government subsidies to conduct R&D to develop its new model of aircraft. Boeing has waged a continual campaign to reduce subsidies granted to Airbus, believing that those subsidies make it difficult to compete with Airbus and to earn sufficient cash flow and profits to fund the development of its own larger, new-generation jets. Nevertheless, Airbus has continued to launch new aircraft models and to gain significant global share. Boeing has survived in the aircraft industry for over 65 years, with capable and experienced management that has guided it through previous recessions in a cyclical industry. The company now faces the challenge of maintaining parity with Airbus's development of product-line breadth and attractiveness to customers.

Airbus Industrie is a multinational consortium consisting of two state-owned enterprises, France's Aerospatiale (37.9 percent of Airbus) and Spain's CASA (4.2 percent of Airbus); the semiprivate Deutsche Airbus from West Germany (37.9 percent); and the wholly private British Aerospace (20 percent). All of them receive subsidies for aircraft development and customer financing of aircraft sales.

THE COMMERCIAL JET TRANSPORT INDUSTRY

The industry has been characterized as a "Sporty Game," in which introducing each new aircraft involves betting the continued survival of the company. The industry is now a duopoly, with Boeing and Airbus being the only manufacturers of large civilian jets. They work hand-in-glove with three aircraft engine manufacturers: GE (and its French joint venture GE/Snecma); Pratt & Whitney (a subsidiary of United Technologies), and Rolls-Royce, a British company. New airframe models typically require new engines. Estimated development costs of new airframes and engines are about $4 billion to $5 billion apiece, with total investment in the aircraft exceeding between $6 billion and $7 billion five to six years after the launch of a model. However, the Airbus A380, the largest civilian jet ever, is estimated to cost in excess of $10 billion to develop.

Development of new aircraft requires long lead times, with eventual sales volume amounting to one or two aircraft a day in a good year. Planning the introduction of a new aircraft involves looking ahead about 20 years: 5 years for the planning and a product life of 15 years or more. Hence, considerable market forecasting abilities are required, particularly because airline demand is highly cyclical.

Once an aircraft model moves beyond development into production, the cost of producing initial batches of aircraft will be far higher than, say, the 300th unit manufactured, owing to learning curve–driven cost reductions. Therefore, it is vital that the gamble represented by development of a new aircraft model be transformed into continuing sales. Commercial aircraft manufacturing can be highly profitable, as operating leverage beyond breakeven is high. It is the possibility of demand growth fueled by rising world incomes, trade, and airline traffic that attracts firms to this industry. If an aircraft model is successful, as in the case of Boeing's 747 (with virtually no competition for much of its life), profits can be enormous.

Introducing derivative aircraft models pushes back the payback period even further. Additional development costs are incurred, although they extend the life of the model. Thus, a company seeking to make commercial jets must be prepared to wait ten years or more to recover its investments—and even longer to make a profit. Price cutting by a less profit-oriented competitor will reduce margins and contribution, thereby pushing back the break-even point further. That practice affects the willingness of top management to approve funding for the development of new-generation aircraft. At the same time, lower prices and margins reduce cash flow and prejudice the ability of a firm to fund new aircraft development from internal sources.

Few aircraft have yielded sufficient volume sales to generate profits for their manufacturers. The De Havilland Comet, the pioneer jet introduced in 1952, sold only 112 units, while the Boeing 707, introduced in 1958, sold nearly 1,000 units. Given a break-even volume of about 600 units for the smaller jets, Boeing has achieved profitability with its 707 (1,010 sold), 727 (1,831 sold), and 737 (5,965 sold). In addition, the 747, with over 1,400 units sold, is profitable given its far higher unit price of over $250 million and higher margins due to its erstwhile monopoly position. (As a consequence, break-even volume on the 747 is lower, at about 300 units.) Airbus may have reached breakeven with its A332/321 model (over 5,400 ordered through 2010), though development costs of extending the product family may have raised the break-even volume significantly. Total orders for the A330/340 have reached about 900 planes, but it, too, has incurred development costs for several derivative models. At best, it is likely to achieve moderate financial returns. Despite those erratic results, Airbus has been able to develop its newest A380 model at an estimated cost of $10 billion.

Future growth and the bulk of the market for commercial aircraft would appear to lie overseas. U.S. traffic is expected to represent only about one-third of world traffic, with Europe and the rest of the world representing another third each. Thus, foreign airlines will be the major customers for aircraft manufacturers, with government-owned airlines representing a significant share of the customer group. Political pressures could significantly affect a sale and hinder a private company that cannot obtain government help.

HOW DO AIRLINES BUY PLANES?

Airlines sell perishable commodities. An empty seat is revenue that is lost forever. Airlines would like to fly their planes with every seat sold, meaning they would like aircraft with different passenger capacities for different routes based on traffic demand patterns. Routes also vary in distance, with major transcontinental routes such as New York to Tokyo and London to Sydney requiring long-range aircraft. In addition, the gradual development of international hub-and-spoke systems means that different-sized but short-range aircraft may be needed depending on passenger density within each hub-and-spoke system.

Further, the larger the plane, the heavier the engine needs to be. Matching engine thrust to aircraft size determines fuel economy and speed, which become important as more airlines seek nonstop flight schedules. As the price of oil exceeded $65 a barrel in 2005, fuel costs approached 30 percent of total operating costs and aircraft buyers presumably placed a higher priority on fuel economy. Aging aircraft fleets are another factor where the costs of replacing fully depreciated aircraft must be balanced against fuel and maintenance costs that are comparatively higher with the older aircraft. Environmental controls and noise abatement provisions complicate this trade-off as freedom to operate older, noisier aircraft over crowded cities is gradually limited. Technical obsolescence of an existing fleet, with improved safety arising from advanced avionics, also colors demand for new jet aircraft.

If existing models of planes are sufficiently discounted and cheap fuel reduces the economic gains to be had from the more expensive new-generation aircraft, airlines might prefer to buy the (cheaper) older models, hoping to squeeze the manufacturers into financing the aircraft at low risk to the consumers (the airlines). Thus, airlines buying jet aircraft are guided by their route structure and the balance of fuel versus labor versus capital costs. They would probably prefer a family of aircraft (of differing ranges and passenger capacity) from one manufacturer in order to economize on flight crew training, inventory of spare parts, spare engines, maintenance, and related expenses. However, the business cycle and outlook for traffic growth influence the willingness of airlines to buy expensive new aircraft and add large amounts of long-term debt. Therefore, offering attractive aircraft financing and flexible delivery of aircraft becomes important. As in any new product launch, firms gamble that the product will appeal to the market. The risks of being wrong are magnified in the commercial jet market because the costs of development are so high.

In sum, aircraft product offerings from manufacturers must cater to market segments. Those markets are defined by the confluence of range, passenger capacity, and engine choices, with the requisite speed, fuel economy, and personnel savings—all at a reasonable and competitive price, while also matching financing terms offered by competitors.

AIRBUS AND BOEING: COMPETING PRODUCT PORTFOLIOS

Airframe manufacturers work within their customers' decision calculus to design and manufacture aircraft, relying on forecasts of expected modal route ranges and passenger densities. Current and proposed product offerings represent the outcome of that course of analysis. Table 9-6 sets out the current product portfolios of the two competing manufacturers. Commercial jet aircraft models—the A320 family, the A330, the A340, the A380, and the A350 (all from Airbus) and the Boeing 787 and 777, the extended range 767s, and the 737 derivatives—can best be understood in light of two dimensions: range and passenger capacity. Other factors such as speed, fuel economy, number and type of engines, number of required flight crew, aircraft reliability, and financing terms also influence the choice between competing aircraft. However, range and capacity are central to demarcating broad product segments within which the factors mentioned here can play a further role.

Table 9-6 • Competitive Product Offerings from Boeing and Airbus

Features	Size: Passengers	Range: Nautical Miles	Boeing: Model	Airbus: Model	Size: Passengers	Range: Nautical Miles	Features
737s can cruise at 41,000 feet. Convertible freight version plane is also available.	110 to 132 126 to 149 162 to 189 177 to 189	3,200 3,200 3,200 3,200	737-600 737-700 737-800 737-900	A320 A321 A319 A318	150 185 124 107	3,000 3,000 3,700 3,250	Airbus's most successful "fly-by-wire"
First launched in 1969. Latest version in 2011.	416	7,260 8,000	747-400 747-800	A380	550	8,000	Long-range, double-deck aircraft; spacious and efficient
Two- or three-class configuration; freighter has 60-ton capacity with international capability	181-224 218-269 245-304	6,600 6,105 5,645	767-200ER 767-300ER 767-400ER	A300-600 A310	266 220	4,050 5,200	The original "Airbus" intended for European routes and European airlines
Fills gap between 767 and 747; stretched configuration; first delivery of three-class was in January 2006; freighter version in 2008	305 368 365 301	7,730 5,955 7,880 9,420	777-200ER 777-300 777-300ER 777-200LR	A330-300 A340-300 A340-500 A340-600	335 295 313 380	5,650 7,400 9,000 7,900	To compete with the Boeing 747, but longer range and smaller passenger capacity
Launched in 2003; GE and RR engines; production began in 2006 with entry into service in 2011	223-259 223-259 296	8,500 8,300 3,500	787-8 Dreamliner 787-9 Dreamliner 787-3 Dreamliner	A350-800 A350-900	253 300	8,800 7,500	Estimated delivery in mid-2013 to compete against the 787 launched two years earlier

Four groups emerge, although with some overlap, as follows:

- A crowded short-haul, short-capacity segment (the A320/Boeing 737 families).
- A competitive medium-haul, medium-sized segment (the A300/310 family and the Boeing 757/767 family).
- A long-range segment created by the Boeing 747, with competitors emerging after a long period, from the Airbus A380 with the higher passenger capacity and the A330/340 with fewer passengers. The Boeing 777 may also be seen as competing at the lower end.
- A fourth segment consisting of planes with 225 to 300 seats and flying extremely long distances, comparable to the 747 but with about 40 to 50 percent fewer seats. This segment includes the A350 and the Boeing 787. The smallest-capacity Boeing 777 and A340 may also be competitive in this segment.

Boeing

Boeing has been successful because of its product forecasting ability. Its first product, the 707, was a success despite the fact that it came several years behind the British Comet. Since then, Boeing has offered jets to meet demand in a variety of segments, as follows:

- The 727 and 737 provide short-range, small-capacity routes. They compete against Airbus's A320. The 727 and 737 are two of the most successful aircraft ever introduced, with sales of about 1,800 and 6,000 units, respectively. The 727 has been withdrawn from production because of its outdated design, inefficient fuel consumption, and noise. The 737 is still in production, with several derivative model aircraft having been introduced—all in response to competition from Airbus.

Table 9-7 • Boeing and Airbus Aircraft Orders in Units by Market Segments

Aircraft Segment	1970–1980	1981–1990	1991–2000	2001–2011	Total Order from Model Inception to May 2011 or end of model production
Short-Range, Small-Capacity					
Boeing 727 (first introduced in 1960)	960	50 (last order received was in 1983)			1,831
Boeing 737 (first introduced in 1965)	690	1,881	2,250	1,144	8,000
Boeing total for segment	1,650	1,931	2,250	1,144	9,831
Airbus A320 family (first introduced in 1984)		680	2,120	840	5,400
Medium-Range, Medium-Capacity					
Boeing 757/767 (launched in 1978)	207	938	738	130	2,013
Airbus A300/A310 (launched in 1974)	300	435	155	69	959
Long-Range, Large-Capacity					
Boeing 747 (launched in 1966)	378	503	276	71	1,404
Airbus A330/A340 (launched 1988)		227	569	277	1,073
Airbus 380 (launched 2008)				234	234
Boeing 787 (first delivery scheduled for late 2011)				835 (commiments)	835 (commitments)
Airbus 350 (first delivery scheduled for mid 2013)				571 (commitments)	571 (commitments)

- The 747 is used for large-capacity, long-range routes. Boeing pioneered this segment at the insistence of Pan Am, nearly bankrupting itself in the process. The aircraft is high-priced, currently at $250 million to over $300 million each. It provided profit margins of 25 percent or more, principally because Boeing had a monopoly in this segment. The emergence of newer offerings such as the A330/340 and the gigantic A380 provide competition in this segment, consequently eroding margins and profits. A further development is the Boeing 777, which is a competitive response to longer-range Airbus 330/340 aircraft.

- The 757 and 767 offer medium-range, medium- and small-capacity long-range routes. They were developed by Boeing in response to the Airbus A300/310 aircraft. They have a smaller capacity than the Airbus aircraft but are two-engine fuel-efficient aircraft. The 767 gradually carved out a role in long-distance trans-Atlantic and trans-Pacific flights over water.

- As mentioned previously, a new segment contains the Boeing 787 and the proposed Airbus 350.

As Airbus introduced planes to cover the principal market segments, Boeing's market share dropped in segments where competition from Airbus intensified. Table 9-7 breaks out orders by segments for each of the three manufacturers and further tracks orders over distinct time frames.

The market segments identified are not rigid, chiefly due to the ability to vary seating capacity on a particular model of aircraft. Airlines have some flexibility in adapting capacity by offering one class or multiple classes of seating and by putting seats closer together. Aircraft manufacturers can adapt airframes by stretching them, literally extending the fuselage to hold more passengers. Further adaptations include upgrading the engines to provide more thrust for the now-heavier aircraft and redesigning the wings, using winglets, to increase aerodynamic efficiency and fuel burn.

Developing such *derivative* aircraft is less costly and, therefore, less risky. Boeing used this approach in offering the 747-400. Boeing's goal was to protect its monopoly position in the 747 segment and extend the product family, while conserving cash and reducing risk associated with developing a brand new plane.

Sticking to derivative aircraft, while safe, can allow a bolder competitor to pioneer a new aircraft model for a new market segment and develop a monopoly position, much like Boeing did with the 747. For example, Boeing was unable to prevent Airbus from gaining a significant presence in the 150-seat segment of the market. The launch success of Airbus's A320 may be traced, in part, to Boeing's strategy of delaying the launch of its competing similar-sized aircraft that utilized new technology, the 7J7, and ultimately canceling the project.

The 7J7 represents an interesting case of product development. Boeing decided to cancel the launch of the 7J7 for several reasons:

- Low fuel prices reduced the incentive to buy an expensive aircraft such as the 7J7 because its promised fuel economy was less attractive economically.
- Price was a factor because the 7J7 would compete with Boeing's own 737-400 and with Airbus's A320. Boeing estimated that the 7J7 should be priced at about $27 million (1987 dollars), about the price at which the 737 was being offered. Airlines seemed unwilling to pay more for the new technology under existing economic conditions. They did not want to commit the traditional one-third advance payment over the four-year development period.
- Airlines disagreed on the desired passenger capacity for a new aircraft, seeking somewhere between 150 and 170 seats.
- The version of the UHB engine's unducted fan that GE was to provide could not accommodate a stretched version of a 170-seat jet, which Boeing would have been likely to use. Therefore, waiting until the UHB engine was better defined seemed prudent both to Boeing and its customers.
- Because Boeing's backlog was high and employment was at almost 140,000 people, scarcity of human resources that could be committed to the 7J7 program became a constraining factor.

Instead, Boeing launched a derivative version of the 737, the 737-500. It had seating for between 100 and 125 passengers and had a range of between 1,700 and 2,800 nautical miles. In this segment of the market, Boeing faced competition from companies it did not usually consider its rivals. Those competitors were the manufacturers of small passenger jets: the Fokker F-100 and the BAE 146. However, those aircraft were intended mainly for short-range regional airline flights. Commuter airlines are becoming affiliates and subsidiaries of major carriers, the principal role of commuter airlines being that of providing feeder traffic for longer routes. The purchase of these smaller aircraft is subject to approval by the major airlines' partners. Commuter airlines began to use the small jet aircraft rather than turboprops. In response, other new manufacturers of small jets have emerged, such as Bombardier and Embraer.

Airbus

Airbus's product strategy has been one of catching up, and then surpassing, Boeing. Airbus's two central goals are to

- Match Boeing's broad product range by providing an Airbus family of aircraft to meet a variety of range and passenger capacity needs: single-

and twin-aisle aircraft for short-, medium-, and long-range flights. That is, Airbus had to grow beyond its two initial models (A300 and A310) and develop aircraft that could match Boeing's offerings across the entire product line.

- Utilize advanced technology, including the so-called "fly-by-wire" avionics and more fuel-efficient engines and airframe design. Those advances made Airbus's offerings efficient and attractive. In addition, the new aircraft could be flown by two-man crews. (The use of advanced cockpit instrumentation in the A300 and the follow-on A310 allowed the aircraft to be certified with a minimum crew of two pilots. That eliminated the need for a flight engineer and led to cost reductions in personnel.)

The Original Airbus: A300/A310

Airbus's initial product offerings were the A300 and the A310. The A300 was designed to meet a gap in the market for twin-engine medium-size aircraft designed for the routes needed by major European airlines. The 310 was a longer-range derivative introduced in 1978. Both aircraft were designed to suit the needs of European airliners. (Their routes did not cover long distances, but they needed passenger capacities of about 250 seats—hence, the term *airbus*.) Cost reduction was achieved using the same jigs and tooling as the 300/310 program and a shared assembly line. However, the aircraft did not share the wing (one of the most expensive components). This initial focus on a narrow market reduced the appeal of the Airbus to U.S. airlines, which generally fly longer routes.

Hence, Airbus launched two derivatives, the long-range 310-300 with a fuel tank in the horizontal stabilizer and a stretched A300-600. With about 950 of the 300/310 aircraft sold, these programs have barely exceeded breakeven.

The A320

Despite average A300/310 sales, Airbus moved on to the 150-seat market with the A320, undergoing certification with fly-by-wire controls. "Fly-by-wire" refers to the use of computer-based controls of the aileron, rudder, and other aircraft mechanisms, replacing the more traditional mechanical controls. The A320 is a short-haul twin-engine aircraft, seating between 150 and 180 passengers in a single-aisle configuration. It uses tried and tested engines and achieves fuel economies with design innovations.

Given the lack of cash flow and profits from the A300/310 program, the A320 was entirely dependent on government funding for its development. But market prospects looked attractive as airlines would be replacing the aging DC9s and 727s. Airbus executives termed it "the hole in the sky." Because Boeing was deep in the launch of the 757/767 model family, it would be less able to launch yet another program for a new 150-seat aircraft model.

Airbus has been successful with the A320. It received 439 orders for the A320 by the time of its maiden flight on February 22, 1987, including 262 firm orders, 157 options, and 20 commitments. It followed up with the derivative launch of both larger and smaller versions of the A320. The A321 carried about 180 passengers; the A319 carried 124 passengers, competing directly with Boeing's newest 737-500 aircraft. The A320 and the follow-on derivatives gathered more than 3,600 orders, thus becoming the first aircraft in the Airbus family to achieve commercial success. Even more importantly, airlines did not see Boeing's derivative 737s as fully matching the A320s fly-by-wire and other advanced technology capabilities. The A320 helped Airbus gain credibility as a technology leader.

The A330/340 Series

With the 150-seat and midsize (200–250 seats) segments covered, Airbus launched the high-capacity long-range A330/340 series. Again, the company shared design elements: the twin-aisle cross-section of the A300/310, a variable camber high-efficiency wing, and a new final assembly line. Airbus's existing A300/310 aircraft needed new wings to improve range and efficiency; adapting the same wing to the A330 and A340 could further reduce development costs.

The A330, a high-capacity medium-range jet, can carry about 330 passengers. The jet has a range of about 5,500 miles. It was intended as a twin-engine replacement for aging wide-body tri-jets (three-engine jets) such as the DC-10 and the L-1011, with sufficient range to operate on transatlantic routes. The A340 was designed as a four-engine long-range aircraft for 260 to 290 passengers. It was capable of flying 7,650 nautical miles (or nonstop from New York to Hong Kong).

The A330/340 program was subsidized. While it is difficult to estimate the extent of subsidies made available to Airbus, total subsidies over the 1970–1990 period (covering the A300/310, the A320, and the A330/340 series) were between $12 billion and $15 billion, including launch. Airbus was certain of receiving government subsidies, and it had an early commitment from the French government to buy several newer models. Those facts may have emboldened Airbus to gamble on its obtaining enough unit volume to derive profits from launches of new aircraft, despite the presence of Boeing, or perhaps Airbus reasoned that its government backing could enable it to sustain losses. Airbus's success with aircraft sales, particularly with the A320, complemented the subsidies, allowing it to lower total costs through economies of scale, thus enhancing its competitive position.

NEW PRODUCT DEVELOPMENT

The pace of new product development in the commercial jet industry might seem glacial compared to other fast-paced technology-intensive industries such as computers and networking. The necessary scale of R&D funding and the time to develop new jets explain why both Boeing and Airbus launch only one or two new models a decade. Since about 1990, only four new aircraft have been launched by the two competitors, with a fourth model on the verge of formal launch.

The B-777 Aircraft

Boeing's product-development effort during much of the 1990s was focused on developing and launching the Boeing 777. Airbus's A330/340 long-range but medium-capacity aircraft, which carried about 350 passengers, was first to market. (The A330/340 had less capacity than the 747, but a somewhat similar range.) It may have focused on the needs of the emerging Asian airlines. The response by Boeing was for its 777 to be the world's largest twinjet. In its initial version, the aircraft carried between 375 and 400 passengers, with a range of 4,200 nautical miles. Boeing intended the 777 to be positioned between the 767 and the 747, with an initial delivery scheduled for mid-1995. The 777 was planned as the widest and most spacious airline in its class, having great interior flexibility. Airlines could easily add, remove, and shift lavatories and galleys and change seating configuration as needed. The 777 was designed with folding wingtips so it could be parked at older airports. In building the 777, Boeing used Japanese suppliers. Mitsubishi, Kawasaki, and Fuji built about 20 percent of the airframe. Frank Schrontz, Boeing's then-CEO, noted, "We would rather have the Japanese with us than with Airbus."

United was the launch customer for the 777, buying 34 aircraft to replace its aged DC-10s. The initial version could replace tri-jets on U.S. domestic routes, on short transcontinental routes such as New York to London, and on regional routes in the Far East. Compared to the A330-300, the 777 would be more fuel-efficient and would carry more passengers. Cathay Pacific is typical of the airlines that ordered the 777. Offering several long flights from its hub in Hong Kong, Cathay Pacific ordered both the 777 and Airbus A330.

The "Superjumbo" Airbus A380

One of the interesting questions facing Boeing and Airbus was whether its customers, the airlines, needed planes that could carry more than 500 passengers, the outer limit of the Boeing 747. As Asian economies grew, demand from their larger populations could result in the need to carry more people at a time across Asian capitals separated by water, such as Singapore to Tokyo and Shanghai to Sydney. However, larger planes had to be filled with people to operate profitably, and airlines might be concerned about their ability to fill 550-seat and larger planes at 75 percent capacity (the level at which the route would be profitable). Those planes would be heavy, require new engines, and incur large R&D costs (estimated at about $10 billion). Boeing decided not to pursue such an option, perhaps constrained by the need to deliver financial returns to its shareholders. Airbus did launch such a plane, the A380, making the announcement in 2002. The plane is a double-decker capable of carrying 550 passengers and flying 8,000 nautical miles nonstop. It is designed for long, high-density routes. For example, one of its customers is a start-up Indian airline, Kingfisher Airlines, which will operate the A380 with 496 seats in a three-class configuration from Mumbai (Bombay) to New York. Lufthansa, another customer, will use the A380 on high-density routes from Germany to cities such as New York, Singapore, Bangkok, and New Delhi. Other early customers are Thai Airways, Malaysia Airlines, and Qantas. The A380 had its maiden flight in April 2005. The first commercial deliveries to Singapore Airlines were in 2008, along with a freighter version.

The Boeing 787 Dreamliner

In 2003, Boeing launched a new aircraft, the 787 Dreamliner. It represented a different development direction from that of Airbus's A380. While the A380 can carry over 500 passengers and fly nearly halfway around the world nonstop, the Dreamliner 787 is fuel-efficient and about half as large in terms of passenger capacity. The 787-8 Dreamliner and 787-9 airplanes can carry 223 to 259 passengers in tri-class configurations on routes of 8,500 and 8,300 nautical miles, respectively. A third 787 family member, the 787-3 Dreamliner, can accommodate nearly 296 passengers in a two-class configuration, optimized for routes of 3,500 nautical miles. With its price of $120 million, Boeing promised a 20 percent improvement in fuel efficiency per passenger. The 787 is aimed at replacing the 757 and the 767 and is intended to compete with the aging A300 and A330. Most initial orders for the 787 have come from outside the United States. The two largest orders were placed by ANA (50 planes) and Japan Airlines (30 planes). By May 2011, Boeing had received orders for over 800 of the Dreamliner 787 planes.

The A380 and the Boeing 787 represent different bets on the future direction of air travel. Airbus expects a major market of large-capacity planes that fly long distances. On the other hand, Boeing is banking on airlines and their customers wanting to fly long nonstop routes between smaller capitals and regional cities; however, there will be fewer passengers. This suggests that the international hub-and-spoke system will become less prevalent and that airlines and their customers will prefer to fly direct over long distances. Airlines can also reach breakeven with fewer customers when flying the smaller 787s.

Airbus's Proposed A350

Airbus's proposed A350 is estimated to enter service in mid-2013 with over 570 orders booked by early 2011. Airbus plans two versions of the A350, the A350-800, which will seat 253 passengers and fly 8,800 nautical miles, and the A350-900, which will seat 300 passengers and fly up to 7,500 nautical miles. The aircraft will feature some of the innovations pioneered in the A380: a fuselage made of aluminum/lithium and carbon fiber wings, making it lighter

Table 9-8 • Growth of Airline Passenger Traffic by Region

	North America	Asia Pacific	China	Europe	Latin America	Middle East	Africa
Percentage Growth Rate							
2004–2023	4.2	6	8.2	5.2	4.9	7.1	4.5

Source: Airbus Global Market Forecast 2004-2023.

Table 9-9 • Manufacturers' Forecasts of Aircraft Market Size, 2005–2024

Manufacturer	Boeing (Forecast 2005–2024)	Airbus (Forecast 2004–2023)
Global Traffic Growth	4.8% per year	5.3% per year
Aircraft Demand (Number of Units)	25,700	17,328
Aircraft Demand (2004 Dollars)	$2.1 trillion	$1.9 trillion
Number of Aircraft in Fleet Beginning of Forecast Period	16,800 planes (2004)	10,838 passenger aircraft (end of 2003) and 1,506 freighter aircraft
End of Forecast Period	35,300 planes	21,759 passenger aircraft and 3,616 freighter aircraft

Source: Boeing Market Outlook 2004 and Airbus Global Market Forecast 2004-2023.

in weight and leading to greater fuel efficiency. Both aircraft will offer spacious cabins with larger windows and more headroom, e-mail connectivity, and mood lighting. Airbus noted that it would carry "30 more people eight percent more economically/seating than its closest competitor."

LOOKING TO THE FUTURE: THE GLOBAL AIR TRAFFIC ENVIRONMENT

Aircraft product cycles can easily extend beyond 20 years. Hence, aircraft manufacturers have to consider how the air traffic market will evolve over the long term. The major industry trend is faster growth outside the United States. Table 9-8 summarizes growth trends in global airline traffic.

As is the case of many other industries, higher rates of growth are occurring outside the United States. Table 9-9 summarizes long-term market forecasts prepared by Boeing and Airbus. Both airlines see significant growth in orders over the next several years.

Oversupply of Aircraft Capacity Relative to Demand

Is there a current oversupply of planes? Between 1985 and 1990, world traffic grew at 7 percent a year, aircraft orders rose at 30 percent a year, and production increased at 16 percent a year. Hence, airlines developed excess capacity. When recession hit Asia in 1997 and when a global recession unfolded in 2001, airline traffic dropped dramatically. As a consequence, domestic and international airlines reduced their capital spending, requesting aircraft delivery postponements. American, European, and Far Eastern airlines all implemented budget reductions. Despite subsequent recovery, airlines have been cautious in adding capacity and ordering new aircraft, preferring, instead, to fly older planes that have higher capacities.

Pacific-based airlines became the biggest source of aircraft orders as major U.S. airlines were noticeably reticent about ordering new planes. Bankruptcy of four of the major U.S. airlines diminished their ability to order new aircraft. Forecasts suggest that by 2015, about half of all wide-body jets will be flying Pacific routes, and those routes will account for 70 percent of all wide-body seats. (The average number of seats on Pacific routes is likely to be around 350.) This boom in demand for aircraft that offer larger passenger capacity is reflected in the many orders that have come from the Pacific region. Airbus has received large orders from China and other Asian markets for its A380.

Financing Difficulties

Airline financing became harder to secure as airline balance sheets deteriorated. Reduced cash flow from a traffic decline due to terrorism fears and economic recession forced airlines and lenders to cut their capital spending budgets. Lenders became less willing to finance the purchase of aircraft to be flown on competitive routes, where rates of traffic growth and yields are low. However, funding is available for aircraft purchase for new routes in stable markets. Leasing of aircraft has also become more costly.

Upgrading Older Aircraft Instead of Replacing Them

Airlines have the option of cutting aircraft spending by upgrading older aircraft (retrofitting) and by using hush kits, thus preserving capacity without buying new aircraft. For example, Delta retrofitted 80 of its older 727-200 and 737-300 aircraft. Delta retrofitted its 727s with Honeywell's glass cockpit avionics and Rolls-Royce's Tay 670 engines, thus reducing crew from three to two. By doing so, Delta saved $400,000 per year per plane in labor and overhead. Retrofitted hardware costs between $15 million and $17 million compared to $30 million for a new aircraft. Such retrofitting meets noise reduction requirements and yields 10 to 15 percent in fuel savings, provided the aircraft still has 12 or more years of economic life. In other words, about 35,000 to 40,000 cycles must still remain for the retrofitting to be economically viable.

When a major airline such as Delta proceeds to upgrade older aircraft, it legitimizes retrofitting as an alternative to buying in a poor economy. Of course, a sudden change in oil prices could make all of the older aircraft fuel obsolete and revive the demand for aircraft offering new technology.

Responding to Subsidies Given to Airbus

In the face of competition from Airbus, Boeing has sought help from the U.S. government in limiting the subsidies for product development and export financing given to Airbus by the consortium member governments. Boeing has attempted to prevent Airbus gains in market share, particularly with long-established Boeing customers. In addition, Boeing has launched new aircraft models such as the 787. There were ongoing legal battles between Boeing and Airbus and their respective governments throughout the early 2000s resulting in complaints to the WTO. Both sides claimed extensive government subsidies.

As the aircraft market recovers, continued government support has enabled Airbus to continue to develop new aircraft models. That has forced Boeing to consider how to counter new aircraft models offered by Airbus and how to fund and allocate R&D. Airbus has emerged as a viable competitor with a full product line. The global aircraft market is changing, with the Far East (especially China) becoming more important. Pressures from major markets such as China to conduct more in-country manufacturing are also affecting the nature of the aircraft industry. Understanding the changing world environment and responding to those changes will determine whether Boeing can continue to compete successfully in the global market.

Case developed for in-class discussion by Ravi Sarathy, Northeastern University. ©2005–2011. All rights reserved.

Questions and Research

1. What are the market segments within the commercial aircraft industry? How have Boeing and Airbus approached those segments?

2. Is Boeing the strongest company in the industry in terms of product line? Explain.

3. Compare Boeing's and Airbus's competing products.

4. Trace how Airbus has filled out its product line. Can its product introductions be seen as competitive responses to Boeing? Explain.

5. How do customers influence the aircraft product line?

6. What factors influence an airline's buying of jet aircraft?

7. What should Boeing do in response to Airbus's launch of the A380? Will its 787 be enough?

8. Will new competitors be entering the aircraft industry? If so, where will they come from and how should Boeing deal with this potential development?

NOTES

1. "About Swatch" (http://www.swatch.com/zz_en/about/history.html), accessed March 24, 2011.
2. T. Levitt. "The Globalization of Markets," *Harvard Business Review* 61, no. 3 (May–June 1983): 93–102.
3. Ibid., Exhibit 1.
4. "Machines for the Masses," *Wall Street Journal*, December 9, 2003.
5. John S. Hill and Richard R. Still. "Effects of Urbanization on Multinational Product Planning," *Columbia Journal of World Business* (Summer 1984): 62–67.
6. "For Coca-Cola in Japan, Things Go Better with Milk," *Wall Street Journal*, January 20, 1997.
7. See Chapter 7 for a more detailed discussion of global per capita income figures.
8. "China Steams Ahead with World's Fastest Train," *The Telegraph*, February 12, 2010 (http://www.telegraph.co.uk/news/worldnews/asia/china/7230137/China-steams-ahead-with-worlds-fastest-train.html), accessed April 20, 2011.
9. "Germany Joins EU in Tying Car Fees to Emissions," *Spiegel Online International*, January 27, 2009 (http://www.spiegel.de/international/germany/0,1518,603798,00.html), accessed April 13, 2011.
10. "Nonalcoholic Beer Hits the Spot in Mideast," *Wall Street Journal*, December 6, 1995.
11. "Why Heinz Went Sour in Brazil," *Advertising Age*, December 5, 1988.
12. Marc Meyer and J. M. Utterback. "The Product Family and the Dynamics of Core Capability," *Sloan Management Review* (Spring 1993): 1–19.
13. Johannes I. M. Halman, Adrian P. Hofer, and Win van Vuuren. "Platform-Driven Development of Product Families: Linking Theory With Practice" *Journal of Product Innovation Management* 20 (2003): 149–162.
14. Researchers Robertson and Ulrich address the different perspectives of differentiation and commonality inherent in a platform approach to product development. They note that a platform-based product plan incorporates attention to the entire portfolio and timing of the introduction of its various components. A platform-based plan also offers detailed differentiation—how the various products in the family are different internally (within the firm) and externally (in the eyes of the customer and the market). Similarly, a commonality plan lays out the extent of shared technology, modules, subsystems, software, interfaces, and standards. See D. Robertson and K. Ulrich. "Planning for Product Platforms," *Sloan Management Review* 39, no. 4 (1998): 19–31.
15. Howard R. Moskowitz and Sam Rabino. "Sensory Segmentation: An Organizing Principle for International Product Concept Generation," *Journal of Global Marketing* 8, no. 1 (1994): 73–93.
16. S. Prokesch. "Mastering Chaos at the High-Tech Frontier: An Interview with Silicon Graphics' Ed McCracken," *Harvard Business Review* 71, no. 5 (November–December 1993): 134–144.
17. Stefan Thomke and Eric von Hippel. "Customers as Innovators," *Harvard Business Review*, 80, no. 4 (April 2002): 74–81.
18. Charles Morris and C. H. Ferguson. "How Architecture Wins Technology Wars," *Harvard Business Review*, 71, no. 2 (March–April 1993): 86–96; Carl Shapiro and Hal Varian, "The Art of Standards Wars," California Management Review 41, no. 2 (Winter 1999): 8–32.
19. Benny Evangelista. "SGI No Longer Is a Dinosaur" *San Francisco Chronicle*, March 30, 2011, p. D1.
20. John Quelch and David Kenny. "Extend Profits, Not Product Lines," *Harvard Business Review* 72, no. 5 (September–October 1994): 153–160.
21. For background on this technique, see S. Kalagnanam and S. K. Schmidt. "Analyzing Capital Investments in New Products," *Management Accounting* (January 1996): 31–36.
22. The factors listed draw on the report by Kalagnanam and Schmidt.
23. Teruo Yamanouchi. "Breakthrough: The Development of the Canon Personal Copier," *Long Range Planning*, 22, no. 5, (1989): 11–21.
24. Sigwald J. Harryson. "How Canon and Sony Drive Product Innovation through Networking and Application-Focused R&D," *Journal of Product Innovation Management* 14 (July 1997): 288–295.
25. Rajan R. Kamath and J. K. Liker. "A Second Look at Japanese Product Development," *Harvard Business Review* 72, no. 6 (November–December 1994): 154–158.
26. Stephen Green, M. Ann Welsh, and Gordon E Dehler. "Advocacy, Performance, and Threshold Influences on Decisions to Terminate New Product Development," *Academy of Management Journal* 46, no. 4 (2003): 419–434, Figure 1.
27. Eric von Hippel, and Ralph Katz. "Shifting Innovation to Users via Toolkits," *Management Science* 48, no. 7 (July 2002): 821–833.
28. H. Takeuchi and I. Nonaka. "The New New-Product Development Game," *Harvard Business Review*, 64, no. 1 (January–February 1986): 137–146.
29. K. Kim, J. H. Park, and J. E. Prescott. "The Global Integration of Business Functions," *Journal of International Business Studies* 34 (July 2003): 327–344.
30. Robert Pearce and M. Papanastassiou. "R&D Networks and Innovation: Decentralized Product Development in Multinational Enterprises," *University of Reading, Discussion Papers in International Investment and Business Studies*, Volume VIII, Series B, Number 204, October 1995.
31. Arnoud de Meyer. "Tech Talk: How Managers Are Stimulating Global R&D Communication," *Sloan Management Review*, 32, no. 3 (Spring 1991): 49–58; Roman Bouteiller, Olivier Gassmann, and Maximilian von Zedtwitz. *Managing Global Innovation* (New York: Springer-Verlag, 2000).

chapter 10 International Branding and Promotion

Branding, advertising, personal selling, sales promotion, and public relations are the major categories of the promotion mix. As a firm expands internationally, these critical marketing tasks must be addressed within the context of the international business environment.

The main goals of this chapter are to •••

1. Discuss the characteristics of a global brand and the approaches to establishing and maintaining a global brand.

2. Discuss how languages, regulations, and infrastructure impact promotion.

3. Show how media diversity and media developments affect the options available in a market.

4. Present criteria useful in selecting promotion agencies in those cases where a firm seeks outside help.

5. Explore the ways in which personal selling varies in world markets, requiring different methods of recruitment and management of a sales force.

6. Describe how different national cultures and requirements affect the possibilities for sales promotion in foreign markets.

7. Detail special forms of sales promotion, such as trade fairs.

8. Explain the role of public relations in effective global promotion.

9. Discuss promotion budgeting and strategy.

Global Branding

•••

Sooner or later the international marketing manager has to decide how important branding will be in the overall marketing mix. Brands allow for differentiation and premium pricing, and they create customer loyalty, leading to repeat purchases. Further, the profits from premium pricing, coupled with steady market share and repeat purchases, result in measurable cash flow, which is at the heart of brand equity calculations. Because acquiring customers is costly for a firm, loyal customers who buy regularly are valuable. However, developing a global brand represents a major challenge for the international marketing manager.

The Relevance of Brands

Once developed and recognized, a brand can have a long life. Major brands such as Lipton, Ivory, Gillette, and Coca-Cola have been popular for decades. An important question, then, is how to build brand recognition in international markets. Brands can be built up through advertising, but advertising merely builds on the brand's foundation, which rests on quality, innovation, superior service, customer satisfaction, and value. With regard to consumer products, brand personality is also relevant; namely, how a brand creates and reinforces a buyer's self-image in products such as designer clothing brands, cars, and shoes. Furthermore, brands provide customers with a guarantee of value and quality, making customers' choices easy. It frees them from the confusion and message fatigue endemic to a competitive marketplace. Brands become a shortcut to consumption, allowing customers to make safe choices. Customers are secure in knowing that by purchasing the brand, satisfaction and value will result. Conversely, breaking this compact with the customer can quickly result in a brand's decline.

But developing and maintaining a brand's position is costly, particularly as the number of major international markets proliferate. A manager has to decide

- Whether to aim for a global brand for the product and product line.
- Whether to offer one international brand or different national brands for a given product.
- What the role of private branding is in international marketing.
- Whether to use multiple brands in the same market to target different customer segments (though this results in higher costs).

The main question is whether to promote local country-specific brands or to establish global and regional brands with appeal across countries.[1]

Table 10-1 sets out the major branding choices in international marketing and summarizes their advantages and disadvantages.

Global Brands: Why the Move to Global Brands?

"A brand is a promise that has to be fulfilled everywhere, at any time."[2]

Building a global brand is inherent in marketing a standardized product.[3] Its success depends on a growing convergence of consumer tastes and the coordination of global advertising and promotion. Mass media and telecommunications make it easy to communicate a single message simultaneously, effectively, and efficiently to a large number of geographically dispersed markets; for example, the simultaneous transmission of the Summer Olympics around the world. In such cases, because the same transmission is received around the world, firms benefit when the brands featured are familiar to the entire audience. Also, the growing importance of the youth market and its convergence of tastes and purchasing power motivate a reliance on global brands. Global branding also offers

Table 10-1 • A Perspective on Branding

Advantages	Disadvantages
NO BRAND	
Lower production cost	Severe price competition
Lower marketing cost	Lack of market identity
Lower legal cost	
Flexible quality and quantity control	
BRANDING	
Better identification and awareness	Higher production cost
Better chance for product differentiation	Higher marketing cost
Possible brand loyalty	Higher legal cost
Possible premium pricing	
PRIVATE (DISTRIBUTOR OR RETAIL) BRAND	
Better margins for dealers	Severe price competition
Possibility of larger market share	Lack of market identity
No promotional problems	
MANUFACTURER'S BRAND	
Better price due to more price inelasticity	Difficulty for small manufacturer
Retention of brand loyalty	with unknown brand or identity
Better bargaining power	Brand promotion required
Better control of distribution	
MULTIPLE BRANDS (IN ONE MARKET)	
Market segmented for varying needs	Higher marketing cost
Creation of competitive spirit	Higher inventory cost
Lower inventory cost	Loss of economies of scale
Avoidance of negative connotation of existing brand	
More retail shelf space gained	
No damage to existing brand's image	
SINGLE BRAND (IN ONE MARKET)	
Marketing efficiency	Market homogeneity assumed
More focused marketing permitted	Harm to existing brand's image
Elimination of brand confusion	when trading up/down
Advantage for product with good reputation (halo effect)	Limited shelf space
LOCAL BRANDS	
Meaningful names	Higher marketing cost
Local identification	Higher inventory cost
Avoidance of taxation on international brand	Loss of economies of scale
Quick market penetration by acquisition of local brand	Diffused image
Variations of quantity and quality across markets allowed	
WORLDWIDE BRAND	
Maximum marketing efficiency	Market homogeneity assumed
Reduction of advertising costs	Problems with black and
Elimination of brand confusion	gray markets
Advantage for culture-free product	Possibility of negative connotation
Advantage for prestigious product	Quality and quantity consistency
Easy identification/recognition for international travelers	required
Worldwide uniform image	LDCs' opposition and resentment
	Legal complications

Source: Sak Onkvisit and John J. Shaw, "The International Dimensions of Branding: Strategic Considerations and Decisions," *International Marketing Review*, 6 (1989): Table 1, 24.

the emotional value of identifying with a well-known global brand to people who want to belong to a group that cuts across countries. Global branding can also be cost effective, providing economies of scale by reaching a large number of potential consumers with the same message. In addition, a global brand can serve as an umbrella brand, support line extensions, and lend a halo to local and national brands intended for a different market segment. For all those reasons, global companies need both a global brand and local brand. Further, the overall quality of the global-brand-based marketing campaign can benefit from cross-border learning by transferring successful best practices and approaches from one market to another. This is possible because all markets are based on the same global brand.

The advantages of global branding include economies of scale in advertising. The uniform image can appeal to globe-trotting consumers. Global brands are also important in securing access to distribution channels. In cases where shelf space is at a premium, as with food products, a company has to convince retailers to carry its products rather than those of competitors. Having a global brand may help persuade retailers because, from the retailers' standpoint, a global brand is less likely to languish on the shelves. Finally, a hidden benefit of a global brand is that it adds to the reputation and image of the company, makes the company better known, and may help attract marketing managers and other executives who want to work for a global company.

What Characterizes a Global Brand?

There are seven common features to a global brand, as follows:

- The brand is strong in the home market. That strength and cash flow from repeat sales fund the push into new foreign markets and the investment in creating a global brand.

- Geographic balance exists; that is, the brand has reasonable levels of sales in at least some of the key markets of North and South America, Europe, Asia-Pacific, and increasingly Africa. A brand cannot be considered global unless people in different parts of the world have heard of it.

- The product addresses a similar need worldwide, providing a basis for a standardized message delivered globally.

- Every global brand has a country of origin that is part of the global brand's identity. If consumers do not place high value on a brand's country of origin, a firm will have difficulty creating a strong intangible attribute for the brand.

- The brand's main focus is on a single broad product category, such as IBM, Coca-Cola, Sony, and BMW.

- Consistent positioning occurs so the brand represents the same set of practical and emotional attributes everywhere.

- There is a link to the corporate brand, with the global brand name and the corporate brand often being the same.

How to Build a Global Brand

As Figure 10-1 suggests, a global brand follows standard, uniform brand positioning (and a strategy) across all its key markets. That is achieved through four building blocks: advertising copy tone and content, brand slogan, brand logo, and brand icons such as packaging. Together, the four components form an integrated communication plan that needs to be executed and then maintained over many years (perhaps decades) to build on the global brand. The communication plan is

Figure 10-1 ● Building Global Brands

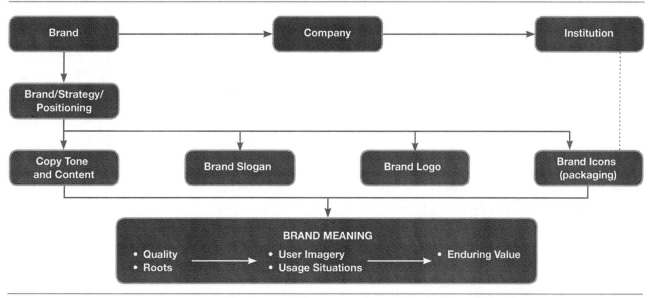

Source: John Quelch, "Global Brands: Taking Stock," *Business Strategy* Review 10 (1). Spring 1999, Figure 1, page 5.

then linked to users and desired users: who they are, how they look and behave, and in what situations the product or service is used. As Figure 10-1 illustrates, heritage, quality, user images, and user situations stress the enduring values that must be associated with a brand to build a bond with the customer, leading to brand loyalty, repeat purchases, and the long-lasting value of a global brand.

WHAT PRODUCTS ARE MOST SUITED TO A GLOBAL BRANDING APPROACH?

Some products, such as food, are harder to brand globally because they are more culturally dependent. Industrial products with relative product uniformity more easily lend themselves to global advertising. So, too, does the luxury goods market, where consumers are a select upper income group that cuts across country markets to form a distinct multicountry segment.

DANGERS OF GLOBAL BRANDING

Global branding does have some negatives. Managers, particularly in subsidiaries, may complain about too much standardization, rigid control from headquarters, and the inability to make allowances for the stage of market growth in each country (proving that there may be a divergence between the country's market evolution and the brand's overall worldwide development). Such possible divergence is particularly important when an established global brand begins entering emerging markets such as India or China. A firm may also have difficulty imposing the same brand image that underlies the global brand campaign in all markets. Markets in developing countries may want more practical attributes stressed, whereas higher-income markets may welcome a campaign built around intangible attributes that stress status, style, and well-being. Global brands can also be seen as a metaphor for the policies of the home-country government, attracting protests and even acts of terrorism.

A global brand also comes with risks as seen in attacks on Starbucks stores.

VARYING BRAND IMAGE

In developing global brands, a marketing manager has to decide what brand image to project across markets. For example, Reebok blends lifestyle and athletic prowess in its U.S. ads, whereas its European image is focused mainly on athletics.

To learn more about brand image, research has examined the links between a country market's cultural and socioeconomic factors and the nature of brand image chosen, whether functional or sensory.[4] Studies have related those choices to product performance in the market, after adjusting for a firm's experience with the market, the nature of competition, and the choices made by the firm across the marketing mix. Findings show that in countries such as China, France, and Belgium, where the degree of separation between high- and low-power-status individuals is high (essentially cultures that score high on the Hoftsede power distance index), brand images should stress social and sensory needs. Similarly, in countries where individualism is low, as in much of Asia, brand images that stress group membership and affiliation are likely to be more successful.

Creative approaches to building brand recognition are helpful. A distributor of British skiwear, Nevica USA, offered photographers free skiwear and a fee each time one of their photographs was published in a ski magazine showing Nevica-clad skiers. Similarly, Franklin Sports Industries built name recognition by giving batting gloves to baseball players. The Franklin name appeared in large letters on the back of the gloves, making them visible to television viewers when a camera focused on a batter. When photographs of batters appeared in newspapers or on the cover of magazines such as *Sports Illustrated*, the Franklin name was often visible.

Branding is a difficult task even in the domestic arena. One study of best practices suggests firms must constantly evaluate their own brands, and that this brand "report card" provides insight into the present and future value of the brand.[5] Only valuable domestic brands can be extended successfully into the international arena. For an example of evaluating a firm's brand, see "LEGO's Brands and Global Expansion."

Walmart is the number one most valuable retail brand in the United States.

A Brand's Value

A strong brand is a valuable asset for a firm. It builds customer loyalty, which leads to stronger sales. A strong brand becomes a competitive barrier helping a firm to maintain or grow market share. Interbrand Design Forum conducts research to estimate the value of brands. It publishes "The Most Valuable U.S. Retail Brands," which includes the ranking of top U.S. retailers and the value of each brand. As explained in the company's report; "Brand functions as an asset. If a brand plays a role in choice and the consumer must choose between competitors, then the brand contributes to earnings and profit."[6]

The results of Interbrand's research are shown in Table 10-2. The number one U.S. retailer brand, Walmart, is estimated to have a brand value of over $154 billion. Walmart clearly dominates in its brand power. Its brand value is over six times greater than the nearest competitor, Target, at $25.5 billion. This strong value helps explain Walmart's dominance in the retail sector.

What helps create brand value? Landor Associates also conducts research into the strength of brands.[7] It has identified five elements that contribute to brand strength:

- Share of mind (awareness and familiarity)
- Share of heart (high regard)
- Value (value for money)
- Momentum (potential for future growth or success)
- Singularity (business choice)

Table 10-2 • The Most Valuable U.S. Retail Brands, 2010

Rank	Brand	Brand Value (US $ billions)
1	Walmart	154.1
2	Target	25.5
3	Best Buy	17.8
4	The Home Depot	17.0
5	Walgreens	14.3
6	CVS	14.1
7	Sam's Club	10.5
8	Dell	10.3
9	Coach	8.9
10	Amazon.com	7.9
15	Costco	5.5
20	Tiffany & Co.	4.0
26	Netflix	2.3
34	T.J. Maxx	1.2
38	Whole Foods	0.926
49	Abercrombie & Fitch	0.484
50	Macy's	0.472

Source: Interbrand Design Forum, New York.

••• LEGO's Brands and Global Expansion

LEGO had developed numerous line extensions, including clothing, shoes, and amusement parks, but was losing money, so it decided to restructure its brand architecture and product portfolio. LEGO is known as a toy company, the maker of colorful interlocking bricks that children can turn into creative constructions, including castles, space stations, and pirate islands. Drawing on that heritage, LEGO divided its products into four brand portals as follows:[8]

- *DUPLO* is aimed at the preschool market.
- *Bricks & More*, which is the traditional LEGO brick, constitutes the pure construction category where children build things and building is playing.
- *Play Themes* is based on action toys, story lines, and role playing. Children build action figures, the Bionicle action figure family, and then play with them.
- LEGO *Next*, which is more abstract, allows children to build robots from Mindstorm kits and then program the robots to determine and control how they will act.

LEGO has taken pains to get its employees to understand and accept the brand restructuring. The company began with an internal process to gain an understanding of how employees saw the company. Franco Ciccolella, the senior vice president for global branding, said, "If our (brand)

LEGO recognized its brand had become confused in the marketplace and launched a global brand restructuring.

identity was to be the real thing, we had to believe in it first." Only then did LEGO approach consumers to learn about their views of the LEGO brand, bringing the information back to the company to work with employees on the brand restructuring.

The new brand portfolio facilitates orderly brand extensions, especially tie-ins with movies and video games. LEGO has taken the Bionicle brand of action figures into movies with the film *Bionicle: Mask of Light*. Another natural continuation is comic books and trading cards. An additional untapped segment for LEGO is girls over the age of six. Hence, LEGO launched a female-oriented brand, Clikits, a range of arts and crafts materials from which girls can make jewelry, picture frames, and hair and fashion accessories.

Because the United States is the world's largest toy market, LEGO naturally concentrates on that market, having built its third amusement park in California. However, with Japan as the second-largest market, LEGO is looking to enter the Japanese market for the long haul. A cultural divide may be at work, however. LEGO construction toys have no rules; children use their creativity to assemble the bricks. LEGO wonders if that approach fits into a culture that emphasizes rules and conformity. Not surprisingly, some of the early adopters of LEGO's newer Mindstorm line are young Japanese adults.

Further, LEGO is making LEGO kits available to schools in Moscow and Madrid as part of its education mission. However, the company has to balance education with fun. Children have fun with LEGOs and learn at the same time, while parents and adults need reassurance that LEGOs are educational toys.

The toy market is competitive. Large firms such as Mattel, Hasbro, and Bandai sell toys worldwide; makers of video games compete for the time and wallets of children from a very young age. LEGO has to innovate, to market effectively, while keeping at its core the fundamental values of creative play, of fun and education. How LEGO manages its brand, its identity, will affect everything it does in the next few years.[9]

Such research is helpful in understanding the power of brands and in determining the value of brands—brand equity. For instance, a survey of Latin American brands shows that brands from companies such as Bimbo (Mexico: bread and snacks), Brahma (Brazil: beer) and Maseca (Mexico: tortillas and corn flour) enjoy high recognition and sustainability.[10] In Holland, both local and global brands are in the top ten strongest brands, which included Google and Microsoft as number one and two, Ikea as number three, and Efteling (a local theme park) as number four.[11] See "Branding and China" for more examples of branding efforts overseas.

China's rapid economic growth has been driven by Chinese manufacturers adept at making a large variety of high-quality, low-cost goods for Western companies in a number of industries. But the manufacturers found that they became dependent on the marketing success of their clients for repeat orders and that margins declined as manufacturing capacity and competition increased. Two solutions that a number of Chinese firms have adopted is to acquire or license Western brands and to establish direct relationships with retailers such as Walmart and Home Depot.[12]

As an example, Techtronic Industries of Hong Kong used to make vacuum cleaners for the Cleveland, Ohio, U.S.-based Royal Appliance Mfg. Co., which owned the popular Dirt Devil brand. As Royal faced difficulties competing in the United States, it turned to Techtronic for lower-priced products, including the Broom Vac (which sold 800,000 units for $40 apiece via two-minute infomercials advertised during Super Bowl games). When Royal became available for sale, Techtronic had to make a quick decision on whether to acquire Royal, which it did. The U.S. subsidiary now handles most U.S. marketing, but Techtronic's head-office staff in Hong Kong is more involved with product design and marketing. Other brands Techtronic has acquired include Ryobi power tools and Homelite outdoor products from Deere. Techtronic is not unique in this regard, and other companies have similarly acquired or licensed well-known brand names. For instance, Grande Holdings, Ltd. acquired consumer electronic brands, including Nakamichi, Akai, and Sansui.

Instead of acquiring brands, Chinese firms have developed their own.[13] Chinese multinationals have developed brand names and captured market share in U.S. and European markets. For example, with its own brand, the Haier Group has captured half the U.S. market for small refrigerators. Brands have been difficult to establish in China because of regional income disparities, infrastructure inadequacies that make national distribution difficult, and dominance of Chinese markets by state-owned companies. But newer Chinese multinationals, hybrids with a combination of state and private ownership, are developing major international brands.

Implementing Global Branding: Organizational and Team Issues

Successful implementation of a global branding is a complex process. It relies on cross-cultural teams that need to understand both the global corporate needs and local market needs. A successful strategy requires recognizing organizational and team issues, including[14]

- Procedures to obtain and share insights and best practices from different markets. This means providing motivation for people to share and use information; creating a culture that promotes sharing of information; and utilizing practices such as regular meetings of brand executives, a global branding "university" (such as "Motorola University"), intranets, and field visits, as well as shared international marketing research.

- A global planning process—a set of steps that encompasses the target segment, brand identity, brand equity goals, brand-building programs, and measurements used to judge success and achievements. The process should begin with an analysis of the brand and its associations, as well an analysis of competitors and customers. A brand audit is the starting point. A brand manual for outlining common approaches for communicating brand identity is useful, answering questions such as these: What does the brand stand for? What are the timeless elements of the brand? The brand equity measurement effort should help managers judge the profitability of the global branding effort, a brand-based profit and loss statement that takes into account market share and repeat business. The process should also help tie the global brand effort with steps taken by local managers, thus ensuring consistency and progress.

- Identification of who will be responsible for managing the global branding effort. Companies can and have used many approaches, including creating a Brand Champion, a Global Brand Manager, a Global Brand Team, and a Business Management Team. In the Business Management Team approach, a product category is managed by a team with representatives from R&D, manufacturing, and marketing, whereas the other organizational structures put marketing people in charge.

- A balance of a global approach with departures from the global standard to take into account local differences so as to create "brilliant" global brand efforts.

BRAND EXTENSIONS

Brand extension allows a firm with an existing presence in overseas markets to quickly establish its new products. Using a well-known brand name with a reputation for quality can extend an image of high quality to the new product. Brand extension can allow the new product to be introduced with lower incremental advertising expenditures. The comfort level and familiarity associated with a well-known brand can motivate customers to choose the new product over a competitor's. Brand extensions can include launching the same product in a different form, adding a brand name to related products often used together ("companion" products), building on company image and expertise, and communicating unique or designer attributes. However, there are dangers. The original brand and product may be damaged when the brand image is extended to undesirable products and settings. There must be a fit—some complementarity— between the original product and the proposed product/brand extension.[15]

Hewlett-Packard, for one, was successful in extending its brand image to the home computer market. Because Hewlett-Packard's inkjet printers were cheap and allowed low-cost color printing, the company first obtained a foothold in this segment by selling them to home computer users with children. It helped that Japanese firms that dominated the previous generation of dot-matrix printers stuck with them too long, slowing down their entry into the inkjet market because of Hewlett-Packard's strong patent position. With its strong brand association in the home segment due to its printer sales, Hewlett-Packard was able to launch multimedia personal computers intended primarily for the home market. It was able to get retail shelf space because it already supplied retailers with large numbers of inkjet printers. This allowed for the bundling of personal computers with printers. Finally, Hewlett-Packard's size and extended product range in addition to high margins from inkjet cartridge sales meant that the company could undercut home computer prices, even accepting losses in the interest of building long-term market share.[16]

Brand Protection: When and Where?

Given the value of brands, competitors may choose to develop their own competitive brands. A shortcut is to copy a brand name, making slight modifications

Counterfeit products are a concern globally, resulting in significant lost sales.

in logo or spelling, in the hope of "free riding," or capturing sales from deceived customers. Those actions hurt the original brand and bring it into disrepute. Hence, managers seeking to develop and maintain global brands must vigorously protect the brands from being copied and pirated. For a firm, brand piracy can result in sales lost to imitators, who are seen as competing unfairly. In turn, the reduced sales and cash flow reduce investment in innovation. (See "Pirates at Large" in Chapter 3.) Consumers may ultimately suffer from a lack of new high-technology and innovative products. Countries dependent on technology, such as the United States, will see their exports decrease, and job losses can result in the affected industries. U.S. firms will lose overseas sales to foreign companies that copy technology, brand names, or copyrighted material with impunity. In the short run, foreign industry and foreign consumers are the beneficiaries.[17] Overall, welfare worldwide is likely to decline unless regulations allow for a fair return to investments in technology and product differentiation.

Protecting a brand in international markets can begin with registering the brand with the appropriate authorities in the countries of interest. Blanket registration in all countries may be wise when the costs of registration, which can be significant, are within the budgetary means of the firm. Smaller firms may choose to be more selective.

Brand protection can come about through use of the brand name in common law countries or through legal registration of the brand name in code law countries. However, use should follow registration and vice versa. Although a firm must incur registration costs—primarily legal fees and administrative payments—use costs are higher. Use costs involve importing material quantities of a product and the development of distribution channels and marketing campaigns. Less-than-diligent registration and use of a brand name or trademark may result in a firm having to buy back the rights to its name (sometimes at an inflated sum), depending on the emerging market potential in the country. (See "Protecting Brand Names and Trademarks" for more examples of the challenges with international trademark protection.)

••• Protecting Brand Names and Trademarks

Timberland is a U.S. company with a reputation for rugged outdoor-use footwear and clothing. Its logo is a tree, and its name and logo have developed a strong image connoting high quality and durability. When the company began registering its name and logo around the world, it found that a Brazilian company, Samello, was using the Timberland name on its products. Timberland sued to prohibit Samello's use of the name. However, because winning such suits is difficult, Timberland's lawyers chose an unusual approach. Instead of requesting that the product name be protected, they argued that Timberland was the actual name of the company, and hence, as a trade name, was protected even without registration.[18]

The fear of losing rights to brands is not an idle one. South Africa's Supreme Court ruled that McDonald's did not own the rights to its trademark in South Africa because it had not used its name there in the previous five years. McDonald's had registered its name in South Africa and had renewed its rights but had not opened operations there because of apartheid sanctions (which were lifted in 1991). The judge also decided that McDonald's trademark was not well known among South Africa's majority black population. Therefore, two small South African companies that

wanted to open their own McDonald's restaurants in Durban and Johannesburg were free to do so.[19]

A similar problem faced Grand Met, which marketed Smirnoff vodka worldwide, selling 5 million cases and spending $10 million annually in promoting the brand. Its right to the Smirnoff name came under attack in Russia from Boris Smirnoff, a descendant of Pyotr Smirnoff, who founded the Smirnoff vodka business over 100 years ago. With the Bolshevik Revolution, the Smirnoffs lost their business, as did most holders of private property. In the 1930s, Grand Met's Heublein division acquired the rights to the Smirnoff name from one of Pyotr's sons, Vladimir. A lawsuit by Boris Smirnoff claimed that Vladimir had no right to sell the name. In December 1995, the Russian Patent Office Chamber of Appeals invalidated Heublein's trademarks. Grand Met pointed out that it had spent millions over the past 50 years, building the value of the Smirnoff brand, and that when Heublein acquired the name, total U.S. sales were only about 5,000 cases. Grand Met estimated the brand's value to be about $1.4 billion, and the brand's value could diminish if Grand Met could not claim to be the "Official Purveyor to the Russian Imperial Court." [20]

Another problem is the local reaction to well-known international brands. Phonetic equivalents of English-language brands may not translate well into foreign languages, sometimes resulting in an undesirable meaning. An example is the U.S. candy bar Snickers, which is similar to the commonly used British word *knickers*, meaning ladies undergarments.

A third problem may be that the English brand name is too similar to an existing brand name in the local language. For example, Sears, when spoken by a Castilian Spanish speaker, sounds remarkably similar to Seat, the Spanish automobile company. To avoid confusion, the solution was to use the full Sears Roebuck name. Sometimes a brand name will be changed to make it easy for the native speaker to pronounce. Ocean Spray cranberries, for example, when translated into Chinese characters that are pronounced as "Hoshien Pei," have the added advantage of meaning "healthy refreshment." When first entering the U.S. market, Matsushita could not use its National brand because the name was already taken. In addition, the name of the Japanese parent company was deemed too difficult for U.S. consumers to pronounce. A new brand name, Panasonic, was created and promoted.

Private Branding

In private branding, which is common in consumer goods marketing, a manufacturer cedes control over marketing to a retailer or distributor. That is, the manufacturer supplies goods, but the retailer sells those goods under its brand names. Thus, a marketer such as Limited Brands might order quantities of dresses, linens, towels, lamps, and accessories, all to be sold under The Limited, Gap, and related brand names. Most of those purchases are from Far East clothing subcontractors, principally in China. The original manufacturer's identity is lost, and its margins tend to be lower on sales of private brands.

Private branding provides a quick and relatively low-cost approach to penetrating foreign markets, though the seller fails to establish any relationship with the ultimate buyer and, therefore, has little control over the marketing relationship. The manufacturer has no say on the prices charged and receives little direct feedback from the market. Nor can service and after-sales support be used as a means of forging long-term ties with the ultimate buyer. However, private branding is a useful means of test-marketing products in markets whose potential is likely to grow in the future. Positioning is also important in selling those private brands. Low prices alone are not enough, however, because profitability is restricted due to lower profit margins. The goals are to match branded product quality and to offer prices that are sufficiently below that of branded products to convince customers to switch to the private label. For manufacturers who supply firms such as Sears, careful sourcing is necessary to lower procurement costs without diminishing quality, while also meeting delivery deadlines and supplying the quantities contracted for.

When buyers provide product specifications, sales of private brands become a window on an emerging market, allowing the manufacturer to better position itself for future direct entry. Companies such as The Limited and Sears benefit from their name becoming a well-known brand.

However, that experience with a private label may not easily transfer across national markets. For example, Britain's largest supermarket operator, Sainsbury's, has been successful in the UK, selling private-label products such as smoked salmon and its own brand of champagne. When Sainsbury's expanded into the United States, it decided not to push its private-label approach until it learned how private-label products in those product categories would be evaluated by U.S. consumers.

An interesting trend is the proliferation of private brands in supermarkets and chain stores in Europe. Most sales in the German low-price food chain ALDI are its private brand of food products. ALDI contracts the manufacturing of basic products such as flour, rice, and noodles and aims for margins of about 12.5 percent, lower than the 16 percent margin typical in French hypermarkets or the 25 percent margin of British supermarkets. At the same time, ALDI concentrates on quality equivalent to brand-name products, but at a lower price. As neighborhood shops disappear across Europe and more customers shop at chain stores and hypermarkets, such private branding could increase.

How serious is the threat to established brands from private labels? Private-label sales are increasing in importance, accounting for about 15 percent of U.S. supermarket sales, more in recession years. The proportion is considerably higher in Europe, where large grocery and supermarket chains such as the Sainsbury's and Tesco dominate and, accordingly, provide more shelf space to their in-house private brands. Sainsbury's, for example, had Cott Corporation manufacture its Classic Cola and was able to capture 15 percent of the U.K. cola market, accounting for 65 percent of cola sales within Sainsbury's.

Private labels have increased in prominence because their quality has improved. Premium private labels have emerged, such as Loblaws President's Choice line of over 1,500 grocery items. With private labels available for a wide variety of goods, consumers may be willing to buy them over higher-priced national brands. As those European retailers begin to expand into the United States, private-label merchandise could increase in importance in the U.S.

Store brands and private labels are more of a threat when national brands do not command high market shares uniformly across a national market. In those cases, efficient retailers can win market share for their private label or store brands depending on the following:[21]

- Demographics of the local markets.

- Scale and scope economies of the retailer.

- Retailer pricing, promotion, and assortment (product range) tactics.

- Retailer expertise in the category (frozen foods, soft drinks, and so on).

- Extent of competition in the local retail sector.

- Extent of competition from all brands in the category.

- Promotion and advertising strategies of national brand manufacturers.

However, manufacturers of branded goods have fought back with the following tactics:[22]

- Convincing retailers of the greater overall profitability of carrying branded goods—greater turnover and more repeat buying make up for lower retailer margins.

- Reducing the price gap between the national brand and the private label, while realizing that some premium is necessary to pay for brand advertising and for the greater reassurance of quality and performance that a brand conveys.

- Combining brand marketing with complementary sales promotions and enhanced channel relationships.

- Continuing to improve the brand so it offers value commensurate with pricing; in other words, manufacturers continuing to invest in and build up brand equity.

International Promotion

Promotion in international marketing plays the same role as it does in domestic operations—that is, communication with a firm's audiences to achieve certain goals. Advertising, selling, sales promotion, and public relations are examples of promotion. Due to differences from country to country, the promotion task is not the same in every market. How promotion is conducted will vary in terms of company goals, the target audiences, and means of communication. Additionally, a firm must decide on what "nationality" to promote: a local, foreign, or multinational company.

Promotion Tools

Advertising is the paid communication of company messages through impersonal media. The messages may be audio, as in radio; visual, as in billboards or magazines; or audiovisual, as in the Internet, television, or movies. Advertising is used everywhere to achieve various marketing goals, which include paving the way for a sales force, gaining distribution, selling products, and improving brand image. In every country, advertising is just one element of the marketing mix. Its role depends on the other elements of the mix in that country. **Personal selling** is direct contact with a potential buyer or group of buyers for the purpose of making or influencing a sale. Personal selling is also paid communication, but

advertising
The paid communication of company messages through impersonal media.

personal selling
A promotional tool that involves personal and direct contact with a potential buyer or group of buyers for the purpose of making or influencing a sale.

Advertising is a common promotional tool in international marketing.

public relations

The effort to influence the opinion or attitudes people have toward a company, brand, product, or service.

sales promotion

A broad category of activities intended to promote the company, brand, product, or service including coupons, directed e-mail and traditional mail, sponsorship of events, and many other means of communicating with people.

it can be altered quickly and targeted at specific individuals or small groups of people. Selling is the most individualized promotion because it involves personal contact.

Public relations (PR) is the effort to influence the opinion or attitudes people have toward a company, brand, product, or service. The goal of a PR campaign may be to obtain a favorable product review or for the press to favorably publicize a product or service. As contrasted with advertising, a company does not pay for such promotion—at least not directly. However, there are indeed significant costs associated with effective public relations. These are the professional PR staff (employees or a PR firm) and costs associated with PR events such as a product launch media event.

Public relations has the benefit of being among the most powerful promotional tools. Those targeted (the media, bloggers, even politicians) view the people providing the message as impartial and, therefore, trustworthy. (People believe *Consumer Reports* because it accepts no paid advertising, for example.) The challenge with public relations is that the message people receive cannot be easily controlled, if at all, by a firm.

Sales promotion includes many things and is sometimes referred to as the "all other" category of promotional tools. It includes coupons, directed e-mail and traditional mail, and sponsorship of events, among many other means of communicating with others. All these promotional tools will be discussed in more depth.

International Promotional Environment

The international promotional strategy of a firm will be constrained by the international business environment. Before developing its strategy, a firm must identify these constraints. They include languages, economies, media availability, government controls, competition, and the availability of outside agencies. In addressing these challenges, a firm must also work within its own internal constraints such as resources and expertise. Figure 10-2 illustrates some of the constraints on international marketing promotion.

LANGUAGES

Although some languages are used in more than one country, there are many more languages than countries. The international marketing manager does not have to know all the languages of all markets, but the firm's promotion must

Figure 10-2 • The International Business Environment and Its Constraints on International Marketing Communication

communicate in those languages. Even in the few cases in which a product and its promotional appeals are universal, the language is not. In an attempt to minimize costs, in one promotional strategy, firms produce an advertisement or another promotional vehicle in one language and then dub it into another language. Mistakes have been made using this strategy, but studies show that it can be effective if applied carefully.[23]

Technical accuracy or perfect translations are insufficient. Persuasive messages must speak the "language of the heart," and for that to occur, intimate local knowledge is required. Local help is of two kinds: (1) national personnel in countries in which a firm has subsidiaries and (2) the advertising agency located in the market. In both cases, a company benefits from having employees in whose language the company wants to promote itself and its products. In other markets, a firm may rely more heavily on intermediaries for promotional assistance.

Another market factor is language overlap from market to market. One world language would obviously facilitate uniform international advertising. Fortunately for those who use the English language, English fills that role in many places. Of course, the present role of English does not allow universal international campaigns in English, except perhaps in the promotion of certain industrial goods or selected luxury items.

Although language overlap among countries does not allow for global campaigns, a few multilanguage areas do facilitate multinational advertising on a less-than-global basis. Examples are found in Europe, where the German language covers Austria, most of Switzerland, and Germany; and where the French language covers parts of Belgium, Switzerland, Luxembourg, Monaco, and France. More important examples include

Global advertising campaigns must be translated into the local language.

- The English-speaking world, covering up to 600 million people in dozens of nations.

- The French-speaking world, including the former French colonies (including Quebec, Canada), in addition to the European countries just mentioned.

- The Spanish-speaking world, including most of the Americas south of the United States and the many Hispanic markets located throughout the U.S. Even though not all residents of these areas are fluent in the dominant language, the role of the language is large enough to facilitate the internationalization of advertising.

Two examples illustrate the practical importance of language overlap. Unilever introduced its Radion detergent into Germany with a heavy ad campaign. Because several German media overlap into Austria, Austrian consumers sought Radion in Austrian stores. Because Radion had not yet been introduced into Austria, Unilever lost the benefit of the free advertising carryover.

In another example, Anheuser-Busch, a heavy advertiser of Budweiser beer in the United States, began marketing "Bud" in Canada, hoping for a 1 to 2 percent market share. It was pleasantly surprised to gain almost 8 percent of the market in a few months. One reason was the big carryover of U.S. television commercials for "Bud" into the Canadian market. Table 10-3 summarizes some considerations when translating promotional campaigns.

Table 10-3 • Translation Tips

» In international campaigns, use language at a fifth- or sixth-grade vocabulary level so translations are direct and relatively easy.

» Avoid slang or idioms.

» Keep copy short because other languages may take more time or space to say what the original language version says.

» Incorporate visual images (pictures and illustrations) that minimize the need for translation.

» Use local experts because language usage varies even between countries that share a common language such as Spain and Mexico.

MEDIA AVAILABILITY

Some of the media used by advertisers in the home country may not be available abroad. Two factors are at work here. One is government regulation, which may limit commercials on specific media, such as radio, television, cell phones, or the Internet. Another variable is the communications infrastructure. For example, newspaper availability includes one daily paper per 2 people in Japan, one daily paper per 5 people in the United States, one daily paper per 16 people in India, one daily paper per 45 people in Peru, and extreme cases such as one daily paper per 200–400 people in much of Africa.[24]

As another example, personal computer ownership ranges from more than 90 percent of the population in the United States and Taiwan, 50 percent in Italy, 30 percent in Malaysia, 10 percent in China, and less than 10 percent in India.[25] Media availability will be discussed in more depth later in this chapter.

GOVERNMENT CONTROLS

A problem for marketers everywhere is government regulation of promotional activities. U.S. marketers often find foreign countries more restrictive of different forms of promotion than their home market. Government regulations can affect the media, the message, the budget, and agency ownership. The following are specific limitations:

- Due to government regulation, some media are not available or are very limited for commercial use.

- Advertising messages have a variety of restrictions. Many countries regulate the languages that can be used. Countries also have limits on comparative advertising and may require preclearance of certain commercials.

- Some countries restrict ownership of ad agencies. One study found that 17 countries allowed only minority foreign ownership; Indonesia, Nigeria, and Pakistan allowed none.[26]

All governments have laws governing promotion. They are similar in some respects and quite different in others. For example, they are often similar in intent—to protect consumers. Therefore, it is common to see rules about truthful and credible promotional messages. Increasingly, tobacco, liquor, guns, and pharmaceuticals are regulated product classes with regard to promotion.[27, 28] Many nations have privacy laws that dictate who may be contacted and when and how they may be contacted. Certain laws dictate how marketers can collect, store, and use data about potential consumers.

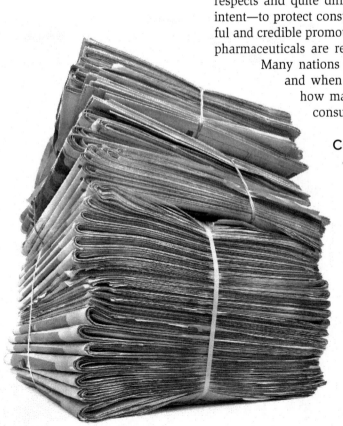

COMPETITION

The competitive situation is another environmental variable. In some markets, an international company competes against other international companies. In other markets, the competition is purely national. Sound promotional strategy in one market is not necessarily sound in another market facing a different set of variables. Furthermore, the approach of an international company provokes different reactions. In some countries, an international company causes national competitors to follow its course of action. For example, when a large competitor such as Walmart enters a new market, established national competitors typically increase their advertising. During an economic crisis, some firms change their appeals, emphasizing the cheapness of their products, whereas others reduce their advertising budgets, not wanting to devalue their brand.

AGENCY AVAILABILITY

Another constraint on the international advertiser is the availability of advertising, promotion research, and promotion agencies in different countries. Countries may have only a very limited number of agencies available to assist with local promotional campaigns. But frequently the agencies are affiliates of the large international agencies, so the service may be better than the limited numbers suggest. At the other extreme are countries with literally hundreds of agencies and semi-independent firms that specialize in specific media, promotional services, industries, or geographic areas.

Strategic Promotion Decisions

After environmental factors have been considered, the international marketing manager must develop the firm's promotional strategy within the environmental constraints. A number of strategic issues would be considered, including (1) selecting the agency (or agencies), (2) choosing the promotion message, (3) selecting the media, (4) measuring media reach and effectiveness, (5) setting the international promotion budget, (6) and selecting the appropriate promotional tools.

Selecting the Agency

Many marketing functions are performed within a company. In the case of promotion, a firm often relies on expertise from an outside advertising or promotion agency. Agency selection is an important decision. Two major alternatives are available: (1) an international agency with domestic and overseas offices or (2) a local agency in each national market. Modifications of those alternatives are often available, especially with the formation of promotion conglomerates (for example, Omnicom Group Inc.). Many larger agencies are acquiring local agencies to achieve global economies of scale and the ability to provide globally coordinated promotional campaigns for their clients yet still provide the local expertise that many companies demand. (See Tables 10-4 and 10-5.)[29, 30, 31]

Table 10-4 ◦ Promotion Holding Companies

Name	Headquarters	2009 Revenues (US $1,000)
WPP Group	London	13,600,000
Omnicom Group	New York	11,720,000
Publicis Groupe	Paris	6,290,000
Interpublic Group	New York	6,030,000
Dentsu	Tokyo	3,110,000

Source: "World's Top 50 Agency Companies," Advertising Age, Agency Family Trees 2010 (http://adage.com/agencyfamilytrees2010/#405), accessed August 14, 2010.

Table 10-5 ● Top U.S. Advertising Agencies

Name	Headquarters	2007 Revenues (US $1,000)
McCann Erickson Worldwide	New York	409,000
BBDO Worldwide (ad only)	New York	472,000
JWT	New York	315,500
Y&R	New York	307,000
DDB Worldwide	New York	290,800

Source: Adweek Agency Report Cards 2008 (http://www.adweek.com/aw/content_display/special-reports/report-card/3i9797ecafefe6fc8b5b4a7feb271b553a), accessed August 14, 2010.

AGENCY SELECTION CRITERIA

Naturally, a firm should choose the agency or agencies that can best help it achieve its goals. Because that criterion is not easy to determine, a firm may want to identify criteria to aid in its choice. First, agency alternatives should be identified. For example, what agencies are located in each market, and which agencies are preempted by competitors? Second, each agency should be evaluated using the following criteria:

- **Market coverage.** Does the particular agency or package of agencies cover all the relevant markets?

- **Quality of coverage.** How effective is the job that the package of agencies does in each market?

- **Market research, public relations, and other marketing services.** If a firm needs these services, how do the different agencies compare in their offerings?

- **Relative roles and compatibility of company and agency.** Some firms have large staffs that do much of the work of preparing promotional campaigns, whereas others have fewer in-house resources or expertise, leaving more to the agencies to perform.

- **Communication and control.** When a firm wants frequent communication with agencies in foreign markets, it is inclined to hire a domestic agency that has overseas offices. The internal communications system of this agency network facilitates communication for the international marketer.

- **International coordination.** Does a firm want its advertising tailor-made to each market? Or does it want coordination of national advertising with advertising done in other markets? One of the major differences among agency groups is their ability to aid in international coordination.

- **Size of company's international business.** The smaller a firm's international promotion expenditures, the less there is to be divided among different agencies. A firm's promotion volume may determine agency choice in order to ensure some minimum level of service. A small volume multiplied by a number of markets could interest an international agency even if it is of no interest to an agency in any one market.

- **Image.** Does a firm want a national or global image? If a firm wants local identification, it might choose a local agency rather than an international agency.

- **Company organization.** Compnies that are very decentralized, with national profit centers, might want to leave agency selection to the local subsidiary.

- **Level of involvement.** In joint-venture arrangements, the international firm shares decision-making responsibilities. The national partner may have experience with a national agency, which could be the decisive factor. In licensing agreements, promotion is largely in the hands of the licensee. Selling through distributors also reduces the control of the international company. Generally, international marketers can choose only the agencies for the promotion paid for by their firms. Where a

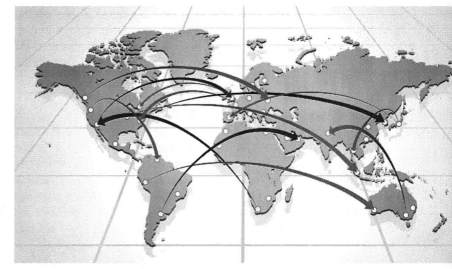

London-based WPP Group is the world's largest promotion holding company.

firm has a cooperative program with its distributors, it may have some voice in agency selection.

GLOBAL VERSUS LOCAL AGENCIES

The growth of multinational agencies puts pressure on agencies that serve only one market. For example, mid-sized British agencies faced tough choices in planning for an integrated European market after 1992. They either had to forge a European network or had to sell out to one if they wanted to keep their clients who would be operating in the market. Similar integration pressures under NAFTA led U.S. agencies to acquire a number of Canadian agencies. Misfortunes have befallen single-country agencies that have multinational clients. Volkswagen advertising in the United States, for example, was handled very successfully by Doyle Dane Bernbach. When this U.S. agency opened an office in Germany, Volkswagen dropped its national agency and gave the account to the office of Doyle Dane Bernbach in Germany.

National agencies are an alternative for the international marketer for several reasons. Although international agencies offer multimarket coverage, their networks are not always of even quality. Offices in some markets may be very strong, whereas offices in other markets may be only average. When a firm needs high-quality advertising in all its markets, it may decide to use the best local agency in each market, even if it does not belong to an international family.

Also, when a firm does not require coordination of its advertising in different markets, it has less need to employ an international agency. Similarly, the coordination provided by international agencies is often more apparent than real. Other reasons for choosing local agencies include the desire for local image and the desire to give national subsidiaries responsibility for their own promotions.

There is one more reason why local agencies survive in some countries: nationalism. Many countries resent the role that foreign firms play in their economies and restrict the firms in various ways. The restrictions often apply to the promotion industry, too. In the Philippines, for example, national agencies pressured the government to ban foreign agencies. They claimed that the multinationals would come to dominate the industry and that in spite of the qualifications of local agencies, the internationals' affiliates would win the major accounts because of their global ties with multinational clients. Thus, along with a dozen other countries, the Philippines allows only minority foreign ownership of agencies. Indonesia, Nigeria, and Pakistan allow no foreign ownership. Such protectionism is a barrier to the growth of multinational agencies.

Notwithstanding the benefits of national agencies, global companies continue to rely heavily on the use of international agencies. Although there will always be room for a certain number of quality independent agencies in each market, their relative importance is likely to decline.

Choosing the Promotion Message

A major decision for an international marketer is whether the firm should use national or international promotional appeals—a localized or standardized approach. The goal in either case is to fit the market. Although people's basic needs and desires are the same around the world, the way those desires are satisfied may vary from country to country.

LOCALIZED OR STANDARDIZED?

In the preparation of promotional campaigns, valid arguments exist for both a national and an international approach. In general, two groups tend to be biased in favor of a separate national approach: management of the local subsidiary and the independent local agency. In each case, the argument depends in large part on the special local knowledge the agencies contribute. The more practical it is for an international firm to treat its international market like other markets, the smaller the role of the local subsidiary and the independent local agency. Because of this vulnerability, management of both the local subsidiary and the agency tend to be defensive about the uniqueness of the market and the need for special approaches therein. Both will argue in terms of objective factors, but their position is influenced by their perceived vulnerability.

Often the argument of local or globally standardized refers to the promotional message, but there is evidence that even something as targeted as personal selling can be standardized, at least to some extent.[32]

By way of clarification, the terms *localized* and *standardized* refer to the two extremes of the international promotion spectrum. Completely localized promotion has little similarity among countries. Completely standardized promotion is identical in all markets. Typically, neither extreme is practiced. The issue for a firm is the degree to which it should move toward one end or the other of the spectrum.

BUYER MOTIVATION

For a product that is used the same way and that meets the same needs from country to country, standardized promotional messages are more feasible than localized campaigns. The international success of Coca-Cola, which takes a standardized approach in its advertising appeals, suggests that the product meets similar consumer desires everywhere. That is true for other consumer goods, too. A famous example is Nike's use of the swoosh symbol to promote its products globally.

Another consideration is the similarity of buying motives from country to country. The same product may be purchased for a mixture of functional, convenience, and status reasons, but with a different combination of motivations in each country. The more alike buying motives are, the more desirable the use of common messages. This is often the case with industrial goods, but it is less common with consumer goods. Procter & Gamble learned that decay prevention was an important motive for buyers of its fluoride toothpaste in Denmark, Germany, and the

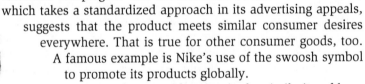

Netherlands. In England, France, and Italy, however, cosmetic considerations were more important. The Ford Motor Company promotes the same vehicles, using safety as the primary focus in some markets, fun and sportiness in others, and comfort in still others.

INTERNATIONAL MARKET SEGMENTS

Another factor is the existence of international market segments; that is, certain markets in a nation often have counterparts in a number of other nations. In many ways, the markets resemble their counterparts in other countries more than they do other markets in their own country. Wealthy people have similar motivations and tastes across national boundaries, for example. The youth market, made up of two segments (the adolescent group and the college age group), is another prominent instance. The concerns of college students on all continents are remarkably similar. Such similarities among age groups can provide a truly global segment. There are numerous examples of successful appeals to national market segments that, together, constitute an international market for a product.

A final market consideration is the gradual development of the world or regional consumer. What is already seen in certain market segments will gradually expand to broader segments of the world's population. Advances in communication, transportation, and production will lead to an international democratizing of consumption. People are not alike, but market segments will become more international in scope, resulting in greater use of similar appeals in advertising. The EU is accelerating the emergence of the European consumer. In the United States, marketers speak of market segments on a national basis. They usually do not separate Michigan consumers from Maine or Missouri consumers. The United States, in a sense, is merely one of the first of the regional groupings. Similarly, advertising campaigns have been coordinated for groupings of countries. Industrial marketers such as Dell, Nokia, and Hyundai organize one campaign for a group of industrialized country markets and another campaign for a group of developing country markets.

TECHNOLOGY

If the same media (the Internet, television, radio, print, and so on) were available everywhere, international campaigns would benefit greatly. The fact that that situation does not currently exist hampers an internationally similar approach. A campaign prepared for a website probably would not be identical to one prepared for radio or print media. The lack of media uniformity does not, in itself, prevent international campaigns, however, as is evidenced by domestic campaigns that use the same appeals simultaneously in several different kinds of media.

Similarity in international media conditions is increasing steadily. The Internet, satellite radio and television, and cell communications have become international media, bringing events such as the Olympic Games and the World Cup to the whole world. Print media is also international. *Reader's Digest* is printed in 21 languages with 50 separate editions;[33] other magazines and newspapers also have international coverage—for example, the *New York Times*, *Financial Times*, *Wall Street Journal*, and *Economist*. Media internationalization will contribute to the internationalization of advertising messages.

Software that allows companies to manage consumer information—including contact information (e-mail addresses), purchase patterns (children's movies), frequency (more than once a month), and amounts (average purchase of $50 per order)—are able to direct messages tailored to very small segments of a target market. The more specialized the message, the more likely consumers are to read it and respond to it.

CULTURE

Language, which was mentioned previously, plays a large role in communication. But as described in Chapter 4, culture encompasses more than language. The allure to Western (European and American) goods was high when Communism was practiced in Russia and other former Soviet Union nations. However, today's Russians do not appreciate Western advertising because those creating the messages typically present ideals and images and make assumptions about gender roles and other important cultural traits that are incongruent with Russian culture. At best, the intended messages either are not received or are misinterpreted, or they are perceived as offensive or ridiculous, at worst.[34]

Television advertisements and language tend to get most of the research attention, but researchers are now studying the effects of other cultural traits on newer media. For example, one project studied the interactivity of websites, using Hofstede's cultural dimensions (see Chapter 4), in Japan, South Korea, the UK, and the United States. Among the findings was the fact that Western websites tend to emphasize consumer-to-firm interactivity, whereas Eastern websites highlight consumer-to-consumer interactions.[35]

REGIONAL OR GLOBAL PRODUCT INTRODUCTIONS

Companies are resorting to more uniform campaigns as they develop products for a regional or global market, introducing them simultaneously (or sequentially) in the region or the world. Adobe and, in particular, Microsoft have turned the announcement of new products into worldwide media events. Harry Potter books were delivered to retailers in armored cars, and Amazon.com had to hold deliveries of new releases to coincide with brick-and-mortar retail releases. Whether planned or not, every small, medium, and large company that posts a website is communicating on a global scale with potential customers.

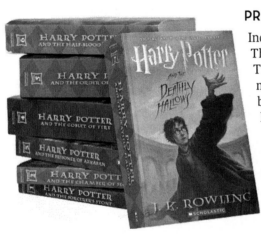

Companies use uniform campaigns globally when possible. The release of Harry Potter books was always under great security, regardless of the country

PRODUCT TYPE

Industrial products are generally more homogeneous than consumer goods. The appeal is generally rational and transcends personal tastes and needs. Therefore, marketers of industrial goods and services can generally implement standardized global campaigns. For example, Siemens of Germany has been working on internationally coordinated advertising in 52 foreign markets since 1955. By contrast, IBM did not run a globally integrated campaign until 1995. That ad was for its AS/400 computer workstation aimed at the industry segment.

Selecting the Media

A critical decision in international advertising is the selection of media for each market or market segment. The desirable media are those that reach the target markets efficiently. The target markets—the purchase decision influencers—are not always the same individuals or groups as in the domestic market. The relative roles of different family members in consumer buying or of the purchasing agent, engineer, or president in industrial procurement vary from country to country.

Those most familiar with the local scene—the agency and the company representative within the country—do much of the local media selection. Studies have found the greatest role of subsidiaries in advertising is in media selection. To the extent that subsidiaries do the job, international managers need not get involved. However, international managers might want to have some voice in local media selection. Through their experience in many countries, they may have insights to contribute.

Managers may also want to use international media alongside or in place of strictly national media. Because international media cover a number of markets, this combination requires some centralization. Then, too, international managers may be able to contribute sophisticated techniques of media selection. International managers can ensure that those techniques are made available to all company operations in a truly integrated marketing communications system.

MEDIA DIVERSITY

International media selection is complicated by international differences in media availability. A successful media configuration cannot be taken from domestic operations and applied abroad because the same facilities often are not available. For instance, in nations where few people go to school and, therefore, are unable to read, the usefulness of print advertising is limited. When it is difficult to obtain addresses, direct mail may not be possible. Due to differences in media availability, how media are used for advertising also differs.

Media expenditures vary by countries. Some may favor television or radio, whereas other countries spend more on print.

Promotion expenditures in various countries, as shown in Table 10-6, help illustrate media diversity. Television's share of advertising dollars spent ranges from US $1,014.4 million in Argentina to US $53.9 billion in the United States. Online advertising spending, in contrast, ranges from US $800,000 in Indonesia to US $16.2 billion in the United States. The amounts spent in each media category relative to the other categories are interesting as well. Many assume that television accounts for the majority of ad spending, but in the United States, 33 percent of ad dollars was spent on television and 37 percent was spent on print. A similar pattern can be seen in the UK and France; while in Germany, print media absorbed 62 percent of all ad spending. Contrast these percentages with Mexico, which spent 73 percent on television (US $3.7 billion of a total $5 billion).

DIRECT MARKETING

An important component of many companies' promotional strategy is the use of direct marketing—direct promotion to buyers through websites, e-mail, electronic and printed catalogs, and telemarketing. Direct marketing contributes substantially to sales figures, and the impact can be measured more directly than with other media. In the United States, direct marketing accounts for more than 8 percent of GDP, according to the Direct Marketing Association. In 2009, nearly $150 billion was spent on direct marketing, accounting for nearly 55 percent of all U.S. advertising expenditures.[36] Technology is driving down direct marketing costs drastically. Thus, despite laws regulating e-mail and other consumer contacts and all the counter-technology spam and adware, companies are likely to continue spending a large proportion of their promotion budgets on direct marketing.

MEDIA AVAILABILITY

Table 10-7 provides statistics relative to media availability in selected countries. Interpreting the data requires knowledge of local media customs. Few television sets in a country does not necessarily mean that few people watch television. Potential consumers (marketers think of people consuming entertainment as potential consumers) may gather in friends' homes or outside electronics stores

Table 10-6 • Promotion Expenditures, Relative Importance of Media

Media Expenditures, 2009 ($US Millions)

Country	Television		Radio		Print	
North America						
Canada	2896.7	(32%)	1383.9	(15%)	2734.4	(30%)
Mexico	3713.4	(73%)	424.9	(8%)	934.4	(18%)
United States	53973.0	(33%)	16528.0	(10%)	60301.0	(37%)
Asia						
India	2730.0	(39%)	119.1	(2%)	3623.5	(51%)
Indonesia	1476.4	(51%)	94.4	(3%)	1152.7	(40%)
Japan	20227.3	(42%)	1631.9	(3%)	12904.0	(27%)
Europe						
France	5745.2	(34%)	1255.7	(8%)	5833.8	(35%)
Germany	5543.1	(25%)	835.2	(4%)	13772.3	(62%)
Sweden	578.4	(20%)	85.7	(3%)	1392.1	(47%)
United Kingdom	4858.0	(24%)	662.8	(3%)	7680.7	(38%)
South America						
Argentina	1014.4	(47%)	53.9	(3%)	760.2	(35%)
Brazil	9539.0	(64%)	648.8	(4%)	3622.6	(24%)
Peru	255.0	(55%)	44.6	(10%)	96.7	(21%)

to watch television, and those people may pay more attention to the advertisements than people in areas with many televisions. Instead of owning personal computers, many people use computers found in local Internet cafés, which are located in nearly every city of the world. A nation reporting that it has many newspapers, magazines, or radio stations is not necessarily a good thing. It may mean that there are many competitors in a fragmented market, and to reach a broad audience, the marketer must advertise through all the newspapers, magazines, and radio stations.

Many consumers no longer listen to the radio or watch television. People may just as easily watch a webcast of a news item on their cell phone or listen to music on their iPod. New technologies that have allowed mass customization of products are also part of media. Providers of entertainment have more outlets today than ever before, and those outlets tend to be targeted at audiences with better-defined characteristics. All those factors make it more difficult to measure the effectiveness of media and complicate promotion budget decisions.

INTERNATIONAL MEDIA OR LOCAL MEDIA?

When media availability differs from market to market, international marketers may have to decentralize media selection and adapt to local possibilities. Because local managers cannot follow media patterns used elsewhere, they must find the local media that reach their markets effectively.

	Cinema		Outdoor		Online		Total
	...		399.0	(4%)	1578.6	(18%)	8992.6
	...		...		...		5072.7
	732.0	(0.5%)	7249.0	(4%)	23060.0	(14%)	161843.0
	104.0	(1%)	305.2	(4%)	163.9	(2%)	7045.7
	1.3	(0.04%)	182.3	(6%)	0.8	(0.03%)	2907.9
	...		3945.4	(8%)	8609.8	(18%)	47318.4
	161.5	(1%)	2038.2	(12%)	1630.9	(10%)	16665.3
	129.2	(1%)	1031.1	(5%)	1060.6	(5%)	22389.5
	12.6	(0.4%)	129.8	(4%)	755.4	(26%)	2954.0
	333.7	(2%)	1169.7	(6%)	5300.9	(26%)	20005.8
	27.9	(1%)	215.3	(10%)	81.8	(4%)	2153.5
	...		339.5	(2%)	775.7	(5%)	14925.6
	6.4	(1%)	53.1	(11%)	9.6	(2%)	465.4

Notes: The total amount shown does not equal total media expenditure because cinema and other categories are not included for some countries. Categories other than those listed still account for only less than 3 percent of media expenditures. Percents provided as rough illustration of varying patterns of media expenditures.

Source: Euromonitor Passport Reference and Markets; 1. Cinema Adspend: Euromonitor International from World Association of Newspapers; 2. Online Adspend: Euromonitor International from World Association of Newspapers/Jupiter research; 3. Outdoor Adspend: Euromonitor International from World Association of Newspapers; 4. Print Adspend: Euromonitor International from World Association of Newspapers; 5. Radio Adspend: Euromonitor International from World Association of Newspapers; 6. TV Adspend: Euromonitor International from World Association of Newspapers (http://www.portal.euromonitor.com/Portal/), accessed April 8, 2010.

In Peru, for example, it is more common to use a wide variety of media, ranging from newspapers, television, and radio to cinema and point-of-purchase materials. Outside the capital, Lima, using billboards makes sense because taxes on billboards are lower in the provinces. On the other hand, the use of cinema in the provinces is not very effective. A multinational marketing manager sometimes has the alternative of using national media or media that cover several markets; both print and broadcast media, for example, have multimarket coverage. Print media with international market coverage include U.S. general-interest magazines such as *Reader's Digest* and *Time*, which reach most of the world's major markets. In addition, *Paris Match* and *Vision* reach several European and Latin American markets, respectively. *Elle*, the French women's magazine, has more than 30 editions worldwide, each with localized websites. Numerous technical and trade publications in the engineering, chemistry, electronics, and automotive industries also have an extensive and influential worldwide circulation. The amount of advertising in national media is greater than that in international media because national media offer certain advantages. National media offer

Table 10-7 • Media Availability

Country	Media (per 1,000 people)			
	Television	Radios	Daily Newspapers	Internet Users
North America				
Canada	716	1,077	3,380	768
Mexico	272	330	3,175	323
United States	803	2,109	5,230	741
Asia				
India	65	120	5,316	102
Indonesia	69	159	1,920	154
Japan	686	956	867	724
Europe				
France	598	950	1,426	591
Germany	567	948	4,647	785
Sweden	520	932	10,148	836
United Kingdom	522	1,445	1,808	836
South America				
Argentina	223	681	2,873	310
Brazil	219	427	2,675	452
Peru	124	269	2,270	269

Source: Television, Radio, Newspaper from UNESCO UIS Data UNESCO Institute for Statistics—Television receivers (per capita) (most recent); Radio receivers (per capita) (most recent) by country; Daily Newspaper: Newspapers and periodicals, Number of titles, Daily (per capita) (most recent) by country (http://www.nationmaster.com/), accessed August 14, 2010. Internet users: Euromonitor Passport Reference and Markets, "Internet Users: International Telecommunications Union/World Bank/Trade Sources/Euromonitor International" (http://www.portal.euromonitor.com/Portal/Statistics .aspx), accessed August 14, 2010.

more possibilities, ranging from newspapers, magazines, direct mail, cinema, and billboards to the broadcast media. National media use local languages and provide greater flexibility in market segmentation and test marketing. In general, local media do a better job of reaching and adapting to the local market, especially for consumer goods.

Disadvantages, however, occasionally arise in using local media. Although industrialized countries frequently offer the same media quality as that found in developed nations, in many other countries, print reproduction may be poor, rates may not be fixed, and audited circulation data may not be available. The need to place the advertising as well as pay for it locally can be a drawback when a firm has centralized control. Nevertheless, those disadvantages are not sufficient to seriously limit the use of local media.

Most companies do most of their advertising in the local media of the foreign market. Generally, the more decentralized a firm, the more it uses local campaigns; and the more a firm relies on local ad agencies, the more it uses local media.

Colgate knows how to use the local media in its foreign markets. It is credited with creating the Mexican soap opera, one of the more popular programs broadcast in Mexico. Thus, the company successfully carried to Mexico a form more commonly associated with its competitor, Procter & Gamble, in the United States.

Measuring Media Reach and Effectiveness

Another factor hampering media decisions in many countries is the lack of reliable information on circulation and audience characteristics. Advertisers in developed nations are accustomed to having audited data about the size of the audience that various media reach. In addition, advertisers often get a breakdown on audience characteristics, such as age, occupation, gender, education, and income level. Some media types are nearly impossible to measure. Word of mouth, text messaging and blogs, and so-called ephemeral media are based on the contact lists and perceived authority of the sender, relying in part on the gullibility of and acceptance by the recipient.[37] Online promotion is also difficult to measure or quantify. (When should page views, click-through-rates, and hits be used?)[38] The availability and reliability of media data decreases rapidly with the level of economic development. The reliability of data is directly related to a nation's level of economic development—generally, the more developed a nation, the more reliable the data. Whether data is available is also related to economic development. Generalizing, the richer a nation, the more likely it is to collect data. Poorer countries tend to spend money on more essential needs. In many countries, the only figures are those supplied by the media themselves. Such unaudited figures are suspect.

Another consideration complicating media evaluation is that whatever figures are obtained for the circulation of a medium do not necessarily indicate the medium's true coverage. In countries where data can be obtained as to the number of televisions or radios, as mentioned, the true audience may be much larger than the figures suggest. For example, in countries with low literacy rates, the average number of viewers per television set is likely to be at least twice as large as in the United States. That principle also applies to the number of radio listeners, especially in less-developed countries, where a few receivers may reach a whole village. Media measurements often rely on samples of message recipients; for example, statements about television show viewership in the United States that are provided by Nielson are based on data from a small number of American homes. Technology has reached the point where some experts are suggesting moving away from samples and taking a census—that is, collecting data on the entire population.[39]

Even with print media, average readership varies from country to country. In less-developed countries, one literate villager will read a newspaper or magazine to illiterate neighbors. In developed countries, one issue may pass from the initial purchaser to several other readers.

This lack of accurate media information makes media selection difficult. This also means it may be difficult calculating the cost per contact, an important measure of media effectiveness. The answer in the long run is to expand media auditing services. In the short run, advertisers must depend on their own ingenuity. As firms gain experience in a market, they learn about the relative effectiveness of different media. Comparative analysis of similar markets can, again, be useful.

Setting the International Promotion Budget

Among the controversial aspects of promotion is determining the proper method for setting the budget. This is a problem domestically, as well as internationally.[40] But because an international marketer must try to find an optimum outlay for a number of markets, the problem is more complex on the international level. In theory, it is not difficult to state the amount of money a firm should put into promotion. In each of its markets, a firm should continue to put more money into promotion as long as the promotion cost returns more than the expenditures for it. In practice, that principle is difficult to apply because of the impossibility of measuring the returns accurately, not only from promotion, but also from other company outlays.[41]

Because of the difficulty in determining the theoretically optimum promotion budget, companies have developed more practical guidelines. This section will examine the relevance of those guidelines for the manager. Although the principle noted previously is difficult to apply, it must, nevertheless, serve as an initial rough guide. In other words, a promotion budget is not set in a vacuum, but is just one element of the overall marketing mix. Therefore, it is necessary to have some idea as to whether a sum of money should go into advertising, personal selling, price reductions, product or package improvements, or something else.[42]

PERCENTAGE-OF-SALES APPROACH

> **percentage-of-sales approach**
>
> A method for determining the amount to spend on promotion in a country whereby the promotion budget is based on a specific percentage of sales, typically based on the percentage of sales spent on promotion in current markets.

An easy method for setting the promotion appropriation in a country is the **percentage-of-sales approach**, which establishes the promotion budget based on percentage of sales. Besides its convenience, this method has the advantage of relating promotion to the volume of sales in a country. This approach, perhaps the easiest to justify in a budget meeting, appeals to financially oriented managers who like to think in terms of ratios and costs per unit. And when a firm is selling in many markets, the percentage-of-sales approach has the further advantage of appearing to guarantee equality among them. Each market seems to get the advertising it deserves.

For a firm that centralizes control over global promotion, the percentage-of-sales approach is attractive. A manager at headquarters would have difficulty using any other budgeting approach for 50 or 100 markets. The Europeans favor this approach as much as the Americans do.

Despite its positives, however, this approach has limitations. The purpose of promotion is to bring about sales, but this method means, ironically, that the volume of sales determines the amount of promotion. When sales are declining, promotion declines, although long-range considerations might suggest that promotion should be stepped up. When a firm is entering a foreign market, it may need a disproportionate amount of promotion to break into the market. Limiting the promotion to the same percentage-of-sales figure used elsewhere would be undesirable during a firm's first years in the market.

The same is true in the introduction of new products into a market. As firms expand, they introduce more products into their markets. The promotion budget for those introductions should relate to the introductory needs, rather than to some percentage of sales applied to existing products—or to the same products being sold in other countries. Significant promotion outlays are usually required of firms that want to expand their presence in world markets.

When Panasonic tried to launch its batteries into the U.S. market, it set an ad budget that was a small fraction of those of its competitors. Its success was limited. By contrast, when Nike and Reebok entered Europe, they each had a promotion budget approximately twice that of the well-entrenched Adidas. They succeeded in sharing 50 percent of the market in a few years.

The major weakness in applying a standard percentage-of-sales figure for promotion in foreign markets is that this method does not relate to a firm's situation in each market. The examples given—entering a market and introducing new products—are just two illustrations of the need for special treatment in special situations. In some countries, a firm may be well established with no strong competitors; in other countries, a firm may have difficulty getting a consumer franchise. Promotional needs are different in those two instances. For example, European firms increased their promotion budgets for the entire EU when the EU became a reality.

Until more sophisticated techniques are made operational, many companies will continue to use the percentage-of-sales method, despite its limitations. That is not necessarily bad if company experience shows the percentage to be reasonably successful and if the method is somewhat flexible, allowing different percentages to be applied in different markets according to need.

COMPETITIVE-PARITY APPROACH

Some companies use the **competitive-parity approach**, which is simply matching competitors' advertising outlays. Although the competitive-parity approach may offer a firm the feeling that it is not losing ground to competitors, the merit of this approach should be challenged, particularly in international marketing. As a practical matter, in most markets, a firm cannot determine competitors' promotion budgets or allocations.

Another danger in following the practice of competitors is that they are not necessarily right. In fact, an international firm is almost always a heavier promoter than national firms in the same industry. If anything, an international firm sets the standard for national competitors to follow, rather than the reverse. That was evident in Procter & Gamble's entry into Europe, for example. The fact that different competitors employ different promotional mixes also hampers the use of this approach. In the United States, for instance, Revlon is a heavy advertiser, whereas Avon relies more on personal selling. Who should follow whom?

A final limitation to the competitive-parity approach in foreign markets is the difference in the situation of the international firm. Because it is a foreigner in the market, its relationship with consumers may differ from that of national companies. This would be reflected in its promotion. Its product line and marketing program are also likely to differ from those of national competitors. For those reasons, it is improbable that matching competitors' outlays would prove to be a sound strategy in foreign markets.

competitive-parity approach
A method for determining the amount to spend on promotion in a country whereby the promotion budget is based on matching the amount spent by competitors in that country.

OBJECTIVE-AND-TASK APPROACH

The weaknesses of the prior approaches have led some marketers to the **objective-and-task approach**. It begins by determining the promotion objectives, expressed in terms of sales, brand awareness, or something else; then ascertaining the tasks needed to attain those objectives; and finally estimating the costs of performing the tasks. If this approach includes a cost-benefit analysis, relating the objectives to the cost of reaching them, it is a desirable method. The objective-and-task approach is as relevant for markets abroad as it is for the home market. It logically seeks to relate the promotion budget to a firm's situation in a country and for the firm's goals there. To use it satisfactorily, however, a firm must know the local market so it can set appropriate objectives. Unfortunately, except where it has local subsidiaries, a firm does not have intimate knowledge of the market, so setting specific objectives and defining the task of promotion may be difficult. In those cases, a percentage-of-sales method may be more feasible.

objective-and-task approach
A method for determining the amount to spend on promotion in a country whereby the promotion budget is based on how much it costs to achieve specific promotion objectives (e.g., level of sales or brand awareness).

COMPARATIVE-ANALYSIS APPROACH

Between applying a uniform percentage to all markets and letting each market determine its own budget lies a middle ground: the **comparative-analysis approach**, in which markets are grouped into categories according to characteristics relevant to promotion. This method yields more flexibility than the uniform approach and more control than the local approach. Categories might be based on size (markets with over $1 million in sales and markets with under $1 million in sales), media situation, or other pertinent characteristics. A firm might try different budgeting methods or percentages for each group. One country could

comparative-analysis approach
A method for determining the amount to spend on promotion in a country whereby the country is grouped into a category with other markets according to characteristics relevant to promotion (e.g., language, availability of media types, market size) and markets in the same category have similar promotion budgets.

serve as a test market for its group. This technique can be useful for a firm with a large number of markets.

Selecting the Appropriate Promotional Tools

Marketers have a variety of promotional tools at their disposal. As mentioned earlier, when people hear the word *marketing*, they often think of advertising, but advertising is only one tool. There are also personal selling, public relations, and sales promotion, all of which have advantages and disadvantages. Selecting the proper tool and allocating promotional funds among the tools are other parts of a firm's strategy. The tools and their basic advantages and disadvantages are summarized in Table 10-8.

Table 10-8 ● Promotional Tools

Tool	Description	Advantages and Disadvantages	Conditions Conducive to Specific Tools
Advertising	Nonpersonal, sponsor-paid communication using mass media	Inexpensive per contact, nonpersonal (requires similar needs and fulfillment characteristics)	Big, homogeneous, and dispersed markets
Personal selling	Sponsor-paid communication that is personal (one-on-one, or one-on-few)	Expensive, but can be tailored to individual needs and the message can be changed quickly; immediate response, but dependent on salesperson's (perhaps inconsistent) skills	Expensive, new, and industrial products in concentrated markets
Public relations	Nonpersonal, medium-paid communication using mass media	Effective and persuasive, but not easily controlled and effectiveness is difficult to measure	Damage control or introduction of new products
Sales promotion	Sponsor-paid communication in mass media as well as direct-mail; generally short-term; an "all else" category	Nonpersonal but effectiveness is easy to measure; technology making increasingly personal	Heavy brand switching, price-sensitive products with mass appeal

Advertising

Advertising is generally described as paid promotion of mass media messages. The concepts have changed little in some respects, but in other respects, advertising is quite different from what it was just a decade ago. Marketers are now able to remove much of the "mass" from "mass media." One term used in manufacturing, *mass customization*, can also be applied to advertising. Technology in printing, programming, and Internet advertising allows a marketer to customize a message to ever smaller groups of people (and in the case of the Internet, almost down to the individual level). So although advertising is still a tool for which marketers must pay, the mass media message may no longer be one of the drawbacks of this tool.

The international marketing manager must make many decisions with regard to advertising. Some of those decisions have already been highlighted, such as what media to select and whether a firm should use a standard global approach or an adapted or local approach. There are many other decisions, though, some of which are strategic in nature; others are more tactical. The strategic issues tend to focus on decisions regarding the appeal (the message of the advertising; for example, should the appeal be emotional or rational?).

Tactical issues focus on media selection and implementation. For example, a firm may be able to develop an advertising campaign internally if it has the expertise, or it may seek additional outside help. The more markets a firm enters and the more diverse those markets are, the more likely the firm is to use outside expertise in developing an advertising campaign. Other decisions include the question of whether to use some form of cooperative advertising (as might be seen with a department store and a perfume manufacturer around big holidays), the timing of ads (for instance, windshield wiper blades when it is raining or toys around Christmas and other large gift-giving holidays), and the spokesperson (a character such as Garfield or a company president). Legal and cultural issues must be considered as discussed in "The Wrong Message". Such decisions are not unique to global marketing, but global campaigns complicate the decisions. For example, when Nike wants to identify its products with a sports figure, it must consider the national sport (baseball, soccer, skiing, and so on) and identify a person who will have instant name and face recognition. The top soccer player in one country may go unrecognized in another.

••• The Wrong Message

A car drives through a winding, rain-soaked country road at a high rate of speed, but the driver is evidently in full control. The announcer's voice confidently states "our new tires are safe in all kinds of weather."

Ronald McDonald appears on the television screen, holding up a new grilled chicken sandwich. The commercial shifts to a group of people sitting around a table, talking and enjoying the new sandwich. The announcer states that three out of four people surveyed prefer this chicken sandwich over KFC's grilled chicken sandwich.

While those ads might be perfectly normal in the United States, they are not acceptable elsewhere. Some nations' laws about comparing products are so strict that no comparisons can be made between competing products. At one extreme, a tire company was sued because it made the claim that its tires were "strong as steel"— sued not by another tire manufacturer, but by the nation's steel industry because the statement put a negative light on steel products. Researchers have found that negative and comparative advertisements are perceived differently around the world. One study found that East Europeans (in Poland, the Czech Republic, and Hungary) did not respond well to advertisements with negative or disparaging messages about competitors or their products.[43]

As a firm develops its advertising, some guiding principals may help improve its effectiveness. The following tips would not apply for advertisements in all markets and all industries, but they are a useful starting point.

- Use simple language.
- Avoid complicated sentence structures.
- Use the active voice.
- Avoid humor.
- Use graphics to help communicate written concepts.
- Avoid complicated and unnecessary graphics.[44]

Personal Selling •••

Although advertising is often the most prominent element in the promotional mix of an international marketer, for some firms, especially those in industrial marketing, it is a minor form of promotion. Another major promotional tool is personal selling (probably better stated in this context as professional selling). Selling is often more important in foreign marketing than in domestic marketing campaigns. The major advantages of selling are its effectiveness and immediate feedback. The sales budget may be a larger percentage of the promotion budget for two reasons: (1) Restrictions on advertising and media availability may

Personal selling is a major form of promotion and can be more important in foreign marketing than domestic campaigns.

limit the amount of advertising a firm can do, and (2) low wages in many countries allow a company to hire a larger sales force. The second reason is especially applicable in less-developed nations.

The experience of Philip Morris in Venezuela illustrates the role personal selling can have. Low wages permitted the sales department to hire 300 employees. However, only one-third were salespeople. The rest were assistants who helped with deliveries, distribution of sales materials, and so on. The younger sales assistants were provided with bikes. The supporting activities of the younger sales assistants provided a very effective complement to the regular sales force.

National, Not International

Personal selling in a firm's foreign markets cannot really be called international personal selling. As relates to advertising, international campaigns and media are appropriate frameworks, but personal selling involves personal contact and is more culture-bound than advertising. As a result, even though international business has expanded tremendously in recent decades, personal selling activities are still conducted primarily on a national basis. In fact, many national markets are divided into sales territories served by salespeople recruited only from their respective territories. The salespeople do not even cover a national market.

A limited amount of personal selling does cross national boundaries, most commonly for industrial goods and high-cost products. However, even very global IBM still uses national sales representatives in its markets. Although the growth of regionalism should encourage more international personal selling, economic integration is not the same as cultural integration. Experience in the EU shows that personal selling activities are very slow to cross cultural-political boundaries.[45] There are cultural boundaries that restrict personal selling efforts, too. For example, in Japan, individual recognition of sales representatives is still at odds with the cultural focus on group and team efforts. In Saudi Arabia, finding qualified sales representatives is difficult because of a labor shortage and the low prestige of selling. In India, sales force management is difficult in a market fragmented by language divisions and the remnants of the caste system. Studies have also shown that training of a sales force is likely to differ from country to country, while hiring practices are likely to be similar from market to market.[46]

One task of the manager is to determine the role personal selling should play in each market. After the role of personal selling has been decided, administration of the sales force would have similar functions to that in the home market. This would include recruitment, selection, training, motivation, supervision, and compensation. However, as the sales task varies by country and personal selling takes place on a national basis, sales management must be decentralized to the national market. International marketers do not have a sales force; instead, they generally serve as advisors to national operations. For example, Manufacturing Data Systems, Inc. (MDSI), a producer of computer software, found that a sale in the United States requires an average of two calls per firm. In Europe, there are frequent callbacks, each involving a higher level of management. That means more time and higher costs. In Japan, MDSI's selling requires even more time than in Europe. In other Asian markets, Electrolux finds its direct sales force requires an average of only 5 demonstrations to make a sale in Malaysia, but 20 demonstrations are needed in the Philippines.

Recruiting and Selecting the Sales Force

Three problems may arise in trying to find and retain salespeople in certain markets: (1) selling is a low-status occupation in many countries; the most attractive candidates seek other employment; (2) finding people with the desired characteristics is often difficult; and (3) keeping or retaining productive salespeople is difficult because they are in short supply and demand is high. When a firm is dealing with salespeople and their customers, it is important to recognize that the same motivation to sell or buy is different from culture to culture. Also, very often extra training is required, especially when a firm and its products are new to market.

As an aid in recruitment and selection of salespeople, many companies develop job descriptions and specification lists. Both may vary internationally. In a foreign market, the sales job will be a function of a firm's product line, distribution channels, and marketing mix. Thus, the job will not be exactly the same in all markets. The greater the carryover from country to country, the more international direction is possible.

A question arises as to whether a universal "sales type" exists, even for one industry. As job descriptions and market situations vary from country to country, so do other cultural influences. In many markets, a variety of religious, educational, and racial or tribal characteristics must be considered. When markets are segmented along those dimensions, the sales force may have to be segmented as well.

In some parts of the world, a particular group is the major source of businesspeople, as were the Jews throughout Europe prior to World War II. The Chinese are prominent merchants in many Asian nations. Within the nation itself, a particular group or tribe may play this role. In many countries, the important commercial role played by a minority group, such as the Chinese, is resented by the majority. Laws may be passed that force greater hiring of the major national group.

Although recruitment and selection are done in the host country, international marketers can make contributions. For example, they may introduce tests or techniques that have proved successful in domestic operations or in other subsidiaries. Each country is not completely different from all others, and some carryover of those techniques is possible. For example, when TGI Fridays recruited staff for its first London restaurant, the company continued the practice from the United States of using games and role playing to select individuals who were particularly outgoing and enthusiastic. Through analysis of company experience and by collaboration with subsidiary personnel, international marketers should optimize the use of those experiences in local operations.

When industrial marketers enter a foreign market, they often find the lack of a local sales force to be an important barrier. To accelerate and ease their entry, they may find it desirable to join with or acquire a local firm for its sales force capability. In Japan, where relationships are so important, personal selling is especially critical. When Merck wanted to expand in Japan, it acquired Banyu Pharmaceutical, which enabled it to field a sales force of more than 1,000 people immediately.

TRAINING THE SALES FORCE

The training of salespeople is done primarily in the national market. The nature of the training program is determined by the demands of the job and the previous preparation of the sales force. Those vary from country to country. Nevertheless, the international marketing manager has a voice in local training. Because of the similarity in company products from market to market, national training programs have common denominators.

Drawing on the firm's multinational experience, the manager seeks to improve each training program. Examples include supplying training materials, program formats, and ideas to each country. International meetings of subsidiary personnel responsible for sales training can also promote the exchange of best practices. Technology allows firms to train its sales force on new products and initiatives without taking employees to headquarters or to plant locations. Internet-based programs are an alternative that allow employees the flexibility to learn new skills and earn higher-level degrees that often lead to advancement in the company. While motivation differs among various cultures, providing challenges and the opportunity to learn is a benefit that may mean the difference between a qualified and motivated sales force and a less effective sales force.

Bristol-Myers Squibb gives special attention to sales training in developing countries. Training programs are developed by the corporate medical affairs division and product planning division. The company has medical directors in its Latin American, Pacific, Indian, and Middle East regions who help in subsidiary training programs. All national salespeople receive basic training in anatomy, pharmacology, and diseases, as well as in sales. Then they receive detailed information on drug products, including contraindications and possible complications.

Another training technique is the traveling team of experts from regional or international headquarters. As a company finds new product applications, adds new products, or enters new market segments, the sales task might change. The new selling task usually requires additional training, which can be accomplished at a regional center, by a traveling team of experts, or via the Internet.

When a firm sells through independent distributors or licensees, it has little control over the sales force, except in the initial selection of the distributor. Firms have found, though, that using intermediaries to manage their foreign sales force is a quick and less expensive alternative to developing the sales force on their own. In those cases, it is not unusual for firms to provide specialized training to the sales staff of their distributors or licensees. This is generally done at no charge and turns out to be a profitable expenditure because of its contribution to sales as well as to relations with the licensee or distributor. A firm faces some challenges when using independent intermediaries, perhaps the most important of which was already mentioned—loss of control over the distribution network. Researchers have identified key areas that help ensure that a firm's relationship with sales force intermediaries is successful.[47] Careful evaluation of potential partners is one of those key factors.

As was mentioned previously, the demand for good salespeople is a particular problem that multinationals face in many markets. The best-trained sales staffs tend to be "raided" by companies within the industry, as well as by noncompeting firms. That means firms must train more salespeople than they need or find some way of keeping their sales force, usually through higher compensation.

MOTIVATING AND COMPENSATING THE SALES FORCES

Motivation and compensation of the sales force are closely related to hiring and retaining good salespeople. Attractive compensation is often a primary motivator. Motivation can be more of a challenge abroad than at home for two reasons: (1) the low esteem in which selling is held and (2) the cultural reluctance of prospective sales representatives to talk to strangers, especially to try to persuade them—two essential elements of selling.

Although compensation is a prime motivator, there are other ways to motivate. Because much depends on cultural factors, motivation must be designed to meet local needs. In countries where selling has especially low status, a firm must try to overcome this handicap. Training, titles, and nonmonetary rewards are all helpful, as are financial awards. In addition, special recognition can help a salesperson's self-image. For example, Philip Morris in Venezuela publicizes the achievements of its best salespeople and gives them financial and other awards. Periodically, the company gives a special party and banquet for its top salespeople.

Foreign travel is another kind of reward employed by international companies. Few members of a sales force in foreign markets could afford significant international travel. Their ability to earn such a trip through good performance is a strong incentive. In addition to providing access to tourist attractions, the company usually entertains the visitors at headquarters. International companies are able to do that because of their size and because their internal logistics facilitate such efforts. They also gain economies of scale by entertaining sales representatives from a number of countries at the same time.

In motivating and compensating a sales force, one challenge is to find the mix of monetary and nonmonetary rewards appropriate for each market. Some nonmonetary factors are training, counseling, supervision, and the use of quotas and contests. In monetary compensation, the question usually arises as to whether payment should be a part of salary or a commission.

In many countries, salespeople are reluctant to accept an incentive form of payment such as a commission. They believe that it reinforces the cultural conflict and the negative image of personal selling. In those markets, a firm tends to rely on a salary payment rather than a commission.

Some companies, however, have been able to introduce incentive elements into their sales representatives' remuneration package, even in those markets. NCR, for example, pioneered the use of commission selling in Japan, a country where incentive payments were considered to be against the cultural pattern. However, a decade of experience in which NCR sales quadrupled and sales representatives were increasingly satisfied showed cultural norms were changing. In fact, the evidence convinced others to follow. In addition to foreign firms such as IBM, even Japanese firms began to model commission systems on the NCR example.

CONTROLLING THE SALES FORCE

Traditional control techniques include establishing sales territories, setting itineraries and call frequencies, using quotas, and reporting arrangements. Because the techniques must reflect local conditions, they must be determined, in part, at the local level. For example, when some territories are less attractive than others, a firm may offer extra rewards to ensure equal coverage. Philip Morris did that in Venezuela, offering higher commissions in rural provinces.

Even though the activity is decentralized, international managers should participate in establishing control techniques. They have contact with domestic operations, which are probably most sophisticated in using the techniques, and their experience can be a source of know-how for foreign markets. They can advise on establishing sales territories, norms for sales calls, and reporting arrangements.

The local knowledge of national management is complemented by the international knowledge of the international manager. A comparative analysis of similar markets provides a better idea of what range of performance is possible. Thus, international managers can aid local managers in setting appropriate norms. Especially in the introduction of a new product, local management can learn from experience in the firm's other markets. In the United States, firms make comparisons among sales territories. With appropriate modifications, the same kind of comparative analysis should be conducted for foreign markets. The comparisons should be among groups of similar countries. That is one way managers can realize the benefits of multinational experience in sales force management.

EVALUATING SALES FORCE PERFORMANCE

Evaluation of foreign sales personnel is important for two reasons. First, the performance of the sales force helps determine a firm's success in a market. International managers want to be sure that local management is getting good performance. To do that, international managers help locals apply the best techniques of evaluation, including measuring the degree to which the sales force has achieved the various objectives set for them. They can also assist with ideas, reporting forms, ratios, and other criteria used elsewhere in the company.

The second interest in evaluating performance is in making international comparisons. It is important to know not only how each country is performing in its local context, but also how it compares with other markets. Such comparisons identify the countries needing help. They can be used to motivate below-average markets to improve their performance. Some criteria used to compare countries include personal selling cost as a percentage of sales, number of salespeople per $1 million sales (to eliminate differences in wage costs), and units sold per sales representative.

Obviously, many differences hinder such comparisons. It is better that the comparisons be made explicitly, on the basis of criteria that take account of relevant differences. For example, the European division of Singer developed such a comparative framework for its 16 European subsidiaries, including such diverse countries as Sweden and Spain. That framework became operational in the sense that it was understood and accepted by management in the 16 subsidiaries.

In instances where discipline or even the firing of an employee is required, care must be taken to remain compliant with local laws. Many countries have laws that are very strict as to the preconditions that must be met before dismissing an employee. Even when such conditions have been met, significant financial payment may be necessary. Cultural considerations are also important, which includes how the disciplinary action should be communicated and what level of management should be involved.

Sales Promotion

Sales promotion is defined as "those selling activities that do not fall directly into the advertising, public relations, or personal selling categories, such as the use of contests, coupons, sampling, premiums, cents-off deals, and point-of-purchase materials." As an example, see "McDonald's Tray Liners." In the United States, sales promotion budgets have been larger than advertising budgets since 1980. The factors that created that situation are coming to other world markets, too. For example, in Colombia, two-thirds of spending goes to sales promotions and only one-third to media.

Sales Promotion and International Constraints

A firm is interested in promotional approaches that persuade customers to buy. Firms that use sales promotion in the United States generally find it as effective in other markets, if not more effective. When incomes are lower, people are usually more interested in "something for nothing," such as free samples, premiums, or contests.

Apart from economics, other constraints affect the international use of sales promotion, one of which is legal restrictions. Laws in foreign markets may restrict both the size and nature of the sample, premium, or prize. The value of the free item is often limited to a percent (say, 5 percent, as in France) of the value of the product. In other cases, the free item must be related to the nature of the product purchased, such as cups with coffee but not steak knives with detergent. Such restrictions are limiting but not always crippling. For example, *Reader's Digest* successfully used contests in Italy, even though they are taxed there, giving away prizes such as automobiles. Vicks was able to distribute over 30 million samples of Oil of Olay in many countries.

McDonald's worked hard to train customers to clear their own tables. Today, when fast-food customers dine in and finish their meals, they take their trays to the trash bin, throw away the remains of the meal, and place the used tray in the receptacle above the trash bin. Although it is difficult to say how much money the fast-food industry saves by not having to hire workers to clean up after patrons (although workers still have to wipe down tables and sweep the floor), it is likely to be substantial. Part of the cleaning process is the tray liner—it makes cleanup fast and leaves less mess on the tray. Because so many people like to read while they eat, the tray liners also provide a vehicle for sales promotion.

Over the past half century, McDonald's has used the tray liner in many ways. Tray liners have served as a form of amusement for children, with games and puzzles printed on them; they have been used to announce new products; and they have been used to promote the image of McDonald's as a good corporate citizen. One example was when Mexico McDonald's wanted to promote pride in being Mexican and printed the Mexican flag on tray liners. That idea did not work so well—drippings from food would fall on the tray liner, leading to comments from patrons that it was a desecration of a national symbol. More recently, in an effort to gain acceptance among Japanese (who were reluctant to try McDonald's menu items), the company included information about the caloric content of items. For example, the caloric content of a cheeseburger or a six-piece McNugget pack was compared to that of more traditional Japanese items, such as tonkatsu (fried pork) and gyodon (a beef, onion, and rice dish).[48]

Another constraint is cultural.[49] The premiums or other devices used must be attractive to the local consumer. For example, for many years, Procter & Gamble successfully used nativity scene characters in packages of detergent in the Spanish market. Premiums may require even greater adaptation than products.

Another problem involves the capabilities of local retailers. Many sales promotion activities require some retail involvement—that is, processing coupons, handling odd-shaped combination or premium packages, posting display materials, and so on. Getting retailers to cooperate may be difficult when they lack appropriate facilities. Problems that arise with small retailers are that the retailers are difficult to contact, they have limited space, and they often handle the materials in a way that the producer did not intend.

For a variety of legal and cultural reasons, sales promotions are primarily national rather than international. Even in Europe, for example, differences in advertising rules are not as great as differences in sales promotion rules. Thus, one sees more pan-European advertising than pan-European sales promotions.

Sales Promotion Strategies

The competitive situation in a market can also affect a firm's choice of sales promotion strategies. GE provides an illustration: In Japan, GE had noticeable success in breaking into the air conditioning market. Two factors behind the successful entry were offering (1) overseas trips as prizes to outstanding dealers and (2) a free color television set to purchasers of high-priced models. The result was that the Japanese trade association drew up rules banning overseas trips as prizes for sales of air conditioners and setting a limit on the size of premiums that could be offered. Those rules were approved by the Japanese Fair Trade Commission. Company complaints led to a modification of the rules—no overseas trips as prizes for home electric appliance dealers.

An international firm should have some advantages over its national competitors in sales promotion. For example, economies of scale may exist in generating ideas and buying materials. Ideas and materials may be suitable for several markets. One country can be used as a test market for other similar countries. Analyzing the company's experience in different markets helps in evaluating sales promotion and setting budgets. Though sales promotion was discussed as a separate item, it obviously is part of overall promotion.

The use of technology to support the sales promotion strategy is becoming widespread and is taking on some unique properties.[50, 51, 52] A firm may send confirmation of an order to a customer via e-mail and include a "coupon" (typically a number that is to be entered on subsequent orders) or an invitation to participate in special sales events. Those examples of sales promotion are more highly focused than coupons generated by registers that customers might receive in a grocery store. (Coupons generated in that fashion are often for products that relate to or compete with items that are scanned.) Consumers' inability to access computers will limit the use of electronically generated coupons, some voucher systems, and customer loyalty programs more commonly found in developed markets. A market's infrastructure and laws related to consumer privacy and the Internet must also be taken into account.

Sponsorships, promotional events, sales, and other forms of sales promotion are similarly constrained for cultural, legal, and economic reasons. There are some very creative contests and events. Walmart Germany developed an event that quickly spread across the country: singles night. Sales increased 15 percent between 6 p.m. and 8 p.m. on Friday nights (the scheduled day and time of these events). Perhaps as important, Walmart received a lot of publicity for the stunt, which brought in even more customers—for which it did not have to spend a cent.[53] (Ironically, Walmart was never really able to establish itself in the German market and in 2006 sold its chain of 85 stores at a loss of $1 billion.[54])

Trade Shows

Trade shows are an effective sales promotion tool. Some shows are primarily focused on business-to-business promotion, such as industry trade shows. These shows are typically organized by trade associations. An example is the International Consumer Electronics Show, which is organized by the Consumer Electronics Association (CEA). Trade shows may also be directed at consumers and offer an excellent opportunity to both promote and perhaps sell products to buyers. As first discussed in Chapter 8, trade shows can either be vertical (primarily focused within a single industry) or horizontal (focused across a wide spectrum of industries but typically within a single market or region). See "International Trade Shows: Tips for Success" for additional information regarding trade shows and related promotional issues.

Public Relations

Public relations (PR) is concerned with images. A firm attempts to present itself in a favorable light with one or more of its constituencies. Too often that has meant telling the world how good the company is or explaining away the company's mistakes. In an ideal sense, good public relations is corporate diplomacy—a firm seeking to relate constructively to its various stakeholders to the benefit of both parties. PR benefits can be numerous, including a means of stretching the promotional budget, strengthening a firm's competitive position,

Trade shows (also known as trade fairs) can be a significant promotional expenditure, particularly international trade shows, given the extra travel and related costs. Planning must be handled well in advance of the shows. Following are some tips to ensure the expenditures are as effective as possible.

Preplanning

Most industries have a number of trade shows. Companies must prioritize which shows they will participate in to maximize limited budgets. One good way to determine how good a match a show is with a firm's global plan is to "walk" the show before exhibiting. This means visiting the show first as an attendee, not an exhibitor, to see the types of exhibitors and participants at the show. It also helps to provide useful information such as floor layout and traffic flow for when the firm does decide to participate.

Meet with Show Organizers

Trade shows have dedicated sales staff to promote the show and help exhibitors with planning. Many of the larger trade shows have dedicated staff in other countries to assist current and future exhibitors. Deutsche Messe, which, among others, operates the Hannover Messe in Germany, has more than 50 representative offices throughout the world, including the United States.[55] These offices can be very helpful in learning about their shows, profiles of exhibitors and attendees, as well as logistics support.

Go Alone or with Others?

Most trade shows offer country pavilions in which all the booths within a particular area of the show are from the same country. These country pavilions, such as the USA, UK, or Japan pavilions, can be powerful partners because attendees are often drawn to the pavilions seeking new technologies or product releases. The cost in these pavilions can also be lower than an independent booth. Sometimes even states organize a pavilion, such as an Illinois pavilion within the USA pavilion.

Reserve Early

For the best booth location, a firm may need to register as much as a year in advance. Some shows hold their booth allocation (sales) for the next year during the final days of the current year's show, meaning potential exhibitors need to be at the show the year before they want to exhibit. Shows often sell out months in advance. The earlier a firm confirms its booth, the better chance of a good booth location with plenty of attendee traffic.

Plan Logistics Early

Not only can booth space be difficult to reserve without adequate planning, but hotel space may also be at a premium. Hotels for

continued

Continued

the Hannover Messe are notoriously difficult to obtain, and many attendees stay in Hannover homes and apartments rented out by the locals. Even those can be difficult to obtain close to the show date, meaning that attendees need to stay in nearby towns and take the train to the fair each day.

Leverage State and Federal Resources

Large industry trade shows are often supported by a state office of international trade or federal offices, such as the U.S. Commercial Service. These resources can be tremendous allies in assisting in the planning for a trade show, as well as assisting with setting up appointments during the show with prequalified buyers or potential partners such as distributors or agents. State or federal trade agencies also manage various pavilions that may offer discounted exhibit space.

Booth Size and Design

Booth space at large international trade shows can be quite expensive. Firms typically match the booth size to their needs. When a firm is simply looking for new partners and has little current business in a territory, a small, simple booth with a table and room for one or two participants may suffice. As sales grow, the firm can justify a much larger booth with various meeting spaces. Booth design can vary also, from simple signage indicating key products or the competitive advantages of the firm to sophisticated custom-made booths with multiple levels. Some even have built-in cafes and hospitality rooms. Trade fair organizers also offer complete show packages that include assistance with booth setup, such as lighting and signage.

Foreign Language Concerns

Some of the basic promotional material should be translated into the primary local languages of attendees. This would include product literature, corporate history and overview, and business cards. Firms may also want to consider hiring a translator during the show. Show organizers and trade assistance organizations can help in finding suitable translators.

Review the Trade Fair Website

One of the best resources for any trade show is the fair's website. It typically includes extensive exhibitor and participant information, including lists of previous exhibitors, profiles of attendees, costs, and logistics support. For a list of trade fair websites, visit http://www.biztradeshows.com.

clarifying core competencies, and providing independent and objective positive comments. Thus, public relations involves more than corporate communications; it requires appropriate corporate behavior. (See Chapter 5.) Public relations is often more important in a foreign market than it is domestically.[56]

Public relations is not marketing, but good relations with the public are essential to marketing success. A firm that is seen as a bad citizen may find itself despised in the marketplace, perhaps leading to a boycott of its products, as seen with BP gasoline during the BP gulf oil spill in 2010. In another sense, public relations can be considered as the marketing of a product, the product being the firm itself. A firm's products can enjoy continued success only because of their performance. The image of the products cannot be maintained if product performance is inconsistent. The same reasoning applies to the image and behavior of a firm. Public relations cannot be more effective than the corporate behavior behind it.

Obviously, a firm must behave in a legal manner in all its markets. It also must be perceived as behaving in an ethically correct and environmentally friendly way. (See Chapter 5.) A problem can arise because what is "ethically correct" and "environmentally friendly" may be defined somewhat differently by different observers. Those observers include a firm's various publics.

The publics of a firm are broader than its market. They include all those who are affected by a firm's operations and all those who can have an effect on a firm's success. These publics, stakeholders, or constituencies include customers, suppliers, employees, intermediaries, stockholders, the general public, activist and special interest groups, governments, the financial community, and the media. The importance of any particular group varies from country to country. A firm's level of involvement in a market also affects the publics with which it must deal.

The Public Relations Task Today

Just as the first job of marketing is to become familiar with the market, so the first task of international public relations is to become familiar with the firm's various publics in each market. This involves two processes: (1) seeing others as they see themselves, rather than using a foreign viewpoint or stereotype; and (2) seeing the company as others see it. Thus, public relations should begin with market intelligence. By being informed, a firm can be proactive rather than be forced into reactive measures after serious trouble has developed. Too often public relations is used to "fight fires" rather than prevent them. Inadequate intelligence can lead to many problems.

RESPONSE TO THE PUBLIC

The purpose of intelligence gathering is to serve as a basis for action. The appropriate action depends on the nature of the intelligence. Occasionally, the appropriate action involves a statement or press release by a firm, for instance, when false statements are circulating. In other instances, it may be a change in the behavior of the firm. When change is inevitable, initiating the change voluntarily is preferable to being forced to accept it. For example, Nestlé was reluctant to change its baby food marketing in developing countries. (See Case 11.1.) That led to a boycott of its products. On the other hand, Procter & Gamble immediately withdrew its Rely tampons from the market when unwanted side effects were discovered. That quick action minimized the problem and maintained customer goodwill. Avon Products took a proactive response to the rise of consumerism: (1) It created the Avon Cares Network to respond to inquiries and complaints, (2) it published consumer information pamphlets, (3) it sought out consumer leaders and groups, (4) it held conferences on consumer issues, (5) it invited consumer leaders to meet Avon managers, and (6) it sought guidance from experts.

Noting host-country complaints about a "foreign" company is a helpful way to identify problems with which a firm must deal. In addition to problems that are peculiar to individual countries, certain complaints tend to appear in foreign markets. The complaints arise primarily because the international firm is a foreigner in the market, and the common thread is that the foreign firm takes unfair advantage of the host country and otherwise abuses its position as a guest. Those complaints are often expressed in emotional language, such as "imperialistic exploitation." A reasonable statement of the kinds of things a host country wants from a foreign firm is provided in Table 10-9.

Table 10-9 • International Public Relations: Things to Do

1. Maintain a high degree of local autonomy in decision making.
2. Retain some earnings within the country.
3. Allow and encourage exports.
4. Process the natural resources of the country locally.
5. Conduct research and development locally.
6. Search out and develop local sources of supply. (Use local content.)
7. Offer equity to national investors.
8. Provide employment and career opportunities at all levels.
9. Maintain fair prices locally and in transfer pricing.
10. Provide information and maintain transparency in company operations.

Source: Based on an advisory of the Canadian government.

The best defense is a good offense. An imaginative public relations program is the best way to reduce the probability of reaction against a company. There are numerous ways to learn about good corporate citizenship, which is defined as promoting ethically and socially responsible behavior. The mission of the World Bank's Corporate Governance and Corporate Social Responsibility division is to help firms meet those objectives. (The division even offers an online course). The OECD and the UN have multiple documents related to corporate codes of conduct—related to bribery, environmentalism, employment practices, economic development, corruption, and a host of other issues. The UN Global Compact, as discussed in Chapter 5, is another useful platform to support a firm's public relations campaign, especially as related to corporate social responsibility.

ORGANIZATIONAL ASPECTS

Because of its need to be sensitive to local publics, a firm must rely heavily on local staff. A firm can centralize policymaking, but day-to-day operations must be left to people in the local market. A firm has nationals on its staff and may use a local public relations agency. The international corporate communications manager ensures consistency from country to country and acts as a clearinghouse of ideas and experience. Aiding in this task is the increasing availability of international public relations firms. Such groups can aid coordination, much like the multinational agency does in advertising.

Effective public relations is critical to the global success of a company.

Public relations is important to effective marketing, but the two functions should be organizationally separate. Although public relations is a profitable activity, its purpose is not immediate sales. By grouping the public relations and marketing functions together, a firm runs the risk that public relations might take a short-run view, focusing on the annual profit-and-loss statement. Public relations should be sufficiently independent to be able to consider the interest of the public as well as the long-run interests of the firm.

Marketing Mix as Promotion

The principal elements of promotion have been discussed: advertising, personal selling, and sales promotion. The purpose of those activities is to induce consumers to purchase a company's products. As marketers well know, however, other factors also help persuade customers to buy—or not to buy—a firm's products. All elements of the marketing mix influence the sale of goods and services. Because the elements of the mix have a different influence from country to country, the appropriate mix for a given market should have some degree of individuality. Some of the following issues are also discussed in Chapter 11 as it relates to a firm's supply chain.

Product

Although the quality of a product is presumably the major reason a consumer buys it, consumers' desires for a given product often differ from country to country. By modifying products for national markets, a firm can persuade more customers to buy. Affluent markets may demand more style and power or a larger size. Poorer markets may require smaller sizes, durability, and simplicity.

Food products vary in the degree of sweetness or spiciness desired. Further differences are found in the form, color, and texture of products. In Britain, for example, Ocean Spray had to mix cranberry juice with black currant juice to gain acceptance. (Chapter 9 discusses this in more detail.)

PACKAGE

For many goods, the package is an important element of the product. Adapting packaging to the market may be effective promotion. In Latin America, Gillette sells Silkience shampoo in half-ounce plastic bubbles. In the Far East, Procter & Gamble sells most of its shampoo in single-use packets. In some markets, dual-use packages attract the consumer because they can be retained for some other use. Plastic containers are popular in some markets, whereas metal and glass are preferred elsewhere. Form and color are important, too. Ocean Spray, for example, had to change from bottles to juice boxes in Britain. The label on the package should also serve a promotional role in its design and color, in the language used, and in the text printed on it.

Bulk packing of a product is another consideration for the international marketing manager. The rigors of long-distance shipping and multiple handling of master cartons mean the international packing may need to be strengthened, reinforced, or perhaps redesigned.

BRAND

Brand policy can affect a product's attractiveness. For some goods, an international brand name is more prestigious and trusted than a national brand. On the other hand, for many products, such as food and household items, individualized national brands are favored by international companies. Johnson Wax and CPC International are examples of firms that pursue primarily a national brand policy. Table 4-1 in Chapter 4 shows P&G's branding in Poland.

WARRANTY AND SERVICE

Many companies use warranties defensively; that is, they meet competitors' warranties. Warranties, however, can also be used aggressively to promote sales. If an international company offers better quality and a more reliable product than its competitors, it may gain a promotional edge through a more liberal warranty. Many producers of electrical and mechanical products have used a strong warranty as part of their entry strategy into foreign markets. When Chrysler reentered Europe, it offered a generous three-year/100,000-kilometer warranty.

Consumers everywhere are concerned about product service, which includes delivery, installation, repair and maintenance facilities, and spare parts inventories. International firms are handicapped in some markets because they are not represented well enough to offer service that is as good as what national firms offer. A weakness in this area can offset strengths in other areas. By the same token, a strong service capability can be effective promotion—a strength of Singer and IBM in many markets and of the German and Japanese auto producers in the U.S. market.

Distribution

Managers are aware of the promotional implications of different distribution strategies. When convenience is important to the buyer, a firm must have widespread distribution. Where dealer "push" is important, more selective distribution is necessary. The same considerations apply to foreign markets. When an international firm sells through distributors, it usually provides an exclusive franchise to encourage support. This exclusive franchise is almost always necessary to get a distributor to cooperate.

When a firm goes from an indirect to a direct channel, the distribution system bears a greater part of the promotion. The more direct the channel, the greater the push it gives a product. Going direct can have a special significance for an international firm's level of involvement in a market. An indirect channel means that many intermediaries exist between producer and consumer. In international marketing, an indirect channel is exporting. The way for a firm to go more direct in export markets is to establish its own presence there with a marketing subsidiary. As with any more direct method, the firm's cost will increase. Many benefits are associated with such a move, however, one of which is a favorable promotional effect. One way of illustrating the benefits is to note the disadvantages of exporting, which are usually overcome by establishing a local subsidiary. Chapter 8 discusses entry mode and its implications on distribution in more detail.

Price and Terms

The idea behind the demand curve and the elasticity concept is that buyers are sensitive to price. By changing the price, the marketer affects the attractiveness of a product. In other words, pricing has promotional aspects. If consumers in different countries have differing degrees of price sensitivity, the marketer should try to adjust prices accordingly, if costs permit.

Price may be used promotionally in other ways. On products for which there is a price-quality association, a firm might want to price above its competitors to gain the quality image. Of course, that is most meaningful when the product actually has a quality advantage. In countries where purchasing power is low, prices might be reduced through modification of the product (for example, giving it fewer features and greater simplicity) or use of smaller sizes. Chapter 12 discusses pricing and promotion in more detail.

SUMMARY

As companies grow internationally, they often move toward a global brand. The advantages of a global brand include economies of scale in advertising, stronger influence of the sales channel, and improved reputation and image of the company.

An important decision in international markets involves brand policy. The major question is whether to opt for local brands or global brands. Global brands are consistent with a standardization approach to world markets.

Issues important to brand policy in international markets include protecting against brand piracy, paying attention to the cultural connotations of brand names, and dealing with government regulations that pertain to brands and trademarks.

Another decision is whether to use private branding. Although this approach may facilitate sales, a company has little contact with the ultimate consumer and learns little about changes at the consumer level.

Several factors affect international promotion. Because languages vary by market, promotion must be in the local language. That requires local help from a local ad agency or subsidiary of the firm. Media availability (television, radio, and newspaper) varies between countries, requiring a marketer to adjust. Governments place limits on advertised products, appeals, media use, and agency ownership. Competition in the local market influences a firm's promotion.

Agency availability differs between markets for political and economic reasons. That can hinder a firm's ability to find a good agency or to get international coordination.

Major decisions involve selecting the agency, message, and media; determining the budget; evaluating the effectiveness of the promotion efforts; and determining the degree of centralization or decentralization that is appropriate.

Using its own international marketing criteria, a firm must choose an agency for each foreign market. The trend is to use multicountry agencies that are gaining market share. However, some good local agencies survive in most markets. In choosing a message, the issue is whether a firm should use local or international campaigns. The use of internationalized campaigns is affected by language requirements, the existence of international market segments, the use of local versus international agencies, and the degree of decentralization in the firm. To maximize similarities, many firms use a pattern, or prototype, approach.

A firm's media configuration often varies from country to country because of government restrictions or media infrastructure in the country. Some firms use international media for multicountry coverage, but local media predominate for most international marketers. It is difficult to apply the various formulas for determining the ad budget for a firm's foreign markets. Therefore, the percentage-of-sales approach is the most common formula used. The ad budget for a country is a function of its overall promotional mix there, local media availability, and the firm's own level of involvement in the country.

Evaluating promotion effectiveness is more difficult in foreign markets than at home. For that reason, firms frequently use sales as a measure of effectiveness. The internationalization of research and advertising agencies is helping on this score.

A firm also must decide how to advertise in markets where it is represented by independent licensees or distributors. Should it rely on them, go it alone, or cooperate? Cooperative programs with the local licensee or distributor appear to be the most common and effective approach.

Personal selling is often more important in the promotional mix abroad than in the domestic market. Although personal selling is done almost entirely on a national basis, management at headquarters can contribute something to most of the tasks of sales force management in the firm's foreign markets: recruitment and selection, training, motivation, compensation, control, and evaluation. Successful techniques can be transferred from the home market to similar foreign markets. Economies of scale can be realized for some tasks. A firm will also frequently train or assist distributors' or licensees' sales forces. And international comparisons help in evaluating and, thus, improving international performance.

Public relations is a very important and sensitive task for international marketing. The first step in successful public relations is conducting research so a firm becomes familiar with all the constituencies that can affect its success in the market. The second is designing a company program and behavior appropriate to the market. Firms should not only respond to the communication environment, but also try to manage it, thus achieving more favorable outcomes in the marketplace through political power and public opinion.

KEY TERMS

advertising	competitive-parity	percentage-of-sales	public relations
comparative-analysis	approach	approach	sales promotion
approach	objective-and-task	personal selling	
	approach		

NASBITE CGBP TOPICS COVERED IN THIS CHAPTER

Note: For full details of the alignment of each chapter with the NASBITE CGBP, be sure to review the information provided in the section "Studying for the NASBITE CGBP Exam."

CGBP Rubric	Topic
02/02/01:	laws and regulations that impact the marketing plan (e.g., entity law, promotional restrictions, distributor requirements, corruption)
02/03/01:	impact on market selection of...promotion
02/03/02:	how to find laws and regulations that impact the market selection (e.g., promotional restrictions)
02/05/01:	budgeting processes
02/08/01:	sales promotion mechanisms (e.g., trade shows and trade missions, horizontal vs. vertical trade show)
02/08/02:	technological tools for promotion (e.g., Internet activities such as e-mail, websites, e-commerce; video-conferencing, virtual trade fairs)
02/08/03:	trade assistance resources in support of global promotion
02/10/01:	sales techniques (e.g., pull vs. push), sales knowledge, and business travel (Note: Pull versus push is discussed in Chapter 8 as part of distribution strategy. This chapter includes the discussion of other selling issues.)

QUESTIONS AND RESEARCH

1. What are some approaches to brand policy in international markets?
2. Should a firm have one brand worldwide? Explain. Would your answer change depending on the product (for example, perfume, photographic film, credit cards, and computers)?
3. Why are trademark piracy and brand piracy important? How can a firm protect itself against these actions?
4. What are the pros and cons of private branding in international markets? Discuss government controls and agency and media availability as constraints on the international advertising manager.
5. Assume a manufacturer of home care products has just opened a marketing subsidiary in Spain. The company has been selling in 12 other European countries since 1950. The advertising manager at European headquarters must choose between the Madrid office of a large U.S. agency and a leading Spanish agency. What questions would you ask in advising the company?
6. Why have international agencies been growing so strong?
7. What factors encourage standardization of international advertising?
8. Why is it difficult for an international advertising manager to use the same media configuration in all markets?
9. Why does personal selling often play a proportionately larger promotional role in foreign markets than in the domestic market?
10. Why is personal selling done largely within national boundaries rather than internationally?
11. Because most of the task of sales force management must be done within the national market, what contributions can an international marketing manager make?
12. Explain how a multinational firm may have an advantage over local firms in training a sales force and evaluating its performance.
13. Discuss the potential competitive advantages of a multinational firm in sales promotion activities in foreign markets.
14. How does the establishment of local operations aid a firm's promotion in foreign markets?

15. What are the elements of a sound public relations program?

16. What is the relationship of public relations to marketing?

CHAPTER 10 TEAM PROJECT ASSIGNMENT: Branding, Advertising, and Promotion Strategy

The team project for this chapter addresses the current branding and promotion strengths of your client; plus, it develops suggestions and strategies to be integrated into the final international marketing plan.

BRANDING AND PROMOTION ASSESSMENT

Begin by doing a branding and promotion assessment of your client's current capabilities in this area. This analysis may build on strengths and weaknesses relating to branding and promotion already discussed from Chapter 1 work. Specifically address these issues:

- Does your client already have a global brand(s)?
- How strong is the brand within the industry in which your client operates?
- How does the brand strength of your client compare to its competitors?
- Assess the current international promotion activities of your client. Which tools identified in this chapter does your client use to implement its promotion policy?
- What strategy does your client use as regards to standardization or adaptation of its promotional message in its current international markets?
- What media does your client currently use to support its promotion strategy?
- How does your firm sell its products or services? Is its sales force a competitive advantage?
- What are the current strengths or weaknesses of your client's current international public relations activities?
- Does your client have any recent public relations challenges?
- Review the "Marketing Mix as Promotion" section in this chapter. To what extent has your client addressed these issues in its international markets.

BRANDING AND PROMOTION STRATEGY AND RECOMMENDATIONS

Based on the findings from the preceding assessment, and on the best practices and issues discussed in this chapter, develop an international branding and promotion strategy for your client. You may want to begin with an international branding and promotion strategy to be used for all markets—meaning the common aspects of the branding and promotion that will be deployed in all foreign markets. Examples would include use of global brands, common promotional messages, and common PR approach. Then, for each of the markets recommended for expansion to be included in the final international marketing plan, detail branding and promotion issues unique to each market. These individual market strategies and recommendations should take into account local conditions that would require adaptation to the global branding and promotion strategy due to local differences.

CASE 10.1 Nestlé: More Trouble in the Baby Market

On October 12, 1988, the International Organization of Consumers Unions (IOCU) called for a renewal of the boycott against Nestlé, a Swiss firm. The boycott had been called in 1977 because of the deaths of babies in developing countries that were alleged to be related to the use of infant formula and reported unethical marketing practices. In 2000, abysmal sales for Nestlé's snack and juice products for children led to the products' withdrawal from the UK market; the 23-year-old boycott was blamed for the poor sales.

Shortly after the boycott was organized, Nestlé changed its marketing practices for infant formula, working with the industry and the World Health Organization (WHO) on a code for marketing infant formula and forming a prestigious committee to investigate the claims and advise Nestlé. By 1984, the company was perceived as a leading firm in support of the WHO code, and the boycott was dropped.

Calls for a renewed boycott arose because some observers claimed that Nestlé and other firms were breaking the spirit of the code by supplying large amounts of free formula to hospitals in developing countries, with the result that too many mothers became dependent on formula and lost the ability to nurse their babies. Nestlé's response was that the WHO code allows for free distribution of supplies to hospitals that request it and that the amounts supplied were not excessive.

NESTLÉ IN THE U.S. BABY MARKET

The U.S. market for infant formula was over $1.6 billion, and until 1988, none of it belonged to Nestlé. (Abbott and Bristol-Myers had 90 percent of the market between them.) In June 1988, Nestlé introduced Good Start H.A., which it said could prevent or reduce fussiness, sleeplessness, colic, rash, and other worrisome ailments because it was hypoallergenic—which the labels indicated in bold type. Carnation, Nestlé's U.S. subsidiary, introduced the product and called it "a medical breakthrough."

The market entry strategy for Good Start H.A. included the product differentiation feature of being hypoallergenic while having a taste similar to other infant formula products. By contrast, Nutramigen, another hypoallergenic product, had a distinctive, less pleasant taste. Good Start H.A. was priced competitively with the leading infant formula brands, although Bristol-Myers' hypoallergenic Nutramigen, a niche product, cost twice as much as Good Start H.A. To further speed market entry, Carnation broke with industry practice and publicized the hypoallergenic feature directly to parents without waiting for pediatricians to recommend it.

About three months after the introduction of Good Start H.A., there were scattered reports of severe reactions. Some mothers of severely milk-allergic babies tried the formula and reported that their babies vomited violently and went limp. Nestlé's competitors helped to publicize those incidents. Some leading pediatricians criticized Nestlé's marketing as misleading, and the American Academy of Pediatrics strongly protested against advertising directly to mothers and bypassing physicians. James Strain, then director of the academy, said, "These ailments (fussiness, colic, etc.) happen to 90 percent of all babies and aren't really symptoms of anything. The advertising just raises the level of anxiety in mothers about something being wrong with their babies." One mother, Elizabeth Strickler, was interviewed by the *Wall Street Journal*. Because her son, Zachary, had not tolerated other formulas well, she was eager to try Good Start H.A. After two weeks of use, Zachary experienced severe vomiting. She discontinued usage, but for two months, she had to feed him Maalox to soothe his gastrointestinal tract. "If you call something hypoallergenic, that means a lot to me," she said. "I thought it was the best thing, and that's why I bought it."

William Spivak, pediatrician and Mrs. Strickler's doctor, said, "My concern is that long after physicians realize that this formula isn't as hypoallergenic as claimed, parents with milk-allergic babies will be grabbing it off the shelf because of its attractive hypoallergenic labeling, and thereby exposing their babies to a potentially dangerous formula without physician supervision." Other pediatricians pointed out that while Good Start was easier to digest than ordinary milk-based formulas, it was not mild enough for the approximately 2 percent of babies who, like Zachary, were severely allergic to cows' milk. The mothers of those babies were most likely to be attracted by the hypoallergenic claim.

Good Start had received preliminary approval from the FDA before introductory marketing, but the FDA had asked for more data backing up the formula's extra claims that it could reduce allergies. After the severe reactions were reported, the FDA began a new investigation of the company's claims as well as of the six reports of severe reactions.

Following the widespread publicity given to the cases of severe reactions to the Good Start formula, several state attorneys general also began an investigation of Nestlé's Good Start marketing. The company had to submit copies of Good Start's print, radio, and television advertising that had appeared in California, New York, and Texas. It also had to provide scientific studies supporting the formula's health and nutrition claims as well as studies showing consumer perception of the term *hypoallergenic*.

Robert Roth, an assistant attorney general in New York, said, "This case is a little unusual in that it involves the health of infants. We are pursuing it more urgently than we would a matter which is purely economic."

In responding to the publicity and the criticisms, Nestlé and Carnation pointed out that all formulas have isolated cases of bad reactions. They argued that severe reactions to Good Start resulted from its misuse with highly milk-allergic babies. Pierre Guesry, then a Nestlé vice president in Switzerland, said, "I don't understand why our product should work in 100 percent of cases. If we wanted to say it was foolproof, we would have called it allergy-free. We call it hypo- or less-allergic."

A PRODUCT FROM EUROPE

Nestlé, which has the largest share of the infant formula market outside the United States, had introduced Beba H.A., a version of Good Start H.A., in Germany two years before bringing it to the U.S. market. While mothers are in the hospital after giving birth, Nestlé supplies them with information about hypoallergenic formulas and infant allergies. It does not name the company or the product, but Beba H.A. is the only major hypoallergenic brand available. Other formula makers also distribute information to mothers, but some critics say Nestlé goes too far. Judith Phillipoa of the Geneva Infant Feeding Association, an anti-Nestlé activist group, said, "In Europe, Nestlé is blowing up the allergy problem as a way of creating demand for their product. Now they're exporting this system to the U.S."

Pierre Guesry said that Good Start was introduced in the United States because "we felt American babies should have the same rights to a good formula as German, Belgian, or French babies." He pointed out that no problems were reported in Europe as occurred in the United States and that most of the 40,000 U.S. babies who had tried Good Start had no problems with it.

NESTLÉ RESPONDS

Nestlé's first response to the publicity and criticism was to remove the term *hypoallergenic* from the front of the can where it had been displayed in large type. Some critics were not satisfied because H.A. was still in the product name—Good Start H.A.—and hypoallergenic was in the fine print on the back of the can. Also, Good Start was still advertised in medical journals as a "breakthrough hypoallergenic infant formula."

In July 1989, Nestlé reached a settlement with nine states' attorneys general about its Good Start marketing. The agreement specified that (1) Carnation could not use the word *hypoallergenic* in advertising Good Start, (2) it could not use expert endorsers that had been paid by the company, and (3) it could not make claims that were not scientifically supported. Carnation also agreed to pay $90,000 to cover the costs of the investigation.

Nestlé also hired Ogilvy & Mather's public relations unit to help its relations with the FDA and the other publics involved. Among Ogilvy's proposals were these:

1. Get people into the groups organizing and supporting the boycott. This was meant to be an early warning system for Nestlé.
2. Create a Nestlé positive image campaign—a daily 12-minute news program to reach 8,000 high schools. This was not to advertise, but to buy public service time such as a "Nestlé News Network."
3. Create a Carnation image campaign to inoculate the Nestlé subsidiary from any negative effects of the boycott.

The game plan included a Carnation National Homework Help Line and a foster care fund for children with AIDS.

Nestlé had a special section on its website devoted to public relations on this topic and on which its Infant Formula Policy was posted:

Breastfeeding is best for babies. Chemist Henri Nestlé stated this in his Treatise on Nutrition soon after founding our company in 1867, and it is still true today.

The company does:

- encourage and support exclusive breastfeeding as the best choice for babies during the first months of life.
- warn mothers of the consequences of incorrect or inappropriate use of infant formula.
- believe that there is a legitimate market for infant formula when a safe alternative to breast milk is needed.
- believe that parents have the right to choose how their babies are to be fed on the basis of adequate and objective information.
- comply with both the letter and the spirit of the World Health Organization's International Code of Marketing of Breast Milk Substitutes.
- support efforts by governments to implement the International Code through legislation, regulation, or other appropriate measures.

The company does not:

- advertise infant formula to the public.
- permit staff whose responsibilities include the marketing of infant formula to make direct contact with mothers, except in response to consumer complaints.
- give incentives to its staff based on infant formula sales.
- use pictures of babies on its infant formula packs.
- distribute free infant formula samples to mothers.
- give financial or material incentives to health professionals for the purpose of promoting infant formula.
- allow educational material relating to the use of infant formula to be displayed publicly in hospitals and clinics.
- donate free infant formula for use by healthy newborn babies except in exceptional social cases (e.g., where the government policy allows manufacturers to respond to a specific medical request, for example if the mother dies in childbirth).

Furthermore, the company included the following statements: "Nestlé will take disciplinary measures against any Nestlé personnel who deliberately violates this policy. Nestlé invites government officials, health professionals, and consumers to draw to its attention any Nestlé infant formula marketing practices in developing countries which they consider are not in conformity with the above commitment."

Source: Nestlé website (http://www.nestle.com/Our_Responsibility/Infant_Formula/Charter/ The+Charter .htm); *Wall Street Journal*, February 16, 1989, p. A1; *Wall Street Journal*, February 24, 1989, p. B6; 3 *Wall Street Journal*, March 13, 1989, p. B6; *Wall Street Journal*, July 7, 1989, p. B4; "Nestle's New Milk Run Reignites Old Debate," *Marketing Week*, June 27, 2002, p. 20.

Questions and Research

1. This case details one of the most famous PR challenges of the recent past and helps demonstrate the complicating factors when the issues involve more than one country. Analyze the problem Nestlé encountered and its public relations response. How would you evaluate the company's PR response? Was it effective?

2. Discuss the complicating factor in this case that Nestlé was an international company.

3. Conduct further research on this case and the related boycott. What further insights does your research provide as to the PR challenge facing Nestlé. Discuss your results.

4. Suggest a program for Nestlé to deal with its public relations problems, for example, the renewed boycott and the negative publicity about Good Start. Would you use the Ogilvy & Mather recommendations? Explain.

5. Visit Nestlé's website at www.nestle.com. What lingering evidence is there of this dispute in material presented on the website?

NOTES

1. Sak Onkvisit and John J. Shaw. "The International Dimensions of Branding: Strategic Considerations and Decisions," *International Marketing Review*, 6 (1989): 22–34.
2. BMW CEO Helmut Panke as quoted in the *Wall Street Journal*, November 20, 2003.
3. John Quelch, "Global Brands: Taking Stock," *Business Strategy Review*, 10 (1999): 1–14.
4. Martin S. Roth, "The Effects of Culture and Socioeconomics on the Performance of Global Brand Image Strategies," *Journal of Marketing Research* (1995): 163–175.
5. Kevin Lane Keller, "The Brand Report Card," *Harvard Business Review* 78, no. 1 (2000): 147–157.
6. The Most Valuable U.S. Retail Brands (New York: Interbrand, 2010): 3.
7. www.landor.com
8. Lego Corporate Website, About Us – Lifelong Play (http://www.lego.com/eng/info/default.asp?page=lifelong), accessed September 1, 2010.
9. Ruth Mortimer, "Lego: Building a Brand Out of Bricks," *Brand Strategy* (April 2003): 16–19.
10. "Staying Power," *Business Latin America*, November 23, 1998.
11. "Dutch Strongest Brands Top 10," Ranking the Brands, 2010 (http://www.rankingthebrands.com/The-Brand-Rankings.aspx), accessed August 12, 2010."Oman's Auto Distributors Gearing Up for Ramadan," *Times of Oman*, September 1, 2002.
12. "After Years Behind the Scenes, Chinese Join the Name Game," *Wall Street Journal*, December 26, 2003.
13. Ming Zeng and Peter J. Williamson, "The Hidden Dragons," *Harvard Business Review* (October 2003).
14. David A. Aaker and Erich Joachimsthaler, "The Lure of Global Branding," *Harvard Business Review* (November–December 1999).
15. David Aaker, "Brand Extensions: The Good, the Bad, and the Ugly," *Sloan Management Review* (Summer 1990): 47–56.
16. "Hewlett-Packard: Big, Boring, and Booming," *Economist*, May 6, 1995.
17. Steven Globerman, "Addressing International Product Piracy," *Journal of International Business Studies* 19, no. 3 (Fall 1988); Richard S. Higgins and Paul Rubin, "Counterfeit Goods," *Journal of Law and Economics* (October 1986); M. Harvey and I. Ronkainen, "International Counterfeiters: Marketing Success without Cost or Risk," *Columbia Journal of World Business* (Fall 1985).
18. "U.S. MNC Wins Some Rounds against Trademark Pirates," *Business International*, June 8, 1992.
19. "Hunting the Big Mac in Africa," *Economist*, November 11, 1995
20. "Who Owns the Smirnoff Name?" *Business Week*, January 15, 1996.
21. Sanjay K. Dhar and Stephen Hoch, "Why Store Brand Penetration Varies by Retailer," *Marketing Science* (Fall 1997).
22. S. Hoch and S. Bannerji, "When Do Private Labels Succeed?" *Sloan Management Review* (Summer 1993): 57–67; John Quelch and D. Harding, "Brands versus Private Labels: Fighting to Win," *Harvard Business Review* (January–February 1996): 99–109.
23. Albert Caruana and Monica Abdilla, "To Dub or Not to Dub: Language Adaptation of Global Television Advertisements for a Bilingual Community," *Journal of Brand Management* 12, no. 4 (April 2005): 236–249.

24. UNESCO UIS Data—UNESCO Institute for Statistics, "Newspapers and periodicals, Daily Circulation per capita," 1997–2000, (http://www.nationmaster.com/graph/med_new_and_per_cir_dai_percap-periodicals-circulation-daily-per-capita#source), accessed August 14, 2010.

25. Euromonitor Passport Reference and Markets; Personal Computers (PCs) in Use, 2009 (http://www.portal.euromonitor.com/Portal/Statistics.aspx), accessed August 14, 2010.

26. J. J. Boddewyn, "Barriers to Advertising," *International Advertiser* (May–June 1989): 21, 22.

27. "Health (Government Urged to Implement Anti-Smoking Laws)," *Financial Times Information*; Global News Wire, Pakistan Press International Information Services Limited, May 11, 2005.

28. "Helping Consumers Make an Informed Choice," *Financial Times Information*; Global News Wire, Asia Africa Intelligence Wire; The Indian Express Online Media Ltd.; Financial Express, December 10, 2004.

29. "Still in the Hunt," *Business Week* (July 7, 2003): 42–44.

30. "Sir Martin's Shopping Spree," *Business Week* (October 4, 2004): 102–104.

31. "Predator to Prey," *Economist*, September 25, 2004, pp. 78–79.

32. Anne Macquin, Dominique Rouzies, and Nathalie Prime, "The Influence of Culture on Personal Selling Interactions," *Journal of Euro Marketing* 9, no. 4 (2000): 71–94.

33. "Our Business," Reader's Digest website (http://www.rda.com/our-company/our-businesses), accessed March 29, 2011.

34. Irina Six, "What Language Sells: Western Advertising In Russia," *Journal of Language for International Business* 16, no. 2 (2005): 1–11.

35. Chang-Hoan Cho and Hongsik John Cheon, "Cross-Cultural Comparisons of Interactivity on Corporate Web Sites: The U.S., the UK, Japan, and South Korea," *Journal of Advertising* 34, no. 2 (Summer 2005): 99–116.

36. Direct Marketing Association (http://www.the-dma.org/aboutdma/whatisthedma.shtml), accessed November 6, 2010.

37. "The Unmeasurable," *PR Week, Media Monitoring*, September 23, 2005, page 25.

38. "Interim Online Ad Measures," *New Media Age*, September 22, 2005, page 14.

39. "A New TV Ratings Method: Bag Sample, Take Census," *Adweek*, July 18, 2005.

40. Gila E. Fruchter and Shlomo Kalish, "Dynamic Promotional Budgeting and Media Allocation," *European Journal of Operational Research* 111, no. 1 (November 16, 1998): 15–27.

41. Boonghee Yoo and Rujirutana Mandhachitara, "Estimating Advertising Effects on Sales in a Competitive Setting," *Journal of Advertising Research* 43, no. 3 (September 2003): 310–321.

42. Richard C. Vancil, "Marketing Budgets Are Earned, Not Granted," *B to B* 90, no. 4 (April 4, 2005): 36.

43. Ulrich R. Orth, Peter P. Oppenheim, and Zuzana Firbasova, "Measuring Message Framing Effects Across Europe," *Journal of Targeting, Measurement and Analysis for Marketing* 13, no. 4 (August 2005): 313–327.

44. Vern Terpstra and Lloyd Russow, *International Dimensions of Marketing*, 1999, Mason, OH: South-Western College Publishing, p. 16. [Adapted from Laura Morelli. "Writing for a Global Audience," *Marketing News* 32, no. 17 (August 17, 1998).]

45. Sergio Roman and Salvador Ruiz, "A Comparative Analysis of Sales Training in Europe: Implications for International Sales Negotiations," *International Marketing Review*,20, no. 3 (2003): 304–327.

46. Earl D. Honeycutt Jr., John B. Ford, Robert A. Lupton, and Theresa B. Flaherty, "Selecting and Training the International Sales Force: Comparison of China and Slovakia," *Industrial Marketing Management* 28, no. 6 (November 1999): 627–636.

47. Thomas N. Ingram, Thomas R. Day, and George H. Lucas, Jr., "Dealing with Global Intermediaries: Guidelines for Sales Managers," *Journal of Global Marketing* 5, no. 4 (1992): 65–80.

48. McDonald's website, history (http://www.media.mcdonalds. com/secured/company/index.html), "McDonald's Comes Clean," Yahoo! Financial News (http://biz.yahoo.com/fool/051025/ 113027388625.html?.v = 1), accessed October 26, 2005.

49. Michel Laroche, Maria Kalamas, and Qinchao Huang, "Effects of Coupons on Brand Categorization and Choice of Fast Foods in China," *Journal of Business Research* 58, no. 5 (May 2005): 674–675.

50. "Coupons and Samples 'Key' to E-Marketing," *Marketing Week*, January 27, 2005, p. 17.

51. "Vouchers: Coupons Can Be Cutting-Edge," *Marketing Week*, June 23, 2005, p. 45.

52. Jeanette Best, "Online Coupons: An Engaging Idea," *Brandweek* 46, no. 18 (May 2, 2005): 20.

53. "Everyone Agrees Singles Night Is a Good Way to 'Drive Sales,'" *Business and Industry*, MMR 21, no. 20 (December 13, 2004): 110.

54. "Wal-Mart Gives Up Germany," *New York Times*, July 28, 2006 (http://www.nytimes.com/2006/07/28/business/worldbusiness/28iht-walmart.2325266. html), accessed August 14, 2010.

55. For more details of the Deutsche Messe organization, visit its website: http://www.messe.de.

56. Suman Lee, "The Emergence of Global Public and International Public Relations," *Public Relations Quarterly* 50, no. 2 (Summer 2005): 14–17.

chapter

11

Supply Chain Management and International Marketing

Supply chain management has seen significant changes over the past decades. Managing a firm's supply chain has gone from "How does a firm get its products to its customers?" to "How does a firm leverage its supply chain better than its competitors to create a competitive advantage?" Essentially, supply chain management has transformed from simply being a "problem" to be solved into an opportunity to be more competitive. Today's international marketing manager needs to understand how to leverage the firm's supply chain into competitive advantage by including supply chain issues in the firm's strategic planning and integrating the supply chain with other functional departments.

The main goals of this chapter are to ●●●

1. Define supply chain and supply chain management and clarify their important role in supporting a firm's competiveness.

2. Discuss supply chain issues unique to the international marketing manager.

3. Delineate the range of strategic decisions a firm would make in managing its global supply chain.

4. Illustrate the role of third-party logistics companies and their role in supporting supply chain management.

5. Discuss global sourcing decisions and the variables affecting those decisions.

6. Detail the role of distribution and warehousing in support of global operations.

7. Highlight common international documents used for international trade.

8. Discuss compliance with export controls.

9. Discuss marketing mix issues and supply chain management including packaging, labeling, and warranties.

339

What Is Supply Chain Management?

supply chain

The sum of activities related to the moving of goods from their source (raw materials, components) to the final consumer (finished goods). A firm's supply chain includes purchasing, manufacturing, logistics, warehousing, tracking of goods, the supply of goods to buyers, and reverse logistics.

reverse logistics

A range of activities associated with customer support, including product returns, warranties, and repairs.

supply chain management

The management of all the events within a firm's supply chain.

A firm's **supply chain** is composed of all the activities related to moving goods from their source (raw materials, components) to the final consumer (finished goods). As shown in Figure 11-1, this all-encompassing view of a supply chain includes purchasing (raw materials, components, perhaps even finished products), manufacturing (full manufacturing, assembly), logistics (transportation, warehousing, tracking of goods), the supply of goods to the sales channel (distributors, retailers, end users), and reverse logistics. (**Reverse logistics** is a relatively new term referring to range of activities associated with customer support, including product returns, warranties, and repairs.)

Supply chain management is the management of all the events within a firm's supply chain. It includes a range of strategic decisions a company must make to ensure its supply chain becomes a competitive advantage—not simply a cost area that needs management. Best practice in supply chain management means a firm is continually addressing how it can be more competitive through decisions made about its supply chain. As once observed by the CEO of Whirlpool, it's no longer enough to sell global with global brands and global manufacturing; a firm also has to leverage its whole capabilities so that the "company as a whole is greater than the sum of its parts."[1]

This competitive and strategic view of supply chain management has important management implications. It means that all departments within a firm must be involved in supply chain decisions—from procurement and manufacturing to sales and customer service. This company-wide involvement may mean other departments have a managerial stake in supply chain decisions and must take responsibility for its effectiveness.[2] It also implies that the corporate information system (IT system) may need to offer a common platform for all departments so the elements of the supply chain are visible to all departments and information can be easily shared.[3] For example, pharmaceutical company GlaxoSmithKline (GSK) found that it consistently has higher inventory levels than its major competitors. For a firm with over 51 brand groups and 1,200 product types, even small improvements in inventory management can result in big financial gains. As a result, GSK is analyzing the benefits of using specialized supply chain software so that it can use data from its supply chain to help determine appropriate levels of inventory and better forecast demand.[4]

As a company expands globally, supply chain management becomes even more complex. Rather than shipments of perhaps just a few hundred miles, shipments are thousands of miles. Rather than just one set of government policies, multiple government rules and regulations need to be recognized. These differences include numerous challenges such as time differences, cultural barriers, multiple currencies,

Figure 11-1 • Illustration of a Firm's Supply Chain

Raw materials → Manufacturing → Warehousing → retail → End user → Customer returns

A firm's supply chain is composed of all the activities related to moving goods from their source (raw material) to the final consumer including customer returns (eg. warranty claims, repairs).

documentation differences, and cost differences. Essentially, the whole of the global business environment, as first discussed in Chapters 2 through 5, contributes to a more challenging supply chain management task for a global firm.

Supply Chain Management and the International Marketing Manager

The extent of involvement of the international marketing department in supply chain management decisions will vary between companies. At the very least, the international marketing manager must be aware of supply chain issues because ultimately they will impact sales levels. The marketing department may do an excellent job with foreign market identification, entry, partner selection, and ultimately foreign sales. However, all efforts will be greatly hampered if supply chain problems mean foreign customers cannot buy products or have problems handling after-sales issues such as warranty repairs. More and more, retailers look to their supply chain partners (e.g., the chain from manufacturer to distributor to retailer) to help them improve brand image and reputation as well as increase sales and profits.[5] This further emphasizes the importance of the manufacturer in helping the ultimate retailer get the product in the hands of consumers. Given this interdependency between marketing and supply chain management, the marketing department of a firm would likely at least have some influence in supply chain decisions.

Companies seek to ensure supply chain decisions are fully integrated into their strategic goals across all departments including marketing. When these decisions are successful, firms can turn something that may be a problem into a success. For example, customers often had to wait for the latest Apple product. But by linking customers to the company's supply chain partners, Apple turned waiting for the product into an adventure as customers tracked their new purchase from China to their home. See "Keeping Waiting Customers Happy" for more details.

• • • Keeping Waiting Customers Happy

Expecting high demand for its iPhone 4, Apple started accepting pre-orders two weeks prior to the phone being available in retail outlets. However, demand was not just high—it was overwhelming, with over 600,000 pre-orders on the first day alone. As a result, many consumers had to wait for their iPhones to arrive, often direct from the manufacturing facilities in China.[6]

Eager customers who paid for a product that they do not yet have in their hands can become angry customers. However, thanks to Apple's supply chain technology, those customers waiting for their iPhones quickly found a new way to pass the time until their iPhones arrived: They tuned in to the tracking statuses and updates on their phones' current location and progress from China to their doorsteps. Instead of getting angry, customers obsessively followed their phones' progress, even tweeting updates about their phones and comparing the shipping paths for their phones on Apple's Support Communities website and discussion board (https://discussions.apple.com) with other iPhone buyers.[7,8]

Although demand outweighing supply put extra strains on Apple's supply chain, the company's integration of the supply chain and ability to share information between links in the supply chain ultimately allowed customers to feel as if they were a part of their phones' journey. Thus, Apple turned a problem (no phones available) into a success (creating excitement and involving the customers in their products' path through the supply chain).

Supply Chain Strategic Decisions

Regardless of the international marketing department's direct involvement, the range of strategic decisions a firm would make in managing its supply chain include:

* **Suppliers.** How many suppliers should the firm use? Should the firm have at least one supplier in its home market?

* **Location of production.** Associated with supplier management is the locating of manufacturing. Though manufacturing decisions are primarily driven by demand and location-cost issues, supply chain consideration also play a role. The location of a facility that is geographically close to buyers may justify a decision to manufacture in a city or region that otherwise has higher manufacturing costs. An example would be manufacturing in Germany versus Greece.

* **Transportation.** What transportation methods should the firm use: air, ocean, rail, truck? (See Table 11-1 for an overview of transportation modes and methods.) Does the firm use more than one company to solve its logistics needs?

* **Warehousing.** Where does the firm warehouse? Does its have one centralized warehouse per international region, one per country, or perhaps more than one per country? Does the firm own warehouses or outsource them?

* **Technology.** Part of the recent revolution in supply chain management has been increased use of technology. Logistics partners now provide tools that customers can integrate into their website or corporate management information system. Technology solutions range from modeling transportation costs using different warehouse scenarios to real-time tracking of packages.

* **Outsource or in-house.** As discussed in the next section, an important decision is which supply chain activities are kept internal to the firm (such as warehousing) and which are outsourced to a partner (such as transportation). This decision helps a company remain focused on its core competencies and leverage the expertise and resources of outside partners.

* **Management of delivery times.** Of course, if cost were not an issue, firms would ship products by air so buyers could get products as fast as possible. But air is not always an option. Cost, weight, and size are all factors that favor alternate modes of transportation such as ocean or truck. A part of supply chain management that firms must always evaluate is total supply chain needs, and they must balance the cost of different transportation options versus customer needs.

* **Long-term needs versus short-term needs.** Effective supply chain management must also address market needs today versus those of the future. This means understanding demand forecasts, cost forecasts, political and economic conditions, and new logistics solutions from vendors. All these issues must be continually addressed.

* **International compliance.** An important international supply chain issue is staying compliant with all the various government regulations. Ignoring these issues can result in significant fines and penalties, and may even require withdrawal from a market.

The selection of transportation method is one of many issues a firm must research as part of its supply chain management.

Table 11-1 • Major Transportation Modes and Methods

Mode/Method	Major Benefits	Cost	Comments
Truck	Primary method to pick up and drop off goods at facilities. Trucks can go anywhere there are adequate roads.	Relatively high versus rail or ocean.	Truck is generally the most common starting mode and ending mode for most international shipments.
Rail	Very efficient and ideal for multiple containers.	Low versus other modes.	This method relies on availability of rail between needed shipping points.
Barge	Efficient water transportation mode for rivers.	Low versus other modes.	Barge is most commonly used for bulk commodities such as coal, grains, or oil. Strong interest in increasing the use of barges for containerized freight.
Ocean (Freighter/Ship)	Most efficient method of shipping goods internationally over long distances.	Low versus other modes especially if goods are containerized.	This is the preferred method for moving international goods when time of delivery is not critical. Transit times between countries can be weeks.
Air	Fast and reliable. Able to ship goods to anywhere internationally within one to two days.	High especially for goods that are relatively large.	This is not a good option for low-value, high-weight goods. Consolidation of freight helps lower costs.
Containerization of freight (also known as consolidation)	Lowers overall freight costs by moving freight in standardized containers. Most common truck/rail/ocean containers are 20 or 40 feet long. Air containers vary by aircraft.	Most efficient way to move freight. Noncontainerized freight (for example, equipment too large to fit in a container or commodities such as corn or oil) is much more expensive to ship internationally.	Generally, international shippers want to have freight containerized when possible. This method not only lowers costs, but also lowers the chance of damage because goods are more protected.
Intermodalism	Moving freight in standardized cargo containers by ocean, air, rail, or truck.	Use of intermodalism has been the primary method to lower international freight costs.	This method works only for goods/products that can be containerized. Most international freight is shipped via intermodalism.

Moving goods internationally typically involves more than one mode (type) of transportation, as shown in Table 11-1. Understanding transportation options is important to effectively manage a firm's supply chain to minimize costs while remaining efficient and meeting customer needs.

Third-Party Logistics (3PL)

As the role of supply chain management has become more critical to the success of companies, so has the use of outside companies to provide supply chain solutions. **Third-party logistics (3PL)** is the use of companies to outsource specific functions of supply chain management. Examples of these functions include transportation, warehousing, packaging, customer support, warranty repairs, consulting, technology solutions, and cost control. 3PL providers include UPS, FedEx, CAT Logistics, and literally hundreds of transportation and freight companies. 3PL has become critical to global companies. As the previous Apple iPhone discussion highlighted, 3PL firms increasingly must offer strong information technology capabilities so that users of 3PL can integrate information from 3PL into their own systems for tracking shipments.[9]

> **third-party logistics (3PL)**
>
> The use of companies to outsource specific functions of supply chain management. Examples include transportation, warehousing, packaging, customer support, warranty repairs, consulting, technology solutions, and cost control.

Warehousing is one of many functions provided by third-party logistics companies.

Using the services of a 3PL provider means a company can consider supply chain options that otherwise might be too costly or risky. For example, a firm seeking to offer a centralized distribution facility (warehouse) in Europe faces considerable costs. It has to rent or purchase a building, equip the building with the required facilities including equipment, hire distribution staff, incorporate technology and security solutions, and then operate the facility. This process implies significant start-up costs, increased political and economic risk, and potentially high operating costs, especially if transaction volumes are low. Use of a 3PL company means the same solution can be achieved with little to no fixed costs and potentially even lower variable costs. 3PL services are typically invoiced on an "as-used" basis—meaning a company pays only for the services it actually used, such as the amount of inventory space in a month or total number of shipments. 3PL is a good short- to medium-term solution until the firm can justify an in-house, company-owned solution.

freight forwarders
Companies that provide services to support the transportation and movement of goods. Standard services include reserving freight space on carriers, handling international documentation, arranging shipping insurance, and providing outsourced logistics services such as warehousing.

Related to 3PL providers are **freight forwarders**—companies that provide services to support the transportation and movement of goods. In this way, freight forwarders are very much like travel agents for international freight. They can find suitable transportation options, calculate the cost and insurance, reserve the space with a transportation carrier such as an ocean shipping line or airline, and assist with international documents. Freight forwarders provide consolidation services as mentioned in Table 11-1. Many freight forwarders also provide 3PL services or can assist with finding a suitable 3PL provider in a foreign market.

Procurement: The Role of Global Sourcing

If low-cost, timely development and high-quality, state-of-the-art components are desired, global sourcing is often a necessary step. The international marketing manager's understanding of what drives the need for global sourcing is important because global sourcing is increasingly a strategic decision with wide-ranging implications for the firm, such as increased financial performance and improved customer responsiveness.[10] Product decisions, costs, and features are all impacted by these sourcing decisions.

Global Sourcing Decisions and Factors

Global sourcing tends to be driven by two fundamental decisions: (1) Companies manufacturing products in a country must continually decide whether to procure raw materials or components from the home market where the plant is located or from another country in order to lower costs while maintaining quality; and (2) companies that have established foreign manufacturing facilities either need to supply those facilities with raw material and components from their home market or source them in the country or region where the foreign facilities are located. An example of the first decision would be whether a U.S. auto parts manufacturer buys all its needed raw materials from U.S. suppliers or decides to purchase some goods from foreign suppliers. An example of the second decision would be if that same auto parts manufacturer were to build a factory in China, it would have to decide whether some of the needed components should be exported from its U.S. factory to China or it should purchase all of them within China or Asia.

A number of studies look at the strategic role of global sourcing by multinationals.[11] They point out that a firm which shifts from supplying a market through exports to supplying through a manufacturing plant in the market's country also has to rethink its component sourcing decisions. New choices must be made because of tariffs, transportation costs, lower costs from local supply sources, and greater familiarity with new local-supplier capabilities.

Several variables affect global sourcing decisions:

* Tariff and non-tariff barriers

* Nationality of the parent multinational

* Stage of the product in the product life cycle

* Exchange rate

* Transportation costs

* Production costs

* Growth of sales in the local market

* Profitability in the local market

Thus, firms will be motivated to begin local sourcing in a foreign manufacturing facility because of high tariff barriers; mature products or components; an appreciating exchange rate in the parent country; high transportation costs; low local-market production costs; and an attractive local market, as reflected in growth rates and profitability. However, manufacturers are likely to continue supplying foreign facilities with products made in their primary facilities for components that require specialized assets, such as proprietary software or machinery. Overall, technology intensity—measured by the levels of R&D spending—affects the transfer of equipment and components between units of a multinational firm.

Global Sourcing and the Supply Chain

As seen from the earlier discussion, supply chain issues have an important impact on global sourcing decisions. Products may be manufactured overseas at a lower per-unit cost, but if the logistics costs are not sufficiently low, the overall costs may not be lower. Thus, when companies analyze their global sourcing options, they must do so within the context of their supply chain.

Trends in the past couple of decades have favored global sourcing. An important trend has been lower overall international transportation costs mostly due to the ever-increasing size of ocean container ships. The largest of these ships can hold as many as 9,000 20-foot containers or their equivalent.[12] This would mean nearly ten million cubic feet of freight on a single ship. A second trend has been lower import tariffs mostly driven by ongoing trade negotiation within the World Trade Organization (WTO), as discussed in Chapter 2, and the

The use of container ships has helped reduced international transportation costs

many bilateral trade agreements between countries. Lower transportation costs and tariffs mean more and more products can be sourced globally that otherwise would not have been cost effective.

Global sourcing is not without its challenges, however. A clear example is the disruption in automobile manufacturing after the March 2011 earthquake and tsunami in Japan. Manufacturers that relied on auto parts made in Japan and with no other immediate source of supply found they had to dramatically reduce automobile production. A good example was Toyota, which was forced to reduced its worldwide production capacity by 60 percent. Competitors took notice and raised prices in anticipation of the decreased projected supply of autos.[13] The Toyota experience is a good illustration of the risks of global sourcing.

Quality and product safety are other examples of issues associated with global sourcing and a firm's supply chain. The toy industry has been fraught with product safety concerns relating to products made in China. Well-known toy manufacturers have had to recall products, including Easy-Bake Ovens from Hasbro and wooden train sets from Thomas & Friends. The recalls have led to parents expressing frustration and wishing government regulators would do more to ensure children's safety.[14]

Notwithstanding concerns, the need to remain competitive will continue to drive companies to source globally. The key is to use best practices and remain vigilant over supply chain issues, including supplier relationships, and maintain strict oversight of quality and safety issues.

Distribution and Warehousing

distribution

The sum of activities that move products from a firm to its customers.

Distribution is the sum of activities that move products from a firm to its customers. At its core, distribution is about transporting and storing products. The structure of distribution within companies varies by industry. For a manufacturer of consumer products, the distribution model will be highly focused on the consumer, ensuring the firm's products are available for purchase when and where they are needed. The distribution system must react quickly to demand changes such as a large snow storm dramatically increasing the immediate demand for snow blowers. Companies in the consumer products industry must also take into account their retail structure, which may have hundreds or even thousands of stores that need supplying.

Distribution for industrial product manufacturers may look very different. It is likely focused on fewer customers that may have a long order lead time. Boeing knows its production schedule months and even years ahead because airlines place their orders much in advance of their actual delivery. Industrial product manufacturers may also have closer communication with buyers to discuss demand expectations. Shipments of industrial products are likely grouped together, such as a hundred electrical components being shipped to an assembly plant.

However, these distinctions are generalizations and will not apply to all companies. Indeed, distribution within firms may look different between competitors within the same industry. The challenge of effective distribution is essentially the same regardless of the structure: how to maximize the effectiveness of a firm's distribution system in meeting customer needs while remaining cost competitive. This need has led to an important trend in distribution: flatter distribution networks. Increasingly, companies are removing layers in their distribution channel. In the past, a product might go through to multiple locations such as manufacturer to wholesaler to distributor to retail store to consumer. Today, manufacturer direct to consumer is not uncommon, such as Dell's strong reliance on direct consumer computer sales and L. L. Bean's extensive direct-purchase website for clothing.

Firms are increasingly simplifying their supply chain by removing layers in their distribution channel. One means to do this is to cut the layers of distribution between the manufacturer and the consumer. In the flower industry, the traditional supply chain starts with the grower who sells the flowers to a wholesaler who sells the flowers to distributors who sell the flowers to retailers (e.g., florists or grocery stores) who sell them to the final customer. This process is costly because each level in the supply chain earns a profit on the sale of the flowers, but it is also quite lengthy for a perishable product with a limited shelf life.

ProFlowers has modified this traditional supply chain to provide only a single intermediary (ProFlowers) between the growers and the end consumers. When a customer orders flowers at ProFlowers.com, the order is routed to a grower who ships the products directly to the consumer via a third-party logistics provider such as FedEx or UPS. One major challenge is keeping the products cold, causing ProFlowers to call this the "cold chain"—a system of refrigerated warehouses and trucks as well as boxes that can have cold air blown into them.[15]

To be successful, ProFlowers has to develop and cultivate relationships with growers, not just in the United States but all around the world. For example, the company works with tulip growers in the Netherlands and rose growers throughout South America. In addition to developing worldwide relationships with growers, ProFlowers focuses on ensuring that growers maintain proper environmental and labor standards. For example, ProFlowers states that its growers provide to their employees earnings above minimum wage; reasonable working hours; and sometimes transportation to and from work and healthy, no-cost meals. ProFlowers ensures these standards are met through regular audits of farms that grow flowers for the company.[16]

In addition to the challenges of sourcing worldwide, ProFlowers also sells globally. While in the United States third-party logistics providers such as UPS can deliver to almost any door, delivery providers vary significantly by country. In some cases, this has caused ProFlowers to alter its delivery policy from a specific date to a window of within two days of the promised delivery date. Further, in some countries, ProFlowers requires the recipient to be home at the time of delivery.

ProFlowers: Global Sourcing, Distribution, and Sales

Dell and L. L. Bean are good examples of the challenge for a firm as it grows internationally. The distribution strategy in the home market may not be as effective in an international market. Direct computer sales rely on affordable, reliable, and efficient methods to track shipping such as offered by FedEx and UPS within the United States. Although both companies have expanded internationally, the affordability and depth-of-delivery network are not yet comparable in all international markets. Companies that otherwise depend on such distribution strategies may find they need to adapt that strategy for particular international markets. See "ProFlowers: Global Sourcing, Distribution, and Sales" for another example.

Warehousing is storing materials or products in one location for further distribution at a later date. Warehousing is a critical tool in distribution because it allows consolidation of products in larger shipments to be broken down later for smaller shipments. Going back to the snow blower example, the manufacturer could position quantities of snow blowers in warehouses throughout key regional cities generally affected by snow. These initial shipments might be made

warehousing

The storing of materials or products in one location for further distribution at a later date.

••• Cross-Docking at Office Depot

There is a trend to avoid the reliance on warehousing through the use of **cross-docking**—moving products immediately from one delivery vehicle at a logistics facility to another vehicle in the same facility that will then take the products directly to a retail store (or even consumer). Use of cross-docking eliminates the intermediate step of warehousing. The term comes from the concept that multiple trucks or delivery vans would be "docked," or parked along a long series of docks, and then the products are placed in the appropriate truck depending on its destination.

Office Depot is the world's largest office supply company with 1,600 retail stores and annual sales of over $12 billion.[17] It uses cross-docking to help keep its stores stocked on an as-needed basis while minimizing freight costs and shipping delays. It operates a cross-dock facility in Jackson, Mississippi, which serves 74 stores in Mississippi, Louisiana, Arkansas, Tennessee, and the Florida panhandle.[18] The facility allows for shipments to be received and then

quickly moved (or "crossed over") to the appropriate dock for the particular retail store. Use of technology means each store knows what to expect with each shipment before the shipment actually arrives.

The use of cross-docking helps eliminate the need for warehousing and lowers supply chain costs.

cross-docking

Moving products immediately from one delivery vehicle at a logistics facility to another vehicle in the same facility that will then take the products directly to a retail store or to the buyer. Use of cross-docking eliminates the intermediate step of warehousing.

by a single full truck of snow blowers, making the per product shipping costs relatively affordable. Then, depending on where a storm hits, the warehouse would direct the snow blowers to specific stores on a weekly or even daily basis. Though these shipments may not be full truckloads, and therefore at a higher shipping cost per unit, this tool offers flexibility to ensure the snow blowers get to the stores that need them most during a specific time period. (See "Cross-Docking at Office Depot" for a trend away from warehousing.)

Internationally, warehousing can be critical. Shipping small quantities of a product would be expensive, especially if the overall value is not very high versus weight. (Imagine sending snow blowers for consumer use by international air: The cost per unit would be higher than the snow blower itself.) To lower overall freight costs, manufacturers would ship one or more containers of products via ocean. The products would then be stored in an overseas warehouse and later shipped to distributors, retail stores, or consumers. For international firms, selecting the location of such warehouses can be challenging. A firm might choose to have multiple warehouses within a market (country or region) to keep transit times low for shipments from the warehouse to the buyer or retail store. But this also increases costs.

Figure 11-2 highlights this issue. The left scenario shows the use of a single warehouse to serve both France and Germany. Using a single warehouse saves on warehouse costs because only one location is involved. But it would need to be located either in France or Germany, which increases shipment distances and delivery times. The alternative approach is to locate warehouses in both France and Germany, placing them closer to each country's stores. This option lowers shipping distances and delivery times. But which option is overall less expensive? There is no easy answer because the choice depends on the location of the proposed warehouses, location of retail stores, frequency of shipments, and logistics costs. Companies must also balance customer needs: Are sales at risk if the supply chain is not able to respond immediately? This is why 3PL companies offer technologies and solutions to address this dilemma. (See Case 11.1,

Figure 11-2 • Alternative European Warehouse Scenarios

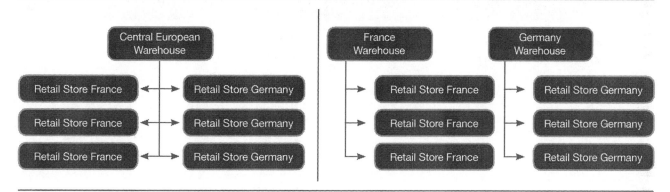

"UPS Logistics Technology and MobileCast®.") For the international marketing manager, it is important to recognize that supply chain decisions will impact marketing efforts.

International Documentation and Compliance

Part of the task of effective supply chain management is to ensure international shipments have the proper documents and are compliant with the appropriate government regulations. The international marketing department plays a critical role in both tasks. The international sales department is likely the first step in ensuring whether the potential sale is allowable under local export laws. The sales department also creates many of the required documents, such as the commercial invoice. Knowing the basic purpose of international documents is important to ensure a firm provides accurate international documentation and complies with the associated laws.

International Documentation

Not all international shipments use the same documents. However, two documents are almost always included: the commercial invoice and bill of lading. For shipments with multiple products, a packing list is typically also included.

COMMERCIAL INVOICE

The **commercial invoice** is a critical document for international shipments. The document is created by the company selling the goods to confirm to the buyer the sales price and payment terms of the shipment. (See "Common Elements of a Commercial Invoice" for a listing of the types of information included.) It is also the document the importing country will use to determine value for the purposes of any applicable tariffs and taxes. Often the commercial invoice is accompanied by a **packing list**—a document that details each product included with the shipment and which box.

BILLS OF LADING

A **bill of lading** is issued by the transportation carrier. It serves as a receipt for the shipment, a contract for the transportation, and as a document of title (ownership). When used for ocean-going shipments, the document is called the ocean bill of lading. When used with air shipments, it is called the air waybill. Bills of lading are particularly important if the payment method is a letter of credit or documentary collection (see Chapter 12) because these payment methods use the bill of lading to endorse ownership of the shipment from party to party (such as a bank to the final buyer).

---

commercial invoice

A shipping document issued by the seller identifying key sales information, including the buyer, products or services sold, payment terms, shipping date, mode of transport, and prices.

packing list

A shipping document that details each product included with a shipment and in which box.

bill of lading

A shipping document issued by the freight carrier (shipping company) that acts as a receipt for the cargo, contract for the transport of the cargo, and as a document of ownership (title).

••• Common Elements of a Commercial Invoice

1. Name and address of the buyer
2. Name and address of the seller
3. Name and address of the consignee
4. Marks (wording on the outside of boxes)
5. Invoice number
6. Date
7. Name and address of the notify party (the company to be notified when the shipment arrives—generally, the buyer)
8. Date shipped
9. Transportation details (This section should actually include a number of details regarding the mode of transportation, including carrier, vessel, voyage number, and bill of lading [for ocean]; air carrier and air waybill number [for air].)
10. Terms of sale, including Incoterm
11. Quantity and description of the goods
12. Unit price
13. Extended price
14. Manufacturer's or producer's name and address
15. Gross and net weights of packages or units
16. Total cubic measurements and individual measure of each package or unit
17. Country of origin of goods
18. Reference to letter of credit, if required
19. Certification statement
20. Signature (Make copies first and then sign each individually.)[19]

OTHER INTERNATIONAL DOCUMENTS

Numerous other documents may be included or required for an international shipment:

---

quotation

A document issued by a seller to a potential buyer to confirm the cost of a product.

---

pro forma invoice

A document issued before shipment to confirm sales information that will later be contained on the commercial invoice.

---

certificate of origin (COO)

A document most generally issued by a manufacturer to confirm the country of origin of a product.

---

insurance certificate

A shipping document issued by the seller, an insurance company, or a freight forwarder to confirm insurance was obtained for the shipment.

---

electronic export information (EEI)

A U.S. electronic form completed by the exporter; it contains basic information about the shipment, including the shipper, products, values, buyer, and country of destination.

- **Quotation.** This is often the first document used. A quotation is issued by a seller to a potential buyer to confirm cost of a product. It may also include expected payment method and warranty information.

- **Pro Forma Invoice.** A pro forma invoice is essentially a preview copy of the commercial invoice—meaning it contains much of the same information but is not the actual commercial invoice. It is most commonly requested by foreign buyers either to obtain an import license from their local government or to open a letter of credit (see Chapter 12).

- **Certificate of Origin (COO).** Certificates of origin are often required to confirm the country of origin of the products. They are mandated for some shipments between countries within a free trade agreement. For example, the NAFTA Certificate of Origin is required for shipments between the United States, Canada, and Mexico that qualify for duty-free status. When a COO is not required, the commercial invoice would include a statement confirming the country of origin for each product.

- **Insurance Certificate.** This certificate may be issued by the seller, an insurance company, or a freight forwarder to confirm insurance was obtained for the shipment.

- **Electronic Export Information (EEI).** The EEI is a U.S. data file required to be completed for any shipment in which the value of a particular commodity is $2,500 or more. It contains basic information about the export, including the shipper, products, values, buyer, and country of destination. The EEI was formerly known as the Shippers Export Declaration. The EEI is filed online through the government website AES Direct (www.aesdirect .gov). Other governments have similar regulations, such as the Canadian Automated Export Declaration (CAED). These export data files are used both to maintain export trade statistics and for export compliance regulations as discussed in the next section.

Incoterms

Related to the topic of international documents are **Incoterms**—a set of 11 transportation-related terms used worldwide in sales contracts. Incoterms are developed and issued by the International Chamber of Commerce (ICC) in Paris, with the latest version known as Incoterms 2010. Incoterms identify the specific responsibilities of the seller and the buyer so that each accepts its role in the international transaction. Examples of responsibilities assigned by each term to either the seller or buyer would be clearing goods for export, arranging international freight and insurance, clearing goods for import, paying import duties, and arranging freight from the import location (city or port) to its final destination. International sales quotes and invoices should use Incoterms to avoid confusion or, worse, legal disputes. All Incoterms are a three-letter code and are followed by a named place. For example, "FCA Chicago O'Hare Airport" illustrates the use of the Incoterm "FCA"—meaning "free (to) carrier." The responsibility of the seller is to get the goods, cleared for export, from its premises to Chicago O'Hare International Airport. The responsibility of the buyer is for all other activities after that point, including the international air freight, importation into the foreign country, and all duties and taxes. In contrast, "DDP London" uses the Incoterm "DDP"—meaning "delivered duty paid." In this case, the seller has all responsibilities for the international freight and insurance, and the buyer has none. (For more details on Incoterms, including training videos, visit Global Edge Resource Desk at http://globaledge.msu.edu/resourcedesk.)

> **incoterms**
>
> A set of 11 transportation-related terms issued by the International Chamber of Commerce (ICC) and used worldwide in sales contracts. Incoterms identify the specific responsibilities of the seller and the buyer so that each accepts its role in the international transaction.

Compliance with Export Controls

The U.S. government has a number of agencies that control the export of products. They include the U.S. Department of Commerce and its Bureau of Industry and Security (BIS), which controls the export of products that could threaten U.S. security. Another is the U.S. Department of the Treasury, which enforces U.S. economic and trade sanctions. (See "Export Controls" in Chapter 3 for a more complete list.) Other countries have similar regulations, such as the European Union's Community General Export Authorisation (CGEA), which controls the export of dual-use products similar to the BIS.

Guns fall within U.S. export controls. Exporters must receive an export license prior to any exports of guns.

The purpose of export control regulations is to promote national security as well as cooperation between countries to combat terrorism, drug cartels, nuclear proliferation, and weapons of mass destruction. Violating export compliance regulations can be costly and even result in criminal charges leading to imprisonment. (See Case 3.2, "U.S. Export Controls.)

It is important to remember export controls are not necessarily the absolute prohibition on export of a particular product. The purpose of export controls is that, when required, the government is notified of the potential shipment, and the exporter receives authorization to ship. This authorization is done via an **export license**—approval by the federal government to make a shipment in cases where either the product is under export controls, or the buyer must be approved prior to shipment. Clearly, some exports will not be approved, such as exporting to an embargoed country. But in other cases, after the potential shipment has been approved, the export will receive an export license and may proceed with the shipment.

Effective export compliance means companies must be aware of the appropriate export controls and train staff to be directly involved in ensuring compliance. As seen from Case 3.2, ignorance of the law is not an excuse. To ensure compliance, companies may develop trade compliance procedures and manuals to document the proper handling of trade transactions. Larger companies

> **export license**
>
> Permission by the U.S. government for a company to make a shipment or shipments to a foreign buyer that otherwise would be illegal without the license. Export licenses are not required for all shipments but are required if the product or the foreign buyer is subject to export controls.

would assign compliance responsibilities to an individual or an entire department. In fact, "trade compliance officer" is a fast-growing career segment in international business. The International Compliance Professionals Association (www.icpainc.org) is an organization of over 1,500 individuals focused on best practices, training, and networking among the trade compliance community.

Supply Chain and the International Marketing Mix

Supply chain management also includes product and customer service issues such as packaging, labeling, and warranties. This section discusses these issues.

Packaging

As discussed in Chapter 10 regarding the marketing mix and promotion, packaging is an important part of a product's attributes. Companies expend considerable effort developing packaging that is recognizable and distinctive, as well as functional. Following are some examples of factors that require packaging adaptation:

- Changes in climate across countries require more protective packaging against extremes of cold and heat.
- Lengthy, difficult transportation and logistics networks require that packaging protect goods against breakage and damage.
- Lengthy periods on retailers' shelves before final sale require that packaging be protective and maintain freshness.

- Varying sizes of packaging are needed, with smaller sized packages required in lower-income countries to make the products more affordable. Smaller size may also be common in countries where frequent shopping trips are made and shoppers carry their purchases on foot back to their dwellings.
- Differences in packaging are needed because of consumer preferences; for example, toothpaste sold in squeeze tubes versus upright cans and fruit juices packaged in glass containers versus cardboard boxes.
- Utilization of standard packaging helps a product be recognized, such as Heineken's "keg" cans.
- With a growing environmental consciousness on the part of consumers, purchasers attempt to persuade firms to use biodegradable and/or recyclable packaging materials that cause the least harm to the environment.

Packaging adds bulk to a product and takes up more space during shipment. It might be more economical to ship the products in bulk and package them upon arrival at the destination markets. These would be supply chain decisions. Whether that practice is feasible depends on the capabilities of the local packaging industry, particularly in terms of quality, use of advanced-technology packaging and printing processes, cost and timely delivery, and availability of quality materials. 3PL providers are another option because many provide outsourced packing services.

Labeling

International labeling decisions go much further than simply translating labels. Regulations in many countries require that detailed product composition and nutritional information be provided. Also required are warning messages for products that may be harmful or hazardous. Firms may also want to provide instructions for the proper use of a product, in which case readability and quality of communication matter. Merely translating text from the home country's language may not be sufficient. Country regulations may require that information be presented in all of a country's or region's official languages. In Europe, this means compressing information in small type on the exterior of packages or including an insert with detailed information and instructions inside packages. This information is necessary for products such as consumer electronics devices, tools, pharmaceuticals, and food products. In those cases, the manufacturer wants to communicate detailed information about setup, energy consumption levels, recommended dosages, and recipes. Language complexities lead manufacturers to use icons, diagrams, and cartoons to instruct consumers in the use of their products. Those pictorial descriptions transcend language and make it easier for firms to introduce products into new markets.

There are a number of resources to find the labeling requirements for local market packaging. The Country Commercial Guide at www.export.gov is one source. Another is Global Edge at http://globaledge.msu.edu. Two private sector sources are the Bureau of National Affairs (www.bna.com) and the *Dun & Bradstreet Exporters' Encyclopedia*.

Warranty and Service Policies

When customers buy products, they are purchasing a specific use, function, and performance as much as image and status. With products that have a clear function or utility (such as washing machines, hair dryers, hiking boots, and cars), customers want reassurances that the products will work as promised. As discussed in Chapter 9, companies seek to standardize or adapt their products depending on local needs. Companies must make a similar decision with regards to warranty and service policies. This involves an important question: Do firms offer the same warranty worldwide or change the terms of the warranty for specific countries or regions? A related question is that of matching or exceeding the competition: Should warranties be used as a differentiating factor in gaining market share against the competition? Should warranties be used to overcome other product attributes that may hinder international market share, such as a negative country-of-origin effect?

STANDARDIZATION

Several conditions encourage the standardization of warranties, as follows:

- Multinational customers may not accept warranties with lower standards compared to warranties they receive in other, perhaps more advanced, industrial markets.

- Goods purchased in one market may be used elsewhere. For example, cars purchased in Germany are often driven across Europe. If different levels of warranty exist in different European countries, customers may decide to switch models.

- Some products affect human health and safety, such as aircraft, pharmaceutical drugs, and food products. In these cases, for ethical reasons, a firm cannot justify offering a lower level of warranty.

When a firm offers standardized products worldwide, warranty standardization is likely to follow.

LOCALIZATION

Warranties may be adapted to different local markets in several cases:

- Competition is weak, and firms do not feel pressure to incur the additional costs that a standardized warranty policy might entail. This is likely in near-monopoly markets. Examples involve travel policies and denied boarding compensation to passengers on foreign routes with little competition.

- When multiple sources of production exist, different quality levels may make offering uniform warranties difficult. This reflects a weak response to a flaw in a firm's sourcing policies, however.

- A product may fail sooner because it is used differently. Warranties may be adapted to make allowances for such use. For example, warranties differ for cars used as taxicabs compared to cars used as private vehicles.

- A lack of an international service network can make meeting warranty promises difficult. Cutting warranties in this case would be an inadequate response. A preferable approach would be to build up service capabilities worldwide so that uniform warranty policies could be offered and met.

Stronger warranties may be offered in markets in which a firm is new. This may be done to overcome customer unfamiliarity with the product and to build an installed base and market share against entrenched incumbents. The higher warranty levels would typically revert to the worldwide norm after an introductory period.

After-Sales Service

Whereas warranties represent the front end of a marketing promise with customers, the ability to follow up and deliver on the implied warranty promise is facilitated by a company's after-sales service network. Thus, a strong level of consistency must exist between a company's warranty policies and its worldwide after-sales service network. Building that network requires choosing locations from which to offer the service; investing in physical facilities, equipment, and parts; staffing and training qualified service technicians; and instituting a logistics and information network to keep track of service performance and customer complaints so that they are handled in a satisfactory manner.

After-sales service is an important supply chain issue. Caterpillar promises to get replacement parts to international customers quickly to decrease equipment down-time.

Providing and proving the existence of a service capability may ensure that a firm wins new clients in overseas markets in industrial product settings. Clients worry, justifiably, about committing resources and critical processes to products from a distant supplier with an unproven record in the marketplace. Caterpillar has built up a strong international market position by promising to deliver service parts within 48 hours anywhere in the world. That promise is appreciated by users of expensive earth-moving equipment, for whom equipment failure can mean being late in completing a project—the result being serious negative financial consequences.

A central issue here is goal congruence. Are distributors interested in investing the necessary capital for building up a strong service network, or are they interested in short-term sales gains before moving on to the next hot product? Given distributors' capital shortages and lower commitments to long-term market share, firms may have to offer their distributors both financial and technical support to ensure a high level of service capability. That support could include carrying a supply of parts to ship to distributors, as needed, or offering ongoing training to a distributor's service personnel at the firm's expense.

Offering ongoing training raises practical questions such as where to conduct the training, how often to conduct it, how to ensure effective training, in what language to offer the training, whether to use online computer-based support to service personnel in distant locations, and whether to offer incentives to enhance motivation and quality of the service personnel. Offering efficient service does not mean maintaining multiple service sites in every major market and city, however. Using operations research techniques and modeling the demand for services, multinational firms can develop optimal configurations of parts depots, service centers, and levels of staff. Doing so ensures that targeted service efficiency levels can be met for a minimum investment while high levels of customer satisfaction are maintained. An interesting development is the offering of graded service plans to customers. Clients can choose the level of service they want, with higher charges accompanying higher levels of service. That practice is illustrated by the computer software business. "Basic service" may mean a few free hours followed by a per-minute charge for phone consultation. "Total service" may mean a blanket lump-sum, fee-based, year-round, onsite service for all of a firm's users and all of its installed bases of computers. The difficulty is striking a balance between offering the requisite level of service to stay competitive and keep customers and offering higher levels of fee-based services for customers who use a product or service more intensively and see economic value in paying for premium service.

SUMMARY

A firm's supply chain is composed of all the activities related to moving goods from their source (raw materials, components) to the final consumer (finished goods). They include purchasing (raw materials, components, perhaps even finished products), manufacturing (full manufacturing, assembly), logistics (transportation, warehousing, tracking of goods), the supply of goods to the sales channel (distributors, retailers, end users), and reverse logistics.

Supply chain management is the management of all the events within a firm's supply chain. It includes a range of strategic decisions companies must make to ensure its supply chain becomes a competitive advantage—not simply a cost area that needs management.

As a company expands globally, supply chain management becomes even more complex. The whole of the global business environment contributes to a more challenging supply chain management task for a global firm.

The range of strategic decisions a firm would make in managing its supply chain include the number of suppliers, location of production, which transportation options to use, how to warehouse, how to leverage technology, whether to outsource or use in-house activities, how to manage delivery times, the choice between long-term versus short-term needs, and how to remain compliant with government regulations.

Third-party logistics (3PL) is the use of companies to outsource specific functions of supply chain management. Examples of these functions include transportation, warehousing, packaging, customer support, warranty repairs, consulting, technology solutions, and cost control.

Global sourcing decisions tend to be driven by two fundamental decisions: (1) Companies manufacturing products in a country must continually decide whether to procure raw materials or components from the home market where the plant is located or from another country in order to lower costs while maintaining quality; and (2) companies that have established foreign manufacturing facilities either need to supply those facilities with raw material and components from their home market or source them in the country or region where the foreign facilities are located.

Factors that affect global sourcing decisions include tariffs and non-tariff barriers, transportation costs, production costs, local market conditions, and overall profitability.

Lower transportation costs and tariffs mean more and more products can be sourced globally that otherwise would not have been cost effective.

Distribution is the sum of activities that move products from a firm to its customers. At its core, distribution is about transporting and storing products. The structure of distribution within companies varies by industries.

Warehousing is storing materials or products in one location for further distribution at a later date. Use of warehousing is a critical tool in distribution because it allows the consolidation of products in larger shipments to be broken down later for smaller shipments.

Companies must ensure international shipments have the proper documents and are compliant with the appropriate government regulations. The commercial invoice is a critical document. It is created by the company selling the goods to confirm to the buyer the sales price and payment terms of the shipment. A bill of lading is issued by the transportation carrier. It serves as a receipt for the shipment, a contract for the transportation, and as a document of title (ownership).

Other international documents include the quotation, pro forma invoice, certificate of origin, insurance certificate, and Electronic Export Information (EEI) record.

Incoterms are a set of 11 transportation-related terms used worldwide in sales contracts. Incoterms are developed and issued by the International Chamber of Commerce (ICC) in Paris.

The purpose of export control regulations is to promote national security as well as cooperation between countries to combat terrorism, drug cartels, nuclear proliferation, and weapons of mass destruction. Violating export compliance regulations can be costly and even result in criminal charges leading to imprisonment.

Companies may need to adapt their product packaging for a number or reasons, including climate, long transport times and distances, long periods of time on retail shelves, varying needs in terms of packing size, consumer preferences, and the growing concern about green issues.

Product labeling for international markets is more than just language translation. It includes meeting government labeling disclosure requirements, warnings, and usage issues. Companies often use icons, diagrams, or cartoons to go beyond language barriers.

Companies must decide to standardize or localize warranty and service policies. Factors encouraging standardization include whether the goods are used in multiple countries and if they affect human health and safety. Factors that encourage localization include having multiple sources of production and differing levels of quality or different uses for products between markets.

Firms must decide whether to offer the international service capability themselves, offer it through their distributors and agents, or contract it to independent third parties. Given distributors' capital shortages and lower commitments to long-term market share, firms may have to offer their distributors both financial and technical support to ensure a high level of service capability.

KEY TERMS

bill of lading	distribution	insurance certificate	supply chain management
Certificate of Origin (COO)	Electronic Export Information (EEI)	packing list	third-party logistics (3PL)
commercial invoice	export license	pro forma invoice	warehousing
cross-docking	freight forwarders	quotation	
	Incoterms	reverse logistics	
		supply chain	

NASBITE CGBP TOPICS COVERED IN THIS CHAPTER

Note: For full details of the alignment of each chapter with the NASBITE CGBP, be sure to review the information provided in the section "Studying for the NASBITE CGBP Exam."

CGBP Rubric	Topic
01/06/01:	export license compliance
02/06/05:	where to find packaging, labeling, and marketing requirements
02/06/06:	after-sales service and support requirements (e.g., manuals, warranties, technical support, recycling)
02/06/07:	product liability implications
03/01/01:	all transportation modes and costs
03/01/09:	resources (freight forwarders)
03/02/02:	third-party logistics providers (3PLs)
03/03/01:	standard export and import documents for goods and services (e.g., pro forma invoice, commercial invoice, transport documents, documents relating to services contracts)
03/03/02:	U.S. export regulations for involved countries and seller-buyer document requirements
03/03/03:	U.S. import regulations and sources for involved countries (e.g., Bureau of Industry and Security)
03/03/04:	Incoterms
03/03/05:	U.S. legal and regulatory requirements regarding documentation for goods/services (e.g., export/import control regulations, export declaration)
03/03/06:	where to find foreign language documentation requirements when applicable
03/05/01:	advantages of global sourcing

QUESTIONS AND RESEARCH

1. What is a firm's supply chain?

2. What is supply chain management, and what is its role in supporting the competitiveness of a firm?

3. What are key supply chain decisions? Pick two and discuss the implication for the international marketing manager.

4. What would be the likely transportation mode for Rolex watches? Why? How would the transportation decisions of Rolex be different from those for Evian and its water?

5. How would a firm use the services of a 3PL provider internationally?

6. What variables affect global sourcing decisions? Pick a well-known multinational company and assume it is operating in a foreign country. How would the variables affecting global sourcing affect that firm?

7. Refer to Figure 11-2. What are the implications from that figure? How might a firm decide between either scenario?

8. What is the purpose of the commercial invoice in an international transaction?

9. What are bills of lading, and how are they used?

10. What is the EEI? When is it required?

11. Discuss the statement "A product covered by export controls may still be exported."

12. What are examples of factors that impact packaging and labeling in international markets?

13. How might a firm decide between having standardized warranty and service policies versus localized policies?

CHAPTER 11 TEAM PROJECT ASSIGNMENT: Supply Chain Management

This chapter discusses supply chain management and its impact on a firm's international expansion. Depending on your client, these issues may be of significant concern. For your team project, discuss which of the key issues in this chapter will most impact your client as it expands internationally. Specifically, address the following questions:

1. How can your client use best practices in supply chain management to be more competitive internationally?

2. What role might 3PL providers have to support your client?

3. How important will global sourcing be for your client?

4. What role will distribution and warehousing play in supporting the global activities?

5. Are there packaging, labeling, warranty and service policy, or after-sales service issues that may have an important effect on your client?

CASE 11.1 UPS Logistics Technology and MobileCast ®

UPS is well known as the company with all the brown trucks delivering packages around the world. In fact, the color brown it uses is trademarked! Founded in 1907, UPS is now the world's largest package delivery company with operations in over 200 countries. UPS is also a third-party logistics company (3PL) that offers a number of services and technologies to help other companies increase the effectiveness of their supply chain. Through its UPS Logistics Technology division, UPS offers a range of products and services focused on supply chain challenges. Customers include Frito-Lay Corporation, Häagen-Dazs, and Nestlé. An example of these technologies is the MobileCast® product family. Using cell phones or handheld devices with Global Positioning System (GPS) capabilities, companies can keep track of where their vehicles are and can record precise arrival and departure times. The information is captured on the MobileCast service—essentially a centralized database accessible by the companies using the technology. This allows companies to monitor all pickup or delivery routes with real-time, up-to-the-minute updates.

UPS promotes a number of benefits from using MobileCast technology:

- **Real-time route execution.** This capability shows how effective the delivery network is with actual versus planned data, plus customer arrival and departure times.

- **Increase driver productivity.** Because the system uses GPS tracking, companies obtain reliable data to track driver activity.

- **Manager by exception.** This capability allows a dispatcher to handle interruptions in the planned delivery schedule.

- **Proactive customer service.** By having real-time delivery status, companies can update customers ahead of time should there be any anticipated disruptions or changes in delivery.

- **Automatic integration.** The data collected through the MobileCast technology can be integrated into a firm's management information system for better decision making.

- **Management reports.** Companies can view reports of actual versus planned delivery activities, such as route exceptions and driver performance.

A number of industries rely on daily delivery of products to retail stores or consumers. Beer distributors are an example. Daily, drivers make numerous stops, picking up and dropping off products. Distributors need to effectively manage this process or risk becoming less competitive either due to high costs or lack of customer service.

Tucson-based Golden Eagle Distributors realized that developing the delivery-tracking capability in-house would be too expensive and likely not represent the latest technology, so the company adopted the MobileCast technology for its 26 trucks and 14 vans. Overall, it calculates the cost savings of outsourcing the technology to UPS at $100,000. In addition, the company eliminated one sales position and canceled two vehicle leases—mostly due to the 10 to 12 percent reduction in mileage driven.

Associated Food Stores provides another example. Headquartered in Salt Lake City, the company delivers groceries to 600 stores throughout the Midwest. The company had already implemented a freight-tracking/routing system but recognized its complexity was a challenge to getting the most efficiency. The older system was replaced with solutions from UPS, resulting in the elimination of two to three daily routes and an overall reduction of 400,000 miles. The company's on-time performance was improved to 96 percent. Associated Food Stores combined the MobileCast technology with other UPS technologies including Roadnet (a vehicle-routing planner) and Territory Planner (a "what-if" scenario planner) to optimize delivery routes.

UPS has taken its technology global for international customers. Over 14 countries within Central and Latin America offer the MobileCast technology, as do many in the Asia-Pacific region. Europe and the Middle East also have access to the technology, including the GPS-enabled solutions. The applications have been translated for easier use by non-English-speaking customers into 15 languages, including Spanish, German, Arabic, and Simplified Chinese. The MobileCast technology portfolio joins other UPS global supply chain solutions, including warehousing, warranty returns, customs brokerage, and distribution support.

Source: www.ups.com.

Questions and Research

1. What problems did UPS address in creating the MobileCast technology?
2. Visit www.ups.com and navigate to the UPS Logistics Technologies website. What are other examples of companies using the MoblieCast technology? How has the technology assisted with their supply chain management?
3. Using the preceding website, research the Roadnet and Territory Planner solutions. What services do they provide? How would a company use the technology in support of its supply chain?
4. Visit www.ups.com and navigate to the business solutions international trade section. Research the Distribution Center Bypass and UPS World Ease services. How would an international company use these services to improve its supply chain?
5. How do the examples from UPS illustrate the concepts discussed in this chapter?
6. UPS is not alone in providing these types of technologies and services. Find another 3PL provider. Research its products and services to compete with UPS. How are their services similar? How are they different?

NOTES

1. R. F. Maruca. "The Right Way to Go Global: An Interview with Whirlpool CEO David Whitman," *Harvard Business Review* 72, no. 2 (March–April 1994): 124–136.

2. Theodore P. Stank, Beth R. Davis, and Brian S. Fugate. "A Strategic Framework for Supply Chain Oriented Logistics," *Journal of Business Logistics* 26, no. 2 (2005): 27–45.

3. For further discussions of this company-wide involvement in the supply chain, see J. B. Houlihan. "International Supply Chain Management," *International Journal of Physical Distribution and Materials Management* 15, no. 1 (1985): 22–28.

4. Jennifer Shang, Pandu R. Tadikamalla, Laurie J. Kirsch, and Lawrence Brown. "A Decision Support System for Managing Inventory at GlaxoSmithKline," *Decision Support Systems* 46, no. 1 (2008): 1–13.

5. Shankar Ganesan, George Morris, Sandy Jap, Robert W. Palmatier, and Barton Weitz. "Supply Chain Management and Retailer Performance: Emerging Trends, Issues, and Implications for Research and Practice," *Journal of Retailing* 85, no. 1 (2009): 84–94.

6. Marguerite Reardon and Erica Ogg. "Preparing for iPhone 4 Launch Day (FAQ)." CNET News, June 23, 2010 (http://news.cnet.com/8301-30686_3-20008509-266.html), accessed May 5, 2011.

7. Apple Support Communities (https://discussions.apple.com/index.jspa), accessed May 5, 2011.

8. Steve Kovach. "From China with Love: What Your iPhone Went Through to Get to You," *Business Insider*, March 23, 2011 (http://www.businessinsider.com/from-china-with-love-what-your-iphone-went-through-to-get-to-you-2010-11), accessed May 5, 2011.

9. Fujun Lai, Dahui Li, Qiang Wang, and Xiande Zhao. "The Informational Technology Capability of Third-Party Logistics Providers: A Resource-Based View and Empirical Evidence from China," *Journal of Supply Chain Management* 44, no. 3 (2008): 22–38.

10. Injazz J. Chen, Antony Paulraj, and Augustine A. Lado. "Strategic Purchasing, Supply Management, and Firm Performance," *Journal of Operations Management* 22, no. 5 (2004): 505–523.

11. Janet Y. Murray, Masaaki Kotabe, and Joe Nan Zhou. "Strategic Alliance-Based Sourcing and Market Performance: Evidence from Foreign Firms Operating in China," *Journal of International Business Studies* 36 (March 2005): 187–208; Masaaki Kotabe and K. S. Swan, "Offshore Sourcing: Reaction, Maturation, and Consolidation of U.S. Multinationals," *Journal of International Business Studies* 25, no. 1 (First Quarter 1994): 115–140; Jane Murray, M. Kotabe, and A. R. Wildt, "Strategic and Financial Performance Implications of Global Sourcing Strategy: A Contingency Analysis," *Journal of International Business Studies* 26, no. 1 (1995): 181–202; P. Swamidass and M. Kotabe, "Component Sourcing Strategies of Multinationals: An Empirical Study of European and Japanese Multinationals," *Journal of International Business Studies* 24, no. 1 (1993): 81–99.

12. " World-wide Largest Container Ship 'XIN LOS ANGELES' Succeeded in Her Virgin Sailing to Tianjin," China Shipping Container Lines Co. Ltd corporate website (http://www.cscl.com.cn/ctrl/news/detail?id=060628004611), accessed April 29, 2011.

13. "Quake Still Rumbles for Carmakers; With Japanese Firms Hobbled, Price Tags Are Up and U.S. Rivals Seek to Grab Market Share," *Los Angeles Times*, April 27, 2011, Part B, p. 1.

14. "As More Toys Are Recalled, the Trail Ends in China," *New York Times*, June 19, 2007, Section A; p. 1.

15. Jane Roberts. "Valentine's Day—11th-Hour Flowers—Memphis is the 'Last Man Standing' in Dot-Com Floral Business." *The Commercial Appeal*, February 14, 2008, p. C1.

16. "Our Commitment to Ethical Labor Standards" (http://www.proflowers.com/EthicalLaborStandards.aspx), accessed May 5, 2011.

17. "About Office Depot," Office Depot Media Relations website (http://mediarelations.officedepot.com/), accessed May 2, 2011.

18. "Office Depot Expansion Brings Jobs to Jackson, MS," Office Depot Media Relations website (http://mediarelations.officedepot.com/phoenix.zhtml?c=140162&p=irol-newsArticle&ID=983815&highlight=), accessed May 2, 2011.

19. Information drawn from James F. Foley. *The Global Entrepreneur*, 2nd ed. (La Verne, TN: Jamric Press International, 1994), pp. 368–371.

12 International Pricing

This chapter examines price setting in international markets. International pricing is complex. It is influenced by differences in consumer behavior across markets, the strategic goals of a firm, competitive responses, a firm's cost structure and profit targets, and government regulation. Fluctuations in exchange rates further complicate the issues.

The main goals of this chapter are to ●●●

1. Establish a framework that covers the broad principles governing international pricing. Determine the influence on pricing of foreign market variables such as competition, government, inflation, local demand, and costs.

2. Discuss how a firm deals with the pressure to cut costs and prices caused by international competition.

3. Discuss international pricing strategies available to companies.

4. Discuss pressures for uniform pricing in international markets.

5. Discuss how fluctuations in exchange rate challenge international pricing decisions.

6. Explore the special roles and problems of transfer pricing in international marketing.

7. Compare payment method options that balance the risk between seller and buyer in international transactions.

8. Analyze the different types of foreign exchange risk and tools to mitigate those risks.

9. Explore the dimensions and implications of currency inconvertibility and the use of countertrade as a possible solution.

Factors in International Pricing

Pricing is part of the marketing mix. Therefore, pricing decisions must be integrated with other aspects of the marketing mix. Price is just one attribute of a product. Others include quality, reliability, features, technology, service, and user satisfaction. But it is not likely all attributes can be maximized and still remain price competitive. A product with the best possible quality, reliability, features, and so on, may not be price competitive. A trade-off between price and other product (or service) attributes must be made. The following factors must be considered when developing a firm's international pricing strategy:

* Relating price to a firm's costs and profit goals.

* Setting strategic objectives for a market and monitoring their influence on pricing. Examples would be market skimming versus market penetration strategies.

* Monitoring price-setting behavior by competitors and assessing their strategic objectives.

* Evaluating consumers' ability to buy in the various country markets.

* Understanding the product-specific factors that may affect pricing, including the product life-cycle stage. Generally, prices are reduced on mature products as they become more commodity-like and face increased competition.

* Recognizing differences in the country environment and their role in governing prices in each national market—factors such as differences in the legal and regulatory environment, the volatility of foreign exchange rates, market structure (especially distribution channels), and competitive environment.

* Analyzing the need to coordinate pricing in multiple foreign markets. This includes choosing between standardizing prices and charging different prices in different markets.

Each of those differences influences a firm's price-setting behavior in its markets.[1] As illustrated in Figure 12-1, three factors influence a firm's international pricing strategy: firm-level factors, market-specific factors, and product-specific factors. These factors in turn are used to help make international pricing decisions.

Firm-Level Factors

As a firm develops its international pricing strategy, an initial review should be made of factors specific to the firm. These factors include their strategic objectives, competitive pressures, and the firm's cost structures. They are discussed next.

Price, Strategic Objectives, and Competitive Pressures

Pricing affects demand, which affects sales. Hence, pricing is an influential tool in gaining market share. Or thinking in reverse, strategic objectives toward gaining market share determine pricing. Therefore, as market share and competitive positions differ from country to country, so do prices. A research study comparing U.S. and Korean price-setting practices considered market conditions and the importance of competitive position versus cost of goods sold in determining price. The study also considered how firm characteristics and export market characteristics, together with cost complexity, influenced pricing and,

Figure 12-1 • Framework for International Pricing Strategy

Firm Level Factors

Strategic Objectives and Competitive Pressures
Market Share, Profits
Marketing Mix Elements: Segmentation, Product Positioning

Cost Structure
Fixed Costs: Amortization of R&D, Manufacturing and Marketing Fixed Costs
Manufacturing Costs: Productivity, Experience Curve, Scale Economies
Marketing and Related Costs: Inventory Levels, Promotion and Service
Shipping/Distance Costs: packing, freight, tariffs
Firm's Target Price
Forecasted Sales Volume, Cost Allocation
Transfer Pricing

Market-Specific Factors

Consumer's Ability to Buy
Icome Levels, Ability to Buy, Information Seeking, Global Account Managment

Government Intervention
As Buyer: Countertrade Demands, Price and Profit Controls, Transfer Price Controls, Barriers to Trade, Quotas, Tariffs, Non-tarrif Barriers, Subsidies

Distribution Channels
Multiple Channels and Price Differentiation, Channel Control, Commission Structure
Local Advertising and Promotions: Local Cooperative Advertising
Macroeconomic Factors: Business Cycle Stage, Inflation

Local Competition and Price Cutting Pressures
Market Share Distribution, Competitive Goals
Inflation
Gray Markets: Product Flow between Markets

Effects of Exchange Rate
FX volatility and impact on prices
Currency of Quote
Short-Term Hedging
Long-Term Impacts: Sourcing Reassessment

Product-Specific Factors

Demand
Market Skimming
Penetration Pricing

Life Cycle Stage
Product Adaptation Costs

Product Line
Other Product Attributes: Quality, Delivery, Service
Place in Product Line
Financing: Terms, Period, Interest Rate Subsidies
Price Unbranding: What is Included in Price

International Market Price-setting: Decision Choices

Differential versus one global price

Market-based pricing

Cost-based pricing

Extent of exchange rate impact: pass-through versus dampening

Outsourcing and shift to low-cost manufacturing

Product redesign to lower costs

Product adaptation to balance priceband product attributes

Product families: low to high end

Transfer price setting and administration

Focus on ownership costs over product life

Pricing for multinational clients

Global account management policies

Client-specific pricing

Discounting

Designing price band cafeteria pricing

Differential pricing by channel based on value-added services: volume discounts

Initiating countertrade and leasing

As in domestic markets, international pricing is an important determinant of demand for a product.

thus, performance. U.S. firms seem to place priority on cost and profit factors when setting price, whereas Korean firms appear more focused on pricing competitively. The study suggests that Korean firms seek market penetration in setting prices, whereas U.S. firms may be setting prices to emphasize the contributions from export markets.[2]

Strategic objectives do not always demand that prices be lowered. In an oligopolistic environment with few competitors, for example, a company may attempt to head off ruinous price cutting by signaling its intent to keep prices steady or even raise them. A case in point is an airline that files a fare increase in a computer reservation system to see whether its competitors raise prices, too. That signaling is part of the role prices play in affecting competitive position. (Firms, though, must also be concerned about legal concerns related to price fixing, as discussed in Chapter 3 and the ADM violations.)

Firms that are faced with competitive price cuts may need to respond with a coordinated strategy in which pricing decisions are only one aspect of an overall marketing mix. In other words, lower prices alone are not the answer. Procter & Gamble, the giant U.S. manufacturer of products such as soap, detergent, shampoo, and food, had a minor presence in India while it focused on selling brandname, higher-priced products in the United States and European markets. As India's economy showed sustained economic growth and the number of middle-class families began to increase, Procter & Gamble wanted to develop a stronger presence and market share there. Its initial strategy was to lower prices sharply (for example, cutting the prices of its detergent in half). However, it had to cope with a vigorous response from entrenched market leaders such as Unilever.

Unilever's subsidiary, Hindustan Lever, matched Procter & Gamble's price cuts in detergents and lowered its shampoo prices as well. In addition, Hindustan Lever launched products suited to Indian consumers' needs, such as a cleaning powder that worked well with two buckets of water rather than the normal four, an important issue in a country in which running water is scarce in large cities. Hindustan Lever pioneered the use of small, affordable packets and sachets of detergent, shampoo, and toothpaste, which could sell for as little as a penny apiece. The sachets provided a means for introducing Unilever products to low-income consumers across India. Lever also enjoys a vast distribution system in India, built over many decades of Indian operations. It employs 20,000 wholesalers and distributors, who may, at times, make deliveries by bicycle. It reaches 2.5 million retail outlets across India in small, remote cities and rural areas. It began employing women, over 6,000 of them, to sell Unilever products door-to-door, planning to expand that sales force to 25,000 within two years. (Procter & Gamble has only about one-third the number of distribution points.)

Lever also has a scale economy advantage with low manufacturing costs since it is ten times larger than Procter & Gamble in India, with $2.2 billion in Indian sales. Unilever's advertising is localized, with heavy use of Indian

"Bollywood" stars. However, as a large global multinational, Procter & Gamble has the means to invest in India and to develop a similar marketing mix breadth adapted to Indian conditions. Procter & Gamble has no choice if it wants to develop a significant position in an Indian market expected to have 300 million middle-class consumers by about 2015, with a forecasted market for consumer goods (soap, detergent, and snack foods) of about $20 billion.[3]

In summary, the intensity of competition, along with strategic objectives, determines a firm's pricing strategies. Differentiating a product to command a higher price is more of a strategic positioning approach to reduce competition to gain greater leeway in setting prices.

Price and a Firm's Cost Structure

The cost to produce a product, provide a service, market those products and services, and deliver goods to the final consumer also influences price. The higher these costs, the higher the pricing needs to be for the firm to be profitable. For international companies, identifying the specific costs for goods and services can be difficult.

MANUFACTURING COSTS AND SERVICE DELIVERY COSTS

When products sold in a market are also produced there, determining manufacturing costs is no problem. Questions arise, however, when a market is served by other production sources: How should fixed R&D and product development costs be allocated? If a firm has several plants, which plant's costs should be used? Should variable or full cost be used? What does "full cost" mean for a product coming from a plant in another country; that is, what portion of that country's costs should be allocated? Obviously, some costs, such as local advertising and marketing research, do not apply to products sold in another country.

Similarly, it can be difficult to identify the specific costs to provide a service such as insurance, consulting, or financial services. These services may utilize cross-border teams that multitask on a number of projects at any given time. They may leverage corporate resources including staff and technology, whose costs also have to be allocated. All these factors can make accurate accounting of service delivery costs difficult for global companies.

International freight costs add additional expenses that must be considered when determining overseas pricing.

MARKETING COSTS

Distribution and marketing costs also must be covered in the foreign market price. Because tariffs can be an important part of delivered cost, a subsidiary tends to prefer a source from a country having favorable tariff relations with its own. Thus, a subsidiary in the EU usually chooses another EU subsidiary because no tariff barriers exist. Marketing costs in the foreign market price are generated primarily within the market by the national subsidiary. Occasionally, however, a firm incurs costs for marketing research or other services rendered by a regional division (or international division) for the subsidiary. Local marketing costs vary from one country to another. That variation derives, in part, from different product lines, service offerings, and company goals in each market.

SHIPPING AND TRANSPORTATION COSTS

International logistics adds additional costs specific to international pricing. These added "distance" costs, if passed on as price increments, are a deterrent to the gaining of market share in overseas markets. These costs can be particularly high for products that must be shipped in relatively small quantities resulting in high per-unit freight costs. Such costs are also significant if the transportation infrastructure in the foreign market is not well developed, which also leads to high costs.

Market-Specific Factors

Consumers' Ability to Buy

Incomes, cultural habits, and consumer preferences differ from country to country. Thus, for the same price in two different country markets, there may be demand for different amounts of products. The importance of pricing is seen in General Motor's attempt to capture minivan market share in China. A minivan priced at $5,000, the Wuling Sunshine, was manufactured in a joint venture (34 percent owned by General Motors) with Shanghai Automotive Industry Corporation (SAIC; 50.1 percent) and Liuzhou Wuling Automotive Company (15.9 percent). The car got 43 mpg in city driving. The low price was made possible by using less powerful engines (one-fourth the horsepower of U.S. minivans), leading to weaker acceleration and a top speed of 80 mph, as well as thinner seats. Customers were mainly small businessmen who used the minivan to carry goods and transport their families.[4]

However, shoppers in country markets that lack price competition and cut-priced distribution channels, for example, may not have formed the habit of comparing prices when shopping or waiting for sales when making large purchases.

Government

Governments also influence a firm's pricing in a variety of ways. When buyers choose winning bidders on government contracts, governments can dictate the acceptable price. Some influence is exerted via tariffs, non-tariff barriers, quotas, taxes, and competition policy. Some governments have specific legislation, such as that governing resale price maintenance or restraint of trade. Governments also have the power to control prices directly if they so choose, such as with public utilities (electricity, water, etc.), and they may use their power in varying degrees.

Government controls obviously limit a firm's freedom in setting prices. They raise the cost of price administration by requiring more record keeping and management time. Government price controls are often limited to select product groups. Some products are perceived as being more strategic or sensitive and are more susceptible to government regulation. Pharmaceuticals, for example, are frequently subject to price controls.

Distribution Channels

A determinant of a firm's price to consumers in a foreign market is its distribution channels in those markets. The costs and margins of a given channel are not the same from country to country, suggesting that a channel decision may also be a pricing decision. A firm may be forced to choose a particular channel in a market to get the final consumer price it needs, such as direct-to-consumer Internet selling versus retailing.

Distribution channels also may differ across countries in the countries' relative demand for discounts. Customary business practices and long-standing relationships in a country may mean a series of additional discounts that reduce the ultimate price realized by the firm.[5] Firms grant a variety of discounts for a number of reasons:

- Order size
- Co-op advertising
- Response to competitive price cuts
- Shipping charges
- Early payment Special customer relationships
- Cumulative volume
- Product-line promotions

Such discounts need not be offered to all customers in all markets. It is useful, however, to monitor the various discounts offered in each market and to establish norms under which the discounts are granted. Otherwise, the customer who negotiates additional discounts is the one who knows when and whom to call, asking for discounts. A firm that develops information on its price waterfall—the sequence of discounts leading to the pocket price—can more easily decide which customers are to be rewarded and which distribution channels should get the most discounts. Research suggests that careful analysis can result in an overall reduction in discounting and significant gains in the pocket price achieved by the firm. Its sales margins will, therefore, be enhanced.[6]

Local Competition and Price-Cutting Pressures

Comparative-advantage concepts indicate that developing nations, with their lower labor costs, are likely to have an advantage in world competition in labor-intensive products. Those advantages also arise when local companies gain higher productivity as product volumes increase. The resulting cost advantage means local firms may have a significant market share versus foreign competitors. The challenge for foreign firms is how to price its products versus domestic competitors. Does it attempt to match pricing or focus instead on product differentiation such as quality or features? Depending on the specific circumstances, this may or may not be possible, such as when a product has become commoditized with little differentiation between competitors (domestic or foreign).

Foreign firms must constantly monitor the prices in a market charged by both their domestic as well as other foreign competitors and understand the reasons why prices are lower. Are the price cuts of a temporary nature, designed to aid in initial market penetration? Or do they represent the net cost advantage enjoyed by competitors? In other words, price cutting is the symptom. The correct response to price cuts requires understanding the cause.

Local firms may have a significant market share versus foreign competitors, as well as price advantage.

Inflation

Most countries face some gradual increase in prices over time. However, continuing strong inflation characterizes a limited number of countries such as Ethiopia, Venezuela, or Ukraine, each with 25 percent or more inflation.[7] In those markets where price levels rise by 20 percent or more every year, pricing presents some different issues. Selling in an inflationary market might well appear to be a marketer's dream. People are eager to exchange their money for real assets that do not depreciate quickly. Indeed, it would be a good situation for sellers if it were not for other factors that usually accompany high rates of inflation. First, costs may go up faster than prices. Second, countries with high rates of inflation are usually those with strong price controls. Third, countries with rampant inflation usually have strict controls over foreign exchange. Profits earned in those countries may not be remittable, at least not until they have been eroded by the devaluations that usually accompany inflation.

Pricing for inflationary markets requires accounting for changing values over time. Material and other costs of a product must be recovered (plus a margin for profit) at the time of sale—or at the time of payment if credit is extended. If prices are stable, pricing can be a simple process of addition. If prices are rising rapidly, addition of the various cost elements at the time they were incurred will not ensure that the current value of the costs is recovered.

GRAY MARKETS

An additional pricing problem in international marketing is the buying incentive that the consumer price differential between countries creates for a given product in a country with lower prices. For example, it was common for planeloads of Japanese tourists (in times of economic prosperity in Japan) to take weekend shopping trips to Taiwan and Hong Kong. The tourists bought goods such as consumer electronics, perfumes, and clothes to take advantage of price differentials.

In international marketing, when a product can be manufactured in more than one location, currency fluctuations may make gray marketing profitable. **Gray marketing** is the unauthorized importing and selling of products intended for one market in another higher-priced market. When the dollar was appreciating in the early 1980s, dealers found it profitable to bring in unauthorized imports of Caterpillar tractors from Europe because of the weak European currency. In those cases, even after shipping and tariffs, the landed cost in the United States of the imported Caterpillar tractors was less than the price charged for U.S.-made Caterpillar tractors.[8]

The major problem with gray marketing is that established distributors lose motivation to sell their products because they see their margins eroded by low-overhead gray marketers. Meanwhile, the gray marketer is primarily interested in quick sales and short-term profits. Over time, a manufacturer could lose markets because the gray marketer competes only on price and drives away customers who seek after-sales service and other forms of support. This issue is particularly serious for industrial products.

Ultimately, gray marketing arises because of unsustainable price differences between two markets. Companies must carefully examine their pricing policies in different markets and their attempts to maintain a price differential. Otherwise, gray marketing is merely an efficient market response to attempts to charge higher prices in certain markets.

> **gray marketing**
>
> The unauthorized importing and selling of products intended for one market in another higher-priced market.

Product-Specific Factors and Their Relevance to Pricing

Demand

Demand for a firm's product or service will generally differ across markets. One implication of differing demand is that a firm may need to charge different prices in each market. Firms may have to choose between market skimming and penetration pricing. **Market skimming** involves setting prices at a high level and accepting lower sales volumes with higher margins per unit sold. That strategy assumes that as the market grows and evolves, prices will be cut gradually to make the product affordable to larger segments of the consuming population. Such a strategy also relies on the likelihood that costs will fall with accumulated volume production. Thus, margins can be held at attractive levels, with lower prices matched with lower costs. The opposite strategy, **penetration pricing**, begins with lower prices, assuming that the lower prices will attract larger numbers of consumers and that the higher unit volumes will result in larger total profits even though margins per unit are lower. The strategy also relies on unit costs falling rapidly as sales volume grows, thus increasing margins as total volume increases. An additional benefit of the penetration pricing strategy is that a firm captures significant market share, making it difficult for competitors who enter the market later to capture equivalent market shares.

Demand for a firm's products is a function of the number of consumers; their ability to pay; their tastes, habits, and attitudes relating to the product; and the existence of competing products. Demand is also related to price elasticity of demand—the quantity demanded of a good or service relative to its price. That is, demand of a product or service will generally be higher at lower pricing rather than higher pricing. Patterns of demand can also change in reaction to cyclical economic conditions within a country. Consider the evolution of U.S. goods and pricing in Japan. Imported U.S. goods such as brand-name sweaters, cosmetics, and software have all been set significantly higher than U.S. prices. Part of the reason for higher Japanese prices has been the higher local costs of rent, sales force, advertising, and multiple-layered distribution margins. However, when Japan underwent a deep recession, depressed incomes led Japanese buyers to seek bargains. Discounting and value-pricing strategies took hold. Gray market pressures and increased public consciousness of high Japanese prices also led to lowered prices, with U.S. companies following the general trend.[9]

> **market skimming**
>
> Pricing policy that involves setting prices at a high level to trade off lower sales volumes with higher margins per unit sold.

> **penetration pricing**
>
> Pricing policy that involves setting prices at a low level to trade off higher sales (attracting a larger number of consumers) with lower margins per unit sold.

Price and the Product Life Cycle

A product's price may be set with the goal of maximizing profits over the product life cycle rather than at every stage of the product's marketing. A company may deliberately price below costs in anticipation of reducing costs through increases in manufacturing volume, a variation of penetration pricing discussed previously. A classic example is the Japanese use of that method to penetrate the motorcycle industry.[10] Japanese firms gambled on gaining learning- and experience-curve efficiencies to produce long-run profits.[11] Note that price has several universal connotations as an indicator of quality and as a proxy for prestige. Negatively, price connotes with value consciousness, suggesting that high prices are not as desirable as equivalent quality with lower prices.[12]

Price and the Product Line

Products within a product line with less competition may be priced higher to subsidize other parts of the product line. Similarly, some items in the product line may be priced low to serve as loss leaders and induce customers to try the product, particularly if the company and its products are recent entrants into a country market. Another variant of such strategies is price-bundling—that is, setting a certain price for customers who simultaneously buy several items within the product line (for example, a season ticket price or a personal computer package with software and printer). In such cases, a key consideration is how much consumers in diverse country markets want to save money, to spend time searching for the "best buy," and so on.

International Pricing Strategies

Given the preceding influences on pricing from firm-level factors, market-specific factors, and product-specific factors, what international pricing strategies do companies implement? The specific strategy depends on the specific situation and which of the preceding factors are seen as most critical to the international success of a firm.

Pricing Strategies

The strength of competition and a firm's objectives interact in determining how the firm sets its international prices. There are several types of pricing strategies.

MARKET SHARE PRICING

One strategy for pricing focuses on attaining significant market share by setting low prices to increase overall volume. The firm expects that elasticity of demand will result in increased volume so that overall contribution from the product (volume in units × margin per unit) is sufficient to meet profit and contribution targets for the product or product line. If the firm already has a large installed base and enjoys scale economies, this strategy hinders the competition from becoming strong.

PRICING AT A PREMIUM TO THE MARKET

The strategy to price at a premium takes the opposite approach to market share pricing. By pricing at a premium to the market, companies avoid the commodity end of the market and cater to niche segments where a higher price is acceptable to customers in return for features and product characteristics that they need and want. Rolls Royce is an example of pricing at a premium.

PRICING ON A COST-PLUS BASIS

Overall costs and a desired profit margin determine the level of prices. In the long run, prices should cover costs to yield a reasonable return on investment. Hence, in making a long-term decision such as whether to proceed with a new product proposal, the cost-plus pricing approach may play a role; that is, it may determine at what level prices should be set in order to earn a given rate of return (often the hurdle rate). In practice, this approach is possible only in industries with limited competition, such as regulated utilities.

Figure 12-2 • Target Pricing and Product Development

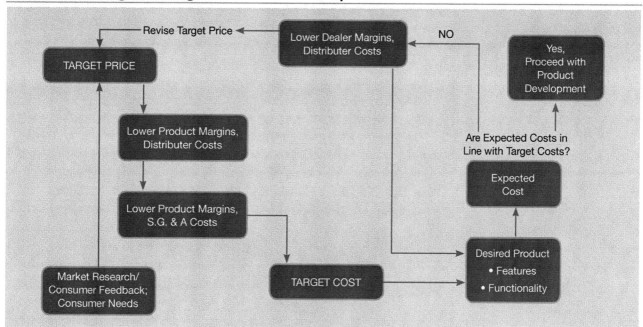

TARGET PRICING

Target pricing takes the approach that a product's pricing needs to be at a specific target price, and then the product is designed to meet that price. This approach, as discussed in Chapter 9, was implemented by Canon in developing a personal copier for under $1,000. Similarly, Olympus used target pricing to determine the price points for its new cameras when faced with digital cameras eroding its market for high-quality single-lens reflex cameras (SLRs).[13] These companies' decision to use the target price approach guided the entire product-development process. Such target pricing is a long-term pricing strategy because it envisions modulating the entire design, procurement, and manufacturing process to meet the target price. Implicit in the idea of a target price is the notion that the price is for a product for a certain market segment and that the product can achieve long-term profitability at the target price. See "Tata Motors and Target Pricing" for another example of target pricing strategy.

Figure 12-2 illustrates how a target-pricing approach interacts with product design and manufacturing to iteratively set product functionality and features so that target prices can be met. If careful study shows that target prices may have to be adjusted upward, the firm can then rethink whether satisfactory markets exist at the new target price. If not, it may consider canceling the particular product development effort.

Price Standardization: Pressures for Uniform Pricing in International Markets

An important issue for companies as they set their international pricing strategies is pressure from buyers in foreign markets for uniform pricing. Customers of multinationals, for example, who pay different prices in different countries for essentially the same product or service can be expected to press for a global

Tata Motors and Target Pricing

● ● ●

Another example of using target pricing comes from India's Tata Motors Ltd., which made headlines in early 2008 when it announced that it was going to produce and market the world's cheapest car. Tata Motors analyzed the Indian market for automobiles and saw a high level of unmet demand of customers who want automobiles but could not afford the higher-priced models currently available in India.

Tata's ultra-low-priced car, the Nano, took six years of development. The company worked backward from the target price of 110,000 rupees (roughly $US 2,500) to determine which features were priorities and which features were only "nice to have." One priority is that Tata wanted a car that was safe to drive in bad weather. Air-conditioning and power windows are two examples of previously "standard" features that were left out of the Nano. Further, Tata Motors offers the Nano in only three colors (red, yellow, and silver). To build scale economies, Tata Motors plans to unveil the Nano in the European and U.S. markets in coming years.

Tata's "target pricing" approach is iterative, and products cannot always be designed to meet both the target price and the desired functionality at an acceptable cost. In fact, some critics claim the car is too cheap and does not appeal to its target market. Tata's efforts, however, demonstrate an approach to integrating product development, pricing, and targeted market share.[14]

Tata Motors Ltd. used a target pricing strategy when developing its Nano car.

uniform price. Better information systems and sharing of data across national subsidiaries allow multinationals to see when different pricing exists, allowing them to pool their purchasing to command a single price and even volume discounts. In response, suppliers have begun a move to uniform pricing. A policy of keeping price variations across countries within a limited range also prevents gray marketing, such as when U.S. distributors ship products to Europe to take advantage of price differentials between the United States and Europe. Those approaches have been formalized in many companies through a program of global account management.

Uniform pricing also allows a firm to set pricing policy centrally and to decide the role that price should play in the overall marketing mix. Headquarters may then decide that the company will not indiscriminately cut prices to win market share. Doing so prevents inconsistencies from cropping up under which one subsidiary might cut prices excessively, whereas another might prefer to cater to fewer clients at a higher margin.[15] Uniform pricing also reduces the need for country-specific marketing research, which can be costly.

Research suggests that pricing in a global setting consists of resolving the tension between the desire to charge different prices and the pressure to charge one price in all markets.[16] Multinational clients who want to buy all of their product needs at the lowest price prevalent within a group of countries and gray marketers indulging in price arbitrage are the two forces leading to a uniform price. Consumers in different markets may have different elasticity of demand, however, with some groups willing to pay higher prices.

Equally important, consumers may differ in the values and features they perceive in a product, which could justify pricing differences between markets. Marketing research among a number of foreign markets would allow a firm to measure the differences in perceived value. Coupling that information with differing elasticities can justify higher prices in certain markets. The solution may be to set up an "international price corridor," within which band prices can vary across countries. The width of the band would be set centrally at headquarters. If some low level of gray marketing ensues, the firm can tolerate it. One study emphasizes that "a global product and local price are incompatible". If low income and positioning strategies suggest that different prices need to be charged, then a multiple brand policy can prevent the low price from diluting the brand equity of the higher-priced brand.

Setting uniform prices across markets (that is, standardizing prices) is seen by some researchers as being influenced by the degree of similarity between home and host country—when viewed in terms of customer characteristics, legal environment, economic conditions, and stage of the product life cycle. Whether to standardize or adapt price may depend on:

* Macro environmental factors (convergence of economic, legal, cultural, physical, and demographic factors).

* Micro environmental factors such as similarity of customer characteristics; attitudes and behavior; structure and nature of competition; and availability, cost, and competence of intermediaries.

* Firm-specific factors including degree of centralization, international experience, strategic orientation, and subsidiary ownership structure.

* Product and industry factors such as life-cycle stage, nature of product, product uniqueness, conditions of use, technology, and customer's degree of familiarity with the product.

Similarities of the economic environment, legal environment, distribution infrastructure, customer characteristics, purchasing behavior, and stage of product life cycle are most influential in determining the standardization of prices.[17]

Pricing too Low: Dumping

Firms sometimes respond to lower-priced international competition by making allegations of dumping. **Dumping** occurs when a firm is judged to be pricing its products below costs to gain market share. Under U.S. international trade law, firms can petition the United States International Trade Commission (USITC) to declare that foreign competitors have "dumped" their goods in the U.S. market by selling their goods in the United States at below fair value. If the U.S. firms can prove such dumping before the USITC panels, the firms can request relief in the form of imposition of antidumping or countervailing duties. In recent years the USITC has imposed a number of such duties, including lumber from Canada, orange juice from Brazil, wooden bedroom furniture from China, and minivans from Japan.[18]

Allocating Cost Strategies

As discussed as part of firm-specific factors and pricing, companies must allocate costs so pricing strategies can be more aligned with their true cost structure. This involves the allocation of a firm's variable and fixed costs. Assume a firm with little to no current international sales is already profitable through its domestic sales, meaning its income is greater than its expenses. These expenses would include **variable costs** (costs directly related to making and selling a product, such as materials, labor, or marketing) and **fixed costs** (overhead costs that generally don't change, such as management, R&D, or buildings). In setting its domestic pricing policy for a particular product, the firm would generally

dumping

Selling products in foreign markets at prices lower than those in the producer's home market or at prices lower than cost.

variable costs

Costs directly related to the making and selling of a product (e.g., materials, labor, or marketing).

fixed costs

Costs that will be incurred regardless if a particular product is manufactured, such as overhead costs, management, R&D, and buildings.

allocate the product's variable costs plus a share of the firm's fixed costs (or overhead costs).

It must allocate these fixed costs so all products (or services) bear their share of the fixed costs. This is known as **full-absorption pricing**—calculating the price for a product or service that includes its full share of fixed (overhead) costs. When this firm sets its international pricing, it must make the decision to what extent its international sales also will cover their share of the firm's overhead costs.

To be more competitive internationally, the firm may begin with a policy of **variable pricing**—calculating the price for a product or service that includes only the variable costs associated with making or offering the service, with no allocation of fixed costs. Clearly, a policy of variable pricing cannot be sustained over the long term as international sales increase. As a firm's international sales increase, they must eventually share in the firm's overall cost structure, meaning international sales must bear their share of fixed costs. However, especially in a firm's initial international expansion, or for a particular market in which its pricing is otherwise uncompetitive, a firm may elect variable pricing to be more competitive.

---

full-absorption pricing

Pricing strategy in which a firm calculates the price for a product or service that includes its full share of fixed costs (e.g., overhead).

variable pricing

Pricing strategy in which a firm calculates the price for a product or service that includes only the variable costs associated with making or offering the product or service with no allocation of fixed costs (e.g., overhead).

••• Transfer Pricing at Hewlett-Packard

Transfer pricing plays a key role in coordinating numerous and distant profit centers at Hewlett-Packard (HP), a multinational firm that gets over half of its sales from outside the United States. The company's transfer pricing objectives include (1) motivating local managers who want to show large profits, (2) minimizing the chances of a tax audit, (3) moving profits to low-tax jurisdictions while satisfying tax authorities of the business reasons for those moves, and (4) potentially reducing the total taxes paid to tax authorities in both the home and host country.

Hewlett-Packard's accounting and finance manual describes the basis for transfer pricing using either a list price minus a discount or a cost-plus method. The company typically uses cost plus 10 percent as the desired company rate of return. The Internal Revenue Service (IRS) generally advises corporations to base transfer pricing markups on a return-on-assets method. Hewlett-Packard believes, however, that the return-on-assets method is more appropriate to capital-intensive and machinery-based industries. Hewlett-Packard and other high-tech companies spend an enormous amount on R&D, which is often expensed. Thus, capital assets may be understated. Hence, Hewlett-Packard argues that using a cost-plus method allows adequate return to R&D. Hewlett-Packard's tax department breaks down the profit from each product line and shows how it is allocated among R&D, manufacturing, and sales.[19]

However, to avoid ongoing conflicts with the IRS over transfer pricing, Hewlett-Packard has considered whether to adhere to the new approach to transfer pricing, called advanced determination rulings (ADRs). The ADR method suggests that rather than wait for an audit to rule on the acceptability of a formula already in use, companies should submit proposed transfer pricing plans to determine whether they comply with IRS regulations. However, Hewlett-Packard believes that the ADR approach needs to be modified to make it more attractive.[20]

Transfer pricing has increasingly caught the eyes of government tax agencies which argue that some transfer pricing policies are simple tax-avoidance schemes. For example, Japanese tax officials have become more aggressive in looking at transfer pricing as fewer and fewer multinationals were paying Japan's 30 percent corporate tax rate. In fact, HP found itself defending its transfer pricing policies and appealing a ruling requiring the company to pay $270 million in "unpaid" taxes to the government of Japan.[21]

HP is a good example of a global firm that must comply with transfer pricing rules.

Transfer Pricing in International Marketing •••

Transfer pricing (intracorporate pricing) is an area that has special implications for international marketing. It refers to prices on goods sold within the corporate family—that is, from division to division or to a foreign subsidiary. (See "Transfer Pricing at Hewlett-Packard.")

> **transfer pricing**
>
> The prices used on goods sold between related parties—such as from division to division or parent company to its subsidiary.

Product Division to International Division

The transfer price paid by an international group to the producing division should have certain characteristics if it is to optimize corporate, rather than divisional, profit. For the producing division, the price should be high enough to encourage a flow of products for export. The transfer price does this if sales to the international division are as attractive as sales to other parties. The price to the international division may be even lower than to other parties if the services the international division renders (market research, promotion, and so on) warrant it.

For the international division, the transfer price should be low enough to enable it to be both competitive and profitable in the foreign market. Obviously, there is room for conflict. The producing division wants a high price, and the international division wants a low price. The transfer pricing mechanism must be such that the overall corporate interest is not ignored in the divisional conflict. A profit margin that is unattractive to one or the other division (or to both) may be worthwhile from the overall corporate viewpoint.

Assume that the producing division makes a product at a full cost of $50. It sells that product to outside buyers for $60, but the transfer price to the international division is $58. The producing division may be unhappy because the markup is 20 percent lower to the international division ($8 versus $10). The international division adds its various export marketing expenses of $10, for an export cost of $68. For competitive reasons, the international division cannot sell the product for more than $72, or a $4 return. Because that is less than 6 percent of sales, the international division is also unhappy. However, the return to the corporation is $12 on $72, or almost 17 percent ($8 from the producing division plus $4 from the international division). The corporation may find that amount attractive, even though both divisions are unhappy with it.

Different approaches can be taken to solve that problem. One solution is to eliminate one division as a profit center. The producing division can be judged on the basis of costs and other performance criteria instead of profit. Then the producing division can sell to the international division at a price enabling it to become competitive in foreign markets. Market pricing will not be handicapped by internal markups of the transfer pricing process, and the total corporate profit will be given greater attention.

On the other hand, the international division can operate as a service center rather than as a profit center, thus eliminating one source of conflict. A question arises, however, about whether a selling organization can be as efficient and motivated when it is not operating under a profit constraint. A related possibility is to have the international division act as a commission agent for the producing divisions. When the international division is not a profit center, its expenses can be allocated back to the product divisions.

Transfer pricing can be established in three ways: at manufacturing cost, at arm's length, and at cost-plus.

TRANSFER AT MANUFACTURING COST

When profit centers are maintained, several alternatives are possible. At one extreme (and favoring the international division) is the transfer at direct manufacturing cost. This is the lowest cost, probably well under what the producing division could obtain from other customers. The producing division dislikes selling at manufacturing cost because it believes it is subsidizing the international division and thereby taking a loss when compared with other profit centers. A firm may offset this by an accounting or memorandum profit to the producing division on its sales for export. Such memorandum profits, unfortunately, are never as satisfactory as the real thing. When the product division is unhappy, the international division may get sluggish service because the product division is servicing more attractive domestic opportunities first.

TRANSFER AT ARM'S LENGTH

The other extreme in transfer pricing is to charge the international division the same price any buyer outside the firm pays. This price favors the producing division because it does as well on internal as on external sales, sometimes even better. The services rendered by the international division and the elimination of the credit problem can make export sales especially profitable.

If the product has no external buyers, however, a problem occurs in trying to determine an arm's-length price. An artificial price must be constructed. Further difficulties arise because that price fails to take into account the services performed by the international division and because the international division may be noncompetitive with the price. Finally, there is no real reason why the price to foreign buyers should be determined by the domestic market.

TRANSFER AT COST-PLUS

Between the transfer pricing extremes, just discussed, is a range of prices that involve a profit split between the producing and international divisions. Starting from the cost floor, cost-plus pricing attempts to add on some amount or percentage that will make the resulting price acceptable to both divisions. The "plus" may be a percentage negotiated between the divisions, a percentage of product division overhead, or a percentage return on product division investment. Further variation can be caused by using different definitions of cost. In any case, the pricing formula is less important than the results obtained. A good transfer pricing formula should consider total corporate profit and encourage divisional cooperation. It should also minimize the time that executives spend on transfer price disagreements and keep the accounting burden to a minimum.

Other factors affecting the transfer price charged include whether there are restrictions on capital outflows from a market; what level of customs tariffs exist in each market; and whether the two transacting parties are wholly owned by the firm or whether one of the two entities is a licensee, a joint-venture, or a minority-owned partner.

Transfer Pricing and Tax Regulations

When countries have different levels of taxation on corporate profits, firms may want to accumulate profits in countries with low taxes. They would like to use a low transfer price to subsidiaries in low-tax countries and a high transfer price to subsidiaries in high-tax countries. U.S. companies, for example, may be tempted to sell at low transfer prices to countries that have lower corporate tax rates than the United States. The IRS, however, is on guard against this behavior because it does not want to lose taxable income to other countries. Therefore, it carefully scrutinizes the transfer prices of international companies to ensure that they are not too low. The same scrutiny is applied by other government taxing authorities on the transfer pricing activities of its international companies.

One specific demand of the IRS is that export prices bear a share of domestic R&D expenses. The IRS wants to be sure that an equitable portion of the income remains under U.S. tax jurisdiction. Transfer pricing cases can drag on for years. Therefore, corporations and the IRS have begun to establish procedures whereby firms set out the transfer pricing scheme they want to pursue and try to get the IRS to agree that the scheme results in a fair price. At the same time, the firms are eager to prevent too much sensitive financial information from being handed over to the IRS. Similar problems confront firms using transfer pricing in other tax jurisdictions, especially when the tax authorities of various countries begin to share transfer pricing data and attempt joint regulation of transfer pricing.

International Payment Methods

How a company sets its payment policies for international transaction is generally the responsibility of the financial staff within a firm. It is essentially an accounting and credit management function. However, payment policies do impact the international marketing function. Payment policies that ignore the needs of foreign buyers may place the firm at a competitive disadvantage.

Balancing the Needs of the Seller versus the Buyer

When a firm makes a sale, the seller would prefer a payment method in which the seller is paid when the sales contract is signed. This ensures that the seller gets paid for the sale before the product is shipped. (Or in the case of a service, payment is made before the service is provided.) It also means the seller has access to any needed working capital to fulfill the sales contract because it receives the money before shipping. The buyer, on the other hand, would prefer to pay for the product after it has been received, and perhaps even later. Paying after the product is received ensures the seller fulfills the sales contract. The buyer also does not have to finance the transaction with its own money. This highlights the fundamental dilemma in selecting the payment method: Sellers want prepayment, and buyers want delayed payment. Thus, in selecting a payment method, the seller wants the opposite of the buyer. This is especially true in international transactions in which the delay between shipping a product and receiving the product could be weeks, if not months, due to shipping and customs delays.

Types of Payment Methods

Selecting the payment method must balance the needs of the seller and buyer. A firm that only accepts payment in advance of shipping may reduce its sales potential, especially if competitors offer more flexible methods. Yet offering payment methods that always favor the buyer could lead to commercial losses if the buyer does not pay. Fortunately, there are compromise payment methods that offer some protection for the seller and buyer to help balance the needs of both. The task is to choose payment terms that satisfy importers yet safeguard the interests of the exporter. Following are discussions of the most common international payment methods.

International payment methods must balance the needs of the seller and buyer.

CASH IN ADVANCE/PREPAYMENT

As previously discussed, an exporter would favor prepayment, that is, cash in advance of shipment—or even in advance of production for custom products. Though importers dislike bearing the financial burden implied in cash-in-advance terms, sometimes this payment method is justified. The most common reason is that the exporter is well known and respected by the buyer. The buyer has little concern that the exporter will not ship the product after receiving payment. Though the risk is still there, the importer is willing to accept the risk to receive the goods. Another reason would be that the overall size of the transaction may be small. This means the overall risk to the buyer is also small. Finally, the exporter

Table 12-1 • Letters of Credit Terminology

Letters of credit (LC): A commitment by a bank to pay the seller as long as the seller fulfills the terms of the LC. LCs are issued by banks.

Applicant: The foreign buyer (importer).

Beneficiary: The seller (exporter).

Issuing bank: The foreign bank that opens (creates) the LC. It is generally located in the country of the buyer. It may be a foreign subsidiary of the buyer's bank.

Advising bank: The bank (generally in the country of the seller, or at least trusted by the seller) that verifies that the LC is authentic.

Confirming bank: The bank (generally the same as the advising bank) that adds its own guarantee to pay in addition to the guarantee to pay promised by the issuing bank.

Discrepancies: Problems with the paperwork submitted for payment that lead to payment delays and extra costs.

Irrevocable letter of credit: An LC in which the terms cannot be canceled or modified. Exporters would always want irrevocable LCs.

Confirmed letter of credit: An LC in which a confirming bank adds its additional guarantee to pay as long as the seller fulfills the terms of the LC. Exporters use confirmed LCs when they are concerned the payment risk of the issuing bank (foreign bank) may be too high, or there is high political risk in the foreign country.

SWIFT

The Society for Worldwide Interbank Financial Telecommunication (SWIFT) is a worldwide collaboration of banks that allows secure, trusted communication between members, such as wire transfers of funds.

letter of credit (LC)

A common form of export financing where the buyer's bank agrees to pay the seller (exporter) as long as the seller fulfills the terms of the LC.

may simply have a policy that initial sales to any foreign buyer must be prepaid until a credit relationship can be established with the buyer.

Important advantages of prepayment are their low cost and minimal documentation. Prepayment is generally done through a bank-to-bank wire transfer through the Society for Worldwide Interbank Financial Telecommunication (SWIFT) network. **SWIFT** is a worldwide collaboration of banks that allows secure, trusted communication between members. In some respects, a SWIFT account (known as a SWIFT code) is like an e-mail account within a closed, encoded e-mail system. One SWIFT member bank receiving a transfer from another SWIFT member bank can "trust" that the transfer is valid. Companies can actually do their own international wire transfer using software provided by their bank. The cost of an international wire transfer can be low and generally not related to the size of the transfer. Fees range between $30 and $75 per transfer. Both the buyer and seller pay a transfer fee, known as the outgoing and incoming wire fee, respectively. The incoming wire transfer fee is generally lower than the outgoing fee.

The international marketing manager should be aware that when a firm insists on prepayment, doing so could put the company at a competitive disadvantage. If competitors offer more generous payment methods, buyers may avoid a firm that requires cash in advance. The situation depends on the relative strength of the seller versus the buyer. As a firm grows internationally and develops a network of buyers, it likely migrates from prepayment to other payment methods to be as competitive as possible.

LETTERS OF CREDIT (LCs)

Letters of credit are a common international payment method because they offer the most protection to both the seller and the buyer. A **letter of credit** (LC) is a commitment by a bank to pay the seller as long as the seller fulfills the terms of the LC. The most important term the seller must fulfill is that it ships the goods as detailed in the LC by the date as specified in the LC. The attraction of an LC to sellers is that this guarantee to pay is from the bank, not the buyer. So as long as the seller trusts the bank to pay, there is generally little risk to the seller. Meanwhile, the bank also guarantees to the buyer that it will not pay the seller until it provides the required documentation proving it has shipped the specific products and within the time frame required by the LC. As long as the buyer trusts the bank, it is also protected. Terms relating to LCs are listed in Table 12-1.

There are some important considerations when using LCs. Because the issuing bank is giving its guarantee to pay the LC if the seller ships, the issuing bank may require that the buyer deposits the full value of the LC with the issuing bank as collateral. This would mean that although the buyer's funds are not at risk, they are still unavailable to the buyer during the time (weeks or months) of the LC. This arrangement could have important cash flow implications for the buyer. However, if the buyer has a line of credit with the issuing bank, the amount of the LC will be deducted from the buyer's line of credit.

Another consideration is commercial disputes. Under an LC, the issuing bank pays when it receives the required documents from the seller, and all the documents are accurate. The bank does not guarantee it has actually seen or inspected the shipment. LCs are paid (negotiated) in bank offices, not shipping docks. Both sellers and buyers need to be aware that there is still the potential for commercial disputes such as damaged goods. Commercial disputes must be handled separately from the LC according to the terms of the sales contract. Pre-shipment inspections may be required as a condition in the LC to better ensure the buyer receives what it ordered.

Cost is also an important consideration. LCs can be expensive, especially if the LC is confirmed. There is a cost to open an LC and a cost to receive funds from the LC. Generally, the costs to open is paid by the buyer ($300 to $400), and the cost to receive the funds is paid by the seller ($200 to $400). Regardless of which party pays, the overall transactional cost can be US$500–$800. Plus, some fees, such as to confirm the LC, are based on the overall value of the LC. This means for a large, confirmed LC, costs can be quite high. Nevertheless, LCs remain an important international payment method given the balance of risk offered to each party.

DOCUMENTARY COLLECTIONS

Documentary collections (DCs) is a payment method in which the seller uti-lizes a foreign bank to collect payment for a transaction, with the understanding that the buyer will not receive the goods until payment has been made. The role of the foreign bank under documentary collections is very different from its role under an LC. With a DC, unlike an LC, the foreign bank does not promise to pay, nor do banks verify the documents. The bank will simply "act in good faith" to receive payment before the necessary paperwork is released to the buyer so the buyer can receive the goods. DCs are less complicated than LCs and less expen-sive. They are a good option when the seller has some trust the buyer will pay.

> **documentary collections**
>
> A payment method in which the seller (exporter) utilizes a foreign bank to collect payment for a transaction with the understand-ing that the buyer will not receive the goods until payment has been made.

OPEN ACCOUNT

In **open account** sales, the seller extends credit to the buyer. This means payment for the goods is not made in advance of shipment but some time later, typically 30, 60, or 90 days. The buyer and seller agree to the specific terms. Open account terms involve less paperwork and give more flexibility to both parties. However, the legal recourse of the exporter in case of nonpayment is less satisfactory than with the methods discussed previously. Open account sales are more attractive to the importer. But because of the risks to the exporter, open account sales tend to be limited to foreign subsidiaries, joint ventures and licensees, and foreign customers with whom the exporter has had a long and favorable experience.

> **open account**
>
> A payment method whereby the seller (exporter) extends credit to the buyer such that the buyer typically does not have to pay for the goods in advance but instead some time later (e.g., 30, 60, or 90 days).

One method to lessen the risk associated with open account sales is for an exporter to obtain foreign receivables insurance. These policies insure foreign receivables against potential loss due to nonpayment by the buyer. Govern-ments and private companies offer foreign receivables insurance. In the United States, the Export-Import Bank (a U.S. government agency) offers the insurance, as does COFACE, a private company.[22]

CONSIGNMENT

In a **consignment sale**, the exporter retains title (ownership) until the importer sells the goods, meaning the buyer does not pay the seller until the buyer sells the product on to the next buyer (perhaps the final consumer). Because ex-porters own the goods longer in this method than in any other, their financial burdens and risk are great. In addition, recovering losses can be lengthy and expensive if the importer fails to always act in good faith, such as keeping the inventory in good condition or doing its best efforts to sell the goods. Because

> **consignment sale**
>
> Export transaction whereby the exporter retains title (ownership) of the goods until the importer sells the goods, and thus the importer does not pay the exporter until the importer sells the product to the next buyer.

In a consignment sale, the exporter retains ownership of the product until the importer sells the goods.

of those problems, exporters tend to limit consignment arrangements to their subsidiaries abroad or foreign partners that are well trusted.

When exporters want to introduce goods to a new market, a consignment arrangement may be necessary to encourage importers to handle the merchandise. Furthermore, when exporters want to retain some control over the foreign market price, they can do so under a consignment contract. They can set the price when they own the goods, as they do under a consignment contract.

Impact of Foreign Exchange on Pricing

Foreign exchange (FX) rate instability presents one of the central challenges to a firm in its price-setting strategies in international markets. As exchange rates change between currencies, this change can have an important impact on how much a firm eventually receives in its home (domestic) currency or what the final consumers pay in their home currency. The more unstable the rate is between two currencies, the harder for a firm to hold prices stable.

Table 12-2 shows how FX rates for four major currencies changed in value against the U.S. dollar over the years 2005 through 2009. The U.S. dollar lost value against the euro and yen but gained in value against the Mexican peso and British pound. The gains and losses were not consistent. The lost against the euro was 17.3 percent, but 21 percent against the yen. The gain against the peso was nearly 23 percent, but only 6 percent on the pound. The gains and losses were also not a trend that held throughout the four-year period. Within two years, at the end of 2007, the British pound had gained considerably against the U.S. dollar (13.4 percent) only to give up the gain by the next year. Changes can also be quite sudden, as seen with the Mexican peso. The peso was losing some value against the dollar in 2006 and 2007, but it took a major devaluation in 2008, which held through 2009.

There are some important insights to be gained from the preceding examples. First, currencies do not move in unison, meaning a country's currency may be strengthening against one currency but weakening against another. This can be seen in the euro (the U.S. dollar lost value over the four years) versus the British pound (the U.S. dollar gained). Second, changes are in no way predictable and trends do not necessarily hold. For example, the British pound was

Table 12-2 • Exchange Rates: U.S. Dollar versus Other Currencies

Country	12/30/2005	12/29/2006	12/31/2007	12/31/2008	12/31/2009	Amount of Local Currency Required to Purchase $100 in 2005	Amount of Local Currency Required to Purchase $100 in 2009	Percent Change US $ over Four Years
Euro	1.1842	1.3197	1.4603	1.3919	1.4332	84 euros	70 euros	−17%
Mexican Peso	10.6275	10.7995	10.9169	13.8320	13.0576	1,063 pesos	1306 pesos	23%
British Pound	1.7188	1.9586	1.9843	1.4619	1.6167	58 pounds	62 pounds	06%
Japanese yen	117.8800	119.0200	111.7100	90.7900	93.0800	11,788 yen	9,308 yen	−21%

Source: Foreign Exchange Rates 2000 to Present (Spot Rate); Federal Reserve Bank of New York; http://www.federalreserve.gov/releases/H10/hist/; accessed October 22, 2010.

steadily gaining value in 2006 and 2007, only to lose all gains in 2008. From both insights, it is clear that exchange rate changes for a currency against another currency cannot be predicted, neither in the short nor long term.

The data from Table 12-2 presents an interesting decision for exporters. Assume a company was exporting to Japan in 2005 with products priced in U.S. dollars. A good that sold for $100 in 2005 would require 11,788 yen to purchase the product. But by 2009 it would require only 9,308. This means the product likely would be much more competitive in Japan in 2009 than it would have been in 2005. Yet the opposite would be true for the same product sold in Mexico. In 2005 the $100 product would require 1,063 pesos, but by 2009, 1,306 pesos. This means over a four-year period, an identical product that is more competitive in Japan is less competitive in Mexico, all due to actions outside the firm's control.

How should the firm respond? To be more competitive in Mexico, the firm may decide to lower pricing, which also lowers profits. It might also raise prices for exports to Japan to capture some of the "profits" otherwise being "passed" onto the Japanese importers. And regardless of what a firm does, at any time the exchange rates can change, reversing the effects of any price changes.

This scenario helps illustrate that because exchange rate movements are outside the control of a firm and unpredictable, companies need to recognize their FX risks and implement strategies to deal with those risks. (See "Fast Food and Foreign Exchange" for some specific examples of the impact FX changes can have on a firm's profits.) The next sections identify the specific risks associated with FX changes and strategies to mitigate those risks.

Types of FX Risk

FX rates between currencies are constantly changing and are an important consideration as companies trade internationally. A firm may mistakenly decide that by always pricing its products its home currency, it is avoiding FX risk. However, all firms conducting international trade between countries with different currencies face some type of FX risk. Foreign exchange risk is generally divided into three types: transaction, economic, and translation FX risk.

Foreign exchange (FX) rate instability presents one of the central challenges to a firm in its price-setting strategies in international markets.

Fast Food and Foreign Exchange

• • •

U.S.-based fast-food restaurant companies are one example of an industry that has been dealing with foreign exchange problems due to increased volatility worldwide. Weaker demand in the United States caused many fast-food franchises, such as McDonald's and Starbucks, to look overseas for growth markets.

However, moving overseas has increased these firms' exposure to foreign exchange risk. For example, Burger King recently reduced its earnings outlook by 10-cents-per-share as a result of declining currencies in Europe, Turkey, Australia, New Zealand, and Mexico. Yum! Brands, whose brands include KFC, Pizza Hut, and Taco Bell, stated that they expect a $25 million reduction in revenue as a result of foreign exchange rate fluctuations. With over 60 percent of its revenue coming from overseas operations, Yum! Brands must look carefully at its exposure to foreign exchange risk and how to manage its risk.[23]

TRANSACTION RISK

transaction risk

The risk that results from changes in the value of foreign currency such that the exporter will receive less domestic currency than anticipated and thus diminish the exporting firm's financial results.

Whenever a sale occurs in which the buyer and the seller operate in different currencies, there is foreign exchange **transaction risk**—the risk that the seller will receive less domestic currency than anticipated or that the buyer will pay more domestic currency than anticipated. For a particular sale, one party must have transaction risk—either the seller or buyer. The seller has the risk if it priced the sale in a currency different from its domestic (home) currency. Similarly, the buyer has transaction risk when it purchases a product priced in a currency different from its domestic currency. (FX transaction risk would also apply to services.) The risk is that when the foreign exchange is eventually completed, it results in less domestic currency (for either the seller or buyer) than anticipated. Companies may naively think that by always pricing in their domestic currency (such as U.S. exporters always pricing in U.S. dollars) they are avoiding transaction risk. Though they are avoiding such risk directly, they are simply pushing that risk onto their buyer. The buyer has to make a judgment that unless it hedges (removes) the risk, it may end up paying more in its domestic currency than anticipated.

ECONOMIC RISK

foreign exchange economic risk

The risk that, over time, a firm will lose profits or become less competitive in its international sales due to foreign exchange rate changes.

As a firm expands internationally, it will be selling into multiple countries. Very likely, these countries will not share the same currency. Over time, as exchange rates vary between currencies, a firm may find that its products or services are becoming more competitive in a foreign market due to FX rate changes. This would be the case if the firm's home currency is depreciating (losing in value) versus the currency in the foreign market. Given such a stronger competitive position, the firm may choose to focus more on markets where exchange rates make its pricing more competitive. However, as discussed earlier, FX rates can change and are not predictable. Thus, if eventually the firm's domestic currency appreciates, the firm may find it is no longer competitive in particular foreign markets. This is the basis for **foreign exchange economic risk**—the risk that over time, a firm will lose profits or become less competitive in its international sales due to FX rate changes. Because economic risk is related to how competitive a firm is, it is also known as competitive risk.

All firms conducting international trade have some economic risk. The risk is particularly high if a firm has concentrated most of its international sales into a limited number of countries. Should the firm's home currency appreciate, and many or all of the currencies in which the firm operates depreciate, the firm may find it is no longer competitive. This would have been the case for a firm in

2005 if it had sales only to Mexico. As previously discussed from Table 12-2, by 2009 the U.S. dollar had appreciated 23 percent versus the Mexican peso, making U.S. products in Mexico more expensive. This would put tremendous pressure on the firm to lower pricing to be more competitive. If unable to do so, the firm may lose sales to Mexico or even have to discontinue sales. But if the firm was also selling into Japan or Europe, it would find its products more competitive because the dollar lost value versus the euro and yen. If the firm was diversified beyond Mexico, the overall impact of the peso FX rates changes would be less.

TRANSLATION RISK

The third type of foreign exchange risk applies to companies with overseas subsidiaries. Companies must translate (or "convert") the financial statements of their subsidiaries from the foreign currency used in the subsidiaries to their domestic (home) currency so the data can be incorporated into the parent financial statements. Examples of items to be converted from foreign currency to the domestic currency include assets (foreign building, fixtures, inventory), invoices to be paid (foreign liabilities), or monies yet to be received (account receivables). **Foreign exchange translation risk** is the risk that when foreign financial statements are restated (translated) into the home currency of a firm, this action reduces profits. How companies translate financial statement of a foreign subsidiary are governed by accounting rules, which is why translation risk is also known as accounting exposure or reporting risk. The greater the amount of assets or liabilities denominated in foreign currencies, the greater the translation risk.

> **foreign exchange translation risk**
>
> The risk that, when foreign financial statements are restated (translated) into the firm's home currency, this action reduces the firm's profits.

Hedging FX Risk

As a firm expands its international business, its level of FX risk, or exposure, is also likely to increase. A company with only a small level of international sales, with no overseas subsidiaries, and all pricing in its home currency, has very little FX risk exposure. But as the firm grows its international sales, adds more foreign markets, and eventually opens an overseas subsidiary, its FX risk exposure may be significant. The core competency of a company is generally not to make or lose money based on foreign exchange rate changes. Companies instead strive to minimize their FX risk exposure, while maintaining their competiveness.

Hedging is a general business term used to describe a number of techniques used to reduce risk. **Foreign exchange hedging** is the specific term for techniques that are used to reduce or eliminate FX risk. **Foreign exchange hedging tools** are the specific financial products banks and other institutions offer to hedge FX risk. Examples include currency forward contracts and currency options. Table 12-3 summarizes the most common FX hedging tools. Depending on the type of FX risk, a firm may use one or a combination of hedging tools.[24]

> **foreign exchange hedging**
>
> Techniques used by firms operating internationally to reduce or eliminate foreign exchange risk.

> **foreign exchange hedging tools**
>
> Specific financial products offered by banks and other financial institutions to firms to reduce or eliminate the firm's foreign exchange risk.

FORWARD CONTRACT

A forward contract fixes the exchange rate that will be used on a specific date in the future. The forward contract is tied to a specific date (for example 30, 60, or 90 days out), the specific rate (also known as the forward rate—for example, 12 Mexican pesos exchanged for one U.S. dollar), and a specific amount of currency (for example, 500,000 Mexican pesos). By purchasing a forward contract, a firm has the security of knowing exactly the exchange rate that will be applied when it converts the specific amount of money on a specific date in the future. The advantages of forward contracts are that they are available for relatively small amounts of money and fees are low. The disadvantage is that after a firm purchases a forward contract, it can generally not be canceled or sold to another party. The firm is essentially obligated to make the foreign currency exchange

Table 12-3 • Foreign Exchange Hedging Tools

Hedging Tool	What It Provides	Advantages	Disadvantages	Cost
Forward Contract	Locks in a future exchange rate. The future exchange rate is known.	It is available for most currencies and for small or large amounts of currencies.	The contract must be executed. It generally cannot be canceled or sold.	Relatively low.
Currency Options	Locks in an exchange rate until the option expires.	The foreign exchange does not have to be completed; it is an option but not an obligation.	This tool is not as flexible as forward contracts because the options generally have to be purchased in specific amounts.	High relative to forward contracts.
Currency Swaps	Provides simultaneous buy and sell of a fixed currency amount; locks in exchange rates.	For the right purpose, this tool is affordable.	This tool works best when there is a short-term need to swap between two currencies.	Low relative to currency options.

when the forward contract is due. Even if the current exchange rate on the day the forward contract is due would otherwise be in favor of the firm, it is still obligated to use the rate from the forward contract, not that day's current rate.

Forward contracts are commonly used to eliminate transaction risk. Assume a U.S. firm invoices a buyer in Mexico 500,000 Mexican pesos for a transaction to be paid in 90 days. If the firm wants to eliminate the FX transactional risk, it could purchase a forward contract for 500,000 pesos to be converted into U.S. dollars in 90 days. When the customer in Mexico pays the invoice, the U.S. firm would use it against the forward contract to receive its U.S. dollars at the exchange rate specified in the forward contract, regardless of what the actual exchange rate may be that day.

CURRENCY OPTIONS

As with a forward contract, a currency option locks in an exchange rate to be used in the future. However, unlike a forward, the **currency option** may be exercised up until the option expires, or not at all. In this way, a currency option is the right but not the obligation to exchange a fixed amount of foreign exchange at a fixed rate. The exchange must be made before the option expires. Currency options may appear to be more flexible than a forward contract given that it can used during a range of dates or not used at all. However, currency options generally have to be purchased in large, fixed amounts of foreign exchange. Rates and fees can be relatively high.

CURRENCY SWAPS

A currency swap is essentially two parties "swapping" a set amount of foreign exchange for a period of time. For example, a U.S. firm may swap $1,000,000 for a corresponding amount of euros, only to then exchange the euros back into U.S. dollars at a set date in the future. Fees take into account interest rate differences between the two currencies. In this way a currency swap is the simultaneous purchase (today) and sale (set date in the future) of a given amount of two currencies. As with other hedging tools, a currency swap locks in the exchange rates to be used. Swaps are useful when a firm has a need to both pay a supplier in foreign currency today but expects to receive that same foreign currency from a buyer in the future. Currency swaps can be customized, including a staggered repayment of the swap between parties.

Matching FX Risk with Hedging Tools

Forward contracts, currency options, and currency swaps are three of the most common hedging tools, though increasingly financial institutions are creating

currency option

A tool to hedge foreign exchange risk whereby the owner of the currency option has the right but not the obligation to exchange a fixed amount of foreign currency at a fixed rate.

more customized products. Which hedging tool a firm uses depends on the specific circumstances. All three of the preceding tools are appropriate for transactional risk. However, for a small hedge, a forward contract would likely be used given the higher costs associated with options and swaps. The decision may also be based on the size of the hedge and the two currencies because not all tools are available for all currencies. All the preceding tools could also be useful to hedge FX translation risk, though options and swaps would be more common than forward contracts.

To manage foreign exchange economic risk, companies would not use hedging tools because the risk is not tied to a specific transaction or collection of foreign assets. The most effective hedge against economic risk is market diversification. A firm has high FX economic risk exposure when its foreign sales are overly concentrated in only a few markets. To lower their

Foreign exchange hedging tools can be an effective way to help mitigate foreign exchange risk.

economic risk, the firm needs to continually invest in new markets to build a stronger, more diverse foreign market. Because currencies do not always change in unison, as previously discussed in Table 12-2, this lowers their overall competitive risk to currency changes.

Currency Inconvertibility

Most free-market economies follow a policy of freely floating exchange rates with complete convertibility of the currency. However, many countries, including key emerging markets such as China, still have restrictions on the convertibility of their currencies, allowing the governments to maintain artificial exchange rates that may diverge significantly from a freely floating or black-market exchange rate. Such currency inconvertibility also poses problems for multinationals seeking to integrate myriad multinational operations and transfer payments for goods and equipment supplied, as well as payment of dividends and capital repatriation.

Pepsi faced currency inconvertibility issues in China and used a number of methods to work around the challenge.

The Impact of Currency Inconvertibility

Figure 12-3 provides an example of different approaches Pepsi used in China. Shown are some of the stresses and creativity that currency inconvertibility fosters. China's exchange controls are due to its desire to conserve scarce foreign exchange and use it for approved purposes such as imports of capital equipment and essential raw materials. The Chinese government prefers that multinationals become self-sufficient in foreign exchange by exporting sufficient amounts to generate the foreign exchange needed to pay for their imports and foreign exchange outflows. Figure 12-3 shows some alternatives developed by Pepsi to handle exchange controls.[25]

Model A of Figure 12-3 shows how Pepsi can use surplus cash generated in one Pepsi subsidiary to fund the capital needs of another Pepsi subsidiary, thus obviating the need to send additional foreign exchange capital contributions into China. However, this runs up against the desire of Chinese states to conserve capital for use within the states. Thus, a state could prevent Pepsi from

Figure 12-3 ● Pepsi in China: Dealing with Currency Volatility and Inconvertibility

The problem: Inconvertibility of Chinese currency (Renminbi) makes it difficult to remit dividends, repartriate capital, and import needed materials, parts, and capital goods.

The Chinese government solution: Earn export revenues sufficient to pay for imports and foreign currency outflows (dividends, imports, and capital repatriation).

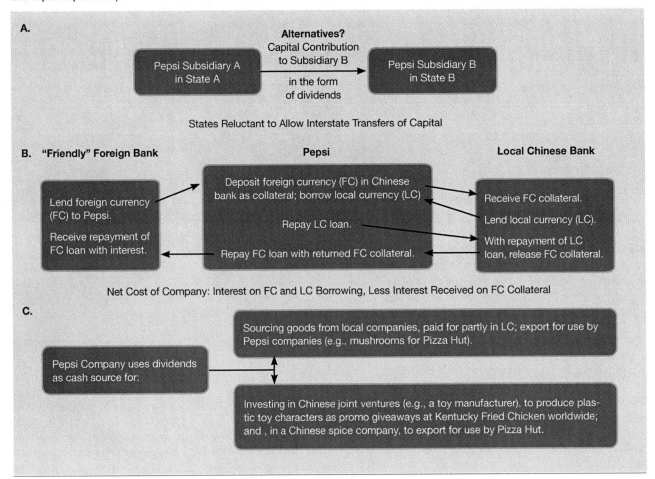

Source: Derived from "Learn from Russia," *Business China,* September 5, 1994, 1–3.

transferring out capital. More generally, such a solution works only as long as a multinational can use local funds to continue to expand within the country. Imports of machinery and components still have to be paid for with additional foreign exchange. In Pepsi's case, it needs to expand across China because soft drink consumption is still at low levels, and there is considerable room for growth. Other companies, however, may not find enough attractive investment opportunities.

Model B shows how Pepsi can tap additional local currency sources to meet its capital needs without having to bring in foreign exchange. In this instance, Pepsi relies on its connections with foreign banks to borrow hard currency (HC), which it then uses as collateral to borrow local currency from a Chinese bank. **Hard currency** is a currency widely traded globally, and trusted, such as the U.S. dollar or the euro. As Pepsi's units generate funds from operations, the local currency loans can be paid off. Paying off those loans releases the HC collateral, which, in turn, can be repaid to the foreign bank. The cost is higher because Pepsi has to pay interest on two loans: both the HC and the local currency loans. However, this method prevents Pepsi from having to make additional HC contributions to its Chinese operations.

> **hard currency**
>
> A currency that is widely traded globally and thus is widely trusted.

Model C is an illustration of how Pepsi might use surplus local currency funds to source goods in China that can be used by Pepsi subsidiaries overseas. For example, Pepsi might use surplus local currency to buy ingredients such as mushrooms for its international chain of Pizza Hut shops. Alternatively, Pepsi can use its surplus local currency funds to invest in joint ventures with Chinese partners to start up new operations that supply goods to Pepsi's overseas subsidiaries or to use for general export purposes. China prefers this third alternative because it deepens China's business base and capabilities. As the three models in Figure 12-3 show, getting paid becomes at least as important as making the basic pricing decision in major emerging markets. Pricing executives need to carefully consider how the foreign exchange situation can affect their pricing flexibility.

Countertrade

Related to the issue of currency inconvertibility is **countertrade**—the exchange of goods for goods rather than for money. It is also widely known as barter. However in barter, the exact item to be exchanged is specified, such as oil for machinery. In countertrade, a range of specified goods can be taken in exchange for exports from a Western supplier. For example, Catalyst Research of Maryland began selling specialized batteries for pacemakers to Tesla, the Czech electronics collective. In 1986, Tesla bought the rights to manufacture the pacemaker battery, with Catalyst selling the equipment, supplies, and raw materials needed. As part of the agreement, Catalyst Research started buying product inventions from the Czech Academy of Sciences to fulfill its countertrade obligations.

> **countertrade**
> Also known as barter; a trade in which good or services are exchanged for other goods or services rather than money.

A typical transaction might be as follows: A Polish apple juice factory may need new equipment, but it is unable to buy from a U.S. supplier because no U.S. bank will lend it money. However, an Austrian bank is willing to guarantee the factory's debt; hence, the order goes to an Austrian manufacturer. The Austrian bank undertakes to buy a large portion of the apple juice produced for resale to Western markets. It is able to do that because most Austrian banks have their own in-house trading companies. (Austria's proximity to the Eastern European countries has led to a concentration of countertrade expertise in Vienna.) Through this convoluted chain, the Polish factory gets the equipment, the Austrian manufacturer gets an order, and the bank makes fees from the loan guarantee and commissions on sale of the apple juice.[26]

There are several forms of countertrade, as described next.

BARTER

The simplest form of countertrade is **barter**—the direct exchange of goods for goods. It is cumbersome because each party must have goods in the exact quantities that the other party wants. It is the least attractive form of countertrade.

> **barter**
> The simplest form of countertrade whereby parties to a transaction directly exchange goods for goods.

COUNTERPURCHASE

Counterpurchase is reciprocal buying to be fulfilled over some future time period, with flexibility as to the actual goods to be purchased. In these transactions, a majority of the purchase price is paid in cash. An example of this is the way in which Lurgi, a European construction and engineering firm, built a methanol plant in what was then East Germany. In return for the 400 million DM contract to build the plant, Lurgi took back 408,000 tons a year of methanol, out of its

> **counterpurchase**
> A form of countertrade whereby the seller agrees to receive goods or services over some future time period as payment for goods or services provided.

total capacity of 800,000 tons. At the time the contract was signed, there was an excess supply, which eased only gradually as older, environmentally unacceptable plants were closed in Western Europe.[27]

OFFSET

Offset is similar to counterpurchase and is more likely at the government level. When dealing with government buyers, the other party has a generalized commitment to buy a certain percentage of the initial export transaction from the country. Thus, when Boeing sold AWACs to the British defense department, it agreed to buy 130 percent of the value of the transaction in British goods. Another example of an offset deal was in South Africa, which purchased over $5 billion worth of arms from foreign defense companies on the condition that the suppliers would, in turn, "invest or spend on South African goods . . . three times as much as the weapons cost to buy."[28]

BUYBACK

Buyback occurs when capital equipment sales are sold with a counterpurchase clause that can be fulfilled by a firm buying some of the output of the plant that is set up with the imported capital equipment.

SWITCH TRADING

Switch trading involves a third party, usually a specialized trading house with expertise in certain industrial sectors and with certain countries, usually centrally planned economies. Austria and Switzerland are two sources of expertise; several switch trading firms are located in those two countries.[29]

BEST PRACTICES IN COUNTERTRADE

Before deciding to enter into countertrade, an exporter should scout firms in the targeted country to decide whether reliable suppliers (of raw materials or components) can be developed. It also should be willing to help upgrade the manufacturing capability of potential suppliers so that useful raw materials and components are obtained at reasonable prices as a result of the countertrade opportunity. Otherwise, the firm is likely to be stuck with poor-quality goods that are difficult to trade. A firm considering countertrade must also recognize the challenges of buying and selling products in which it may not have direct experience. That increases the challenges associated with utilizing countertrade.

Countertrade, then, should be viewed as the initiation of a long-term relationship between a country and its firms. That, in turn, will satisfy the needs of the countries that resort to countertrade. Typically, such developing nations use countertrade for several reasons:

* They lack foreign exchange.

* They want as partners multinationals that will help sell their goods overseas.

* They hope that successful technology transfer will take place as multinationals work with domestic firms to transform them into reliable suppliers of high-quality raw materials and components.

* All of this, they hope, will increase domestic employment and incomes and lead to economic development.

Three factors influence a firm's international pricing strategy: firm-level factors, market-specific factors, and product-specific factors. These factors influence international pricing decisions.

Firms that are faced with competitive price cuts may need to respond with a coordinated strategy in which pricing decisions are only one aspect of an overall marketing mix.

The cost to produce a product, provide a service, market those products and services, and deliver goods to the final consumer also influence price. The higher these costs, the higher the pricing needs to be for the firm to be profitable.

Distribution and marketing costs also must be covered in the foreign market price. These costs include international freight, import duties and taxes, and foreign marketing costs.

Factors affecting pricing that are market specific include consumers' ability to buy, government regulations and restrictions, and distribution channel costs such as order size and discount expectations.

Local competition entranced in foreign markets can be formidable competitors, especially if they enjoy significant cost advantages to their foreign competitors. New firms entering the market may find strong pressure to reduce their prices to be competitive.

Demand for a firm's products is a function of the number of consumers; their ability to pay; their tastes, habits, and attitudes relating to the product; and the existence of competing products.

International pricing strategies include market share pricing, pricing at a premium to the market, pricing on a cost-plus basis, and target pricing.

There is strong pressure for firms to offer standardized pricing among its international buyers. Uniform pricing also allows a firm to set pricing policy centrally and to decide the role that price should play in the overall marketing mix. However, consumers may differ in the values and features they perceive in a product, which could justify pricing differences between markets. Marketing research among a number of foreign markets would allow a firm to measure the differences in perceived value. Coupling that information with differing elasticities can justify higher prices in certain markets.

Setting pricing too low (below a firm's cost) may result in accusation of dumping. If such behavior is proven, foreign government may impose anti-dumping or countervailing duties.

As discussed as part of firm-specific factors and pricing, companies must allocate costs so its pricing strategies can be more aligned with their true cost structure. This involves the allocation of a firm's variable and fixed costs. Firms can select full-absorption pricing or variable pricing.

Transfer pricing (intracorporate pricing) is an area that has special implications for international marketing. It refers to prices on goods sold within the corporate family—that is, from division to division or to a foreign subsidiary.

Companies must select international payment methods that balance the needs of the seller (which prefers being paid as early as possible) and those of the buyer (which prefers the opposite—waiting weeks or months until paying). Use of intermediaries, such as banks, is often the solution.

Four payment methods are commonly used with international trade: (1) Cash in advance is the most risky method for the buyer, the least risky for the seller. (2) Letters of credit are a common compromise. (3) Documentary collections are more risky to the seller than letters of credit, but they are less expensive and a good option when there is some trust of the foreign buyer. (4) Open account is the most risky for the seller and the more preferred by the buyer. Use of foreign receivables insurance from government agencies or the private sector can help mitigate the risk to the seller.

In a consignment sale, the exporter retains title (ownership) until the importer sells the goods. Because exporters own the goods longer in this method than in any other, their financial burdens and risk are great.

Foreign exchange (FX) rate instability presents one of the central challenges to a firm in its price-setting strategies in international markets. As exchange rates change between currencies, this change can have an important impact on how much a firm eventually receives in its home (domestic) currency or what the final consumers pay in their home currency. The more unstable the rate is between two currencies, the harder for a firm to hold prices stable.

There are three most commonly recognized foreign exchange risks: transaction risk, the risk associated with a single transaction; economic risk, the risk that over time a firm will be less competitive in a foreign market due to foreign exchange rate changes; and translation risk, the risk that when the financial statements of a foreign subsidiary are translated in the home currency of the parent company, losses will be incurred.

As a firm expands its international business, its level of FX risk, or exposure, is also likely to increase. A company with only a small level of international sales, with no overseas subsidiaries, and all pricing in its home currency has very little FX risk exposure. But as the firm grows its international sales, adds more foreign markets, and eventually opens an overseas subsidiary, its FX risk exposure may be significant.

Companies use foreign exchange hedging tools to reduce FX risk. The most common are forward contracts, currency options, and currency swaps. Each in its own way offer ways to lock in an exchange rate to be used in the future. Market diversification is the most effective way to reduce FX economic risk.

Countertrade is the exchange of goods for goods rather than for money. It is also widely known as barter. Countertrade is a common tool when foreign currencies are inconvertible.

KEY TERMS

barter	fixed costs	foreign exchange	open account
consignment sale	foreign exchange	translation risk	penetration pricing
counterpurchase	economic risk	full-absorption pricing	SWIFT
countertrade	foreign exchange hedging	gray marketing	transaction risk
currency option	foreign exchange hedging	hard currency	transfer pricing
documentary collections	tools	letter of credit (LC)	variable costs
dumping		market skimming	variable pricing

NASBITE CGBP TOPICS COVERED IN THIS CHAPTER

Note: For full details of the alignment of each chapter with the NASBITE CGBP, be sure to review the information provided in the section "Studying for the NASBITE CGBP Exam."

CGBP Rubric	**Topic**
01/05/01:	country risk (e.g., political risk, economic risk, expropriation)
01/05/02:	commercial risk
01/05/04:	credit assessment and mitigating techniques (e.g., export credit insurance, international finance)
01/07/02:	revenues and expense uncertainties
01/07/03:	transfer pricing
02/03/01:	impact on market selection of (price)
02/06/02:	product life cycle implications (or strategies)

02/06/08:	legal/regulatory requirements for pricing
02/07/01:	cost structures, including marginal and fixed
02/07/02:	tariff and non-tariff barriers and incentives
02/07/03:	quoting methods
02/07/04:	resources for global pricing strategies (e.g., current revision of International Chamber of Commerce publications [e.g., Incoterms, UCP, URC], U.S. government agencies, and websites)
02/07/05:	how local market conditions could impact pricing
04/01/01:	political and economic risks causing late and/or non-payment from overseas markets (e.g., cancellation/failure to grant U.S. export license, civil unrest, foreign currency delays/shortage)
04/01/02:	cultural issues of buyer's country which may impact payment methods, money trans mission methods, language used, credit control procedures, level of governmental control, corruption issues, and sources of finance
04/02/01:	foreign exchange risk mitigation techniques and required documentation (e.g., hedging tools, currency option contracts, transfer pricing)
04/03/04:	methods of payment (e.g., letters of credit, documentary collections, cash in advance, sight draft)
04/03/05:	mitigating techniques (e.g., credit risk insurance from Overseas Private Investment Cor poration (OPIC) and U.S. Export-Import (Ex-Im) Bank)
04/04/01:	methods and costs of payment (e.g., letters of credit, documentary collections, cash in advance, time draft, banker's acceptance)
04/04/05:	types of letters of credit (e.g., confirmed/unconfirmed, irrevocable, transferable, stand by, with a time draft)
04/05/01:	terms and conditions of purchase or sale (e.g., countertrade, consignment, payment terms)
04/05/02:	resources: banks, U.S. government agencies, International Chamber of Commerce

QUESTIONS AND RESEARCH

1. What are some of the major factors affecting international pricing? In particular, how are prices influenced by a firm's strategy, a firm's competition, consumers' ability to buy, a firm's cost and market structure, and the complete product line?

2. What should be the relationship between export and domestic prices?

3. What are the consequences of charging an export price below the domestic market price?

4. Are there reasons why export prices should be higher than domestic prices? If so, what are the marketing implications of export price escalation?

5. How might government policies affect international pricing strategies in a foreign market?

6. What is gray marketing, and what is the implication for international pricing?

7. Provide an example when a firm would likely use market share pricing as its international pricing strategy for a particular foreign market. What are examples for other pricing strategies such as pricing at a premium to the market, pricing on a cost-plus basis, and target pricing?

8. Discuss the pressure for uniform pricing in international markets. Provide examples illustrating when uniform pricing would not be justified.

9. What is transfer pricing? Why is it a consideration in international pricing? What are some useful formulas in setting transfer prices?

10. What is gray marketing? How does it affect international marketing and price setting?

11. Discuss what a seller wants as an international payment method. Contrast that with what the seller wants.

12. For each of the four most common international payment methods, provide an example of an international transaction that would be appropriate for each payment method.

13. Refer to Table 12-2. Discuss the implications for a Mexican exporter selling products to a U.S. buyer during the years 2006 through 2009.

14. How do exchange rates affect international pricing? Why might a firm with an appreciating currency not raise its export prices?

15. Is quoting export prices only in a firm's domestic currency a viable strategy to avoid the impact of exchange rates?

16. What are the different risks that a firm marketing its products internationally faces because of exchange rate fluctuations?

17. For each of the three most common foreign exchange hedging tools, provide an example illustrating when a firm might use each tool.

18. What is countertrade? Why should firms be willing to consider countertrade arrangements in their international marketing efforts?

19. Why do countries seek countertrade? How can a firm assess the profitability of a proposed countertrade transaction?

 CHAPTER 12 TEAM PROJECT ASSIGNMENT: Trade Finance

This chapter discussed how companies develop their international pricing strategies, along with examples of those strategies. It also discussed payment methods and foreign exchange risk.

For your team project for this chapter, think about these issues as they relate to your client. The goal is to first identify the issues and then develop an initial pricing strategy.

PRICING ISSUES

Research your client's international activities (if any). In addition, think about the countries your client has proposed for global expansion. Use these questions to frame a discussion of the issues that may impact your client as it develops its international pricing strategies:

• What are firm-level factors that will affect your client's pricing strategy?
• What are market-specific factors that will affect your client?
• Are there significant product- or service-related issues?
• Will competitors have an important impact on how your client sets its pricing strategy?

Discuss your findings.

DEVELOPING PRICING STRATEGIES

Discuss recommended strategies for your client. Link these strategies to the key issues just discussed. The goal is not to recommend specific *prices*, but to recommend pricing *strategies*.

Consider these two questions as you develop pricing strategy recommendations:

• What are the specific pricing strategies you recommend, such as market share pricing, pricing at a premium, target pricing, and so on?
• Do you recommend a global pricing strategy or adapted strategies for each market?

The outcome of your research and discussions will be incorporated into the final international marketing plan.

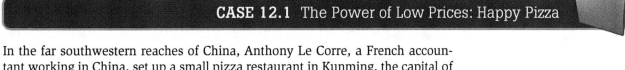

CASE 12.1 The Power of Low Prices: Happy Pizza

In the far southwestern reaches of China, Anthony Le Corre, a French accountant working in China, set up a small pizza restaurant in Kunming, the capital of Yunnan Province and a gateway to the Silk Road, close to the borders of Burma and Vietnam. He charged between $2.50 and $5.00 for pizzas, a relatively high price, making the pizza unaffordable for the masses. He sold that restaurant and opened another pizzeria in Chongqing, to the north and east of Kunming. Chongqing is a large port city at the confluence of the Yangtze and Jialing rivers and one of China's largest cities. Le Corre's second restaurant, experiencing a similar fare, closed after a year, unable to be distinctive in a competitive local market. Two years later, Le Corre opened a third restaurant in Shanghai, at the estuary of the Yangtze River. Shanghai is China's largest industrial city, as well as its largest financial and commercial center. This time Le Corre made some changes in the way he sold pizza. The Shanghai pizza restaurant, Hello Pizza, sold nine-inch pizza for 10 yuan, about $1.20. His most expensive pizzas sold for $4.20, still below the price of inexpensive pizzas sold at comparable restaurants, as shown in the table below. In addition to three restaurants, Le Corre also has three pizza delivery locations, a bakery, and a catering business.

Restaurant	Hello Pizza	Pizza Hut	Pizza Italia	Gino Cafe
Cheapest pizza ($)	1.2	5.4	6.6	4.3
Most expensive pizza ($)	4.2	6.6	9.0	9.2
Number of restaurants	3.0	28.0	3.0	12.0

Low prices are an essential component of Le Corre's business model. But to make a profit with low prices, he also has to achieve low costs, while maintaining quality. Le Corre learned his formula from reading a book about McDonald's, which achieved its success by combining low prices with consistent quality and service.

Le Corre's objective in Shanghai was to make inexpensive pizza that the Chinese could eat every day. In the evening, his staff chops green peppers and stores them in tiny resealable bags that hold exactly 30 grams of peppers. Similar small bags hold chopped eggplant, onions, sausage, and other ingredients designed to be used in making single pizzas. Salad boxes are prepared with lettuce, carrots, and a packet of salad dressing. Another employee rolls pizza crusts. All of those items are delivered to the restaurants the next morning.

The restaurants, seating about 25 customers, operate with four employees. One employee assembles the premixed salads while another employee sprinkles ingredients from the resealable bags onto the premade pizza crusts and begins baking them. A third employee serves the customers; the fourth employee is the cashier. Men on electric bicycles make deliveries, which are about half the business. The small staff, needing a limited skill set, can be well trained. To reduce turnover, the restaurants hire migrants from neighboring provinces who are likely to stay while they save money to take back on their visits home. Wage costs are $140 to $180 a month, nearly all are local employees except for a French baker. Average Chinese urban income in 2003 was about 8,500 yuan, or a little over $1,000 a year.

Aside from low prices, Le Corre is careful to change menus and introduce new pizzas regularly, to cater to different tastes, and to offer new varieties to regulars, thus providing fewer reasons to go to other restaurants. His challenge is to grow the company and add restaurants while sticking to his formula and continuing to provide quality, low prices, and good service. Competition is intense, though, as noted previously. The other foreign pizza establishments aim for a higher price point. By 2005, Pizza Hut had opened 160 restaurants across China in 40 cities. Young Chinese are attracted to those chains for the setting and the lifestyle it represents. Pizza Hut opened a Chinese call center in Hong Kong with an investment of HK$30 million (Hong Kong dollar) to help increase carry out sales by 20 percent. Two hundred workers take calls, which, at peak times, can number 10,000 per hour. Pizza Italia in Shanghai offers set menus to complement its pizza and pasta.

Hello Pizza is a departure from the normal foreign company approach that concentrates on higher-priced luxury products and brand names catering to the premium segment of the market. That segment may be narrow and competitive as all foreign companies occupy it, ignoring the masses of Chinese with moderate incomes. While margins may be higher in the premium segment, market share may be lower and growth circumscribed by the smaller size of the high-income segment. Offering low prices with quality and choices may represent a strategic alternative with considerable long-term promise.

Source: "Lessons from a $1.20 Pizza," *Wall Street Journal*, February 10, 2004; "Pizza Hut Accelerates Expansion in China," *China Daily*, February 14, 2005.

Case prepared by Professor Ravi Sarathy for use in class discussion, © 2005. All rights reserved.

Questions and Research

1. How important was pricing in the strategy of Happy Pizza's China expansion? What challenges did the company encounter?

2. Beyond its pricing strategy, what did Happy Pizza do in China to compete?

3. Since this case was developed, Hello Pizza has continued its expansion in China. Research its current operations. Discuss your findings. What new competition in the pizza industry is now in China? Has Hello Pizza continued its low-price strategy?

CASE 12.2 Tuna and Mango Prices in Japan: Price and Value

As connoisseurs of fish, the Japanese are finicky about the quality of the raw fish used to make sashimi, a national favorite. Tuna is one of the major fish varieties used in sashimi. With both yellowfin and bigeye tuna found off the coast of Australia in the Coral Sea, the Australians have been encouraged to export chilled fresh tuna to Japan for consumption as sashimi. Chilled tuna must be exported by air, but auction prices in Japan are attractive—about A$80 (Australian dollar) per kilogram (in 1987) in Japan versus A$1 per kilogram in Australia. Clearly, the economic incentive is high. Australian exports of tuna have been low, however, even while Japanese fishing boats have been active in the waters.

The Australian fishing industry was discouraged by the high variation in prices received at the Tokyo fish auctions. Those price differences led them to believe that Japanese auction buyers colluded to keep Australia's imported fish out of the market, thereby favoring the Japanese fishing fleet in the Coral Sea. As a result, Australian researchers meticulously studied auction prices for 27 days in October 1985, attempting to relate prices (in yen per kilogram) to factors such as fish meat color, freshness, condition (degree of carcass damage, bruises, and so on), weight of the whole fish, and origin (whether the tuna was caught in the waters off Japan, the Philippines, Taiwan, or Australia). Because sashimi is eaten raw, consumers are willing to pay more for "good" meat color, such as the absence of a concentration of red meat pigments in the flesh of the tuna. They also want the freshest fish possible. (The degree of freshness can be measured by the presence of breakdown products such as adenosine triphosphate, which increase with length of time.)

Aside from the importance of freshness and color, the study found that auction prices were lower for bigeye tuna caught in non-Japanese waters. However, research could not determine the reason. Because bigeye tuna have a high fat content, one possibility was that the food organisms found in the particular feeding grounds off the waters of Taiwan and the Philippines are absorbed into the fat, yielding flavors that are less acceptable to the discerning Japanese palate. The main conclusion of the study, however, was that Japanese consumers choose raw fish for their sashimi on the basis of its appearance. Hence, buyers at auctions are willing to pay more for tuna that has good color. The implication, then, is this: If Australians want to get high prices, they must select tuna of the requisite freshness and meat color for export to the chilled tuna auction in Tokyo.

The researchers also found that although the Tokyo market accounted for nearly 60 percent of all chilled bigeye tuna sold in Japan, two other markets, Nagoya and Osaka, accounted for about 40 percent of all chilled yellowfin tuna, as compared to the Tokyo market's 16 percent. Thus, because of lack of information, the Australians were erroneously concentrating on the Tokyo market alone.

The market for tuna in Japan may be of little interest to most people. The principle that emerges from the study, however, is important: The price that people are willing to pay for a product depends on the value perceived. Careful market research can uncover what consumers in different countries look for in a product. The price set for a particular country market must be appropriate to the value delivered in that market if the company wants to avoid over- or underpricing the product.

Another Australian study focused on prices paid in Japan for wild shrimp exported from Australia to Japan. Wild shrimp are harvested at sea and used to be sold primarily to high-priced Japanese restaurants. Then Taiwanese research led to the cultivation of pond-reared, high-yield shrimp similar in taste to the Japanese kuruma ebi (a favorite among Japanese consumers), with about 25 to 30 shrimp per pound. The lower shrimp prices resulting from pond culture and higher yields increased Japanese demand considerably, with Japanese homemakers buying shrimp for home cooking and consumption. In 1990, Japan imported 287,000 tons of shrimp valued at $3.6 billion.

A direct consequence was that new producers, such as shrimp farmers from Vietnam, entered the market, and wild shrimp prices began dropping. Australian wild-shrimp fishing costs increased, while prices for their catch dropped 25 percent in Tokyo. Even so, wild shrimp prices were double farmed shrimp prices. While connoisseurs could distinguish between wild and farm shrimp, few consumers could, especially because shrimp is often cooked in spicy sauces, further masking the taste.

Australian shrimp producers began considering an advertising campaign to build a brand image for Australian shrimp. The campaign stressed that the shrimp was wild; that it had been harvested at sea in clean, cold, unpolluted waters; and that it had a distinctive and superior taste. The question was whether the expense of an advertising campaign could lead to a differentiated image for Australian shrimp and convince Japanese consumers that Australian-origin shrimp justified a higher price. The Australian producers also considered other alternatives, including switching their export focus to less competitive markets in the United States and Europe. Doing so would further reduce Australian market share in Japan because Japanese shrimp dealers would not look kindly on suppliers who walked away from long-standing business arrangements. Another alternative was to form a Japanese distribution joint venture and sell directly to higher-priced Japanese restaurants whose chefs might be willing to pay higher prices for larger and more distinctive-tasting shrimp.

Another study on Japanese preferences for imported mangoes provides similar insights. The authors address the role of pricing in influencing the attractiveness of a new fruit unfamiliar to Japanese households and palates. Because most mangoes imported to Japan come from the Philippines and Mexico, Australia could be a new source. How can a new importer use price to compete against established import sources? Japanese consumers want premium quality and are willing to pay for it. Australian mangoes are relatively expensive in Japan and are positioned as "gift fruit"; if they were priced less expensively, home use would increase.

Source: "Yukiko Miyauchi and Chad Perry, "Marketing Fresh Fruit to Japanese Consumers: Exploring Issues for Australian Exporters," *European Journal of Marketing* 33, no. 1/2 (January 1, 1999): 196–205; Stephen C. Williams and John W. Longworth, "Factors Influencing Tuna Prices in Japan and Implications for the Development of the Coral Sea Tuna Fishery," *European Journal of Marketing* 23, no. 4 (1989): 5–24; and Steve C. Williams, "Prospects for Promotion of 'Wild' Shrimp in Japan: Implications for Australian Exporters," *European Journal of Marketing* 26, no. 10 (1992).

Questions and Research

1. What were the issues researchers tried to resolve as pertains to the Japanese market for sashimi? Why was this research important for Australian exporters?

2. What are the lessons from this case as relates to how a firm should develop its international pricing strategy?

3. Using this case, illustrate how particular industries used the pricing strategies discussed in this chapter in their own pricing strategies.

4. Though foreign exchange was not a significant issue in this case, research the exchange rates today between the Australian dollar and the Japanese yen. What implications would today's exchange rates have on the examples in this case?

NOTES

1. For reviews of pricing, see Kent Monroe, Lan Xia, and Jennifer L. Cox, "The Price Is Unfair! A Conceptual Framework of Price Fairness Perceptions," *Journal of Marketing*, 68 (2004); Scott Davis, Akshay Rao, and Mark Bergen, "How to Fight a Price War," *Harvard Business Review* (March–April 2000);Vithala R. Rao, "Pricing Research in Marketing: The State of the Art," *Journal of Business*, 57 (1984); and Gerard J. Tellis, "Beyond the Many Faces of Price: An Integration of Pricing Strategies," *Journal of Marketing* 50 (October 1986).

2. Mary Anne Raymond, John F. Tanner, Jr., and Jonghoon Kim, "Cost Complexity of Pricing Decisions for Exporters in Developing and Emerging Markets," *Journal of International Marketing* 9, no. 3 (2001): 19–40.

3. "Unilever, P&G Wage Price War for Edge in India," *Wall Street Journal*, August 11, 2004.

4. Keith Bradsher, "G.M. Thrives in China With Small, Thrifty Vans," *New York Times*, August 9, 2005.

5. Michael Marn and R. L. Rosiello, "Managing Price, Gaining Profit," *McKinsey Quarterly*, no. 4 (1992).

6. ibid

7. Countries with the Highest Inflation Rates (http://www.aneki.com/inflation.html), accessed March 1, 2011.

8. F. V. Cespedes, E. Raymond Corey, and V. Kasturi Rangan, "Gray Markets: Causes and Cures," *Harvard Business Review* (July–August 1988).

9. "Luxury Prices for U.S. Goods No Longer Pass Muster in Japan," *Wall Street Journal*, February 8, 1996.

10. See "Note on the Motorcycle Industry," Harvard Business School Case Services, Number 578–210.

11. Boston Consulting Group, Perspectives on Experience, 1972, Boston: BCG; Robert Dolan and Abel Jeuland, "Experience Curves and Dynamic Demand Models: Implications for Optimal Pricing Strategies," *Journal of Marketing* (Winter 1981).

12. Karen M. McGowan and Brenda J. Sternquist, "Dimensions of Price as a Marketing Universal: A Comparison of Japanese and US Consumers," *Journal of International Marketing* 6, no. 4 (1998): 49–65.

13. Robin Cooper and W. Bruce Chew, "Control Tomorrow's Costs through Today's Designs," *Harvard Business Review* (January–February 1996): 88–97.

14. "Ultracheap Tata Nano Debuts," *The Nikkei Weekly*, March 30, 2009 (accessed via LexisNexis Academic, November 8, 2010).

15. "Is the Price Right?" *Business Europe* (February 6–12, 1995): 6–7.

16. Hermann Simon, "Pricing Problems in a Global Setting," *Marketing News*, October 9, 1995.

17. Marios Theodosiou and Constantine S. Katsikeas, "Factors Influencing the Degree of International Pricing Strategy Standardization of Multinational Corporations," *Journal of International Marketing* 9, no. 3 (2001): 1–18.

18. Top 10 Title VII Cases in Terms of the Value of Imports Covered, Fiscal Years 1980–2008; United States International Trade Commission Office of Investigations (http://www.usitc.gov/trade_remedy/documents/historical_case_stats.pdf), accessed November 5, 2010.

19. "Hewlett-Packard: Making Transfer Pricing Work," *Business International*, November 12, 1990.

20. "Hewlett-Packard: Jousting with the IRS over Transfer Prices," *Business International Money Report*, June 11, 1990.

21. "Authorities make $270 million claim against HP," *Transfer Pricing Weekly News*, August 13, 2010 (http://www.tpweek.com/Article/2651314/Authorities-make-270-million-claim-against-HP.html), accessed November 8, 2010.

22. For further information on foreign receivables insurance, visit ExIm Banks resource page (www.exim.gov) or Coface (www.coface.com/).

23. Sarah E. Lockyer. "Global Brands Adjust Plans as Strong Dollar Gouges Profits: Volatile Currency Markets Dent McD, Yum, BK revenues," *Nation's Restaurant News*, February 23, 2009. http://findarticles.com/p/articles/mi_m3190/is_7_43/ai_n31414961/?tag=content;col1, accessed November 8, 2010.

24. For an interesting discussion of foreign exchange from the view of the marketing department, see Richard T. Hise and James W. Kolari, "The Outcomes from Foreign Currency Exchange Decisions Can Be Improved If Marketing Partners with Finance," *Marketing Management* (May/June 2008): 46–50.

25. "Learn from Russia," *Business China* (September 5, 1994): 1–3.

26. Stephen S. Cohen with John Zysman, "Countertrade, Offsets, Barter, and Buybacks," *California Management Review* 28, no. 2 (Winter 1986): 43.

27. George Melloan, "Countertrade Suits Metallgesellschaft Fine," *Wall Street Journal*, August 2, 1988.

28. "Gunning for Profit," *Economist*, November 22 2001.

29. Countertrade has become sufficiently important that DeBard, a Swiss company operating in Britain, has published *The Oxford International Countertrade Directory*, listing participants in the business worldwide.

13 Global Marketing of Services

Trade in services is growing faster than the international trade in goods. Examples of services include consulting, banking, tourism, personal services, and retailing. Services have unique characteristics that pose special problems in international marketing.

The main goals of this chapter are to ● ● ●

1. Identify the characteristics that distinguish services from goods and that influence the way services are marketed internationally.

2. Determine the basis of comparative advantage in service industries.

3. Define the roles played by governments and World Trade Organization (WTO) in the service trade.

4. Discuss examples of services industries including sports, airlines, retailing, and financial services.

5. Identify critical success factors in the global marketing of services.

What are services? Industries such as wholesaling and retailing, communications, transportation, utilities, consulting, banking and insurance, tourism, and business and personal services are all service industries. Services account for the largest portion of output and employment in advanced industrialized countries. Services typically become more important as an economy becomes more developed. Thus, U.S. employment in service industries was 24 percent of total employment in 1870, 31 percent in 1900, 55 percent in 1950, and 72 percent in 1985, reaching 80 percent by 2009. Similar increases were recorded in Japan, Germany, France, and Britain.[1] The service industry as a whole has been increasing in importance in advanced industrialized nations for almost a century.

Given their importance in national economies, it is not surprising that services are becoming increasingly important in world trade. Trade in services accounts for about 20 percent of all world trade.[2] For the U.S., trade in services is a significant competitive strength. As compared with the ongoing trade deficit in manufactured products, the U.S. has a trade surplus in services. Table 13-1 provides a summary of the U.S. trade in services. U.S. direct exports of services is shown in column A. Services sold to foreign markets through affiliates of U.S. companies is in column B. Together these two columns represent services provided to foreign markets. Note that the amount of services provided to foreign markets in all cases exceeded what foreign firms sold to U.S. markets, which are listed in columns C and D. (Column C shows the direct import of services from firms outside the U.S., and Column D shows the amount of services provided in the U.S. by subsidiaries of foreign owned companies.) In 2009 for example, even with the weaker economy, the U.S. still directly exported nearly $150 billion more in services than it imported (column A versus C). Also note that the U.S. has generally enjoyed significant annual growth in its services exports. For the five years just prior to the economic downturn in 2009, there were annual increases generally above 10 percent. Table 13-1 also demonstrates the importance of foreign direct investment as an entry mode to provide services to foreign markets. From 1996 onwards, U.S. companies sold more services through foreign affiliates (offices, subsidiaries, joint ventures) than what was sold directly from firms in the U.S. By 2004, over twice the amount was through overseas affiliates. (Column A versus B.)

Services that have been exported include the following:

- Banking and financial services
- Construction, design, and engineering services
- Computer software and data
- Entertainment, music, film, and sports
- Franchising
- Hotel and lodging services
- Insurance
- Legal and accounting
- Management consulting
- Training and education
- Transportation services, including airline, maritime, and passenger and cargo services

As the list indicates, countries export a wide variety of services. It is interesting to note, however, that some major service sectors are not represented in the list. For example, the utility sector, auto repair services, and personal services (laundry, barbershops, home cleaning) are not well represented in service exports.

Table 13-1 • Services Supplied to Foreign and U.S. Markets through Cross-Border Trade and through Affiliates

	To Foreign Markets				To U.S. Market			
	(A) Through cross-border trade (U.S. exports)	% Change	(B) Through foreign affiliates of U.S. companies [1]	% Change	(C) Through cross-border trade (U.S. imports)	% Change	(D) Through U.S. affiliates of foreign companies	% Change
	Billions of dollars							
1986	77.5		60.5		64.7		n.a.	
1987	87.0	12.2%	72.3	19.5%	73.9	14.2%	62.6	
1988	101.0	16.0%	83.8	15.9%	81.0	9.5%	73.2	17.0%
1989	117.9	16.8%	99.2	18.4%	85.3	5.3%	94.2	28.7%
1990	137.2	16.4%	121.3	22.2%	98.2	15.1%	109.2	15.9%
1991	152.4	11.1%	131.6	8.5%	99.9	1.8%	119.5	9.5%
1992	164.0	7.6%	140.6	6.8%	103.5	3.5%	128.0	7.1%
1993	171.6	4.6%	142.6	1.5%	109.4	5.8%	134.7	5.3%
1994	186.7	8.8%	159.1	11.6%	120.3	9.9%	145.4	8.0%
1995	203.7	9.1%	190.1	19.4%	128.7	7.0%	149.7	2.9%
1996	222.1	9.0%	223.2	17.4%	138.8	7.8%	168.4	12.5%
1997	238.5	7.4%	255.3	14.4%	151.5	9.1%	[2] 223.1	[2]
1998	244.4	2.5%	286.1	12.0%	165.6	9.4%	245.5	10.1%
1999	261.8	7.1%	[3] 353.2	[3]	180.5	9.0%	293.5	19.6%
2000	279.5	6.8%	413.5	17.1%	203.4	12.7%	344.4	17.3%
2001	268.6	-3.9%	421.7	2.0%	200.6	-1.4%	367.6	6.7%
2002	275.8	2.6%	423.5	0.4%	206.0	2.7%	367.6	(*)
2003	284.9	3.3%	452.5	6.8%	218.2	5.9%	374.1	1.8%
2004	328.9	15.4%	[4] 684.9	[4]	252.5	15.8%	[4] 540.9	[4]
2005	358.9	9.1%	795.6	16.2%	270.9	7.3%	571.2	5.6%
2006	400.1	11.5%	889.8	11.8%	305.3	12.7%	648.3	13.5%
2007	469.9	17.4%	1,019.2	14.5%	335.1	9.7%	683.8	5.5%
2008	517.9	10.2%	1,136.9	11.5%	363.5	9.1%	727.4	6.4%
2009	483.9	-6.6%	n.a.		334.9	-8.4%	n.a.	

Source: "U.S. International Services," 2009, U.S. Bureau of Economic Analysis, (http://www.bea.gov/international/international_services .htm#summaryandother); accessed November 24, 2010.

n.a Not Available

* A non-zero value between -0.05 and 0.05 percent

1. For 1986-88, the statistics, for the purposes of this presentation, have been adjusted to be consistent with those for 1989 forward, which reflect definitional and methodological improvements made in the 1989 Benchmark Survey of U.S. Direct Investment Abroad to exclude investment income from sales of services by affiliates in finance and insurance.
2. Beginning in 1997, sales by U.S. affiliates were classified as goods or services based on industry codes derived from the North American Industry Classification System (NAICS); the statistics for prior years were based on codes derived from the 1987 Standard Industrial Classification (SIC) System. This change resulted in a redefinition of sales of services by affiliates and a net shift of sales from goods to services. See SURVEY 79 (October 1999): 61. (http://www.bea.gov/)
3. Beginning in 1999, sales by foreign affiliates were classified as goods or services based on industry codes derived from NAICS rather than the SIC system, which resulted in a redefinition of sales of services and a net shift of sales from goods to services. See SURVEY 81 (November 2001): 58. (http://www.bea.gov/)
4. Beginning in 2004, services provided by bank affiliates and by the nonbank affiliates of U.S. banks are included in the statistics. Also beginning in 2004, the statistics are presented as "services supplied" rather than "sales of services." Compared with sales of services, services supplied adds, 1) wholesalers' and retailers' distributive services, 2) insurers' premium supplements, and 3) banks' implicitly-charged services; it subtracts a proxy measure of insurers' expected losses. For more information, see SURVEY 89 (October 2009): 37. (http://www.bea.gov/)

Note: The statistics on cross-border trade for 1999-2008 and services supplied through affiliates for 2007 are revised from those released in October 2009.

Services: How Are They Different from Products?

Services have been defined as "those fruits of economic activity that you cannot drop on your toe: banking to butchery, acting to accountancy." Indeed, services are mostly intangible.[3] The distinguishing characteristics of services include intangibility; heterogeneity; perishability; and, often, simultaneous production and consumption.[4] Measuring service quality is also problematic as cultural differences impact expectations, which impacts the consumer's impression of quality. These characteristics of services are outlined in Table 13-2 and discussed in detail next. Because of these characteristics, services are more difficult to price and measure than are products.

Intangibility

Services are often performances, such as conducting an audit, designing a building, and fixing a car. In that sense, they are intangible. Intangibility makes selling services overseas more difficult because the buyer must take the quality of service on faith. Corporate brand name and reputation sometimes help. Questions pertinent to the intangibility of services include whether (1) actions are being performed on people (for example, education) or things (for example, air freight), (2) the customer needs to be physically present during the service or only at initiation and termination of the service, and (3) the customer can be just mentally present—that is, can the service be performed at a distance?[6]

Heterogeneity

Different customers going to the same service company may not receive the same service. This quality of heterogeneity occurs because different people perform the service. Therefore, it is impossible to make sure that the service is performed the same way each time. One salesclerk may be less polite or amiable than another, resulting in consumer dissatisfaction. The implication of heterogeneity is that quality is difficult to control.

A logical response is to attempt to standardize the service. One way is to develop a detailed blueprint of the steps involved in providing the service, then analyzing results as the steps are taken to ensure that quality standards are maintained. This may mean changing the way the service is performed to reduce complexity and the possibility of divergence between different service providers. However, it is very difficult to standardize services when the personnel providing them must exercise a high degree of judgment. When a firm's advantage is based on customizing a service, any attempt at standardization means that the fundamental strategy of the business is being changed.

When extending the service to international markets, there is also the question of whether the service standardized for one national market will satisfy customers in other markets. For example, one way to standardize a service is to personalize the interaction between customer and service provider

Table 13-2 • Services Characteristics and Their Implications for Globalization Service[5]

Intangibility: How to differentiate the service? Advertise mainly through word of mouth: Who are the influential opinion makers in each market? Validity of a follow-the-client strategy in entering international markets. Manage corporate image in multiple markets.

Heterogeneity: How to reduce across-country variations in service quality influenced by variations among service providers? Can all service personnel in several countries be trained to the same level and quality of performance? Impact of cultural differences affecting extent and kind of training in each market. Develop ownership and control stake sufficient to influence recruitment and training.

Perishability: Can excess capacity in one market be used to satisfy demand in another? How to forecast service demand patterns in different markets? Are there similarities in the model for service demand across countries? Can standardized incentives be used to manage demand across countries? Create cross-country databases, raise switching costs, employ ownership, and franchise strategies.

Simultaneous production and consumption: Can service be provided at a distance internationally? Enhancing role of technology and electronic delivery (for example, ATMs—automatic teller machines). How much of service production can be placed in the "back office?" Sharing of back-office functions across markets. The need to find service providers places a constraint on the pace of international expansion. If technology cannot facilitate service exporting, then franchising, licensing, joint venture, and foreign direct investment are better avenues.

Service quality and consumer participation in service creation/delivery: How do consumers determine quality of service? It is a matter of consumer perceptions. Moreover, are customers in all markets equally willing to participate in the service creation process? What turns off the customer? (What are the variations in customer defection rates across markets?) How to ensure customer loyalty and repeat business? Developing market-specific plans to maintain customer loyalty. Customer perceptions of service quality may be affected by culture.

by training retail salespersons to greet customers by name and use certain standard conversational remarks. However, when employees must follow "scripts," cultural factors demand a somewhat different "script" for each country market.

The pressure to standardize on manufacturers of products can often be quite high, especially if the fixed costs associated with producing the products are also high. But in offering services, companies tend to have lower fixed costs. This may help service companies address the issue of market heterogeneity through adaptation to local market needs.

Perishability

Services are perishable in that they cannot be inventoried, saved, or stored. Thus, a plane seat that sits empty when the flight takes off is lost forever. The perishability of seats makes it harder to adjust the supply of a service to fluctuating demand, es-

Intangibility of services is a challenge for global service companies. Customers must trust that the service will be acceptable.

pecially during times of peak demand. Therefore, service companies seek innovations that allow the service to be "inventoried" in some fashion or that allow demand to be managed so that the supply of services is adequate and can be provided economically. An example is providing a restricted number of reduced-fare, advance-purchase seats on flights, with the number being increased if seats on the flight do not appear to be selling as forecast.

Simultaneous Production and Consumption

Production and consumption of a service often take place at the same time; that is, the producer and the seller of the service are often the same person. Moreover, the customer must often be present for the service to take place. Unlike products, services usually cannot be physically transported across borders in the way that goods can be exported. So, international marketing means that the service must be performed by the firm in the country market, whether through franchising, licensing, a direct investment, or an acquisition. Thus, the country in which the service is offered may affect the desirability of the service provider. Does the country of origin matter to consumers when they select services? The answer may depend on the type of service being consumed. Specifically, customers seem to prefer core services from their home country (for example, medical care and travel). Supplementary services such as a warranty are more important when the country-of-origin effect is less favorable. Further, brand name recognition can make the country of origin less important, and cultural sensitivity can be an important adjunct of the country of origin of services.[7]

While the country of origin may be important, the fundamental question is whether the service can be performed at a distance. If not, how should a firm position itself in a distant market when offering a service? An example is the use of automated teller machines (ATMs), which allow customers to conduct certain banking transactions without a teller being present.

Measuring Service Quality

Service quality is difficult to measure, particularly in cross-cultural settings. This is primarily because customer expectations of quality can vary between cultures making direct comparisons difficult.[8] It is often unclear what the consumer expects. Quality is a matter of meeting customers' expectations—yet quality depends on consumer perception. These perceptions are determined by the following:[9]

- The person doing the service.

- The technical outcome of the service.

- The overall image of the company whose employee is carrying out the service.

Technical quality may be amenable to traditional quality-control approaches borrowed from a manufacturing setting, but only if the service process is standardized. If corporate image affects the perception of quality, the firm must decide whether the same corporate image is needed in all countries. Should all employees wear the same uniforms? Should the physical facilities look the same in all national markets?

Consumer dissatisfaction may result from unrealistic expectations. Other reasons for the gap between desired quality and perceived quality include a lack of understanding about what consumers expect from a service, an inability or unwillingness to meet customer expectations, problems with delivering the service, and communication gaps when a firm fails to communicate realistic expectations about what quality will be offered.[10] Quality of service is difficult to measure in cross-cultural settings.

Benchmarking allows service firms to assess performance gaps relative to their competitors and remedy those gaps in service quality. However, customers may change their perceptions of what attributes of service quality matter most. Responding to changing customer needs and perceptions of service quality, service providers must ensure continuous improvement. One study applied a dynamic benchmarking approach to luxury hotels in Seoul. It showed that hotels can improve customer desirability by using analytical hierarchy analysis to spot changes in customer perceptions of attributes considered important to overall service quality and then improve their service along those lines.[11]

Marketing and Selling Services Internationally

The previous issues discussing the characteristics of services versus products have an impact on how services are marketed and sold internationally. Three important areas are branding, advertising, and the role of customer loyalty.

BRANDING SERVICES

How services are branded should differ depending on whether the services are chosen based on comparative search and evaluation (purchasing an expensive, durable service such as a university education), previous experience (deciding on a restaurant), or established credibility (choosing a doctor). Some services may be chosen using multiple criteria. One service branding model, set out in Figure 13-1, suggests that services' branding will depend on how the brand is presented and perceived in the marketplace.[12]

ADVERTISING SERVICE OFFERINGS

From branding services, it is a short and necessary step to advertising the services. The principal functions include making the services tangible, showing the service encounter, encouraging word-of-mouth communication (by satisfied users) and building the brand image. How are services best advertised—by word of mouth, direct mail, satisfied customer referrals, or ads in newspapers or on television? How important is the Internet and social media? Are there national differences in the relative appeal of the different forms of advertising of services? What should be the focus of advertising? Which is more important—the image

Figure 13-1 • Services Branding Model

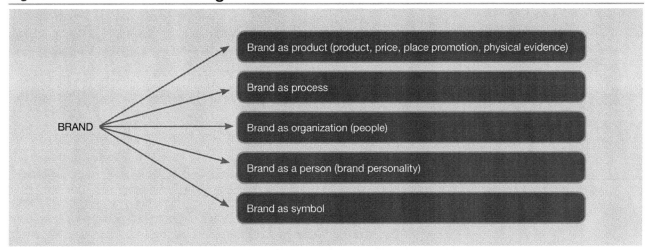

BRAND

Brand as product (product, price, place promotion, physical evidence)

Brand as process

Brand as organization (people)

Brand as a person (brand personality)

Brand as symbol

and name of the company providing the service or facets of the service being sold? Those questions must be answered for each country market.[13]

The traditional view of advertising services focuses on making the service tangible, representing the service encounter, encouraging word-of-mouth communication, and building a strong brand image. In contrast, when advertising agencies were asked about advertising services, they emphasized that the advertising objective was what mattered. Agencies believed advertising was more influenced by the service being utilitarian (insurance) or experiential (leisure travel) than by the customer's level of involvement with the service.[14]

IMPORTANCE OF CUSTOMER LOYALTY TO SERVICES

Because services cannot be stored, a basic marketing strategy is to ensure repeat business by generating loyalty in existing customers. Devices such as frequent-flier plans may be used to reward customer loyalty. However, given that consumers have different characteristics in different countries, are such plans necessary for all national markets? Or should they be shaped mainly by competitive variations in each market? Loyalty can also be maintained and rewarded through pricing. The question for each national market is whether volume discounts and membership strategies work equally well in all markets.

Because services generally involve close interaction between the service provider and the customer, cultural variables affect user satisfaction and loyalty to specific service providers. Cultural variables also affect service design and the nature of interaction with the customer. In collectivist cultures, such as Thailand, consumers seem less likely to switch service providers, particularly when they received special benefits in return for their loyalty. Studies suggest that service providers need to make special efforts in collectivist cultures to provide special benefits, such as making appointments at the last minute and nurturing close relationships with specific service providers.[15]

Comparative Advantage and the Service Industries

As previously discussed, the U.S. has a comparative advantage in offering services internationally, as shown by its trade surplus in services. Other developed countries also dominate the services industry. This leads to the question of what factors help a nation and its firms to have a comparative advantage in services? Having attained a comparative advantage, how do nations and firms sustain that advantage? These issues are discussed next.

The Basis for Comparative Advantage

Clearly, each service industry is distinct, having a different production function; that is, each service industry uses technology, labor, capital, and management in different proportions to deliver its service. Still, certain factors of production play a role in service industries. Those factors of production leading to a national competitive advantage tend to be labor, capital, and technology. There are also firm-specific factors such as management skills and reputation.

LABOR

Service industries are generally labor-intensive, with both highly skilled and un-skilled labor being used. Labor in retail stores, barbershops, and florists, for ex-ample, may not need much training and is likely to be low-paid. Countries with low labor costs have an advantage. At the other extreme are legal and account-ing services that require highly educated and highly paid personnel. Advanced countries would likely have an advantage in offering those services. However, high-level skills may be country-specific and may not be easily transferable to other countries. Expertise in U.S. tax law may not be meaningful to tax practices in Europe. However, the methodologies used by U.S. law firms to research and argue tax issues may, indeed, be pertinent to the practice of tax law in advanced nations.

CAPITAL

Traditionally, services have low capital-to-labor ratios. Lower amounts of capital are used per worker in service industries than in manufacturing industries. Ser-vice productivity has been lower than in manufacturing, and the future growth of service industries will require larger amounts of capital per worker to raise productivity and quality. In banking, for example, widespread use of comput-ers results in more productive workers, faster transactions, and more satisfied customers. If the trend continues, countries and firms with lower costs of capital will gain an advantage in international markets.

TECHNOLOGY

Technology is a key driver for suc-cess in many services industries. A country with a strong technology base helps make service industries more competitive.

The ability of a firm to offer quality services is generally linked to the firm hav-ing excellent technology resources. Services such as airlines and shipping, de-veloping computer software, and banking all utilize high levels of technology to be globally competitive. Clearly, the capital investment in R&D that resulted in the technology-based services application leads to a comparative advantage for a company—and for a country. Both can use the technology to enter the global maintenance industry in a new fashion, by-passing former barriers.

FIRM-SPECIFIC FACTORS

Beyond national comparative advantages, firm-specific factors also contribute to the competitiveness of companies offering servic-es internationally. One important factor is the management skills of a firm specific to servic-es industries. Given the challenges of taking a service internationally, while ensuring that service meets local cultural and quality needs, the ability of management to execute their global plan is critical. Studies also show that a firm's size and reputation have a significant influence. Finally, a firm's global reputation

Figure 13-2 • Creating Sustainable Competitive Advantage in Service Industries[16]

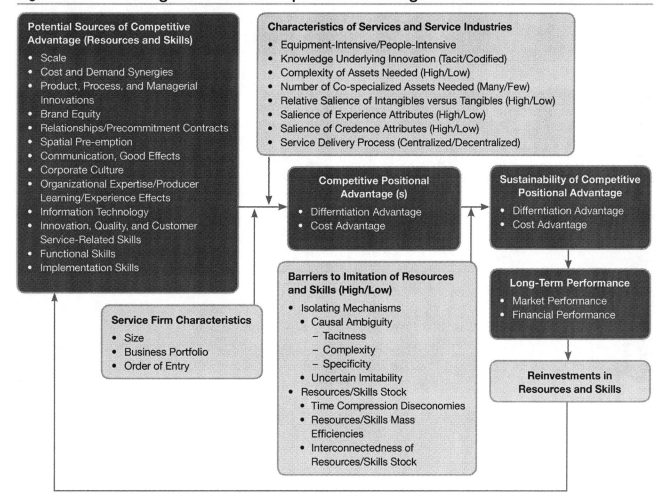

Potential Sources of Competitive Advantage (Resources and Skills)

- Scale
- Cost and Demand Synergies
- Product, Process, and Managerial Innovations
- Brand Equity
- Relationships/Precommitment Contracts
- Spatial Pre-emption
- Communication, Good Effects
- Corporate Culture
- Organizational Expertise/Producer Learning/Experience Effects
- Information Technology
- Innovation, Quality, and Customer Service-Related Skills
- Functional Skills
- Implementation Skills

Characteristics of Services and Service Industries

- Equipment-Intensive/People-Intensive
- Knowledge Underlying Innovation (Tacit/Codified)
- Complexity of Assets Needed (High/Low)
- Number of Co-specialized Assets Needed (Many/Few)
- Relative Salience of Intangibles versus Tangibles (High/Low)
- Salience of Experience Attributes (High/Low)
- Salience of Credence Attributes (High/Low)
- Service Delivery Process (Centralized/Decentralized)

Service Firm Characteristics

- Size
- Business Portfolio
- Order of Entry

Competitive Positional Advantage (s)

- Differntiation Advantage
- Cost Advantage

Barriers to Imitation of Resources and Skills (High/Low)

- Isolating Mechanisms
  - Causal Ambiguity
    - Tacitness
    - Complexity
    - Specificity
  - Uncertain Imitability
- Resources/Skills Stock
  - Time Compression Diseconomies
  - Resources/Skills Mass Efficiencies
  - Interconnectedness of Resources/Skills Stock

Sustainability of Competitive Positional Advantage

- Differntiation Advantage
- Cost Advantage

Long-Term Performance

- Market Performance
- Financial Performance

Reinvestments in Resources and Skills

also contributes to its success. This is especially obvious in services where reliability and dependability are particularly important to consumers, such as with airlines, banking, or the insurance sector.[17]

The U.S. software industry is a good example of firm-specific factors contributing to global success. U.S. firms have been able to dominate the world software industry because of the experience and management skills developed over the years of being in business. Those skills include transforming custom software into packages that have the widest customer appeal and supervising the development of complicated software within large teams of programmers. The strong reputation of firms such as Microsoft has also assisted in its significant global expansion.

In short, services can be more or less technology-intensive and capital-intensive and have greater or lesser reliance on skilled labor. Advanced industrialized nations such as the U.S. and France are likely to have a comparative advantage in service industry sectors that are more capital-intensive, skilled labor-intensive, and technology-intensive.

Sustainable Competitive Advantage in Services

Having achieved success internationally, companies seek to build a sustainable competitive advantage in order to enhance long-term performance. Figure 13-2 shows a framework for creating a sustainable competitive advantage in service industries. The model links the resources and capabilities of a service firm with the nature of the service offered and with certain characteristics of the firm. The result is a competitive positioning advantage. Whether the advantage can be sustained depends on whether barriers exist to the diffusion and imitation of firm-specific capabilities and resources.

Government Intervention in the Services Trade

International trade in services is subject to government interference and protection just as with trade in products. The goal of government intervention varies, but most often is linked to protecting domestic industries, protecting national security, and maintaining sovereignty (control) over issues of national importance. Government actions in the services trade can include the following:

* Business formation and ownership limitations (meaning the right to establish a branch or subsidiary in a foreign country; for example, many nations ban ownership of media companies by foreigners).

* Trade barriers, including limitations on the proportion of a market that a foreign company can serve and discriminatory taxation of services provided by a foreign company.

* Foreign exchange controls; limits on remitting profits from service businesses.

* Government procurement barriers because government buys services only from "national" companies or enacts preferential financing, and political or regional bias in public procurement.

* Technical issues that serve to keep out foreign firms, such as the use of standards and certification conditions.

* Licensing regulations that impose unreasonable terms of entry or insist on licensing as the only mode of entry.

* Restrictions on professional qualifications, including ban on entry of qualified service company personnel.

* Tolerance of commercial counterfeiting.

The aviation sector and cell phone markets are examples of an industries where governments can be influential. (See "Government Control in the Brazilian Service Sector.") Governments may set control entry, limit competition, set prices, and favor "national champions."

Global Agreement toward Fair Trade in Services

As services grow more important in world trade, nations have begun seeking a consensus on fair trade practices with regard to services. The World Trade Organization (WTO) has paid special attention to protecting Intellectual Property (IP) rights. It has also addressed the issues of barriers to trade in services, national treatment of foreign firms, allowance of FDI in services without undue restrictions, temporary admission of foreign service workers, international agreement on the regulation of international data flows and ownership rights in international databases, and importation of materials and equipment necessary for providing services. Other challenges addressed by the WTO include establishing a framework to control restrictive licensing practices and the right of "nonestablishment," which is growing increasingly important as service firms deliver their services via

**Government Control
in the Brazilian
Service Sector**

As Brazil's economy grows, the growth is driven partly by services. The Heritage Foundation estimates that more than 60% of Brazil's GDP is based on services, and this sector is growing. However, Brazil's government continues to enforce restrictions on foreign investment and participation in some of Brazil's most attractive service industries such as energy, health services, and aviation.[18] Despite these restrictions, the U.S. Commercial Service rates Brazil's aviation sector as one of the "best prospects" for U.S. firms and the fifth largest aviation market in the world.[19]

Brazil is not the only country in the world to keep tight control on air services. Domestic air routes remain heavily regulated by most nations, although governments are increasingly opening up routes to improve foreign airlines' access to international flight services. Brazil recently signed an air services agreement with the U.S. that expands passenger flights by 50% between the two countries and eliminates government restrictions on which airlines fly which routes. Not only will U.S. air carriers get more flights (from 105 to 154) but five additional Brazilian cities will be open to U.S. carriers. Restrictions on cargo flight services will also be reduced.[20] Brazil also is talking with the other countries, like Jamaica, as well as economic zones such as the EU about broadening access to air services. Meanwhile, increased competition, growing demand, and reduced fares are helping Brazil's air services industry to thrive.

Success in opening the air services industry to growing foreign investment and competition provides a roadmap to reducing restrictions in other promising service sectors including telecommunication, transportation, and financial services.

electronic means or through the mail without being physically present in a country. The WTO regulations govern the conditions under which a foreign firm can be said to have established a presence in a foreign market. That, in turn, may determine whether the foreign firm qualifies for treatment as a domestic firm. Similarly, establishing a domestic presence is often necessary to qualify for protection under the laws of IP rights in a country.

The U.S. government offers specialized help to service industries. Within the Department of Commerce, the Office of Service Industries has divisions covering specific industry sectors such as information, transportation and tourism, and finance and management.

Foreign Market Entry Mode for Service Industries

As contrasted with the direct exporting of products, service companies tend toward entry modes that involve foreign direct investment. Through experience, firms have learned that because services are intangible, exporting them is often unfeasible without also exporting the personnel to provide them. Hence, FDI, licensing and franchising, and joint ventures are common vehicles for providing services in international markets.

Another factor is that financing the overseas expansion of services can be difficult, with the cost structure leaning toward fixed costs. Although heavy capital investments may not be necessary, working capital may be high initially, especially in regards to the personnel required to provide the service. That is another reason why joint ventures and strategic alliances are also common when a firm seeks to sell services overseas.

Because direct interaction between buyer and service provider is essential to the marketing of services, cultural differences must be accounted for in seeking

••• The Globalization of Sports

Sports is an area of the entertainment industry that is rapidly becoming globalized, partially because of the media industry itself. Global media providers combined with technology (e.g., satellite television, the Internet, and worldwide editions of print and broadcast media) enable sporting events to be broadcast globally. For example, ESPN gains additional revenue by broadcasting U.S. sports, for which it already has obtained rights (such as NFL games) to overseas audiences. The leagues themselves are also broadcasting content via the Internet and satellite television. As a result, local teams can appeal to and build global fan bases as well as expatriate fans of a local team living far away.

One example is the global popularity of the "American pastime" of baseball. Baseball is broadly popular in Asia, particularly in Japan and South Korea. In 1992, the U.S. affiliate of Nintendo Corporation, a Japanese firm, bought the Seattle Mariners. While Seattle is home to a significant Japanese population, the Mariners also market the team back in Japan by signing Japanese league stars such as Ichiro Suzuki and Kenji Johjima. The team includes Japanese-language advertisements on its television broadcasts, and the Mariners' Japanese players are well-supported for Major League Baseball's annual All-Star team by Internet voting from Japan.

Sports leagues themselves continue to expand internationally. The U.S.-based National Football League (NFL) created a European league for American football in 1991 and annually plays a game in the UK at London's Wembley Stadium. David Stern, commissioner of the U.S. National Basketball Association (NBA) noted that the NBA was "the world's largest provider of reality programming" due to the global popularity of basketball.[21] Football (or soccer, as it is called in the U.S.) is perhaps the most global of sports with a truly worldwide event: the World Cup. Other worldwide sporting events such as the Olympics also continue to perform well, with television ratings outperforming high profile American dramas in the U.S. market.[22]

buyer satisfaction. For that reason, establishing a local presence and using local personnel are usually recommended. If the service must be adapted to a foreign market, the interaction between buyer and foreign provider takes on additional importance because direct contact can facilitate cooperation and result in more appropriate adaptation.

Selected Service Industry Sectors ••••

The remainder of this chapter examines the global marketing of a variety of service industry sectors. Those sectors include the global media and entertainment industries, music and sports, the airline industry, hotels, professional services, and retail.

International Airline Industry

International marketing in the airline business consists mainly of offering air transportation services on foreign routes. However, foreign governments have traditionally regulated foreign competitors' access to domestic routes. Foreign governments have also regulated the rights of foreign airlines to offer service to international passengers. Such traffic rights have generally been subject to bilateral negotiation between governments.

Governments have also regulated what fares may be charged, what routes airlines may fly, and what airlines will be allowed to compete in the market.

Many countries have one or two dominant airlines, either being owned by the government or enjoying quasi-public status. Those "flagship" carriers are given preference in the allocation of new routes, finances, and fare increases. Examples of those airlines are Lufthansa, Air France, Japan Air Lines, Royal Jordanian, and Air India. Thus, if a U.S. airline wants to compete for foreign passenger traffic, it has to wait for the U.S. government to negotiate a bilateral agreement.

Deregulation of the U.S. airline industry facilitated entry by foreign airlines and led many of them to seek a portion of U.S. air traffic. For example, KLM acquired a stake in Northwest Airlines and a joint marketing agreement was attained between British Airways and American Airlines. In that agreement, each airline agreed to use the other airline for ongoing service on complementary routes. The airlines also agreed to list each other's flights in their computer reservation system, which is the heart of competitive advantage in the industry. (Airlines that own such systems can more easily fill seats on flights.) Those agreements have gradually evolved into a series of formal global marketing coalitions. Examples include Star Alliance, whose members include United Airlines, Lufthansa, Air China, and Singapore Airlines; SkyTeam, which includes Air France/KLM, Delta Airlines, and Korean Air; and Oneworld, which includes American Airlines, British Airways, Quantas, and Cathay Pacific. Each of those global airlines attempts to provide seamless service by using alliance partners. The result is that they gain customer loyalty and market share and offer frequent-flier reward points for use across the alliance. See "A Day in the Life of a Star Alliance Traveler" as an example of how these benefits can make a difference.

The major industry trend is for faster growth outside the U.S. In such a regulated industry, the dilemma for U.S. airlines is how to obtain and increase market share in the fast-growing overseas markets when host governments seek to favor their domestic flagship carriers.

Table 13-3 summarizes growth trends in global airline traffic. Note that although the North American market is forecasted to grow at 2.5%, it will register the lowest estimated rates of growth, while Africa and the Middle East will have some of the highest growth rates. Hence, airlines around the world will be seeking route authority to permit them to fly passengers on these routes. Of course, factors such as airspace congestion and airport capacity limitations also hinder efforts by airlines to expand routes, yet government regulation will not disappear overnight. Therefore, U.S. and other airlines must seek alliances with carriers from around the world while requesting U.S. government help in obtaining fairer access to burgeoning markets.

Service quality is a particularly important issue for passengers choosing between airlines. Studies find that European and U.S. Passengers differ in their expectations of service quality and in their assessment of whether airlines (European as well as American) meet their expectations. In general, European passengers seem to have higher service quality expectations and think that European airlines are closer to meeting those expectations. The authors speculate that those perceptions could be useful if "open skies" allow European airlines greater

Table 13-3 • Air Passenger Traffic Forecast by Region (Percent Growth)

	World	North America	Europe	Africa	Asia/ Pacific	Latin America Caribbean	Middle East
2009 Actual	-2.0	-3.9	-3.9	-3.3	-0.2	0.9	9.1
2012 Forecast	4.9	2.5	2.7	7.7	4.9	5.6	11.5

Source: ICAO passenger traffic forecast by region: 2010 to 2012; Centre for Asia Pacific Aviation & ICAO; (http://www.centreforaviation.com/news/2010/07/19/global-air-traffic-to-surge-64-in-2010-growth-easing-to-47-in-2011--icao/page1); accessed November 13, 2010.

••• A Day in the Life of a Star Alliance Traveler

The growing use of strategic alliances among airlines is impacting the international traveler. Here is an example of one trip from Chicago, IL to Christchurch, New Zealand and the benefits from using a global airline alliance. Our traveler, consultant Johnny, is taking a trip to Christchurch to meet with his distributor. Johnny flies United Airlines over 50,000 miles per year. This means he has attained United Airlines Mileage Plus status as a Premier Executive. This also gives him Star Alliance Gold status, a critical benefit for his New Zealand trip:

Chicago, IL to Christchurch, NZ

Monday 3pm: Leaves on United 973 from Chicago O'Hare to San Francisco for his connecting flight to Auckland. During his 2 hour layover Johnny wishes he could get away from the loud noise at the gates and seek refuge in an airline club. But his company won't pay for membership in such clubs. No problem. As a Star Alliance Gold on an international trip, he gets free access to Star Alliance lounges. He walks into the United Airlines Red Carpet Club to get some needed email done before the long trip to New Zealand.

Monday 7:15pm: Getting ready to board UA 9543 flight to Auckland. Realizes the flight is a codeshare—it is actually an Air New Zealand flight. Johnny has a large piece of hand luggage and worries he'll not board in time to secure a great overhead spot since he has never flown Air New Zealand. No problem: As Star Alliance Gold he gets priority board before most of the other passengers. Luggage secured!

Wednesday 5:55am: Arrival into Auckland. Johnny has a long layover since the only confirmed flight on to Christchurch is not until 1pm. If only he could wake up with a

nice shower! No problem. As a Star Alliance Gold he has access to the Air New Zealand Koru Lounge, which has a shower. Johnny forgets about his long 13 hour flight he just completed. Grabs some fresh coffee and checks his email.

Wednesday 9:30am: Johnny sees there is an earlier flight to Auckland and asks if he can standby for the flight? He is able to use a dedicated check-in line normally reserved for first and business class passengers but also allowed for Star Alliance Gold member. He quickly talks to an agent. No problem—in fact as a Star Alliance Gold he gets priority waitlist.

Wednesday 10am: Johnny boards his Air New Zealand flight leaving 3 hours early. His Star Alliance status put him in front of the group of college kids trying to get back to Christchurch. Johnny smiles and remembers his college days and no status on airlines!

Wednesday 11:30am: Johnny arrives in Christchurch. His luggage is among the first to come out of the Air New Zealand carousel, having been tagged by United Airlines way back in Chicago as Star Alliance Priority handling.

Johnny agrees his loyalty to United Airlines is paying off, even though most of this trip had little to do with United Airlines. But with United's membership in the Star Alliance, Johnny gets benefits around the world. During the visit, he buys more stuff than can fit in his two pieces of luggage. He smiles: As a Star Alliance Gold he gets three checked pieces of luggage for free. Things are going so well he just might use some of his United Airlines Mileage Plus miles and upgrade on the flight back home to business class! No problem. Even though he's not flying United Airlines, Air New Zealand allows him to use his miles to upgrade. Life is good!

access to U.S. markets and to U.S. airline customers. The research also suggests that global airline code-sharing alliances such as Star Alliance and OneWorld may face problems if service quality differs among the members of the alliance. Customers from different countries might rate members of the same alliance differently, causing dissatisfaction with the alliance as a whole.[23]

International Retailing

Retailing, one of the major sectors of any economy, typically requires contact between retailer and seller. It is generally a labor-intensive and geographically diffused activity, with considerable national and regional variation in business practices. It is also an industry subject to government regulation. In addition, it is a major generator of jobs that requires substantial time and attention from management.

Retailing globally has been changing considerably in the last three decades. In 1987, 3 percent of Taiwan's population shopped in modern supermarkets and grocery stores. Today over half of all shopping is done in modern department stores and supermarkets. All across Asia and Latin America, as incomes rise and more two-income families emerge, time has become scarce for consumers. Shopping at modern stores that offer large assortments of goods, fairly priced and fresh, and amenities such as debit card shopping and home delivery has caused a major shift in people's shopping habits and preferences. As shopping volumes increase, prices can be lowered as fixed costs of warehouses and computerization can be spread over a larger sales base. The net result is a virtuous cycle wherein low prices, convenience, more choices, and high quality combine to attract more customers, allowing owners to continually upgrade the shopping conveniences that attracted shoppers initially. Western-style enclosed shopping malls, with their temperature-controlled, safe, well-lit ambience, offer variety and entertainment, attracting former patrons of small street-side shops.

China, for example, has seen the opening of stores by the Japanese chains Isetan and Yaohan and the Hong Kongbased chain A. S. Watson. There has also been an increase in local chains, such as Giordano. Those chains are adapting to the local culture, such as the traditional Chinese preference for "wet" markets, where shoppers can inspect live fish and chickens. Taiwan's local chain, Dairy Farm International, has seen competition from the European retailers Makro and Carrefour. Those two retailers stress the hypermarket model, offering a huge assortment and accepting very low margins. Makro, for example, sells groceries in bulk, office supplies, and computers to individuals as well as local wholesalers and small retailers. Regional integration has seen similar cross-border forays. Promodes from France has opened stores across Spain; and Walmart, partnering with Cifra, is populating the Mexican countryside. One consequence of the proliferation of large chains is the gradual seeping of power from manufacturers to retailers. That is exemplified in rising sales of private, or store-brand, items, with the foremost exponents of private brands being the U.K. chains Tesco and Sainsbury. (See the discussions on private label versus branded goods and the implications for brand equity in Chapter 9, "Global Products and Global Branding" and Chapter 10, "Global Product Policy and New Product Development.")

How do foreign firms expand their presence in these growing retail markets globally? A common entry method is to obtain control of retailing channels through direct investment. Joint ventures and franchises are examples. For an example of franchising, see "McDonald's in Hungry, Russia, and Brazil." The key objective is to have a degree of control over the retailing channel and to obtain from retailers as much information about consumers as possible. That control is often linked to a vertical integration strategy. However, retailing offers attractive returns in its own right as a means of participating in the growth of an economy. From that angle, a foreign retailer hopes to bring a competitive edge to the domestic industry in the form of more efficient management, greater worldwide purchasing clout, and superior retailing technology and information systems. "Best Practices in Global Retailing Expansion" highlights some of the best practices demonstrated by successful global firms in the retail sector.

Retailing is an important but challenging international services sector.

••• McDonald's in Hungary, Russia, and Brazil

McDonald's began operations in Budapest, Hungary, on April 30, 1988. On its first day of operation, it broke a McDonald's record for the most transactions. Today it is one of the busiest McDonald's in the world.

Plans to establish a McDonald's in Hungary began with a joint-venture agreement in November 1986. McDonald's is a 50 percent owner, its partner being Hungary's Babolna Agricultural Cooperative. McDonald's supplied all of the restaurant equipment, including equipment to established supply sources, such as a bakery to make hamburger buns. McDonald's also contributed something intangible: a standard of quality for the fast-food industry. It had to develop a supplier infrastructure by introducing new food-processing techniques and forcing development of new products in Hungary, as well as insisting on the improvement of existing products to meet worldwide standards of quality. Products such as hamburger buns, the kind of cheese used in the cheeseburgers, and orange juice concentrate were unavailable in Hungary. Ketchup was available, but it did not meet McDonald's quality standards. It took over a year to develop supply sources. McDonald's experts in purchasing and quality control then worked with suppliers on a monthly basis to get the desired product and quality.[24]

Locally produced food products are used by most McDonald's restaurants worldwide. The exceptions are McCormick spices, which are used by McDonald's around the world, and sesame seeds, which cannot be grown in Hungary. Paper products, such as paper cups, are imported. McDonald's opened with 7 partially trained managers and another 20 employees loaned from stores in other countries. Most of those employees returned home after a month, with the exception of a U.S. manager who stayed on as an advisor and trainer. New employees had training, but little experience. They had to learn while on the job, in the middle of huge crowds. During the first few days, a line wound outside the store. Some of the training focused on instilling attitudes of customer service. In a country of shortages, where people were accustomed to waiting, customer service was, to some degree, an unfamiliar concept. McDonald's found it impossible to hire part-time help, which it relies on in most countries.

After its Hungarian experience, McDonald's natural response was to turn to Russia. McDonald's Russian entry was shepherded by its head of Canadian operations, George Cohon, who had made initial contact with some Russian delegation members during the Montreal Olympics in 1976. But the joint-venture agreement was not signed until April 1988 because of intervening events, one being the U.S. Olympic boycott. McDonald's Russian venture had some unusual features. McDonald's joint-venture partner, with a 51 percent ownership, was the food service department of the Moscow City Council. Normally, McDonald's worked with entrepreneurs, but in Russia in the late 1980's, the company had no choice but to work with a leading entity within the Communist party. The joint venture was also a "rubles-only" joint venture at a time when the ruble was inconvertible. That meant that McDonald's would sell its hamburgers to Russians for rubles and would buy mostly local supplies paid for in rubles.

As in Hungary, the company had difficulty maintaining its reputation because of the poor-quality local supplies. Ultimately, McDonald's had to invest over $40 million in setting up a raw material processing plant to supply the requisite buns, French fries, hamburger patties, etc. Amortizing that large injection of foreign capital at a time when the ruble was rapidly devaluing meant that McDonald's was making no money in the short run. It might well have been selling Ray Kroc's original dream of 15-cent hamburgers. Overall, McDonald's is hugely profitable overseas and losing money for a few years seems a reasonable investment to ensure front-row seats for the Russian renaissance.[25]

By 2003, McDonald's had about 1,600 restaurants in Brazil. The Brazilian restaurants introduced interesting innovations, such as stand-alone ice cream kiosks. However, devaluation of Brazilian currency raised the price of dollar-linked ingredients such as bread and meat. As their prices rose, profits declined. McDonald's also became a luxury to a significant portion of the Brazilian population as unemployment rose and real incomes dropped. Disappointed franchisees began suing McDonald's management, complaining of high rents, oversaturation of the market, and general economic discontent. McDonald's began buying back distressed franchisees in order to help bring the Brazilian operations back to life and closed other stores.[26] Even as the economy improved, McDonald's began to face pressure in Brazil about the healthfulness of its food. In 2010, a Brazilian judge ordered McDonald's to pay $17,500 to one of its employees because he gained 62 pounds as a result of eating McDonalds food everyday.[27] This high profile case highlighted growing concern about the healthiness of the restaurant's food.

1. An understanding of the market obtained by careful observation over an extended period of time or through pilot expansion.

2. A measured pace of expansion within constraints of capital and management.

3. A clearly defined role for local partners after careful consideration of whether they are needed.

4. The importance of planning the assortment of goods to be carried, which should vary with the preferences of each local market. Stores such as Marks & Spencer carry a core of best-selling products across borders, supplemented by products adapted to local preferences.

5. The extent to which goods are sourced locally, which is affected by local quality and availability considerations, as well as exchange-rate volatility. For example, cost reduction pressures move Benetton toward centralization, with customization for individual markets happening at the last minute. At that point, up-to-date point-of-sale information is used to dye clothes in the colors that sell best in each market. Of course, that can work only if the basic product concept—namely, the style and design—have strong multicultural acceptability.

6. Scale economies, as evidenced by the merger of Kingfisher, a UK consumer electronics retailer, and Darty, a leading French retailer of consumer electronics and appliances (white goods) through warehouse-style stores, with 12 percent market share at the time of the merger.

7. The development of local management for day-to-day supervision as well as strategic expansion.

8. Reduction in cycle time, particularly with time-sensitive goods such as perishables and fashion items. Balancing in-house design and manufacture with outsourcing and just-in-time manufacturing shaped by information technology investments allow a firm to react quickly to changing market signals, such as shifts in fashion.

International Financial Services

International financial services is another rapidly globalizing service. A number of factors influence global competitiveness in this industry: availability of low-cost capital, creative ideas for innovating financial services, world-class technology, and high quality service. Specific services offered include twenty-four-hour trading, international bank lending, global foreign exchange trading, and the hedging of products to manage interest and currency exposure as discussed in Chapter 12. The U.S. and UK represent a significant portion of global international bank lending making New York City and London major financial centers. Other key financial centers are Frankfurt, Hong Kong, and Tokyo, with Shanghai increasing in importance.

GLOBAL BANKING

Table 13-4 lists the world's largest global banks by assets. As in years past, banks located in developed western countries continue to dominate the top twenty banks. However, the full list of the top 1000 banks worldwide reveals an important shift away from the developed countries to emerging economies. The Banker annually publishes its list of the top 1000 largest banks. Since their rankings began forty years ago, research has shown the share of banks increasing in developing economies, such as China and Brazil, while reducing in the countries of the West. In 1990, of the 1000 top banks, 222 were in the U.S. By 2010, this had reduced to 199. Whereas in Asia, excluding Japan, there were 150 banks in

2010, a significant increase over the 104 in 1990. China alone had an increase from nine to 84 over the same time period. These changes help demonstrate the significant shift in the global banking system away from a dominance of banks in the West to a more balanced global banking system.[28]

Another aspect of banking is private banking, in which banks tailor their services to wealthy individuals. It is a labor-intensive business, with highly qualified and specialized employees developing customized financial packages for each client. Numerous banks (large and small) are aggressively pursuing this opportunity, using their global networks to win clients by offering opportunities for investing globally and minimizing taxes.

INTERNATIONAL INVESTMENT BANKING

Investment banking and brokerage services are another attractive international services industry. Companies seek investment banking service to ensure that investment portfolios are diversified internationally for optimum performance. That means there is a need for information about and access to investing in foreign stock markets around the world. The question for international brokerage houses is how to go about selling brokerage services globally in the face of intense competition from local brokerage houses with extensive retail networks. It is expensive to do business in most world financial centers, where costs are significant. With high salaries, rent, and overhead costs, large volumes of business are needed to break even and to make a profit.

Foreign firms can concentrate on a specialty or, if they are large, offer a breadth of global investment opportunities. Accordingly, some large firms offer institutional clients the options of investing in government securities, trading in futures and options, hedging currencies, and investing in major stock markets of the world. Smaller companies usually specialize.

As with other international service industries, cultural issues are important. Local employees can be particularly effective in addressing such issues as they can leverage their professional and personal contacts. These relationships lead to stronger sales. However, this also means global firms need to allow their local financial services branches significant autonomy, especially as relates to marketing, sales, and customer service. The global firm brings to the branch world-class technology, systems, procedures, and marketing intelligence.

INTERNATIONAL INSURANCE MARKETS

Insurance is another important global market for services. Though insurance had historically been dominant in industrialized countries, it is increasingly important in emerging markets. Table 13-5 shows the global market for insurance. Industrialized markets account for 87% of total worldwide insurance premiums, led by the U.S. as the number one market for insurance. However, the growth opportunities are in emerging markets such as China, India, and Brazil. Already China has become the seventh largest market with India and Brazil in the top 15. These would

Table 13-4 • World's Major Global Banks

	Bank	Country	Tier 1 Capital (U.S. $M)
1	Bank of America Corp.	U.S.	160,387.8
2	JPMorgan Chase & Co.	U.S.	132,971.0
3	Citigroup	U.S.	127,034.0
4	Royal Bank of Scotland	U.K.	123,859.0
5	HSBC Holdings	U.K.	122,157.0
6	Wells Fargo & Co.	U.S.	93,795.0
7	ICBC	China	91,110.5
8	BNP Paribas	France	90,648.4
9	Banco Santander	Spain	81,577.8
10	Barclays Bank	U.K.	80,586.7
11	Mitsubishi UFJ Financial Group	Japan	77,218.1
12	Lloyds Banking Group	U.K.	77,034.0
13	Credit Agricole Groupe	France	75,504.3
14	Bank of China	China	73,667.0
15	China Construction Bank Corp.	China	71,973.9
16	Goldman Sachs	U.S.	64,642.0
17	UniCredit	Italy	56,244.9
18	Groupe BPCE	France	54,141.2
19	Societe Generale	France	49,989.9
20	Deutsche Bank	Germany	49,576.4

Source: "1000 World Banks," *The Banker* (page 9; July 1, 2010)

be critical markets for expansion as seen in their growth in insurance premiums. Though globally insurance premiums were lower in 2009, due to the economic recession, premiums actually rose by 10% in Southeast Asia and over four percent for all emerging markets.[29]

The growth of insurance in emerging markets shows that the potential for future growth lies primarily outside of developed countries. In emerging markets, incomes are rising and individuals and heads of families are beginning to purchase insurance.

Marketing Services Overseas: Major Findings

The previous discussions of the airline, retailing, and financial services industries help illustrate the challenges and opportunities in globalizing services. Critical success factors can be summarized as: [30]

- Overcoming barriers to trade in services while leveraging increasing access to markets through multilateral and bilateral trade agreements.Trade barriers, including limitations on the proportion of a market that a foreign company can serve and discriminatory taxation of services provided by a foreign company.

- Indentifying the bases of international competitive advantage in services unique to the firm.

- Understanding and overcoming (or leveraging) country-of-origin effect in services.

- Understanding how culture affects service processes and service delivery.

- Understanding how information content related to services is presented across cultures, especially between high-context and low-context cultures.

- Using appropriate modes of entry in delivering services.

- Forecasting and managing demand across markets.

- Deciding whether to standardize or adapt services.

- Understanding how service quality dimensions and their perceived importance vary across countries.

- Conducting market research across nations in services industries.

Table 13-5 • Global Insurance Market

Bank	2009 Global Ranking by Insurance Premium Volume	US $ Billion (Percent of Global)
Industrialized Countries:		**$3,533** (87.0%)
United States	1	$1,140 (28.0%)
Japan	2	$506 (12.0%)
United Kingdom	3	$309 (8.0%)
France	4	$283 (7.0%)
Germany	5	$238 (6.0%)
Italy	6	$169 (4.0%)
Hong Kong	24	$23 (1.0%)
Emerging Economies:		**$533** (13.0%)
China	7	$163 (4.0%)
India	12	$65 (2.0%)
Brazil	15	$49 (1.0%)
Russia	19	$40 (1.0%)
Mexico	29	$17 (0.4%)
World		$4,066

Source: "World Insurance in 2009," Swiss Re (http://www.swissre.com/media/media_information/pr_sigma2_2010.html); accessed November 24, 2010.

SUMMARY

Services industries include wholesaling and retailing, communications, transportation, utilities, banking and insurance, sports, media and entertainment, tourism, and business and personal services. Services account for the largest portion of output and employment in advanced industrialized countries.

Services are becoming increasingly important in world trade. Trade in services accounts for about 20 percent of all world trade. As compared with the ongoing trade deficit in manufactured products, the U.S. has a trade surplus in services.

Services that have been developed globally include construction, banking, insurance, accounting, software, entertainment, consulting, transportation, and franchising.

Services are different from products in primarily five ways: Services are intangible, have heterogeneity consumers, are perishable, are simultaneously produced and consumed, and perceptions of service quality and delivery will vary by cultures.

Service quality is difficult to measure, particularly in cross-cultural settings. Consumer dissatisfaction may result from unrealistic expectations. Benchmarking allows service firms to assess performance gaps relative to their competitors and remedy those gaps in service quality.

The challenge of marketing services globally is directly related to the differences of services versus products. This has an important impact on how firms brand services, and advertise their availability.

Nations have competitive advantages in offering services primarily due to labor, capital, and technology.

Firm-specific factors also contribute to competitive advantages in offering services. Factors most important are management skills, firm size, and reputation.

International trade in services is subject to government interference and protection, just as with trade in products. The goal of government intervention varies, but most often is linked to protecting domestic industries, protecting national security, and maintaining sovereignty (control) over issues of national importance.

As services grow more important in world trade, nations have begun seeking a consensus on fair trade practices with regard to services. The WTO has paid special attention to protecting Intellectual Property (IP) rights. It has also addressed the issues of barriers to trade in services, national treatment of foreign firms, allowance of FDI in services without undue restrictions, temporary admission of foreign service workers, and international agreement on the regulation of international data

Service companies tend toward entry modes that involve foreign direct investment. FDI, licensing and franchising, and joint ventures are common vehicles for providing services in international markets.

Working capital requirements to offer services internationally may be high. Hence, joint ventures and strategic alliances are also common when a firm seeks to sell services overseas.

NASBITE CGBP TOPICS COVERED IN THIS CHAPTER

The NASBITE CGBP standard does not specifically call out services as a separate learning objective. Instead references are to "product and/or service." As such, there are no topics singularly associated with offering services internationally.

QUESTIONS AND RESEARCH

1. What are services? Why are they important in industrialized nations?

2. Which service industry sectors are important in the U.S. economy? How do these sectors vary from the industry sectors in other countries? Discuss your findings.

3. What are the major service-exporting nations? What might explain the number of advanced industrialized nations that appear on that list?

4. Explain the steps by which McDonald's was able to initiate operations in Hungary. What difficulties did the company face, and how did it solve them? What generalizations can you make from the McDonald's example?

5. What are some distinguishing characteristics of services? Explain why these characteristics make it difficult to sell services in foreign markets.

6. Discuss how culture can affect the sale of services overseas.

7. What are the bases of comparative advantage in services? Provide two or three examples of global services companies that are more competitive because of these comparative advantages.

8. Why and how do governments intervene in services? How is the WTO attempting to create freer trade in services?

9. Sports in a growing global service. Find an example of a successful global sport. Discuss the strategy the sport has used to increase its awareness internationally.

10. What are opportunities and challenges facing the global airline industry?

11. The text discusses some examples of global retailing. Research a retail firm that has expanded internationally. What were some challenges it faced? What lessons can be learned from that firm's experiences?

12. Insurance is one of the fastest growing services internationally. Pick an insurance firm that has expanded internationally. Discuss its strategy. What are the future prospects for this firm to continue its international expansion?

CHAPTER 13 TEAM PROJECT ASSIGNMENT: International Services

If your client is a services company, review the topics in this chapter as they relate to your client. Use the topics to help identify opportunities and challenges for your client specifically as it relates to offering services globally? Also research the comparative advantage of the home country of your client. How does this comparative advantage support the global growth of your client?

Integrate the findings of this research either into the overall international marketing plan, or develop a special section of the marketing plan that address issues specifically to offering services internationally.

CASE 13.1 Baseball: The Japanese Game

This case from 2005 is an interesting example of how a U.S. sport was expanded into Japan. It offer insights into the challenges and opportunities to global services.

Babe Ruth toured Japan with an All-Star team in 1931. Professional baseball resumed in Japan after the war in 1950. Japanese teams play each other all the time. There are 12 professional teams divided into two leagues, the Pacific and the Central. The champion from each league plays in an end-of-season playoff, a Japanese "World Series." The teams are as follows:

CENTRAL LEAGUE	**PACIFIC LEAGUE**
Yomiuri Giants	Nippon Ham Fighters
Yakult Swallows	Orix BlueWave
Chunchi Dragons	Chiba Lotte Marines
Hanshin Tigers	Seibu Lions
Hiroshima Toyo Carp	Fukuoka Softbank Hawks
Yokohama Bay Stars	Kintetsu Buffaloes

Four of those teams are located in Tokyo, and four are located in Osaka; all of the teams are owned by corporations. The Yomiuri Giants are owned and run by Japan's leading newspaper chain, the Yomiuri. The Yokohama Bay Stars are owned by TBS, a Tokyo television station. The Chunichi Dragons are owned by another newspaper chain. Two teams are owned by railroads: Hanshin and Kintetsu. Other team owners include Nippon Ham, a meat producer; Lotte, a Korean department store chain; Yakult, a yogurt and soft drink company; and Toyo Tire, which owns the Hiroshima Carp. The Central League is more popular, with an attendance of 12 million compared to 7 million for the Pacific League. The Yomiuri Giants are on television five or six nights a week, and all 65 of their home games and most of their away games are covered. Similarly, both Yokohama and Yakult have television connections; therefore, fan loyalty is strong and home attendance is high.

Japanese baseball stresses fundamentals. Bunting is common, and wa, or team spirit, is important. Managers are authoritarian, and teams practice extensively, working on fielding, covering bases, throwing to cutoff men, etc. Japanese players are small in size. They become professional baseball players the traditional way. They begin to play in high school, then moving on to Japan's only minor league team or to four years of college. Once in college, they cannot be drafted for four years. Japanese players know that American baseball players are better paid. They also accept that U.S. players are bigger, stronger, and faster and that U.S. players hit with more power than most Japanese players. Mike Lum, a hitting coach with the Kansas City Royals who played in Japan, noted, however, that Japanese pitching is good. It helps that the Japanese strike zone is wider and deeper—from below they player's belt to the armpits. Japanese pitchers pitch deeper into the game and, on average, pitch more innings over the course of a season.

As in the U.S., television has a strong influence on baseball. The Yomiuri Giants have a national following because of television. With Sadaharu Oh (who has 868 career home runs), the team won nine straight national championships between 1965 and 1973. The team plays in the Tokyo Dome (which is modeled after the Metrodome in Minnesota), sharing it with the Nippon Ham Fighters.

Built by the Korakuen Corporation for about $280 million, the new Tokyo Dome produced first-year revenues of over $325 million. It draws on a population of nearly 30 million in a 100-square-mile radius (due to Japan's public transportation system). The 56,000-seat arena also hosts track meets, bicycle races (on which big bets are placed), rugby matches, and events as diverse as Michael Jackson concerts and Mike Tyson boxing matches.

To combat the greater financial strength of the Central League, the Pacific League began importing U.S. players. The practice is now standard in both leagues. Each team can have two active foreign players. Additional "imported" players are in the minor leagues and can be called up in case of injury. Japanese baseball offers an opportunity for young U.S. ballplayers who *almost* make the U.S. major league teams.

An example is Alfonso Soriano, the New York Yankee and Texas Ranger star. In 1984, he signed with the Hiroshima Toyo Carp at age 16. He went to Japan not knowing the language and knowing nothing about the country. In 1988, he came back to the U.S., speaking Japanese and playing better baseball, and signed with the Yankees. His tutelage in Japan helped him become the first second baseman to hit 30 home runs and steal 30 bases, starting for the American League in the 2003 All Star game.

The foreign players, *gaijin senshu*, are well paid, with a strong yen making Japanese salaries look better. For example, in May 1998, Mike Easler signed with the Nippon Ham Fighters to play one year, making $975,000. He had been cut by the Yankees and, at age 37, saw Japan as his only chance to continue playing in the majors. Easler had played ten seasons of winter ball in Mexico and Venezuela, resulting in his becoming comfortable with foreign cultures. Other notable U.S. players who played in Japan include Orlando Merced, Kevin Mitchell, Tony Fernandez, and Reggie Jefferson. Managers such as Charlie Manuel (who played for six years in Japan) and Bobby Valentine have coached for Japanese teams, then moved on to coach U.S. major league teams.

Salaries for U.S. baseball players are high when compared with the average salaries for Japanese players. However, the pay difference is not a problem with the Japanese player. He knows that he is a company employee and that the company that owns the team will absorb him into the company culture, finding him a position if he decides to quit baseball.

The pay is good, but life is not easy for a U.S. ballplayer in Japan. For one thing, the entire team relies heavily on him. For another, although teams hire an interpreter to work with him, he and his family must adjust to the culture and deal with the scarce housing and the expensive way of life. Then there are the playing fields. The Tokyo Dome is first-class, as are three other stadiums that have artificial turf, but the remaining clubs have all-dirt infields and grass outfields or just all-dirt fields. When it rains, the field can be like a swamp. In contrast, playing during the hot season has been compared to playing on a basketball court. The work ethic, quintessentially Japanese, is often the undoing of an aging U.S. baseball player who comes to Japan expecting easy money. Faced with the demand to believe that the company or team is what matters and that the manager must not be questioned, many U.S. players quit after a year.

Randy Bass's story is an example of the culture gap. He became Japan's leading slugger, winning the Triple Crown in 1985 and 1986. He became the highest-paid player in Japan, but he left the Hanshin Tigers for San Francisco in May 1988, when his son was hospitalized. He was violating the Japanese cultural code that puts loyalty to the company above personal considerations. When he did not return to Japan by June 17, as he had agreed, he was released.

Unlike U.S. baseball, Japanese teams play each other frequently because each league has only six teams. Pitchers learn about batters. A pitcher's chief weapons are his curve, slider, and forkball—in other words, control. After facing a hitter so many times during the Japanese season (and studying him carefully), the pitcher has a distinct advantage. As Easler put it, "They know everything about you—what you can hit, what you can't. Before the game, you have a video of each team that you play. We go over everything in great detail. The practice habits and work habits here are just exceptional.... It's like spring training every day." One other difference is the stress on pitching complete games. Easler thinks that this builds confidence because the pitcher learns to bail himself out. "Patience is the key to hitting in Japan. You are definitely going to have to hit the ball the other way. If you don't, you'll die here." Easler, who used to be a dead pull hitter (that is, a right-handed batter hitting to left field) returned to the spray hitting style (that is, hitting to all parts of the field, not just to left field) that he learned under Walter Hriniak with the Boston Red Sox.

JAPANESE PLAYERS TO THE U.S.

Most baseball fans have heard of Ichiro Suzuki. He plays for the Seattle Mariners, the first Japanese position player to sign with a major league club. Formerly a player for the Orix BlueWave, he broke George Sisler's 1920 record for most hits in a season, getting 262 hits in 2004—a sign of the extraordinary bat control that he possesses. He is only the first in a line of top Japanese baseball players who have begun to make an impact in the U.S. major leagues. Hideki Matsui is a mainstay slugger for the New York Yankees. Hideo Nomo has zig-zagged across the U.S. professional baseball landscape, pitching no-hitters and getting shelled.

A TRUE WORLD SERIES

What of the future? Because of the strong yen, Japanese clubs can bid more dollars for better U.S. players if they choose to do so. The concentration of teams in Tokyo and Osaka may hinder attempts to expand baseball in Japan by adding new teams in other cities. On the other hand, the success of the Tokyo Dome points to the possibility of moving franchises and creating expansion teams linked to new major league-quality stadiums. In March 2006, players competed for their home countries in the World Baseball Classic, the first 16-nation world championship. Professional players will participate, making the event different from the Olympics, which allows only amateurs. Thus, Albert Pujols, Vladimir Gurrero, David Ortiz, and Pedro Martinez could all be playing for the team from the Dominican Republic. That type of international tournament will create a greater awareness of baseball globally and raise the quality of baseball elsewhere. Japan might consider increasing the size of team rosters from the present 25 men and raising the current ceiling for foreign players. Other nations might start larger and better-funded professional baseball leagues, thereby increasing market size for the better baseball players, bringing in more advertising dollars, and augmenting the economic stature of professional baseball.

BASEBALL TRADE OPPORTUNITIES

Selling U.S. baseball to the world is an "export" possibility. The popularity of Japanese players in the U.S. raises the audience for major league baseball games because Japanese fans want to see their favorite Japanese players succeed on the U.S. stage. Television rights for baseball games to be shown in Japan bring yen-based revenues for U.S. entrepreneurs. U.S. Major League Baseball announced a $275 million six-year deal selling TV rights to its games to the Japanese advertising company Dentsu (three times what Major League Baseball received in its previous contract with Dentsu). Promotional opportunities for ballplayers in Japan are underexploited, currently under control of the company owning the team, and if baseball can be exported, can ownership rights be far behind? Would Sony buy a U.S. baseball team? After all, the owner of Nintendo was given permission by U.S. baseball team owners to purchase the Seattle Mariners when the team was up for sale. If the two richest markets in the world are baseball crazy, opportunities surely exist for further trade in baseball between those nations and others.

Case prepared by Ravi Sarathy for use in classroom discussion. © 2005, all rights reserved. Based on Robert Whiting, "*The Samurai Way of Baseball: The Impact of Ichiro*," Warner Books 2005; "Major League Baseball Agrees to $275 Million Deal in Japan," *Wall Street Journal*, October 31, 2003; Warren Cromartie, "Slugging It Out in Japan," *Kodansha*, 1991; and a three-part series by Larry Whiteside, *Boston Globe*, July 17, 18, and 19, 1988. Also see http://baseballguru.com/bbjp1.html.

Questions and Research

1. How is Japanese baseball marketed? How is that different from the way U.S. baseball is sold?

2. How would an aging U.S. baseball player market himself to a Japanese team? What about a rookie?

3. How is the growing popularity of baseball in Japan likely to affect U.S. baseball?

4. Does U.S.–Japanese collaboration change the market for U.S. and Japanese baseball players? How should the Major League Baseball Players Association (the union) react to protect its members' interests?

5. Why would U.S. entrepreneurs and agents be interested in Japanese baseball players?

6. Why would someone in Japan want to buy a U.S. baseball team? What are the implications of an internationalization of the baseball scene?

7. How can trade in baseball be seen as an example of trade in services?

8. Research how baseball has continued to expand between the United States and Japan since this case was developed in 2005. What have been ongoing challenges? What are examples of further successes?

CASE 13.2 Sony Corporation

This case is the first of three cases that track Sony Corporation during two decades of growth. The first two are in this chapter (Cases 13.2 and 13.3) and focus on Sony's major expansion into the entertainment industry. The final case is in Chapter 15. Following the issues and challenges during these many years provides useful insights into the expansion of a global company in products and services.

This first case discusses the business environment for Sony that led to its significant change in strategy, culminating in its acquisition of CBS Records.

Sony has long been known for its innovative consumer electronics products, such as the pioneering Walkman. Sony is an international corporation, with 70 percent of its sales coming from outside Japan and non-Japanese owners owning 23 percent of its stock. Sony manufactures about 20 percent of its output outside Japan. As of 1986, its sales mix was video camera recorders (VCRs), 33 percent; audio equipment (CD players), 22 percent; televisions (the Trinitron), 22 percent; and other products (records, floppy disk drives, and semiconductors), 17 percent. Sony has always emphasized R&D, spending about 9 percent of sales on it.

THE BETAMAX EXPERIENCE

Sony has seen increased competition from other Japanese companies and from countries with lower labor costs, such as Taiwan and South Korea. Its strategy of inventing new, advanced-technology products and then waiting for the market to buy seemed to be faltering. However, Sony's biggest failure was the VHS format. Having invented the Betamax format for VCRs, Sony refused to license the technology to other manufacturers. Betamax was higher-priced, and recording times were somewhat shorter than those of the competing VHS format, although image quality was better.

Sony's competitors—Matsushita (Panasonic), Hitachi, and Toshiba—all banded together around the VHS format. They licensed the format to any manufacturer who wanted it. Consequently, the total number of VHS sets produced and sold was far higher than the Betamax-format VCRs. That meant lower retail prices for the Betamax because of accumulated volume and resulting economies of scale. Also, far more "software" was available for the VHS format; that is, movie producers were more likely to use VHS tapes to make copies of their films available for purchase and rental. That further increased demand for VHS-format VCRs. The net result was that Betamax gradually faded. Sony stopped its production in 1988.

RETHINKING BASIC STRATEGY

The difficulty of selling advanced technology, coupled with the speed of imitation and the impact of lowwage country competitors, led Sony to change its basic corporate strategy. The CBS/Sony Group, Inc., a 50-50 joint venture between Sony and CBS, Inc., has grown dramatically over a 20-year period to become an industry leader in the multibillion yen Japanese music industry.

On CD and other formats, the company releases recordings in Japan, Hong Kong, and Macau of popular Japanese artists as well as foreign artists. Therefore, Sony's diversification into the global music industry is not unexpected. In January 1988, it agreed to buy CBS Records for $2 billion, but subsequent moves have dramatically transformed Sony as it moves to become more of a service company. Table 13-6 summarizes the major entertainment industry acquisitions made by Sony since 1988.

Table 13-6 • From Electronics to Entertainment: Sony's Acquisitions since 1988

Date	Company Acquired	Price
October 1989	Gruber-Peters Productions	$200 million
September 1989	Columbia Pictures	$3.4 billion
January 1989	Tree International (country music publishers)	$30 million
January 1988	CBS Records	$2 billion

Source: Sony Corporation news releases.

SONY'S DIVERSIFICATION INTO THE ENTERTAINMENT INDUSTRY

The acquisitions are large, totaling over $5 billion, or about half of Sony's total assets. More interesting is the reasoning behind Sony's decision to acquire a slew of entertainment companies. A summary of the acquisitions follows.

- **CBS Records:** For $2 billion, Sony acquired control of the world's largest record company, CBS Records. CBS Records, Inc., consists of CBS Records (Domestic), CBS Masterworks, CBS Records International, CBS/Sony, Columbia House, and CBS Music Video. The acquisition gave Sony an immediate international presence in the music industry. Traditionally selling music hardware, Sony was one of the world's largest producers of CDs, tape recorders (including the phenomenally successful Walkman), and stereo television, but all of those products were subject to competition because innovative ideas could be imitated and prices could be cut. Sony realized that being in the music business allowed it to take advantage of the entire installed base of CD players around the world, not just those it manufactured. Imitation was impossible because each musical performance was unique. However, managing such a creative business required great cultural sensitivity and the use of local managers rather than predominantly Japanese management.

- **Columbia Pictures:** The major attraction of Columbia Pictures was its large library of movies, which earn revenues every time they are shown at cinemas and on video around the world. Columbia also had a profitable television production and syndication business, thus, through the acquisition, Sony could sell products to owners of television sets and VCRs (similar to providing music on record and tape for owners of CD players and tape recorders).

There are two other reasons Sony found Columbia Pictures attractive. First, television in Japan is being liberalized, with the number of television stations and on-air time doubling because of the launch of satellite television. There will be a sudden increase in demand for products such as films and television shows to fill air time on Japan's satellite stations. Sony will be in a position to supply those products at premium prices in yen at a time when demand is increasing. The second reason is hardware-related. Sony has been trying to establish its 8 mm camcorder format, competing with the VHS-C-based format from Japanese producers. This standards battle is reminiscent of Sony's experience with Betamax. This time, however, Sony realizes the need to build the installed base. Hence, it has licensed the 8 mm technology to other producers and is willing to manufacture the camcorders for others to sell under their brand names. Thus, Sony is making sure that volume sales of the 8 mm camcorder will be achieved, resulting in economies of scale and lower prices. The next step is to stimulate demand by making a variety of movies available in this format. Sony can do this by putting the entire Columbia Pictures catalog on 8 mm video, thus giving consumers a reason to buy the camcorder, which can also be used as a video player. Making the movie catalog available will be crucial to the success of Sony's newly introduced 8 mm video Walkman. The pocket-sized portable color television will appeal to consumers as long as videos are available to use with it.

With the acquisitions of CBS Records and Columbia Pictures, Sony becomes one of the world's major producers of entertainment hardware and software: a producer of records and CD players, a leading manufacturer of television sets, and an owner of a library of classic films.

- **Guber-Peters Productions:** When Sony purchased Columbia Pictures, it obtained a film library as well as a film production studio. Columbia had gone through four producers in five years, however, and needed more capable film production management. The logical step was to take over one of Hollywood's most successful film production companies, Guber-Peters Company (formerly Barris Productions). The company had produced Batman, one of Warner Communications' all-time best-selling films. In fact, Guber-Peters had signed a five-year exclusive agreement with Warner to produce movies on its behalf. Guber-Peter's expertise lay in spotting hot properties, signing them, and then convincing major studios to bankroll the films and distribute them. Guber-Peters had a unique culture-specific talent for working in and with Hollywood, producing successful films for the huge U.S. television and film audience. Sony acquired Guber-Peters for over $200 million, or about five times Guber-Peters's latest-year revenues. The two key producers, Peter Guber and Jon Peters, received about $50 million for their stock in Guber-Peters, a 10 percent stake in future profits at Columbia Pictures, 8 percent of the future appreciation of Columbia Pictures' market value, and about $50 million in total deferred compensation.

Warner immediately sued Sony for acquiring Guber-Peters and refused to release Peter Guber from his long-term contract. Of course, Sony and Warner ultimately settled out of court, exchanging valuable assets such as a share of the movie studio and video rights. Clearly, Sony wanted the management talent—Americans who knew Hollywood and could hire the right people; who had the appropriate financial and creative contacts; and, most importantly, who knew how to make hit films.

- **Tree International:** Through CBS Records, Sony also acquired ownership of Tree International, the premier country music publishing company. Owning rights to several generations of hit country songs guaranteed a steady stream of revenue, especially as the catalog became popular around the world through Sony's music and video production divisions. This was a minor acquisition, but it may point to a trend toward acquiring other music publishing companies as a means to further control the software end of the entertainment business.

SONY'S FUTURE

Looking to the future, Sony's heavy involvement in new hardware technologies such as advanced high-definition television, computer workstations, and compact disc interactive technology will require further research and development. Consumer acceptance of those products will depend on the availability of software products that showcase the new hardware products. Sony's long-term plans focus more on services and entertainment. Paradoxically, that focus will help the company become a stronger hardware company and reduce risk by smoothing revenue fluctuations and providing the stability of recurring earnings from sales of music, film, and videotapes. (The Sony case is continued with Cases 13.3 and 15.1).

Sources: "Sony Sees More Than Michael Jackson in CBS," *The Economist*, November 28, 1987; "A Changing Sony Aims to Own the Software That Its Products Need," *Wall Street Journal*, December 30, 1988; "Sony Sets Pact with Coca-Cola for Columbia," *Wall Street Journal*, September 28, 1989; and "Dynamic Duo: Producers of 'Batman' Stir Whammo Battle over Future Services," *Wall Street Journal*, October 20, 1989.

Questions and Research

1. What threats were facing Sony?
2. Trace the various entertainment industry acquisitions made by Sony. Why did Sony make these acquisitions? Have they helped the company compete more effectively in international markets?
3. What are the risks of Sony's strategy of buying U.S. entertainment companies?
4. What would you recommend that Sony do next? How do you think Sony's Japanese competitors might respond to its action?
5. Is Sony becoming a global company, or is it becoming a company with products adapted for each specific country market? Explain.
6. Based on Sony's experience, what generalizations can you make about the global service industry?

CASE 13.3 Sony in 1996

This case is the second of three cases that track Sony Corporation during two decades of growth. The introduction to Case 13.2 discusses the background to the cases.

This second case discusses a turbulent time for Sony and its entertainment divisions. This case tracks the activities of the company's new president, Mr. Nobuyuki Idei, in working toward the convergence of entertainment, consumer electronic products, and computers. It ends with a summary of the key decisions that needed to be made to address the relatively poor performance of the company.

In December 1994, Sony announced that it was taking a $2.7 billion write-off in connection with its 1989 acquisition of Columbia Pictures. Furthermore,

Sony Pictures reported a loss of $500 million for the year. The combined losses of $3.2 billion were some of the largest losses incurred in Hollywood. Shortly thereafter, Matsushita, which had copied Sony by buying MCA, announced that it was selling MCA to Seagram, incurring a large loss in the process. MCA's top management had threatened to leave because Matsushita did not want to invest additional funds into MCA. MCA's main film-producing partner, Steven Spielberg, would have accompanied MCA's management and stopped distributing his films through MCA.

Meanwhile, back in Japan, an appreciating yen made Sony's consumer electronics products more expensive in its export markets. Sony was facing competition from producers in South Korea and Taiwan that could offer a basic VCR in U.S. stores, such as Circuit City, for $99, a price at which Sony could not compete.

CHANGES AT THE TOP

Major changes occurred within Sony's top management ranks. Mr. Morita, Sony's founder, had suffered a stroke and was no longer involved in management. Mr. Ohga, the CEO, who had undergone a bypass operation, missed being able to chat with his mentor, Morita. The gradual decline in Sony's fortunes led him to think about what sort of person should lead Sony into the Twenty-First Century. Years earlier both Morita and Ohga had agreed to step down as president of the company at age 65. It was assumed that an engineer, Mr. Minoru Morio, the president of Sony's audiovisual products and head of Sony's DVD efforts, would step in. Ohga, however, turned to a marketer, Mr. Nobuyuki Idei, as Sony's next president. Idei had worked for Sony in overseas locations and had been in charge of marketing Sony's audiovisual products. In 1990, Idei had become head of Sony's Design Center, responsible for Sony's merchandising and product promotions and corporate communications. As such, he represented Sony across the world at major trade shows and industry gatherings. His appointment signaled a major change in Sony's strategic direction and corporate vision. Idei was an enthusiastic proponent of digital video and saw opportunities for Sony in the convergence of entertainment, consumer electronics products, and computers.

THE DIGITAL VIDEO ERA

Digital video could be to VCRs and films on videotape what CDs were to older analog long-playing records (LPs). Digital video allows entire films to be stored on CD-ROM-sized discs, accessed at any point, manipulated, and reused. Sony had been working with the Dutch company Philips in developing a DVD standard that would be used in digital video devices. Sony's standard called for a single-sided disc containing about 3.7 gigabytes of information, equal to about 135 minutes of video.

Establishing an industry standard can be enormously profitable, as can be seen in the examples of Intel and Microsoft. Sony (and Philips) earned a nickel in royalties for each CD sold, but in 1993, Sony learned that Toshiba and Time Warner were working on a DVD standard of their own. Their Super Density, (SD), format would use both sides of the disc and store 5 gigabytes on each side. Time Warner was also able to get the attention of movie studios in Hollywood, learning what performance criteria they expected from DVD. (In contrast, Morio, who headed Sony's DVD effort, spoke little English and came from an engineering, not a marketing, background.) With mounting competition from Toshiba and Time Warner, Idei was asked to formulate a new DVD strategy, which he crafted by stressing the role of DVD as a format for multimedia computers. By January 1995, Matsushita had joined Hitachi, Pioneer, JVC, Thomson, and Mitsubishi in supporting the Toshiba SD standard. Possibly with the Betamax fiasco in mind, Sony ultimately compromised and agreed to work out a unified DVD standard.

NEW BUSINESS DIRECTIONS

One of Sony's successes has been the Sony PlayStation, which competed against the Nintendo and Sega 16-bit game machines. However, it offered superior video and sound and faster speed through 32-bit processors. Planning for the PlayStation began in 1988. Ken Kutaragi, who was designing Sony workstations using advanced chips, realized that the price of the chips would fall to the point that it made sense to build a game machine around the 32-bit semiconductors. Features such as a CD-ROM input device and a superior graphics screen could also be added. However, game machines sell because customers want hit games that are exclusive to the platform. Hence, an executive from Sony Music, which was a distributor of Nintendo machines, suggested that Kutaragi think about building reusable modules that programmers could use to create entertaining and impressive new games quickly. Based on that suggestion, Kutaragi built a dictionary of images that could be combined on the fly to build game characters who exhibited subtle and lifelike movements, while cutting game development time by half. Sony also created a joint venture within the company with Sony Music to focus on selling hardware (the PlayStation) and software (newly developed games). That allowed the PlayStation to be priced at $299 in the U.S., a full $100 below the competing Sega Saturn. (Sony's expectation was that a growing installed base would offer a fertile and captive market for the sale of high-margin hit games; the typical Nintendo owner purchased 6 to 12 games for a machine).

In 1995, Sony's PlayStation became the best-selling 32-bit game machine in Japan and the U.S. About a year later, when Nintendo introduced its N64 machine, both companies reduced prices of their game machines to under $150. Loyal Nintendo fans bought the new Nintendo machine in large numbers, but Sony's lead and bigger selection of games meant that it continued to hold a larger market share over Nintendo in the new-generation video game segment of the market.

Under Idei's leadership, Sony entered into an alliance with Intel to make multimedia computers that he termed "Intelligent television." He visualized "the intelligence of computers, the access power of on-line communications, and the visual power of full-motion video integrated into a new form of viewing experience." Other new products that Sony targeted for the age of digital television included wide-screen living room TVs that could access the Internet using web browsers, eyeglasses onto which television and e-mail could be projected using wireless technology, and low-cost computers acting as web browsers. The new Sony computers could include PlayStation game-playing abilities as well as the ability to access digital television programs and use screen savers featuring images and sound from Sony films and music acts. Moreover, Sony's library of 3,000 films and over 35,000 hours of television programs would be a valuable resource for an age of digital television.

Outside the U.S., Sony saw strong growth possibilities in satellite television. It formed a joint venture with Singapore-based Argos Communications to launch a Hindi satellite television channel beamed to India. The channel featured Indian-produced shows and movies, as well as films and programs from Sony's library. Initially, the channel was offered free to cable television operators who would redistribute it. Sony expected to generate revenues from sale of advertising time. Sony also became a partner in Home Box Office (HBO) Olç, a Spanish broadcast aimed at Latin America.

MANAGEMENT SHAKE-UP IN THE U.S.

Mr. Schulhof, a physicist and jet pilot (like Ohga), was the head of Sony's U.S. operations and a close ally of Morita and Ohga. He had authorized payment of $200 million to buy Guber-Peters Entertainment and to buy out Guber's and Peter's contracts with Warner Brothers. He allowed Guber and Peters to choose their managers, sometimes resulting in the appointment of friends and associates. (Guber named his lawyer as the number two executive.) That may have resulted in an atmosphere where politics and the people one knew was important.

Guber and Peters had little experience in running a studio, but spent lavishly, updating the Culver City studios at a cost of $200 million. There were no cost controls, and several new film releases were expensive failures (Last Action Hero, Hudson Hawk, Geronimo, and Frankenstein). Schulhof also backed Sony's entry into programs for radio syndication and into theme parks featuring Sony characters and goods. He did not agree with the move into computers, which he characterized as a low-margin business with rapid change and short product cycles—an environment in which Sony had no experience. By the end of 1995, Schulhof had resigned from Sony as Idei moved to reestablish control by Japanese headquarters over Sony Pictures and U.S. operations.

SONY'S FINANCES

Table 13-7, below, summarizes Sony's financial performance between 1986 and 1995. Sales grew dramatically, from $7.7 billion to over $46 billion. Sales in 1995 were nearly evenly distributed across Japan, the U.S., and Europe, with sales of $12.3 billion, $13.9 billion, and $10.2 billion, respectively. However, net income was half the profitability levels of 1986 and long-term debt grew tenfold. In allocating its cash flow, Sony had to choose between the entertainment division and the support of R&D in the hardware divisions. In 1995, sales of television, audio, and video equipment were about 58 percent of total sales (compared to about 20 percent from music and films). In 1995, U.S. revenues from consumer electronics actually exceeded U.S. revenues from music and film.

ALTERNATIVES FOR SONY'S U.S. ENTERTAINMENT OPERATIONS

Matsushita's sale of MCA immediately raised questions as to whether Sony should do the same. Idei remarked that Matsushita was shortsighted in selling its film division. In a digital age, content and copyrights can be distributed in many formats, and the large film library that came with the acquisition of Columbia Pictures was a valuable and scarce asset. Few Hollywood film studios remain for sale to media companies, wanting to enter into the software or content-generation side of the business. When Idei took over as president of Sony, he indicated that he wanted to hold on to the entertainment division in the U.S. His priority, however, was to restore profitability to Sony Pictures. He wanted to see more pictures made with lower budgets, stressing cost controls. When Schulhof, head of Sony's U.S. operations, mentioned that Sony's market share was rising, Idei remarked that he was more interested in profits.

If Sony were to sell, several choices existed: Should it sell all of the entertainment business? If so, who should it sell to, mindful that it did not want to create a strong competitor down the road. Interested parties included GE, which owned NBC-television; News Corporation, which already had Fox Studios; and overseas buyers such as Polygram and Bertelsmann, neither of which had a

Table 13-7 • Sony Corporation: 1986-1995 Financial Statements ($Billions)

	1986	1987	1988	1989	1990	1991	1992	1993	1994	1995
Sales	7.7	10.7	17.1	20.5	26.1	29.6	32.2	34.8	40.4	46.2
Operating income	0.2	0.4	1.2	2.1	2.1	1.4	1.0	0.9	-1.7	2.3
Net income	0.245	0.269	0.562	0.717	0.827	0.904	0.292	0.143	-2.97	0.683
Long-term debt	0.88	1.58	1.67	4.1	4.91	6.65	7.65	9.36	10.49	8.47
Net worth	3.7	5.2	6.9	9.1	10.4	11.6	12.4	12.6	11.7	10.7

major Hollywood studio. Another alternative was to sell only part of the U.S. entertainment business. Options included selling a portion in a U.S. public stock offering or selling a stake in the company to a strategic partner.

Idei had specific ideas on how Sony should be run. He expressed little interest in buying media channels like Disney did with ABC. In his words, "Buying a network in a digital age with so many channels won't bring any benefits to us." He disliked the idea of selling the U.S. music and film business and taking on a partner. His fear was losing control and having to put up with interference from U.S. owners with different perspectives. "I also want to set a new future direction for our R&D so that it is not merely trying to extend our current business, but attempting to identify new opportunities for the 21st century. And of course DVD is a very high priority because setting a format standard energizes the company."

For a 2005 update on Sony, see Chapter 15, Case 15.1: Sony in 2005.

Sources: "Ouster of Schulhof Leaves Focus Fuzzy at Sony Entertainment," *Wall Street Journal*, December 6, 1995; "Sony Heads Down Information Highway and Decides Not to Go It Alone," *Wall Street Journal*, April 14, 1995; "Sony President Rules Out Buying American Network," *Wall Street Journal*, November 21, 1995; "Sony May Sell Stake in U.S. Operations," *Wall Street Journal*, October 30, 1995; "Sony Resignation Brings Speculation about Possible Suitors for Movie Unit," *Wall Street Journal*, December 7, 1995; "Sony Unit Plans Venture to Launch Hindi-Language television Channel in India," *Wall Street Journal*, August 14, 1995; "Sony President Seeks to Quash Rumors about Sale of U.S. Entertainment Unit," *Wall Street Journal*, January 15, 1996; "Sony's Heartaches in Hollywood," *Business Week*, December 5, 1994; "It's Nobuyuki Idei's Sony Now," *Business Week*, December 18, 1995; "Sony on the Brink," *FORTUNE*, June 12, 1995; "Lonesome Samurai," *Financial World*, May 23, 1995; and "Sony Outside, Intel Inside," *Financial World*, January 2, 1996. Case prepared by Ravi Sarathy for use in classroom discussion. © 2006. All rights reserved.

Questions and Research

1. Evaluate the performance of Sony's U.S. entertainment division. Why did it do so poorly?

2. What were the challenges facing Sony in 1996? Assess its strategy for coping with those challenges.

3. Looking back, would Sony have been better off not buying into the U.S. film and music businesses? Explain your answer.

4. What do you think of Mr. Idei's approach to running Sony?

NOTES

1. For historical data: Victor R. Fuchs, The Growing Importance of the Services Industries, National Bureau of Economic Research Occasional Paper, No 96, New York, NBER, 1965. Current data: US Bureau of Labor Statistics International Labor Comparison "Percent of Employment in Services"; (http://www.bls.gov/fls/flscomparelf/lfcompendium.pdf); accessed November 21, 2010.

2. "Services: Rules for Growth and Investment"; World Trade Organization; (http://www.wto.org/english/thewto_e/whatis_e/tif_e/agrm6_e.htm); accessed November 21, 2010.

3. "Services Area in a Fog," *The Economist*, May 23, 1987.

4. Zeithaml, V., A. Parasuraman, and Leonard L. Berry, "Problems and Strategies in Services Marketing," *Journal of Marketing*, Volume 49, Spring 1985.

5. Source: Adapted from R. Sarathy, "Global Strategy in Service Industries," *Long Range Planning*, Volume 27, Number 6, 1994.

6. Lovelock, C. H. and George Yip, "Developing Global Strategies for Service Businesses," *California Management Review*, Volume 38, Issue 2, 1996, pp. 64–86; Lovelock, Christopher, "Classifying Services to Gain Strategic Marketing Insights," *Journal of Marketing*, Volume 47, Summer 1983.

7. Javalgi, R. G., Bob D. Cutler, and William A. Winans. "At Your Service! Does Country of Origin Research Apply to Services?" *Journal of Services Marketing*, Volume 15, Issue 7, 2001, pp. 565–582.

8. Smith, Anne M. and Nina L. Reynolds. "Measuring Cross-Cultural Service Quality: A Framework for Assessment," *International Marketing Review*, Volume 19, Number 5, 2001, pp. 450–481.

9. Groonroos, C, "A Service Quality Model and Its Marketing Implications," *European Journal of Marketing*, Volume 18, Number 4, 1984.
10. Parasuraman, A., V. Zeithaml, and Leonard L. Berry, "A Conceptual Model of Service Quality and Its Implications for Future Research," *Journal of Marketing*, Volume 49, Fall 1985.
11. Min, Hokey, Hyesung Min, and Kyooyup Chung, "Dynamic Benchmarking of Hotel Service Quality," *Journal of Services Marketing*, Volume 16, Issue 4, 2002, pp. 302–321.
12. Moorthi, Y. L. R., "An Approach to Branding Services," *Journal of Services Marketing*, Volume 16, Issue 3, 2002, pp. 259–274.
13. Mortimer, Kathleen, "Integrating Advertising Theories with Conceptual Models of Services Advertising," *Journal of Services Marketing*, Volume 16, Issue 5, 2002, pp. 460–468; Mortimer, K. and B. P. Mathews, "The Advertising of Services: Consumer Views vs. Normative Guidelines," *Service Industries Journal*, Volume 18, Number 3, 1998, pp. 14–19.
14. Mortimer, Kathleen, "Services Advertising: The Agency Viewpoint," *Journal of Services Marketing*, Volume 15, Issue 2, 2001, pp. 131–146.
15. Patterson, Paul G. and Tasman Smith, "Relationship Benefits in Service Industries: A Replication in a Southeast Asian Context," *Journal of Services Marketing*, Volume 15, Issue 6, 2001, pp. 425–443.
16. Bharadwaj, S. G., P. R. Varadarajan, and J. Fahy, "Sustainable Competitive Advantage in Service Industries: A Conceptual Model and Research Propositions," *Journal of Marketing*, October 1993, pp. 83–99.
17. Javalgi, R. G., D. A. Griffith, and D. Steven White, "An Empirical Examination of Factors Influencing the Internationalization of Service Firms," *Journal of Services Marketing*, Volume 17, Issue 2, 2003, pp. 185–201.
18. Terry Miller and Kim R. Holmes, *2010 Index of Economic Freedom*, The Heritage Foundation and the Wall Street Journal, 2010. Also available online at: http://www.heritage.org/index/country/Brazil.
19. *Doing Business in Brazil: 2010 Country Commercial Guide for U.S. Companies*, U.S. and Foreign Commercial Service and the U.S. Department of State, 2010. (http://www.buyusainfo.net/docs/x_6282408.pdf); accessed November 29, 2010.
20. Brian Straus, "US, Brazil Reach Expanded Air Services Agreement." *Air Transport World*, June 27, 2008. (http://atwonline.com/international-aviation-regulation/news/us-brazil-reach-expanded-air-services-agreement-0626); accessed November 29, 2010.
21. John L. Wettheim, "The Whole World Is Watching." *Sports Illustrated*, June 14, 2004, p. 76.
22. Gary Levin, "Ratings Surge for Olympics, Thanks to Live Events, Web." *USA Today*, February 25, 2010. (http://www.usatoday.com/life/television/news/2010-02-25-olyratings25_ST_N.htm) accessed November 29, 2010.
23. Sultan, Fareena and Merlin Simpson, Jr., "International Service Variants: Airline Passenger Expectations and Perceptions of Service Quality," *Journal of Services Marketing*, Volume 14, Issue 3, 2000, pp. 188–216.
24. "Joint Ventures in Hungary," *CW Informatika Ltd. (Budapest)*, Volume 2, Number 1, 1989, pp. 9–10;
25. Peter Foster, "McDonald's Excellent Soviet Venture," *Canadian Business*, May 1991.
26. "McDonald's Faces Revolt in Brazil." *Wall Street Journal*, October 21, 2003.
27. "Judge Fines McDonald's for Obese Employee in Brazil." FoxNews.com, October 28, 2010 (http://www.foxnews.com/world/2010/10/28/judge-fines-mcdonalds-obese-employee-brazil/) accessed November 29, 2010.
28. "New World Order," *The Banker* (July 1, 2010), (www.lexisnexis.com); accessed November 23, 2010.
29. "New Swiss Re sigma study "World Insurance in 2009" Reveals Slight Premium Dip But Improved Capital," *Swiss Re*, (http://www.swissre.com/media/media_information/pr_sigma2_2010.html); accessed November 24, 2010.
30. The list draws on concepts contained in this article: Javalgi, R. G. and D. Steven White, "Strategic Challenges for the Marketing of Services Internationally," International Marketing Review, Volume 19, Number 6, 2002, pp. 563–581.

14 Global Marketing Strategy

This chapter explores how companies formulate their international marketing strategy. After a carefully developed strategy is implemented, a company can better ensure it maximizes and sustains its global competitive advantage.

The main goals of this chapter are to ●●●

1. Identify a framework in which a firm may develop its global strategy.
2. Discuss strategy issues specific to global marketing.
3. Identify the foundational analysis used to develop a global strategy: organizational, structural, and country/regional analysis.
4. Discuss the relationship between competitive advantage and a firm's value chain and address their impact on global strategy.

5. Detail the way a global marketing strategy is implemented and various strategic perspectives that may be used in support of that implementation.
6. Identify the impact of competitors and global strategy.
7. Discuss the pressure to standardize or adapt the global marketing strategy.
8. Discuss how the global marketing system must be coordinated.

As a firm develops its global marketing strategy, it must consider a number of factors. Some highlights include

- How should the global marketing strategy be linked to the overall corporate strategy?
- Which markets should the firm enter?
- Should products and services be standardized across all markets or adapted to meet consumer needs?
- How does the firm leverage its competitive advantage in each foreign market?
- What is the role of the firm's global value chain and its impact on strategy?
- What impact will government policies have on implementation of the marketing strategy?

Some of these issues have been addressed in previous chapters, such as foreign market selection (Chapter 7) and product standardization or adaptation (Chapter 9). This chapter primarily focuses on issues related to a firm's global marketing strategy not yet addressed as well as a general review of strategic planning goals.

Global Strategy: A Framework

Figure 14-1 sets out a framework for developing a firm's global strategy based around multiple product or service lines. The model details the three fundamental areas of analysis required to set the marketing strategy: organizational, situational, and country/region-specific analysis. The model implies it is an incremental process. Indeed, a firm would likely begin with its organizational analysis (internal), followed by the situational analysis (external or industry focus), and then move to the strategy for each country or region. But the process is also interrelated, with each analysis impacting the other. As the model shows, it is also an ongoing process that involves feedback after a period of time, and strategy reexamination and revision (shown as the final step in the model). The next sections look at each type of analysis in more detail.

Creating the global marketing strategy begins with an internal review of the firm and should involve all key departments.

Organizational Analysis

Creating the global marketing strategy begins with an internal review of the firm. As shown in the model in Figure 14-1, a broad range of company departments and functions must be involved in developing the global strategy. They would include decisions and policies regarding technology, product or service issues, marketing capabilities, financing, personnel, and organizational structure. The involvement of key departments helps ensure that all have a voice in setting the global strategy. It also better ensures each department fully supports and implements the strategy.

This initial situational analysis should identify strengths and weaknesses for the firm as it grows internationally. Examples of strengths would be management expertise, Intellectual Property (IP) rights

Figure 14-1 • Developing a Global Strategy

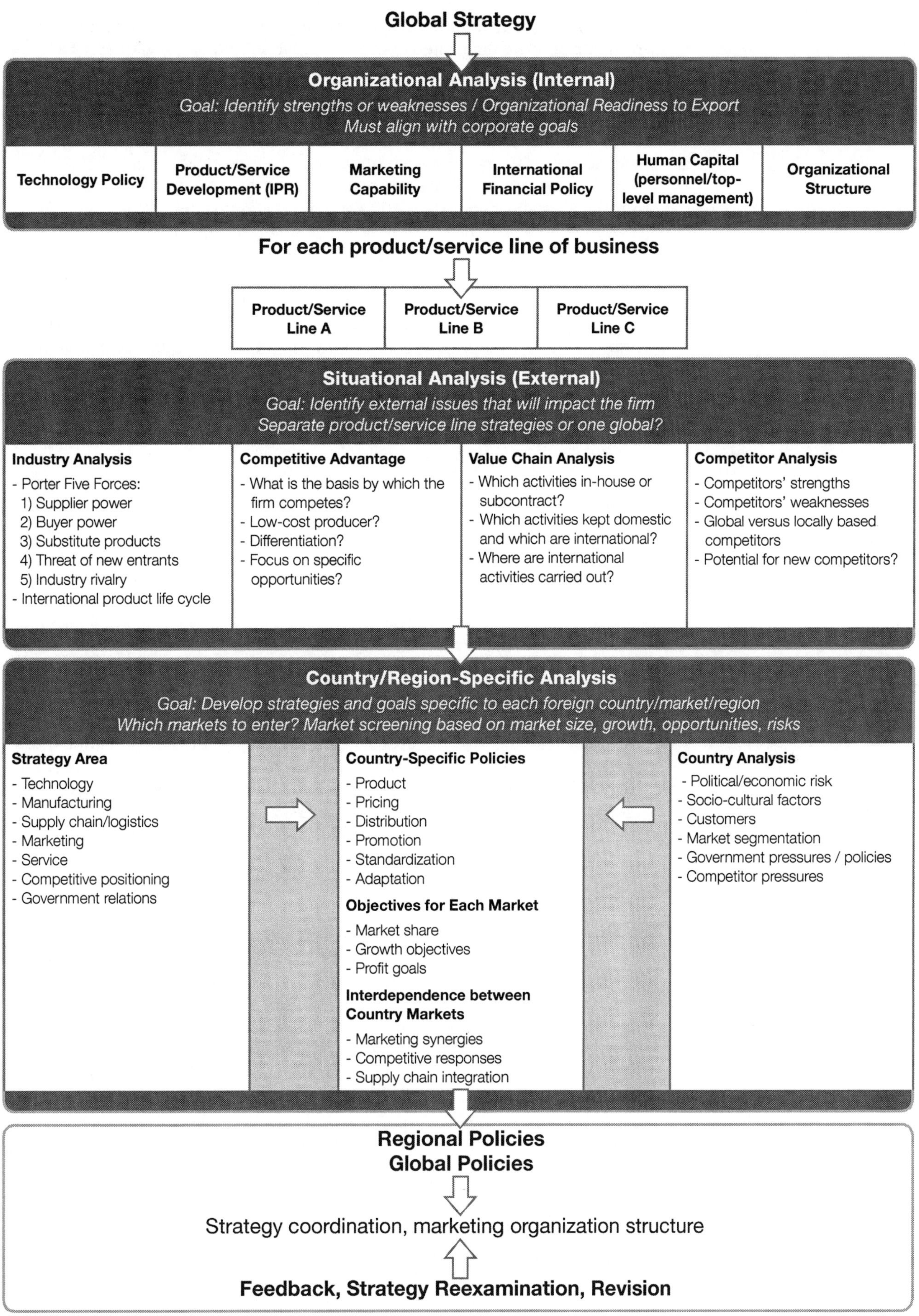

Global Strategy

Organizational Analysis (Internal)
Goal: Identify strengths or weaknesses / Organizational Readiness to Export
Must align with corporate goals

Technology Policy	Product/Service Development (IPR)	Marketing Capability	International Financial Policy	Human Capital (personnel/top-level management)	Organizational Structure

For each product/service line of business

Product/Service Line A	Product/Service Line B	Product/Service Line C

Situational Analysis (External)

Goal: Identify external issues that will impact the firm
Separate product/service line strategies or one global?

Industry Analysis
- Porter Five Forces:
  1) Supplier power
  2) Buyer power
  3) Substitute products
  4) Threat of new entrants
  5) Industry rivalry
- International product life cycle

Competitive Advantage
- What is the basis by which the firm competes?
- Low-cost producer?
- Differentiation?
- Focus on specific opportunities?

Value Chain Analysis
- Which activities in-house or subcontract?
- Which activities kept domestic and which are international?
- Where are international activities carried out?

Competitor Analysis
- Competitors' strengths
- Competitors' weaknesses
- Global versus locally based competitors
- Potential for new competitors?

Country/Region-Specific Analysis

Goal: Develop strategies and goals specific to each foreign country/market/region
Which markets to enter? Market screening based on market size, growth, opportunities, risks

Strategy Area
- Technology
- Manufacturing
- Supply chain/logistics
- Marketing
- Service
- Competitive positioning
- Government relations

Country-Specific Policies
- Product
- Pricing
- Distribution
- Promotion
- Standardization
- Adaptation

Objectives for Each Market
- Market share
- Growth objectives
- Profit goals

Interdependence between Country Markets
- Marketing synergies
- Competitive responses
- Supply chain integration

Country Analysis
- Political/economic risk
- Socio-cultural factors
- Customers
- Market segmentation
- Government pressures / policies
- Competitor pressures

Regional Policies
Global Policies

Strategy coordination, marketing organization structure

Feedback, Strategy Reexamination, Revision

(patents, copyrights, trademarks), brand equity, excellent marketing and public relations, and existing international distribution and sales channels. Examples of weaknesses may include inadequate international experience, poor financing or access to capital, and a weak competitive position. If the firm has limited international experience, this analysis should also look at management's commitment to internationalize. A firm is not likely to have significant international success if management does not fully back the expansion.

This initial internal assessment is often referred to as determining the "organizational readiness to export." Various models to systematically measure readiness to export have been developed. For small- to mid-sized companies, these assessments can be a useful way to identify issues that may both help and hinder the firm as it expands internationally. Company Organizational Readiness to Export, or CORE™, was first developed at Bradley University (Peoria, Illinois) in the mid 1980s. This computer-based assessment offered a benchmark for a firm to rate its own readiness to export. The program would identify strengths (such as IP rights, past international sales, management commitment) versus weaknesses (lack of experience, poor management commitment, and so on). Its development continued at Michigan State University and is now part of the GlobalEdge website export tools.[1] The U.S. Commercial Service offers readiness assessment at www.export.gov.

The organizational analysis should also include matching the global strategy with corporate goals. This would include asking questions about fundamental corporate principles that likely need to be taken into consideration. Examples would be the dominant corporate orientation. Is it short term or long term? Another would be profit and return on investment (ROI) goals. Can profits be lower in the short term in return for a higher market share? These are important questions to ensure corporate goals are retained (or perhaps modified) as a firm sets its global strategy.

Situational Analysis

In the development of a global marketing strategy, the situational analysis is used to identify external issues that will impact the firm. These issues are primarily related to the global environment and industry influences such as trends, competitive pressures, and consumer behavior. As shown in the model, the situational analysis may be done separately for each product line should the firm have lines sufficiently distinct to warrant separate situational analysis.

INDUSTRY ANALYSIS

A starting point for the situational analysis is the industry analysis. Any number of frameworks could be used, such as Porter's Five Forces: (1) supplier power, (2) buyer power, (3) substitute products, (4) threat of new entrants, and (5) rivalry (competition) within the industry.[2] The goal is to identify what industry-specific issues and forces will have an impact on the firm as it grows internationally. Basic industry analysis is necessary to establish the product line's stage of growth, future prospects, and barriers to entry. This process would identify key competitors and their current international position. It would also look at the consumers in the industry and their needs, behaviors, and preferences. This would be an important point to identify consumer or industry trends that will also impact the global strategy, such as technology changes.

Another industry analysis tool is the international product life cycle, which may be at different stages in different national markets. For some markets, the product may be new with relatively low sales. For others, the same products may be maturing and sales growing—perhaps quickly. Yet in others, the product may have become standardized, and sales levels may even be declining. In each case, the stage of the product's life cycle will impact strategic decisions in that market. These differences will also impact the ideal location to manufacture the product, with the main implication that as a product becomes more standardized, the more likely it would be manufactured in low-labor-cost markets.[3]

COMPETITIVE ADVANTAGE

Having conducted the industry analysis, the firm must look at its competitive advantage within that industry. **Competitive advantage** is the basis of a firm's ability to compete. As presented by Porter's theory of competitive advantage, a firm generally has three strategic options: (1) becoming the lowest-cost producer and competing on the basis of low prices, (2) providing a differentiated product and competing on the basis of providing unique value to the customer, or (3) focusing on specific opportunities based on market segmentation or competitive issues.[4] See "Understanding the Basis for Competitive Advantage" for more explanation of these three options.

> **competitive advantage**
>
> In the context of firm-level strategy, this reflects the firm's basis or ability to compete, generally by becoming the lowest cost producer, providing a differentiated product or service, and/or focusing on a niche opportunity.

••• Understanding the Basis for Competitive Advantage

As defined by Michael Porter in his strategy book *Competitive Advantage*, companies have three fundamental strategies to compete.

Competing as a Low-Cost Producer

If a firm has an overall lower cost structure and can produce its product or service at a lower cost than competitors, it can lower its prices and still make an adequate profit (assuming comparable quality). On the other hand, it can charge the same prices as its competitors and make higher profits because its costs are lower.

Low-cost production is typically linked to high-volume production, a technology advantage, or low-cost overhead. Economies of scale reduce costs; learning and experience curve factors also lead to cost reduction. Learning curve economies result from workers becoming more productive as they work at a job longer and learn from experience. Similarly, experience curve economies result from learning to better manage a line of business. As accumulated production grows, a company can manage its machines better and reduce overhead; it typically finds that average cost per unit declines with each doubling of accumulated volume of production. Low cost and high market share are closely linked because the large market share allows for large-volume production.

Competing with Differentiated Products/Services

Some firms rely on attracting customers with products that their competitors do not offer. Such differentiated products may have superior design or better performance, better quality and reliability, or more durability; they may be backed by better service, or they may simply appeal more to the consumer for aesthetic and psychological reasons. Similarly, a service company may have superior quality, professionalism, benefits, or technology that attracts customers.

Firms competing on that basis must monitor world markets to ensure that the benefits and features that differentiate their products or services have not been copied by competitors. They must constantly work on new benefits because what is a differentiated offering today will soon become a commodity. A global competitor must constantly stay ahead of the pack; otherwise, the basis of its competitive advantage disappears. Once a product or service has become a commodity, the lowest-cost competitor will win.

Focusing on Specific Opportunities

The third strategy exploits specific opportunities based on market segmentation or competitive issues. Examples would be targeting a specific demographic of consumers, such as marketing primarily to one age segment of the population. Another would be

Airlines is an example of a firm using its low-cost structure as its basis to compete. By keeping costs as low as possible and not offering services that are expensive, such as first class, it can compete primarily by offering low fares

focusing on areas in which competitors ignore, such as a computer company that competes only in the very high-end, power-user consumer segmentation. Having a focus strategy allows a firm to not necessarily have the lowest cost or the most differentiated products because it offers consumers other benefits related to their needs.

Table 14-1 • **Perspectives on Global Marketing Strategy**

Perspective	Basic Logic	Key Variables	Antecedents	Effects
Standardization perspective	Scale economies Low-cost Simplification	Product standardization Promotion standardization Standardized channel structure	Convergence of cultures Similarity of demand Low trade barriers Technology advances Orientation of firm	Efficiency Consistency Transfer of ideas
Configuration-coordination perspective	Comparative advantage Interdependency Specialization	Concentration of value-chain activities Coordination of value-chain activities	Low trade barriers Technological advances Orientation of firm International experience	Efficiency Synergies
Integration perspective	Cross-subsidization Competitive delocation Rationalization	Integration of competitive moves Global market participation	Low trade barriers Orientation of firm International experience Integrated markets	Effectiveness in competition Competitive leverage

Source: S. Tamer Cougill and Shaoming Zou, "Marketing Strategy Performance Relationshihp: An Investigation of the Empirical Link in Export Market Ventures," *Journal of Marketing*, Volume 58, January 1994, Table 1.

This analysis helps the firm understand why the firm should be able to make a profit in its chosen line of activity in the face of competition and why customers should buy its product or service. Competitive advantage can come from many sources: a firm's proprietary technology, its superior manufacturing, its skills in marketing, or its overall management talent and organizational capabilities.

COMPETITIVE ADVANTAGE AND THE VALUE CHAIN

value chain

The sum of activities a firm performs to create value (profitability).

Related to the issue of competitive advantage is a firm's **value chain**: the sum of activities a firm performs to create value (profitability). The value chain is made up of all the activities (departments) of a firm, including research and development, purchasing, manufacturing, marketing and sales, and logistics, as well as its relationship with external partners (suppliers, resource companies, customers, and so on). The analysis of the value chain helps identify which activities the firm would keep internally and those it would subcontract. An example would be a drug company that has as its main competitive advantage pharmaceutical patents. As the firm primarily creates value by focusing on developing new drugs, it may choose to have a third party do all manufacturing. A firm with a competitive advantage in one or more activities that constitute the value-added chain is able to make a long-term profit by specializing in those activities.

When expanding internationally, companies should perform the same analysis but within a global context. This leads to the basic questions: (1) which activities? and (2) where?

Table 14-1 illustrates the application of the value-added chain to a hypothetical global firm.

- **Which activities?** The firm decides what activities it will specialize in and what activities it will subcontract, thus adopting a make-or-buy decision on each of the activities that constitute the value-added chain. For example, a firm in the running shoe business might decide to develop a new type of running shoe in-house in its laboratories, using its own equipment and scientists. Then it might provide product specifications and ask another company to manufacture the product. After receiving delivery of the shoes, the firm might carry out its own marketing campaign in major markets around the world. Thus, it controls the technology and marketing activities while subcontracting the manufacturing value-added activity.

- **Where?** The firm must also decide where it will carry out the value-added activities it has chosen. In this regard, principles of comparative advantage come into play in deciding what activities are most appropriately carried out in what countries. A country typically has a comparative advantage in activities that use large amounts of its abundant factor of production. For example, a country with large quantities of unskilled labor might be an appropriate site for manufacturing products that use unskilled labor, such as garments or shoes.

Returning to the example of the running shoe company, suppose that the company decided to let another independent company manufacture the shoes based on its technology and design. With the addition of the country factory, the company could decide not to subcontract the manufacturing of shoes, instead deciding to manufacture the shoes itself in another low-wage country by making an investment and managing a running shoe factory. The company could add manufacturing to its value-added chain by carrying out the activity in a different country. Moreover, if the company decides to continue to subcontract the manufacturing, it must decide which country's manufacturers to use as a source of supply. In choosing between competing subcontractors in different countries, the company will consider low delivery costs, quality, timely delivery, and low risk of supplies being interrupted. Companies within the same industry can take different approaches to the value-added chain. See "HP versus Dell: A Study of Two Value Chains."

SEPARATE PRODUCT STRATEGIES OR ONE GLOBAL STRATEGY?

As part of its situational analysis, a firm needs to address whether it should be developing separate product strategies or one global strategy for all products (or services). The decision to develop separate strategies by product line would

---

HP versus Dell: A Study of Two Value Chains

The laptop industry offers a good example of how two firms in the same industry configure different value chains.[5] Hewlett-Packard (HP) designs its laptops and subcontracts the manufacturing to Taiwan-based Quanta Computer Inc. HP often identifies the location from which specific components should be sourced, orders the components, and has them shipped to Quanta's assembly locations. Thus, HP buys microprocessors from the United States (Intel, AMD, and others); graphics processors from the United States and Canada; hard-disk drives from Japan, Singapore, and (increasingly) China; memory chips from South Korea, Taiwan, the United States, and Germany; LCDs for the computer screen from South Korea, Japan, Taiwan, and China; and power supplies and magnesium casings from China. In turn, Quanta has moved all its laptop assembly operations to China to take advantage of low-cost but increasingly skilled labor. Quanta ships the assembled computers to a U.S. hub such as Memphis. There the individual laptops are packed to be sent directly to the customers.

In contrast, Dell Computer prefers to perform the final assembly itself, after buying partly built laptops from contract manufacturers. Dell's laptop manufacturing approach is dictated by its business model, which relies on building laptops and computers to each customer's individual specifications, developed at Dell's website. Dell's ability to meet each customer's configuration may rest partly on having significant control of the final assembly step. Thus, in the same industry, two prominent manufacturers have split up the value chain differently, based on their chosen strategy.

be based primarily on how different the product lines are. The more varied the marketing needs of each product line, the greater the justification for separate product strategies. Examples would include product lines with a different customer base, different sales cycles, or different channels—essentially different market mixes. The more homogeneous the product or service line offerings of a firm, the stronger the justification for a single, global strategy.

Country/Region-Specific Analysis

After the organizational and situational analysis, a firm must begin to consider individual markets. Global marketing involves the consideration of all of a firm's foreign markets and understanding commonalities and synergies between them. However, a decision must be made as to whether the strategy will be the same in all markets or whether aspects of strategy, including global marketing strategy, will be adapted to fit individual countries. In part, this decision depends on the goals set for a product line within a particular country market. In some markets, a firm may seek market share, planning to obtain profits after market share has been established. In other cases, the goal may be to challenge strong global competitors as a means of preserving competitive balance across countries. In still other markets, a firm may simply want to establish a small market presence and wait until the market becomes more attractive. In more mature markets, a firm may actively seek profits and set up return-on-investment targets.

Next, the firm must analyze whether it should change its marketing policies in a specific market because of government restrictions, competitive pressures, or differences in customer needs that may arise from economic and cultural differences. This choice between standardizing policies across markets or adapting them and becoming locally responsive is fundamental to international marketing. Not all aspects of global strategy need to be adapted for each market. Local responsiveness can vary across the marketing mix. Promotion and distribution may be tailored to individual national markets, while the same basic product and price strategies may be used for all markets. The country/regional analysis would also include setting specific goals for each country or market, including market share, growth objectives, and profit goals.

The interaction between product-line goals and environmental analysis affects strategies in a variety of areas, including technology, manufacturing, marketing, customer service, competitive policy, and management of government relations. As shown in the model, linkages exist between marketing strategy and strategies in other areas. The firm's consideration of these linkages leads to a more integrated strategy and, thus, more successful international marketing.

In addition, the interdependence and potential synergies of many national markets must be considered. This leads to questions such as when do changes in one market dictate changes to marketing strategy in other markets? When can similar marketing mix decisions between a collection of national markets lead

The automotive industry's European launch of GPS navigation is an example of the use of a regional strategy over a global strategy.

to increased efficiencies and enhanced competitive advantage? Not all marketing mix decisions must be similar across multiple markets. Perhaps only one or two common strategies are used. For example, a firm may develop standardized global policies for a product line in some aspects of strategy, such as making antilock brakes standard on all cars that it sells, but when it comes to introducing newer technologies, a firm may adopt a regional policy of first introducing the technology into a select group of countries. For example, automobile firms tended to first include GPS-based navigational systems on luxury cars—a strategy used in all EU countries. In other areas of the marketing mix, such as advertising and promotion, the same firm would adopt national policies tailored to each market's profile.

Strategy Implementation

Strategies must be implemented if they are to be effective. How well they are implemented depends on organizational structure and personnel assigned to a given country. After implementation has begun, feedback on results is essential to monitor the plan and to decide when and how it should be changed. In Figure 14-1, this is shown as the final section on the bottom. To improve the global strategy, continuous assessment must be done involving all departments of a firm associated with the strategy.

Ongoing strategy implementation requires evaluation of the firm's value chain. The firm must constantly assess the shifting nature of comparative advantages across countries and its own competitive advantage when compared to that of its competitors. The global environment will change over time as economies grow and acquire technology, capital, and skilled labor. Companies must respond by changing their value-added configuration. If wage costs are important to a firm's competitive advantage and wages rise in its present manufacturing location, the company must consider whether to shift manufacturing to another lower-cost location. A firm can stay globally competitive only when it constantly reexamines and then changes its global strategy as needed.[6]

Strategic Perspectives

As a firm develops its global marketing strategy, it may find the overall structure of the strategy fits one of three overarching perspectives: market-extension, multidomestic, or global. These perspectives may be useful models as a firm develops its international marketing strategy.

- The **market-extension perspective**, which is typically the way in which a small firm becomes involved in international marketing, represents an unplanned and short-term exploitation of foreign markets while the domestic market remains the focus of the company. Products developed for the home market are sold in one or more overseas markets to obtain incremental revenue, with little planning of the role of foreign markets in the firm's overall strategy.

- A **multidomestic perspective** represents a careful consideration of foreign markets, but with a clearly separate orientation toward each country market. That is, the firm approaches each market on its own terms, and little effort is made to capitalize on interdependencies between various markets. Such an approach may be consistent with the nature of consumers and line of business.

- A **global perspective** is one in which the firm directs special attention to the interdependence among national markets and competitors' actions in those markets when formulating its own strategic plans. Such an approach can lead to economies of scale in technology development, manufacturing, and marketing and in making the appropriate competitive responses.

---

market-extension perspective

A firm's international expansion philosophy highlighted by unplanned and short-term exploitation of foreign markets while the domestic market remains the focus of the company.

multidomestic perspective

A firm's international expansion philosophy highlighted by careful consideration of foreign markets and with a clearly separate orientation toward each country market.

global perspective

A firm's international expansion philosophy highlighted by formulating its strategic plans in order to direct special attention to the interdependence among national markets and competitors' actions in those markets.

Despite the theoretical and conceptual emphasis on globalization, few of the world's largest multinationals have been successful in marketing globally. One research project analyzed the geographic distribution of sales of 320 large multi-nationals. It showed that over 80 percent of sales, on average, came from the home regions (the United States, Japan, or the EU) of these companies.[7] Additional research has shown that firms have better profitability on sales inside their home region than outside their home region.[8] This implies that in practice the world's multinationals end up practicing a regional strategy, even though their intent is global. That result suggests that even the world's largest firms have a long way to go before they achieve true globalization in their marketing activities and that limits exist to the extent of globalization for most firms.

These perspectives also have important implications on both configuration and implementation of a firm's strategy. Configuration refers to the decision about where a firm's value-added activities are carried out. When the activities have been spread out (configured) in different countries, the firm must coordinate the activities to manage them effectively. Configuration decisions can result in a company having a presence in more than one national market.

••• Whirlpool: Configuring and Coordinating the Global Value Chain

For most of its existence, Whirlpool was a U.S.-based manufacturer headquartered in rural Benton Harbor, Michigan. It focused mainly on selling to the U.S. market. Despite acquisitions within the United States to enter the premium (KitchenAid) and the value-oriented (Roper) market segments, Whirlpool saw little market share growth and slim margins in the United States. However, the formation of the EU gave Whirlpool the impetus to consider expanding into the European market, with Asia as its second priority. Entering Europe and Asia presented opportunities for growth but also new challenges configuring and coordinating Whirlpool's value chain across the globe.

Whirlpool believed that being an "insider" in Europe was essential, with established distribution and local market knowledge, and, in 1989, Whirlpool initiated a joint venture with the Dutch Philips company. In 1991, Whirlpool acquired the firm from Philips, instantly transforming itself into a company that was rapidly globalizing. A plus was that Philips had a strong international presence with worldwide operations and sales, including China.

Whirlpool was then faced with the challenge of integrating European operations into a global framework. Then–Whirlpool CEO, David Whitwam, described the need to unify two "parochial margin-driven" companies into "customer-focused organizations."[9] Whirlpool's competitive advantage was in understanding how customers viewed their products and developing products that customers value, but the company needed a way to apply these competencies globally as well as take best practices wherever they arose and integrate them across its worldwide organization.

Drawing from worldwide quality best practices, Whirlpool created the "Whirlpool Excellence System," which helped the company meet pressures for both standardization and localization. Whirlpool developed common technology and manufacturing processes to meet standardization pressures but also allowed regional manufacturing and marketing organizations to adapt product features and dimensions to local needs. A key element of this approach was the formation of cross-border product development teams. Three examples shed light on Whirlpool's approach—and its successes.

One example is how Whirlpool created a usability lab in Italy to learn what customers wanted in a microwave, leading to the introduction of its best-selling VIP Crisp model.[10] Another example is how Whirlpool's pan-European design teams worked with U.S. designers on products sharing common platforms. That allowed distinct products such as the high-end Bauknecht and the utilitarian Ignis to share common interior components, saving costs. Another example of this approach is the CFC-free refrigerator, which was developed with insulation technology from Europe, compressor technology from Brazil, and manufacturing and design expertise from the United States. The fundamental change was in organizational culture, convincing employees that they needed to learn to think globally.

This global but local approach helps Whirlpool coordinate its value chain across borders while also increasing Whirlpool's profit potential. Whirlpool is now the world's leading appliance manufacturer with 67 manufacturing and technology research centers worldwide and sells to consumers in nearly every country worldwide.[11]

Competitors and Global Strategy

Throughout the strategic planning process, firms need to address the current and future threat from competitors. This requirement is even greater for global firms, as contrasted with wholly domestic firms, because they will encounter other global competitors and local competitors in each foreign market. Ignoring the competitive threat may lead to a loss of a firm's competitive advantage and potentially risk the viability of the firm. (See "Apple and the PC Industry" as an example.) Thus, firms need to continually understand their competitive position and the potential for new competitors.

••• Apple and the PC Industry

Apple had long distinguished itself in the personal computer world by making and selling computers based on a proprietary operating system standard. However, the company was unwilling to license its operating system to other manufacturers seeking to manufacture Apple-compatible clones. Because it had no clone competitors to innovate hardware and software advances, it had to spend more on research and development to keep up with developments in the industry. Apple must spread its R&D costs over the unit volume of computers sold; because Apple held less than 9 percent of the total personal computer market as of 2010, its unit R&D cost was high.[12]

Apple's early technological lead of a graphical user interface, the suitability of desktop publishing, the use of images, and digital video production and editing allowed the company to charge premium prices. However, as the Microsoft Windows standard began catching up and offering roughly comparable performance at lower prices, Apple found it hard to convince customers to pay a higher price for the privilege of using the Mac standard.

Apple's Strategic Problems

For Apple to recover market share in global markets, it had to address solutions to several issues:

- Apple's R&D costs as a percentage of sales were high in relation to the Windows-compatible PCs.
- Apple incurred high marketing costs to push and sustain the Apple brand.
- Differentiation was being reduced as Microsoft's Windows products became as easy to use as the Apple operating system.
- Computers, in general, were becoming a commodity; as a result, margins were falling.
- Apple had been forced to cut prices in the United States and elsewhere to compete, cutting margins despite higher costs. As a result, its gross margins were under pressure.
- When customers were lost to the Windows-compatible PCs, they did not come back because of lower prices

and the investments in software and learning. They also became accustomed to the multiplicity of vendors from whom they can buy products and software.

- Apple was weak in the business market, a higher-end market segment with greater likelihood of repeat purchases and product upgrading.[13]
- On occasion, Apple experienced shortages of units in the retail channel at crucial selling seasons because it had underestimated demand.[14]

As Apple declined through the 1990s and into the new millennium, the company went through several CEOs before calling back founder Steve Jobs (for the third time) as its new CEO. Jobs spun off several Apple products, including Newton, a handheld palmtop organizer, and concentrated on a newly designed Mac that would parallel the performance of the PC-compatible world. His bold new design, with transparent housing, green-gray color, and overall radically innovative look, coupled with a competitive price, won back many Apple fans.

Fresh off the success with the new Mac, Apple introduced its iPod and the iTunes service, both of which have been enormous successes. Next, Apple introduced the iPhone and iPad, which, like all Apple products, are elegant and easy to use.

These new consumer products allowed Apple to once again charge high prices and command attractive margins, thus regaining profitability while diversifying away from its exclusive focus on PC-type computers. The heart of its marketing has been differentiation to the point of uniqueness, protected by proprietary standards and patents, and products that meet consumer needs. That combination is difficult to achieve, but the company is capable of obtaining huge success (and profits) when done right. In a dramatic turnaround, Apple is now the computer industry's largest firm (by market capitalization) and is the world's largest PC maker (with a market share of 25 percent), if you count the popular iPad.

Assessing Global Competition

Global strategy must include a careful study of sources of competition and the likely responses of individual competitors in global markets. That analysis usually begins with an assessment of a competitor's strengths and weaknesses, its goals, and the way it should respond to the firm's actions. Much depends on the balance of competitive power—that is, whether the competitor is a leader in a particular product/market area. The same firm may hold a dominant market position in one national market and play catch-up in another; within the same country/market, a firm may be a leader in one product line and hold a minor market share in another product line. Thus, how a firm reacts depends on its market position—whether it is a market leader; whether it seeks to challenge the market leader; or whether it is a follower, holding a small market position and using niche strategies to hold on to its market share.

national champions
Firms that have dominant positions in their national markets and often receive government support.

A special place in global competition is held by **national champions**—firms that have dominant positions in their national markets and often receive government support. In the European auto industry, Fiat in Italy and Peugeot and Renault in France enjoy such a position, with their dominant market share in their home markets partly attributable to regulations that restrict Japanese auto imports. With continuing European integration, the position of nationally dominant firms becomes less secure as it becomes harder for national governments to justify favored treatment of national companies in a unifying Europe. National champions are also lightning rods for claims of unfair government subsidies, such as the battle taken to the WTO by the United States that European countries were subsidizing Airbus, the most significant global competitor to Boeing.

Where Do Global Competitors Originate?

New firms are constantly adding to the pool of potential competitors. They do so through market extension, extension of product lines into new market segments,

Throughout the strategic planning process, a firm must identify current and potential competitors and their impact on the firm's ability to compete. This is especially true in highly competitive industries such as shoes, which has both strong global and local competitors in most markets.

and forward or backward integration by suppliers. Competitors often emerge from their domestic markets to begin challenging established firms in major foreign markets. Firms from countries such as South Korea have begun competing in a variety of consumer industries, where companies such as Kia, Samsung, and the LG Group have gained market share in automobiles, color televisions, cell phones, flat-panel displays, and semiconductors. South Korean firms, previously manufacturing partners for companies in the West, are now competitors. They used market extension as the basis for the entry, extending their reach to global markets after solidifying their position at home.

Firms may also diversify into new product markets to emerge as potent competitors. Examples abound in the biotech area, which is rich in small R&D-oriented start-up companies. It takes years to complete the research and to shepherd new drug applications through the governmental approval process. Once approved, and if highly effective, the drug may be marketed as a high-priced pharmaceutical. Large companies such as Pfizer have their own R&D labs. However, they are aware that their pace of innovation has slowed while it has become more costly and time-consuming to develop new blockbuster drugs. At the same time, the likelihood exists that a start-up biotech research outfit will develop innovative new drugs. Hence, it is becoming common for major pharmaceutical companies to take stakes in new biotech firms, often acquiring them if their research and development results in successful new drugs with sizable markets.

Existing competitors may also extend their product lines to enter new market segments. Japanese auto firms in the United States have followed that policy. Honda was the first; its high-priced Acura was marketed for the luxury car segment in the United States. Honda's action was promptly followed by Nissan and Toyota, with their Infiniti and Lexus lines, respectively. Such product extension moves by the Japanese auto industry affect the market share of both U.S. and European automobile manufacturers.

Finally, competition can also develop from forward or backward integration by suppliers. That is happening in semiconductors. Manufacturers of memory chips and microprocessors are incorporating their semiconductor components into board-level and systems products, thus selling complete systems as opposed to components. Such firms are using forward integration (getting closer to the final consumer product) to increase their competitiveness at the expense of what were previously customers of those same firms. Backward integration (manufacturing a product in-house that was previously purchased) also creates new competitors as the firm may sell its newly produced product to buyers that were otherwise customers of the previous supplier. (For details on how to research competitor activities, refer to Chapter 6.)

Global Marketing Strategies

Clearly, global marketing strategy cannot be separated from overall corporate strategy. Decisions about technology, new product development, and manufacturing inevitably affect marketing decisions and marketing success. Thus, a corporate strategy focused on time-based competition and speedy innovation requires a marketing division to plan for continued introduction of new products and to relay timely feedback on customer information to the product development department to help speed the innovation process. If a firm decides to focus on being the lowest-cost producer, low selling price becomes an essential element of the global marketing mix.

Standardization or Adaptation: Impact of Differences among National Markets

Keeping in mind the linkages between a firm's overall global strategy and global marketing strategy, the firm must decide between standardization and adaptation of marketing strategies to local markets. Management complexity is reduced when a completely standardized marketing mix is applied without change to all national markets. Usually, some local adaptations are necessary to accommodate differences in consumer tastes, income levels, government regulations, differences in distribution channels, and structure of competition. Research indicates that whether a firm will standardize or adapt largely depends on the specific circumstances of a particular foreign market at a specific point in time.[15]

When trying to decide what degree of adaptation is appropriate, the firm must consider the factors that distinguish between different national markets:

- Buyer profiles differ across countries; taste, income, culture, and buying decision processes are different.
- The marketing infrastructure differs from country to country, different kinds of media are available in different countries, and differences exist in what products and messages are acceptable in advertising.
- Variations in countries' transportation and communications systems affect marketing approaches, such as the use of mail order. Different legal provisions may govern conditions of sale.
- Distribution systems differ in the number of layers and in ease of access; differences in the physical environment of various national markets may dictate changes in product design and sale.

Some Adaptation Is Necessary

The real question is not whether to adapt, but how much to adapt. Some elements of the marketing mix are more likely to be standardized than others. The basic product probably needs to be standardized in order to permit economies of scale in its manufacture. Firms are also likely to standardize brand names and the basic advertising message. Adaptation is more likely in areas such as packaging, pricing, sales promotion and media decisions, distribution channels, and after-sales service. Although management is motivated to standardize to reduce costs and management complexity, satisfying consumers in different markets and responding to competition should be the main criteria. Government restrictions can also limit the degree of standardization possible.

Coordinating the Global Marketing System

Coordination of global marketing activities is as essential as configuring marketing activities across national markets. Table 14-2 summarizes various coordination issues, highlighting the adaptation-standardization dichotomy for various elements that enter into formulating a global marketing strategy.

Such coordination can take place in the following ways:[16]

- **Using similar methods to carry out marketing activities across countries.** Examples include Avon's door-to door sales of cosmetics in different markets and companies' use of similar standards for warranty and after-sales service across countries.

- **Transferring marketing know-how and experience from one country to another.** This is particularly true in transferring information gained in lead markets to other countries.

- **Sequencing marketing programs**. This ensures that successful elements are gradually introduced into different markets, often in conjunction with evolution of the product life cycle in the various markets.

- **Integrating efforts across countries.** This ensures that international clients with operations in many countries can be offered the same service in each country. For example, a client may want to use the same computer equipment or software at all its international subsidiaries. Closing that sale could require coordinating the sales effort in key markets where the largest subsidiaries are located. A clincher might be offering worldwide service with a maximum response time of 48 hours.

Beyond considering its global marketing strategy, a firm must also determine whether its strategy is effective or requires modifications as the business environment changes. These steps are discussed in Chapter 15, "Planning, Organization, and Control of International Marketing." Such ongoing analysis is needed to ensure the firm moves toward and achieves the goals outlined in the international marketing strategy.

Table 14-2 • Global Marketing Strategy Choices

	Total Standardization				Complete Adaptation
New ProductDevelopment/Product Line	X				
Marketing Mix					
Product Positioning				X	
Market Segmentation		X			
Brand Policy	X				
Packaging				X	
Advertising and Promotion		X			
Distribution Channels					X
Pricing			X		
Customer Service		X			
Country Markets					
Market 1	X				
Market 2		X			
*					
*					
*					
Market *n*					X

X = a hypothetical firm's choice

Source: Adapted from John Queilds and E. Holl, "Customizing Global Marketing," *Harvard Business Review*, May–June 1986.

Global marketing strategy must form part of and be consistent with a firm's overall global strategy. Establishing a firm's international marketing strategy is therefore linked directly with the formation of the firm's overall global strategy.

Developing the global strategy begins with a foundational analysis of three areas: an organizational analysis (internal analysis); situational analysis (external analysis); and country- or region-specific analysis (to develop strategies and goals specific to each country and/or region).

The organizational analysis is used to identify the strengths and weaknesses of the firm as related to its international expansion goals. It forms a part of the firm's readiness to export. The analysis must be aligned with the overall goals of the firm. The review should be across the whole of the firm, including but not limited to technology policy; product or service development; marketing capabilities; international financial policy; personnel issue; and organizational structure.

The situational analysis is an external analysis of the global business environment in which the firm will operate. The goal is to identify issues that will impact the firm. These issues include an analysis of the industry, the firm's competitive advantage, the value chain of the firm, and the competition.

The country and/or region specific analysis is used to develop strategies and goals specific to each foreign market. They include decisions such as which markets to enter, how to enter the markets, and specific policies established for each market. These policies include the product or service mix and standardization or adaptation requirements. These decisions would be made within the context of the firm's overall strategy policies (technology, manufacturing, value chain, and so on), as well as an analysis of each country (risk assessment, demand assessment, competition).

As part of the foundational analysis, the firm must look at its competitive advantage, which is the basis of a firm's ability to compete. A firm generally has three strategic options: (1) becoming the lowest-cost producer and competing on the basis of low prices, (2) providing a differentiated product and competing on the basis of providing unique value to the customer, or (3) focusing on specific opportunities based on market segmentation or competitive issues.

A firm's value chain is the sum of activities a firm performs to create value (profitability). The analysis of the value chain helps identify which activities the firm would keep internally and those it would subcontract. In a global context, the global value chain can be used to determine which activities are kept in the home market and which are conducted in foreign markets.

As part of the situational analysis, the firm needs to address whether it should be developing separate product strategies or one global strategy for all products (or services). The decision to develop separate strategies by product line would be based primarily on how different the product lines are.

Some of the variables firms must consider in adopting a global perspective include differences in global markets, customers, and competition; different host-government policies; technology; production resources; and the time factor.

A successful strategy implementation depends on organizational structure and personnel. Feedback on results is essential to monitor the plan and to decide when and how it should be changed. A firm must constantly assess the shifting nature of comparative advantages across countries and its own competitive advantage when compared to that of its competitors.

As a firm develops its global marketing strategy, it may find the overall structure of the strategy fits one of three overarching perspectives: market-extension, multidomestic, or global.

Global competitors emerge by (1) diversifying out of national markets that they dominate, (2) diversifying into new products, or (3) extending their product lines into new product segments; and (4) forward or backward integration by suppliers.

A decision must be made between standardization and adaptation of marketing strategies to local markets. Management complexity is reduced when a completely standardized marketing mix is applied without change to all national markets. Usually, some local adaptations are necessary to accommodate differences in consumer tastes, income levels, government regulations, differences in distribution channels, and structure of competition.

Coordinating the global marketing system is a complex task. Some common methods include using similar marketing approaches across countries, transferring marketing know-how and experience, sequencing marketing programs across countries, and integrating approaches to multinational clients.

KEY TERMS

competitive advantage
global perspective

market-extension
perspective

multidomestic perspective
national champions

value chain

NASBITE CGBP TOPICS COVERED IN THIS CHAPTER

Note: For full details of the alignment of each chapter with the NASBITE CGBP, be sure to review the information provided in the section "Studying for the NASBITE CGBP Exam."

CGBP Rubric	Topic
01/03/01:	environmental factors affecting international strategies (e.g., political, legal/regulatory, sociocultural, cost and competitive factors, appropriate levels of technology)
01/03/03:	elements of a global business plan
02/01/01:	internal resources (e.g., export readiness assessment, goals and preferences of senior management, experiences and capabilities of employees, technical and production capabilities)
02/01/02:	external environment (e.g., economic and physical geography, competitive analysis, regulatory, cultural, technological issues, currency fluctuations, and protected industries and sectors)
02/01/08:	SWOT analysis related to global marketing
02/06/09:	trade assistance resources in support of providing products and services

QUESTIONS AND RESEARCH

1. How is marketing strategy linked to global strategy?
2. What are some factors that affect global strategy at the level of a firm?
3. How can management attitude affect global strategy?
4. What are some factors that influence global strategy at the product-line level?
5. What is the value-added chain? How is it relevant to a firm in formulating a global strategy?
6. What are some goals that a firm might set for itself in individual country markets?
7. What are the three fundamental strategies to compete?
8. Select a well-known company that operates globally. Describe its competitive advantage. Discuss examples of how it has leveraged that advantage in world markets.

9. Using Porter's five forces, describe the attractiveness of the fast-food industry in the United States. Contrast that with the fast-food industry in China. How would such an analysis assist in a U.S. firm developing its international marketing strategy?

10. What factors affect strategy implementation? How are these factors further complicated for a global firm?

11. Explain and contrast the three strategic perspectives: market-extension, multidomestic, and global.

12. What are national champions? Find an example in each of three foreign markets. How are their national market positions similar? How are they different?

13. Where do global competitors originate? What is the implication for a global firm?

14. Discuss instances in which a firm would select a standardized marketing strategy for a group of countries? Discuss instances in which an adapted approach would be required.

15. What are some issues associated with coordinating the global marketing system?

16. Select a large global company. What are some examples of how it coordinates its global marketing strategy?

 CHAPTER 14 TEAM PROJECT ASSIGNMENT: Coordination and Control of Global Marketing

At this point, you should begin assembling the final international marketing plan for your client. Using the research results from prior chapters, you should write the international marketing plan in the format assigned either by your instructors or as suggested in Chapter 1. If a presentation is also to be developed, the team would typically develop this after the majority of the written report has been finalized. This ensures the presentation directly reflects the international marketing plan.

This chapter discusses how a firm would develop its global marketing strategy, and some of these topics should be integrated into your report. Some of the topics, such as the internal and external analysis, were a part of your research in Chapter 1. But you may want to review that research within the context of its discussion in this chapter to see whether a more in-depth discussion of the foundational strategy analysis (organizational, situational, and country/region-specific) should be included. At the least, you should think about your client's competitive advantage and the value chain plus any implications for the global marketing plan. Also, think about how your firm will implement its global strategy as discussed in this chapter. Discuss whether you believe one of the three strategic perspectives should be followed by your client: market-extension, multidomestic, or global. Also, discuss any significant issues as related to your client's competitors. Finally, you should also address the issue of strategy adaptation or standardization, as highlighted toward the end of the chapter.

The preceding topics could either be integrated as part of each country analysis or individual country marketing plan, or they could be discussed as a stand-alone section titled "Global Marketing Strategy." Your instructor can provide further details. Regardless of how this material is included in your report, highlights of these issues would normally be included in any international marketing expansion plan. As part of the next chapter's team project, you will discuss planning and control issues and fully complete the project.

In the summer of 2003, Charlie Davila-Bond was at yet another crossroads. As the general manager of a major sweater exporter, Davila & Bond, Inc., based out of Quito, Ecuador, he was facing a number of international strategic issues. Since 1999, his importer in Chile had lost interest in Davila & Bond products, and there was a serious future risk of a continued sales decline in Chile. The Chilean dilemma stemmed from stiff international competition in the Chilean market. The economic crisis in Argentina had trickled over to Brazil, and the devaluation of the Brazilian real to the U.S. dollar (now Ecuador's currency) had made the continuation of sales to Brazil unprofitable. Due to extremely high fixed costs (such as loan payments on new equipment and employee salaries), Davila-Bond's factory in Ecuador needed to operate at a high level of capacity to maintain profitability. A drop in sales would have a major impact on Davila & Bond's performance. To diversify his international sales portfolio, Davila-Bond's decided to place more emphasis on Mexico, a large and potentially lucrative market. Sales to Mexico instantly jumped to over 25,000 sweaters (about 12 percent of total sales), which was promising.

Yet as Davila-Bond looked at the numbers, he noticed that his firm's reliance on the Ecuadorian market was still extremely heavy. Over 50 percent of the firm's sales were coming from Ecuador. The climate in the Ecuadorian mountains was ideal for lightweight sweaters.[1] However, the economic uncertainty of the country was, at times, mystifying. Ecuador was also corrupt and was experiencing political unrest.

Would increased sales to Mexico help alleviate some of the uncertainty that Davila & Bond was experiencing? And were there underlying issues related to Ecuador's adoption of the U.S. dollar that could dampen the potential in the Mexican market? Davila-Bond knew that the time had come to redefine his international strategy. For years, he and his family had dreamed of exporting to the U.S. Yet with limited plant capacity and intensely narrow margins, it seemed unrealistic. Perhaps Mexico could be a solid stepping stone toward the ultimate goal of entry into the U.S. market.

COMPANY HISTORY

In 1974, Fernando Davila, a native of Ecuador, and his Scottish wife, Rosalind Bond, opened a factory in a valley just east of Quito, the national capital. They made high-quality yarn. Fernando had studied textile management at the University of Leicester, where he met Rosalind. They named the yarn manufacturing company Hilacril, which still exists today. Their idea was to take various sizes of high-quality imported acrylic yarn and spin it into a professionally woven product that could be used by other firms for clothing, upholstery, and car seat covers. By 1980, in order to increase sales, Hilacril began exporting to Colombia. Although the margins were not very favorable, the company began to turn a reasonable profit.

After struggling with tight margins for a number of years, in 1990, Fernando and Rosalind decided to open a weaving department. The objective of the weaving department was to utilize Hilacril yarn to create finished products, which would eventually be sold directly to consumers and retailers. The strategy proved effective, and in 1997 (now with their three sons home from university), Davila and his wife created the retail firm Davila & Bond to take further advantage of stronger margins by getting closer to the consumer.

*Case prepared by Professor Christopher Robertson (Northeastern University) for use in classroom discussion, with assistance from Mr. Charlie Davila-Bond. Copyright @2005, all rights reserved. Reprinted with permission.

While Fernando continued to head up the Hilacril arm of the family business, Rosalind assumed the position of president of the final product-oriented Davila & Bond. Charlie, the oldest son, served as production manager for Hilacril and general manager for Davila & Bond. He spent the majority of his time in the factory, designing new products and ensuring that the firm's quality standards were being met. As his parents began to step aside, preparing for retirement, Charlie essentially took over the leadership position of the firm. Eduardo, the second son, was the salesman of the family. He headed up all sales-related activities for both Hilacril and Davila & Bond. The youngest son, Fernando, a lawyer by training, was in charge of the Davila & Bond upholstery division. The final member of the management team was Jorge Perez, a veteran accountant and the CFO of the firm.

It was Charlie's energy, vision, and zeal that brought Davila & Bond into international markets. While spending eight years in Scotland between prep school and university, Charlie became anxious to return home and expand the family business. It took only four years for Charlie's vision of a more integrated firm to come to fruition. And since the inception of the sweater retailer Davila & Bond, Charlie was instrumental in signing franchise agreements and pushing the product into new international markets.

As a manager, Charlie had many strengths. He was upbeat and energetic and could be found joking with employees on the factory floor. Yet at the same time, he commanded respect due to his intricate knowledge of the retail sweater business. He used that knowledge and his open communication style to motivate workers. Charlie was also extremely creative, and the majority of the firm's sweater designs were based on Charlie's ideas. He made a point of attending industry conferences, many in Europe, where he could learn about new manufacturing, design, and marketing techniques. Despite the fact that Davila & Bond was located in a poor developing country with chronic economic problems, Charlie ran the company as if it were located in Milan, New York, or Paris. As a result of his accomplishments in Ecuador, Charlie was recognized in 2003 as an industry expert and appointed to a seat on the Ecuadorian Board of Textile Producers.

BACKGROUND OF THE ECUADORIAN MARKET[2]

Ecuador has been a presidential democracy since 1979, but its institutions have been fragile. Economic deterioration helped undermine the functioning of democracy. Lucio Gutiérrez, backed by left-wing and indigenous organizations, was inaugurated as president on January 15, 2003, taking over for Gustavo Noboa. At one point in 1999, the country held four different presidents in one 24-hour period. Despite reforms designed to prevent the proliferation of forces, the country had a fragmented and polarized political system with numerous parties. Ecuador's largest political parties in terms of congressional representation are the centre-right PSC, the PRE, and the centre-left Izquierda Democrática (ID). All have held power at some time since the transition to democracy in 1979.

ECONOMIC CONDITIONS/BUSINESS ENVIRONMENT

Ecuador had a long road in becoming a stable international investment target. To that end, Ecuadorian officials recently made important developments regarding economic openness. They also pursued a strategy that included improving competitiveness and efficiency and matching their goals to international requirements. The Ecuadorian government also tried to consolidate its policy of openness by improving microeconomic management strategies in the productive and financial sectors, opening the real estate sector and the financial system to foreign investment, fostering a transparent privatization process, improving the administration of the state sector, and eliminating state interventionism.

Ecuador is a member of the Andean Community, which consists of Bolivia, Colombia, Ecuador, Peru, and Venezuela. The Andean Community was in the process of formally establishing a free-trade zone. The Ecuadorian government signed complementary economic agreements with several Latin American countries: Argentina, Uruguay, Chile, Brazil, and Cuba.

U.S.-Andean Free Trade Agreement negotiations were under consideration, the goal being to sign a deal by the end of 2004. The accord would benefit the Andean nations by more permanently locking in the special access to the U.S. market that Andean nations enjoyed under the Andean Trade Preference Act, which was set to expire in 2006. The free-trade agreement also would encourage reforms for attracting investment to the region and would allow the Andean nations to remain competitive with other nations in the U.S. market.

Mexico and Ecuador started free-trade negotiations in 1996. The same year they drafted an agenda of issues related to market access, rules of origin, customs procedures, technical regulations, safeguards, and unfair trade practice. Ecuador withdrew from the talks, saying the terms of the agreement were not favorable. Both countries planned to restart talks to negotiate a free-trade agreement.

THE GROWTH OF DAVILA & BOND

By September 2003, Davila & Bond was exporting sweaters and other woven items to five other countries in Latin America: Colombia, Mexico, Brazil, Bolivia, and Chile. At the same time, the firm had also pursued an aggressive retailing strategy with a combination of company-owned and franchised stores. Fourteen Davila & Bond retail stores (eight firm-owned) were operating in Ecuador, Colombia, and Bolivia. Three additional stores were scheduled to open in Ecuador by the end of 2004. As a result of the strong brand image and reputation that Davila & Bond built through its high-quality sweaters, a number of franchising opportunities developed. In addition to the seven retail shops in Quito, Davila & Bond also owned a store in Ambato, a small city about 50 miles south of Quito. In Cuenca, a colonial city in southern Ecuador, two stores were owned under a franchise agreement. Franchised retail stores were also present in other markets: three in Colombia and one in Bolivia. Reflective of Davila & Bond's high-quality image, the stores were tastefully decorated with a European ambiance accentuated by British flags and classical music.

The basic terms of a franchise agreement were as follows: $40,000 was required up front for 120 days worth of merchandise; a $15,000 fee was charged to use the Davila & Bond name for four years; and approximately $20,000 to $30,000 was needed to set up the retail stores according to company standards (typically, Davila & Bond would front the store setup money with the promise that the store would repay within four years). In addition, Davila & Bond charged franchisees 3 percent of purchases for monthly publicity.

Refer to the graph and table that follow on page 454 for Davila and Bond's 2000–2002 profit and loss information.

A decision was made in 2000 to gradually reduce emphasis on yarn production as a raw material and to place more emphasis on finished product sales, primarily sweaters and shawls. From 2000 to 2002, yarn sales dropped from 42 percent of total sales to 4 percent. Sweaters and shawls experienced significant increases over the same period, with sweaters jumping from 40 percent to 57 percent and shawls up from 7 percent to 33 percent. The theory was that through vertical integration and the sale of finished products, profits would increase over time. Yet it was production costs that increased due to the labor-intensive nature of sweater manufacturing, and profits remained relatively flat.

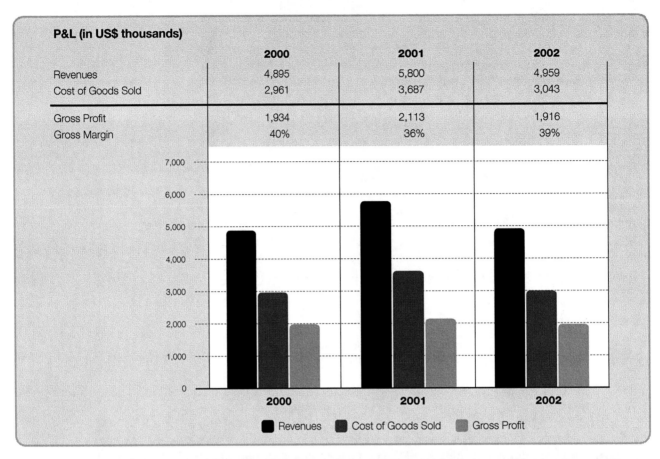

P&L (in US$ thousands)

	2000	2001	2002
Revenues	4,895	5,800	4,959
Cost of Goods Sold	2,961	3,687	3,043
Gross Profit	1,934	2,113	1,916
Gross Margin	40%	36%	39%

Legend: ■ Revenues ■ Cost of Goods Sold ■ Gross Profit

Products	Year 2000					Year 2001					Year 2002				
	Units Sold (000)	Net Sales (US $000)	Cost of Goods Sold (US $000)	Gross Profit (US $000)	Gross Margin	Units Sold (000)	Net Sales (US $000)	Cost of Goods Sold (US $000)	Gross Profit (US $000)	Gross Margin	Units Sold (000)	Net Sales (US $000)	Cost of Goods Sold (US $000)	Gross Profit (US $000)	Gross Margin
Sweaters	199	1,952	1,011	941	48%	253	2,405	1,417	988	41%	285	2,816	1,647	1,169	42%
Chales	42	319	155	164	51%	230	1,797	1,075	722	40%	215	1,622	1,026	596	37%
Fabrics	201	536	325	211	39%	237	406	283	123	30%	96	310	211	99	32%
Yarns	454	2,088	1,470	618	30%	268	1,192	912	280	23%	51	211	160	51	24%
Total		4,895	2,961	1,934	40%		5,800	3,687	2,113	36%		4,959	3,043	1,915	39%

Davila & Bond's marketing budget was close to $100,000, or 2 percent of total sales, during the last few years. Since 2004, the company has added new products to its Ecuadorian stores. That new approach involved other products that were not manufactured at their own factory—Cumberland jackets, chinos, and women's shirts. Charlie noted that the company was trying to leverage its name recognition in the home market. He also considered more of a push in the teenage market, primarily through magazine and television advertising.

International sales hovered between 40 percent and 50 percent between 2000 and 2002. The one major change was a sixfold increase in sales to Mexico and a 10 percent decline in Colombian sales. Still, Colombia was the top export destination, accounting for 24 percent of sales in 2002, followed by Mexico with 12 percent, Brazil with 3 percent, and Chile and Bolivia with 2 percent each. Political unrest and a weak economy in Bolivia meant an end to that market in the short run, poor economic conditions throughout Latin America made market entry risky and complicated.

The increase in sales in Mexico highlighted the potential of that market and how important it was to future growth. In 2003, Davila & Bond had only one store, with the company engaged in developing distribution channels. In 2004, Charlie said the following:

> We are developing our distributors. One of them sells with our brand name (Davila & Bond) and also with their private label to big wholesale chains like Liverpool, Palacio de Hierro, Costco and Wal-Mart.[3] Our second distributor tackles the lower market all over Mexico, which has given us a great boost on sales. We have not decided on franchises yet. We sell over 90,000 items a year to the Mexican market. For the year 2005 we expect a sales increase of 20 percent for this market.

The relevance of the Mexican market would imply a new approach in regards to the production strategy. In that respect, Charlie mentioned, "We have had some talks on the possibility in producing in Mexico, but nothing is definite yet. Mexico's labor costs are pretty similar to the Ecuadorian's, but labor laws are very difficult to handle."

Although Davila & Bond was clearly the market leader in Ecuador, Charlie perceived a number of small threats within the country. First, importation of sweaters from China, South Korea, and Taiwan was on the rise. Producers in those countries had a major competitive advantage in labor costs, yet the quality of their sweaters was typically below that of Davila & Bond's. One local competitor, Fashionlana, had made a minor surge by copying the business model and manufacturing technique of Davila & Bond. Fashionlana had the same supersoft technology that Davila & Bond utilized and had recently opened three retail stores in Quito.

PRODUCTION

Technology was a key ingredient to Davila & Bond's success. Through keen long-term vision, the firm decided to purchase sophisticated weaving machines from Germany. Each machine cost over $100,000. However, in the mind of Charlie, the investment was well worth it since the machines ran 24 hours a day, 364 days a year (every day but Christmas). Davila & Bond had plans for expanding its knitting department in 2004 by acquiring six new machines from the German firm Stoll. Charlie commented, "The whole knitting project will increase our production 20 percent with a total investment of U.S. $600.000." That investment was to be financed directly by the German supplier over a period of three years. Also, for the year 2005, the company planned to buy a new weaving machine at a cost of $250,000. The machine would increase yarn production another 20 percent.

The raw synthetic yarn was also imported (typically from Peru or Germany), which enabled the firm to produce a high-quality range of products. Using supersoft technology and materials, the Davila & Bond's sweaters that looked and felt like cashmere, yet could be washed in a washing machine due to their synthetic nature. Moreover, Charlie and his staff of sweater designers traveled to seminars and fashion shows in the U.S. and Europe to generate ideas for new designs. The company also purchased a new state-of-the-art computer software design program to enhance the creation and production of new styles. Quality was a huge priority for Davila & Bond. Each final product went through a seven-point quality check prior to shipment to ensure that the company's excellent reputation and positive image were maintained.

In the factory, the firm employed 130 workers in the Davila & Bond knitting department, another 50 in weaving, and 70 in the Hilacril yarn division. In addition, about 40 employees worked in the company-owned retail stores around the country. The typical factory worker worked 50 hours a week and earned $250 a month ($300 to $350 if production goals were met). That compared well to the local minimum wage of just under $150 a month, and turnover was virtually nonexistent.

THE MEXICAN MARKET[4]

Charlie was convinced that with just over 100 million consumers and a rising per capita income, Mexico would be an excellent market for the company's sweaters. The plan to open a Davila & Bond store was in place, and the potential to engage in franchising looked promising. Charlie was extremely pleased with the distributor he had selected and agreed to take on a second distributor for "lower-end sales."

Mexico was the largest trading nation in Latin America and the eighth largest in the world. GDP growth had been strong since 1996. In addition, FDI had surged, partly due to Mexico's friendly investment climate, competitive labor costs, fully convertible currency, low taxation, and duty-free access to the U.S. and Canada. Investment had been particularly strong from major multinational manufacturers who set up operation in Mexico to supply the U.S. market free of duty. More investment was expected with the recent entry into the EU/Mexico Free Trade Agreement. Mexico was now uniquely positioned to supply the two largest markets in the world tariff-free, the EU and North America.

Investors had few restrictions, and investment approaches ranged from a branch office to a fully owned subsidiary. Most investors set up a corporation (S.A). That required a minimum share of capital, at least two shareholders, and registration in the public register. All foreign investments had to receive prior authorization from the Ministry of Foreign Affairs.

Labor costs in Mexico were very competitive. Skilled and semiskilled labor was plentiful. However, some pressure came from the border regions with the U.S., with their many job vacancies and high turnover of staff. There were no controls on the remittance of profits or the repatriation of capital. In some strategic areas of the economy, such as the oil industry, satellite communications, postal services, and minting, foreign investment is prohibited.

There were no restrictions on a foreign investor's access to capital. Most financing from local sources was obtained from privatized commercial banks. Interest rates were very high by international standards. Most investments, however, both domestic and foreign, were sourced from private capital.

Mexico had a number of important ports on both its Atlantic and Pacific coasts, including Altamira, Ensenada, Mazatlan, Progreso, Salina Cruz, and Veracruz. There were plenty of warehouse facilities at most ports. Joint-venture contracts were easily set up in Mexico. Those contracts did not create a business entity, and operations were carried out by the active party. However, income and losses were divided between the two partners according to the contract.

With respect to patents and trademarks, Mexico was a signatory to the 1983 Union of Paris Convention for the Protection of Industrial Property. Patents are protected for a term of 20 years from filing. Nonuse (unless justified by technical or economic reason) may result in the issue of a compulsory license. Trademarks are registered for ten years, renewable for further ten-year periods indefinitely. Mexico did have a significant problem with piracy in the music, alcoholic beverage, clothing, and software industries and some counterfeit/contraband difficulties with other consumer goods.

LOOKING TO THE FUTURE

Although Charlie Davila-Bond knew that the emphasis on international sales was an important factor in the growth of his firm, he also acknowledged that the Ecuadorian market was a mature cash cow. He clearly stated, "First, Davila &

Bond must maintain its number one position in the Ecuadorian market." Yet at the same time, he went on to say, "We must also expand our image overall and increase our international sales." Indeed, the trade-off between balancing the risk of relying too heavily on Ecuador with aggressively pursuing international sales while possibly losing ground at home was the key to the future.

As Charlie examined his existing markets, he thought more growth in Mexico was almost a certainty. With a market of 100 million people and an income per capita triple that of Ecuador, the potential of selling more sweaters in Mexico was promising. Charlie mentioned that he even had talks with a Mexican producer about the possibility of manufacturing there. But he was somewhat concerned about the complexity of Mexican labor laws. Elsewhere in Latin America, Brazil and Argentina seemed like viable possibilities. Being relatively large, wealthy nations with a European fashion sense and an amenable climate, those markets looked like reasonable places to bolster future sales. For the moment, Charlie wanted to determine the best possible strategy for further penetration into the Mexican market. Would finding a stronger distribution partner there be essential? What were the benefits and drawbacks of getting involved in manufacturing in Mexico, possibly through one of the Mexican maquilas? Compared to other potential markets in the world, Mexico's profile seemed to be an excellent fit, both culturally and economically, with Davila & Bond's international.

Finally, the production issue was something Charlie had to address. Typically, all of the sweaters for the year were sold by August. Expanding the plant was certainly an option, yet labor costs in Ecuador had been creeping up and were no longer a competitive advantage. Did it make sense to outsource some part of production to Mexico? If so, could Davila & Bond's quality reputation be maintained? Also, franchising had gone well in recent years, and the potential for establishing stores in Mexico, Europe, and elsewhere remained strong. As the end of 2003 approached, Charlie knew that the time had come to take Davila & Bond to another level. The decisions he made would set the firm's trajectory for years to come.

Notes: 1. In Quito, the people say that there are four seasons in every day: morning is like spring, noon is like summer, early evening is like fall, and midnight is like winter. 2. Part of this section has been drawn from The Economist Intelligence Unit Research. 3. WalMart is the most important retailer in Mexico. Sales in 2003 were $11.8 billion, and 671 units were distributed over 68 cities nationwide. It employs approximately 110,755 people, has 24,378,536 square feet in supermarket space, and has 60,342 restaurant seats. 4. Part of this section was based on research drawn from the UK Trade and Investment Office.

Questions and Research

1. Would increased sales to Mexico help alleviate some of the uncertainty that Davila-Bond was experiencing?

2. To develop an international expansion strategy, Davila-Bond would need to complete a situational analysis. What types of questions should be asked? What might be some of the answers to those questions?

3. What were the benefits and drawbacks of getting involved in manufacturing in Mexico, possibly through one of the Mexican maquilas?

4. Did it make sense for Davila-Bond to outsource some part of production to Mexico?

5. What is Davila-Bond's primary competitive advantage?

6. Which of the three strategic perspectives in this chapter would you recommend for Davila-Bond?

NOTES

1. http://globaledge.msu.edu/diagtools/
2. For a discussion of Porter's Five Forces, see his book *Competitive Advantage* (New York: The Free Press, 1985).
3. For more information, see R. Vernon and L. T. Wells, *The Economic Environment of International Business*, 4th ed. (Upper Saddle River, NJ: Pearson Education, Inc., 1986).
4. Michael Porter. *Competitive Advantage* (New York: The Free Press, 1985).
5. "The Laptop Trail," *Wall Street Journal*, June 9, 2005.
6. For more discussions on shifting value chains, see C. Samuel Craig and Susan P. Douglas. "Configural Advantage in Global Markets," *Journal of International Marketing* 6, no. 1 (2000): 6–25; M. Porter, "Competing in Global Industries: A Conceptual Framework." In M. Porter, ed. *Competition in Global Industries* (Boston: Harvard Business School Press, 1986), Chapter 1.
7. Alan M. Rugman and Alain Verbeke. "A Perspective on Regional and Global Strategies of Multinational Enterprises," *Journal of International Business Studies* 35, no. 1 (2004): 3–18.
8. Gongming Qian, Theodore A. Khoury, Mike W. Peng, and Zhengming Qian. "The Performance Implications of Intra- and Inter-Regional Geographic Diversification." *Strategic Management Journal* 31, no. 9 (2010): 1018–1030.
9. Regina Fazio Maruca, "The Right Way to Go Global: An Interview with Whirlpool CEO David Whitwam," *Harvard Business Review* (March/April 1994): 134–145.
10. Patrick Oster and John Rossant. "Call It Worldpool," *Business Week*, November 28, 1994.
11. "Whirlpool Corporation," *The Global and Mail (Canada)*, September 29, 2010.
12. "iPad Makes Apple Top U.S. 'PC' Maker," *Techweb*, October 18, 2010.
13. "Apple's Likely Loss May Spur Cutbacks, Merger," *Wall Street Journal*, December 18, 1995.
14. "Apple Is Facing Widespread Shortages of Its Products," *Wall Street Journal*, August 11, 1995.
15. Marios Theodosiou and Leonidas C. Leonidou. "Standardization Versus Adaptation of International Marketing Strategy: An Integrative Assessment of Empirical Research," *International Business Review* 12 (2003): 141–171.
16. Hirotaka Takeuchi and Michael Porter. "Three Roles of International Marketing in Global Strategy." In M. Porter, ed. *Competition in Global Industries* (Boston: Harvard Business School Press, 1986).

chapter

15 Planning, Organization, and Control of International Marketing

With global strategy covered in the preceding chapter, this chapter focuses on how the separate functional tasks of organization, planning, and control are blended together into an effective international marketing mix. A common theme throughout the chapter is balancing the needs of headquarters versus those of foreign markets and subsidiaries.

The main goals of this chapter are to ● ● ●

1. Identify the elements of the planning process.
2. Describe how firms develop and coordinate plans for national markets.
3. Describe the nature and role of long-range planning.
4. Identify the variables that affect organizational design for international marketing.
5. Describe the alternative designs available for international marketing organizations.

6. Identify issues relating to staffing international operations.
7. Discuss the role of a firm's headquarters in planning and control.
8. Discuss how companies control international marketing.
9. Explain the role of the information system in international control.

Planning for Global Marketing

Planning for global marketing consists of identifying systematic steps that will help a company formulate detailed actions to implement broad strategies. Thus, the stages of planning should mirror the steps used in formulating strategy, as set out in Figure 14-1 in Chapter 14. Planning can be for the short or long term. Typically, firms plan for three to five years, revising the long-term plan annually. The year immediately ahead then becomes the short-term plan, which involves more detailed strategies.

There is an advantage to having the annual plan be part of a longer planning horizon. It keeps planners from becoming shortsighted by forcing them to consider the impact of each year's operating plan. The short-range plan for international marketing can be composed of several elements, including, for example, a marketing plan for each foreign market, plans for individual product lines, and a plan for international product development.

There are several elements of the marketing plan:

- **Situation analysis.** Where are we now? The company must analyze its current environment in each market: What are the important characteristics of demand, competition, distribution, law, and government? What problems and opportunities are evident in the current situation? What are the firm's internal strengths and weaknesses—globally and in each foreign market?

- **Objectives.** Where do we want to be? Given an understanding of the firm's current situation in markets around the world, management can propose objectives that are appropriate for each country, market, and region. Although those objectives should be challenging, they also need to be reachable; they must be specific if they are to be operational.

- **Strategy and tactics.** How can we best reach our goals? After the firm has identified concrete objectives for foreign markets, it must prepare a plan of action to meet these goals. The approach includes assigning specific responsibilities to marketing personnel and to the marketing functions.

These three basic elements—situation analysis, objectives, and strategy and tactics—provide a framework for discussing the planning needs of the international marketing manager. The short-range planning task of the international marketer has two basic parts: (1) developing a plan for each foreign market and

The complexity of a firm's supply chain is one of a number of factors influencing the need for formal business planning.

Figure 15-1 • A Model of Global Strategic Planning Formality

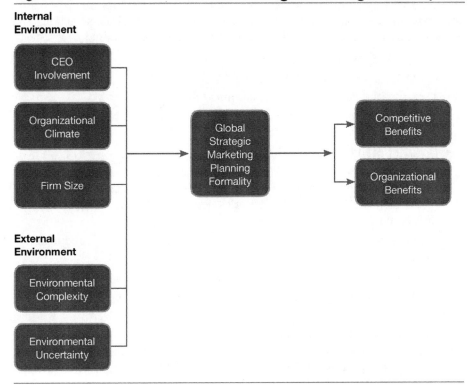

Source: Myung-su Chae and John S. Hill,"Determinants and Benefits of Global Strategic Marketing Planning Formality," *International Marketing Review*, Volume 17, Issue 6, 2000, pages 538–562.

(2) integrating the national plans into a coherent international plan, both regional and global. Planning needs will also be affected by the entry mode used in each market.

What factors influence whether a firm formally develops strategic marketing plans? As Figure 15-1 shows, a number of issues influence the need for formal planning, but some factors are more influential than others, including

- A corporate culture that believes in and is supportive of planning

- Supply chain complexity

- Complex and uncertain foreign environments

- Greater levels of governmental involvement with, and impact on, the business environment

- Greater levels of competition

All of those factors influenced the degree of planning formality. The external environment tends to impact the need for formal planning more than the internal environment. Research has shown that involvement by CEOs and firm size were factors not as important as the external environment. Furthermore, such formal planning generated competitive and organizational benefits.[1] There is also an increase in the need for formal planning when there is direct involvement in a foreign market—for example, having a subsidiary in the market as opposed to direct export only.

Developing Plans for Individual Markets

As outlined in Chapter 14, a firm must first evaluate the environment in which it plans to operate and its industry context, which can be unique for each foreign market. It must also clarify the governmental actions and role that may affect the foreign partners or subsidiaries and determine what competitors are up to—their strengths and weaknesses, the threats they pose, and their strategic actions and tactics. The firm can then set detailed market objectives, including

- Target sales, in units, in local currency, and in the parent company's home currency, possibly at a predetermined exchange rate
- Target market share by product and line of business
- Goals for distribution channel penetration, coverage, and extension to new distributors and channels
- Goals for brand image creation and awareness
- New product introduction plans, as appropriate, with detailed marketing plans for launch, covering issues such as pricing, positioning, channels, media plans and spending, target sales, logistics, and marketing service and support
- Export and international marketing plans, including countries and regions to be addressed
- Marketing research goals and specific programs
- Marketing personnel training, hiring, and motivation, including sales force plans

Each of the preceding planning goals can be broken down into more detailed targets, with operational plans spelling out details of implementation, budgets, and managerial responsibilities. At this stage, individuals within the marketing department can receive specific assignments, with details sorted out for working with third parties such as advertising agencies, market research firms, value-added distributors, product servicing companies, and so on.

Stages in the Planning Calendar

As a firm develops its planning process, it will typically utilize the following stages:

1. Internal assessment to identify the current strengths and weaknesses of the firm to expand globally

2. Market environment analysis (macroeconomic and industry) to identify opportunities and threats and ways they will affect company objectives

3. Communication of company-wide goals, subsequently broken down into global-, regional-, and country-specific goals and goals for product lines

4. Detailed country and product-manager plans showing how goals such as market share, competition containment, and ROI will be achieved

5. Aggregation of detailed country and product-line plans to determine whether the overall result is compatible with corporate headquarters' goals

6. Translation of plans into budgets, setting out quantitative and qualitative targets in terms of market share, unit volume growth, prices, target-market segments, distribution channels, advertising budgets, new product introductions, and personnel and training needs

7. Actions by product line and country managers based on plans and budgets, which also form the criteria used to judge performance

See "Planning at Avon" as an example of planning in stages.

A firm's planning process involves a number of stages including internal and external assessment, identification of goals, country and product-line plans, and budgets.

Planning at Avon

An example of international planning in stages is Avon's planning process for Latin America. Local executives gather information and develop preliminary country business strategies. Scrutiny of the operating environment is given precedence, focusing on the political, economic, and regulatory environment in each market, as well as making forecasts for the next five years. Next, competitors are identified and their products, market share, strengths, and weaknesses assessed. Avon seeks to learn the sources of its competitors' competitive advantages and compare them with Avon's own competitive advantages. Out of such analysis emerges a plan designed to capitalize on opportunities and competitive weaknesses. Contingency planning is emphasized, the question being, what actions are necessary to achieve planned results in the face of unforeseen events?

The Avon planning process is initiated by top management, which visits each of the firm's key country subsidiaries over a period of two months. While each country's subsidiary's general manager prepares the plan, a planning staff at headquarters, including a planning director, helps key markets with their plans. After all of the plans are completed, they are forwarded to headquarters for review and integration. Country proposals are reviewed and prioritized, and through comparison, headquarters can detect unexploited opportunities and suggest imitation or adaptation of plans currently scheduled for implementation in one country.

Division of Labor in International Planning

Avon's approach, discussed in the box above entitled "Planning at Avon," highlights the importance of organizational arrangements in international marketing planning. How the company is organized will affect the quality of the plan and the likelihood of its implementation. Who contributes what to national operating plans? What are the respective roles of corporate headquarters and the national subsidiaries? Usually, corporate headquarters can contribute planning know-how based on its domestic and international experience. That expertise would include planning guidelines, a planning schedule, and training of subsidiary personnel.

The national subsidiary should do most of the actual planning. Whereas the international parent has planning expertise, only the subsidiary has the intimate local knowledge needed. Most of the data for the plan, therefore, must be supplied locally. The resulting plan is more effective because of the complementary contributions of the two parties.

Nestlé provides an example of interactive planning, but with a bias toward decentralization. Some guidance comes from headquarters, but each national company prepares the annual marketing plan and budget. Once a year each affiliate meets at headquarters in Switzerland to review the plan with specialists. Compromises and adjustments are made at that time.

International Coordination of National Plans

The final role of the international planner is to coordinate the national plans into an international plan. This coordination is not done after the national plans have been completed; rather, it is done at the beginning of the planning process. Otherwise, national plans will make conflicting claims on company resources and require time-consuming revision. Therefore, coordination begins with guidelines sent to each national operation at the beginning of the planning period. National plans may be modified during the planning process, but good communications will ensure that those changes can be coordinated within the overall international plan.

For example, assume that a company begins its planning cycle in August. Each country prepares its plan, which goes to its regional headquarters and then to its international headquarters. Between September and November, continuing exchange of information might occur among the three levels. Final coordination takes place at area-wide meetings in December, where country managers, regional managers, and headquarters staff meet for one or two weeks.

Comparative Analysis for International Planning

As firms increase their multinational presence and the number of subsidiaries increases, regional and headquarters managers begin comparing subsidiaries against one another—by region, by product line, and by stage of evolution of their respective markets. Such comparisons can help determine whether targets set for individual subsidiaries represent challenging but achievable goals. Comparisons can be helpful when the subsidiaries being compared are similar in their markets and competitive environments and when they face roughly the same degree of governmental controls. Thus, it may make sense to compare plans for marketing razor blades in Brazil, Argentina, and Mexico, perhaps extending the marketing plan to Turkey or the Philippines.

Long-Range Planning

long-range planning
Organizational activity that deals with the future of the company over a period of 5 to 10 years and developing forecasts and strategies for the future.

Long-range planning deals with the future of the company over a period of five to ten years. Uncertainty is high, and the level of detail that can be forecast is low. The major concern is determining the shape of future markets and competition. How will the environment change, how will competition change, how will the customer base change, and what will future needs be? A firm seeks to learn enough about the future to prevent unpleasant surprises that can reduce its competitive advantage. See "Long-Range Scenario Building at Shell" for an example of how Shell uses scenarios to deal with long-term uncertainty and to plan for the future.

The overall goal of long-range planning is to address issues such as: What markets should we be in at that time? What products should we be making then? What business and operations methods will be valid then? Long-range plans can be prepared at group headquarters by a planning and development department. They would draw on data assembled by the group's product divisions and foreign subsidiaries. A long-range plan would cover several variables:

Long-range planning tries to answer five- to ten-year-out questions, such as: What markets should a firm be in? What products should they be making?

- Historical trends in the industry
- Forecasts of demand from end-user segments such as cars, trucks, and off-road vehicles
- Forecasts of the political and economic conditions of the countries where the group has current or planned operations
- The competitive situation in those countries
- Possible scenarios which could dramatically impact profitability such as economic, political, climate, or regional disruptions
- Technology trends and forecasts

••• Long-Range Scenario Building at Shell

Shell Oil (Royal Dutch Shell) has long been renowned for using scenarios in its long-range planning.[2] The oil industry requires long-term forecasts when examining investment decisions in new energy and exploration projects. An oil field can yield output for 20 years or more, and long-range scenarios covering that time period are common at Shell. Many oil field locations are in uncertain or potentially volatile areas of the world such as the Middle East, Nigeria, and Venezuela. As a result, Shell's scenarios often study consequences for the oil industry of volatility in these regions. For example, when war broke out in Iraq, Shell's scenarios did not specifically address the war, but they did include unknown events leading to volatility in oil prices and supply uncertainty. Therefore, Shell was able to implement contingency plans immediately—and did so when war broke out.

Shell typically develops global scenarios every two years, developing more detailed regional scenarios as needed. The scenarios address issues important to Shell's senior management. World experts work with in-house staff to develop "branching points" from which the business environment might be changed significantly. Plans are then developed to cope with shifts in the environment. The thinking is that if the business can be prepared to accept and live with major paradigmatic change, it can more easily accommodate lesser degrees of change.[3] For example, scenarios address the growth of the environmental movement and potential opportunities and challenges arising from recent volatility in oil prices. Other interesting scenarios might be China's emergence as the world's second largest oil consumer (af-

ter the United States), and increased real and potential conflict between the West and Muslim countries.

Shell's CEO Peter Voser recently discussed Shell's planning in light of increases in oil prices over the past few years and the impact of these price changes for investment in the medium term (2011–2014) and profitability in the long term (2015–2020). The company plans to invest in 35 new extraction projects worth the equivalent of eight billion barrels of oil. Despite high oil prices, Shell sees a near- and medium-term oversupply in oil refining and retail outlets (gas stations) and thus plans to cut these areas by 15 percent and 35 percent, respectively, over the next five years.[4]

Within scenarios, Shell uses econometrics and system dynamics models to study economic and energy situations in different countries. Users comment on the scenarios as they are developed. As a result, the scenario undergoes several iterations. The final result is a 100-page book for top management that summarizes the key scenarios, statistical data, and strategic implications for Shell's lines of business. For more information on Shell's current scenarios for the future, go to www.shell.com/home/content/aboutshell/our_strategy/shell_global_scenarios/.

Long-range plans should reflect a company's relationship with the plans of its key customer segments. Planners would rely heavily on contacts within customer companies for input to the plan.

Planning May Lead to Alliances or Acquisitions

Integral to the planning process is assessing and responding to new opportunities and evolving competitive threats. Both short- and long-term planning must continually ask the question: Are there strategic alliances, joint ventures, or acquisitions that would make the firm more competitive? Identifying such opportunities is particularly relevant during the planning process, though a firm is likely always to be addressing such issues. Planning involves an assessment of the global business environment, competitive landscape, and individual markets. Thus, an assessment of possible partnerships or acquisitions is particularly timely during the planning process.

WHY ALLIANCES OR ACQUISITIONS?

In a strategic alliance, firms join together in some area of their business to reduce risk, obtain economies of scale, and obtain complementary assets—often intangible ones such as market access, brand names, and access to government procurement. The allure of acquiring technology and the pressures of government are also reasons for such alliances. These alliances are typically formed in one of three broad areas: technology, manufacturing, or marketing. Acquisitions have similar goals but involve the purchase of a company or parts of a company.

Another reason for alliances is that consumers are becoming alike in developed nations. Consumers tend to receive the same information, especially as consumers become increasingly connected through shared social media and entertainment. As a result, tastes are becoming homogenized. As one analyst put it, "Everyone in a sense wants to live and shop in California."[5] No one company can expect to dominate all technologies and create entire product lines for the developing global market. A likely solution, therefore, is to swap products.

Another factor concerning alliances and acquisitions is that fixed costs account for a larger proportion of total costs. Global sales help a firm recover higher fixed costs even when lower prices are charged. (Volume compensates for a smaller contribution per unit.) The reasons firms should lower prices and sell globally are that product life cycles are becoming short, and fixed costs are more likely to be covered by resorting to global markets. It is difficult to exploit worldwide markets without global alliances, however. Short product life cycles mean that firms must move quickly to exploit their technological lead. Such a technology lead is actually a disappearing asset, diminishing in value with the passage of time. Strategic alliances allow a firm to penetrate several key markets simultaneously. Table 15-1 summarizes the motivations for seeking alliances and/or acquisitions as a firm grows globally.

Table 15-1 • Motivations to Form Alliances or Make Acquisitions

Motivations	Results
Complement weakness in the value chain	Obtain complementary competencies in R&D (basic research and/or applications development) and manufacturing (scale/scope economies, new processes, and cost reduction).
Take defensive position to protect market	Achieve stronger market share, stronger competitive advantages.
Be proactive by developing new businesses	Keep pace with new technologies and new customer segments.
Focus on product line or geographic area	Enhance market access to specific countries, brands, distribution channels, and service capabilities; enhance product line with partners possessing complementary products and services.
Think strategically of core and peripheral operations	Reduce dependency on alliance partner and possible hollowing out of the corporation.
React to government-imposed regulations	Offer legally necessary ownership stakes in return for political ties and local influence, as in several Asian private energy infrastructure projects.
Reduce or share risk	Reduce ownership with resulting reduction in share of profits and losses.
Overcome resource scarcity with partner contributions	Obtain resources (materials, components, capital, management, and information technology, such as computer reservation systems in airline and hotel businesses).
Learn from partner	Seek partners from related or unrelated industries, from supplier and customer segments, or from possible multiple partners and coalitions (for example, telecommunications firms bidding for licenses in the wireless industry).
Obtain fit with global strategy alternatives through licensing, foreign direct investment, and acquisitions	Act cautiously because alliances are not the universal panacea (over half of all joint ventures and alliances are dissolved within a few years).

Organizing for Global Marketing

Whatever planning is done will be in vain unless the company is organized to implement the plans. Organizational structure determines who does what, including which employees exercise gatekeeping power in supporting or undermining decisions made by others. Furthermore, organizational structure determines how marketing activities will be implemented. Implementation should flow from strategy; that is, activities are carried out to implement strategy. Thus, a critical element of designing a global marketing organization is to ensure that it is consistent with strategy and leads to activities that help implement strategy.[6] Organizational structure also sets up the rewards that motivate performance and determines the degree to which activities can be integrated. This is particularly important within a global strategy because implementation must be carried out by subsidiaries in different countries without many opportunities for face-to-face communication. Indeed, some of the greatest challenges for international marketers result from the friction between headquarters and foreign subsidiaries.

The basic issue for all organizational structure in global corporations revolves around centralization versus decentralization. Global corporations need strong coordination at headquarters to provide and supervise implementation of global strategy. If local subsidiary managers have different opinions, however, they may pull away from that strategy, or pressures by the local government may require greater local responsiveness, even if it means diverging from global strategy. Thus, the major task for organizational structure is to mediate between the opposing needs for centralization and local responsiveness.[7]

Research has suggested that in some industries where consumers around the world buy essentially the same product, as in consumer electronics, centralization and large-scale manufacturing are the keys to success. In industries in which national consumers have distinct product preferences and much product adaptation, as in branded packaged goods (such as detergents), a large degree of national subsidiary autonomy is needed. Then there are industries in which scale economies demand centralized, large-scale manufacturing, yet consumers have distinct product preferences, as in the telecommunications industry. Here, both centralization and local responsiveness are needed.[8]

A fundamental organizational decision to be made by global firms is the role of headquarters versus their subsidiaries.

Internationalizing the Company: Staffing Issues

Organizing the international marketing function is partly a matter of hierarchies, power, and control, but it is also about finding and putting the best people in key positions. The best planning or optimal organizational structure will not be effective for a global firm if the staffing of the firm is not handled properly.

STAFFING CHALLENGES FOR A GLOBAL FIRM

Staffing international positions raises tricky issues not found in the domestic arena. Foremost is the danger that the executive assigned overseas will get "lost," forgotten by colleagues and bosses. The ability of executives posted overseas to function effectively is heavily influenced by whether their families, spouses, and children adjust well to the extended

overseas assignment. Issues such as health care, education for children, and lifestyle all loom large in family satisfaction. In turn, this may make re-entry into domestic operations difficult. Often the returning expatriate finds no job available that may make use of the incremental international business skills gained during the overseas assignment. Overseas executives also supervise large staffs, enjoy high pay and fringe benefits, and have considerable autonomy. Returning to headquarters may mean lower pay and less prestige. Unless they have a mentor or champion at home who smoothes re-entry and finds them a position commensurate with their new skills, returning managers could believe that their careers are diminished and that the firm does not appreciate them. Former overseas executives may resign, which is a loss to the firm because the international skills are hard-earned and necessary for the corporation to compete successfully in the global arena. Hence, firms need to set up programs that ensure that the best younger managers are selected for overseas assignments and that a clear career path is established, including identifying jobs that will be open and available for returning managers.

Companies that have globalized tend to promote executives with substantial international experience. Senior executives will likely have spent several years overseas, immersing themselves in the culture while running operations. Companies increasingly value experience in emerging markets such as China, India, and Brazil. Language ability may also be valued. See "International Staff: Corporate Examples" for some illustrations of these issues. Companies value internationally experienced managers because they realize that international experience improves the performance of the managers themselves[9] as well as the performance of the company as a whole.[10]

••• International Staff: Corporate Examples

As the global economy continues to become more important, one prerequisite to attaining top management positions at large multinationals is substantial international experience. For example, members of Tupperware's executive committee speak two to four languages and have worked overseas. Samir Gibara, former CEO of Goodyear Tire & Rubber, spent 27 years in management positions outside the United States. The chief operating officer (COO) at the Gillette Company and the CEOs at Outboard Marine Corporation, Case Corporation, and ExxonMobil have all spent over half of their management careers outside the United States. Twenty-eight percent of all senior management searches now require international experience.

Companies have also begun to assign executives from headquarters units to overseas locations based on the executives' origin and their cultural knowledge of those markets. Payless Shoe Source is one such company. It had set its strategy around expansion into Latin America. Payless, with its many U.S. stores in inner-city locations, appealed to Latin American immigrants to the United States who could afford the prices and liked the range of styles. Those people often gave Payless shoes as presents when they returned home to visit relatives. This practice created strong brand awareness and brand loyalty in the local population in these foreign markets.

In 2000, Payless began to expand by opening five stores in Costa Rica, increasing to almost 200 stores scattered throughout Central America, Trinidad, the Dominican Republic, Chile, Peru, and Ecuador. The company informed its U.S. employees of Latin American origin that it was willing to let some of them manage overseas stores in Central and Latin America. Many homesick expatriates were willing to accept such a job offer. One of those employees was Roxana Orellana, who had come to the United States when she was a child, smuggled into the country as a refugee from El Salvador during its civil war. Many years later, she joined Payless, working her way up to manager of an outlet in Los Angeles. When the opportunity arose to go back home, she took it, despite a pay cut from $33,000 to $15,000. She was given charge of a new store in Sonsonate, a regional capital. Customers flocked to the store, which was air-conditioned, carried a full line of popular styles, attractively displayed a full range of sizes, and was decorated with mirrored panels with which to judge the potential new shoe purchases in a retail environment where such modern customer-friendly stores were uncommon. The stores became successful, partly because of the local managers who brought with them knowledge of both the U.S. corporate culture and the local culture.[11]

THE COUNTRY MANAGER

A key element in the growing multinational company is the country manager (CM).[12] What does the CM do? The CM is often given local profit center responsibility, is responsible for multiple functional areas, and is the liaison with regional and headquarters management. Expected to be as much an entrepreneur as a manager, the CM seeks to increase local autonomy.

The role of the country manager is changing over time. Factors impacting the role of a CM include, for example, demands for greater global integration of R&D and manufacturing. Other factors include the subordination of national interests, the rise of product-based global organizations and global customers, and regional integration policies such as the EU and NAFTA. How do those forces impact on the CM? They tend to reduce the CM's local authority to implement global and regional policies in the national sphere. The CM's main focus becomes local sales and distribution, along with local planning, forecasting and budgeting, financial management and control, personnel and labor relations (including training local managers), and government relations. Public relations is another responsibility of the CM, particularly representing the parent company in meetings with local trade and industry officials and in community relations. However, the CM's autonomy may depend on the importance of the local subsidiary. This importance is typically determined by the subsidiary's size, age, and experience; total sales revenues and market position; overall performance; and the ability and effectiveness of local management. The cultural distance of the local subsidiary from its parent is also relevant.

A fundamental issue is how much autonomy should the country manager have? Some products, functions, and marketing activities can be safely left to subsidiary managers. Indeed, companies should seek to create some areas in which autonomy is fostered. The extent to which a foreign subsidiary is allowed to practice greater or lesser independence in designing local marketing strategies is affected by the following:[13]

- The subsidiary's history of relationship with headquarters; for example, how much the subsidiary trusts headquarters, whether the subsidiary believes it is dependent on headquarters, whether the subsidiary believes it is part of the parent organization, how the subsidiary participates in setting local market objectives, and how much cooperation exists between the marketing manager and headquarters' marketing organization.

- Industry conditions; namely, whether the subsidiary is in a local market characterized by market turbulence and market concentration and whether the global industry is characterized by technological turbulence. A subsidiary may have more autonomy when the local market is turbulent. Also, a subsidiary is more likely to follow headquarters' direction when the local market is concentrated and when there is considerable technological turbulence.

- Economic and cultural distance. A subsidiary will have more autonomy when there is greater economic and cultural distance between the local market and the parent country.

Approaches to Organizing International Operations

A company can organize its international operations as a separate international division, with further subunits within the international division consisting of regional and local entities. It may also prefer to create organizational units structured along products and lines of business. A third approach is to create functional units, with distinct global responsibilities for research, marketing, manufacturing, logistics, and other functions. Finally, a company may decide that proper planning and execution of tasks require cooperation between managers, thereby fostering such cooperation by resorting to a matrix organization. In the latter, responsibilities for achieving goals are jointly allocated to managers with country, functional, and product-line responsibilities.

THE INTERNATIONAL DIVISION

Creating a separate organizational unit to focus on international business and operations allows international expertise, personnel, and vision to be concentrated in one part of the company. It creates a unit whose sole focus is on international business; a unit that stands up for international operations and seeks human and capital resources for that activity. Such an approach is more common in companies with relatively limited international operations, where domestic concerns predominate, and where product-line complexity is limited. Figure 15-2 illustrates the **international division structure**.

international division structure
Organizational form with a separate unit to focus on international business that concentrates international expertise, personnel, and vision in one part of the company.

However, a separate international division faces several problems. It may receive a lesser share of resources than its markets warrant, it may be perceived as an outsider that is less relevant to the future of the company, and it may have less political clout in the fight for attention and budget allocations from top management. Resolving international business issues without regard to their integration into the overall company's strategy may result in suboptimization. Thus as a firm's global sales grow, it may evolve to a different organizational structure.

Figure 15-2 • The International Division Organizational Structure

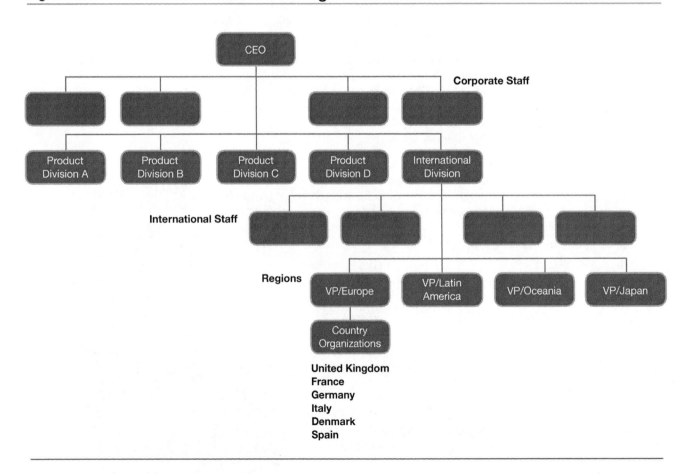

STRUCTURING BY AREA

Rather than have a separate international division, a company may develop an organizational structure with distinct responsibilities for each major geographical area. What is "international" is not relegated to second-division status. Instead, world markets are broken up into a series of geographical divisions, one of which happens to include the company's home, or domestic, market. When the company is structured by area, the primary basis for organization is by divisions for major regions of the world. For example, when CPC International reorganized from an international division to a world company approach, it set up five operating companies: one for Europe, one for Latin America, one for the Far East, and two for North America (consumer products and industrial products). Each may then be divided on the basis of product. A **regional organization** is used primarily by marketing-oriented companies that have relatively stable technology, such as those in consumer nondurables, pharmaceuticals, automotive, and farm equipment.

The growth of regional economic groupings, such as the European Union, favor a regional approach to company organization.

Several factors favor a regional approach to organization. The growth of regional groupings is one. As nations within a region integrate economically, it makes more sense to treat them as a unit. The proximity of countries provides one logical basis for organization. Certain kinds of expertise can be grouped within the region to enhance operations in the individual countries. Communication is easy, and coordination of product and functional know-how can take place in the region. A narrow product line and similarity in technology and methods of operation also favor regional organization.

In spite of its popularity, the regional organization has drawbacks. It ensures the best use of a firm's regional expertise, but it means less than optimal allocation of product and functional expertise. If each region needs its own staff of product and functional specialists, duplication—and inefficiency—may result if the best staff is not available for each region. Inefficiency is most likely when regional management is located away from corporate headquarters. When regional management is housed at corporate headquarters, a centralized staff can serve all regional units, providing some economies of scale. A regional organization may optimize performance within the region, but there is danger of global suboptimization when no coordination takes place among the regions. Each region must blend into a global operation. Figure 15-3 illustrates a regional organizational structure.

> **regional organizational structure**
>
> Organizational form with separate units to focus on major geographical areas.

Figure 15-3 • The Worldwide Product Organizational Structure

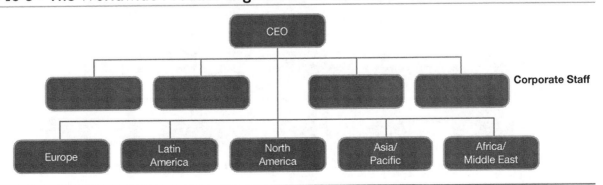

STRUCTURING BY PRODUCT

Organizing by product line means that product groups have global responsibilities for marketing; thus, it is a global company approach by product division. An international division can be organized along product lines, too, but by its very nature, this type of organizational structure also includes area expertise. Structuring by product line is most common for companies with several unrelated product lines because their marketing tasks vary more by product line than by region. As Figure 15-4 shows, the **worldwide product organizational structure** gives each product group essentially its own international division.

Structuring an organization along product lines has the merit of flexibility; a firm can add a new product division if it enters another business unrelated to its current lines. However, the product division approach has several potential limitations. When the domestic market is more important to a product division, international opportunities are likely to be missed. Limited area knowledge is a common weakness of product-structured organizations. Each product division cannot afford to maintain a complete international staff.

Another problem in a product-structured approach is the difficulty of achieving company-wide coordination in international markets. If each product division goes its own way, the firm's international development will encounter conflicts and inefficiencies. The organization must provide global coordination to offset the sometimes contradictory international plans of individual product divisions. For example, it is probably unnecessary for each producing division to have its own advertising agency, service organization, and government relations staff in every market. When foreign plants manufacture products of different divisions, coordination among the divisions also is often a problem for a product organization.

Eaton provides an illustration of how companies with global product organization try to overcome some of its weaknesses. Eaton is highly diversified in the capital goods and automotive industries. It has five worldwide product groups, and each group has a managing director for European operations. To get a better overall corporate understanding and response to European problems in areas such as legislation, labor, and taxes, Eaton formed a European Coordinating Committee (ECC) composed of the five product division managing directors, several European staff members, and one executive from world headquarters. The responsibilities of the ECC's chair rotate among the managing directors, and meetings are held at different European facilities. Eaton established country

> **worldwide product organizational structure**
>
> Organizational form with separate units to focus on major products or services offered by the organization.

Figure 15-4 • The Worldwide Product Organizational Structure

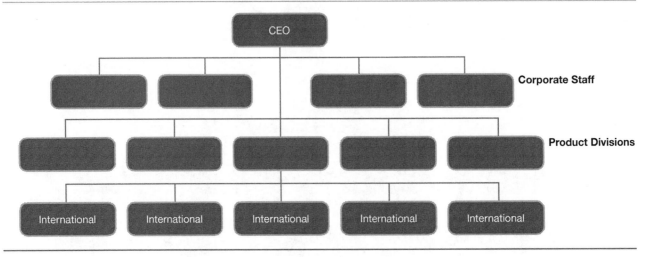

coordinating committees to manage the product groups within each European country. It also formed a Latin American coordinating committee to achieve the same integration in Latin America.

THE MATRIX ORGANIZATION

One of the more interesting organizational developments in recent decades is the **matrix form of organization** (see Figure 15-5). Companies became frustrated with the shortcomings of uni-dimensional organizational structures (product, area) that were noted previously. Therefore, they moved to a more complex organizational form that allowed two dimensions to have more or less equal weight in the organizational structure and decision making. A matrix organization has a dual rather than a single chain of command, meaning that many managers have two bosses. Matrix also involves lateral (dual) decision making and a chain of command that fosters conflict management and a balance of power. Product and market (geography) are the two dimensions receiving equal emphasis in matrix organizations in international business. For example, AGCO Corporation implemented a matrix restructuring that created operational control of sales, marketing, and engineering by geographic brand, with functional supervisory responsibility on a global basis.[14] A matrix can solve some problems of the simple product or area structure, but matrix organizations have many problems of their own arising from inherent conflicts and complexity.

> **matrix organizational form (matrix form of organization)**
>
> Complex organizational form with a dual chain of command where units report to superiors about both product and geographic issues.

Evolving to a Transnational Organization

Generally, multinationals evolve from a structure consisting mainly of domestic operations with some overseas business to the multinational stage in which international business becomes more important. This evolution typically results in independent, locally responsive subsidiaries that display greater sensitivity to local customers, governments, and culture that are headed by local country managers with an entrepreneurial bent. At some point, competitive forces and environmental pressures from globalization of the industry lead headquarters to want greater global integration of relatively autonomous local subsidiaries. One solution is to implement the matrix approach discussed in the preceding section. The problem, however, is that a global matrix organization is both complex and bureaucratic with its two-boss structure. The possible consequence is conflict and confusion with overlapping responsibilities. Negotiation is necessary,

Figure 15-5 • Matrix Organization

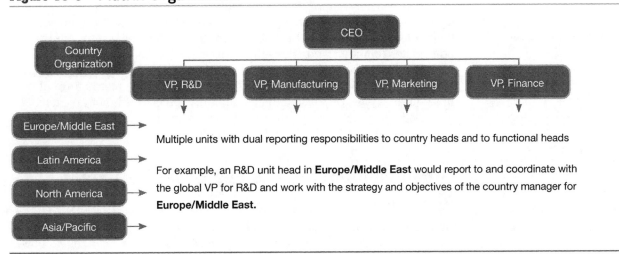

The transnational form of organization attempts to mediate the conflicting needs of headquarters and local subsidiaries.

transnational organizational form (transnational form of organization)

Organizational form that balances conflicting needs of global integration and local responsiveness by centralizing some units and distributing others to product or regional units.

transnational corporations

Organizations that balance the competing needs to standardize and localize products and/or services and thus "think local, act global."

and the organization may become bogged down with information, while multiple time zones and distances render the resolution of face-to-face conflict difficult. Hence, top management attempts to rein in national subsidiaries and begins to eliminate redundancies that may have developed in products, manufacturing sites, and staff functions.

Greater centralization focuses on developing global products and rationalized global manufacturing. Such steps require more central coordination and control. At this point, local managers may resist the dictates of central headquarters, and market forces may lead top management to realize that some local responsiveness and autonomy are necessary. This leads to the emergence of the **transnational form of organization**, with the goal of mediating between the conflicting drives of global integration and local responsiveness. Such an organizational form brings the added benefit of stimulating worldwide innovation because it also facilitates knowledge sharing and transnational cooperation.

Why become transnational? The multinational can achieve scale and scope economies and obtain lower factor costs for raw materials, labor, and capital. At the same time, growing convergence of tastes allows the multinational to concentrate on developing global products and standards, with some local variation. The multinational is better able to confront global competitors with cross-subsidization of weaker or embattled subsidiaries with cash flow from stronger subsidiaries in healthy markets. Such a structure also allows the multinational to respond to environmental volatility, including discriminatory industrial policies by local governments, currency volatility, short product life cycles, economic cyclicality, and cultural differences. Because the environment is constantly changing, the challenge facing the transnational organization is to continue to stimulate worldwide innovation and organizational learning while still maintaining organizational flexibility.[15]

Transnational corporations are the conceptual translation of the rule: "think local, act global." Transnationals often have products that require adaptation to the needs of local markets. At the same time, the size of transnationals results in benefits from the centralization or regionalization of functions such as finance and product development. Because ideas can develop anywhere in the world in a large, far-flung corporation, the transnational form of organization creates communication links that encourage the sharing of information and ideas across entities, whether demarcated by function, geography, or product line. The transnational organization is an evolution of the matrix form of organization; however, responsibility and authority are clarified. For an example of an organization that has implemented the transnational structure, see "Unilever and the Switch to a Transnational Organization."

Organizational Culture and Organizational Structure

● ● ●

As a firm develops its international organization, it must also ensure its organizational culture is globalized. Organizational culture can be a powerful organizational influence. It is deeply embedded in a firm through its history and experiences, and it impacts the way in which the firm approaches problem solving.[16]

••• Unilever and the Switch to a Transnational Organization

In Unilever's transnational organization, product groups are responsible for profits in Europe and North America, whereas geographically based regional organizations have profit responsibility elsewhere in the world. In addition, special strategic groups and task forces help to coordinate efforts across geographic and product divides.

Initially, Unilever was organized as a series of relatively independent country subsidiaries with strong local management (a worldwide regional organization). Later, product groups took over worldwide profit responsibility (a worldwide product organization), which was divided into three major groups: edible fats, frozen food and ice cream, and food and drinks, such as tea and soup.[17]

As markets changed, consumer-driven products such as low-calorie, health, and convenience foods and the use of natural ingredients became important. Unilever's response was to form an executive triad of three board directors responsible for all of Unilever's food businesses. Each director received profit responsibility for a group of countries in a region. Five strategic groups centered around edible fats, ice cream, beverages, meals, and professional markets. Today those groups advise the "food executive," providing product expertise, but they do not have profit center responsibilities.

Unilever's newest transnational organization structure seeks to preserve unity within diversity. It well understands that current trends in major food markets such as global fast food—national foods that cross country boundaries (for example, Chinese and Mexican food)—and purely national foods might require continued organizational evolution, which, in turn, means maintaining a flexible workforce.

Such flexibility is achieved by careful recruitment and training of managers. Unilever's managers constantly watch for young, bright local university graduates and scientists. Recruits go through in-house training programs on a continuing basis, maintaining contact with their peer cohorts around the world. Job rotation across product groups and countries and use of third-country nationals in high-level executive positions in country subsidiaries further cement informal transnational network ties across various country units. Unilever also uses international working groups to handle specific tasks and issues. Twice a year international conferences bring together managers from all over the world to listen to top management plans and to meet and renew old friendships.

A firm's or group's organizational culture consists of processes and values that all group members share. They agree that those values and processes, because they have been successful in the past, should continue to be used to solve problems in the future. The organizational culture determines how members are accepted by the group; how power is gained, exercised, and lost in the group; and how rewards and sanctions will be used by the group to motivate or deter certain behaviors. Such cultures can vary even within a large organization, with subcultures developing around functional roles, geographic or regional locales, professions, business units, and so on. Thus, within a large organization, the marketing culture may be distinct from the organizational culture of an engineering and product development unit or a manufacturing site. Such differences are considerably exacerbated when the firm goes overseas to set up its international marketing organization. Many, if not most, of its employees in its overseas international marketing subsidiaries are likely to be local nationals or third-country nationals. In those cases, the company's organizational culture needs to be communicated and established; further, it needs to coexist with national culture.

For example, marketing departments often use quotas of individual salespeople by territory. Receiving commissions based on sales performance and exceeding quotas can form a large (sometimes the biggest) share of total compensation.

Salespeople may be given considerable autonomy to plan their sales calls and may report back to the head office once a week or less, communicate remotely, and act with a high degree of independence. Salespeople may be expected to be highly productive, optimizing their time while in the field. In some countries, such as the United States and the United Kingdom, such behaviors are consistent with their home-country culture that stresses individualism, material success, performance measurement, risk taking, and independence. However, such practices may be difficult to transfer to more traditional cultures where salespeople feel more comfortable being paid principally with salary, prefer close supervision and direction from sales managers, and are reluctant to initiate sales calls on clients to whom they have not been introduced or with whom they have no previous connection. This suggests that the solution may lie in helping to socialize foreign salespeople gradually to the company's dominant organizational culture, beginning with careful recruitment to select individuals who may be a better fit with the company's values and processes. At the same time, the company should expect to adapt its processes to the changed environment and to the local culture while still maintaining its core values and core ethical stance. Research has proposed that organizational culture differences could be disruptive in the formation and performance of an alliance, particularly when the underlying professional cultures (engineering and software design) were critical to value creation in the alliance.[18]

The Role of Headquarters and Global Organizations

A constant theme running through the various attempts at creating an organizational structure appropriate for global strategy and marketing is the role that the parent company headquarters should take. This is an important decision that will impact the effectiveness of the overall global organization.

THREE ROLES FOR HEADQUARTERS

Corporate headquarters can play three roles in its dealings with subsidiaries around the world: controller, coach, or orchestrator.[19] The specific role selected depends on the needs of the firm:

- **A controller.** This role gives considerable autonomy to subsidiaries and uses measurements, such as profits by a small business unit, to determine when to intervene. This is classic management by exception.

- **The coach.** This role also decentralizes authority to subsidiaries but is available to provide support and advice. This means that the coach will intervene when necessary, attempting to strike the right balance between decentralization and central control.

- **The orchestrator.** This interventionist role has central control and responsibility for activities such as manufacturing, R&D, and finance. Subsidiary managers, therefore, have less autonomy. This style may be appropriate for industries for which global integration is important and investment needs are large, as in oil, steel, mining, and financial services.

CONSISTENCY WITH THE BUSINESS ENVIRONMENT

Company roles should be consistent with the nature of businesses within the global firm. The degree of synergy between the various lines of business in a firm, the level of risk facing the firm, and the intensity of competition determine which headquarters' style is appropriate. Table 15-2 summarizes these points.

If a company's lines of business are such that both high and low risk are present, the task of headquarters becomes blurred. For a high-risk business, headquarters may have to play the role of orchestrator; for a low-risk business, a

---

controller

The role of corporate headquarters in dealing with subsidiaries in which headquarters gives considerable autonomy to subsidiaries and uses measurements to determine when to intervene.

coach

The role of corporate headquarters in dealing with subsidiaries in which headquarters decentralizes authority to subsidiaries, but is available to provide support and advice.

orchestrator

The role of corporate headquarters in dealing with subsidiaries in which headquarters is an interventionist with central control and responsibility for activities such as manufacturing, R&D, and finance.

Table 15-2 ⚬ **Headquarters' Roles and the Business Environment**

	Controller	Coach	Orchestrator
Synergy	Little/None	Medium	High
Risk	Low	Medium	High
Competition	Stable	Open	Intense

Source: M. Goold and A. Campbell, *Strategies and Styles*, United Kingdom: Ashridge Management Centre, 1987.

controller role is more appropriate. Unless the company restructures so that only one kind of business line profile prevails, the firm must live with multiple roles. This implies that no one organizational structure is appropriate for a global firm with many lines of business. This is the reason that large global firms seem to be constantly changing their organizational structure. As the profiles of the various lines of business change, new organizational structures are necessary.

The level of risk is one factor that may determine the role of headquarters.

The Informal Organization

Regardless of which organizational structure is chosen, the central problem is that organizational structure is static, whereas the environment is dynamic. How can a multinational preserve strategic and organizational flexibility? The answer is to go beyond the formal organization. Beyond organizational structure, the firm must focus on communication channels, interpersonal relationships, and changing individual perceptions. The goal should be to let the informal organization bloom.

Overall, an environment of intense competition, overcapacity, and technological change means that companies will succeed because of their clarity of corporate purpose, effective management processes, and ability to develop people—employee capabilities and perspectives. Instead of sweeping strategic visions, employees who believe in what the company is trying to achieve are more likely to move the company to success.[20] Firms must also recognize how its organizational structure impacts working with outsiders, including suppliers and customers. See "Informal Organization and Boundary Spanning" for details.

Conclusions on Organizational Structure

From the preceding discussion, three generalizations can be made about organizational structure:

- The structure must be tailored to the situation and needs of the individual firm. No standard model exists.

- Changing conditions require the firm to adapt; as a result, organizational structures are in almost continual evolution.

- Perhaps the most important conclusion, though, is that firms are now recognizing that organizational structure can never be a complete and satisfactory means of coordinating their international operations. Accordingly, they are now trying to incorporate the product, geographic, and functional dimensions into their decision making without changing their organizational structure. In other words, other approaches besides organizational structure can be used to coordinate international business.

••• Informal Organization and Boundary Spanning

Another facet of organizational structure is how a company is organized to deal with outsiders. As companies begin to work closely with entities such as suppliers and customers, a network approach is becoming more common. Such network linkages go beyond purely commercial links; they encompass a larger relationship wherein the two partners attempt to share resources and to harmonize competitive strategies for competitive advantage. Such networks can include key suppliers, customers, governments, unions, universities, research institutes, and trade associations. At times, even competitors may be included. Individuals who play key roles in linking the company to this network are called boundary spanners due to their role in crossing organizational boundaries.

One example of such networks is in technology-based industries where companies form an informal network around a common technological standard such as those for high-definition televisions. Coalescing around a technological standard reduces risk because there is greater assurance of larger market size. In addition, the web of informal linkages allows individual firms to focus their strategy and to concentrate on relatively narrow segments of the value chain. The trade-off is whether to increase the size of the network by freely giving away the standard or to attempt to capture profits while reducing the size of the network.[21]

A firm's supply chain is another example of a critical informal network. Informal networks operate alongside formal communication channels as a means to provide information on the design, manufacture, and delivery of key components. Recent advances in communication technology (e.g., e-mail and Internet telephone services) and the way in which people connect with each other (e.g., social networks such as Facebook and LinkedIn) have altered the way in which these networks develop and grow. As a result, informal networks are bigger than before and increased communication fosters greater trust among network members. Recent research suggests that these changes allow innovations to "hop" or move more freely to different parts of the value chain and thus improve the performance of the value chain as a whole.[22]

Controlling International Marketing ••••

Companies market internationally to attain certain corporate goals. The purpose of control is to direct operations to achieve desired objectives. Considered that way, control is the essence of management, consisting of establishing standards, measuring performance against the standards, and then suggesting and implementing corrective action for deviation from standards and plans.

Control is inextricably related to the previous topics—planning and organization. Planning and organization can be seen as prerequisites of control systems. Planning involves setting standards and goals, the first step in the control process. The organization of a firm establishes the hierarchy, the division of labor, and the communications channels for management control. Furthermore, the degree of decentralization affects the control task. General control principles are as valid internationally as they are domestically. Special problems arise from different environments in which the operations occur. Communication gaps— distances between firms' different markets and differences in language, nationality, and culture—are the major causes of difficulty. Problems also arise from differences in financial and monetary environments. For example, government supervision, exchange controls, and differing rates of inflation may limit a firm's ability to control prices, remittances, and market entry strategies; that is, the economic environment limits where the firm may buy and sell internationally.

Special Measurement Techniques

In addition to regular reporting, specialized techniques exist for evaluating marketing performance. Two of the most noteworthy are distribution cost analysis and the marketing audit.

Distribution cost analysis is a technique used to analyze the profitability of different parts of the marketing program. It can be used to study product lines, distribution channels, customers, or territories. Through comparative distribution cost studies of markets, international marketers can recognize weaknesses in marketing programs and find solutions to recommend to markets having problems.

The **marketing audit** is a methodical examination of the total marketing effort, often by some outside expert.[23] Such an audit may be done by international marketing managers for each market every few years. Certainly, the audit would add to management's understanding of the firm's foreign marketing and aid in improving it. A marketing audit is especially useful when a firm is changing its involvement in a country. At a higher level, an audit may be made of the total international marketing of a firm.

> **distribution cost analysis**
>
> Technique used to to evaluate marketing program performance in which different parts of the marketing program are analyzed by comparing costs and profitability of the marketing program across product lines, distribution channels, customers, or territories.

> **marketing audit**
>
> Technique used to evaluate marketing program performance by conducting a methodological examination of the total marketing effort, often by an outside expert.

Organization and Control

The purpose of organization is to facilitate management control. The organizational structure shows the lines of authority—the hierarchy of control. Going beyond organizational structure, organizational context can be a means of maintaining strategic control.[24] In respect to maintaining strategic control, organizational context means that administrative mechanisms exist (apart from changing the organizational structure) that allow headquarters to maintain control in changing environments and circumstances. Table 15-3 gives an overview of these administrative mechanisms. The implication is that headquarters must maintain strategic control if international operations are to be optimized. To achieve this, organizational context (the administrative mechanisms) is more effective than structural change.

For example, in executive placement, it may be necessary to consider the propensity of individual managers to take a headquarters/business perspective versus a subsidiary/market perspective. Reporting relationships may be created to encourage greater or lesser local autonomy. Management accounting and reward systems may be used to enforce a strong national profit center mentality or to create an international perspective. Membership in critical committees may be adjusted to recognize either global or foreign national concerns. Critical functional staff groups may be centralized at headquarters or attached to local operating units.

Budget

The budget is the basic control technique most multinationals use. The control offered by the budget is essentially negative: It may prevent excessive

Table 15-3 ▪ Administrative Mechanisms for Strategic Control

Data Management Mechanisms	Managers' Management Mechanisms	Conflict Resolution Mechanisms
1. Information systems	1. Choice of key managers	1. Decision responsibility assignments
2. Measurement systems	2. Career paths	2. Integrators
3. Resource allocation	3. Reward and punishment systems	3. Business teams
4. Strategic planning	4. Management development	4. Resource allocation
5. Budgeting process	5. Patterns of socialization	5. Coordination committees
		6. Issue resolution process

Source: Yves L. Doz and C. K. Prahalad, "Headquarters' Influence and Strategic Control in MNCs," *Sloan Management Review* (Fall 1981): 16. Copyright 1981 by the Sloan Management Review Association. All rights reserved.

expenditure, but it does not ensure that goals will be reached. Furthermore, if the foreign subsidiary is substantially independent financially, control from headquarters can be difficult. In that case, the administrative mechanisms, as discussed previously, become especially important.

Budgets are a basic control technique for multinationals—though they can be perceived negatively by subsidiaries.

Subsidiaries as Profit Centers

One way to minimize the control burden on corporate headquarters is to have each subsidiary operate as a profit center. Profit centers can take on varying degrees of responsibility. With a high degree of delegation, the subsidiary handles most control problems. Headquarters may enter the scene only when profits are unsatisfactory. Most U.S. companies operate their foreign subsidiaries as profit centers, but with differing degrees of decentralization.

The profit center approach to controlling subsidiaries has several advantages. It maximizes the use of local knowledge and on-the-spot decision making and minimizes the frictions of absentee management. It is good for subsidiary morale because local management likes to have local control.

On the negative side, local management, evaluated on short-term profitability, may act in ways that endanger long-term profits. Autonomous subsidiaries are difficult to integrate into a coherent international operation. Therefore, a high degree of decentralization is most feasible when the subsidiaries are self-contained in buying and selling and have minimal reliance on the corporation for other inputs.

Information Systems for Control

Information is needed to plan, assess performance against plans, and monitor changes in the competitive and client environment. The company's planning and organizational structure determine what information is gathered and how it will be channeled through the organization. The amount of information collected can be enormous.

Without information, global corporations cannot be integrated efficiently. Mattel, a U.S. toy company, is a good example. Toy sales are concentrated around the Christmas season, with significant sales occurring between late September and mid-December. Toy makers must stock sufficient quantities of the best-selling toys in order to do well. Mattel produces most of its toys in plants in the Far East and needs to be able to change production plans to take advantage of new sales forecasts, which are based on sales figures. That is, if a certain toy sells out in early November, Mattel needs to know so it can increase production in Hong Kong and then ship the toy where demand is greatest. Equally important, if a toy is not selling well, the company needs to know so it can stop production. Otherwise, the company may have to write off inventory.

Mattel also needs updated figures on toy inventory at its warehouses around the world so that it can shift excess inventory from slow-selling areas to high-demand markets. This requires a global computer and communication system that can track production of several thousand toys, inventories at warehouses in various countries, and all retail stock. Mattel built a global information system linking headquarters with distribution centers and its plants in the Far East. Now the company knows what finished goods are due from which plant on a daily basis and where inventory is located. This allows for better alignment of the production schedule, market forecast, and real orders. Another benefit is that engineers can quickly communicate product specifications to plants, reducing the time it takes for an idea about a toy to become a finished product.

The global information system allows Mattel to update inventory, production schedules, and engineering specifications in a day, as opposed to between 7 and 30 days formerly. In addition, the system allows Mattel to reduce inventories significantly. Without this system, global strategy and its implementation would remain a dream.

When such networks are in place, they can be used for other purposes. Communication through e-mail and videoconferencing allows for closer coordination of international marketing, making both local autonomy and centralized coordination achievable. Such systems also allow for close monitoring and the exchange of information about competitors from around the world, which can be invaluable in determining competitive response.

SUMMARY

Planning consists of identifying systematic steps that will help a company formulate detailed actions to implement broad strategies. Thus, the stages of planning should mirror the steps used in formulating strategy.

The short-range plan for international marketing can be composed of several elements, including, for example, a marketing plan for each foreign market, plans for individual product lines, and a plan for international product development.

The basic elements of a marketing plan include the environment and the company situation in each market, the firm's objectives, and the strategy and tactics that will help the firm achieve its objectives.

Plans have a short-range and a long-range component. They should be developed for each foreign market and within the context of a global plan, integrating country markets and other areas of activity, such as manufacturing, technology planning, and R&D.

A comprehensive operating plan is necessary to help a firm achieve its short-term objectives. The plan should include elements such as detailed sales and market share targets, planned new distribution outlets, brand awareness goals, plans for new product introduction, test-marketing plans, and other market research activities. A planning calendar typically requires reconciliation of national plans with headquarters' goals. After headquarters accepts the plan, budgetary targets are derived and become the basis for managerial action and evaluation.

Broad company-wide plans must be adapted to individual markets. Local participation is necessary, and additional information-gathering and analysis will ensure a plan that is better adapted to individual market realities.

Long-range planning deals with the future of the company over a period of five to ten years. The focus is on developing scenarios in basic areas such as technology, market growth, competitive change, and a firm's resources. The goal is to be prepared for contingencies and to be alert for major opportunities.

Responding to competitive moves is another essential aspect of planning. This is contingency planning, with a firm deciding how it will react if the competition cuts prices, launches a new product, or strikes up a strategic alliance.

The planning process includes assessing and responding to new opportunities and evolving competitive threats. Firms must continually ask the question: Are there strategic alliances, joint ventures, or acquisitions that would make the firm more competitive? Identifying such opportunities is particularly relevant during the planning process.

Beyond hierarchies, power, and control of a firm's global growth, internationalization also includes the challenge of finding and placing the right staff. Challenges include ensuring executives assigned overseas do not get "lost" and that their re-entry to the home market is relatively easy. Determining which individuals are assigned to international duties can also be a challenge.

The country manager can be a key element in the global growth of a company. However, issues include what the country manager does, how much authority and autonomy he or she has, and how much profit center responsibility is given. The role of the country manager is changing due to regional economic integration and demands for greater overall company coordination across borders.

Planning cannot work without a well-designed organizational structure to implement plans. The basic choice is between centralization and decentralization; in some cases, manufacturing may be centralized, with technology development, product adaptation, and marketing decentralized.

Multinational organizations can be structured along four approaches: by international division, by areas (geographic), by product, or through a matrix structure. As the environment changes, organizational structure also must change.

The challenges associated with a matrix structure may lead to the emergence of the transnational form of organization, with the goal of mediating between the conflicting drives of global integration and local responsiveness.

A central issue is the role that headquarters should play. One approach is to view headquarters as controller, coach, or orchestrator.

Further, headquarters' style must be consistent with the nature of the firm. Firms may be grouped according to three criteria: synergy between lines of business, level of risk, and intensity of competition facing the firm.

Headquarters can affect the quality of implementation, taking a stance that ranges from informing to persuading, coordinating, approving, and directing subsidiary actions. Headquarters must decide how much autonomy to grant subsidiaries. In some cases, it may want to direct new product development while using persuasion in the area of pricing.

Control is necessary to monitor progress against plans and budgets. The chief control tasks are establishing performance standards, measuring performance against standards, and taking corrective action in the case of deviations. Marketing audits are useful in looking at the performance of foreign markets.

The purpose of organization is to facilitate management control. The organizational structure shows the lines of authority—the hierarchy of control. It can also be a means of maintaining strategic control.

Global information systems are a necessary component of international planning. A wide variety of information can be gathered and, if usefully organized, can help a firm increase sales and manage global factories and inventories, ultimately giving the firm a competitive edge.

 **KEY TERMS**

coach
controller
distribution cost analysis
international division
   structure
long-range planning

marketing audit
matrix organizational
   form (matrix form of
   organization)
orchestrator
regional organizational
   structure

transnational
   corporations
transnational
   organizational form
   (transnational form of
   organization)

worldwide product
   organizational
   structure

NASBITE CGBP TOPICS COVERED IN THIS CHAPTER

Note: For full details of the alignment of each chapter with the NASBITE CGBP, be sure to review the information provided in the section "Studying for the NASBITE CGBP Exam."

CGBP Rubric	Topic
01/03/01:	environmental factors affecting international strategies
01/03/03:	elements of a global business plan
01/07/02:	revenues and expense uncertainties
02/01/01:	internal resources (goals and preferences of senior management, experiences and capabilities of employees)
02/05/01:	budgeting processes
02/05/02:	reporting requirements

QUESTIONS AND RESEARCH

1. What is planning, and what is its role as a firm expands internationally?

2. What basic elements should be included in a company's international marketing planning?

3. What distinguishes a short-range plan from a long-range plan? What sorts of activities are appropriate for inclusion in a short-range plan?

4. How should a marketing plan be integrated with other aspects of the firm—for example, technology and manufacturing?

5. What elements would you include in a firm's operating plans for international markets?

6. What is the appropriate relationship between a national subsidiary's marketing plans and headquarters' broad goals?

7. Why should headquarters' broad plans be adapted uniquely to individual country markets?

8. Why should future scenarios be incorporated into a firm's long-range marketing plan?

9. How does competition affect international marketing planning?

10. Why would a firm consider forming a partnership with competitors?

11. How is a firm's organizational structure relevant to its international market planning?

12. Explain this statement: Organizational structure is essentially a choice between headquarters' centralization and local autonomy.

13. What are examples of staffing challenges for a firm as it grows internationally?

14. What is the role of the country manager and how is it changing?

15. What are the various organizational options for a firm as it grows internationally? Discuss the pros and cons of each.

16. Research the organizational structure of a multinational company. What type of structure has it implemented? What evidence is there that this structure is a good fit for the firm? What organizational challenges might the firm be experiencing due to its structure?

17. How can headquarters influence the implementation of plans? Under what conditions will headquarters be more or less directive?

18. What is control? How is control related to multinational planning?

19. What are some measurements that could be useful in controlling a multi-national marketing subsidiary?

20. What is a marketing audit? How might such an audit be useful in international markets?

21. What are the components of a global information system? How do such systems fit in with international market planning?

CHAPTER 15 TEAM PROJECT ASSIGNMENT: Putting It All Together— The International Business Plan

Because this is the final chapter, the team project task is to complete the international marketing report and/or presentation. Please refer back to the team project details in Chapter 1 for guidelines for the report or defer to the instructions given by your instructor.

There are some additional issues relating to this chapter that may be addressed in your plan. Specifically, they include

- What type of organizational structure does your client currently use, if any?
- What type of organizational structure would be ideal given the current state of globalization for your client?
- Should the client use a different structure as it grows internationally?
- What recommendations do you have for your client as they relate to staffing its international growth? Do the specific issues relate to the need for country managers?
- What are your recommendations for your client relating to effective control of its international marketing and global growth?

CASE 15.1 Sony in 2005

In January 1997, as previously discussed in Chapter 13, Sony's stock was at $33.70. In August 2005, almost nine years later, Sony's stock price was $33.62. Over that period of time, Sony introduced new products such as the successful PlayStation computer game-playing console. Sony's stock price peaked at $111.50 in April 2000, before gradually declining back to early 1997 levels.

Sony is one of the best-known brand names in consumer electronics and is well regarded for its digital cameras, camcorders, TV sets, and computer game consoles. However, as its stock price performance suggests, Sony has not been able to achieve consistent growth and profits. As Tables 15-4 and 15-5 show, net income margins improved slightly. However, it is still low, at 2.3 percent for fiscal year 2005, with return on equity at approximately 6 percent. Those figures are not indicators of stellar performance.

Sony continued to invest in developing technology, with R&D spending averaging 7.5 percent of sales in the 2004 and 2005 fiscal years, up from 6.4 percent in 2003. Sony sold in markets all around the world, with sales split as follows: Japan (29.3 percent of sales), the U.S. (27.6 percent of sales), Europe (22.6 percent of sales), and the rest of the world (20.5 percent of sales).

Table 15-4 • Sony Corporation's Income Statement ($Millions)

Year Ended March	2005	2004	2003	2002	2001
Sales	66,912.0	72,081.0	63,264.0	57,117.0	58,518.0
Cost of Sales	40,673.0	42,175.0	40,672.0	34,993.0	38,901.0
Gross Margin	26,239.0	29,906.0	22,592.0	22,124.0	19,617.0
SG&A	18,856.0	22,152.0	15,402.0	16,612.0	13,071.0
EBITDA	7,383.0	7,754.0	7,190.0	5,512.0	6,546.0
Depreciation and Amortization	6,057.0	6,462.0	5,621.0	4,498.0	4,743.0
EBIT	1,326.0	1,292.0	1,569.0	1,014.0	1,803.0
Other Income	644.0	377.0	379.0	−301.0	79.0
Interest Expense	230.0	268.0	231.0	275.0	344.0
Minority Interest	15.0	23.0	56.0	−122.0	−123.0
Pretax Income	1,740.0	1,401.0	1,717.0	438.0	1,771.0
Income Taxes	150.0	507.0	684.0	491.0	924.0
Special Income/Charges	0.0	0.0	0.0	0.0	233.0
Net Income	1,575.0	871.0	978.0	70.0	970.0
Effect of Accounting Change	−44.0	−20.0	0.0	45.0	−836.0
Total Net Income	**1,531.0**	**851.0**	**978.0**	**115.0**	**134.0**
Net Income as a % of Sales	2.3%	1.2%	1.55%	0.2%	0.2%

Table 15-5 • Sony Corporation's Balance Sheet ($Millions)

Year Ended March:	2005	2004	2003	2002	2001
Cash	7,269.0	8,165.0	6,036.0	5,154.0	4,858.0
Receivables	10,385.0	10,806.0	9,463.0	9,367.0	10,362.0
Inventory	5,890.0	6,409.0	5,297.0	5,076.0	7,543.0
Other Current Assets	9,635.0	6,960.0	5,904.0	5,556.0	5,057.0
Total Current Assets	7,269.0	8,165.0	6,036.0	5,154.0	4,858.0
Net Plant and Equipment	12,804.0	13,125.0	10,821.0	10,640.0	11,474.0
Intangibles	4,394.0	5,057.0	4,645.0	4,242.0	4,211.0
Other	38,249.0	36,888.0	28,690.0	21,662.0	19,119.0
Total Noncurrent Assets	55,447.0	55,070.0	44,156.0	36,544.0	34,804.0
Total Assets	**88,627.0**	**87,410.0**	**70,857.0**	**61,696.0**	**62,624.0**
Accounts Payable	6,965.0	7,809.0	7,315.0	6,554.0	6,460.0
S-T Debt	9,668.0	12,056.0	7,247.0	8,455.0	10,251.0
Other Current Liabilities	9,578.0	8,810.0	6,050.0	4,276.0	4,463.0
Total Current Liabilities	26,211.0	28,675.0	20,613.0	19,283.0	21,174.0
Long Term Debt	6,335.0	7,477.0	6,835.0	6,321.0	6,749.0
Other Noncurrent Liabilities	28,404.0	27,248.0	22,568.0	16,848.0	14,624.0
Total Noncurrent Liabilities (including deferred taxes, minority interest)	35,635.0	35,870.0	30,936.0	24,548.0	22,926.0
Total Equity	**26,780.0**	**22,865.0**	**19,308.0**	**17,866.0**	**18,524.0**
Total Liabilities and Stockholder Equity	88,626.0	87,410.0	70,856.0	61,699.0	62,624.0

SONY'S VARIOUS LINES OF BUSINESS

Sony had five major businesses:

- Electronics
- Sony Pictures
- Sony Music
- Games and Entertainment
- Financial Services division (a major cash generator)

Table 15-6 provides sales and operating profits for Sony's key lines of business.

Some of Sony's top products and well-known brands include the PlayStation, the Wega and Bravia LCD, high-definition and projection TVs, the Walkman, the Vaio line of PCs, and the Handycam video camera. Sony expected that in the future, it could link its various devices, offering consumers access to entertainment irrespective of their location; in other words, consumers did not need to be at home. For example, in the future, customers could wirelessly connect their digital cameras to TVs at home, access stored digital photos from anywhere, and share photos via connection to a proprietary Sony network site.

Sony also initiated a number of joint ventures, including the Sony Ericcson mobile phone manufacturing venture. In mobile phones sold, the joint venture sold about 43 million handsets. The GSM Association voted Sony's V800 model the best 3G handset. Sony also launched a Walkman phone and planned to draw on the company's entertainment assets to offer preloaded music and film clips on the phone.

In its TV business, Sony developed a joint venture with Samsung to source LCD panels to make largescreen LCD TVs. Sony also sourced parts from China to manufacture rear projection-screen TVs and high-definition TVs. (Seventy-five percent of products would support high definition by 2007.) Sony and BMG Music formed a music joint venture leading to a 25 percent global market share. Sony also formed a joint venture in semiconductors with Samsung to jointly produce amorphous thin film transistor LCD panels for new-generation big-screen TV sets. To make up for its inexperience in software, Sony set up operations in Bangalore, India, hiring 150 engineers initially and then rapidly increasing the number to over a thousand as it gained confidence in and success with developing critical software overseas.

Table 15-6 • **Sony's Sales and Operating Revenue by Line of Business**

Year Ended March 31 ¥ Millions Sales	2003	2004	2005
Electronics	5,095,079	5,042,319	5,021,647
Games	955,031	780,220	729,754
Music	466,338	440,306	249,105
Pictures	802,770	756,370	733,677
Financial Services	537,276	593,544	560,557
Other	261,145	268,317	254,427
Operating Income			
Electronics	65,939	(6,824)	(34,305)
Games	112,653	67,578	43,170
Music	−28,261	−5,997	8,783
Pictures	58,971	35,230	63,899
Financial Services	22,758	55,161	55,490
Other	(28,316)	(12,054)	(4,077)

SONY APPOINTS AN AMERICAN CEO

Sir Howard Stringer, a Welsh-born American, was appointed as CEO of Sony Corporation in April 2005. Following Nobuyuki Idei, who had been CEO since 1995, Stringer's appointment was unusual in that few large Japanese companies have foreign CEOs, with top management and boards dominated by senior Japanese executives. However, Stringer's appointment seemed consistent with Sony's maverick tradition. The company had been started in the rubble of World War II by Akio Morita and Masaru Ibuka, the inventor who led Sony into cassettes, Trinitron color TVs, and the Walkman. Morita, Sony's first CEO, had appointed Norio Ogha, an opera singer and symphony conductor, to succeed him. Ogha, in turn, appointed Idei as his successor. However, Ogha did not relinquish power and influence completely. He continued as chair and as a member of Sony's board of directors. At one point, in 1995, Sony had 40 directors, most of whom were insiders (that is, Sony executives). The appointment of Stringer, who did not speak Japanese, was a marked contrast to Sony's Japanese origins and tradition, and a shock to the largely Japanese employee base in the company's Japanese operations. It may also have been intended as a message from Idei to the Sony Japanese unit, underlining that business could not continue as usual.

In an address in New York, Stringer outlined how changing its organization could help increase Sony's competitiveness. (See Figure 15-6)

Stringer also announced a major restructuring at Sony to reduce the number of products by 20 percent, to reduce head count by 10,000 employees worldwide, and to reduce total costs by ¥200 billion. Sony would incur restructuring costs of ¥210 billion for closing down plants and related severance costs. In addition, Sony would attempt to sell nonstrategic surplus assets to raise ¥120 billion.

Sony's critical problems included:

- A silo organizational structure.
- Product lines that were becoming commodities.
- New products that customers found difficult to use, that were not widely adopted by customers, and that did not result in continued loyalty. (The exception was the PlayStation game machines.)
- Uncoordinated divisions that were acting semiautonomously, making competing versions of the same product. For example, Sony's new PSX and another device named Sugoroku in Japan both included a combination of computer game and digital video recorder (DVR).
- Frequent changes in technology development strategy.

SONY'S ELECTRONICS DIVISION

The heart of Sony was its electronics division. That division had the highest sales; a strong global brand; and a variety of products ranging from color TVs, LCD TVs, flat panel TVs, and projector TVs to other products such as DVD players, camcorders, digital cameras, and commercial cinematography equipment. The division's strength was a well-regarded global brand, global marketing and advertising prowess, a strong global distribution system, and technological depth. The division's problem was that its technological advances were often quickly copied by competitors from Korea and China. That led to prices dropping quickly, making it difficult for Sony to maintain a premium pricing policy and to maintain higher operating margins in its electronics sector. Many of the division's innovations quickly became commodities, an arena in which scale economies and volume are critical to success. Those areas did not mesh well with Sony's competitive advantages. The division also had a number of fiercely independent, competitive businesses that did not cooperate well in developing new products—instead, often working at cross-purposes to each other. For example, Sony was developing the new PSP handheld game console, which could also store video, films, and music. However, another business in the electronics division developed the Sugoroku line, competing with the hybrid game player DVD recorder from the computer game division.

Part of Sony's restructuring was to merge such organizations so the company could focus on external competitors and develop a successful new product, rather than continue the in-fighting. The same organizational silos led to the introduction of a digital Walkman that could not directly play the common MP3 music files. A review of the new Walkman noted that its users were expected to

Figure 15-6 ● **Proposed Changes to Sony's Organization**

Current and New Organizational Structure

Our proposed streamlined organizational structure eliminates pre-existing silos and strengthens the horizontal planning functions.

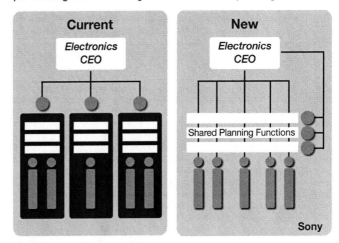

Source: Sony, Howard Stringer, CEO, corporate strategy presentation, New York, September 2005 (http://www.sony.net/SonyInfo/IR/info/Strategy/2005/Stringer/pre_index.html).

use the SonicStage software (included with the digital Walkman) to convert the MP3s into a proprietary format, ATRAC3, the only format the Walkman could play. That conversion was a slow process that consumed precious hard disk space. The review also reported dissatisfaction with the user interface.

Figure 15-7, below, outlines some of the problems that Sony's electronics businesses faced.

Figure 15-7 • Causes of Problems with the Electronics Line of Business

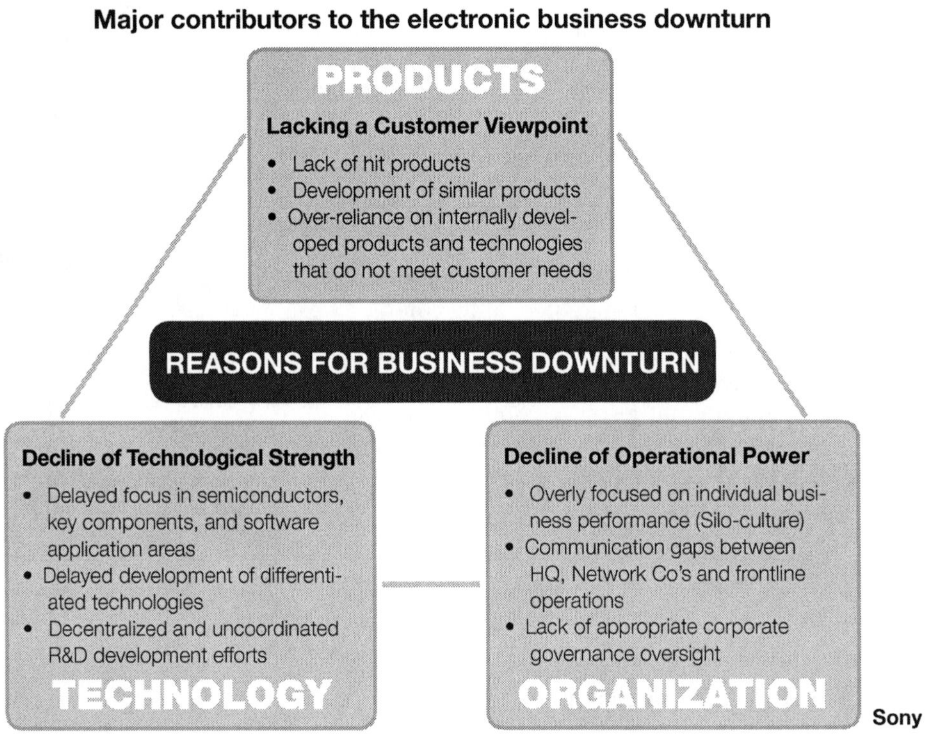

Major contributors to the electronic business downturn

PRODUCTS
Lacking a Customer Viewpoint
- Lack of hit products
- Development of similar products
- Over-reliance on internally developed products and technologies that do not meet customer needs

REASONS FOR BUSINESS DOWNTURN

Decline of Technological Strength
- Delayed focus in semiconductors, key components, and software application areas
- Delayed development of differentiated technologies
- Decentralized and uncoordinated R&D development efforts

TECHNOLOGY

Decline of Operational Power
- Overly focused on individual business performance (Silo-culture)
- Communication gaps between HQ, Network Co's and frontline operations
- Lack of appropriate corporate governance oversight

ORGANIZATION

Sony

Source: Sony, Ryoji Chubachi, President and Electronics CEO, corporate strategy presentation, New York, September 2005 (http://www.sony.net/SonyInfo/IR/info/Strategy/2005/Chubachi/pre_index.html).

Executives of the electronics division discussed the following:

- The need for product interoperability and an attempt to shape industry standards.
- The consequent need to develop competence in software and networking, not just hardware.
- The need to divest of nonstrategic assets and businesses that were performing poorly.
- The need to work within the Japanese culture and organization while becoming and continuing to be a global company.
- The importance of emphasizing mobile entertainment.

Sony's top management recognized the importance of revitalizing the electronics business, Sony's largest. Many new ideas developed, such as the Connect initiative, to better integrate electronics, software, and service. The end result was Sony's emergent ability to provide location-independent TV and other products, such as its combination DVR and game console.

Hence, Ryoji Chubachi, the CEO of Sony's electronics division, outlined his proposed approach to solving the division's problems. (See Figure 15-8.)

Part of the solution involved reorganizing the organizational structure of the electronics division to overcome the consequences of silos. (See Figure 15-9.)

Figure 15-8 • A "Solution" for Electronics

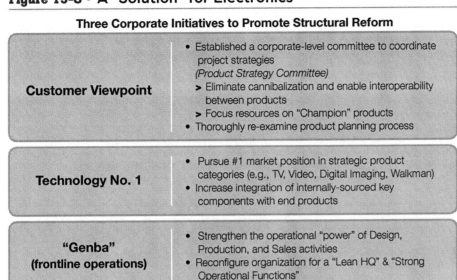

Three Corporate Initiatives to Promote Structural Reform

Customer Viewpoint
- Established a corporate-level committee to coordinate project strategies
  (Product Strategy Committee)
  > Eliminate cannibalization and enable interoperability between products
  > Focus resources on "Champion" products
- Thoroughly re-examine product planning process

Technology No. 1
- Pursue #1 market position in strategic product categories (e.g., TV, Video, Digital Imaging, Walkman)
- Increase integration of internally-sourced key components with end products

**"Genba"
(frontline operations)**
- Strengthen the operational "power" of Design, Production, and Sales activities
- Reconfigure organization for a "Lean HQ" & "Strong Operational Functions"

Sony

Source: Sony, Ryoji Chubachi, President and Electronics CEO, corporate strategy presentation, New York, September 2005 (http://www.sony.net /SonyInfo/IR/info/Strategy/2005 /Chubachi/pre_index.html).

Figure 15-9 • The Proposed New Electronics Organization

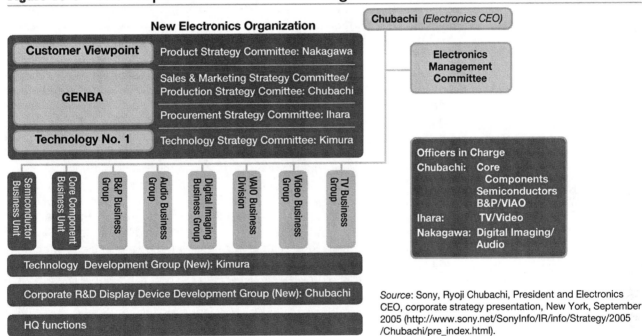

Source: Sony, Ryoji Chubachi, President and Electronics CEO, corporate strategy presentation, New York, September 2005 (http://www.sony.net/SonyInfo/IR/info/Strategy/2005 /Chubachi/pre_index.html).

SONY'S COMPUTER GAME BUSINESS

Sony's "newest" line of business was its computer game business, anchored by its PlayStation and PS2 game machines. This business was a start-up within Sony, led by another maverick, Ken Kuratagi, who received Idei's assent to develop a game machine to challenge Nintendo, then the industry leader.

The computer game business was developed in a separate organization, independent of Sony's mainstream electronics business. Kuratagi's vision was to develop a proprietary chip for the game console and game software that would leap-frog Nintendo in game-playing quality and experience. Sony's games would be faster and more complex; players would have the ability to play games on the Internet against other Internet opponents. The PlayStation was successfully introduced with considerable marketplace demand, but Sony had difficulty manufacturing adequate quantities of the complex semiconductor chip, resulting in large losses in 2000. However, once the manufacturing difficulties were resolved, Sony began to dominate the computer gaming industry, gathering over 60 percent of the market share. Sony launched new products to compete with Microsoft, which entered the industry with its Xbox, and with Nintendo, the previous industry leader. By 2005, 200 million PS and PS2 models were shipped, accompanied by over 1.8 billion games. The PlayStation Portable, launched in late 2004, shipped over 6 million units. Sony's newest game machine, the PS3, would be launched in March 2006 to compete with Microsoft's latest Xbox model.

The computer entertainment (game) division's newer products included the PSX, containing a combined DVD recorder and game player. Sony planned to develop complex new-generation semiconductor chips in a joint venture with IBM and Toshiba for use in new-generation game machines and in other electronics products. The new semiconductor initiative, Cell, with IBM and Toshiba, was a supercomputer on a chip. It had 10 times the processing power of a standard computer and was designed for initial use in PS3, Sony's newest PlayStation game machine. Later applications would include real-time high-definition media processing. The computer entertainment (game) division, not the electronics division, would house the Cell development center under the leadership of its chief technology officer (CTO).

SONY PICTURES AND MUSIC

Sony's third major business was Music and Entertainment. Based almost entirely in the U.S., it included Sony Pictures and Sony/BMG Music. The division had over 7,500 films in its library, "about half of all color films ever made." The film library included hits such as the James Bond series, Spider Man, and The Wizard of Oz. However, sales declined as customers purchased fewer CDs and downloaded more music from the Internet, often for free. As a major producer of music and films, Sony was torn between embracing the delivery of digital media and opposing alternative forms of delivery for fear of rampant piracy of music CDs and films on DVD. Because Sony Pictures had recently acquired MGM and its film library, it saw an opportunity for synergies between computer games, films, and music; for example, a computer game drawing on the Spider Man film.

Sony saw promise in developing new ways of packaging and marketing film and music together. However, its film and music business, as well as its electronics business, had to cope with establishing new standards for the distribution of film and music on DVDs. Sony and its allies had developed the Blu-ray DVD format and were involved in a standards fight with the opposing and alternative standard, Toshiba's HD-DVD. While Microsoft had backed the Toshiba standard, Sony was attempting to establish its Blu-ray as the industry standard. As in a previous standards war with Toshiba over the VHS and Betamax standards for videotape, the prevailing standard will be determined by market forces. Toshiba "won" with its VHS standard because consumers liked it, therefore purchasing and renting more films in the that format.

SIR HOWARD STRINGER'S YEARS AT SONY

Stringer had his roots in the media and entertainment industry, having come to Sony with a background in TV news production. He headed Sony Theaters and Sony's U.S. real estate divisions, then was appointed head of the film studio and music division before taking over as head of the music and pictures businesses. Idei said that Stringer was an excellent general manager and that he did not have to be an individual from the creative side of the business. Stringer was successful in cutting costs at the U.S. operations by over $600 million by 2005, an achievement that brought him to the forefront as a possible successor to Idei. When announcing Stringer's accession to the CEO position, Idei also revealed that he and six other insiders would be stepping down from Sony's board, that the board would be reduced in size, and that outside directors would now dominate the board by an 8 to 3 margin. The difficulty for Idei had been that Ogha, the former CEO, had continued to exercise influence from his position on the board, often undercutting Idei's attempts at change. For example, when Idei announced that Sony Insurance in Japan would be sold to GE Capital for $5 billion, the insurance business executives opposed the sale and enlisted Ogha's help. His opposition to the sale forced the board to reverse its decision.

FOREIGN CEOS IN JAPAN

Another foreign CEO in Japan, Carlos Ghosn, who headed Nissan, noted that not speaking Japanese meant that all communication had to take place through translation. He added that change was possible in Japan, but for that to happen, it had to be clear what change was intended and how the change would be made. In addition, the CEO had to commit to results that would ensue from making the change. Ghosn emphasized that regardless of language, numbers were the same in any language and that performance spoke volumes, implying that achieving results helped support making changes.

THE CHALLENGE FOR SONY

After Stringer took over as CEO of Sony, he announced that about 10,000 jobs would be cut, 4,500 coming from Japan. He noted that because Japanese investors were against layoffs, he did not go as far as he would have liked. He pointed out that he had put several businesses on probation because those managers had promised results that never happened. Stringer had given the managers a year to show results, holding off further restructuring.

The broad challenge to Sony (and to many of its biggest competitors) came from the convergence of digital media across several forms of delivery. Modes of delivery included the TV, the PC, mobile phones (cell phones), music players, game machines, storage devices such as DVD players, and Tivo-like products. Digital content included the following: movies, new and old; music; digital pictures and digital video; data (business and personal); books, magazines, and newspapers; Internet content such as blogs and podcasting; and game software.

Convergence stems from the ability of content and modes of delivery to connect through the Internet, through broadband transmission across Internet networks, often wirelessly. The companies that can dominate that bridging can reap market share and profits and avoid the threat of commoditization. Microsoft is one such company. Its Windows software dominates. Microsoft is also attempting to use different versions of Windows in cell phones and in home electronics such as TV sets. Its hope is to achieve the success and dominance it has seen with Windows in the computer world.

Sony wanted to emulate Microsoft's success in leveraging its Windows platform. Sony could use Windows, but doing so would give some control to Microsoft, and Sony would have to pay license fees to Microsoft. Sony would be at greater risk from commoditization at the delivery device end. That explains Sony's attempts to develop advanced semiconductors (the Cell), a microprocessor and design distinct from Intel's Pentium architecture, and to develop Linux-based software for this microprocessor, relying on Linux's open source tradition.

The challenge for companies, such as Sony, is to mediate how such digital content is made available through the Internet broadband network to the variety of hardware delivery alternatives, as Sony puts it: How to capture a major role in the "broadband network society" of the Twenty-First Century.

Sources: Sony's Sledgehammer Strategy" and "Sony Chief Wields His Ax with Sensitivity," *Financial Times*, September 26, 2005; "At Sony, Rivalries Were Encouraged, Then Came iPod," *Wall Street Journal*, June 29, 2005; "Inside the Shake-up at Sony," *Fortune*, April 4, 2005; "Sony, Lagging behind Rivals, Hands Reins to a Foreigner," *Wall Street Journal*, March 7, 2005; "Videogame Whiz Reprograms Sony after a 10-Year Funk," *Wall Street Journal*, September 2, 2004; "Sony's Digital Walkman Doesn't Best Apple's iPod," *Wall Street Journal*, July 28, 2004; "Sony: The Complete Home Entertainer," *The Economist*, March 1, 2003; "Sony Redreams Its Future," *Fortune*, November 25, 2002; "Sony Is Grooming Games Maverick for the Next Level," *Wall Street Journal*, April 18, 2002; Sony Corporation's web site (http://www.sony.net/SonyInfo/IR/info/Strategy/index.html).

Case prepared by Prof. Ravi Sarathy, ©2005. For use in class discussion.

Questions and Research

1. Diagnose Sony's problems. How would you evaluate its performance?

2. Why did Sony succeed in the computer game business?

3. How does Sony's organization contribute to its difficulties?

4. What is your assessment of Mr. Chubachi's planned changes for the electronics division?

5. Why was Howard Stringer appointed CEO of Sony? What is he expected to achieve?

6. Why did Ken Kuratagi, Sony's "videogame whiz" not get the post of CEO?

7. If you were to advise Howard Stringer, what would you recommend?

8. What are the cultural and other difficulties Stringer is likely to face in turning Sony around?

NOTES

1. Myung-su Chae and John S. Hill. "Determinants and Benefits of Global Strategic Marketing Planning Formality," *International Marketing Review* 17, no. 6 (2000): 538–562.

2. Paul J. H. Schoemaker. "Scenario Planning: A Tool for Strategic Thinking," *Sloan Management Review* (Winter 1995): 25–40.

3. "Shell Pioneers Use of Scenarios to Enhance Its Long-Range Planning," *Business International*, November 12, 1990.

4. Alex MacDonald. "Shell Sees Oil Prices Rising," *Wall Street Journal*, March 15, 2010.

5. Kenichi Ohmae. "The Global Logic of Strategic Alliances," *Harvard Business Review* 67 (March–April 1989): 143–154.

6. Douglas W. Vorhies and Neil A. Morgan. "A Configuration Theory Assessment of Marketing Organization Fit with Business Strategy and Its Relationship with Marketing Performance," *Journal of Marketing*, no. 67 (January 2003): 100–115.

7. See Christopher Bartlett, Sumantra B. Ghoshal, and Julian Birkinshaw. *Transnational Management*, 4th ed. (New York: McGraw-Hill, 2004); C. K. Prahalad and Yves Doz, *The Multinational Mission* (New York: The Free Press, 1988).

8. Christopher Bartlett and Sumantra Ghoshal. "Managing across Borders: New Strategic Requirements," *Sloan Management Review* 28, no. 4 (Summer 1987): 7–17.

9. William W. Maddux, Adam D. Galinsky, and Carmit T. Tadmor. "Be a Better Manager: Live Abroad," *Harvard Business Review* 88, no. 9 (September 2010): 24.

10. Mason A. Carpenter, W. G. Sanders, and Hal B. Gregersen. "Bundling Human Capital with Organizational Context: The Impact of International Assignment Experience on Multinational Firm Performance and CEO Pay," *Academy of Management Journal* 44, no. 3 (June 2001): 493–511.

11. "Deep Inside China: American Family Struggles to Cope," *Wall Street Journal*, August 2, 2005; "Repats Help Payless Shoes Branch Out into Latin America," *Wall Street Journal*, December 24, 2003; "Grappling with the Expatriate Issue: Little Benefit to Careers Seen in Foreign Stints," *Wall Street Journal*, December 11, 1989; and "An Overseas Stint Can Be a Ticket to the Top," *Wall Street Journal*, January 29, 1996. "iPad Makes Apple Top U.S. 'PC' Maker," *Techweb*, October 18, 2010.

12. John A. Quelch. "The New Country Managers," *McKinsey Quarterly*, no. 4 (1992): 155–165.

13. K. Hewett, M. S. Roth, and K. Roth. "Conditions Influencing Headquarters and Foreign Subsidiary Roles in Marketing Activities and Their Effects on Performance," *Journal of International Business Studies* 34, no. 6 (2003): 567–585.

14. "AGCO Announces New Organisation Structure as Part of Succession Planning," PR *Newswire European*, February 12, 2004.

15. Christopher Bartlett, Sumantra B. Ghoshal, and Julian Birkinshaw. *Transnational Management*, 4th ed. (New York: McGraw-Hill, 2004); C. Bartlett and S. Ghoshal, "Organizing for Worldwide Effectiveness: The Transnational Solution," *California Management Review* 31, no. 1 (1988): 54–74.

16. Edgar Schein. *Organizational Culture and Leadership* (San Francisco: Jossey-Bass, 1988).

17. Floris A. Maljers. "Inside Unilever: The Evolving Transnational Company," *Harvard Business Review* (September–October 1992): 46–52.

18. David G. Sirmon and Peter J. Lane. "A Model of Cultural Differences and International Alliance Performance," *Journal of International Business Studies* 35 (2004): 306–319.

19. M. Goold and A. Campbell. *Strategies and Styles* (United Kingdom: Ashridge Management Centre, 1989).

20. Christopher Bartlett and Sumantra Ghoshal. "Changing the Role of Top Management: Beyond Strategy to Purpose," *Harvard Business Review* 72, no. 6 (November–December 1994): 79–88.

21. John Hagel III. "A Web That Supports Rather Than Traps," *Wall Street Journal*, March 11, 1996.

22. Joseph Galaskiewicz. "Studying Supply Chains from a Social Network Perspective," *Journal of Supply Chain Management* 47, no. 1 (January 2011): 4–8.

23. Philip Kotler, W. T. Gregor, and W. H. Rodgers III. "The Marketing Audit Comes of Age," *Sloan Management Review* (Winter 1989): 49–62.

24. Yves L. Doz and C. K. Prahalad. "Headquarters' Influence and Strategic Control in MNCs," *Sloan Management Review* (Fall 1981): 15–29.

Studying for the NASBITE CGBP Exam

This textbook has been aligned with the NASBITE CGBP exam, meaning topics have been enhanced or added to chapters to help students or practitioners prepare for the exam. The CGBP is a professional designation offered through NASBITE International, a nonprofit professional association in international trade. To receive the CGBP designation, candidates must pass the CGBP exam and have either two years of college studies in any field or two years of work experience in international trade. For more details of the CGBP qualification, visit www.nasbite.org.

If you are studying for the exam, the material in this textbook will be a useful resource especially within the marketing domain. As shown in the following pages, the CGBP is focused around four domains (functions): Global Business Management, Global Marketing, Supply Chain Management, and Trade Finance. Within each domain are tasks and knowledge statements. Each knowledge statement has a unique six-digit identifier called the rubric. For example, the knowledge statement "components of a mission statement" is *rubric* 01/01/01. Recognizing these rubrics is important so that information and resources can be easily found.

Because this is an international marketing textbook, the primary topics that align with the CGBP are within Domain 2: Global Marketing. However, many topics from the other three domains are included as well. To show this alignment and to help in preparation for the exam, this textbook offers the following guides.

Chapter-by-Chapter Alignment

At the end of each chapter in the book is a section titled "NASBITE CGBP Topics Covered in This Chapter." Within each of these sections is the list of rubrics (knowledge statements) included in that chapter. This list will help reinforce the application of the topics in that chapter to the CGBP exam. Before reading the chapter, students or practitioners may want to review these rubrics as a preview of the CGBP topics that will be discussed.

Full Textbook Overview: Rubric Listing

To see where specific topics within each of four domains are located, readers should review the rubric listing on the following pages. At the end of particular rubrics is the number of the chapter, or chapters, in which that topic is discussed. For example, after rubric 01/02/01 is "(C-4, 5)" meaning that topic is discussed in both Chapters 4 and 5.

Note that not every rubric has been included in the textbook, except for the Global Marketing domain. However, there is extensive coverage of the Global Business Management domain because many of those topics are related to marketing. There is also a strong link between the Domain 3, Global Supply Chain, and Chapter 11, "Supply Chain Management and International Marketing." Chapter 11 is, in fact, a new chapter for this edition and was included partly to support Domain 3 of the CGBP. There is also strong alignment with Domain 4, Trade Finance, and Chapter 12, "International Pricing." Candidates preparing for the exam, seeking to review specific topics, can use the full textbook rubric listing to identify where topics may be covered in the book.

Glossary and Index

In addition to the preceding guides, the glossary will be a useful study tool. It contains many of the topics, agency names, program names, theories, and abbreviations included in the CGBP. The index can also be used to find where similar topics are discussed within the book.

Additional Reading

There are numerous additional resources for candidates preparing for the CGBP exam. Some are listed on the NASBITE website. Three in particular will be useful as companions to this textbook:

Trade Finance Guide—A Quick Reference for U.S. Exporters
Published by the U.S. Department of Commerce, International Trade Administration Available free at http://trade.gov/. This guide is particularly useful for understanding payment terms and finance programs to support export growth.

The Global Entrepreneur—Taking Your Business International
Author: James F. Foley
Published by Jamric Press International
Available through Amazon.com. This book is good for filling in many of the supply chain topics not covered in this textbook; plus, it provides additional reading on the Trade Finance domain.

globalEDGE website: http://globaledge.msu.edu/
The globalEDGE website includes an excellent glossary as well as specific training modules. They are listed as "Online Course Modules" and may be found in the "Academy" section. Many of the modules are related directly to CGBP topics.

CGBP Domains of Practice—Rubric Listing*

01 DOMAIN 1: GLOBAL BUSINESS MANAGEMENT

Develop and/or assist with the strategic and operational planning, development, implementation, and assessment of the international aspects of the business

Task 01/01:	**Develop and/or assist in the creation of a global mission statement for the firm.**
	Knowledge of:
01/01/01:	components of a mission statement

Task 01/02:	**Recognize ethical and cultural issues that are inherent in global activities and contribute to an ethical and cross-culturally sensitive business environment.**
	Knowledge of:
01/02/01:	business ethics as perceived and practiced in the U.S. and in other countries (e.g. cultural relativism, labor laws) *(C-4, 5)*
01/02/02:	culturally appropriate techniques for international business settings (e.g., adaptive behavior, response, and verbal/written language to correspond with local business culture, group vs. individual, ethnocentric vs. monocentric, high context vs. low context) *(C-4)*

Task 01/03:	**Participate in the global business planning and long-term strategic planning processes.**
	Knowledge of:
01/03/01:	environmental factors affecting international strategies (e.g., political, legal/regulatory, sociocultural, cost and competitive factors, appropriate levels of technology) *(C-1, 3, 4, 14, 15)*
01/03/02:	local, state, federal and global support initiatives that are designed to enable global business ventures and expansion
01/03/03:	elements of a global business plan *(C-14, 15)*

Task 01/04: **Contribute to the ongoing internal and external research efforts to determine viability of global ventures.**

Knowledge of:

01/04/01: basic research concepts and techniques (e.g., primary vs. secondary data, basic research methodologies/processes, surveys) and data analysis/evaluation processes (statistical evaluation, quantitative and qualitative analyses) *(C-7)*

01/04/02: data sources for international market data (e.g., U.S. Dept. of Commerce, IMF, World Bank, UN agencies, Country Desks, and private firm data) *(C-6, 7)*

Task 01/05: **Develop and/or assist in risk assessment and the development of risk management policies to support proposed global business activities.**

Knowledge of:

01/05/01: country risk (e.g. political risk, economic risk, expropriation) *(C-3, 12)*

01/05/02: commercial risk *(C-12)*

01/05/03: risks and sources (e.g. Department of State) associated with travel and expatriate activities (e.g. family member's adaptation, reverse culture shock, Centers for Disease Control and Prevention – CDC as source for travel risks) *(C-3)*

01/05/04: credit assessment and mitigating techniques (e.g., export credit insurance, international finance) *(C-12)*

Task 01/06: **Develop and/or assist in internal and external legal and regulatory compliance efforts to support global activities.**

Knowledge of:

01/06/01: general legal liability issues (e.g., product, international contractual disputes, governance issues, export license compliance) *(C-3, 11)*

01/06/02: intellectual property rights (e.g., patent, trademark, copyright), international agreements (e.g., Paris Convention, Madrid System) and practical enforcement levels *(C-3)*

01/06/03: issues related to and sources of information (e.g. Bureau of Industry and Security, United Nations) for offshore regulatory/legal concerns (e.g., bribery/corruption, antitrust, customs, import/export permits, licenses, labor law, currency regulations) *(C-3, 5)*

Task 01/07: **Develop and/or assist in the development, implementation, and evaluation of the global budget.**

Knowledge of:

01/07/01: general budgeting concepts (e.g., basic elements of financial statements, sales forecasts, expense forecasts)

01/07/02: revenues and expense uncertainties *(C-12, 15)*

01/07/03: transfer pricing *(C-12)*

Task 01/08: **Establish and maintain relationships with appropriate external organizations to support global activities.**

Knowledge of:

01/08/01: industry, trade, and investment associations *(C-8)*

01/08/02: government support agencies (e.g., U.S. government agencies, IMF, World Bank,) *(C-8)*

Task 01/09: **Participate in the effective use of technology to support global performance.**

Knowledge of:

01/09/01: commonly used business and communication technologies, advantages of the internet

01/09/02: software tools to support global activities

02 DOMAIN 2: GLOBAL MARKETING

Manage, implement, coordinate and/or assist with marketing, including planning, sales, research and support functions to assess customer needs; evaluate opportunities and threats on a global scale; and meet corporate needs within environmental constraints and corporate goals.

Task 02/01:	**Evaluate the internal and external environment (e.g., economic and physical geography, history, political environment, competitive analysis, regulatory, cultural, and technological issues) to identify potential marketing threats and opportunities.**

Knowledge of:

02/01/01: internal resources (e.g., export readiness assessment, goals and preferences of senior management, experiences and capabilities of employees, technical and production capabilities) *(C-1, 8, 14, 15)*

02/01/02: external environment (e.g., economic and physical geography, competitive analysis, regulatory, cultural, technological issues, currency fluctuations, and protected industries and sectors) *(C-2, 3, 4, 7, 14)*

02/01/03: public and private sources of data and assistance including electronic and print *(C-6, 7)*

02/01/04: major trade agreements, trade law, and customs unions (e.g., NAFTA, European Union, export control regulations, anti-boycott regulations, Foreign Corrupt Practices Act,) *(C-2, 3)*

02/01/05: product certifications and standards (e.g., CE Mark, ISO 9000) *(C-3, 9)*

02/01/06: cultural issues related to marketability of product, translation issues *(C-4, 9)*

02/01/07: assessing technological infrastructures in target markets *(C-6)*

02/01/08: SWOT analysis related to global marketing *(C-14)*

02/01/09: how to research competitor activities internationally (e.g., PIERS, UN Comtrade, Kompass Directory, STAT-USA, USA Trade Online) *(C-6)*

	Develop and implement the global marketing plan:
Task 02/02:	**Conduct market research in order to determine the best potential market.**

Knowledge of:

02/02/01: laws and regulations that impact the marketing plan (e.g., entity law, promotional restrictions, distributor requirements, corruption) *(C-3, 5, 7, 10)*

02/02/02 public and private marketing resources (e.g., International Trade Administration, U.S. Commercial Service and the Country Commercial Guides, freight forwarders,) *(C-6, 7, 8)*

Task 02/03:	**After analysis of the market research, select products and markets to be targeted.**

Knowledge of:

02/03/01: impact on market selection of product, price, place, and promotion (the four P's) *(C-5, 7, 9, 10, 12)*

02/03/02: how to find laws and regulations that impact the market selection (e.g., entity law, promotional restrictions, distributor requirements) *(C-3, 6, 7, 10)*

02/03/03: market segmentation and demand analysis *(C-6, 7)*

Task 02/04:	**Develop and select market strategy to maximize sales and profitability.**

Knowledge of:

02/04/01: foreign market entry methods (e.g., licensing, agency/distributor, sales subsidiaries, international joint venture) *(C-8)*

Task 02/05:	**Develop and implement a marketing budget related to the global activities of the company.**

Knowledge of:

02/05/01: budgeting processes *(C-10, 15)*

02/05/02: reporting requirements *(C-15)*

02/05/03:	basic accounting procedures (e.g., retained earnings, accounts payable, accounts receivable) *(not included in textbook – outside the scope of international marketing)*
02/05/04:	cost of marketing and promotion *(not included as it would be difficult to quantify costs without specific information as regards to the foreign market, entry mode, and industry.)*

Coordinate the marketing mix of goods and services to implement the company's marketing plan:

Task 02/06: **Provide products and services for the targeted markets.**

Knowledge of:

02/06/01:	customer expectations and cultural requirements *(C-1, 4, 8, 9)*
02/06/02:	product life cycle implications (or strategies) *(C-1, 2, 9, 12)*
02/06/03:	(new) product development modification process *(C-1, 5, 9)*
02/06/04:	technical compatibility and product standards (e.g., CE marking) *(C-9)*
02/06/05:	where to find packaging, labeling, and marketing requirements *(C-11)*
02/06/06:	after-sales service and support requirements (e.g., manuals, warranties, technical support, recycling) *(C-11)*
02/06/07:	product liability implications *(C-11)*
02/06/08:	legal/regulatory requirements for pricing (e.g., pricing constraints and controls, fair trade laws, anti-dumping) *(C-3, 12)*
02/06/09:	trade assistance resources in support of providing products and services *(C-3, 6, 7, 8, 14))*
02/06/10:	environmental concerns *(C-5)*

Task 02/07: **Implement, monitor, and adjust the company's global pricing strategies.**

Knowledge of:

02/07/01:	cost structures, including marginal and fixed *(C-12)*
02/07/02:	tariff and non-tariff barriers and incentives *(C-2, 12)*
02/07/03:	quoting methods *(C-12)*
02/07/04:	resources for global pricing strategies (e.g., current revision of International Chamber of Commerce publications [e.g., Incoterms, UCP, URC], U.S. government agencies, and websites) *(C-12)*
02/07/05:	how local market conditions could impact pricing *(C-5, 12)*

Task 02/08: **Initiate and manage global promotion strategies in order to support the global marketing plan.**

Knowledge of:

02/08/01:	sales promotion mechanisms (e.g., trade shows and trade missions, horizontal vs. vertical trade show) *(C-10)*
02/08/02:	technological tools for promotion (e.g., internet activities such as e-mail, web sites, e-commerce; video-conferencing, virtual trade fairs) *(C-10)*
02/08/03:	trade assistance resources in support of global promotion *(C-10)*

Task 02/09: **Analyze and formulate global distribution strategy for products and/or services.**

Knowledge of:

02/0901:	types and roles of distribution channels (e.g., resellers, agency/distributor, joint ventures) *(C-8)*
02/09/02:	impact of local market distribution characteristics and implementation issues, gray marketing *(C-8)*
02/09/03:	contractual issues related to market entry (e.g., common elements found in most distributor agreements) *(C-3)*

Task 02/10: **Establish and manage the global sales activities.**

Knowledge of:

02/10/01:	sales techniques (e.g., pull vs. push), sales knowledge, and business travel *(C-10)*

03 DOMAIN 3: SUPPLY CHAIN MANAGEMENT

Evaluate all supply chain options which result in the best overall solutions to support the international business plan while complying with all rules, regulations, and security issues from sourcing to final distribution.

Task 03/01:   **Optimize supply chain solutions to meet the requirements of the international business plan including evaluation of all modes of transportation, inventory, time to market, landed costs, and customer requirements.**

Knowledge of:

03/01/01:	all transportation modes and costs *(C-11)*
03/01/02:	trade agreements, free trade zones and use of regional value content
03/01/03:	duties and how to read the HTS duty rate table, duty drawback, taxes, and quotas
03/01/04:	product classification regimes (e.g., HTS, Schedule B)
03/01/05:	security issues (e.g., Container Security Initiative [CSI], Customs Trade Partnership Against Terrorism [C-TPAT], warehouse security issues, Customs and Border Protection)
03/01/06:	where to find legal/regulatory packing requirements
03/01/07:	non-regulatory packing requirements (e.g., preservation of cargo, types of containers, packing materials)
03/01/08:	insurance, transportation liability regimes and demurrage
03/01/09:	resources (e.g., freight forwarders, trade associations, Internet resources) *(C-11)*

Task 03/02:   **Evaluate and select the potential intermediaries (e.g., carriers—all modes, 3PL's, forwarders, brokers, contract carriers) necessary to support the international business plan (including evaluation of outsourcing alternatives and/or partners).**

Knowledge of:

03/02/01:	major transportation modes and methods (e.g. consolidation and costs) *(C-11)*
03/02/02:	third party logistics providers (3 PL's) *(C-11)*
03/02/03:	forwarder's role in the transaction
03/02/04:	customs broker and other service providers
03/02/05:	usage of power of attorney
03/02/06:	databases available to search for intermediaries *(C-6)*
03/02/07:	resources available in support of intermediary selection (e.g., WTCs, local trade associations, state and federal government) *(C-6)*

Task 03/03   **Complete the documents required for international movement of product and services.**

Knowledge of:

03/03/01:	standard export and import documents for goods and services (e.g., proforma invoice, commercial invoice, transport documents, documents relating to services contracts) *(C-11)*
03/03/02:	U.S. export regulations for involved countries and seller buyer document requirements) *(C-11)*
03/03/03:	U.S. import regulations and sources for involved countries (e.g., Bureau of Industry and Security) *(C-11)*
03/03/04:	Incoterms (e.g., EXW, FAS, FOB,CFR, CIF) and their impact on transfer of title *(C-11)*
03/03/05:	U.S. legal and regulatory requirements regarding documentation for goods/services (e.g., export/import control regulations, export declaration) *(C-3, 11)*
03/03/06:	where to find foreign language documentation requirements when applicable *(C-11)*
03/03/07:	technology available for document completion (e.g., AES, SNAP, private sources)
03/03/08:	offshore legal and regulatory requirements regarding documentation for goods/services (e.g., certificate of origin, sanitary certificate, export/import control regulations)
03/03/09:	country of origin determination

Task 03/04:   **Coordinate with other departments to calculate the true cost, benefits, and risks of proposed transactions in order to implement risk management policies.**

Knowledge of:

03/04/01:   marine insurance (e.g., delays, losses, claims and other insurances, general average)

03/04/02:   transportation options and documents (e.g., ocean bill of lading versus air waybill, negotiable vs. non-negotiable bill of lading)

03/04/03:   international conventions (e.g., Warsaw Convention and the United Nations Convention on Contracts for the International Sales of Goods - CISG) and international conditions of contract (e.g., Force Majeure, arbitration) *(C-3)*

03/04/04:   packaging for cargo protection and loss prevention

03/04/05:   insurance companies and brokers, consultants, freight forwarders

Task 03/05:   **Facilitate the offshore procurement process.**

Knowledge of:

03/05/01:   advantages of global sourcing *(C-11)*

03/05/02:   cultural considerations affecting supplier/buyer relationships *(C-4)*

03/05/03:   impact of trade agreements

03/05/04:   terms and conditions of purchase or sale

03/05/05:   quality considerations (e.g., ISO9000, industry quality specifications)

03/05/06:   calculation of landed costs

03/05/07:   U.S. Customs regulatory compliance (e.g., product marking)

03/05/08:   import documents

03/05/09:   customs brokers and customs management tools (e.g., duty drawback programs, tariff engineering)

 04 DOMAIN 4: TRADE FINANCE

Evaluate financial risks and methods, select and implement most favorable methods of payment to support global activities and ensure that all related costs are included at the time of quotation. Evaluate quantity and source of finance necessary to implement global activities.

Task 04/01:   **Assess political and economic risks and cultural issues of the target country to establish the financial costs and viability.**

Knowledge of:

04/01/01:   political and economic risks causing late and/or non-payment from overseas markets (e.g., cancellation/failure to grant U.S. export license, civil unrest, foreign currency delays/shortage) *(C-3, 12)*

04/01/02:   cultural issues of buyer's country which may impact payment methods, money transmission methods, language used, credit control procedures, level of governmental control, corruption issues, and sources of finance *(C-3, 4, 5, 12)*

04/01/03:   resources for determining risk (e.g., U.S. government organizations, websites, Moody's, Standard and Poor's, Euromoney, credit bureaus such as Graydon America and Coface Veritas)

Task 04/02:   **After evaluating foreign currency exchange risk, select, implement, and manage risk mitigation techniques to protect the company against fluctuation of foreign exchange.**

Knowledge of:

04/02/01:   foreign exchange risk mitigation techniques and required documentation (e.g., hedging tools, currency option contracts, transfer pricing) *(C-12)*

Task 04/03:   **Research and analyze credit history and payment capacity of the potential buyers/partners to assess the commercial risk of the buyer and maintain credit management and control procedures and documentation.**

Knowledge of:

04/03/01:   sources of credit reports (e.g., credit bureau, D&B, Hoovers, US Department of Commerce, International Company Profile)

04/03/02:   costs, usage and value of credit reports

04/03/03:   commercial risks of late and/or non-payment from overseas buyer

04/03/04:   methods of payment (e.g., letters of credit, documentary collections, cash in advance, sight draft) *(C-12)*

04/03/05:   mitigating techniques (e.g., credit risk insurance from Overseas Private Investment Corporation (OPIC) and U.S. Export-Import (Ex-Im) Bank) *(C-12)*

Task04/04:   **Establish the most appropriate methods and terms of payment and required documentation to ensure timely payment for the sale of goods and/or services and to facilitate external financing.**

Knowledge of:

04/04/01:   methods and costs of payment (e.g., letters of credit, documentary collections, cash in advance, time draft, banker's acceptance) *(C-12)*

04/04/02:   commercial, economic, and political risks of buyer and buyer's country *(C-3)*

04/04/03:   international regulations published by the International Chamber of Commerce (Paris) governing international transactions and methods of payment (e.g., Incoterms, UCP, arbitration, Uniform Rules for Collection)

04/04/04:   methods of funds remittance (e.g., checks, banker's draft, SWIFT transfer,)

04/04/05:   types of letters of credit (e.g., confirmed/unconfirmed, irrevocable, transferable, stand by, with a time draft) *(C-12)*

04/04/06:   types of payment (e.g., sight, deferred, acceptance)

04/04/07:   documentation requirements (e.g., commercial invoices, transport documents and documents relating to services, inspection certificate)

04/04/08:   related financial and legal costs (e.g., bank charges, insurance premiums, legal fees)

04/04/09:   communication of letters of credit, collections, and associated documents electronically via the Internet (e.g., eUCP, SWIFT)

Task 04/05   **Select appropriate methods, terms, and currency of payment to agents, sales representatives, distributors, suppliers, and international joint ventures.**

Knowledge of:

04/05/01:   terms and conditions of purchase or sale (e.g., countertrade, consignment, payment terms) *(C-12)*

04/05/02:   resources: banks, U.S. government agencies, International Chamber of Commerce *(C-12)*

Task 04/06:   **Develop a financial plan to establish whether internal/external international trade financing is required.**

Knowledge of:

04/06/01:   resources (e.g., Ex-Im Bank, SBA, private banks, non-bank private sector lenders)

Task 04/07:   **Identify options for short-term (up to 180 days) pre- and/or post-shipment finance for the seller to ensure lowest cost financing at acceptable levels of risk.**

Knowledge of:

04/07/01:   forms and functions of short-term financing (e.g., credit insurance, government supported finance, discounting, time draft letter of credit, Export Working Capital Program)

Task 04/08: **Identify options for medium- and long-term finance for the overseas buyer (internal/external) to allow buyer extended terms while providing cash payment to seller without recourse.**

Knowledge of:

04/08/01: forms of medium- and long-term financing (e.g., government supported finance, finance provided by banks and financial institutions, lease financing)

absolute advantage   A country's ability to produce a good at a lower cost, in terms of real resources, than another country.

acquiescence bias   The partiality that occurs when interview or survey respondents feel obliged to give responses that will please the researcher rather than state their true opinions or beliefs.

acquisition   The purchase of a foreign producer or firm.

ad valorem duty   A tariff levied as a percentage of the value of the goods.

advertising   The paid communication of company messages through impersonal media.

aesthetics   An element of culture that reflects what that culture considers beautiful and in good taste. Aesthetics are expressed in the arts and in the appreciation of color and form.

agent   An individual or organization located in a foreign market that makes an international sale on behalf of the manufacturer.

arbitration   The use of a neutral third party to resolve contract disputes.

Atlas method   An exchange rate calculation in which the exchange rate is averaged over three years.

attitudes and values   An element of culture that clarifies what people in that culture think is right or appropriate, important, and desirable.

autarky   Self-sufficiency—in this context, in a country's production of goods and services.

balanced scorecard   A method of evaluating firm performance that adds nonfinancial measures (relationship with customers, internal processes, and learning and growth) to financial measures of performance.

balance-of-payments (BoP)   Statements of the economic transactions between one country and all other countries over a period of time, usually one year.

barter   The simplest form of countertrade whereby parties to a transaction directly exchange goods for goods.

beneficiary   The seller (exporter) that receives the funds from a letter of credit.

Berne Convention   A multilateral agreement offering protection of literary and artistic works among member countries.

bilateral trade agreement   Trade agreement between two countries.

bill of lading   A shipping document issued by the freight carrier (shipping company) that acts as a receipt for the cargo, contract for the transport of the cargo, and as a document of ownership (title).

born global   A term used to refer to companies that begin operations with both domestic and foreign sales from the outset.

bottom of the pyramid (BOP)   A group of people within a country (or other geographic, political, economic, or cultural entity) with the lowest level of per capita income.

B-to-C or B2C   See direct sales.

capital account   A specific balance-of-payment account that includes flows such as direct and portfolio investments, private placements, and bank and government loans.

CE mark   A product safety standard of the European Union.

Certificate of Origin (COO)   A document most generally issued by a manufacturer to confirm the country of origin of a product.

choice of law clause   A specific section added to contracts that specifies which country's laws govern the content and enforcement of a contract.

civil (or code) law   A form of law based on an extensive and comprehensive set of laws organized by subject matter into a code. The intention in civil law countries is to spell out the law on all possible legal questions rather than rely on precedent or court interpretation.

coach   The role of corporate headquarters in dealing with subsidiaries in which headquarters decentralizes authority to subsidiaries but is available to provide support and advice.

commercial invoice   A shipping document issued by the seller identifying key sales information, including the buyer, products or services sold, payment terms, shipping date, mode of transport, and prices.

commercial policy   Government regulations dealing with foreign trade.

common law   A form of law English in origin and found in the United States and other countries that have had a strong English influence. Also called case law, it is traditions-oriented and based on the interpretation of what the law means on a given subject and is influenced by previous court decisions and also by usage and custom.

common market   A type of market that includes the features of a customs union but goes significantly beyond it because it seeks to standardize all government regulations affecting trade.

common territory   A form of social organization based on geography, as in a neighborhood, city, or tribal grouping.

comparative advantage   A country's ability to produce a good at a lower cost, relative to other goods, compared to another country; a country tends to produce and export those goods in which it has the greatest comparative advantage and import those goods in which it has the least comparative advantage.

comparative-analysis approach   A method for determining the amount to spend on promotion in a country whereby the country is grouped into a category with other markets according to characteristics relevant to promotion (e.g., language, availability of media types, market size) and markets in the same category have similar promotion budgets.

competitive advantage   In the context of firm-level strategy, this reflects the firm's basis or ability to compete, generally by becoming the lowest cost producer, providing a differentiated product or service, and/or focusing on a niche opportunity.

competitive-parity approach   A method for determining the amount to spend on promotion in a country whereby the promotion budget is based on matching the amount spent by competitors in that country.

completely knocked down (CKD)   A method of foreign assembly in which the product is shipped in components and then assembled in the foreign market.

confiscation   Government seizure of assets without remuneration.

Conservative Judaism   One of four types (denominations) of Judaism. Conservatives attempt to maintain tradition while applying new methods of study.

consignment sale   Export transaction whereby the exporter retains title (ownership) of the goods until the importer sells the goods, and thus the importer does not pay the exporter until the importer sells the product to the next buyer.

consultation   A stage in the WTO process for managing trade disputes between countries whereby the countries have a chance to talk with each other and attempt to resolve the dispute before it goes to a mediator or a panel of experts.

contract manufacturing   The production of a firm's product in a foreign market by another producer under contract with the firm.

controller   The role of corporate headquarters in dealing with subsidiaries in which headquarters gives considerable autonomy to subsidiaries and uses performance measurements to determine when to intervene.

copyrights   Intellectual property protection for artistic or literary works such as books, paintings, music, and software.

corporate social responsibility (CSR)   A firm's commitment and policies regarding global social and ethical behavior.

counterpurchase   A form of countertrade whereby the seller agrees to receive goods or services over some future time period as payment for goods or services provided.

countertrade   Also known as barter; a trade in which good or services are exchanged for other goods or services rather than money.

cross-docking   Moving products immediately from one delivery vehicle at a logistics facility to another vehicle in the same facility that will then take the products directly to a retail store or to the buyer. Use of cross-docking eliminates the intermediate step of warehousing.

cross-section comparison approach   A process by which the known market size of a product in one country is related to some economic indicator, such as disposable income, to obtain a ratio that can be applied to another country.

currency option   A tool to hedge foreign exchange risk whereby the owner of the currency option has the right but not the obligation to exchange a fixed amount of foreign currency at a fixed rate.

current account   A specific balance-of-payment account that includes transactions in manufactured goods and services as well as unilateral transfers.

Current U.S. method   An exchange rate calculation in which the U.S. dollar figures are calculated by converting each foreign currency using a single-year official exchange rate.

customs union   Similar to a free-trade area, but adds the requirement that members also have a uniform tariff on trade with nonmembers.

deficit   In the context of balance-of-payments, the shortfall that results when country-level spending exceeds country-level saving.

direct exporting   A foreign market entry mode in which the manufacturer is the exporter and directly sells to an importer in another country.

direct sales   The type of transaction that occurs when a manufacturer sells direct to foreign buyers; also called B-to-C or B2C.

direct-selling retailers   Firms that use a sales force to make their sales directly to consumers.

distribution   The sum of activities that move products from a firm to its customers.

distribution cost analysis   Technique used to evaluate marketing program performance in which different parts of the marketing program are analyzed by comparing costs and profitability of the marketing program across product lines, distribution channels, customers, or territories.

distributor   An organization located in the foreign market that takes title (ownership) of a manufacturer's product and sells the product.

distributor agreement   Legal document that spells out the responsibilities and interests of both the exporter and the distributor.

documentary collections   A payment method in which the seller (exporter) utilizes a foreign bank to collect payment for a transaction with the understanding that the buyer will not receive the goods until payment has been made.

dual-use goods   Products that have both commercial and military or weapons proliferation applications.

dumping   Selling products in foreign markets at prices lower than those in the producer's home market or at prices lower than cost.

economic unions   An association that includes the features of a common market but also includes a common currency and the coordination of monetary and fiscal policies.

education   An element of culture that includes formal training in schools and the process in that culture for transmitting skills, ideas, and attitudes.

Electronic Export Information (EEI)   A U.S. electronic form completed by the exporter; it contains basic information about the shipment, including the shipper, products, values, buyer, and country of destination.

ethnocentrism   A belief that one's culture is superior to other cultures.

euro   The common unit of currency used by members of the European Union.

exchange control   A scarcity of foreign exchange resulting in a government's rationing it out according to its own priorities.

export license   Permission by the U.S. government for a company to make a shipment or shipments to a foreign buyer that otherwise would be illegal without the license. Export licenses are not required for all shipments but are required if the product or the foreign buyer is subject to export controls.

export management companies (EMCs) Companies that specialize in exporting and handle the export transaction on behalf of the manufacturer.

export trading companies (ETCs) Companies that specialize in international trade, generally organized as vertically or horizontally integrated entities.

expropriation Government seizure of assets with some compensation, usually less than fair market value or the firm's valuation of the assets.

first-mover advantage The advantage associated with being first to market to a particular group of consumers such as establishing a brand and developing strong relationships with buyers.

fixed costs Costs that will be incurred regardless if a particular product is manufactured, such as overhead costs, management, R&D, and buildings.

focus group A group of individuals gathered together to answer specific research questions.

foreign assembly The type of manufacturing that occurs when a firm produces domestically all or most of the components or ingredients of its product and ships them to foreign markets for assembly.

foreign exchange economic risk The risk that, over time, a firm will lose profits or become less competitive in its international sales due to foreign exchange rate changes.

foreign exchange hedging Techniques used by firms operating internationally to reduce or eliminate foreign exchange risk.

foreign exchange hedging tools Specific financial products offered by banks and other financial institutions to firms to reduce or eliminate the firm's foreign exchange risk.

foreign exchange rate The domestic price of a foreign currency.

foreign exchange translation risk The risk that, when foreign financial statements are restated (translated) into the firm's home currency, this action reduces the firm's profits.

foreign manufacturing A foreign market entry mode in which the manufacturer produces a product or service in a foreign market rather than exporting it to that market.

foreign marketing Marketing within foreign countries.

free-trade area A form of economic integration where member countries agree to have free movement of goods among themselves, so no tariffs or quotas are imposed against goods coming from other members.

freight forwarders Companies that provide services to support the transportation and movement of goods. Standard services include reserving freight space on carriers, handling international documentation, arranging shipping insurance, and providing outsourced logistics services such as warehousing.

full-absorption pricing Pricing strategy in which a firm calculates the price for a product or service that includes its full share of fixed costs (e.g., overhead).

Gini index Also known as the Gini coefficient, this is a common indicator of income distribution such that the higher the number, the greater the income inequality between people in a country.

Global Compact United Nations (UN) effort listing ways in which businesses should fight against corruption.

global environment A business environment in which business transactions take place between and within different country environments.

global marketing Coordinating marketing in multiple markets in the face of global competition.

global perspective A firm's international expansion philosophy highlighted by formulating its strategic plans in order to direct special attention to the interdependence among national markets and competitors' actions in those markets.

Global Public Good (GPG) Commodities, resources, services, and systems of rules or policy regimes with substantial cross-border externalities that are important for economic development and poverty reduction, and that can be produced in sufficient supply only through cooperation and collective action by developed and developing countries (World Bank definition).

Gold Key A service provided by the U.S. Commercial Service whereby the USCS prequalifies companies and sets up appointments with potential foreign partners.

gray marketing The unauthorized importing and selling of products intended for one market in another higher-priced market.

greenfield Establishment of a brand new facility built from the ground up.

greenwashing A company's publically claiming to be committed to sustainability and environmental issues, but its actual business practices do not support the claim.

gross domestic product (GDP) Measure of the total domestic value created by resident producers plus any product taxes and minus any subsidies.

gross national income (GNI) Measure of a country's wealth by summing the value added of all resident producers, plus any product taxes (less subsidies) not included in the valuation of output plus net receipts of primary income (compensation of employees and property income) from abroad.

hard currency A currency that is widely traded globally and thus is widely trusted.

high-context culture Culture that places less emphasis on actual verbal communication and more on the relationship and nonverbal communication.

horizontal trade missions Trade mission focused across a wide spectrum of industries but typically within a single market or region.

horizontal trade shows Trade show focused across a wide spectrum of industries but typically within a single market or region.

hypernorms Manifest, universal norms that represent principles so fundamental to human existence that they are reflected in a convergence of religious, philosophical, and cultural beliefs.

Incoterms A set of 11 transportation-related terms issued by the International Chamber of Commerce (ICC) and used worldwide in sales contracts. Incoterms identify the specific responsibilities of the seller and the buyer so that each accepts its role in the international transaction.

indirect exporting A foreign market entry mode in

which the manufacturer is not the exporter; instead, a third party conducts the export transaction.

individualism   The degree to which a culture places emphasis on the individual as opposed to a group of people.

insurance certificate   A shipping document issued by the seller, an insurance company, or a freight forwarder to confirm insurance was obtained for the shipment.

integrative social contracts   Implicit social contracts between companies and stakeholders whereby local ethical expectations guide the relationship.

intellectual property (IP)   Abstract property created in the human mind. IP includes thoughts and ideas that are turned into paintings, music, software, and architectural designs, and the processes used to create products.

intensive distribution   Policy of selling through any retailer that wants to handle the product.

international division structure   Organizational form with a separate unit to focus on international business that concentrates international expertise, personnel, and vision in one part of the company.

international marketing   The act of marketing across borders including marketing between countries as well as within each country.

International Monetary Fund (IMF)   An organization that acts as a forum for monetary and fiscal discussions that affect the world economy and that supplies financial assistance (loans) and technical assistance (economic consultants).

International Partner Search (IPS)   A service provided by the U.S. Commercial Service that connects firms with potential foreign partners.

Islamic law   Law of the religion of Islam. Although it has harsh penalties for adultery and theft, it is not dramatically different from other legal systems with regard to business.

joint venture   Foreign operation in which the international company has enough equity in a new company to have a voice in management but not enough to completely dominate the venture.

kinship   A form of social organization that is based on a shared origin, often the same family.

language   An element of culture that includes the spoken and written word—how a culture communicates verbally and in writing.

legal environment   The nation's laws and regulations pertaining to business that also influence the operations of a foreign firm.

letter of credit (LC)   A common form of export financing where the buyer's bank agrees to pay the seller (exporter) as long as the seller fulfills the terms of the LC.

licensing   An arrangement wherein the licensor gives something of value to the licensee in exchange for specified performance and payments from the licensee.

long-range planning   Organizational activity that deals with the future of the company over a period of 5 to 10 years and developing forecasts and strategies for the future.

long-term orientation   People's belief that wisdom comes from age or longevity, traditions and elders are to be valued, and those rewards come to those who make long-term commitments.

low-context culture   Culture with a very direct communication style in which the message is clear, logical, and specific.

Madrid Agreement   A multilateral agreement offering a single international application for trademark protection.

mail-order retailers   Firms that sell through catalogs and the Internet.

market-extension perspective   A firm's international expansion philosophy highlighted by unplanned and short-term exploitation of foreign markets while the domestic market remains the focus of the company.

marketing   The collection of activities undertaken by a firm to assess and satisfy customer needs, wants, and desires.

marketing audit   Technique used to evaluate marketing program performance by conducting a methodological examination of the total marketing effort, often by an outside expert.

marketing management   The planning and coordinating of activities to achieve a successfully integrated marketing program.

market screening   A means of identifying and ranking foreign market opportunities by using selection criteria to reduce the total number of countries under consideration.

market segmentation   A technique in which a subset of consumers who share common characteristics or common needs is identified.

market skimming   Pricing policy that involves setting prices at a high level to trade off lower sales volumes with higher margins per unit sold.

masculinity   A cultural characteristic of societies that measures the extent to which some societies are male-dominated and a large separation exists between men and women.

material culture   The tools and artifacts (physical things) in a society.

matrix organizational form   Complex organizational form with a dual chain of command where units report to superiors about both product and geographic issues.

merchant wholesalers   Firms that perform the traditional role of buying products and selling to retailers.

mixed ventures   Joint ventures with foreign government entities as opposed to foreign firms.

multidomestic perspective   A firm's international expansion philosophy highlighted by careful consideration of foreign markets and with a clearly separate orientation toward each country market.

multilateral trade agreement   Trade agreement between more than two countries.

multiple-factor index   An indirect measure of market demand calculated by using multiple variables that are closely correlated with the actual market potential.

national champions   Firms that have dominant positions in their national markets and often receive government support.

nationalization   Government seizure of entire industries, regardless of nationality.

national sovereignty   A nation's right to govern itself without outside interference.

new product development (NPD)   The process of bringing a new product or service to market, including research and development, technology commercialization, and product testing. NPD also includes modification of existing products. (See also product-line extensions.)

nondiscrimination   A policy such that each contracting party (government) must grant all others the same rate of import duty; a trade concession granted to one trading partner must be extended to all members.

non-tariff barriers (NTBs)   Trade barriers that include customs documentation, requirements, marks of origin, food and drug laws, labeling laws, antidumping laws, "buy national" policies, and subsidies.

North American Free Trade Agreement (NAFTA)   A free trade agreement between Canada, the United States, and Mexico.

objective-and-task method   A method for determining the amount to spend on promotion in a country whereby the promotion budget is based on how much it costs to achieve specific promotion objectives (e.g., level of sales or brand awareness).

open account   A payment method whereby the seller (exporter) extends credit to the buyer such that the buyer typically does not have to pay for the goods in advance but instead some time later (e.g., 30, 60, or 90 days).

Organization for Economic Cooperation and Development (OECD)   A membership organization of over 30 countries committed to democracy and market economics, with a focus on research and a sharing of policies and best practices.

Orthodox Judaism   One of four types (denominations) of Judaism; orthodox adherents uphold the traditional way of life as detailed in the Torah.

packing list   A shipping document that details each product included with a shipment and in which box.

Paris Union   A multilateral agreement offering trademark and patent protection among member countries. The agreement offers extended time in which to file for IPP in a member country.

Patent Cooperation Treaty (PCT)   A cooperative union for the filing of patents among member countries.

patents   Intellectual property protection for products, technology, and inventions.

per capita income   A measure of income in a country whereby a measure of national wealth (e.g., GDP or GNI) is divided by the midyear population of that country.

percentage-of-sales approach   A method for determining the amount to spend on promotion in a country whereby the promotion budget is based on a specific percentage of sales, typically based on the percentage of sales spent on promotion in current markets.

personal selling   A promotion tool; paid communication that can be altered quickly and targeted at specific individuals or small groups of people.

piggybacking   A form of indirect export in which one product "rides" on the back of another from one national market to another.

point of sale (POS)   The location at which a transaction occurs between buyer and seller.

political environment   Any national or international political factors that can affect the operations of a business.

political risk   The possibility that actions or policies by a government may adversely affect a firm's operations and profits.

political union   An association that often includes the features of an economic union but also adopts a governing structure that supersedes individual national or state interests.

power distance   The degree to which power in a group is shared and is the relative distance between the "most" and "least" powerful person.

predatory pricing   The practice of pricing a product at a very low price, sometimes below cost, to gain market share and take business away from competitors.

primary data   Data gathered firsthand though interviews and field research.

product family   A collection of products built on a common platform of technology, design, architecture, or formula. (See also product platform.)

product innovation   A new or substantially different way of meeting customers' needs through the development of a new product.

product life cycle   When referring to international trade and product patterns, a trade cycle that many markets go through wherein one nation is initially an exporter, then loses its market exports, and finally may become an importer of the product.

product-line extensions   The process of developing a new product (or model) primarily based on an existing product that offers new or enhanced characteristics or benefits.

product platform   A common technology, design, architecture, or formula base on which a line of products is developed. (See also product family.)

pro forma invoice   A document issued before shipment to confirm sales information that will later be contained on the commercial invoice.

public relations   Publicity; a promotion tool that is considered unpaid communication but with certain costs.

pull strategy   A strategy that attempts to gain business by bringing consumers to the manufacturer, often through heavy consumer advertising.

purchasing power parity   Calculation which utilizes an exchange rate that takes into account the relative difference in purchasing power between countries.

push strategy   A strategy that attempts to gain business by incentivizing the channel (wholesalers, retailers) to "push" the product to buyers. This strategy often uses incentives and promotions aimed directly at the wholesalers or retailers.

qualitative data   Information expressed as words often representing opinions, preferences, or behaviors.

quantitative data   Information expressed as a number or statistics.

quotas   Quantitative restrictions that limit the amount of goods that may enter a county.

quotation   A document issued by a seller to a potential buyer to confirm the cost of a product.

reactive market selection   The behavior a firm exhibits when entering a foreign market mostly based on opportunities presented to the firm or following the activities of competitors.

Reconstructionism   One of four types (denominations) of Judaism; this most recent denomination rejects the assertion that Moses received the Torah at Mount Sinai.

Reform Judaism   One of four types (denominations) of Judaism; reformists tend to be more liberal and support the notion that how one lives in accord with the Torah may change over time.

regional economic integration   Economic cooperation within geographic regions to pursue common economic gains.

regional organizational structure   Organizational form with separate units to focus on major geographical areas.

religion   An element of a culture that provides insight into the culture; in general, religion is a set of beliefs about the cause, nature, and purpose of the universe.

resale price maintenance (RPM)   The effect of rules imposed by a manufacturer on wholesale or retail resellers of its own products to prevent them from competing too fiercely on price and thus driving profits down from the reselling activity.

reverse logistics   A range of activities associated with customer support, including product returns, warranties, and repairs.

reverse trade missions   Meetings and seminars for in-bound international visitors at a trade show.

sales channel   Means by which a manufacturer gets a product to market.

sales promotion   Sometimes referred to as the "all other" category of promotion tools; includes coupons, directed e-mail and traditional mail, sponsorship of events, and many other means of communicating with people.

secondary data   Data from published and third-party sources, often quantitative in nature.

selective distribution   Policy of choosing a limited number of resellers in a particular market.

sensory segmentation   Segmenting consumers based on their likes and dislikes especially as related to sensory factors such as taste and smell.

single-line wholesalers   Firms that focus on a specific product line.

social desirability bias   The partiality that occurs when respondents answer questions based on what makes them look good, or is socially acceptable, rather than state their true opinions or beliefs.

social organization   The roles and expectations a group of people place upon themselves and others within the group.

special interest group   A form of social organization in which group members come together as a result of a common cause, interest, or idea.

specialty wholesalers   Firms that carry a very narrow line of products, often to an equally narrow retail market.

specific duty   A tariff levied based on quantity.

strategic alliance   Broad term used to describe a relationship formed by a firm and another partner that covers a variety of contractual relationships, may involve competitors, and usually does not involve equity.

supply chain   The sum of activities related to the moving of goods from their source (raw materials, components) to the final consumer (finished goods). A firm's supply chain includes purchasing, manufacturing, logistics, warehousing, tracking of goods, the supply of goods to buyers, and reverse logistics.

supply chain management   The management of all the events within a firm's supply chain.

surplus   In the context of balance of payments, an overage that results when country-level saving exceeds country-level spending.

sustainability   The environmental impact of a firm's business through the pursuit of corporate goals.

SWIFT   The Society for Worldwide Interbank Financial Telecommunication (SWIFT) is a worldwide collaboration of banks that allows secure, trusted communication between members, such as wire transfers of funds.

tariff   A tax on products imported from other countries.

tariff engineering   A process of minimizing the impact of tariffs by modifying the form in which the product is imported.

technology   Techniques or methods of making and using that which surrounds us.

technology gap   Differences in the ability of two societies to create, design, and use that which exists in nature or to use that which has been transformed in some way.

third-party logistics (3PL)   The use of companies to outsource specific functions of supply chain management. Examples include transportation, warehousing, packaging, customer support, warranty repairs, consulting, technology solutions, and cost control.

time-series approach   A marketing approach that estimates the demand in a second country by assuming that it has the same level of consumption that the first country had at the same level of development.

trademarks   Intellectual property protection for words, phrases, symbols, and designs that distinguish one product from another.

trade missions   Group travel to a foreign market, sometimes led by state or federal officials, to explore business opportunities in that market.

trade secrets   Proprietary company information that is highly secret to the company but not officially registered with a patent, trademark, or copyright.

trade show   Industry- or country-specific events in which many exhibitors introduce their products and services to potential buyers and partners.

transaction risk   The risk that results from changes in the value of foreign currency such that the exporter will receive less domestic currency than anticipated and thus diminish the exporting firm's financial results.

transfer pricing   The prices used on goods sold between related parties—such as from division to division or parent company to subsidiary.

transnational corporations   Organizations that balance the competing needs to standardize and localize products and/or services and thus "think local, act global."

transnational organizational form (transnational form of organization)   Organizational form that balances conflicting needs of global integration and local responsiveness by centralizing some units and distributing others to product or regional units.

uncertainty avoidance   A cultural index that measures a nation's tolerance for risk.

United Nations Conference on Trade and Development (UNCTAD)   A permanent organ of the United Nations General Assembly with the primary goal to further the development of emerging nations.

utilitarianism   A moral principle in which behavior is judged in terms of the costs and benefits to society. It suggests choosing actions that result in the greatest net benefit or that can be implemented at the lowest net cost.

value chain   The sum of activities a firm performs to create value (profitability).

variable costs   Costs directly related to the making and selling of a product (e.g., materials, labor, or marketing).

variable pricing   Pricing strategy in which a firm calculates the price for a product or service that includes only the variable costs associated with making or offering the product or service with no allocation of fixed costs (e.g., overhead).

vending retailers   Firms that maintain traditional brick-and-mortar retail stores.

vertical trade missions   Trade missions focused within a single industry.

vertical trade shows   Trade shows focused within a single industry.

warehousing   The storing of materials or products in one location for further distribution at a later date.

World Bank   An institution whose goal is to promote economic growth, to provide loans for infrastructure development, and to improve the living conditions of the world's population.

World Trade Organization (WTO)   An association of over 150 countries focused on cooperation and agreements concerning the trade of goods and services. Its primary goal is to provide a framework for multilaterial trade negotiations.

worldwide product structure   Organizational form with separate units to focus on major products or services offered by the organization.

Front Matter
pp. i, iii: © geopaul/iStockphoto.com
p. vi: © DNY59/iStockphoto.com
p. ix: © Alex Slobodkin/iStockphoto.com
p. x: © Fontmonster/iStockphoto.com
p. xi: © Alex Slobodkin/iStockphoto.com
p. xii: © Olivier Blondeau/iStockphoto.com
p. xiii: © Terry Morris/iStockphoto.com
p. xvi: © Nicholas Monu/iStockphoto.com
p. xvii: © Joshua Hodge Photography/iStockphoto.com
p. xvii: © corwinsg/iStockphoto.com

Chapter 1
p. 1: © Robert Churchill/iStockphoto.com
p. 2: © Rubén Hidalgo/iStockphoto.com
p. 4: © Catherine Yeulet/iStockphoto.com
p. 6: © Anthony Baggett/iStockphoto.com
p. 8: © Catherine Lane/iStockphoto.com
p. 9: © Ivan Bajic/iStockphoto.com
p. 12: © code6d/iStockphoto.com
p. 14: © narvikk/iStockphoto.com

Chapter 2
p. 23: © Giordano Aita/iStockphoto.com
p. 24: © Peeter Viisimaa/iStockphoto.com
p. 25: © ricardoazoury/iStockphoto.com
p. 27: © Alexander Raths/iStockphoto.com
p. 28: © DNY59/iStockphoto.com
p. 30: © jfmdesign/iStockphoto.com
p. 32: © luminis/iStockphoto.com
p. 33: © Jeremy Edwards/iStockphoto.com
p. 35: © Lachlan Currie/iStockphoto.com
p. 36: © david franklin/iStockphoto.com
p. 37: © ktsimage/iStockphoto.com
p. 41: NAFTA countries map © michal812/Fotolia
p. 43: © Franck Boston/iStockphoto.com

Chapter 3
p. 49: © AFP/Getty Images
p. 50: © Jim Barber/Fotolia
p. 53: © Yong Hian Lim/iStockphoto.com
p. 54: © AFP/Getty Images
p. 58: © dinostock/Fotolia
p. 59: © James Steidl/Fotolia
p. 61: © Thomas Acop/iStockphoto.com
p. 64: © L. Entringer
p. 66: left: © René Mansi-iStockphoto.com;
     right: © Lebazele-iStockphoto.com
p. 68: Hadj in Mecca, © ayazad/Fotolio.com
p. 71: © James Foley
p. 73: © Spectral-Design/iStockphoto.com

Chapter 4
p. 83: © Ricardo De Mattos/iStockphoto.com
p. 84: © slobo/iStockphoto.com
p. 86: © Constance McGuire/iStockphoto.com
p. 87: iStockphoto.com
p. 88: © Okea/iStockphoto.com
p. 88: © narvikk/iStockphoto.com
p. 90: © Catherine Yeulet/iStockphoto.com
p. 91: © Loic Bernard/iStockphoto.com
p. 92: © Holger Mette/iStockphoto.com
p. 95: © kevin miller/iStockphoto.com
p. 97: © Amy Harris/iStockphoto.com
p. 98: © Peter Spiro/iStockphoto.com
p. 98: © Clifford Mueller/iStockphoto.com
p. 98: © William Howell/iStockphoto.com
p. 101: © Alida Vanni/iStockphoto.com
p. 103: © Francisco Romero/iStockphoto.com
p. 104: © Sean Locke/iStockphoto.com
p. 106: © Stan Rohrer/iStockphoto.com

p. 107: © blackred/iStockphoto.com
p. 108: © Neustockimages/iStockphoto.com

Chapter 5
p. 117: Andrew Burton/Getty Images/Getty
p. 118: © P_Wei/iStockphoto.com
p. 121: © Nico Smit/iStockphoto.com
p. 124: © Uyen Le/iStockphoto.com
p. 127: © Sean_Warren/iStockphoto.com
p. 128: © Robert Byron/iStockphoto.com
p. 130: © peng wu/iStockphoto.com
p. 131: © Patrick Duinkerke/iStockphoto.com

Chapter 6
p. 143: © Bloomberg via Getty Images
p. 144: © Selahattin BAYRAM/iStockphoto.com
p. 145: © Eugene Kuklev/iStockphoto.com
p. 147: © James Peragine/iStockphoto.com
p. 151: © Dmitry Ersler/iStockphoto.com
p. 153: © Elena Schweitzer/iStockphoto.com
p. 156: © geopaul/iStockphoto.com
p. 159: © pagadesign/iStockphoto.com
p. 163: © José Luis Gutiérrez/iStockphoto.com
p. 164: © iShootPhotos, LLC/iStockphoto.com

Chapter 7
p. 175: iStockphoto.com
p. 179: © KieselUndStein/iStockphoto.com
p. 182: © Henrik Jonsson/iStockphoto.com
p. 184: © Ermin Gutenberger/iStockphoto.com
p. 186: © Frank Ramspott/iStockphoto.com
p. 187: © Henryk Sadura/iStockphoto.com
p. 189: © Nicola LOPARCO/iStockphoto.com
p. 190: © Dieter Spears/iStockphoto.com
p. 197: © Arthur Carlo Franco/iStockphoto.com
p. 199: © Janine Lamontagne/iStockphoto.com
p. 199: © muratkoc/iStockphoto.com

Chapter 8
p. 207: © Yann Layma/iStockphoto.com
p. 209: © Timothy Hughes/iStockphoto.com
p. 210: © Allar Bernard/iStockphoto.com
p. 211: © Felix Alim/iStockphoto.com
p. 216: © Talaj/iStockphoto.com
p. 218: © Lise Gagne/iStockphoto.com
p. 220: © Feng Yu/iStockphoto.com
p. 224: © Lise Gagne.com
p. 225: © Lise Gagne.com
p. 226: © Paul Mckeown/iStockphoto.com
p. 228: © Oleg Prikhodko/iStockphoto.com
p. 234: © Juanmonino/iStockphoto.com

Chapter 9
p. 251: © iStock inhouse/iStockphoto.com
p. 252: © Giorgio Fochesato/iStockphoto.com
p. 253: © 36clicks/iStockphoto.com
p. 254: iStockphoto.com
p. 256: © 101dalmatians/iStockphoto.com
p. 262: © Victor Martello/iStockphoto.com
p. 265: © Xin Zhu/iStockphoto.com
p. 267: © Laurence Gough/iStockphoto.com
p. 269: © George Peters/iStockphoto.com
p. 271: © rrocio/iStockphoto.com

Chapter 10
p. 287: © Jeremy Edwards/iStockphoto.com
p. 288: geopaul/iStockphoto.com
p. 290: © Chris Hutchison/iStockphoto.com
p. 291: © Jen Grantham/iStockphoto.com
p. 292: © Stacey Newman/iStockphoto.com
p. 293: © Sean Locke/iStockphoto.com